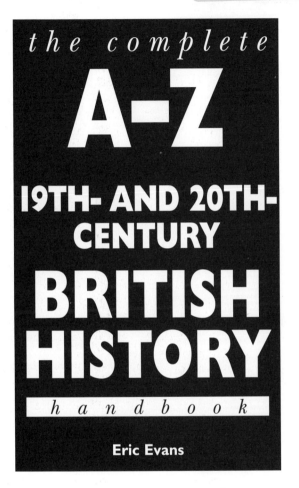

the complete

A-Z

19TH- AND 20TH-CENTURY

BRITISH HISTORY

handbook

Eric Evans

Hodder & Stoughton

A MEMBER OF THE HODDER HEADLINE GROUP

British Library Cataloguing in Publication Data
A catalogue entry for this title is available from the British Library

ISBN 0–340–67378–8

First published 1998
Impression number   10 9 8 7 6 5 4 3 2 1
Year   2002 2001 2000 1999 1998

Typeset by GreenGate Publishing Services, Tonbridge, Kent.
Printed and bound in Great Britain for Hodder and Stoughton Educational,
a division of Hodder Headline plc, 338 Euston Road, London NW1 3BH,
by Redwood Books, Trowbridge, Wilts.

HOW TO USE THIS BOOK

The *A–Z of 19th- and 20th-Century British History* is an alphabetical glossary designed for maximum ease of use. The main individuals, events, themes and issues which you will come across in your study of later modern British history have all been included. You may well be studying a period rather shorter than that covered by this book. Do not worry about this. The index lists will help you find your way around the chronology and it is often valuable to have an outline knowledge of those events which happened immediately before and after the period covered by your syllabus. You will, for example, find a number of entries on British history since the end of World War II. Few A or AS level students make a detailed study of near-contemporary history, but these entries are nevertheless useful. Not only are many entries directly relevant to people who are also studying Politics, 'British Government and Politics' and, indeed, 'General Studies', but they will also give you a secure understanding of how your study relates to the more recent past. Examiners are always impressed by students who can show an awareness of how the past links with the present. Don't forget also that historians are centrally concerned with cause (why things happened), consequence (what happened because of key individuals or events) and the process of change. This handbook will therefore put things in context for you; it also constitutes an important reference work helping you to make sense of the key issues. It will also show you how historians explain things about the past.

Each entry begins with a one-sentence definition. This helps you to gain an immediate understanding of the relevant issues in a precise way. The length of an entry usually relates to its importance and sometimes also to the degree of controversy which the subject matter has excited among historians. In addition to the standard entries on political and diplomatic history, I have taken the opportunity to introduce you to the main themes in social, cultural and economic history. You may be making a detailed study of these themes or you may not. Either way, this book will enable you to see people, issues and events in an appropriately broad context. History does not happen in a narrowly political vacuum. People make their own histories. Much history is made by people who are not powerful, as well as by the Pitts, Peels, Gladstones, Disraelis and Churchills. Illustrations and tables have been provided where they help you better to understand the concept or topic under discussion.

In a subject like history, cross-references are essential. It is in the links and the connections between individuals and events that the subject comes alive. Although each entry has been written to make coherent sense by itself, your understanding will be enhanced if you use cross-references. These are to be found in italics either in the main body of an entry or in brackets at the end of an entry. Use the cross-references as a kind of 'search engine' to gain a deeper or more complete understanding of the issues and themes you are exploring.

This *A–Z* is a glossary which will aid your study of British history. You should not see it as a textbook. You will need to do further reading to strengthen your overall grasp of the subject. Since interpretations of how, and why, things happened in the past are the very lifeblood of history, historians are expected to have different views. You will, therefore, be expected to read more than one book! However, the entries in this book, particularly the more substantial ones, will give you a reliable introduction to the issues and debates with which historians engage while also giving you that firm factual grounding in the subject which examiners like so much.

To help you in your revision, there are towards the end of the book lists of the most important issues and concepts in the main topic areas of nineteenth- and twentieth-century British history. These topic areas have been selected with an eye to the priorities of the main examining boards, whichever syllabus you may be studying. You will also find specific hints to help you tackle the different types of questions which history examiners ask.

I hope that you enjoy using this A–Z on a regular basis and that you will find it an invaluable resource supporting your studies. Perhaps most important, I hope that it will further stimulate your interest in, and enthusiasm for, history – a subject which can help develop so many life skills. Not only is knowledge of the past vital in helping to make sense of the present, history helps you to develop skills of communication, sharpens your thinking powers and generally makes you a better informed and more critical citizen.

Eric Evans

ACKNOWLEDGEMENTS

I am very happy to acknowledge the help of the editorial staff at Hodder and Stoughton who gave me great support throughout a process of creation which has taken longer than I planned, and certainly than they expected. I am very grateful for their forbearance. Kim McGuire helped me devise the list of topic areas and created the referencing system within it. I am most grateful to her for much meticulous work. So many of the entries owe their particular emphasis, line of development, or even existence to the expertise and enthusiasm of the numerous colleagues in both the professional history and the assessment worlds with whom I have worked now for almost thirty years. It would be invidious, even if it were possible, to name them all but both my perception of what is important in history and also of what students find accessible and challenging have been decisively shaped by their insights, kindnesses and collegiality. They have saved me from many misjudgments. Any which remain are, of course, my sole responsibility.

Eric Evans
Lancaster, July 1998

Abdication Crisis: the event which led to *George VI*'s accession to the throne on 11 December 1936. It was caused by *Edward VIII*'s determination to marry a divorcee, the American Wallis Simpson. The *Prime Minister, Stanley Baldwin*, supported by most politicians and by the *Church of England*, took the view that the proposed marriage would contravene the King's coronation oath in respect of his duties as head of the Church of England. Though intense, the crisis itself was short-lived since Baldwin was not officially consulted until November and news of the established relationship between Simpson and the King, fairly common knowledge on the continent, had been kept out of the British press. Edward, faced with overwhelming establishment, though not popular, opposition to his plans, chose to abdicate, marrying Mrs Simpson in France six months later.

(See also *monarchy*.)

Aberdeen (George Gordon), 4th Earl of: *Conservative*, later *Peelite*, politician and *Prime Minister*. Born in 1784 into an aristocratic family, his main expertise was in foreign affairs. He was outmanoeuvred by the vastly more experienced Count Metternich when negotiating for an Anglo-Austrian alliance in 1813, but developed into an experienced, and internationally respected diplomat. His main offices were:

- Foreign Secretary, 1828–30 and 1841–46
- Secretary for War and the Colonies, 1834–35
- Prime Minister, 1852–55

His main achievements included bringing the Anglo-Chinese *Opium War* of 1839–42 to a successful conclusion and helping to negotiate agreed boundaries between the US and Canada in the so-called *Webster–Ashburton Treaty (1842)*. This enabled increasingly close Anglo-American relations to develop. A firm supporter of *Peel*, he left office with him in 1846, becoming *de facto* leader of the Peelites after 1850. In this capacity, he headed a coalition government with the *Whigs* in 1852 which came to grief in 1855 over alleged mismanagement of the *Crimean War*. Aberdeen never held office again and died in 1860. It is regrettable that a level-headed and effective politician's reputation should have been permanently besmirched by army difficulties in the Crimean.

(See also *Graham, James; Palmerston, Viscount; United States*.)

Act of Union, 1800: see *Union, Act of*

Acton, John: historian. He was born in 1844, was educated in Germany and became a *Liberal* MP in 1859 before becoming a peer as Baron Acton in 1869. He researched a very wide number of historical subjects and was responsible for editing the authoritative 'Cambridge Modern History', beginning in 1896. His efforts contributed much to the establishment of separate history degree courses at Oxford and Cambridge. He is best remembered for the famous phrase 'Power tends to corrupt and absolute power corrupts absolutely', first written in a private letter of 1887. He died in 1902.

Addington, Henry (later Viscount Sidmouth): *Tory* politician and *Prime Minister*. Born in 1757, he was a man of limited gifts who owed a succession of offices both to good fortune and to the long period of Tory rule in the first part of the nineteenth century. His major offices were:

- Speaker of the *House of Commons*, 1789–1801
- Prime Minister, 1801–4
- Lord President of the Council, 1805–7 and 1812
- Home Secretary, 1812–22

He was selected by *George III*, somewhat surprisingly, to head the ministry which replaced the younger Pitt's when the latter resigned when George would not permit *Catholic emancipation* as part of the Union settlement with Ireland. Addington helped negotiate the short-lived *Peace of Amiens* and later proved ineffective as leader of the renewed war. He is best remembered as *Liverpool's* Home Secretary during a period of considerable internal unrest from 1815 to 1820. He suspended the Habeas Corpus Amendment Act and, in 1819, drafted the 'Six Acts' which restricted political liberties. Though he lived until 1844, he never held office again after his voluntary retirement in 1822.

(See also *Pitt the Younger, William; Napoleonic Wars.*)

Addison, Christopher: *Liberal*, then *Labour*, politician. First elected to Parliament in 1910, he was a *progressive Liberal* who supported *Lloyd George's* policies. He was Minister for Reconstruction in 1917. As a member of the post-war coalition government he was responsible as Minister of Health for the passage of the Housing and Town Planning Act in 1919. He lost his seat at the 1922 *general election* and joined the *Labour Party*, becoming a peer as 1st Viscount Addison in 1937. He became an influential elder statesman in the Labour Party and died in 1951.

(See also *Addison Housing Act.*)

Addison Housing Act, 1919: this Act inaugurated the era of council housing by introducing for the first time the principle of government subsidy for *housing*. The main terms of the Act were:

- local authorities were required to make a thorough survey of housing needs
- they must plan to provide housing in their area to meet these needs
- rents were to be fixed on the principle of affordability for the working classes rather than by market forces
- costs, beyond that which could be raised locally by a penny rate, were met by central government

The legislation was instituted to fulfil *Lloyd George's* promise in November 1918 to provide 'a fit country for heroes to live in', but the cost proved enormous and had to be scaled down to meet expenditure cuts from 1921.

(See also *Wheatley Housing Act.*)

'Adullamites': description coined by the reformer *John Bright* for those Liberals, led by *Robert Lowe*, who opposed their own party's parliamentary Reform Bill in 1866. The reference is Biblical. The Old Testament's First Book of Samuel (Chapter 22) refers to David escaping from Saul and fleeing to 'the cave Adullam … And everyone that was in distress ... and everyone that was discontented gathered themselves unto him'. The so-called Adullamites were important. Their votes led to *Lord John Russell's* resignation as *Prime Minister*. This was followed by the creation of a minority *Conservative* government which passed a much more radical *Reform Act* in 1867.

(See also *Liberal Party.*)

Africa, Scramble for: the name given to the period during which much of the land mass, especially of southern, western and eastern Africa, was colonised by the European powers during the 1880s and 1890s. Whereas Britain had been the dominant European power in Africa before the last quarter of the nineteenth century, competition both for important resources and international power and prestige caused France, Germany, Belgium and Spain to become increasingly involved. By the end of the nineteenth century, little of central and southern Africa was not under the direct control of a European power. Major British interests were *South Africa, Rhodesia*, British East Africa (Kenya), *Nigeria* and the Gold Coast, while in northern Africa, Britain had effective control over Egypt from 1882.

(See also *Empire, British; imperialism.*)

Agricultural Gangs Act, 1867: legislation protecting certain categories of rural worker. It was similar to the protection which had been advanced for textile and other industrial workers in the 1830s and 1840. It prohibited the employment of:

- all children under the age of eight
- women and children working alongside men in a field-gang

(See also *Factory Acts.*)

Agricultural Revolution: the name frequently given to the changes in land use and capitalisation which took place between 1750 and 1850. Both the periodisation and the term itself are controversial, since some authorities hold that changes took place over too long a period (stretching over 250 years, according to some) to be called 'revolutionary', while others argue that the decisive changes took place in the sixteenth century, rather than the eighteenth and nineteenth centuries. Nevertheless, consensus exists that the pace of agricultural change quickened from the middle of the eighteenth century. The main changes involved were:

- new technology, such as the seed drill (1733) and threshing machine (1784)
- the development of improved drainage systems
- the application of industrial technology, such as iron ploughs and cylindrical clay pipes for drainage, to agricultural use
- selective and scientific breeding of animals to increase weight and improve meat quality
- the development of new crops, such as turnips and sainfoins, as animal feed
- the development of specialist crops for the urban market, such as vegetables and fruit
- improved rotation of crops, reducing the amount of fallow land and increasing crop yield and productivity
- the formation of agricultural societies to disseminate good practice and new ideas and the development of experimental research stations such as

that at Rothamsted (1843) to promote the use of agricultural chemistry to fertilisers
- consolidation of land holdings – more land held by fewer owners
- enclosure of land, either by agreement or by Act of Parliament, thus requiring less communal, and more individual, decision making
- greater investment

A combination of these factors enabled Britain to feed a population almost three times as large in 1850 as in 1730, while also making agriculture a much more profit-conscious activity.

(See also *aristocracy.*)

aircraft, civilian: benefited substantially from the technological innovations and developments which took place during *World War I.* Amalgamated from a number of small, independent airlines, most of which had catered for very small, exclusive clientele, Imperial Airways began trading in 1924 and developed long-haul routes. In 1940 it was split into the British Overseas Airways Corporation (BOAC), which catered for long-distance flights, and the British European Airways (BEA). After *World War II,* civilian use of air transport increased spectacularly, boosted by rising *living standards* and longer, paid, holidays for working people. Package tours, particularly to southern European and North African coastal locations, provided new opportunities for ordinary people to travel long distances. Heavy competition between airlines in the 1960s and 1970s saw heavily discounted fares offered for travel to popular locations in the *United States.* Partly to meet this competition, BOAC and BEA merged in 1969 to form British Airways.

(See also *leisure.*)

aircraft, military: developed rapidly as a means of transport after the first air flight in Britain in 1908. Aircraft proved important in *World War I* when the Royal Flying Corps, founded in 1912, was responsible for defence. The RFC remained under the control of the army. Its successor body, the Royal Air Force, was founded in 1918 and operated as a separate service. Air power was decisive in *World War II,* not only in defending Britain against invasion during the *Battle of Britain,* but in a range of strategic and tactical roles as long-distance bombers, fighters and ground-attack aircraft. The advent of nuclear weapons from 1945 gave even greater strategic importance to military air forces, as carriers of the new weapons.

Alabama Claim: see *United States*

Alanbrooke, Viscount: British military strategist during *World War II.* He was born, as Alan Brooke, into a military family in 1883 and saw service in *World War I,* rising to the rank of Brigadier General. In World War II, he first commanded the *British Expeditionary Force (1940),* became Commander-in-Chief of Home Forces and, from November 1941, Chief of the Imperial General Staff until his retirement in 1946. He was appointed Field Marshal in 1944. A clear-headed strategist, he is credited with tempering some of *Winston Churchill*'s more impetuous ideas, including what would almost certainly have been a premature and futile invasion of France in 1942 or 1943.

(See also *D-Day; Montgomery, Bernard.*)

Albert, Prince: consort to Queen *Victoria.* He was born in 1819, the youngest son of the Duke of *Saxe-Coburg-Gotha,* and married Victoria in 1840. He was given the title Consort in 1842 and Prince Consort in 1857. A man of studious disposition and considerable ability, he gave the young Queen much political advice. He was on good terms with leading politicians, especially *Robert Peel,* but his political interests provoked adverse comment from those who felt he was infringing the constitutional boundaries between the throne and Parliament. Much of his later career was devoted to promoting learning and philanthropy. He was a leading organiser of the *Great Exhibition* in 1851 and did much to promote the development of the Museums of Science and Natural History in South Kensington. He died prematurely of typhoid in 1861. The Queen, who was devoted to him, withdrew into a long period of mourning, neglecting many of her duties.

(See also *monarchy.*)

Althorp, Viscount: *Whig* politician. Born in 1792, he served as Chancellor of the Exchequer in the governments of *Grey* (1830–34) and *Melbourne* in 1834. His succession to the Earldom of Spencer and departure from the Government was one of the reasons for *William IV*'s loss of confidence in Melbourne's government, leading to its dismissal in November 1834. Althorp supported *parliamentary reform* in 1830–32, while assuring the Commons that members elected under the new franchise would still predominantly represent the landed interest. He was a keen agricultural improver and became first President of the Royal Agricultural Society in 1838.

(See also *Liberal Party; Brougham, Henry.*)

Amiens, Battle of (8–12 August 1918): the decisive battle of *World War I* in which British and dominion troops under *Earl Haig,* using tanks, defeated German troops, ending the last German offensive and precipitating a rapid Allied advance which caused Germany to sue for peace.

Amiens, Treaty of (1802): negotiated by *Addington*'s government, it ended the first phase of the wars between Britain and France and produced a truce, lasting for fourteen months, in the otherwise continuous wars of 1793–1814. The main terms were:

- with the exception of Trinidad and Ceylon, all naval conquests by Britain were returned to the powers (French, Spanish or Dutch) which held them at the beginning of the war
- Cape of Good Hope returned to the Dutch
- France agreed to evacuate southern Italy
- both Britain and France agree to quit Egypt, leaving it in Turkish control

(See also *French Revolutionary Wars; Napoleonic Wars.*)

Anderson, Elizabeth Garrett: pioneer woman doctor and politician. She was born in 1836 and qualified as the first woman medical practitioner in 1865. She opened a centre in Euston Road, London, where women and children could be treated. This became, as the Elizabeth Garrett Anderson Hospital, the first to employ only women doctors. She supported the cause of women's *suffrage* and, at Aldeburgh in 1908, became England's first woman mayor.

Andover Scandal: *Poor Law* scandal in Hampshire in 1846. Those opposed to the *Poor Law Amendment Act* of 1834 had been seeking evidence of the inhumanity which the new, centralised system engendered. This scandal proved ideal propaganda material. Harsh implementation of workhouse regulations by the Board of Guardians reduced paupers to gnawing bones. Revelation of the scandal led to the replacement of the Poor Law Commission in 1847 with a new Board more directly accountable to Parliament.

(See also *Poor Laws*.)

Anglo-American War, 1812–15: the last war between the two countries.

Causes of the War

- British reaction to the attempt by US ships to break its naval blockade of France
- border disputes between the United States and British Canada
- impressment of British sailors from US ships
- British support for Indians aiming to block US westward expansion

The main engagements of the War

1812   Britain captures Detroit and defeats a US force at *Queenston Heights*

1813   British prevent US from launching a decisive attack on Canada, but Commander Oliver Perry defeats and captures British ships on Lake Erie; British forces capture Fort Niagra

1814   British burn Washington DC after an attack from Maryland led by Admiral Cockburn and General Ross

1815   US repel British attack on New Orleans, a month after official peace between the two countries had been signed at *Ghent*

Throughout the war, the Americans proved vulnerable to attacks on their north-east coast but neither side could establish decisive advantage around the Great Lakes.

(See also *Napoleonic Wars*.)

Anglo-German naval agreement, 1935: an important element in Britain's developing strategy to appease Nazi Germany. By it, Germany was allowed to build up its navy to 35 per cent of the tonnage of Britain's and, thus, to evade the restrictions placed on it by the *Versailles* peace settlement. Rapid German naval rearmament followed.

(See also *World War II*)

Anglo-German rivalry, 1890–1914: a pronounced feature of the build up to *World War I*. After the Unification of Germany in 1871, the new nation state increasingly saw itself as a rival to Britain. The rivalry took four main forms:

1   **Industrial and commercial:** here Germany sought to exploit Britain's relative economic decline from the 1870s. Many in Britain felt that Germany was able to exploit superior natural resources and a more scientifically and technologically orientated education system to make inroads into Britain's early industrial supremacy. E E Williams's book 'Made in Germany' (1896) symbolised a growing British fear that the country was being outperformed.

2   **Naval:** Germany mounted an effective challenge to Britain's naval supremacy. The building of the Kiel Canal in 1895 gave German battleships a route between the Baltic and the North Sea and Germany diverted much of its defence expenditure towards the building of a large battle

fleet. In response, Britain launched its first *dreadnought* battleships in 1906. A naval race ensued between 1909 and 1912 in which Britain outperformed Germany by building eighteen battleships to Germany's nine. The rivalry continued into *World War I*.

3 **Imperial:** rivalry here was characterised by competition both for territory in Africa and for the support of native peoples, especially in the Congo and Niger regions. Germany sought territorial expansion in part to offset Britain's early colonial supremacy in Africa. The development of German East Africa, for example, was a direct challenge to Britain's colonial presence in the area.

4 **Diplomatic:** Germany's main concern as the dominant power in central Europe was to avoid the threat of encirclement. Attempts to build on the close blood ties between the royal families of the powers came to little, and from 1902 Britain was usually linked with France in *ententes* so as to counter what was perceived as the growing threat from Germany. A dispute between France and Germany over influence in Morocco developed into the full-blown crisis in 1911 when Britain, fearing that Germany would build a naval base at Agadir on the Moroccan coast, supported French claims and threatened war on Germany. While war was averted, the Agadir Crisis led to a close naval agreement between Britain and France, whereby, in any future war, the two nations would be allies, and their fleets would operate in the North Sea and Mediterranean respectively. This agreement represented a direct challenge to Germany and contributed substantially to the build-up of tension before World War I.

Anglo-Irish Treaty: agreement of December 1921. By it:

- the 26 counties of southern *Ireland* became a free state, with dominion status in the British Empire
- the six counties of modern *Ulster*, now called *Northern Ireland*, were given the right (which they exercised) to remain part of the United Kingdom

The treaty ended what had effectively been a war between Britain and Irish nationalists since 1919 and it brought to a conclusion more than half a century of pressure for *Home Rule*. The signing of any treaty owed much to the negotiating skills of the British *Prime Minister, David Lloyd George*. It was accepted by a narrow majority in the Irish dáil (parliament) but led almost immediately to civil war in Ireland (1922–23) between those who accepted the treaty as the best deal available and those who wished the struggle for a united Ireland to continue and therefore rejected it. The former were led by Michael *Collins*, one of its signatories, and the latter by Eamonn de Valera, later President of Ireland. In the 1930s, de Valera emphasised Ireland's separation from Britain. The 1937 Irish Constitution made the Irish Free State a virtual republic and gave it a free hand in foreign affairs, which it exercised by its neutrality in *World War II*.

(See also *Ireland; Ireland Act, 1949; Stormont.*)

Anti-Corn Law League: pressure group for the repeal of *Corn Laws* which restricted the importation of grain into Britain. Formed by businessmen in Manchester in 1838, it argued that trade restrictions hindered prosperity by artificially increasing the price of necessities and therefore restricting opportunities for consumers to buy manufactured goods. Behind this specific argument lay a general belief in the virtues of *free trade* as an economic philosophy. The League used its substantial resources to disseminate propaganda through lecture tours and newspapers, and attempted to secure the election of MPs who supported its arguments. It discovered that by-elections could focus attention effectively on a single issue. The journal 'The Economist' was founded in 1843 to convey the free trade message. Though the League had, in George Wilson, an organiser of genius, and in *Richard Cobden* and *John Bright* articulate and persuasive parliamentary supporters, the League did not directly bring about the repeal of the Corn Laws, which was a political decision taken by *Robert Peel* when the impact of the League was on the wane.

(See also *laissez-faire; Manchester school.*)

anti-slavery movement: pressure group to abolish first the trade in slaves in British ships, and second the institution of *slavery* in all British colonies. Though the conditions in which slaves were transported from Africa to the Americas were the subject of widespread inquiry and condemnation among humanitarians in the second half of the eighteenth century, the focus of pressure for change lay with Anglican evangelical reformers, who banded together in the so-called Clapham Sect. Leading figures were Henry Thornton, Isaac Milner and Charles Simeon, but the best-known advocate of the slaves' cause was *William Wilberforce*, a close friend of the *Younger Pitt*. Despite considerable opposition from commercial and colonial interests, legislation to prohibit the trade (1807) and the institution of slavery itself (The Emancipation Act, 1833) was passed by Whig governments receptive to public opinion on the issues.

(See also *slave trade, abolition of; slavery, abolition of.*)

Ánzio, Battle of (1944): important battle towards the end of *World War II*. It was begun by an amphibious landing 30 miles south of Rome and allied troops then engaged with German forces attempting to prevent them moving inland. The battle lasted from January to May when Allied success led directly to the capture of Rome in June.

appeasement: foreign policy strategy associated with the *National Governments* of *Stanley Baldwin* and *Neville Chamberlain* in the 1930s in their relations with the German and Italian dictators, Hitler and Mussolini. The policy involved making concessions in the face of aggression from the dictators. The two main reasons for the policy were:

1 an increasingly widespread feeling that the *Versailles* settlement ending *World War I* had been too harsh towards the defeated nations
2 a desire to avoid a renewal of war, particularly since World War I had been widely portrayed as a 'war to end wars'

Additionally, the Government knew that public opinion was opposed to a renewal of war, and political leaders, especially Chamberlain, believed that it was possible to reason, and reach agreements, with the dictators. The main occasions upon which appeasement, rather than confrontation, was the preferred policy were:

1935 the Italian invasion of Ethiopia
1935 German remilitarisation in contravention of the Versailles settlement

1936   German reoccupation of the Rhineland
1938   absorption of Austria into the German Reich
1938   German invasion of Czechoslovakia

The policy was abandoned only from the end of 1938. It excited enormous controversy at the time and has remained controversial among historians since. Appeasement was perceived to have failed when war broke out; anti-appeasers such as *Winston Churchill* appeared to have been vindicated in their argument that standing up to the dictators at an earlier stage would not only have averted *World War II* but would have confirmed the supremacy of Britain and France over Germany. Revisionist historians have argued, however, that appeasement was a rational strategy, particularly later in the 1930s. Not only was it an honourable attempt to avert the miseries of a war which would inevitably kill millions, but it bought the Allies time for rearmament in 1938–39. Britain was far less militarily prepared for a war over Czechoslovakia in 1938 than it was for one over Poland in 1939.

(See also *World War II; Halifax, 6th Earl of.*)

Applegarth, Robert: *trade union* leader. Born in 1834, he became leader of the Carpenters' Union in the 1850s. This union was typical of many so-called 'new-model' unions formed to protect the interests of skilled workers against both employers and 'dilution' from unskilled workers. Like other union leaders, Applegarth looked to the Liberal Party to increase the political representation of skilled men and supported the Reform League, formed to press for a new parliamentary Reform Act in the 1860s. He died in 1925.

apprenticeship: the period of training, usually of seven years' duration, in a particular skill or craft. Skilled craftsmen took on young people and provided training in return for payment: a 'premium'. Regulations governing apprenticeship and wage regulation were formulated by the *Statute of Artificers* (1563) and survived into the early nineteenth century, providing a legislative framework within which quality and training might be guaranteed. Such a closely regulated system of long-term training proved increasingly inimical to the recruitment and deployment of a mass workforce during the early stages of the Industrial Revolution. Evasion of the regulations became increasingly common in the later eighteenth century. In 1802, Parliament refused to uphold a petition from weavers in Yorkshire and the West of England to enforce regulations. In 1813 the wage-regulation and in 1814 the apprenticeship clauses of the Statute of Artificers were repealed. *Free trade* in labour thus pre-dated free trade in most goods.

Arch, Joseph: *trade union* leader. Born in 1826, he soon became critical of the Anglican-dominated hierarchy of rural society. He became a *Primitive Methodist* local preacher and in 1872 founded the National Agricultural Labourers' Union, the first attempt to organise a notoriously scattered and often deferential group of workers. An unsuccessful strike movement – the so-called *Revolt of the Field* – followed in 1874 which brought Arch to national prominence. Like most union leaders of his generation, he supported *Gladstonian liberalism* and became an MP for a Norfolk constituency in 1885. He died in 1919.

Arctic convoys: the means whereby the Allies supplied the Soviet Union with armaments during *World War II*. The convoys operated along a route north of Norway to

supply the ports of Murmansk and Archangel. They continued throughout the period of USSR participation in the war (1941–45) and provided approximately four
million tons of supplies. German attempts to cut off this lifeline produced much conflict and heavy loss of life among the British navy and merchantmen.

aristocracy: in nineteenth- and twentieth-century Britain, the description given to
landowners with hereditary titles. For much of the period, the aristocracy exercised
as much political power as social influence, passing that power and influence on to
their nearest relatives according to the principle of hereditary succession. Most members of the *House of Commons* until the 1880s were landowners and many of the most
successful were sons of peers. Aristocrats sat as 'peers of the realm' in the *House of
Lords*. Until 1911, the Lords could permanently block any legislation passed to it by
the House of Commons, and not infrequently did.

It is no exaggeration to say that late eighteenth- and early nineteenth-century Britain
was governed by not more than 200 landed families, many of which – like the Bed-
fords, Derbys and Devonshires – were immensely wealthy. The *Whig* Party, in
particular, was led by some of the richest men in England. The surviving symbols of
the social exclusivity which they enjoyed are the great palaces (Chatsworth, Castle
Howard, Kedleston, etc.) which they built or opulently extended in the eighteenth
and nineteenth centuries. Intermarriage between aristocratic families preserved
social exclusivity, although the British aristocracy was never a closed caste. Successful
soldiers (such as the *Duke of Wellington*), industrialists (Richard Arkwright and
William Armstrong) and diplomats (*Evelyn Baring*) could all be ennobled. Throughout
the nineteenth century, most *Cabinets* contained a clear majority of peers, rather than
commoners. A peer (the *Marquess of Salisbury*) was *Prime Minister* as late as 1902.
Though peers retain the right to sit in the House of Lords (a right which fewer regularly exercised by the late twentieth century), the unchallenged power of the
aristocracy did not survive the medium-term consequences of:

- the *Great Depression* of the last quarter of the nineteenth century, and
- the death duties and other taxes on wealth and high income imposed by
  the *Liberal Party* between 1894 and 1914

Such blows caused many to sell up at least part of their estates, retrench financially
and seek alternative sources of income. Many became increasingly involved in the
worlds of business and finance, in effect marketing their family names as evidence of
a firm's social, if not necessarily financial, soundness. Some recouped part of their
fortunes by making financially advantageous marriages to *United States* heiresses. During the twentieth century, the burden of keeping up massive properties became
insupportable. Many were given over to the *National Trust*. Others were opened to
public view and, not infrequently, vigorous commercial exploitation as theme or
amusement parks. In 1958, the Life Peerages Act undermined the hereditary principle by enabling leading citizens (mostly those nominated by political parties) to serve
in the Lords during their lifetimes. Since then, the great majority of peerage creations have been of life peers, although two successful Conservative *Prime Ministers*,
Harold Macmillan (1984) and *Margaret Thatcher* (1990) accepted increasingly anachronistic hereditary baronetcies.

aristocracy of labour: see *labour aristocracy*

Armstrong, William (1st Baron Armstrong of Cragside): inventor, entrepreneur and armaments manufacturer. One of the most successful businessman in late nineteenth-century Britain, he was born in Newcastle-on-Tyne in 1810 and pioneered new techniques of breech-loading guns which he marketed successfully during and after the *Crimean War*. He employed considerable business expertise in making himself the leading shipyard owner on the Tyne, specialising in producing warships. His firm profited enormously from the naval race between Britain and Germany at the end of the century. In the 1870s, he built a massive Gothic mansion at Cragside, 30 miles north-west of Newcastle, to which he retired and which he furnished with new electronic and telephonic technology, experimenting also with new forms of *water power*. He received his peerage in 1887 and died in 1900.

(See also *dreadnoughts; engineering industry; shipping industry.*)

Arnhem, Battle of (1944): battle towards the end of *World War II*. The Allies mounted the operation 'Market Garden' as a strategy to build a bridgehead across the Rhine two and a half months after the successful Normandy landings. Immediate success would almost certainly have shortened the war, probably ensuring that British and US troops, rather than Russian ones, reached Berlin first. However, despite massive air bombardment in what became the largest airborne battle in the war, German resistance proved very strong and the advance was delayed. British troops had to be evacuated and the main purpose of the engagement was frustrated.

Arnold, Matthew: educationist and critic. He was born, the son of *Thomas Arnold*, in 1822 and worked as an inspector of schools from 1851 to 1886. His working life was committed to an examination of culture and of the roles of education and reason in promoting appropriately critical attitudes. His 'Culture and Anarchy' (1869) offered trenchant criticisms of English life and attitudes, which he viewed as excessively materialistic. He died in 1888.

(See also *Arnold, Thomas.*)

Arnold, Thomas: educationist. Born in 1795, he is best known for his work as headmaster of Rugby School where he did much to reduce the brutality and philistinism of English public school life, offering in the process a model for many public school headmasters to follow as the number of such schools expanded in mid-Victorian Britain. Arnold's educational philosophy and methods were further publicised in the thinly veiled tribute 'Tom Brown's Schooldays' (1857). The school in Thomas Hughes's novel is Arnold's Rugby in all but name. Arnold died in 1842.

(See also *Arnold, Matthew; Clarendon Commission.*)

Arras, Battle of (1917): battle on the Western Front during *World War I* which lasted from 9 to 24 April. British and *Empire* forces under Edmund Allenby achieved some success against German troops but at substantial cost. The battle is best remembered for the Canadian troops' capture of Vimy Ridge.

'Arrow' War, 1856–60: see *Opium Wars*

Artificers' Statute, Repeal of (1813 and 1814): an important stage in the free movement and recruitment of labour during the early part of the Industrial Revolution. Tudor legislation (1563), which had empowered local magistrates to set wage levels and to regulate the supply of labour, had proved increasingly irksome to employers who wished to recruit workers in large numbers to do the kinds of tasks which did not require formal apprenticeship. After a long period during which the legislation was either evaded, ignored or actually repealed in respective of specific trades, the Tory government in 1813 repealed the wage-regulation, and in 1814 the apprenticeship, clauses of the Statute of Artificers. Skilled workers regarded this legislation, with some justice, as deeply injurious to their objectives of maintaining good wages and of restricting entry to trades to those who had been fully trained.

(See also *apprenticeship; labour aristocracy.*)

artisans: *skilled workers*, most of whom had received a formal seven-year *apprenticeship*. These skills had normally been rewarded in the eighteenth century with higher wages and greater job security but the Industrial Revolution posed new challenges in the form of mass recruitment, and thus skill 'dilution' and downward pressure on wages. Highly skilled, many artisans were also literate and increasingly politically aware. In late eighteenth and early nineteenth-century Britain, they were prominent in many radical movements, including the democratic agitation of the 1790s (often called 'artisan radicalism'), pressure for *parliamentary reform* from 1815 to 1832 and *Chartism.* The dominant occupation of the Chartist Conventions was *handloom weaver,* one of the trades most threatened by mechanisation and dilution. Some skills which remained unmechanised during the Industrial Revolution, such as those in building, *engineering* and quality clothing, continued to be well rewarded. These trades were the bedrock of the 'new-model' unionism of the 1850s and 1860s. Other erstwhile artisans, however, lost their privileged status at this time.

(See also *labour aristocracy; radicalism.*)

Artisans' and Labourers' Dwellings Act, 1875: social legislation passed during Disraeli's government of 1874–80. Like most such legislation in Victorian Britain, this was a permissive measure designed to improve the quality of *housing* for working people. Local authorities were given compulsory powers to remove slum dwellings. It had very limited impact, largely because the costs of slum clearance and rebuilding were so huge. *Joseph Chamberlain* used it in Birmingham to create impressive new commercial buildings in the town centre, but this only moved the housing problem a couple of miles away, rather than easing it. Only about one-eighth of the local authorities which could have made use of it chose to do so in the first ten years of operation.

(See also *Torrens Act, 1868.*)

Asquith, Herbert Henry (Earl of Oxford and Asquith): *Liberal* politician and *Prime Minister.* He was born in Yorkshire in 1852 into a family of small manufacturers in the *woollen industry.* He was educated at Oxford University, where he excelled. He then trained as a lawyer and practised as a barrister, becoming a Queen's Counsel in 1890. He always intended a political career, however, and, given his family background, it was natural that he would choose the *Liberal Party.* He became MP for East Fife in 1885 and remained so until defeat in the *general election* of 1918. He was returned for Paisley, which he represented from 1920 to 1924. His major offices were:

- Home Secretary, 1892–95
- Chancellor of the Exchequer, 1905–8

- *Prime Minister*, 1908–16
- Leader of the Liberal Party, 1908–26

He was a good speaker, possessed a mind of great clarity and was a master of detail. *Gladstone* offered him Cabinet office during his last government. With the Liberal Party out of office for ten years after 1895, and split on major issues, Asquith joined the 'imperialist' wing in supporting British involvement in the *Second Boer War*, thus distancing himself from the new leader *Campbell-Bannerman*. His stock in the party rose, however, as a result of his effective attacks on *Joseph Chamberlain* and the *tariff reform* campaign in the years 1903–5, and Campbell-Bannerman was happy to appoint him Chancellor of the Exchequer in his government. He was responsible for drafting the legislation on *old-age pensions*, but had become Prime Minister before it could be enacted. As Prime Minister, he encouraged younger *progressive Liberals* to develop their social reforms in what became a *radical* reforming government in both social and constitutional matters. He was also able to use his political skills and growing authority to keep more conservative figures from rebelling against the leadership at a time of industrial unrest, trouble over *Ireland* and *suffragette* disturbances.

He faced more serious challenges during *World War I*, at first from those *pacifists* in his party who opposed war on principle and later from those who wished to see it pursued more vigorously and more successfully. This led to a coup against him in December 1916 led by his coalition partners, *Bonar Law* and *Lloyd George*. Asquith continued to lead the Liberals outside the coalition but he was deeply bitter at the way he lost power. He continued his vendetta against Lloyd George into a full split at the end of the war, which led to the loss of his own seat and to the installation of the Labour Party as the official opposition from 1918. He persuaded his Liberal followers to support the Labour Party during its first period as a minority government. Having lost his seat in the election of 1924 his interest in politics waned. He accepted a peerage in 1925, finally resigned the Liberal leadership the following year and died in 1928.

Assisted Areas: places defined under the Special Areas Act, 1934 as having experienced particularly acute problems during the inter-war Depression. The Government provided a range of incentives for employers to invest and thus help to regenerate these areas. Most designated under the Act were textile, mining and shipbuilding areas. The policy had limited effect in the 1930s; rearmament at the end of the decade reduced unemployment much more substantially.

Association Football: popular spectator sport. Football had always been a popular pastime but the authorities in mid-Victorian Britain were concerned about the implications for public order of a contact game which had few rules. The development of professional Association Football began in the 1860s. Factors aiding professionalisation were:

- rapid urbanisation which aided the emergence of spectator loyalty
- the formulation of agreed rules and a structure of control to ensure that they were kept
- the development of Saturday half-holidays
- *railways*, which greatly facilitated rapid movement of teams to fixtures
- improved living standards in the last quarter of the nineteenth century, enabling more to pay to see games and some to travel to away fixtures

Many of the early professional teams grew out of amateur boys' clubs or Sunday school organisations. The main competitions in England, the FA Cup (first competed for in 1872) and the Football League (1888) drew large crowds. To the dismay of many who favoured 'rational recreation' some matches were affected by crowd disturbances and violence.

(See also *leisure; social control.*)

Astor, Nancy: *Conservative* politician. Born in the *United States* in 1879, her main claim to fame was that she was the first woman to take her seat as an MP. She did this in 1919 when she took over the constituency of Plymouth Sutton from her second husband, Waldorf Astor, who had inherited a baronetcy and was not permitted under legislation at that time to resign his peerage. She remained an MP until 1944, during which time she sponsored a range of social causes, including the regulation of drink and conditions of *women* and children. She was fiercely opposed to *divorce*. As a member of the *Cliveden Set* in the 1930s, she was strongly pro-*appeasement*. She served as Plymouth's Lord Mayor during *World War II* and died in 1964.

(See also *aristocracy.*)

Atlantic, Battle of the: naval conflict during *World War II*. The conventional title, which was coined by *Churchill* in 1941, is misleading. There was no one 'battle'; the description covers the attempt by the Allies to counter German naval strategy, which was to use 'U-boats' – submarines – and depth mines to stop supplies reaching Britain by sea. The conflict at sea, which lasted from 1940 to 1943, cost about 60,000 lives with roughly equal casualties on both sides, before the Allies, using sophisticated detection systems, fought off the threat from German sea power.

Atlantic Charter: Anglo-American declaration, signed during *World War II* at a secret meeting off Newfoundland in August 1941. The Charter's eight principles, agreed between President Roosevelt and *Winston Churchill*, were concerned with rights of national self-determination and the importance of democratic decision-making. Intended as a statement about post-war settlements, it had three important effects:

- it announced that Britain and the US remained committed to Woodrow Wilson's Fourteen Points of 1918
- although the US was not yet at war, the Charter implied severe criticism of totalitarian regimes
- statements about national self-determination could be read as critical of the continuation of foreign empires. It was heavily implicit (although Churchill denied this) that the US would not support the continuation of an extensive *British Empire* after the war ended

(See also *United States.*)

Attlee, Clement Richard: Labour politician and *Prime Minister*. He was born in 1883 and trained as a lawyer. His early professional life was spent in London, where he was influenced by Sidney and Beatrice Webb and by Fabian politics. He saw active service as an officer during *World War I*. He spent some time in local government before being elected as *Labour* MP for Limehouse in 1922. His major political offices were:

- Chancellor of the Duchy of Lancaster, 1930–31
- Postmaster General, 1931

- Leader of the Labour Party, 1935–55
- Deputy Prime Minister, 1940–45 (also Lord Privy Seal, 1940–42; Secretary of State for the Dominions, 1942–43; Lord President of the Council, 1943–45)
- Prime Minister, 1945–51

Attlee was not a demonstrative politician but a highly effective one. In one of his more spectacular misjudgements, *Winston Churchill* called him 'a modest little man with much to be modest about'. In reality, his downbeat personality and clipped upper-middle class tones concealed both a highly organised mind and steely resolve. He could be brutal in his treatment of those whom he judged, in his characteristic phrase, 'not up to it' but he was a shrewd judge of ministers whom, for the most part, he was happy to leave to discharge their departmental responsibilities. He led the *Labour Party* with distinction during a period of revival after the split of 1931 and held it together despite growing splits between left and right in the early 1950s. In between, he was a very capable deputy to Churchill, holding a succession of important departmental posts.

His reputation is most firmly based on his leadership of the Labour government which passed a succession of important welfare and nationalisation measures. That he got such diverse characters as *Stafford Cripps, Herbert Morrison* and *Aneurin Bevan* to work together in government says much in itself for his abilities, especially since they were operating during a period of severe economic stringency. He was also content for others to claim direct credit for the important reforms passed by his government. Despite less than total enthusiasm at the time, Attlee is now recognised as one of the two or three most impressive *prime ministers* of the twentieth century. He died in 1967.

(See also *National Insurance; nationalisation; welfare state; Wilson, Harold.*)

Attwood, Thomas: banker and political reformer. Born in 1783, his work in banking in Birmingham led him to oppose financial orthodoxy and argue that the issuing of paper currency – the so-called 'Brummagem remedy' – would enable credit to be given more readily, thus mitigating the effects of the frequent slumps in early industrial Britain. He is best known for his advocacy of a greatly increased franchise. He founded the Birmingham Political Union in early 1830, which engendered substantial pressure for *parliamentary reform,* and later, as MP for Birmingham which he represented in the reformed Parliament from 1832 to 1839, he presented the first Chartist petition. He died in 1856.

(See also *Chartism; Cobbett, William; free trade; radicalism.*)

Austen, Jane: novelist. She was born the daughter of a Hampshire rector in 1775 and developed into the most elegant and perceptive novelist of her age. Her novels, which include 'Pride and Prejudice' (1813), 'Emma' (1816) and 'Persuasion' (published posthumously 1818), are comedies of manners which offer ironic and informed analyses of landed and clerical society in the South of England. She painted on a small canvas and only wrote of what she directly knew, but her insights into society and its foibles are of timeless value.

(See also *aristocracy; Napoleonic Wars.*)

austerity: the policy of retrenchment pursued by *Attlee*'s Labour government from 1947 to 1950. It involved severe economic restriction, including:

- restraints on imports
- encouragement to exports, including a 30 per cent devaluation of the pound from $4.03 to $2.40
- even more severe rationing than during wartime

Consistent application of this policy by the Chancellor of the Exchequer, *Stafford Cripps*, combined with the *United States* Marshall Plan from 1948, ensured that the economy remained stable, but almost certainly at the cost of severe loss of electoral popularity.

Australia: successively part of the *British Empire* and *Commonwealth.* The east coast of Australia was discovered by Captain Cook in 1770 and New South Wales developed from 1788, first as a penal colony for those serving terms of transportation. More than 50,000 convicts were living in Australia by 1830. Economic development of the continent, which rapidly marginalised the indigenous Aboriginal population, was dependent on sheep and, increasingly from the 1850s, gold. Other states developed – Tasmania (1812), Western Australia (1827), South Australia (1834), Victoria (1851), Queensland (1858). Under legislation passed in 1850, most states could choose their own form of internal government.

A federal system was created in 1900 by the Australian Commonwealth Act, which also established Canberra as the country's new capital. Australian soldiers played a prominent part during the *Second Boer War* and both World Wars, emphasising the strength of the imperial link. Until the second half of the twentieth century it continued to attract large numbers of British migrants but the country has looked increasingly to the Pacific, and particularly to the states of South-East Asia, both for immigrants and for its wider economic and social development. Although an important part of the British Commonwealth, with the British monarch as its official head of state, many in Australia have argued that recent politico-economic developments suggest that the country should become a republic in the twenty-first century.

(See also *imperialism; monarchy; Wakefield, Edward Gibbon; World War I; World War II.*)

autodidacticism: a form of self-education, especially common in Victorian Britain. Since opportunities for working people to receive formal education in the nineteenth century were so sparse, many literate artisans placed their faith in improving their own knowledge and understanding. They were voracious consumers of the books and newspapers housed in the new *public libraries* for books and newspapers. Throughout the century, autodidacticism went hand in hand with artisan radicalism, and many self-taught men became *Chartist* leaders and trade unionists. It was a central plank in the culture of self-improvement which fell out of fashion in the second half of the twentieth century.

(See also *radicalism; skilled workers; trade unions.*)

B-specials: part-time branch of the *Ulster Special Constabulary*. They were founded by *Lloyd George* in 1920 as a Protestant vigilante group in *Ulster* during the conflict which preceded the Anglo-Irish Treaty. This strongly loyalist element created great hostility within the *Catholic* community which saw them as symbolic of the strong anti-Catholic prejudices which ensured religious discrimination in Northern Ireland after partition. They took action against Catholics in Belfast and Londonderry when violence flared again in 1968, were considered too provocative by the British government and disbanded in 1969.

(See also *Ireland; Northern Ireland; O'Neill, Terence.*)

Baden-Powell, Robert: founder of the Boy Scout and Girl Guide movement. He was born in 1857 and trained as a soldier, seeing service in *India* and during the *Second Boer War*, where he defended *Mafeking* in 1899–1900. Both the Boy Scout (founded 1908) and Girl Guide (1909) movement, which stressed uniforms as necessary dress, placed emphasis upon the development of individual self-reliance, group responsibility and patriotism. With his wife, he established scout and guide camps. Under his leadership, scouting became internationalised as the most famous youth movement of the first half of the twentieth century. He died in 1941.

(See also *Empire, British.*)

Baird, John Logie: inventor. A Scot, born in 1888, his scientific career was devoted to the transmission of live pictures. He gave a demonstration of '*television*' in London in 1926. His system used a revolving disc. Commercial exploitation of television in the 1930s, however, depended upon the development of the cathode-ray tube. He died in 1946.

(See also *leisure.*)

Balaclava, Battle of: battle during the *Crimean War*. This engagement, on 25 October 1854, is mostly remembered as the occasion of the famous *Charge of the Light Brigade* when, after misinterpreting an order from his superior officer, the *Earl of Cardigan* launched a doomed attack on the main body of Russian guns. The battle was begun by the Russians in an attempt to relieve the British siege of Sebastopol.

(See also *Raglan, Baron; Tennyson, Alfred.*)

balance of payments: measure which shows the respective value of exports and imports. A balance of payments surplus is earned if the value of exports exceeds that of imports. Though a technical calculation by economists, it has sometimes – as in the 1960s and 1970s – had political significance since it can be taken as a rough indicator of economic performance. In terms of movement of goods in and out, Britain usually had a negative balance at a time when it was widely regarded as possessing the strongest economy in the world. This was explained by the growing need for imports of both food and raw materials and was anyway offset by large credits from shipping and the sale of insurance – the so called 'invisible exports'. During the twentieth century, and particularly since 1939, Britain has experienced some exceptionally high adverse balances as its relative position in world markets has weakened.

(See also *economic policy; laissez-faire; overseas trade; Wilson, Harold.*)

Baldwin, Stanley (1st Earl): *Conservative* politician and *Prime Minister*. Born in Bewdley, Worcestershire, he made a considerable fortune as an iron and steel manufacturer before becoming an MP in 1908. His major offices were:

- President of the Board of Trade, 1921–22
- Chancellor of the Exchequer, 1922–23
- Leader of the Conservative Party, 1923–37
- Lord President of the Council, 1931–35
- Prime Minister, 1923, 1924–29, 1935–37

He had limited ministerial experience when he became Prime Minister and this, combined with a lack of oratorical flair, gave an impression of the benign, commonsensical country gentleman in politics. He cultivated this image carefully, especially through *radio* broadcasts at which he quickly made himself more expert than any political contemporary. In truth, he was a shrewd operator and ruthless when he needed to be. He plotted successfully to remove *Lloyd George* in 1922, provided unflinching opposition to the *General Strike* in 1926, played a significant role in the formation of the *National Government*, and briskly outmanoeuvred *Edward VIII* during the *Abdication Crisis*. He did not understand economics, however, and quietly went along with treasury orthodoxy on economic and *unemployment* policy. He was also one of the earliest, and most influential, advocates of *appeasement*. He was not to be underestimated but he lacked both the breadth of vision and the clarity of purpose to be a great Prime Minister. He died in 1947.

(See also *Bonar Law, Andrew; Churchill, Winston; economic policy; MacDonald, Ramsay*.)

Balfour, Arthur (1st Earl): *Conservative* politician and *Prime Minister*. He was born in East Lothian (Scotland) in 1848 and was the nephew of the *Marquess of Salisbury*, whom he succeeded as Prime Minister. He first became an MP in 1874 and his major political offices were:

- Chief Secretary for Ireland, 1887–91
- Prime Minister, 1902–5
- Leader of the Conservative Party, 1902–11
- Foreign Secretary, 1916–19
- Lord President of the Council, 1925–29

His prime ministership was wracked by deep divisions within the *Conservative Party* over whether *free trade* or *imperial preference* should be the preferred *economic policy*. Although he persuaded *Joseph Chamberlain* to quit the Cabinet, he was unable to provide sufficiently strong leadership. The *Education Act*, 1902 passed by his government also proved highly controversial because it seemed to favour the *Church of England*'s interests over those of *nonconformity*. In 1906, under his leadership, the Conservative Party suffered an election defeat larger than any other in the twentieth century except that of *John Major* in 1997.

He became Foreign Secretary in *Lloyd George*'s wartime Cabinet government, but gave up active domestic politics when the war ended. Intellectually extremely able, he often gave the impression that he regarded politics less seriously than most of his contemporaries and preferred thinking to administration and government. He died in 1930.

(See also *Balfour Declaration*.)

Balfour Declaration, 1917: declaration of support by the British government for a Jewish national home in *Palestine*. It was made during *World War I* in the form of a letter to the British *Zionist* leader Lord Rothschild. The Declaration became particularly important when Britain was granted the League of Nations mandate to govern Palestine after 1918. Many Jews settled there in the expectation than an independent Jewish state would rapidly be established.

Ballot Act, 1872: instituted a secret ballot at parliamentary elections. Introduced by *Gladstone*'s *Liberal* government, it was designed to put an end to the undue political influence exercised particularly by landlords over their tenants. Most landowners voted *Conservative*. The Act was the second of the *Chartists*' 'Six Points' to be enacted, although it did not put an immediate end to illegitimate influence.

(See also *parliamentary reform; Reform Act, 1867*.)

Bamford, Samuel: *radical*, skilled weaver, poet and journalist. Born in Middleton, Lancashire in 1788, he was an active supporter of *parliamentary reform* and was arrested, along with *Henry Hunt*, in the wake of the *Peterloo Massacre* in 1819, spending a year in prison. His subsequent career was more in journalism, written from a Lancashire base, than in active political agitation. He was suspicious of *Chartism* and hostile to the so-called 'physical-force' men. His autobiography 'Passages in the Life of a Radical' (1841–42) and 'Early Days' (1848–49) give a vivid and sympathetic insight into the life and politics of the weaving communities of Lancashire during the early part of the *Industrial Revolution*. In the 1850s he worked for the Inland Revenue in London, before retiring to Lancashire. He died in 1872.

(See also *parliamentary reform*.)

Bank Charter Act, 1844: measure introduced by *Peel*'s government to increase confidence in the national financial system. By it:

- the *Bank of England* was given dominant powers to issue bank notes
- the Bank's note-issuing powers could not exceed by more than £14m the amount which could be backed by the Bank's reserves of gold. This restriction controlled the money supply
- newly established banks were not permitted to issue their own promissory notes

This monetarist policy did increase confidence but was not proof against severe financial crises in Victorian Britain, especially those in 1847, 1857 and 1866–67.

(See also *economic policy; monetarism*.)

Bank of England: founded in 1694 to help fund England's wars against France, it developed during the eighteenth century by buying government stock and issuing promissory notes ('Bank notes') on the security of these stocks. From 1697 to 1826, it had monopoly status as a joint-stock bank (i.e. a bank in which capital stock is held by people jointly). During the nineteenth century, its status as the central Bank was confirmed, especially after 1833 when its notes were designated as legal tender. It increasingly acted as banker both to the Government and to other banks, managing gold and convertible currency reserves and also the National Debt. The Bank was nationalised by the *Labour government* in 1946.

Bank policy has nearly always erred on the side of financial caution which in the second half of the twentieth century has led to conflict with leading politicians, notably the Chancellor of the Exchequer. It was to reduce the possibility of this that the Labour Chancellor, Gordon Brown, gave the Bank unfettered control over interest rates in 1997.

(See also *Bank Charter Act, 1844; economic policy.*)

Baring, Sir Evelyn (1st Earl of Cromer): diplomat and colonial administrator. He was born into the famous banking family in 1841 but is best known for his rule of Egypt as Consul-General in the years 1883–1907. He restored Egypt's finances and was instrumental in resolving conflicts between Britain and France in North Africa at the end of the century. He received a barony in 1892, an earldom in 1901 and the Order of Merit in 1906. He wrote 'Modern Egypt', a substantial study of the country he knew so well, in 1908. Afflicted by ill-health for the last decade of his life, he died in 1917.

(See also *Empire, British; Scramble for Africa.*)

Barnardo, Thomas: philanthropist. Born in 1845, he trained as a doctor and became increasingly concerned with the problems of poverty. He founded the first of a number of children's orphanages, which became known as Barnardo's Homes, in Stepney in 1870. He died in 1905.

(See also *Hill, Octavia; social policy.*)

Barnett, Henrietta: social reformer. Born Henrietta Rowland in 1851, her early career was much influenced by *Octavia Hill*'s work among the London poor in Marylebone. Most of her work was with her husband Samuel and aimed at improving housing conditions in London. She founded the Hampstead Garden Suburb project as a means of improving mutual understanding between rich and poor. She was also active as a *Poor Law* guardian, in which capacity she took an increasing interest in educational provision for the poor. Like most social reformers of her generation, she believed in improving the poor by persuading them to adopt the habits of the socially concerned better off. Much support was linked to monitoring of behaviour. She died in 1936.

(See also *Barnett, Samuel; social policy.*)

Barnett, Samuel: social reformer. He was born in 1844 and was ordained into the *Church of England*. He married Henrietta Rowland in 1873 and the couple founded Toynbee Hall in 1844. This 'university settlement' was developed to enable socially concerned university graduates to live among, learn about and thus aim to improve the living conditions of, the poor. He and his wife also helped to develop the East End Dwellings Company which rehoused the poor from slum dwellings. He became Canon of Westminster Cathedral and died in 1906.

(See also *Hill, Octavia; housing; social policy.*)

Barry, Sir Charles: architect. Born in 1795, he developed into the most fashionable architect of the early Victorian period, designing the new Houses of Parliament to replace those destroyed by fire in 1834. He began work on this project in 1837 and it was finished seven years after his death. He also designed the Covent Garden Opera House (1858) which, together with several country houses on which he worked, showed the influence of the Italianate style.

Beatles, The: popular music group active in the 1960s. Comprising John Lennon, Paul Macartney, George Harrison and Ringo Starr, this band achieved unprecedented success on both sides of the Atlantic between 1962 and 1969, becoming the first British rock or pop group to exert influence in the highly commercial *United States* popular music market. The success of their distinctive 'Liverpool sound' made them enormously wealthy and also icons of popular culture. Both their influence and their popularity endured through their recordings for the remainder of the twentieth century.

(See also *popular culture; Rolling Stones.*)

Beaverbrook, Baron: *newspaper* proprietor and politician. Born Maxwell Aitken in Canada in 1879, he lived largely in Britain from 1910, becoming a *Conservative* MP in the same year. He made a fortune as owner of the 'Daily Express'. He used his newspapers to campaign for a series of right-wing causes, notably imperial *free trade* and defence of the *Empire* against *decolonisation* in the 1940s and 1950s. In politics during wartime, he proved both a galvanic influence and an effective administrator, working harmoniously with his friend *Winston Churchill.* His main offices were:

- Minister of Information, 1918
- Minister of Supply, 1941–42
- Minister of Production, 1942–43
- Lord Privy Seal, 1943–45

He died in 1964.

(See also *World War II.*)

Bedchamber Crisis: political crisis over a proposed change of ministry in 1839. When *Melbourne* resigned, *Peel* at first agreed to head a Conservative government. He asked for certain ladies at Queen *Victoria*'s court whose husbands were well-known Whigs to be replaced, but the Queen refused. Peel, in turn, refused to form a government since he regarded her decision as an indication of her lack of confidence in the new ministers. The Whigs returned to office.

(See also *Conservative Party; Whig Party.*)

Beecham, Sir Thomas: musician. He was born in Lancashire in 1879 into a family which had made its fortune by manufacturing proprietary medicines. He was Artistic Director of the Royal Opera House in 1933 and founded the Royal Philharmonic Orchestra in 1946. A man of sharp wit and intuitive musical skill, he had a special affinity for the music of *Frederick Delius.* He died in 1961.

Beeching Report: proposals for reducing Britain's *railway* network. The report was written by the Chairman of the British Railways Board, Lord Beeching, published in 1963 and implemented by both Conservative and Labour governments during the remainder of the decade. The so-called Beeching Axe closed many lines, reducing the railway mileage by about 20 per cent and the number of stations by a third. Though widely condemned as too destructive, the proposals did lead to the creation of a network of high-speed 'Inter-City' trains. Overall, however, the report symbolises the defensiveness of the railway network against the increasingly powerful challenge from roads and especially from the new *motorways.*

Beeton, Isabella: writer on cookery. Born in 1837, her reputation is based almost entirely on her cookery manual, 'Mrs Beeton's Book of Household Management'

(1861), which contained 3,000 recipes, explained in simple terms. The book, which first appeared in serial form in a woman's magazine, has remained continuously in print. She died at the age of 28 in 1865.

Bell, Alexander Graham: inventor. Born in 1847 and educated in Edinburgh, he emigrated to Canada before settling in Boston, Massachusetts. His work with the deaf led him to pioneer a system of communication. This led to work on the telephone, and he took out a patent on his invention in 1876.

Benn, Tony: *Labour* politician and diarist. Born Anthony Wedgwood-Benn into an upper-middle class family in 1925, and educated at public school and Oxford, his career has been increasingly on the extreme left of British politics. His campaign against moving to the *House of Lords* when he inherited his father's peerage in 1961 led to the passage of the Peerage Act, 1963 by which peers were enabled to renounce their titles. He was a prominent member of all the Labour governments of the 1960s and 1970s, for most of which time he was not known for left-wing views. His major offices were:

- Postmaster General, 1964–66
- Minister of Technology, 1966–70
- Secretary for Industry, 1974–75
- Secretary for Energy, 1975–79

After Labour's defeat in 1979, he led a left-wing challenge calling for the party to adopt fully socialist policies. His great energies and effective oratory were effective in mobilising support but they also precipitated a Labour split, when some important right-wingers left to form the Social Democratic Party. He was much pilloried in the right-wing press as a dangerous extremist. *Harold Wilson*, no admirer of his move to the left, waspishly remarked of him that he had 'immatured with age'. His political diaries, transcripts of tapes recorded at the end of the working day, have provided an extraordinarily detailed commentary on politics in the later twentieth century.

(See also *socialism.*)

Bentham, Jeremy: political philosopher. Born in 1748, he trained as a lawyer and wrote many works calling for a reform and rationalisation of the complexities of English law. He wrote an 'Introduction to the Principles of Morals and Legislation' in 1789 and 'Constitutional Code' (1827–30). He is best known for developing utilitarianism, a political philosophy which judged systems by their practical utility. Bentham influenced many important political thinkers and administrators in the nineteenth century, notably *David Ricardo, John Stuart Mill* and *Edwin Chadwick.* The controversial *Poor Law Amendment Act* of 1834 was an attempt to put *utilitarian* principles into practice. University College London, where Bentham's preserved body remains on display, was founded to put his educational ideas into practice. He died in 1832.

(See also *laissez-faire.*)

Berlin, Congress of: the peace settlement of 1878 which ended the Russo-Turkish war of 1877–78. Its importance for Britain concerns the country's long-standing fears of Russian expansionism and the need to protect commercial interests in North Africa, especially the *Suez Canal.* Britain therefore sought to bolster the Turks against the Russians. Although the Russians had won the war, combined Austro-British diplomatic activity, co-ordinated by *Benjamin Disraeli,* ensured that the Russians gained little benefit. Britain acquired *Cyprus* as a useful Mediterranean base from which to help the Turks if necessary. Disraeli famously called the settlement 'peace with honour'.

(See also *Salisbury, Marquess of.*)

A BLAZE OF TRIUMPH!

Punch *comments on the Congress of Berlin.*

Besant, Annie: social reformer and secularist. Born in 1847, she co-edited 'The National Reformer' with the atheist *Liberal* MP *Charles Bradlaugh* in the 1870s. Their book on methods of birth control was hugely controversial and both were convicted of obscenity. She joined the Fabian Society in 1885 and was the main organiser of the *Match Girls' Strike* three years later. She emigrated to *India*, where she worked with nationalists in calling for independence. She died in 1933.

(See also *birth control.*)

Bevan, Aneurin: *Labour* politician. Born in South Wales in 1897 he followed his father into the coal mines, first making a name for himself as a *trade unionist*. Becoming Labour MP for the mining constituency of Ebbw Vale in 1929, he rose to become one of the most charismatic and creative politicians of his generation. His passionate oratory, both in the *Commons* and at public meetings, was justly celebrated. He piloted through the Commons legislation which led to the establishment of the *National Health Service* in 1948 and resigned from the *Cabinet* when the Labour government introduced the first charges for prescriptions in 1951. He led the left wing of the party in opposition after 1951, failing to defeat *Gaitskell* for the party leadership in 1955. He became deputy leader in 1959 and led a crusade to commit the Labour Party to the abolition of nuclear weapons. His major offices were:

- Minister of Health, 1945–51
- Minister of Labour, 1951

He died in 1960.

(See also *Attlee, Clement; National Insurance Act, 1946; Wilson, Harold.*)

Beveridge Report: report on Social Insurance and Allied Services, 1942. This proved one of the most influential *social policy* documents of the twentieth century. It was produced by a committee of leading civil servants, asked to enquire into the workings of the existing system and make recommendations for rationalisation and improvement. The report identified five evils: want, ignorance, disease, squalor and idleness, and recommended the implementation of a 'comprehensive policy of social progress' to cope with them. This would include a compulsory system of state insurance (to which employers and employees contributed as well as the State) to cover sickness, unemployment, retirement pensions and support for young families. While the scheme represented a radical extension of earlier policies, it sustained the basic principle of state insurance which had been in operation since 1911.

The report became a best-seller but compromises on important details had to be made before the wartime coalition government incorporated most of its recommendations into a White Paper in 1944. The *Labour* government then produced the *National Insurance Act* of 1946 which is normally seen as marking the origins of the *welfare state*.

(See also *Attlee, Clement; Bevan, Aneurin; Beveridge, William; social policy.*)

TACKLING THE FIRST GIANT

" WANT is only one of the five giants on the road of reconstruction " — T h e Beveridge Report.

Cartoon published in the 'Daily Herald', 2 December, 1942

Beveridge, William: economist and social reformer. Born in 1879, he produced an influential study of *unemployment* in 1909 which argued that unemployment frequently resulted from structural imbalances in the economy rather than individual failings. He thus challenged a central tenet of Victorian belief about *social policy*. He was Director of the Labour Exchanges scheme instituted by the Liberal government, a post he held from 1909 to 1916. Most of his subsequent career was in academic life as Director of the London School of Economics (1919–37) and Master of University College, Oxford (1937–44). He was the author of the *Beveridge Report* (1942). His political beliefs were always *Liberal* and he represented the party in Parliament in 1944–45. He died in 1963.

(See also *Asquith, H H; Attlee, Clement; Bevan, Aneurin; Churchill, Winston; Lloyd George, David; welfare state.*)

Bevin, Ernest: *trade unionist* and *Labour* politician. Born in Somerset in 1881, he left school at the age of eleven. He first came to prominence as a member of the Dockers' Union working in Bristol. From 1922 to 1940 he was General Secretary of the newly amalgamated Transport and General Workers' Union and helped both organise and settle the *General Strike*. As a right-wing Labour MP, he opposed *communist* influence both in the party and trade unions. He also strongly criticised *Ramsay MacDonald*'s governments of 1929–31 and 1931–35 for failing to tackle *unemployment*. His organisational skills brought him to *Winston Churchill*'s attention and he served in his War Cabinet. Under *Attlee*, he became a distinguished Foreign Secretary. He was instrumental in the development of NATO as a counterweight to the growing influence of the Soviet Union and in 1950 he ensured that Britain recognised the People's Republic of China, though he was against *United States* policy. His major offices were:

- Minister of Labour and for National Service, 1940–45
- Foreign Secretary, 1945–51
- Lord Privy Seal, 1951

He died in 1951.

(See also *Morrison, Herbert.*)

Birkbeck, George: pioneer adult educationist. Born in Yorkshire in 1776 he practised as a physician before developing his interest in education for working people. He worked as a Professor of Philosophy in Glasgow where he gave free lectures to adult workers. He founded the London *Mechanics' Institute* in 1824 which later retained its distinctive adult education focus as Birkbeck College of London University. He died in 1841.

(See also *Workers' Educational Association.*)

birth control: although a number of methods of 'natural' birth control, including delayed marriage and extended lactation, were practised from early times, and the upper classes used various forms of primitive sheath in the eighteenth century, widespread use of 'barrier' methods in British society developed only in the nineteenth century. The application of vulcanised rubber enabled condoms to be used from the second half of the century, particularly by the middle and upper classes. Early pioneers of birth control methods were the rationalists *Charles Bradlaugh* and *Annie Besant* in the 1870s and 1880s and, in the early twentieth century, *Marie Stopes*, whose 'Wise Parenthood' (1918) gave precise details of a variety of methods. Stopes also inaugurated the first birth control clinics in the 1920s. The army issued condoms to troops in *World War I* as a protection against venereal disease. Greater knowledge from this source greatly increased the use of sheaths between the wars. Women also began to use pessaries and later the inter-uterine coil. The development of the contraceptive pill in the 1960s revolutionised birth-control practice and helped significantly to reduce the birth rate.

Black and Tans: colloquial name given to the additional recruits to the Royal Ulster Constabulary enlisted by the *United Kingdom* government in the years 1920–22. Most of these recruits were demobilised soldiers and their frequently brutal methods in support of the Protestant majority in *Ulster* provoked much retaliatory violence and contributed to a heightening of tension in *Ireland* before the *Anglo-Irish Treaty* of 1921 was signed. The force was disbanded immediately after the signing of this treaty.

(See also *Ireland; Northern Ireland; Ulster Special Constabulary.*)

Blair, Tony: *Labour* politician and *Prime Minister.* Born in 1953, he trained for the law and qualified in 1976. He became MP for Sedgefield (County Durham) in 1983 and joined the Shadow Cabinet in 1988. He held energy, employment and home affairs portfolios before being elected leader of the party after the sudden death of *John Smith* in 1994. He both inherited, and accelerated, the programme of modernisation and reform begun by Kinnock and Smith, offering to the electorate in 1997 a 'New Labour' programme which most saw as directly critical of 'Old Labour' with its strong *trade union* links and its commitment to *socialism.* A persuasive speaker with an engagingly direct personality, he was perhaps the ideal leader to take on a tired and divided *Conservative Party* on the defensive after policy failures and tainted with sleaze and sexual scandals. He became Prime Minister in May 1997 after the Labour Party gained an overall *general election* majority of 177.

Blake, William: artist, poet and visionary. He was born into a prosperous London trading family in 1757 and studied at the Royal Academy. His verses 'Songs of Innocence' (1789) and 'Songs of Experience' (1794) conveyed strong moral messages which developed in later writings into an extended critique both of conventional morality and conservative politics. His writings and engravings conveyed powerful messages about the evils of industrialism. His most famous poem, 'Jerusalem', argues the need to fight 'the dark satanic mills' which besmirch 'England's green and pleasant land'. The strangeness and power of his imagery became increasingly influential. He died in 1827.

(See also *Industrial Revolution.*)

Blanketeers, March of: name given to a peaceful protest movement by Lancashire weavers who intended to march to London in 1817 to petition the Prince Regent against *unemployment* and low wages in their trade. They were so called because of the blankets they carried with them for warmth. The local yeomanry, fearful of more widespread political disturbance, forcibly halted their march at Stockport.

(See also *handloom weavers; Hunt, Henry; Industrial Revolution; parliamentary reform.*)

Blitz, the: name conventionally given to the air raids by German bombers during *World War II.* It is frequently narrowed to describe the concentrated raids on major British cities, especially London, Liverpool, Manchester and Coventry, between September 1940 and April 1941. Although Hitler lavished large resources on a concerted bombing campaign against civilians, and although these did lower the morale of shattered cities much more than was admitted at the time, the full impact of the raids was reduced by the use of radar by RAF night fighters and by the effectiveness of air raid precautions, including Anderson shelters. The Blitz failed in its main objective which was to shorten the war.

(See also *aircraft*.)

Bloody Sunday, 13 November 1887: name given to the consequence of forcible break-up by the authorities of a protest rally against *unemployment* organised by *socialists* and *trade unionists* in Trafalgar Square, London. Both police and military were involved; one person was killed and several injured. The action failed to halt the growth of trade unionism and probably acted as an incentive to the development of more unions of unskilled workers from 1888 onwards.

(See also *new unions*.)

Bloody Sunday, 30 January 1972: name given to the consequence of the Government's banning of a protest by *Roman Catholic* workers and nationalists in Londonderry. The army, believing itself to be under attack by nationalist snipers, opened fire, killing thirteen civilians and injuring seventeen more. The action destroyed any remaining faith in the British troops and British government by the Catholic minority in *Northern Ireland* and almost certainly stimulated a growth in sectarian violence. The action was also an important factor in the *Conservative* government's decision to suspend the Protestant-dominated Northern Ireland parliament (*Stormont*) and impose direct rule.

(See also *Ireland; Irish Republican Army; Ulster*.)

Bloomsbury Group: collective name for the writers and intellectuals who met and lived near the British Museum in the Bloomsbury area of London, especially during the first 30 years of the twentieth century. Prominent among them were the novelist *Virginia Woolf*, the essayist *Lytton Strachey* and the economist *John Maynard Keynes*. They espoused no clear ideology, though almost all were left of centre in their political views. Many were unorthodox in their sexual activities and preferences, despising conventional morality as confining and Philistine. They were influential in developing the idea that the Victorian period was vulgar, materialistic and derivative.

Blue Books: collective, colloquial name given to published parliamentary papers incorporating the results of enquiries of parliamentary committees in the nineteenth century. Though the enquiries covered a huge range of subjects, the Blue Books are most associated with enquiries into Victorian social issues, such as *factory conditions, public health* and *education*.

bluestocking: colloquial, and mildly derogatory, name given to women of an intellectual, studious or aesthetic disposition. It was first used to describe the circle of women students and admirers who clustered around the writer and social reformer Elizabeth Montagu in the 1750s and came into widespread use at the end of the eighteenth century.

(See also *Women, legal status of*.)

board schools: name given to elementary schools created under the Liberal Education Act of 1870 and controlled by directly elected local boards. Similar legislation brought board schools to Scotland in 1872. Board schools were designed to 'fill up the gaps' left by voluntary provision and aimed to give working-class children a decent, if basic, education. They received government grants but were also support-ed by local ratepayers. The quality of education in board schools varied, but some progressive authorities, especially in London, used ratepayers' money to build schools in the 1870s and 1880s which offered a more extensive education than the Government had intended. Widely seen as a threat to *Church of England* 'national' schools, they were abolished by the Conservative government's *Education Act of 1902* which transferred responsibility for elementary education to *county councils*.

(See also *Conservative Party; Liberal Party; state education.*)

Boer War, First: fought in *South Africa* in 1880–81 between British troops and farmer-settlers, mainly of Dutch descent, in the Transvaal. The Boers, who had rebelled against British rule, defeated a British force at Majuba Hill in February 1881 and *Gladstone* with-drew British forces. The Convention of Pretoria (1881) effectively granted the Boers in the Transvaal independence, although the British continued to claim 'suzerainty'.

(See also *Boer War, Second.*)

Boer War, Second: fought in South Africa between the British and the Boers in 1899–1902. The background to this war was the discovery of extensive goldfields in the Transvaal in 1886. British determination to win back control increased and *Cecil Rhodes* plotted in the 1890s to overthrow its government. When war began, the Boers invaded Cape Colony and Natal, besieged Mafeking, Kimberley and Ladysmith and inflicted defeats on the British at Magersfontein and Colenso in December 1899. After the appointment of Field Marshal Frederick Roberts as Commander-in-Chief and *H H Kitchener* as Chief of Staff, the British mounted successful counter-offensives, and the relief of Mafeking in May 1900 produced scenes of great rejoicing in Britain.

The war was brought to a successful conclusion by the Treaty of Vereeniging (May 1902), whereby the Boer Republics were absorbed into the *British Empire*. The British gave guarantees of eventual self-government which were honoured when the Union of *South Africa* was granted dominion status in 1910. Though eventually successful, the war brought considerable embarrassments for Britain. It took a considerable time for overwhelming numerical superiority to have its effect and British victory owed much to the contribution of white colonial troops. The war suggested the need for army reforms. Also, Kitchener's use of concentration camps to house Boer guerilla troops attracted widespread criticism because of the poor conditions and high mor-tality rate among his captives.

(See also *Rhodesia; Scramble for Africa.*)

Bonar Law, Andrew: *Conservative* politician and *Prime Minister*. He was born in *Canada* in 1858 of Northern Irish and Scottish emigrant parents. He settled in Scot-land from 1874 and worked in the family iron business. He was first elected to Parliament in 1900 and came rapidly to prominence on the opposition benches after the Conservative defeat at the 1906 *general election*. His major offices were:

- Leader of the Conservative Party, 1911–21 and 1922–23
- Colonial Secretary, 1915–16
- Chancellor of the Exchequer and member of Lloyd George's War Cabinet, 1916–18
- Prime Minister, 1922–23

As leader of the opposition, he proved himself a tough debater and especially vigorous in the defence of Protestants in *Ulster* and against *Home Rule*. He successfully reunited the party. He became Prime Minister after agreeing to lead a backbench *Conservative* revolt against the post-war *Lloyd George* coalition. When he became Prime Minister, *Austen Chamberlain* and *Arthur Balfour*, leading Conservative coalition ministers, refused to serve under him. He won the general election of November 1922 but his brief tenure as Prime Minister was ended by ill health in March 1923. He died later the same year. Though his brief tenure of the highest office and his unusual colonial background have earned him the title 'The Unknown Prime Minister', Bonar Law achieved much. He helped to reunite the Conservative Party, winning first Lloyd George's grudging respect and later his enthusiastic endorsement as a dynamic and efficient Cabinet colleague. His contribution in truth deserves to be better known.

Bondfield, Margaret: Labour politician. She was born in 1873 of humble parents and, after an elementary education, became a shop assistant in Brighton. She moved to London where she rapidly took up the cause of women working in sweat shops for very low pay. In 1898 she became Assistant Secretary of the National Union of Shop Assistants and served as an officer of the National Union of General and Municipal Workers for 30 years (1908–38). Such a background frequently led into Labour politics. In 1923, she was both elected MP for Northampton and became the first woman chairman of the *Trades Union Congress*. She served as MP for Wallsend from 1926 to 1931 and is best known as the first woman Cabinet minister, becoming Minister for Labour from 1929 to 1931. After the split in the Labour Party in 1931, she increasingly devoted her time to issues concerning women's employment. She died in 1953.

(See also *trade unions; women: legal status of.*)

Booth, Charles: pioneer social investigator. He was born into a wealthy shipowning family in 1840 and worked for several years as a partner in the family firm. His interests increasingly turned to social enquiry, however, and his 'Life and Labour of the People of London', researched over seventeen years and published in twelve volumes between 1891 and 1903, exposed the extent of poverty in the capital and also classified it into 'primary' and 'secondary' forms. His work also revealed the extent to which poverty was related to the life cycle and he became a leading campaigner for *old-age pensions* to alleviate one aspect of this problem. His ideas influenced *progressive Liberals* anxious to use the powers of the State to tackle social issues.

(See also *old-age pensions; Rowntree, Seebohm; social policy.*)

Booth, William: *nonconformist* leader. He was born in Nottingham in 1829 and, after a conversion experience, became a member of the *Methodist* New Connexion. After marrying Catherine Mumford, who had been expelled from the Connexion for extremism, he also left the Methodists and founded with her the Christian Revival Association in 1865. This organisation changed its name to the Salvation Army in 1878. Always concerned with the practical aspects of religious responsibility, he and his wife published several pamphlets on social conditions, most notably 'In Darkest England and the Way Out' (1890). The Booths, with their son, William Bramwell played an important role both in awakening the social conscience of the nation and in bringing the poorest sections of society within the ambit of the Christian message. He died in 1912.

(See also *evangelicalism; social policy.*)

Boxer Rebellion, 1900: rising in northern China against increasing territorial acquisitions by Western powers, especially Britain, Germany and Russia. Britain had occupied Wei-hai-wei in 1898 in response to Russian occupation of Port Arthur. The rebellion took the form of looting foreign goods and attacking diplomatic areas in Peking (Bejing). Concerted retaliation by the Western powers involved to the looting of Peking and further territorial occupations. The incident proved important in developing both nationalism and anti-imperialism within China and indirectly led to revolution there in 1911.

(See also *imperialism.*)

Braddock, Bessie: *Labour* politician. She was born Liverpool in 1899, the daughter of a bookbinder, and entered Labour politics through the *trade union* movement. She was elected MP for Liverpool Exchange at the Labour landslide of 1945 and held the seat until her death in 1970. She was the first woman MP for a Liverpool seat. A pugnacious and, her opponents said, graceless and uncharitable right-winger of formidable personal aspect, she launched trenchant attacks on the Labour left, notably *Aneurin Bevan* and Michael Foot. She was offered a post in the *Wilson* government of 1964 but refused it, saying that she could serve her Liverpool constituents best from the backbenches.

Bradlaugh, Charles: *radical* Liberal politician. He was born in 1833 and took up journalism early in his career. Using the appropriate pen-name 'Iconoclast', he advocated both republicanism and secularism. He founded the 'National Reformer' in 1865. With *Annie Besant*, he wrote pamphlets advocating contraception. After earlier failures, he was elected Liberal MP for Northampton in 1880 but was debarred from taking his seat for almost six years because he wished to affirm rather than take the normal oath of allegiance on the Bible, and the *House of Commons* would not accept affirmation as valid. An accomplished controversialist, he delighted in the many scandals both his writings and his lifestyle occasioned in polite late Victorian society. He died in 1891.

(See also *Liberal Party.*)

Bright, John: *radical* Liberal politician. Born into a prosperous Quaker carpet manufacturing family in Rochdale in 1811, Bright quickly made his name as an orator supporting full religious liberties for *nonconformists* and the abolition of rates paid to the *Church of England*. He is best known, however, for his part in the *Anti-Corn Law League* campaign against protection for landowners. Unlike some members of the League, he was anxious to use it as a vehicle for a range of anti-aristocratic measures. He first became MP for Durham in 1843 and later represented Manchester until being defeated in the election of 1857 after opposition to the *Crimean War* made him, and many radical Liberals, unpopular. He returned to Parliament as MP for Birmingham in 1858 and served the city with distinction. Other causes he supported included land reform in *Ireland*, further parliamentary reform and full civil and religious liberties for *Jews* in Britain. His opposition to *slavery* made him a strong supporter of the North in the American Civil War. He became President of the Board of Trade in *Gladstone*'s Liberal government of 1868 but only served for two years. He proved much more successful as an agitator and orator than as a minister. Always a supporter of the *British Empire*, he had advocated the Crown's taking over all political responsibilities for the government of India in the late 1850s. Not surprisingly, therefore, he split from the Gladstone Liberals over Irish *Home Rule* in 1886. He died in 1889.

(See also *Ireland; nonconformity.*)

Britain, Battle of (1940): crucial battle in the early stages of *World War II* between the Royal Air Force and the German Luftwaffe. The Germans, having defeated the French, were pressing on towards speedy victory. Their strategy required them to break Britain's aerial defences in order to mount an invasion of Britain. Between July and September 1940, RAF Spitfire and Hurricane fighters under *Hugh Dowding*, Head of Fighter Command, British pilots successfully frustrated a much larger German force and, in effect, deterred Hitler from implementing his invasion plan, *Operation Sealion*, and thus probably prevented British defeat in the war. It was this which caused *Churchill* to deliver his famous judgement: 'Never in the field of human conflict has so much been owed by so many to so few'. Casualties were extremely high. The British lost about 900 aircraft in the battle, the Germans perhaps twice as many.

(See also *aircraft; World War II.*)

British Broadcasting Corporation: founded as the pioneer radio service '2LO' in 1922, the BBC grew into one of the largest, and most respected, broadcasting organisations in the world. It became officially the British Broadcasting Corporation under royal charter issued in 1927. It is funded by annual licence fees, bought first by the owners of radio sets. Under the initial direction of the Scottish Presbyterian John C (later Lord) *Reith*, it aimed to provide both instruction and entertainment. Initial traditions of formality included radio broadcasters reading the news in formal dress while the English spoken on the radio rapidly established itself as 'standard' or 'received' pronunciation. The BBC World Service provided high-quality news and magazine broadcasting throughout the globe and established its international primacy. The BBC retained for Britain a form of world dominance in 'public service' broadcasting at the time the formal empire was in retreat. The BBC maintained a monopoly of television broadcasting from its inception in 1936 until 1955 when the Independent Television Authority was formed to provide competition. Although the BBC remained in public ownership, and funded by radio and television licences, pressures of commercialism, especially since the 1960s, have tilted the balance within the organisation away from public service and education towards greater emphasis on entertainment, diversity and informality. Another important move away from the purity of the 'public service' concept came in 1996 when, under a revised charter, the BBC was permitted to develop a range of commercial services alongside its primary broadcasting function.

(See also *radio; television.*)

British Commonwealth: see *Commonwealth, British*

British Empire: see *Empire, British*

British Expeditionary Force: forces sent to France, amid great optimism, in 1914 with the intention of winning the *World War I* 'by Christmas'. The force was commanded by *Sir John French* and was instrumental in halting the German army's westward sweep through Belgium at the Battles of *Mons* and the *Marne* in August and September, thus inaugurating a prolonged period of static, 'trench' warfare on the Western Front. Highly trained and disciplined, the BEF was nicknamed 'the Old Contemptibles'.

Britten, Benjamin: composer. Born in Lowestoft, Suffolk in 1913, and after studying under Frank Bridge, he developed into one of the twentieth century's most influential composers. His operas, such as 'Peter Grimes' (1945) and 'Billy Budd' (1951) set new standards of musical theatre in the years following World War II. With his long-term partner, the tenor Peter Pears, he established in 1948 a highly influential international music festival at his home town of Aldeburgh on the Suffolk coast. He died in 1976.

Brontë, Charlotte: novelist. Born the daughter of an Anglo-Irish parson in 1816, she lived for most of her life in the remote West Yorkshire village of Haworth. Her most famous novel was 'Jane Eyre' (1847) written under the male pseudonym Currer Bell. She and her sister Emily revealed their true identities in 1848 and she went on to write 'Shirley' (1848), set in Yorkshire during the Luddite period, and 'Vilette' (1850). She died in 1855.

(See also *Brontë, Emily.*)

Brontë, Emily: novelist. Sister of Charlotte and Ann, author – as Acton Bell – of 'The Tenant of Wildfell Hall' (1847); born in 1818. She is remembered almost exclusively for her romantic novel 'Wuthering Heights', published in 1847 under the male pseudonym Ellis Bell and set in the Yorkshire Moors where she spent nearly all her life. The Brontës' novels demonstrated the ability of women to write full-blooded romantic fiction. She died of tuberculosis in 1848.

(See also *Brontë, Charlotte.*)

Brooke, Rupert: poet. Born in 1887, he wrote two of the most famous British poems of the twentieth century: 'The Old Vicarage, Grantchester', which evoked the timeless certainties of pre-war rural England, and 'The Soldier', a paean to romantic patriotism in wartime. He died on active service in 1915.

(See also *Owen, Wilfred; Sassoon, Siegfried; World War I.*)

Brougham, Henry: *Whig* politician, lawyer and writer on government and political economy. Born in Scotland in 1778, he was called to the Scottish bar in 1800 and the English in 1808. He founded the Whig-supporting journal 'Edinburgh Review' in 1802 and entered Parliament in 1810. He proved a very effective opponent of *Lord Liverpool*'s government while espousing a range of reformist causes including *Catholic emancipation* and the abolition of *slavery* in British colonies. He championed Queen Caroline against *George IV* during the divorce scandal of 1820. Always an advocate of parliamentary reform he joined *Grey*'s Cabinet in November 1830 as Lord Chancellor, accepting the title Lord Brougham and Vaux in 1831. He introduced a number of reforms in the Chancery court. He remained in office when *Melbourne* replaced Grey but annoyed him by public revelations about the circumstances of the *Prime Minister*'s dismissal of the Government in November 1834. When Melbourne returned to office in April in 1835, he refused to reappoint Brougham who never held high office again. He died in 1868.

(See also *Liberal Party; parliamentary reform; Whig Party.*)

Brown, George (Lord George-Brown of Jevington): *Labour* politician. Born in 1914, he came to prominence through the Transport and General Workers' Union. He became MP for Belper, Derbyshire in 1945, a constituency he represented until his defeat in the *general election* of 1970. His major offices were:

- Deputy Leader of the Labour Party, 1960–70 (defeated by Harold Wilson in the leadership contest of 1963)
- Head of the new Department of Economic Affairs, 1964–66
- Foreign Secretary, 1966–70

Brown was a clever man and an intuitive politician on the right wing of the Labour Party whose innovative ideas frequently failed to carry through into achievement. He failed to establish the Department of Economic Affairs as an effective counterweight to the Treasury and his time at the Foreign Office was marked by a number of diplomatic incidents when he spoke his mind too plainly, often under the influence of drink. His relationship with the more calculating *Harold Wilson* was neither close nor effective and Brown resented Wilson's lack of trust in him. He took a peerage in 1970, drifted ever further from the Labour mainstream and died in 1985.

(See also *trade unions*.)

Browning, Robert: poet and husband of Elizabeth Barrett. He was born in 1812 into less favourable circumstances than Elizabeth and practised poetry from an early age. His poems cover a range of themes but are characterised by the ability to sustain verse narratives of great length and their philosophical insights. His best known work includes 'Men and Women' (1855) and 'The Ring and the Book' (1869). His poetry evinces similar insights and some of the same bases as the music of his exact German contemporary Richard Wagner. As with Wagner, his work was frequently attacked by contemporaries as incomprehensible. He died in 1869.

Brunel, Isambard Kingdom: engineer. Born in Portsmouth in 1806, he developed a spectacularly varied career including design of the Clifton Suspension Bridge, Bristol (1829–31) and then various harbour and dock developments in the South-West. He worked with his father, Marc, on the first tunnel under the Thames which eventually formed part of the London Underground system. He became engineer to the Great Western Railway in 1833 and developed the famous seven-feet 'broad gauge' to take engines along it. From 1836, he was mainly concerned with shipbuilding and pioneered in 'Great Western' a *steamship* capable of carrying a full load of coals across the Atlantic. He also designed, and helped to see implemented in the Royal Navy, the screw propeller. 'Great Britain' became the first screw-propelled ship. Recognised as the most fertile engineer of the age, he helped organise London's *Great Exhibition* in 1851. His other engineering interests encompassed gun technology and hospital construction. From 1853 to his death in 1859 he worked on further large-scale shipping projects including the monumentally large 'Great Eastern', the biggest steamship yet built although it was not a commercial success on transatlantic runs.

(See also *engineering industry; Industrial Revolution; railways*.)

building societies: organisations designed to help subscribers meet the substantial capital costs needed for house purchase. The first building societies emerged in the 1770s and 1780s in the Midlands and North of England in the form of 'terminating societies'. These had a fixed number of subscribers and wound themselves up ('terminated') when all had been housed. In the nineteenth century, these were replaced by organisations which borrowed from outside. Building societies had to be formally registered under the *Friendly Societies* Act of 1829 and further legislation in 1836 regulated their operations. They came under company law provisions in 1874 and then played a full part, as societies established for members' mutual benefit, in the explosion of owner-occupation from the late nineteenth century onwards. By 1979, the societies had more than five million borrowers. *Conservative Party* legislation in the 1980s encouraged many to shed their 'mutual' status and offer a wider range of banking and other financial services as profit-making organisations responsible to shareholders.

(See also *self-help*.)

Bulgarian Crisis, 1876–78: the Turkish Empire, which ruled much of south-eastern Europe in the nineteenth century, faced increasing nationalist challenges, especially from Christian subjects. In 1875 and 1876 first the Bosnians and then the Bulgars rose in revolt. These risings were put down ferociously which gave rise to controversy in Britain. *Gladstone* published a pamphlet 'The Bulgarian Horrors and the Question of the East' calling for Turkish expulsion from Bulgaria. The *Conservative* government, headed by *Disraeli*, was concerned that a weakened Turkish Empire would lead to increased Russian influence in the Mediterranean, which would threaten British trading and imperial interests in Asia and Africa. The Russians aided the Bulgarians in 1877 and, after defeating the Turks, imposed harsh peace terms at San Stefano (March 1878): a 'Big Bulgaria' was created with a seaboard on the Aegean, which the Russians hoped to dominate, and the Russians acquired additional territory in the area. This provoked a response from other European powers, notably Germany and Britain. The crisis was settled by the *Congress of Berlin* (July 1878). Its main terms were:

- an effectively independent Bulgaria (under nominal Turkish suzerainty) was created, though with less territory than planned at San Stefano
- Russia retained some of its territorial gains in Bessarabia and the Caucasus
- Austria occupied Bosnia–Herzegovina
- Britain occupied Cyprus

Disraeli famously told the Commons in July 1878 that he had 'brought you back peace – but a peace I hope with honour'.

Bulge, Battle of the (1944–45): final attempt by German forces at the end of *World War II* to halt Allied advance on Germany after the *D-Day* landings. After pushing the Germans back, the Allies advanced to the Rhine and thence into Germany itself.

Burdett-Coutts, Angela: philanthropist. Born in 1814 into a wealthy banking family, who supported numerous Victorian charities, especially housing projects and the newly founded National Society for the Prevention of Cruelty to Children. She also played an active role in the Coutts banking firm and was a lavish entertainer, maintaining a correspondence with *Charles Dickens*. She was created a baroness in 1871 and died in 1906.

(See also *social policy*.)

Burma: effectively controlled by Britain from 1824 to 1941 and from 1945 to 1948, it was formally annexed as a territory of British *India* from 1886. Three wars involving the British were fought: in 1824–26, 1852–53 and 1885. During *World War II*, the Japanese occupied the country (1941). British resistance continued led by Orde-Wingate and his 'Chindit' forces. In 1944, General *Slim* won the decisive battle of Kohima-Imphal in 1944 which led to British recapture. Burma became independent in 1948.

(See also *Empire, British.*)

Burns, John: trade unionist and *Labour* politician. He was born in 1858 and trained as an engineer. He came to prominence as leader of the London *Dock Strike* in 1889. He became an inaugural member of the *London County Council* in 1889 and MP for Bermondsey in 1892. He later joined the *Liberal Party*. His major offices were:

- President of the Local Government Board, 1905–14
- President of the Board of Trade, 1914

He was the first working man to achieve *Cabinet* office but left Government in protest against the outbreak of *World War I*. He took no further part in political life and died in 1943.

(See also *trade unions.*)

Burt, Thomas: trade unionist and *Liberal* politician. Born in 1837, he became a coal miner and became Secretary of the Northumberland Miners'Association in 1865. He became one of the first two working-class MPs when elected Liberal MP for Morpeth in 1874.

(See also *Liberal Party; trade unions.*)

Butler, Josephine: feminist and social reformer. Born in 1828 the daughter of John Grey, a leader of the anti-*slavery* campaign, she campaigned for women to have access to higher education but, while living in Liverpool, became interested in improving the conditions of poor women, especially *prostitutes*. She campaigned against the discriminatory *Contagious Diseases Acts*, forming a 'Ladies' Association' for the purpose, and was instrumental in securing their repeal in 1883. She also secured a rise in the age of female sexual consent from 13 to 16 years in 1885. She also championed the cause of female *suffrage* but died in 1906 before it entered its critical stage.

(See also *women, legal status of.*)

Butler, R A: *Conservative* politician. Born in 1902, he was close to the centre of power for most of the period from the early 1940s to the mid-1960s. Indeed, during the later stages of *Churchill's* government of 1951–55, he took the lead in *Cabinet* when the *Prime Minister* was ill. Universally known as 'RAB', he was able and experienced. He was extremely unfortunate not to have become Prime Minister on two, if not three, occasions after the resignations of *Churchill*, *Eden* and, especially, *Macmillan*. Macmillan's campaigning against him from his hospital bed during some fevered and disreputable party manoeuvring in 1963 probably told decisively against him. Known as a formidably efficient administrator, he introduced a crucial *Education Act* in 1944 which secured universal secondary education and, by competitive examinations, access to grammar schools and, through them, to higher education. He also helped rebuild Conservative organisation after electoral defeat in 1945. His main offices were:

- Minister for Education, 1941–45
- Chancellor of the Exchequer, 1951–55
- Leader of the *House of Commons*, 1955–57
- Home Secretary, 1957–62
- Foreign Secretary, 1962–64

He retired from active politics in 1965, accepting a peerage as Lord Butler of Saffron Walden, and died in 1982.

Butt, Isaac: Irish politician. Born in 1813, he trained for the law but soon turned to politics. He opposed the Union with Great Britain but opposed the violent methods of *Sinn Fein*. He founded the Home Government Association in 1870; it changed its title to the Home Rule League in 1873. He became an MP in 1871. He was replaced as leader of the Home Rule Group by *Charles Stewart Parnell* in 1877, many Irishmen feeling that his moderation would not coerce British politicians into action to secure *Home Rule* for *Ireland*.

Byron (George Gordon), 6th Lord: poet. Born in 1788, he became known equally for his Romantic poetry and for his lifestyle, which encompassed a very brief marriage and numerous liaisons, most notoriously with *Lady Caroline Lamb*, wife of the future *Prime Minister Lord Melbourne*. He produced 'Childe Harold's Pilgrimage' in 1813 but produced his later works – including 'Manfred' (1817) and 'Don Juan' in instalments from 1819 – abroad since he left Britain in 1816. He vigorously embraced both Italian and Greek independence movements and died of marsh fever at Missolonghi in 1824 while planning to lead an expedition against the Turks.

(See also *Keats, John; Shelley, Percy Bysshe.*)

C

Cabinet: the name given to the group of senior ministers who direct policy in the British political system. It grew out of the larger, but increasingly unwieldy, Privy Council. By the early nineteenth century, the Cabinet was established as a cohesive group of ministers which had wrested most of the political initiative from the Crown, and monarchs no longer attended meetings. In the 1820s, the *Prime Minister Lord Liverpool* was able to have his wishes about members of Cabinet prevail over the preferences of King *George IV* and since then decisions on Cabinet membership have lain more with the Prime Minister than the *monarch*, although Queen *Victoria*'s strongly expressed preferences had considerable impact in the 1850s and 1860s.

Another feature of Cabinet government is that, whatever disagreements ministers may have in private, these should be subsumed in 'collective responsibility' for policy decisions. Those who cannot accept a collective review are expected to resign. In practice, Cabinet policy often reflects the balance of opinion within the governing party rather than the result of argument within Cabinet, and some prime ministers – notably *Margaret Thatcher* in the early 1980s – have effectively appealed over the heads of Cabinet colleagues for wider support when policies did not command a majority there. From 1937, by the Ministers of the Crown Act, only an agreed number of ministers of the Cabinet may receive a salary and this has usually limited Cabinet membership to a number in the low twenties. By recent convention, all retiring Cabinet members are offered a peerage.

(See also *Commons, House of; Lords, House of; Parliament.*)

Callaghan, James: *Labour* politician and *Prime Minister*. He was born in 1912 the son of a naval petty officer. He worked for the Inland Revenue and came into Labour politics as a representative of a clerical trades union. He became MP for Cardiff South in 1945 and represented that city continuously thereafter until his retirement. He rose quickly, becoming a junior minister in 1947 and continuing to progress while Labour was in opposition. His major offices were:

- Chancellor of the Exchequer, 1964–67
- Home Secretary, 1967–70
- Foreign Secretary, 1974–76
- Prime Minister, 1976–79
- Leader of the Opposition, 1979–80

A politician who nurtured his trade union links and carefully cultivated an image of avuncularity, his extensive career as a senior minister was dogged by controversy and disappointment. His relationship with *Harold Wilson* during the government of 1964–70 was uneasy; neither man trusted the other. Not a trained economist, he often struggled as Chancellor of the Exchequer and failed to prevent a politically damaging devaluation of the currency in 1967 and, forced to resign as Chancellor, then took the fateful decision as Home Secretary in 1969 to put troops into Northern Ireland. He used his acute political skills to prevent radical proposals for trade union reform – supported by *Barbara Castle* and by *Harold Wilson* – from becoming law, thus arguably contriving to sustain the politically damaging dominance of trade unionism within Labour politics throughout the 1970s.

His prime ministership was wracked both by internal Labour divisions and by economic crisis. Albeit at the dictation of the International Monetary Fund, it was his government which began to develop policies which ran counter to *Keynesian* orthodoxy and which *Thatcher* greatly extended. His government lacked a *Commons* majority and was sustained for most of its length by an agreement with the *Liberal Party*. He almost certainly made a fatal error in deciding to delay the calling of a general election when one was widely expected in the autumn of 1978. He had to face rejection of his pay policy by the trade unions, the *Winter of Discontent* and, following the failure of proposals to give greater self-government for Scotland, his government lost a confidence motion by a single vote. The general election which followed saw the Conservatives elected and Callaghan resigned the *Labour Party* leadership shortly afterwards.

(See also *economic policy; Lib–Lab pact.*)

Campaign for Nuclear Disarmament: a spin-off from the Cold War, founded in 1958 with the objective of persuading British governments to renounce the use of nuclear weapons. It was strongly supported by many intellectuals and politicians on the left, including *Bertrand Russell,* J B Priestley, E P Thompson and Michael Foot. It attracted much media attention, largely from annual marches to the Atomic Research Establishment at Aldermaston, but failed to become a genuinely popular movement and was widely, if unfairly, associated with full-scale *pacifism.*

Campbell-Bannerman, Henry: *Liberal* politician and *Prime Minister.* Born in Glasgow in 1836, he became MP for Stirling in 1868 and rose to prominence with the support of *Gladstone.* His main offices were:

- Chief Secretary for Ireland, 1884–85 and 1886
- Secretary of State for War, 1892–95
- Leader of the Liberal Party, 1898–1908
- Prime Minister, 1905–8

Under Gladstone, Campbell-Bannerman supported *Home Rule,* though, in the interests of party unity, he later moderated his position. The vote of censure passed on him for not having equipped the army with sufficient cordite was the occasion of the fall of *Rosebery*'s brief administration. Thereafter, the Liberals were in open disarray over the *Boer War.* Campbell-Bannerman, whose abilities as a conciliator helped him to win the leadership on *Harcourt*'s resignation, needed similar skills to keep party divisions over the Boer War within compass. Nevertheless, he lost the 1900 *general election* badly. The Liberals profited from Conservative divisions over *free trade* and *imperial preference* after 1903 and Campbell-Bannerman agreed to form a government when *Balfour* resigned in December 1905. He almost immediately called a *general election* and the Liberal victory of 1906, the last large Liberal electoral success, proved to be one of the three greatest party-political landslides of the twentieth century, to be ranked alongside the Labour victories of 1945 and 1997. His government, though brief, was very talented, including *Asquith, Lloyd George* and *Edward Grey.* It began the important transition towards 'new liberalism' with an increased emphasis on state intervention. Illness forced 'CB' to retire in April 1908 and he died shortly afterwards.

(See also *Liberal Party; welfare state.*)

Camperdown, Battle of (1797): naval engagement during the *French Revolutionary Wars* in which the British fleet, under Admiral Duncan, defeated a Franco-Dutch force, capturing much of it. The outcome of this battle frustrated plans for substantial French support to be given to the planned Irish rising against British rule.

Canada: colony in the *British Empire* and, later, *British Commonwealth*. British settlers had colonised parts of Canada during the seventeenth century, but the French dominated the territory until defeated in the Seven Years' War (1756–63). Thereafter, British rule was frequently challenged by French and the *Younger Pitt*'s 1791 Canada Act, creating competing territories of Upper and Lower Canada based on Ontario (predominantly British-settled) and Quebec (predominantly French-settled) respectively, did not significantly reduce antagonisms. Rebellions in 1837 brought matters to a head and *Melbourne*'s government sent out *Lord Durham* as Governor-General. His report (1839) led to the Canada Act of 1840 which:

- united the two territories
- created two chambers of government: an elected assembly and a nominated legislative council
- introduced locally responsible government in all matters except defence, foreign policy and overseas trade

This solution proved a model for other British colonies. In 1854, an agreed boundary between Canada and the United States was agreed at the 49th parallel of latitude and in 1867 the British North America Act conferred federal dominion status on Canada with territories encompassing Ontario, Quebec, Nova Scotia and New Brunswick. In 1870–71, British Columbia, Manitoba and Prince Edward Island entered the federation, which became further enlarged, after the late nineteenth century gold rush, with the accession of Alberta and Saskatchewan in 1905.

(See also *Wakefield, Edward Gibbon.*)

canals: the great era of canal building was *c.*1760–1820. The main purpose was to increase the extent of navigable waterways to link rivers and reduce transport costs, and canals were the most important source of speculative investment at the time. Canals proved much more efficient carriers of bulk cargoes than roads and played a crucial role in helping create mass markets in the early stages of the *Industrial Revolution*. They transformed the prospects of places, such as the West Midlands and South Wales, where there were relatively few navigable rivers. The opening of the Grand Junction Canal, linking Birmingham to London, in 1805 consolidated Birmingham's position as Britain's pre-eminent metals and *engineering* town.

In the second quarter of the nineteenth century, canals (which were by 1825 more than 4,000 miles in extent) suffered a double blow: the development of the stage coach travelling fast on new, hard roads, and increasing competition for freight from the *railways*. Although important new canals were opened in this period, notably the Birmingham and Liverpool (1835), the long period of decline had begun. In the second half of the nineteenth century, railway companies began to buy out canal companies and close down previously important sections of the canal network. This process was halted by Railway and Canal Regulation Act, 1873. Perhaps the most famous British canal, the Manchester Ship Canal linking the *cotton* capital of the *Empire* to Liverpool and the west coast, was opened in 1894. Many canals fell into disrepair and disuse. Partial rehabilitation began from the late 1960s when the *leisure* potential of canals began to be more systematically exploited.

(See Figure on page 41. See also *transportation*.)

Canning, Charles John: *Tory* politician and colonial administrator. The son of George Canning, he was born in 1812 and became MP for Warwick in 1836. He worked for the East India Company and was appointed Governor-General of *India* in 1856. He was thus in charge when the mutiny broke out the following year. He discharged a difficult balancing act between the need to break the mutiny, restore order and rebuild Indian confidence. Appointed 1st Viceroy in 1858, after the rising had been put down, he did much constructive work, earning the nickname 'Clemency Canning' before his death in 1862.

(See also *India; Indian Mutiny; India Act, 1858*.)

Canning, George: journalist, Tory politician and *Prime Minister*. He was born in 1770 and brought up by an uncle, a wealthy banker. He became MP in 1794, and his merits quickly earned him promotion under the *Younger Pitt* as Under-Secretary of State at the Foreign Office (1796–99) and a member of the India Board (1800). His journalistic talents were employed at the same time when he edited 'Anti-Jacobin', a strongly anti-reformist newspaper which successfully branded British reformers as lapdogs of a deranged and evil French revolutionary regime. His major offices were:

- Paymaster General, 1800–1
- Foreign Secretary, 1807–9 and 1822–27
- Prime Minister, 1827

Acknowledged on all sides as a brilliant writer and speaker, his career was frequently controversial. Not only did he often disagree with colleagues, and even fought a duel with *Castlereagh* in 1809, but he did not inspire trust. He was also disliked by the Prince Regent (later *George IV*) whose hostility almost certainly delayed his return to high office. He was associated with a foreign policy which supported the nationalist ambitions of territories seeking to throw off old colonial rule, whether the Turkish in south-east Europe or the Spanish and Portuguese in southern America. This was more for commercial and strategic reasons than for ideological ones. Contrasts with the objectives of his foreign policy and that of Castlereagh have been generally overdrawn. A Liverpool MP, he also supported moves in the direction of greater freedom to trade without tariffs or other restrictions. This, and his support for *Roman Catholic* emancipation, put him on the so-called 'liberal' wing of *Liverpool*'s increasingly disunited government in the 1820s. His succession to the prime ministership made obvious divisions which Liverpool's emollient leadership had often papered over. Peel and Wellington refused to serve him and Canning turned instead to the *Whigs*, heading what amounted to a brief coalition government before his premature death in August 1827.

(See also *Conservative Party; Tory Party; overseas trade*.)

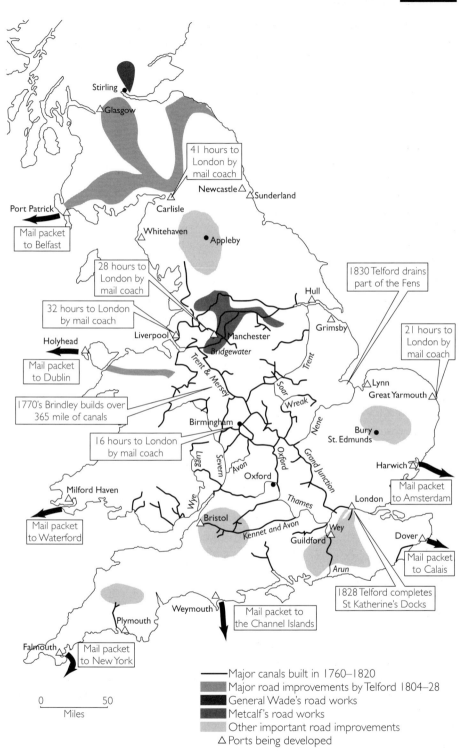

41 hours to
London by
mail coach

Port Patrick

Mail packet
to Belfast

Stirling

Glasgow

Newcastle △ △ Sunderland

Carlisle

Whitehaven

Appleby

28 hours to
London by
mail coach

32 hours to London
by mail coach

Holyhead

Mail packet
to Dublin

1770's Brindley builds over
365 mile of canals

16 hours to London
by mail coach

Milford Haven

Mail packet
to Waterford

Liverpool

Manchester

Bridgewater

Trent & Mersey

Birmingham

Lugg

Wye

Severn

Avon

Oxford

Hull

Grimsby

Trent

Soar

Wreak

Nene

Oxford

Grand Junction

1830 Telford drains
part of the Fens

21 hours to
London by
mail coach

Lynn

Great Yarmouth

Bury
St. Edmunds

Harwich

Mail packet
to Amsterdam

Thames

Bristol

Kennet and Avon

Guildford

Wey

London

Dover

Mail packet
to Calais

Arun

1828 Telford completes
St Katherine's Docks

Plymouth

Weymouth

Mail packet to
the Channel Islands

Falmouth

Mail packet
to New York

0   50
Miles

—— Major canals built in 1760–1820
▓ Major road improvements by Telford 1804–28
■ General Wade's road works
▓ Metcalf's road works
░ Other important road improvements
△ Ports being developed

Canals

capital punishment: execution for specified crimes, by the nineteenth century invariably by hanging. The eighteenth century saw a substantial increase in the number of 'capital' offences as landowners aggressively defended their property interests. Executions for relatively trivial crimes like theft, however, deterred many juries from conviction, frequently to the frustration of judges. Whig reformers, like *Romilly* and *Bentham,* and the administrative expertise of *Robert Peel* combined to reduce drastically the number of capital offences by the 1830s. After 1861, murder, treason, piracy and arson in naval dockyards remained the only capital crimes. Public execution, however, remained until 1868 and executions frequently generated a commercial penumbra as 'dying speeches' were sold to the crowd, impromptu street theatres and peddlers exploited their opportunities. Campaigns against what the Victorians increasingly saw as a degrading spectacle culminated in the abolition of public execution in 1868. Capital punishment continued, however, well into the twentieth century. The last woman was executed in 1956 and the last men in 1964 before the left-wing Labour MP Sydney Silverman piloted abolition through Parliament in 1965. Despite sustained evidence of popular support for its reintroduction, parliamentary opinion has remained substantially opposed to the death penalty.

Cardigan, 7th Earl of: Tory politician and army commander. Born James Brudenell in 1797, he was a *Tory* MP from 1818 to 1834. A famously irascible and incompetent man, he had numerous conflicts with brother officers before the action which made his name. He commanded the Light Brigade at the *Battle of Balaclava* (1854) and, apparently mistaking an order from his commanding officer, *Lord Raglan,* charged down the wrong valley and attacked Russian guns head on. *The Charge of the Light Brigade* was immortalised in verse by *Tennyson* ('Into the valley of death rode the six hundred') and earned a place in the story of extraordinary, but pointless, British heroism under fire.

(See also *Crimean War.*)

Cardwell, Edward: *Peelite* Tory and *Liberal* politician. Born in 1813, he became an MP in 1842, winning junior office under *Peel* in 1845–46. His major offices were:

- President of the Board of Trade, 1852–55
- Chief Secretary for Ireland, 1859–61
- Secretary for the Colonies, 1864–66
- Secretary for War, 1868–74

Like *Gladstone,* he journeyed from the *Conservative Party* through the Peelite group to end his career as a Liberal. Like Gladstone, too, he prized administrative achievement. He was responsible for a *Merchant Shipping Act* in *Aberdeen*'s government in 1854 but is best remembered for his army reforms of 1870 during Gladstone's first ministry. These helped modernise the army after the embarrassments of the *Crimean War.* The main features were:

- short-service commissions and promotion on ability
- reform of army administration
- abolition of purchase of commissions
- abolition of transportation
- creation of an army reserve

He was created Viscount on the fall of Gladstone's government in 1874, did not hold office again and died in 1886.

Carlyle, Thomas: essayist, lecturer and critic. Born in 1795, he made his name with 'The French Revolution', a book published in 1837. This was followed by 'Chartism' (1839) and 'Past and Present' (1843). A constant theme of his writing was the evil of unrestrained capitalism in the modern world, but he was no *socialist*. Rather he looked back to the evangelical prescriptions of hard work, duty, authority and the example of great men as his remedy for the evils of industrial society. His ideas on what he called the 'social question' were a great influence on *Charles Dickens*. He died in 1881.

(See also *Chartism; French Revolutionary Wars; Industrial Revolution; Macaulay, Thomas Babington; social policy.*)

Caroline of Brunswick, Princess, later Queen: she was born in 1768 and married Prince George, later *George IV*, in 1795. Although it produced one daughter, the marriage was a disaster and led to a political scandal when George became King in 1820 and announced his intention to divorce his wife, with whom he had not lived for many years and who (like him) had conducted many semi-public affairs in the meantime. Caroline came back from the Continent and contested the divorce, to the great delight of opposition politicians, *radicals* and anti-government cartoonists, who all had a field day. The affair damaged the *monarchy*, not least when the Queen, attempting to attend George's coronation in July 1821, found herself locked out of Westminster Abbey and noisily went from door to door demanding admittance. She died a couple of weeks later in 1821, thus cutting short one of the most damaging passages in the history of the monarchy.

(See also *Hanoverian dynasty.*)

Carpenter, Mary: philanthropist and humanitarian reformer. She was born in 1807 into a Unitarian household. Strong religious precepts dominated her life. She founded numerous *ragged schools* for the poor in Bristol, where basic education was provided free to the pupils. She wrote of 'Juvenile Delinquents' in 1854, thus coining a phrase which remained the dominant description for disruptive youths, mostly male, well into the twentieth century. She advocated the use of reformatories where behaviour could be improved by a combination of discipline and example. She died in 1877.

(See also *nonconformity; social policy.*)

Carson, Edward: lawyer and *Unionist* politician. He was born in 1854 and made a formidable reputation as an advocate. His cross-examination of *Oscar Wilde* during the latter's libel action (1895) led to the author's downfall and subsequent imprisonment on charges of homosexuality. He became Solicitor General for Ireland (1892). He became MP for Dublin University in 1892 and became leader of the *Ulster Unionists* and the main champion of the campaign against *Home Rule*. He helped organise the *Ulster Volunteer Force* and his slogan 'Ulster will fight and Ulster will be right' deterred the Liberals from pushing ahead with Home Rule proposals in the years before *World War I*. During World War I he became first *Asquith*'s Attorney General and, from 1917, First Lord of the Admiralty in *Lloyd George*'s War Cabinet. He resigned as Unionist leader in 1921, having played a key role in ensuring that a separate, Protestant-dominated *Northern Ireland* would be part of the Irish settlement. He returned full-time to the law and died in 1935.

(See also *Ulster.*)

Cartwright, Edmund: inventor. Born in 1743, he was inventor of the *power loom* (1785) which, after many initial problems, established itself as the key development which enabled the weaving process in making textiles to be fully mechanised. Cartwright was not an effective businessman and had to apply to Parliament to ensure that he got reward for an invention which others had put to such profitable use. The power loom had established itself fully by the 1820s. He died in 1823.

(See also *cotton industry; Industrial Revolution.*)

Cartwright, John: *radical* politician, brother of *Edmund Cartwright*. He was born in 1740 and became one of the earliest advocates of *parliamentary reform* in the 1770s. His speaking tours and numerous pamphlets advocating universal manhood *suffrage* helped to revive the reform cause in the early nineteenth century after the repressions of the 1790s. He vigorously opposed the *slave trade*. He died in 1824.

Castle, Barbara: *Labour* politician and journalist. She was born in 1910 and was elected MP for Blackburn in 1945, a constituency she continued to represent until her retirement from the *House of Commons* in 1979. She was a vigorous upholder of left-wing *socialism*, and a disciple of *Aneurin Bevan*. As a high-profile member of *Harold Wilson*'s Labour governments of 1964–70 and 1974–76. Her main offices were:

- Minister for Overseas Development, 1964–65
- Minister of Transport, 1965–68 (where she introduced the breathalyser)
- Secretary of State for Social Services, 1974–76

Her career had two major setbacks. Her attempt at *trade union* reform 'In Place of Strife' failed in 1969 and her main opponent in that campaign, *James Callaghan*, refused to keep her in office when he became *Prime Minister*. She also argued vigorously against Britain's becoming a member of the EEC in the early 1970s. She accepted a peerage in 1979 and continued to support a range of reformist causes, including improved conditions for *old-age pensioners*. Her long career near the peak of power in the 1960s and 1970s helped to persuade public opinion that it was possible to have a woman Prime Minister, although Castle was a bitter opponent of *Thatcher* and *Thatcherism*.

(See also *social policy.*)

Castlereagh (Robert Stewart), Viscount: *Tory* politician. He was born in *Ireland* in 1769 and entered Parliament in 1790. He came to political prominence in the late 1790s as one of the main engineers of the *Act of Union* between Britain and Ireland after the failure of the 1798 Irish rebellion, an activity achieved with no small effort of bribery and coercion of reluctant Irish politicians. His main offices were:

- President of the Board of Control, 1802–9
- Secretary for War and the Colonies, 1805–9
- Foreign Secretary, 1812–22

Castlereagh's career had some setbacks; he was largely responsible for the disastrous *Walcheren Expedition* in 1809, for example, and he was never an inspiring speaker.

However, his cool brain, diplomatic skills and mastery of detail made him a formidable minister after he first attracted the attention of the *Younger Pitt*. He remained a staunch opponent of *parliamentary reform* throughout his life but his career is mainly noteworthy for his management of the *Napoleonic Wars* and, particularly, for the peace settlement which ended them. This earned him the admiration of Europe's leading diplomats. He committed Britain to a *congress system* whereby the great powers met regularly to discuss matters of common concern. He was no supporter of the narrow reaction against nationalism favoured particularly by the Russians and Austrians after 1815, however. He helped to secure the long-term stability of France by ensuring that the peace was not excessively punitive. He also played a major role in restoring the Bourbon monarchy there. His long-term objective was a stable balance of power on the European continent which would leave Britain free to pursue its commercial and colonial interests. He committed suicide in 1822, certainly troubled by the increasing rift between Britain and the other signatories to the congress system and probably also concerned by unsubstantiated accusations of homosexuality.

(See also *Canning, George; Liverpool, Earl of; trade, overseas; Vienna, Congress of.*)

'Cat and Mouse' Act, 1913: officially known as the 'Prisoners' Temporary Discharge for Ill Health Act', this was passed by *Asquith*'s government to deal with the problems caused by *suffragette* hunger strikes. Force-feeding suffragettes had proved a public relations disaster, so the Government urged prison authorities to release them on licence when they became ill or weak because of lack of food and then to rearrest them to complete their sentences. It was widely condemned as playing 'cat and mouse' with suffragette prisoners. While the Act deflected attention away from force-feeding, many suffragettes proved elusive once released.

(See Figure on page 46. See also *Women's Suffrage and Political Union.*)

Catholic Emancipation Act, 1829: the legislation introduced by *Robert Peel* in *Wellington*'s government of 1828–30 to quieten mounting discontent in *Ireland* because of the success of *Daniel O'Connell*'s Catholic Association from 1823 and in the wake of his election to Parliament for the seat of County Clare. Peel feared the outbreak of civil war in Ireland. The Act proved immensely controversial within the Tory Party, not least because Peel had long been seen as a key champion of the 'Protestant Ascendancy'. Peel was never properly trusted by many right-wingers after his 'treachery' on the issue. By legislation from 1793 when *Pitt* was *Prime Minister*, Catholics in Ireland could already vote and could be members of the universities and the professions there. By the Emancipation Act, however:

- Roman Catholics could sit as Members of Parliament for the first time, and
- they became eligible to hold all public offices except Regent, Lord Lieutenant and Lord Chancellor

Discrimination against Catholics in Ireland continued, of course, and the clause which increased the threshold for voting in parliamentary elections from 40 shillings (£2) to £10 effectively disfranchised most Catholic peasants and small landowners anyway.

(See also *Roman Catholicism.*)

Cecil, Robert Gascoygne: see *Salisbury, 3rd Marquess of*

'Cat and Mouse' Act, 1913

census: counting of *population*. The first official census of the *United Kingdom* was published in 1801 and a full population census has been held at ten-year intervals (except in 1941 during World War II) ever since. The first census included decennial estimates of population from 1701. Early estimates showed how rapidly the British population was growing. It virtually doubled during the eighteenth century (from about 6 million to 10 million) and doubled again in the first half of the nineteenth century (reaching 20 million in 1851). Thereafter, except in *Ireland* (which took almost a century to recover to the 8.3 million population level on the eve of the Potato Famine of 1845–7), population growth increased, albeit at rather slower rates.

Population stood at about 37 million in 1901 and 49 million in 1951. Only from the 1970s, when the population of Britain reached 54 million, have population growth rates slackened markedly. From 1841, 'census enumerators' books', showing names and occupations, were produced. Although these are not invariably accurate, and systematically under-estimate both women's and part-time work, they have been a key source of information for historians, social scientists and planners. Only one official census of religious observance was held, in 1851.

Chadwick, Edwin: public health reformer and administrator. Born in humble circumstances near Manchester in 1800, he worked in a solicitor's office and then became a journalist. Under the influence of *Jeremy Bentham*, he worked first as an investigator for the *Poor Law* Commission (1832–34) and then played a major part in drafting its report. His career is best remembered for two contributions to public policy:

- as Secretary to the Poor Law Commission in 1834, a post he held until 1846, defending the new Poor Law against attack from radicals and humanitarians
- he used his Poor Law position to investigate other social issues, particularly the state of public health. His 'Report on the Sanitary Condition of the Labouring Poor', published in 1842, was influential in focusing attention on the need for state intervention to effect significant improvements. His energetic lobbying also helped to secure a *Public Health* Act in 1848, but the Act contained fewer elements of compulsion than he would have liked

Chadwick's personality, and especially his self-certainty on controversial public issues, alienated many. He might be called the first 'public service expert' but his arrogance made him many influential enemies. In consequence he frequently achieved less than he hoped. His long career in public service was eventually crowned with a knighthood in 1889 and he died the following year.

(See also *social policy; utilitarianism*.)

Chamberlain, Austen: Conservative politician. Born in 1863, the elder son of *Joseph Chamberlain*, he entered Parliament as a *Liberal Unionist* in 1892. His major offices were:

- Chancellor of the Exchequer, 1903–5, 1919–22
- Secretary of State for India, 1915–17
- Member of *Lloyd George*'s inner War Cabinet (as Minister without Portfolio), 1918–19
- Leader of the Conservative Party, 1921–22
- Foreign Secretary, 1924–29

His career was eventful enough. He rose rapidly within the *Conservative Party* in the 1890s and took on the main burden of trying to convert it to tariff reform after his father's illness struck in 1906. He tried, and failed, to keep the Conservatives loyal to the Lloyd George coalition in 1922 and, as Foreign Secretary, negotiated the *Locarno Treaty* (1925). He briefly joined the *MacDonald* coalition government in 1931 in minor office as First Lord of the Admiralty, but retired to the backbenches from where he advised of the need to stand up to Hitler. He never quite fulfilled his early promise, perhaps lacking that acute political sensitivity to party reaction at times of complexity and crisis. He died in 1937.

(See also *Chamberlain, Neville; India; World War I.*)

Chamberlain, Joseph: *Liberal* then *Conservative Unionist* politician. Born in 1836, his was one of the most dynamic, and turbulent, of nineteenth-century political careers during which he was largely responsible for decisive splits in both of the parties he belonged to. He made his money from the Nettlefolds screw-manufacturing firm, which enabled him to follow a political career. He first made his mark in local government, being Lord Mayor of Birmingham (1873–76) where he carried out a number of reforms known colloquially as 'gas and water *socialism*', rebuilding the city centre. After demonstrating his ability as a formidable political organiser for the Liberals in the changed political world after the 1867 Reform Act, he became a Liberal MP in 1876, where he used his influence to advocate increased state involvement in social reform, a policy which reached its climax in the so-called Unauthorised Programme of 1885 which annoyed *Gladstone* and most of his *Cabinet*. His major offices were:

- President of the Board of Trade, 1880–85
- Secretary of State for the Colonies, 1895–1903

Having urged a policy of devolution for *Ireland* in the early 1880s, he nevertheless recoiled at the prospect of *Home Rule* and left both Gladstone and the Liberal Party, joining a Unionist secession group which eventually linked with the Conservatives under *Salisbury*. As Colonial Secretary, he proved a strong supporter of imperialism and directed policy concerning relations with *South Africa* which led to the *Second Boer War*. He became convinced that British interests would be best served by abandoning *free trade* and using the resources of the *Empire* in a policy of *imperial preference*. He resigned from *Balfour*'s government to pursue this cause, fatally weakening the Conservatives in the process. His career was ended by a stroke in 1906 and he died in 1914.

(See also *Chamberlain, Austen; Chamberlain, Neville.*)

Chamberlain, Neville: Conservative politician and *Prime Minister*. He was born the son of *Joseph*, and half-brother of *Austen, Chamberlain* in 1869 and was one of very few leading politicians to have a training in science and *engineering*. After a brief period managing his father's estates in the West Indies, he followed in his footsteps by becoming a Birmingham City Councillor, where he adopted successful slum clearance and housing programmes. He was elected MP for a Birmingham seat in 1919 and represented the seat without a break until his death. His major offices were:

- Minister of Health, 1924–29 and 1931
- Chancellor of the Exchequer, 1923–24, 1931–37
- Prime Minister, 1937–40

Chamberlain's political reputation is indelibly associated with the policy of *appeasement* and especially with his acceptance of Hitler's demands over Czechoslovakia in 1938 when, after the famous Munich Conference, he stated: 'I believe it is peace for our time'. He was forced out of office after the Germans occupied Norway in May 1940. He died later the same year. Chamberlain's reputation perhaps stands unduly low. Appeasement was both a popular policy and one which gained an under-prepared Britain time for rearmament. Chamberlain was never the entire dupe he appeared after Munich. His career as a social reformer and a high-class administrator deserves separate appraisal. He finally put an end to the hated Poor Law and, in the mid-1930s, reorganised *unemployment* relief. Although an efficient, rather than innovative, Chancellor he finally abandoned the shibboleth of *free trade* and began to implement his father's policy of *imperial preference* from 1932.

(See also *National Insurance; social policy.*)

Chanak Crisis, 1921–2: crisis in relations with Turkey when *Lloyd George* ordered a British garrison on the *Dardanelles* strait to defend its position against a resurgent Turkish army. This initiative, which Lloyd George undertook to protect Greek interests, left Britain diplomatically isolated, and an armistice was followed by Turkish reprisals against Greek citizens. The incident was widely interpreted as a humiliation for Britain and it directly prompted a majority of *Conservatives* to withdraw their support from the coalition government, bringing Lloyd George's prime ministership to an end.

(See also *Liberal Party.*)

Charge of the Light Brigade: engagement by a small troop of cavalry under *Lord Cardigan* during the Battle of *Balaclava* (25 October 1854). It happened when Lord Cardigan, misinterpreting an order from his commanding officer, charged the main body of Russian guns. Huge loss of life resulted. It was the most famous of many mistakes during the *Crimean War* which led to pressure for army reforms after the war ended.

(See also *Raglan, Lord.*)

Charity Organisation Society: organisation founded in 1869 to improve the condition of the poor according to systematic principles based on the development of 'case-work'. It was the most famous of numerous Victorian initiatives and was characterised by an attempt to separate the 'deserving' from the 'undeserving' poor. The intention was to give aid to help beneficiaries to help themselves, thus eventually reducing the need for such extensive charity. It did not intend to help the 'residuum' of undeserving, who should be minimally relieved by the State. Its first secretary was C S Loch and the housing reformer *Octavia Hill* was also a prominent member. Its work was increasingly criticised by *Liberal* progressives and *socialists* who argued that it was not possible to make hard-and-fast distinctions between 'deserving' and 'undeserving'.

(See also *housing; Poor Law; social policy.*)

Chartism: working-class political movement active mainly between 1838 and 1850. Its name derived from the so-called 'People's Charter' drawn up by skilled working men in 1836. Its six points were:

- universal manhood suffrage

- equal electoral districts (so that one man's vote would be as valuable as another's)
- payment for MPs (to enable working men to be elected)
- a *secret ballot* (so that voters could not be coerced)
- removal of property qualifications for MPs
- annually elected parliaments (to reduce scope for bribery and corruption)

Although each of these points, except the last, was achieved in stages from 1856 to 1948, Chartism had no realistic chance of success. During the peaks of Chartist activity, in 1838–39, 1841–42 and 1848, threats, accompanied by some violence, alienated many of the middle classes who, in the main, saw closer affinity with the aristocratic ruling class after 1832 than with workers. Chartists themselves frequently disagreed, some arguing for the 'moral force' of argument and propaganda, while others argued that only 'physical force' – the threat or reality of violence – could work. It is easy to write off Chartism as a political failure but this would be to ignore the sheer size of Chartist support at its peak and its ability both to educate and inform working men. Chartism produced in the 'Northern Star' a genuinely popular newspaper of high quality which had lasting influence. Chartism also played a crucial long-term role in improving the self-confidence of working people and in giving them the organisational tools which were crucial in the development of other *radical* and educational organisations, not least trade unions.

(See also *Cooper, Thomas; Jones, Ernest; O'Brien, Bronterre; O'Connor, Feargus; parliamentary reform; socialism; Vincent, Henry.*)

child labour: the work of children had long been integral both to the production of goods in the so-called 'domestic system' of industry and in agriculture. However, with the advent of the Industrial Revolution, attention was increasingly focused on the widespread use of children in factories and in mines where they often worked outside parental supervision and with at least the potential for being exploited by rapacious mill or mine owners. From the late eighteenth century, many orphans and illegitimate children were taken from their parish of origin to work in factories as so-called 'pauper apprentices'. Public consciences were aroused by the work of Jonas Hanway, *Robert Peel senior, Richard Oastler, Michael Thomas Sadler* and the *7th Earl of Shaftesbury*. This led to a spate of legislation designed to protect children, although much of it was of limited effect. The main legislative landmarks were:

1802	Health and Morals of Apprentices Act – pauper apprentices were not to work more than twelve hours a day. No inspectors were appointed to supervise the legislation
1819	Factory Act sponsored by Peel senior: no child under nine to be employed; maximum twelve-hour working day for nine- to sixteen-year-olds, but again no inspection
1833	first inspected Factory Act, applying to textile mills only: no child under nine to work; nine- to twelve-year-olds could work a maximum of eight hours and those aged thirteen to eighteen a maximum of twelve hours. Children under thirteen must have at least two hours education a day
1842	Mines Act: children and women prohibited from working underground
1844	Factory Act: in textile factories, hours of eight- to thirteen-year-olds reduced to 6½ a day and minimum education increased to three hours

1847	Factory Act: women and children could work maximum of ten hours a day
1853	Employment of Children in Factories Act: eight- to thirteen-year-olds could not work before 6 a.m. or after 6 p.m., or on Saturday afternoons
1867	Extension Act: legislation previously covering textile factories was now extended to non-textile factories and industrial workshops. No child under eight could work; eight- to thirteen-year-olds must have ten hours education a week
1867	Agricultural Gangs Act: restricted child labour in agriculture
1875	Chimney Sweeps Act: police had to provide licences for chimney sweeps, thus effectively regulating labour for 'climbing boys' for the first time

(See also *Factory Acts; Industrial Revolution; J R Stephens; Ten Hours Movement.*)

China Wars: see *Opium Wars*

cholera: severe intestinal disease frequently transmitted by drinking contaminated water. Water infected by sewage proved a particularly virulent agency for the spread of the disease. So-called Asiatic cholera reached Britain in 1831, causing more than 20,000 deaths. Further outbreaks in 1848 and 1853–54 killed 52,000 and 25,000 respectively. Particularly since it could be spread through water, to which the wealthier sections of the community in the nineteenth century had disproportionate access, cholera outbreaks acted as a substantial spur to public health legislation, beginning with the Cholera Act, 1832 giving local authorities powers to finance anti-cholera activity from the rates. The last significant outbreak in Britain occurred in 1873. Robert Koch's discovery of the cholera bacillus in 1883 led to the discovery of an effective vaccine soon widely available within Europe.

(See also *tuberculosis; typhus.*)

Church and King Riots: popular disturbances held in several English towns in the late eighteenth and early nineteenth centuries in support of the authorities and against *nonconformists* and political *radicals*. It was widely suspected that these apparent expressions of popular loyalty were either instigated, or at least stimulated, by local authorities, including clergymen. Such is almost certainly the case with the most famous: the Priestley Riot in Birmingham in July 1791. This form of rioting died out after 1815.

Church of England: the official or 'established' Church in England, originally created during the sixteenth century. Its establishment status extended to Ireland and Wales and was characterised by the legal requirement for landowners to pay 'tithes' (10 per cent of agricultural produce) or a monetary equivalent, by the compulsory payment of 'church rates' (until 1868) for the upkeep of the Church and the building of new churches, and by the presence of bishops in the Church of England. The two archbishops are appointed by the Crown on recommendation from the Prime Minister.

In the 1820s and 1830s, a substantial movement to disestablish the Church and place it on an equal footing with other Christian Churches was beaten off by substantial reform of both the parochial and episcopal structure, including the creation of new bishoprics for industrial areas. During the nineteenth century, much hostility was evinced between the Church of England and *nonconformity*, not least in education for the poor where the two competed bitterly. The *Tory Party* was the natural political haven for Church of England supporters while most nonconformists looked to the Liberals for support and anti-discriminatory legislation. The Church of Ireland (the Anglican Church in that country) was disestablished in 1869 and in Wales in 1920.

(See also *disestablishment, Ireland; disestablishment, Wales.*)

Churchill, Randolph: *Conservative* politician. Born in 1849, the son of the Duke of Marlborough, he became MP for what was effectively still the family seat of Woodstock, Oxfordshire in 1874. He came to prominence after the Conservative defeat of 1880 as leader of a reformist group within the party, quickly christened the 'Fourth Party'. He made a number of effective attacks on *Gladstone* during the *Home Rule* crisis of 1885–86 and achieved office briefly under *Salisbury*:

- Secretary for India, 1885–86
- Chancellor of the Exchequer and Leader of the *House of Commons*, 1886

He was, however, an uncomfortable colleague, fond both of criticising 'establishment' Conservatives and of threatening resignation. Salisbury accepted his resignation in December 1886 and he never held office again, going into mental and physical decline, probably caused by syphilis. He died in 1895.

(See also *Churchill, Winston; Primrose League.*)

Churchill, Winston Spencer: *Conservative* and *Liberal* politician, and *Prime Minister*. Born in 1874, the eldest son of Lord *Randolph Churchill*. His early career was as an army officer who saw action under *Kitchener* in the Sudan in 1898. He then became a journalist, reporting on the *Second Boer War* during 1900 before becoming *Unionist* MP for Oldham in 1900. He left the party over free trade in 1904, joining the Liberals. His major offices were:

- President of the Board of Trade, 1908–10
- Home Secretary, 1910–11
- First Lord of the Admiralty, 1911–15, 1939–40
- Minister of Munitions, 1917–19
- Secretary of State for War and Air, 1919–21
- Secretary for the Colonies, 1921–22
- Chancellor of the Exchequer, 1924–29
- Prime Minister, 1940–45, 1951–55
- Leader of the *Conservative Party*, 1940–45

For most of his life he was an intensely controversial figure who inspired much mistrust. A man of ferocious energies, he adopted apparently contradictory positions on many issues. While embracing progressive Liberal policies under *Asquith*, he earned the undying hostility of the working classes of South Wales for what they saw as his vicious action against strikers in Tonypandy. A brilliant writer and speaker, with a range of rhetorical flourishes, he was often accused both of lacking mastery of detail and of committing resources to ambitious schemes which could not be carried through.

During *World War I* he was forced to resign over the failed *Gallipoli* campaign. He served as a member of *Lloyd George*'s coalition Cabinet after World War I and returned to Conservative government in 1924, though labelling himself a 'constitutionalist'. He formally rejoined the Conservatives in 1929. As Chancellor of the

Exchequer he has been widely criticised by economists for taking Britain back to the *gold standard* in 1925 at an uncompetitively high rate of parity against the dollar. He was out of office during the 1930s when his strident defence of the *Empire* and, particularly, his hostility to *appeasement* made him intensely unpopular in the Conservative Party.

Prone to fits of depression, he thought his career effectively over and of himself as a failure before *World War II* brought his own 'finest hour'. His indomitable spirit, inspiring speeches and sheer physical magnetism united the nation as no one else could have done at a time when Hitler's troops were sweeping across Western Europe. He was already into his seventies when the Conservatives lost the election in 1945, but he proved a surprisingly robust leader of the opposition before returning to office as Prime Minister in 1951. By now, however, he was well past his prime. The effects of a stroke in 1953 were concealed from the public by his colleagues and he remained a backbench MP from 1955 to 1964.

Churchill was a considerable writer and wrote a rumbustious and colourful 'History of the English Speaking Peoples'. He was also a more than tolerable artist. He was awarded the Nobel Prize for Literature in 1953. He died in 1965.

(See also *Abdication Crisis; Attlee, Clement; Empire, British.*)

cinema: techniques of moving photography were developed in the 1890s and the first moving pictures were seen in London in 1896, where the first British cinema was opened in 1912. The cinema expanded phenomenally in the 1920s and 1930s, especially after the invention of 'talkies' in 1927. Cinema became one of the most popular leisure activities of the inter-war period, with Hollywood films dominant. However, a substantial British film industry also developed, nurturing the production and directorial talents of Michael Balcon and Alfred Hitchcock. Feature films were the main attraction, of course, but the spin-offs were important. Newsreels, a make-weight in the main cinema programme, nevertheless gave most ordinary citizens their first moving pictures of key political events both in Britain and around the world. Likewise, cinema gave enormous scope to the creative imagination in the advertising industry.

During both the Depression of the 1930s and *World War II* a number of effective British propaganda films were produced, such as 'Sing as we Go' (1934), starring the popular Lancashire singing artiste Gracie Fields, and Noel Coward's 'In Which we Serve' (1942). Two of the peaks of British film came with the so-called 'Gainsborough Dramas' and 'Ealing Comedies' of the later 1940s. During the 1950s the advent of mass *television* began to make inroads into the popularity of the cinema, although the British film industry experienced a revival in the 1960s, associated particularly with the brittle and modish *popular culture* of the period, with social-realist dramas such as 'Saturday Night and Sunday Morning' (1960) and 'Billy Liar' (1963) and with adaptations of nineteenth-century literary classics such as 'Far from the Madding Crowd' (1967).

(See also *leisure.*)

Citrine, Walter: trade union leader. He was born in Liverpool in 1897. He became General Secretary of the Electrical Trades Union and then, from 1926 to

1946, General Secretary of the *Trades Union Congress*. He had been Assistant General Secretary during the *General Strike* and, when promoted, did much to restore trade union confidence when the movement was on the defensive. He was always anxious to keep distance between unions and political parties. He developed links with other trade union movements worldwide. He died in 1983.

(See also *Labour Party; trade unions.*)

Civil Service: professional administrators who put the policy of government into practice. Its structure emerged originally from support for the monarch but, as the functions of government grew during the eighteenth century, many administrators also provided political support for the Government as 'placemen' with seats in the *House of Commons.* Growing opposition to North's government in the 1770s led to legislation designed to reduce such examples of government patronage. The need for a fully professional Civil Service grew with the increase of government functions during the nineteenth century, and the Civil Service Commission was established in 1855 with the aim of increasing the efficiency of government administration by recruiting on merit rather than from patronage. Competitive examination for entry to the higher ranks of the Service was introduced in 1870.

The Service grew very rapidly in the late nineteenth and twentieth centuries as the role, functions and complexity of government administration expanded. The number of civil servants in the Department of Agriculture, for example, expanded from 3,000 in 1914 to 17,000 by 1950 and in the *Post Office* from 9,000 to 255,000. In 1919–20, the Service was organised into different grades: administrative, executive and clerical. In 1968, the Civil Service Commissioners (first established to secure the political neutrality of the service) were absorbed into the Civil Service Department controlled by the *Prime Minister.*

By 1979, the Civil Service employed about 750,000 people and the incoming Prime Minister, *Margaret Thatcher*, attempted to reduce the size of the Service and also to reform it by encouraging the recruitment of senior managers from the worlds of business and industry, by devolving many of its functions and by dispersing some government functions away from London. At the same time, however, the Government's need to have its policies followed through led to the establishment of more governmental organisations needing professional administration. These policies led to widespread criticism that the political impartiality of the Civil Service was being threatened, but it did not significantly reduce the size, or cost, of the service.

Political neutrality within the Civil Service has been a key objective since the early nineteenth century, but the need to provide ministers with detailed information about, and administrative support for, government policy has often led to charges that the Government can 'politicise' the Service, not least by promotions to the most senior positions. Long-lived administrations tend to end with a senior Civil Service staffed by people known not to be broadly favourable to the Government's objectives. A truly neutral Civil Service tends to be found more readily in textbook accounts of the theoretical distinction between politicians and civil servants than in reality.

(See also *Gladstone, William; Northcote–Trevelyan Report.*)

Clarendon Commission: government report of 1861 on the state of the nine great *public schools* of the day. Its purpose was to examine the quality of education in the educational establishments which provided most of the nation's political and administrative leaders. It urged these schools to adopt modern curricula, including training in languages and science, while endorsing the centrality of the classics as the basis for an educated gentleman. It has been criticised for the anti-industrial and anti-technological bias of its recommendations as Britain attempted to meet increasingly potent commercial competition from other industrial nations.

class consciousness: a concept derived from *Marxism* which holds that social groups can be categorised according to their economic origins and that a 'consciousness' of difference, as between *aristocracy, middle classes* and working classes, leads to mutual antagonism. Differences in social structure derived from the basis of income, as in rent (aristocracy), profit (middle classes) and labour (working classes), and Marxist theory held that historical change led to inevitable conflict, first between the middle classes and the aristocracy and later – the aristocracy having been vanquished – between the middle and working classes, which would create the dictatorship of the proletariat.

Historical experience has belied the theory and, although historians have found it useful to employ class-related terminology, they have become increasingly sceptical both about the degree of 'consciousness' and about the inevitability of conflict. In Britain, as in most industrialised countries in the twentieth century, the main shifts in economic 'base' have been away from manual labour and towards the service and professional sectors. Thus, the middle classes have expanded proportionately while the working classes have contracted.

(See also *Industrial Revolution; skilled workers.*)

Cliveden Set: a wealthy group which met for weekend parties in the 1920s and 1930s at the home of Nancy and Waldorf *Astor* in Buckinghamshire. Distinguished as socialites, the group increasingly became associated with policies of *appeasement* and may have been influential in persuading Geoffrey Dawson, editor of *The Times,* to commit his influential newspaper to the policy in the mid-thirties.

coalition government: government in which power is shared between political parties. Coalitions have occurred in British history in two main circumstances:

1 when support for one party in Parliament is insufficient to produce an overall majority, as with the *Aberdeen* coalition of 1852–55
2 at times of perceived national emergency. Britain was ruled by coalitions during most of both world wars, 1915–18 and 1940–45, and also by a *National Government* formed in 1931 to handle the effects of a worldwide economic crisis and which lasted until 1940

Cobbett, William: leading *radical* journalist in the early nineteenth century. Born in Hampshire in 1762, he served in the army and taught himself to read and write. His early career was as a supporter of the authorities during the *French Revolutionary Wars* but he became a radical in 1804, and thereafter became a champion of working people and an advocate of *parliamentary reform*. His background remained agricultural, however, and this coloured much of his writing, not least his account of the hardships of the poor, especially in southern England, 'Rural Rides'. He also produced 'Cobbett's Parliamentary Register', a rival to 'Hansard'. His 'Weekly Political

Register 'was the most influential radical journal during the disturbed years after the *Napoleonic Wars*. He became radical MP for Oldham in 1832, dying in 1835.

(See also *Reform Act, 1832.*)

Cobden, Richard: leading member of the *Anti-Corn Law League*. He was born into a farming family in 1804 but made his fortune in textiles. His main beliefs were:

- repeal of the *Corn Laws*
- free trade to increase national prosperity
- peaceful resolution of disputes between nations

He pioneered political propaganda techniques to increase the League's effectiveness. In particular, he wanted MPs to be elected who would give priority to repeal of the Corn Laws, rather than representing a party. He was MP for Stockport, 1841–7, and county MP for Yorkshire, 1847–57. As a convinced *free trader* he supported the *Liberal Party* after the Corn Laws were repealed and was British representative in 1860 at the talks with France which reduced customs barriers between nations: the Cobden–Chevalier Treaty. He died in 1865.

(See also *aristocracy; free trade; Peel, Sir Robert.*)

Cobden–Chevalier Treaty, 1860: a treaty between Britain and France whereby Britain reduced tariffs on coal, *textiles* and *iron* while France made reciprocal reductions on silks, wines and brandy. The treaty not only stimulated trade between the countries but also helped improve diplomatic relations between them.

(See also *free trade; overseas trade.*)

Cockerton judgement, 1901: key legal decision that the London School Board's use of rates designed for elementary education for the purposes of secondary education was illegal. It left the interpretation of the 1870 Act by many local authorities untenable and hastened a new Education Act the following year.

(See also *Education Act, 1902; elementary schools; local government.*)

Cole, G D H: Fabian *socialist* writer. Born in 1889, he produced a large number of works on socialist theory and labour history, including, with R Postgate, 'The Common People' (1946). He also wrote many articles for the left-wing journal 'New Statesman' and encouraged the development of the *Workers' Educational Association*. He died in 1959.

(See also *Tawney, R H.*)

Coleridge, Samuel Taylor: poet and political writer. Born the son of a clergyman in 1772, he produced numerous powerful polemics against government attacks on citizens' liberties in the 1790s before turning to attacks on the materialism of an industrial society, although he had been for many years supported by the Wedgewood pottery family. He is best known as an early Romantic writer associated with the Lake poets and his most famous work is 'The Rime of the Ancient Mariner' (1798). He died in 1834.

(See also *Wordsworth, William.*)

Collins, Michael: Irish republican politician. Born the son of a farmer from Cork in 1890, he took part in the Easter Rising of 1916 and became Secretary to the *Irish*

Republican Brotherhood. After *Ireland* declared its independence in 1919 he was made Minister of Home Affairs and organised resistance to the British forces. He proved a ruthless and effective commander who later revealed diplomatic skills during negotiations for Irish independence in 1921. He became the first Chief Minister of independent Ireland in 1922, but was killed later that year in an ambush during the civil war which followed between those who supported the treaty and those who could not accept the separation of *Ulster.*

(See also *Anglo-Irish Treaty; Easter Rising; Sinn Fein.*)

Combination Acts, 1799–1800: legislation passed during the *French Revolutionary Wars* which formally declared illegal all 'combinations' of workmen 'in restraint of trade'. Many such combinations were already illegal, but this Act had general applicability across trades. Conceived largely as anti-radical legislation, they also symbolised the Government's increasing reluctance to intervene in relations between employers and employees. The Acts remained in force until 1824.

(See also *radicalism; skilled workers; trade unions.*)

Commons, House of: the lower of the two houses of the British *Parliament.* It evolved over more than 600 years to become by the early nineteenth century the more important House with right to control finance. Before 1832, the procedure whereby men became Members of Parliament was complex and, in some cases, arbitrary. However, the principle that members of the Commons were elected (or at least returned unopposed) by constituents distinguished it from the hereditary *House of Lords. Reform Acts* during the nineteenth and twentieth centuries changed the rules concerning elections and the composition of constituencies, eventually ensuring that Members of Parliament were elected by universal *suffrage* in single-member constituencies of roughly equal size. The number of MPs has varied only slightly in the nineteenth and twentieth centuries. After the *Act of Union* with Ireland in 1801, there were 658 MPs and, though numbers reduced after the Union was dissolved in 1922, they had increased again to 659 by the end of the twentieth century.

General elections were called either on the death of the sovereign (whose advisers, technically, were MPs) during the eighteenth and nineteenth centuries or, from 1716 to 1911, at intervals of no less than seven years. Theoretically, the dissolution of a Parliament is part of the royal prerogative but, in practice, the monarch accepts the 'advice' of any prime minister who can command the confidence of the House of Commons. After 1911, MPs received a salary for the first time and the maximum length of Parliament (except during wartime) was reduced to five years. In 1911, also, the House of Lords lost their veto over Commons legislation, though they could delay its passage for two parliamentary sessions (effectively two years) – a period reduced to one session in 1949.

Common Wealth Party: organisation founded by the *Liberal* MP Sir Richard Acland in 1942, largely to offer an alternative to voters dissatisfied with *Winston Churchill*'s coalition government. It won three by-elections and won one seat at the *general election* of 1945 after which it disbanded as normal party activity resumed.

(See also *House of Commons.*)

Commonwealth, British (of Nations): an organisation of self-governing states, formerly part of the British Empire, which meets periodically to discuss matters of mutual interest and concern. The term 'Commonwealth' was first coined by the Earl of *Rosebery* in 1884 to describe how Britain's colonies were changing in their constitutional relationship with the mother country. In 1926 the *Balfour* Report on the British Empire defined Britain's dominions as 'autonomous communities within the British Empire, equal in status, in no way subordinate to one another … united by common allegiance to the Crown and freely associated as members of the British Commonwealth of Nations'.

The Commonwealth came formally into being under the Statute of Westminster (1931) which conferred independence, though under the Crown, to the major white colonies of Australia, Canada, New Zealand, Newfoundland and South Africa. During the main period of decolonisation from the late 1940s to the late 1960s, almost all the newly independent nations chose to remain within the Commonwealth. Burma declined to join in 1948 and Ireland left the Commonwealth permanently in 1949. South Africa remained outside the organisation during the Apartheid period from 1961 to 1994, Pakistan was not a member in the years 1972–89, and Fiji left in 1987 but returned in 1997 when its government pledged it to return to democracy. *Nigeria*'s membership was suspended in 1995. Only one state, Mozambique, which joined in 1995, had not previously had formal territorial links with Britain. In the late 1990s, the Commonwealth comprised 54 independent nations.

(See also *Empire, British; Decolonisation.*)

Communist Party of Great Britain: organisation founded by splinter socialist groups in 1920, in the wake of the successful Communist Revolution in Russia. The party, which always had close links with Soviet Russia, never achieved mass support. Its maximum membership was about 43,000 during World War II, when Britain was allied to the USSR. With initial *Labour* support, however, it did win two parliamentary seats, in the *general election* of 1922, losing both in 1923 but regaining one from 1924 to 1929. It also won two seats in the election of 1945. It fielded 100 candidates in 1950 but has had no MP since 1951. Its newspaper, called first 'Daily Worker' and later 'Morning Star', has continued publication but with very small circulations. Its most consistent support came from *skilled workers*, especially in the Glasgow area during the 1920s, and from intellectual *Marxists*. Many intellectuals left over the Soviet invasion of Hungary in 1956 and the party limped on, in the face of defection, split and increasing contempt until it renamed itself the 'Democratic Left' after the collapse of the USSR in 1991.

(See also *socialism.*)

Complete Suffrage Movement: organisation founded by Joseph Sturge in Birmingham in 1842 in an attempt to unite *Chartists* and members of the *Anti-Corn Law League* in a concerted effort to put pressure on government to introduce democratic reforms. It had very limited success, since the support of vested interests for the more established groups proved too strong.

congress system: devised by *Castlereagh* and other European statesmen in the *Treaty of Paris* (1814–15) at the end of the *Napoleonic Wars*. It was a means of settling future disputes in regular meetings between the victorious great powers of Austria, Britain, Prussia and Russia. After the first meeting – the *Congress of Vienna* – five further Congresses were held:

1   at Aix La Chapelle (1818), France was re-admitted to international diplomacy and the army of occupation (see *Congress of Vienna*) was withdrawn

Later Congresses, however, saw much greater measure of disagreement, largely between Britain and the other victorious powers.

2 & 3   at Troppau (1820) and Laibach (1821), Britain refused to support action against nationalism in Italy and Greece and signalled its disapproval by sending only junior ministers as observers

4   at Verona (1822), Britain withdrew entirely, fearing intervention by the great powers in Spain, Portugal and Greece and reluctant to see the Congress system as a means of strengthening the old empires and regimes at the expense of new nations and new ideas about government

5   the final Congress, at St Petersburg (1825) was held in Britain's absence. Nothing was decided

(See also *Canning, George; Wellington, Duke of*.)

Conrad, Joseph: novelist. Born in Poland of Ukrainian parents in 1859, he became a merchant seaman before basing himself in Britain from 1894. His naval experience, especially in the Malay archipelago, became a vital source of inspiration. His most famous books – all written in English – are 'Lord Jim' (1900), 'Heart of Darkness' (1902) and 'Nostromo' (1904).

conscientious objectors: name given to those who refuse military service, especially in wartime, on grounds of religious belief or moral conviction. Quakers were the most numerous single group. Many conscientious objectors undertook dangerous work at the front, for example as nursing auxiliaries or ambulance drivers. Although the Government accepted the legitimacy of conscientious objection, many 'conchies' were targeted by the troops for vilification and abuse.

(See also *nonconformity; World War I; World War II*.)

conscription: the compulsory enlistment of citizens into the armed forces. British forces were manned by those who were, at least theoretically, volunteers before *World War I*, although the degree of freedom for those 'press-ganged' into the navy during the 1790s, for example, is highly dubious.

Conscription was introduced by the Military Service Act, 1916 and again in May 1939 during the build-up to *World War II*. From 1943, unmarried women between the ages of 18 and 50 were also liable to forms of war work, including actual military service. Conscription was continued by the *National Service* Act of 1947, which required short-term military service for most youths, and remained in place until 1963.

Conservative Party: the most formidably successful political organisation in modern British history. It grew out of the historical *Tory* Party, originally formed to support Charles II in the late 1670s in his determination to see his Catholic brother succeed him. The Tories were usually out of office after the Hanoverian succession of 1714 but what amounted to an anti-reform coalition under the *Younger Pitt* was formed in 1794. It comprised many old *Whigs*, Tories, 'Pittites' and independent MPs and is often seen as the origin of the modern Conservative Party. The Tories were in office almost continuously from 1794 to 1830 by which time writers were beginning to coin the term 'Conservatives' to describe those who wished to conserve the ancient, unreformed, constitution against all change. It came into more widespread use to describe *Peel*'s attempt to modernise the party in the years 1834–46.

1832–80

After considerable recovery under Peel following a disastrous general election defeat in 1832, the party split over Protection when Peel repealed the *Corn Laws* in 1846. This split gives a clue to the structure of the nineteenth-century party. Its most loyal supporters were English landowners, tenant farmers and *Church of England* clergymen and it was largely the party of England, rather than Great Britain. It tended to do better electorally in smaller towns and well-established commercial centres like Bristol than it did in the new industrial towns. However, anti-Catholic fears and prejudice could be profitably exploited by Conservatives, especially in Liverpool and in some Lancashire cotton towns. Mostly out of office after 1846 when led by the *Earl of Derby*, its fortunes revived from the late 1860s under the dynamic leadership of *Benjamin Disraeli* who presided over a major reorganisation of the party and who also attempted to make the party more attractive to the working-class voters recently enfranchised by the *Reform Act* of 1867. Disraeli appreciated how persuasive patriotism could be as a political rallying cry, especially when linked to policies of social reform. Perhaps the main seeds of later Tory dominance were sown, however, immediately after Disraeli's death and under the leadership of the *Marquess of Salisbury*.

1880–1945

In the 1880s, the Conservatives gained considerable electoral benefit from the split within the *Liberals* over *Irish Home Rule* and accepted a large number of *Unionist* MPs. At the same time, middle-class property owners saw the Conservatives as the better guarantors of property than the Liberals and the party gained in 'villa Toryism' a strong suburban vote which it has rarely lost. The party suffered its second great election defeat in 1906 after a further split over free trade but rapidly won back support. During *World War I* leading Conservatives came back into government as members of *Lloyd George*'s wartime coalition and Conservative success in the twentieth century owes much to its ability to function as the dominant element in the peacetime and wartime coalitions of 1918–22, 1931–40 and 1940–45. For much of the twentieth century, the Conservative Party gained support as the solid, reliable party which (unlike radical Liberal or Labour Socialist opponents) could be trusted not to do anything rash with people's property. *Stanley Baldwin*'s cunning leadership epitomised safety in the 1920s, just as *Winston Churchill*'s did patriotism in the 1940s. From Disraeli onwards, however, the party has never turned its back on reform. One of its main strengths has been its political adaptability to social change and its reputation with the electorate (not always deserved) for efficient economic management.

Since 1945

The party gained many new supporters in the period 1951–64 among the aspirant working classes now able to afford televisions, cars and a wide range of consumer goods. Until the late 1970s, it had the reputation (again not always deserved) of being the non-ideological party which would govern in non-sectarian fashion, guided by common sense and in the interests of the people as a whole. This reputation was enhanced by its willing support of the *Keynesian* economic consensus under *Churchill* and *Macmillan*. It underwent an enormous change under the leadership of *Margaret Thatcher*, who embraced free-market ideology while also alienating many traditional, 'hereditary' or 'one-nation' landowning Tories, especially in the shires, by her stridently expressed beliefs in *laissez-faire*. Nevertheless, her ability to appeal to self-improvers among both the upper-working classes and the lower-*middle classes*, combined with fatal divisions both within and across the other parties, ensured that even an ideologically driven Conservative leader could still win elections. The long-term consequences of *Thatcherism*, combined with electoral alienation with a party which seemed to have lost both direction and a sense of moral purpose, brought about the party's third huge Conservative defeat, this time at the hands of the *Labour Party*, in 1997.

(See also *Butler, R A; Chamberlain, Joseph; Chamberlain, Neville; Eden, Anthony; Heath, Edward; Tories.*)

Conspiracy and Protection of Property Act, 1875: *trade union* legislation passed during *Disraeli's Conservative* administration of 1874–80. By it:

- unions could not be prosecuted collectively for offences when committed by individuals. This protected unions from prosecution for conspiracy
- individuals had the right to picket peacefully: that is, to try to persuade others not to work during a strike

(See also *Trade Union Acts.*)

Contagious Diseases Acts: legislation passed in 1864, 1866 and 1869 to protect men in garrison towns and ports against the spread of *venereal disease*. Prostitutes had to be registered and to undergo regular physical examination. If infected, they could be forcibly detained in hospital. The Acts represented an example of what many women historians have called 'the double standard'. This was neatly indicated by a Royal Commission report in 1871, written wholly by men, which declared that: 'there is no comparison to be made between prostitutes and the men who consort with them. With the one sex, the offence is committed as a matter of gain; with the other it is an irregular indulgence of a natural impulse'. A campaign led by *Josephine Butler* on the grounds that the Acts discriminated against women led to their repeal in 1886.

(See also *sexually transmitted diseases.*)

continental system: economic warfare during the Napoleonic wars. Having failed to invade Britain in 1805, Napoleon attempted to starve Britain into submission by using his massive territorial strength on mainland Europe to block entry of British goods. The British responded with the Orders in Council (1807). Napoleon could not close the whole of Europe, however, and Britain survived a war of economic attrition better than France. The system's effects, however, were very serious leading to shortages and widespread *unemployment* in Britain.

(See also *Castlereagh, Viscount; economic policy; Industrial Revolution.*)

contraception: see *birth control*

Cook, Arthur James: miners' leader during the *General Strike* of 1926. Born in 1885, he supported syndicalism and used his position as President of the Miners' Federation of Great Britain to urge solidarity against the mine owners. Mutual intransigence soured the miners' dispute which led to widespread misery. Cook died in 1931.

(See also *trade unions.*)

Cooper, Thomas: journalist and *Chartist* leader. Born in 1805, he was apprenticed as a shoemaker before he became a Chartist lecturer. He argued strongly against physical force as a means of gaining Chartist objectives, although he was imprisoned for two years in 1843 for urging workers to strike in support of the Charter. He died in 1892.

(See also *O'Connor, Feargus; Vincent, Henry.*)

Co-operative Movement: largely working-class organisation based on principles of trading for mutual benefit. It was strongly influenced by the humanitarian and non-competitive ideas of *Robert Owen* and is generally held to have begun with the Rochdale Pioneer Society in 1844. Twenty-eight working men contributed £1 and set up a fund for the purchase of essential items. The movement grew rapidly after the establishment of the Co-operative Wholesale Society (CWS) in Manchester (1863) and Glasgow (1869). The organisation provided a range of trading and educational benefits for its members and became closely linked both with the trade union movement and the Labour Party, sponsoring MPs with the label 'Co-operative and Labour'. Twenty-five Co-operative MPs were elected in 1945. The organisation declined in second half of the twentieth century in the face of aggressive marketing techniques and the advent of supermarkets. Its direct parliamentary representation also declined sharply from 1983 onwards.

(See also *Labour Party; self-help.*)

Copenhagen, Battle of (2 April 1801): naval battle in the later stages of the *French Revolutionary Wars* fought by Britain under Sir Hyde Parker and Vice-Admiral Nelson. During the battle much of the Danish fleet was destroyed and its capital city was pounded by British guns. The victory ended the 'Armed Neutrality of the North' which was hostile to Britain.

(See also *Napoleonic Wars.*)

Corn Laws: protective legislation designed to give support to British farmers against foreign competition. Corn Laws had been a prominent feature of British commercial policy since 1660 and protective legislation had been enacted against widespread import of European wheat in 1804. The most important protective legislation, however, was the new Corn Law of 1815, passed at a time of rapidly falling domestic prices, which prohibited the import of wheat until the domestic price reached 80 shillings (£4) a quarter. This legislation proved intensely controversial. Opponents argued that it protected the dominant landed interest at the expense of industrialists (who had to compete in world markets without protection) and working people (who had to pay higher prices for their staple food). The government argued that this degree of protection was necessary to keep British farmers in business and supplying the country. The laws were amended in 1828 and 1842 but the basic principle of protection was not abandoned until the laws were repealed by *Peel's* government in 1846 in a move which split his landowner-dominated party.

(See also *Anti-Corn Law League; aristocracy; Derby, 14th Earl of; Conservative Party; Tory Party.*)

Corrupt and Illegal Practices Prevention Act, 1883: electoral legislation which set a limit on the money which parties could expend in each constituency at parliamentary elections.

(See also *Ballot Act; parliamentary reform; Reform Act, 1884.*)

cotton industry: the industry most rapidly transformed by mechanised production during the early stages of the *Industrial Revolution*. The main centres of the cotton industry were Lancashire and Lanarkshire and it was here that spinning, and later weaving, machines were introduced which transformed cotton into the dominant clothing fabric, displacing wool, and made it into the world's first mass-produced, factory-based industry. The totality and speed of the transformation should not be exaggerated. Much production continued in the home. *Handloom weavers* still found work until the 1850s though at depressed rates of pay and most of the factories of the first half of the nineteenth century were small-scale affairs, not the huge, impersonal monsters of legend. About two-thirds of employees in early cotton factories were women and children. Employment in cotton textiles remained one of the main sources of women's employment in Lancashire until after *World War II.*

Although foreign competition became increasingly important, the industry continued to expand substantially until 1914. It was then severely affected both by worldwide depression and by the growth of mechanised and small-scale production in the colonies, especially *India*. In consequence, cotton was one of the main casualties of the inter-war Depression and never recovered its previous importance.

(See also *Child Labour Factory Acts; women, legal status of.*)

council houses: housing provided by local authorities for rent. Few authorities could afford to build council houses before *Addison's Housing and Town Planning Act* was passed in 1919 which provided subsidies for local authorities. Further Acts in 1923 and 1924 also encouraged council house building. More than 600,000 council houses were built in the 1920s and almost 800,000 in the 1930s. These transformed *living standards* for working people in reasonably regular employment and able to keep up the rent. It was worth noting, however, that private house construction considerably outstripped council housing in both decades. Further legislation encouraged council-house building after *World War II* and by 1979 about 30 per cent of the population lived in council houses.

(See also *Conservative Party; housing; Wheatley Housing Act.*)

county boroughs: local government administrative units created under the Local Government Act of 1888. County boroughs were large urban areas which exercised the same powers as the counties of which they formed part. These included public health and roads.

(See also *county councils; local government.*)

county councils: By the Local Government Act, 1888, 66 councils in England and Wales were established and elected by ratepayers on a household franchise. *London County Council* was created as a separate entity and remained so until it was abolished in 1986. The 1888 Act remained the basis of local government until radically reorganised by the *Heath* government in 1972 with the redrawing of county boundaries, the creation and merger of several counties and the establishment of six metropolitan county councils for the six main conurbations.

(See also *county boroughs; local government; Parish Councils Act, 1894.*)

'coupon election': named colloquially given to the *general election* of 1918 when the *Prime Minister, Lloyd George,* and the leader of the *Conservative Party,* Bonar Law, determined to maintain the coalition government into peacetime. This followed a split within the *Liberal Party* between *Asquith* and Lloyd George. Supporters of Asquith either refused to join the coalition or were refused approval as candidates: refused 'the coupon' as it was derisively termed. Most of the *Labour Party* candidates also stayed out of the coalition. The election resulted in a huge majority for the coalition, but almost three times as many Conservative and *Unionist* candidates were returned as Lloyd George Liberals. The Prime Minister in effect became a prisoner of the Conservatives since they had the numbers to remove him from office at any time. Since Labour gained more seats than the Asquith Liberals, it became the official opposition for the first time. The election thus had huge implications for the history of party politics.

(See also *Baldwin, Stanley; Bonar Law, Andrew; Chanak Crisis.*)

Cousins, Frank: *trade union* leader and politician. He was born in 1904 and worked both as a miner and a lorry driver before becoming an official of the Transport and General Workers' Union. As General Secretary of the union he often urged militant policies. He became the most influential trade union leader of the 1960s. He was Minister of Technology from 1964 to 1966 in *Harold Wilson*'s first government but resigned to remain free to campaign on behalf of the unions against Labour's policy of wage restraint. He became a leading opponent of Labour's trade union reform plans in 1969. A forceful trade unionist who lacked political and, especially, ministerial skills he bears some responsibility for the growing perception that trade unions exercised too much power. He died in 1982.

(See also *Callaghan, James; Castle, Barbara.*)

Cranborne, Lord: see *Salisbury, 3rd Marquess of*

Crimean War: fought between the British, French and Turkish troops against the Russians between 1854 and 1856 after Russian forces had occupied Moldavia and Wallachia and destroyed a Turkish squadron. Britain's primary objective was to halt Russian expansion south-east into the area of the Black Sea. The main engagements, at Alma (September), *Balaclava* (October) and Inkerman (November) all took place in 1854. The Allies frustrated Russian objectives and the Treaty of Paris which ended the war in 1856:

- kept the Russian fleet out of the Black Sea, and
- guaranteed the territories of Moldavia and Wallachia under nominal Turkish government but with a high degree of internal self-government guaranteed by the Western powers

The Crimean War is primarily remembered, however, for the high degree of administrative and military incompetence with which it was waged. It proved a logistic disaster. In the severe winter of 1854–55, for example, half the British army was lost, far more as a result of inadequate protection against the cold and poor medical protection against disease than of the Russian army. The war precipitated the fall of Aberdeen's government and led to calls for widespread administrative and military reforms.

(See also *Aberdeen, Earl of; Cardwell, Edward; Charge of the Light Brigade; Cardigan, Earl of; Nightingale, Florence; Raglan, Baron.*)

Cripps, Stafford: *Labour* politician. Born the son of a Conservative MP, he trained as a lawyer and practised at the Bar with great success in the 1920s. He became a Labour MP in 1931. His main offices were:

- Minister of Aircraft Production, 1942–45
- President of the Board of Trade, 1945–47
- Chancellor of the Exchequer, 1947–50

Although he held office briefly as Solicitor General in the Labour government of 1929–31, he refused to join the *National Government* and developed strong left-wing policies within the *Labour Party* and as a member of the Socialist League. He was twice expelled from the Labour Party, in 1937 and 1939, first for working too closely with the *communists* and then for advocating a coalition of dissident MPs to get rid of the *Prime Minister Neville Chamberlain*. He entered the wartime *coalition* after the alliance with the USSR made his pro-communist policies more palatable. His high degree of efficiency was clear both in the wartime coalition and in the *Attlee* Labour government which followed it. He ascetic personality and dry presentation symbolised the 'age of austerity'. He was able to maintain a prices and profits freeze during 1948–9 but was forced to devalue the pound in 1949. He resigned on account of ill-health in 1950 and died in 1952.

(See also *Dalton, Hugh; devaluation; socialism*.)

Crosland, Charles Anthony Raven (Tony): *Labour* politician and theorist. Born in 1918 he became a Labour MP in 1950 and distinguished himself during years in opposition for his reassessment of the future for Labour politics. He published 'The Future of Socialism' (1956) and supported *Gaitskell* in his campaigns against *Aneurin Bevan* and the Labour left. His main offices were:

- Secretary of State for Education, 1965–67
- President of the Board of Trade, 1967–70
- Minister of the Environment, 1974–76
- Foreign Secretary, 1976–77

He contributed substantially to the development of comprehensive schooling in the mid-1960s and brought to all the offices he held a keen intellect and a considerable scepticism of received opinion. He died in office as Foreign Secretary in 1977.

(See also *Callaghan, James; state education; Wilson, Harold*.)

Crystal Palace: large glass building, 1,848 feet long, 408 feet broad and 66 feet high, which housed the *Great Exhibition* of 1851. Both the innovatory design by *Joseph Paxton* and the building's enormous size made it an appropriately striking building to accommodate a great international festival of technology. Originally housed in Hyde Park, it was moved to south London after the Exhibition where it became a venue for concerts and displays. Its vaulted glass arches influenced *railway* station design, notably at London's King's Cross and St Pancras and York. It burned down in 1936.

Curzon (George Nathaniel), 1st Marquess: *Conservative* politician, explorer and administrator. He was born in 1859 into an aristocratic family and became MP for Southport in 1886. He travelled widely, especially in Asia. He became a firm believer in the imperial ideals of expansion, duty and service and served in minor office in *Salisbury*'s governments of 1891–92 and 1895–98. He was created Lord Curzon in 1898, 1st Earl in 1911 and Marquess in 1921. His major offices were:

- Viceroy of *India*, 1899–1905
- Lord Privy Seal, 1915–16
- Lord President of the Council, 1916–19 (and member of the Lloyd George War Cabinet, 1924–25)
- Leader of the *House of Lords*, 1916–24
- Foreign Secretary, 1919–24

He remained in the post-war coalition but his time as Foreign Secretary was frustrating, since *Lloyd George* took many important initiatives against his advice, especially in respect of Turkish policy. He also opposed the *Balfour Declaration*, believing that the British would exert more influence in the Middle East via an Arab protectorate. While his brilliance and grasp of detail were widely admired, his arrogance and aloofness of manner earned him many enemies not least within his own party. This was an important factor in his failure to become *Prime Minister* on the resignation of *Bonar Law* in 1923. The party, certainly, and *George V*, probably, preferred the seemingly more down-to-earth style of *Stanley Baldwin*. Utterly convinced that he had been both born and bred to lead, Curzon died a disappointed man in 1925.

(See also *Empire, British*; *imperialism*.)

Cyprus: Mediterranean island which Britain occupied in 1878 and retained thereafter under notional Turkish sovereignty. It was recaptured by the Turks in 1915 but formally ceded to Britain after *World War I*. The majority of the island's population was Greek and a nationalist movement favouring unity – 'enosis' – with Greece developed in the 1950s led by Archbishop Makarios. An associated terrorist movement, EOKA, was controlled by George Grivas. To cede Cyprus to Greece would outrage the substantial Turkish minority and also destabilise relations in the Mediterranean. Accordingly, the British government resolved the conflict by granting Cyprus independence in 1959, although parts of the island were still used as a British military base. After further tension and violence, the island became effectively partitioned into Greek (southern) and Turkish (northern) zones.

(See also *United Nations*.)

D

D-Day: landings of Allied troops on the beaches of Normandy on 6 June 1944 during *Operation Overlord*. With massive air support, about 130,000 troops were landed to begin the move east which would involve the recapture of France and then the invasion of Germany over the next ten months. The operation involved about 10,000 casualties.

(See also *World War II*.)

'Daily Mail': popular newspaper first issued at a cost of a halfpenny in 1896 and owned by Sir Alfred *Harmsworth*. It launched a new era in newspaper history; its primary aims were liveliness and accessibility for people who did not have a university education. It rapidly achieved a circulation of over 200,000 – much larger than establishment newspapers such as *'The Times'*. The famous jibe of the *Prime Minister* of the day, the Marquess of Salisbury, that it was written 'by office boys for office boys' did not impede its circulation and competitors such as the 'Daily Express' (1900) and the 'Daily Sketch' (1909) soon followed. The newspaper has proved a remarkably staunch ally of the *Conservative Party* throughout its history.

'Daily Herald': newspaper of the *Labour Party*, published from 1911 to 1964. It was for many years funded by the trades union movement. After its demise, its assets were taken over by Rupert Murdoch who re-launched it as a tabloid newspaper with the title 'The Sun'.

Dalton, Hugh: Labour politician and academic. Born in 1887 in South Wales, the son of the Chaplain to Queen *Victoria*, and educated at Eton and Oxford, he became a Labour MP in 1924. He taught at the London School of Economics in the early 1930s, producing 'Practical Socialism' in 1935 as an agenda for a future Labour government which included proposals for widespread *nationalisation*. He returned to government as a member of *Churchill's* wartime coalition. His major offices were:

- Minister for Economic Warfare, 1940–42
- President of the Board of Trade, 1942–45
- Chancellor of the Exchequer, 1945–47
- Chancellor of the Duchy of Lancaster, 1948–50
- Minister of Town and Country Planning 1950–51

As Chancellor of the Exchequer, he was responsible for nationalising the *Bank of England* but was forced to resign because of an incautious word to a journalist about the contents of the Budget just before his Budget Speech. He quickly returned to office where he remained until Labour lost power in 1951. He died in 1962.

(See also *Attlee, Clement; Labour Party; Morrison, Herbert; World War II*.)

Dalton, John: mathematician and chemist. He was born in Cumberland in 1766, the son of a weaver. He performed practical experiments from an early age and became the first man to describe the phenomenon of colour blindness, which became known as 'Daltonism' for a time. He worked on the physics of gases and produced a path-breaking paper in 1801 on 'The Expansion of Gases by Heat'. His most famous contribution, however, concerned the combination of chemical elements. He produced the Periodic Table in 1805 and has a good claim to be considered the pioneer of modern quantitative chemistry.

(See also *Davy, Humphry.*)

Dardanelles Campaign: unsuccessful Allied action in 1915–16 against the Turks in an attempt to remove them from the war and thus strengthen the Russian war effort against the Germans. Supported by the navy, Allied landings in April and August 1915, which included a significant presence from Australians and New Zealanders (Anzacs), were beaten back with heavy casualties. These failures brought about the resignations of *Winston Churchill* from the Admiralty and also *Sir John Fisher* as First Sea Lord.

(See also *World War I.*)

Darwin, Charles: British naturalist. Born in 1809, he studied both medicine and biology before embarking on the 'HMS Beagle's' voyage to South America where he made extensive studies crucial in the development of his theories about evolution. These had been widely discussed within the scientific community from the 1840s, and Alfred Wallace was thinking along similar lines. However, the publication of 'On the Origin of Species by Means of Natural Selection' (1859) caused a sensation in Britain since it directly challenged biblical views about the creation. Its central thesis was that, in the fight for the scarce resources of the earth, only the fittest survived by means of evolution. 'The Descent of Man' (1871) developed the theory by arguing that humans descended from the higher primates. He died in 1882.

(See also *Darwin, Erasmus.*)

Darwin, Erasmus: British botanist and grandfather of Charles. Born in 1731, he studied medicine at Edinburgh and became a member of the English intellectual group The Lunar Society in the Midlands. He produced the influential 'Zoonomia or the laws of Organic Life' (1784–86) which incorporated some ideas about evolution which his grandson would develop further. He died in 1802.

(See also *Darwin, Charles.*)

Davies, Clement: Liberal politician. Born in 1884, he trained as a lawyer, became Liberal MP in 1929 and succeeded Archibald Sinclair as leader of the party after the 1945 *general election.* He served as leader until 1956 through the party's darkest days, seeing its complement decline to six MPs at the election of 1951, when the Liberals won only 2.5 per cent of the popular vote. He bore the inevitable jibes that the parliamentary party could be conveniently transported across London in a single taxi with good humour and fortitude, though the party did not improve its position in 1955. Refusing the office of the post of Education Secretary in *Churchill's* 1951 Cabinet, he thereby prevented the *Liberal Party* from being merged with the Conservatives.

(See also *Grimond, Jo.*)

Davison, Emily: suffragette. Born in 1872, she was a prominent member of the *Women's Social and Political Union* after its formation in 1906. She was imprisoned for militant activity and force-fed. At the 1913 Derby, she threw herself under the King's horse, thus becoming a highly publicised martyr to the suffragette cause.

(See also *suffragettes; Pankhursts.*)

Davitt, Michael: Irish journalist and nationalist politician. Born in 1846, he joined the *Fenian Movement* in 1866 and was sentenced to fifteen years' imprisonment in 1870 for gun running. He was released early and formed the *Land League*, an anti-landlord organisation, in 1879. He was both a strong supporter of Irish Home Rule but also, unlike many Parnellites, a socialist. He was elected an MP on three occasions in the 1880s and 1890s and found that his socialist beliefs ran counter to the political need to keep the Liberals favourable to Irish Home Rule after the resignation of *Gladstone*. He died in Dublin in 1906.

(See also *Ireland; Parnell, Charles Stewart.*)

Davy, Humphry: chemist. Born in Cornwall the son of a wood craftsman in 1778, he worked extensively in the field of electrochemistry, discovering that some compounds could be decomposed into their elements by the use of electricity. This led to the discovery of several key elements, including sodium and potassium. His popular reputation rests on his discovery of the miners' safety lamp (1815). He was also an effective populariser of science. He became President of the Royal Society in 1820 and died in 1829.

(See also *Dalton, John.*)

Dawson, Geoffrey: civil servant and newspaper editor. Born in 1874, he worked in South Africa during the Boer War before moving back to Britain in 1910. In 1912, he became editor of '*The Times*', a post he held, with one break from 1919 to 1923, until 1941. Because of the newspaper's standing, Dawson's opinions carried weight, which he threw behind the establishment. In the 1920s, he supported orthodox financial policies of 'sound money' and when the Abdication Crisis broke in the British press at the end of 1936, he unhesitatingly supported Baldwin's position against the King. 'The Times' also supported Chamberlain over appeasement at Munich. Dawson died in 1944.

decolonisation: the process whereby colonies are reduced in number, most gaining complete independence. In the case of Britain's colonies, the main period was from the late 1940s to the late 1960s, although the old white colonies had achieved independence within the *Empire* as dominions between 1867 and 1931. Decolonisation elsewhere was precipitated partly because of the pressure from nationalist movements, as in India from the 1920s onwards, and also from the growing realisation that the Empire was too large and unwieldy to maintain in the changed conditions of the mid-twentieth century. *World War II* was probably the key factor in accelerating a process which was usually accompanied by terrorist movements and the imprisonment of nationalist leaders, as with Mau Mau and the imprisonment of Jomo Kenyatta in the early 1950s. The outcome of the *Suez Crisis* also weakened the resolve of many British imperialists. The independence of *India*, involving partition to create a separate *Pakistan*, in 1947 was hastily crafted and produced much disorder and loss of life. However, moves towards independence in the late 1950s and early 1960s in Africa were carried out with less bloodshed and relatively less internal turmoil. Most of Britain's larger colonies in *Africa* and Asia had achieved their independence by the end of the 1960s. Independence was given to many smaller colonies (such as Fiji, the Bahamas, St Lucia and Antigua) during the 1970s and early 1980s.

(See also *Commonwealth, British.*)

Defence of the Realm Act, 1914: legislation passed near the beginning of *World War I* giving the State emergency powers to prosecute the war. It became colloquially known as 'DORA'. Among its more important powers adopted were those to:

- requisition the products of arms factories or take over the factories themselves
- control the movement and deployment of labour
- apply censorship to sensitive material

Although these provisions were taken during wartime, they had longer-term significance since they showed how the Government could use powers to effect rapid change. The implications were not lost on politicians seeking to extend welfare and other social provisions after the end of the war.

Delius, Frederick: composer. Born in Bradford into a family of wool merchants of German descent in 1862, he specialised in orchestral pieces which painted in sound scenes from rural life, such as 'Brigg Fair', 'A Song at Sunrise' and 'On Hearing the first Cuckoo in Spring'. He wrote one opera, 'A Village Romeo and Juliet'. After becoming blind he dictated compositions to an amanuensis, Eric Fenby. He died in 1934.

democracy: system of government based on the consent of those governed. Originally developed in ancient Greece, where 'citizens' were carefully distinguished from 'slaves', who had no political rights, it has taken many forms in the modern world. Of the essence of democracy, however, is the concept that mechanisms exist for the orderly and peaceful transfer of power from one group (usually a political party) to another. Britain developed a system of 'parliamentary democracy'. Here, although non-elected constitutional forms survive in the forms of the *monarchy* and the *House of Lords*, power is concentrated in the hands of a parliament now elected by so-called 'universal suffrage', in which almost all adults (excluding peers of the realm, prisoners and those certified insane) are entitled to vote for a Member of Parliament. This system evolved over a long period but the main changes were brought about in the nineteenth and twentieth centuries by parliamentary *Reform Acts*.

(See also *Commons, House of.*)

Democratic Unionist Party: Protestant political party in *Northern Ireland* founded in 1971, and led, by *Ian Paisley*. Most of its followers are staunch Presbyterians. It has taken an uncompromising stance in defence of Protestant supremacy in the province, though it frequently co-operates in Parliament with the official Unionist Party.

(See also *Ulster Unionist Party.*)

Derby (Stanley, Edward), 14th Earl of: *Whig* and later *Conservative* politician and *Prime Minister*. Born in 1799 at the ancestral seat of Knowsley Hall, Lancashire, he entered Parliament as a Whig in 1828. He was quickly appointed to government. His main political offices were:

- Secretary for Ireland, 1830–33
- Secretary for War and the Colonies, 1833–34, 1841–45
- Leader of the Conservative Party, 1846–68
- Prime Minister, 1852, 1858–59, 1866–68

As Colonial Secretary he piloted through Parliament legislation abolishing slavery in the British Empire. After resigning from *Grey*'s government on the issue of using Irish church money for non-ecclesiastical purposes, he left the Whigs and joined the *Tory Party*. He resumed his colonial responsibilities in *Peel*'s government of 1841 but left office because he opposed Peel's repeal of the Corn Laws. Thereafter he led the non-*Peelite* wing of the Conservative Party which was condemned to almost perpetual opposition in the generation after 1846. He succeeded his father to the Earldom of Derby in 1851, the year before he formed the first of three minority Conservative governments. A man of shrewdness and keen intellect, his leadership prevented further splits while he sought means of making his party attractive to both the urban middle and the working classes. To this end, the policy of protection was quietly dropped in the 1850s. During his third government, the second *Reform Act* (1867) was passed. Though Derby famously called it a 'leap in the dark', it indicated the Conservatives' determination not to be considered merely a party of English landowners. Ill-health forced him to resign the premiership in 1868 and he died the following year.

(See also *Disraeli, Benjamin*.)

Derby (Stanley, Edward Henry), 15th Earl of: *Conservative* politician. Son of the 14th Earl he was born in 1826 and followed his father into Parliament. He became Foreign Secretary in his father's 1866 government, a post he held under his successor, *Disraeli*, and held again from 1874 to 1878 in Disraeli's second administration. He prided himself on his realism, arguing that it would be fruitless to oppose the Unification of Germany which Britain was anyway powerless to prevent. He resigned office over the *Bulgarian Crisis* in April 1878, considering Disraeli's anti-Russian policy excessive. He died in 1893.

devaluation: the reduction in the value of a currency, either against gold or against other currencies. Devaluation has often been a politically sensitive issue in Britain, associated – as in 1967 – with the failure of economic policy. Maintaining the international value of currency, however, may be disadvantageous. If the pound sterling is valued highly, then exporters find it more difficult to sell goods abroad. In retrospect, *Churchill*'s decision to return the pound to the *gold standard* in 1925 at a pre-war value of $4.86 to the pound was a mistake since it hindered international trade at a time when British exporters – especially in previous key markets like textiles and shipping – were finding it increasingly difficult to sell. Over the period since 1925, the general trend has been for the pound to depreciate against both the dollar and most other leading currencies. The main government policy devaluations took place in September 1939, at the beginning of *World War II* ($4.03 to the pound); 1949 ($2.80) and 1967 ($2.40). At other periods, the pound has been allowed to 'float', finding its own level in international money markets. Britain came off the gold standard in 1931, and sank as low as $3.30 at one point, while at another it was higher against the dollar than it had been set in 1925. The pound also 'floated' after 1972. The 1970s and early 1980s was a period of considerable volatility. During the financial crisis of 1976, it sank as low as $1.56. It bounced back to $2.39 in 1980 before falling to $1.05 in 1985. Recovery from this historically low point saw the pound normally in the range $1.56 to $1.70 in the late 1980s and 1990s.

(See also *economic policy*.)

devolution: policy aimed at giving the constituent elements of the United Kingdom greater separate powers, although remaining within the Union. In Northern Ireland, *Stormont* (a Protestant-dominated parliament) exercised devolved powers from 1921 to its suspension in 1972 which included the power to raise revenue from taxation. Since 1972, Northern Ireland has been ruled direct from Westminster. Growth in support for nationalism in Scotland, especially, and Wales from the late 1960s led to the establishment of the Kilbrandon Commission which recommended devolution for both Scotland and Wales. In referenda, held in March 1979, the Welsh decisively rejected devolution while the Scots, who retained a separate educational, ecclesiastical and legal system at the Act of Union in 1707, although voting narrowly in favour, failed to reach the required threshold of 40 per cent of the registered electorate declaring for devolution. The failure of devolution ended the informal coalition supporting *Callaghan*'s minority government. The *Conservatives* elected in 1979, were firmly anti-devolution under both *Thatcher* and *Major*, leaving devolution to return to the active political agenda only with the return to power of Labour in 1997.

(See also *Commons, House of; referendum; Ulster.*)

Devonshire (Cavendish, Spencer (Marquess of Hartington)), 8th Earl of: *Liberal*, and later *Unionist*, politician. Born in 1833 into one of the richest aristocratic families in Britain, he was known as Hartington for most of his political career. He became Liberal MP for North Lancashire in 1857, remaining a member of the *House of Commons* with one brief break (1868–69) until 1891, when he succeeded to the dukedom. He was at, or near, the centre of power for most of his career. His main offices were:

- Secretary for War, 1866 and 1882–85
- Postmaster General, 1868–74
- Leader of the Liberal Party, 1875–80
- Secretary for India, 1880–82
- Lord President of the Council, 1895–1903

His varied career involved responsibility for piloting the Ballot Act through Parliament and for despatching General Gordon to Khartoum. He took over as leader after *Gladstone*'s sudden resignation, but stood aside for Gladstone after the 1880 election, informing a disappointed Queen *Victoria* that Gladstone enjoyed much more public support as *Prime Minister* than he could command. He broke with Gladstone over *Home Rule* and, with *Joseph Chamberlain*, formed a Unionist Party which soon joined the Conservatives. In 1886, he twice refused Salisbury's offer that he become Prime Minister in a Conservative and Liberal–Unionist coalition, realising that most Unionists still considered themselves Liberals and were not ready for a coalition. He supported the Conservative leadership over support for free trade in 1903 and died in 1908.

(See also *Ireland; parliamentary reform; Salisbury, Marquess of.*)

Dickens, Charles: novelist and journalist. Born in Portsmouth in 1812, he worked in a blacking factory after his father was imprisoned for debt. He enjoyed considerable success as a journalist and political reporter before 'Pickwick Papers' (1837) secured his fame as a novelist. A stream of colourful novels followed, many of them first appearing in serial form. Some, notably 'David Copperfield', were partly autobiographical.

His novels were romantic and usually sympathetic to the underdog. He exposed many abuses, such as the law's delay in 'Bleak House' and the miseries endured by industrial workers in 'Hard Times'. He was most at home, however, in his depiction of mid-century London which he knew intimately. Though he wrote 'social novels', he was never a socialist. He abhorred working-class violence and strikes and urged working people to improve themselves by education and thrift, the better to take their rightful, and respected, place in a society characterised by social harmony. He died in 1870.

(See also *Industrial Revolution; Gaskell, Elizabeth; Thackeray, William Makepeace*.)

diet: what working people were able to eat was of vital importance not only for their living standards, but on occasion for their very survival. Death rates were very high in the first half of the nineteenth century and inadequate diet produced a higher mortality rate from infectious disease than would otherwise have been the case. Until the last quarter of the nineteenth century, most working people could afford meat only on rare occasions and bread remained the staple diet. Thereafter improvements in living standards, together with the development of *railways* (which could transport perishable goods speedily) and the advent of refrigerated ships, gave them access to a more varied diet, including some meat and vegetables. Mass availability of fish and chips, especially in northern industrial towns, from the 1880s substantially improved labourers' diets. Diets improved in both variety and nutritional value during the twentieth century for those in work. Only from the 1960s did obesity, arising from readily available food of dubious nutritional value, become a greater health hazard than weakness and stunted growth deriving from inadequate food intake by the poorer sections of the community.

Dilke, Sir Charles: *radical* Liberal politician. Born into a successful literary family in 1843, he trained as a lawyer and became MP in 1868. He had been attracted to *republicanism* during the Queen's unpopularity in the 1860s but his continued support for this creed in the 1870s made him many enemies. He became a close ally of *Joseph Chamberlain* as radical liberalism gained in importance in the late 1870s. He became a *Cabinet* minister, as President of the Local Government Board, in 1882 but his career was halted spectacularly by a salacious divorce scandal in which he was cited as co-respondent by a fellow MP. He lost his seat in 1886, returning in 1892 but only to the backbenches. He died in 1911.

(See also *Gladstone, William; Liberal Party*.)

direct taxation: taxes to government paid on income, land or wealth. The essence of direct taxes is that they are paid 'directly' and usually at an agreed rate per pound (income tax at 23p in the pound, for example, means that 23 per cent of income, after allowances, is deducted from an employee's income). *Indirect taxes*, by contrast, are paid on consumption.

(See also *economic policy; income tax*.)

disestablishment involves separating the Church from government. The political unions of Ireland and Wales (though not Scotland) with England had involved incorporating the state *Church of England* into the structure of both nations. The Church of Ireland (the Anglican Church in Ireland) was supported by only about 3 per cent of the population and was disestablished in 1869 as the first of *Gladstone*'s Irish reforms designed to reduce violence and lawlessness in the country. In Wales, Protestant non-conformity had much more support than the Church of England and after a failed attempt in 1905, the Anglican Church in Wales was disestablished by the Parliament Act of 1914. Its implementation was delayed until after the end of *World War I* and finally took effect in 1920.

Disraeli, Benjamin: *Conservative* politician, novelist and *Prime Minister*. Born in 1804 into a Jewish intellectual family, he began writing novels early in his career but took some time to break into Parliament, becoming MP for Maidstone only in 1837. Early in his career he was a leader of the *Young England* movement which upheld rural values and was critical of *Peel*'s leadership. One of his novels of the 1840s, 'Sybil', coined the phrase 'two nations' to describe the vast gulf which separated the rich and the poor. He came to national prominence as the most articulate and effective Tory spokesman against the repeal of the *Corn Laws*, launching several wounding attacks on Peel's leadership. The Conservative split in 1846, quickly followed by the death of *Lord George Bentinck*, made Disraeli the leader of the Protectionist Party in the Commons. His major offices were:

- Chancellor of the Exchequer, 1852, 1858–59, 1866–68
- Leader of the Conservative Party, 1868–80
- Prime Minister, 1868, 1874–80

He served *Derby* loyally and effectively as Chancellor on the rare occasions when the Conservatives were in government in the 1850s and 1860s, though his grasp of financial detail made him no match for Gladstone. The two men developed a personal antagonism which became legendary. He was seen as the natural successor when Derby resigned, although some Conservatives would have preferred a more aristocratic, or a more naturally 'English', successor.

Disraeli's flamboyance, exotic dress and use of language all combined to make him an unusual politician. He proved an extremely effective leader of the party. He made a series of effective speeches attacking *Gladstone*'s first government in its latter years and he developed policies, based on an active foreign and imperial policy and social and labour reform, designed to be attractive to the newly enfranchised voters of 1867. The mixture worked in 1874, when the Conservatives won a large majority, but the amount of social reform Disraeli actually offered was limited. Some of his own ministers were disappointed by the relative lack of initiatives in office. In part, this was because Disraeli was in his late sixties before he became *Prime Minister* with a working majority, and his health was not good. Also, his greater concern was increasingly with foreign affairs and his diplomacy at the *Congress of Berlin* (1878) won widespread praise. Thereafter, however, the *Zulu* and Afghan Wars tarnished the Government's reputation while, at home, agricultural depression and increasing Irish nationalist disruption and violence added to its difficulties.

Disraeli proved no match for the revived energies of Gladstone in the general election campaign of 1880 and the Conservatives were defeated. Gladstone, who had always believed Disraeli shallow and stronger on image than substance, memorably asserted that 'The downfall of Beaconsfieldism is like the vanishing of some vast magnificent castle in an Italian romance'. Disraeli, who had been created Earl of Beaconsfield in 1876, resigned immediately and died the following year. Many see him as the founder of the modern Conservative Party, because of his commitment to 'one nation' and his ability to broaden the base of the Conservative Party. Others, notably Peel and *Salisbury*, have at least an equal claim. However, Disraeli's shrewd party management, extraordinary talents as a parliamentarian and his considerable record as Prime Minister all contributed to reviving Conservative fortunes after a generation spent almost entirely out of office.

(See also *Victoria*.)

dissenter: collective name for Protestants who were not members of the *Church of England*. Otherwise known as *nonconformists*, they originally dissented from the doctrines of the Church as promulgated in the 39 Articles. In nineteenth-century Britain, rivalry (by no means all of it friendly) between Church and Dissent was keen both for membership and for provisional of educational opportunity, especially once the 1851 religious census revealed that nonconformists – mostly Methodists, Congregationalists and Baptists – had as many attendances as the Church of England.

(See also *Methodist Church*.)

divorce laws: divorce in the nineteenth century was prohibitively expensive for all but the most wealthy and church courts lost jurisdiction over marriage only in 1857. The main changes in English divorce law have been:

1857   Matrimonial Causes Act: man could divorce wife on grounds of adultery; woman could divorce man on combined grounds of adultery with cruelty *or* desertion

1923   Matrimonial Causes Act: removed double standard since women could divorce on same grounds as men

1937   Matrimonial Causes Act: permitted divorce also on grounds of incurable insanity, wilful refusal to consummate, pregnancy by partner other than the husband. Wives could institute divorce also on grounds of rape, buggery and bestiality. No petition normally entertained in first three years of marriage

1967   instituted the over-arching category of 'irretrievable breakdown of marriage' – evidence of which might include any of the categories previously indicated

1970   Matrimonial Proceedings and Property Act: courts empowered to order either spouse to make financial provision for the other and asserted concept of shared property in marriage and, thus, rights at divorce

1984   minimum period for divorce reduced from three years to one

The number of divorces increased hugely in the course of the twentieth century. In 1910, only 801 divorces were effected. In 1940 this had risen to 8,300. Thereafter, increase was very rapid: 32,500 in 1950, 62,000 in 1970 and 165,000 in 1990. In the 1990s rather more than one marriage in three ended in divorce.

(See also *women: legal and occupational status of*.)

Dock Strike, 1889: important labour dispute in London which gave impetus to the development of unskilled workers' unions. The dockers struck work, claiming an increase in pay – 'the dockers' tanner' – and improved conditions. The strike generated much favourable publicity and was supported by leading radicals such as

Annie Besant. Its success was one of the factors which transformed the *trade union* movement and led to the development of mass unions in the period 1890–1914.

(See also *strike weapon*.)

dole, the: originally a name for any kind of charitable relief, it became colloquially attached to uncovenanted benefit – state supported for the long-term unemployed who had exhausted their insurance entitlement to relief. This was a common problem during the inter-war period and the Unemployment Insurance Act, 1927 made provision for unlimited benefits rather than having the long-term unemployed apply to the hated *Poor Law*. In 1930, responsibility for the long-term unemployed passed directly to central government, which instituted a means test. The system was further rationalised in 1934 when a clear distinction was made between unemployment benefit (which related to *National Insurance* contributions) and unemployment assistance paid to the long-term unemployed after they had exhausted their insurance benefit. Administration for this latter category of those 'on the dole' passed to a newly created Unemployment Assistance Board. Latterly, the term 'dole' has been widely, if imprecisely, used for anyone on unemployment benefit.

(See also *unemployment; unemployment legislation*.)

domestic service: employment within a house as cook, parlour maid, butler, etc. In Victorian Britain the ability to keep servants was one important indicator of status and respectability and the number of servants grew rapidly. In 1851, 1.2 million domestic servants were employed in Britain; by 1871 this number had increased to 1.9 million. Although the middle and upper classes were the main employers of servants, even skilled workers in regular employment might employ one or two servants, at least part-time. It was much the largest source of employment for women, and particularly the young and unmarried. In 1871, for example, three times as many female domestic servants were in employment as female textile workers (much the largest industrial category of women workers). As opportunities in clerical work began to increase, however, so the numbers of domestic servants dwindled, since the work was generally poorly paid and of low status. Complaints were regularly heard by 1914 that servants were increasingly difficult to obtain and numbers declined even more rapidly after the end of *World War I*.

dominions: See *Empire, British*

Don Pacifico: a Gibraltar-born merchant (properly David Pacifico) who gave rise to an international incident in 1850. His property was destroyed in Athens in 1847 during a nationalist uprising. Pacifico appealed to the Government as a British subject (Gibraltar had been British since 1704) for redress. This gave an opportunity for the Foreign Secretary, *Viscount Palmerston*, to declare that British subjects deserved protection wherever in the world their lives or property might be at risk. He ordered a fleet to Athens and threatened to bombard the city unless Pacifico's claims were met in full. The Greeks capitulated and Palmerston's threat gave rise to the phrase '*gunboat diplomacy*', coined by opponents like *Cobden* and *Bright* at what they considered the crude, and disproportionate, use of force by a strong power against a weak one. Palmerston's famous speech to the Commons on 25 June 1850 likened the rights of a British subject to those of a citizen during the Roman Empire was immensely popular. His analogy was 'Civis

Romanus sum' [I am a Roman citizen]: so also a British subject, in whatever land he may be, shall feel confident that the watchful eye and strong arm of Britain will protect him against injustice and wrong'.

Douglas-Home, Alec (Lord Dunglass (1918–51) and 14th Earl of Home (1951–63)): *Conservative* politician and *Prime Minister.* Born into an aristocratic Scottish family in 1903 he became an MP in 1931 and served without a break until inheriting his peerage. His major offices were:

- Lord President of the Council, 1957 and 1959–60
- Leader of the *House of Lords*, 1957–60
- Foreign Secretary, 1960–63 and 1970–74
- Leader of the *Conservative Party*, 1963–65
- Prime Minister, 1963–64

He developed extensive experience in both the foreign and commonwealth offices from the 1930s to the 1950s and accompanied *Neville Chamberlain* on his famous mission to Munich in 1938. He developed the reputation as a shrewd, smooth diplomat. However, few thought of him as a potential Prime Minister, first because his experience had been so skewed towards foreign affairs, and second because he was a peer. No peer had been Prime Minister since *Salisbury* resigned in 1902. His emergence as Prime Minister from the then opaque processes by which Conservative leaders were selected was, therefore, a surprise. Indeed, on the morning he became Prime Minister, '*The Times*' carried a headline informing its readers that *R A Butler* was to be the new Prime Minister.

Douglas-Home resigned his peerage to become Prime Minister, but his tenure was both brief and troubled. The Conservative Party, which had to face an election within a year, was in disarray after sex scandals and panic reshuffles by the previous Prime Minister, Harold Macmillan. In 1963, several leading Conservatives refused to serve under Douglas Home who was also cruelly attacked by the leader of the opposition, *Harold Wilson*, who used him to paint a picture of the Conservatives led by old-fashioned landowners – the 'grouse–moor' image – whereas he had presented his own party as anxious to use 'the white heat of new technology to forge a modern Britain'. Douglas-Home lost the election of 1964, but only narrowly. His prime ministership can now be seen as a period in which the Conservatives made a considerable recovery. Nevertheless, he resigned the leadership and, for the first time, an election of Conservative MPs was held to choose the next leader. A popular figure within the party, and admired for his honesty in the country, he continued in active politics and served as Foreign Secretary throughout the *Heath* government. He died in 1996.

(See also *Munich Crisis, 1938.*)

Dowding, Hugh: airforce commander. Born in 1882, he served as a pilot in *World War I* and was appointed Head of RAF Fighter Command in 1936. In this position, he supported development of the Hurricane and Spitfire fighter planes and then commanded the RAF during the *Battle of Britain* in 1940. His relations with politicians were usually uneasy, however, and he was removed from Fighter Command after disagreements about air policy in November 1940. He died in 1970.

(See also *Churchill, Winston; Harris, Arthur; World War II.*)

dreadnoughts: class of battleships developed before *World War I.* HMS 'Dread-nought' (launched 1906) was the first ship to be equipped with large guns throughout. It was oil-fired and turbine driven. Thereafter, dreadnoughts were at the forefront of the developing battle for Britain to sustain its naval supremacy against Germany and many further developments to battle cruisers were made, under the supervision of the innovative naval architect and Director of Naval Construction from 1912, Sir Eustace Tennyson D'Eyncourt.

Dunkirk: the site, in May and June 1940, of one of the most famous rearguard actions in *World War II.* German troops overran Holland, Belgium and France in the space of six weeks from mid-May to late June, trapping large numbers of British and French troops who had to be evacuated. About 330,000 troops were taken off the beaches around Dunkirk, most of them British. The operation saved the *British Expeditionary Force* and may even have enabled Britain to continue the war.

Durham (Lambton, John), 1st Earl of: *Whig* politician and diplomat. Born in 1792, he became MP for County Durham in 1818. He became Earl Durham in 1830. His father-in-law was Earl *Grey,* in whose government he served as Lord Privy Seal from 1830 to 1833. In this capacity, he helped frame the *Reform Act* of 1832. After serving as British Ambassador to Russia, Prussia and the Habsburg Empire, he was Governor-General of *Canada* from 1837 to 1838. His famous report on Canada (1839) recommended both the ending of the division of Upper and Lower Canada and also the development of internal self-government with what amounted to dominion status. It was acted upon in the Canada Act, 1840 and set a precedent for Britain's relations with its white colonies into the twentieth century. He died in 1840.

(See also *Empire, British; parliamentary reform.*)

Easter Rising: rebellion in *Ireland*, 25–30 April 1916, to assert Irish independence. It was organised by a group within the *Irish Republican Brotherhood*, although others urged caution and delay until promised German support was more firm. It began when the General Post Office was seized on Easter Monday by Patrick Pearse and James Connolly. The rising was put down after five days of fighting and the leading conspirators quickly executed. However, these executions helped to strengthen the Irish sense of nationhood by making the nationalist rebels into martyrs. In the first election held after *World War I*, the Irish nationalists won 82 of the 105 Irish seats and were unopposed in 55 of these.

(See also *Irish Republican Army; Sinn Fein.*)

The remains of the Liberty Hall, Dublin, 3 May 1916

Eastern Question: the name given to the changing balance of forces in south-east Europe as the Ottoman Empire declined in power and Russia tried to exploit this weakness by increasing its territorial and commercial influence in the eastern Mediterranean. Britain believed that Russian ambitions in this area threatened British commerce, and rivalry between Britain and Russia was evident not only in the *Crimean War* but also in the *Bulgarian Crisis* of 1876–78. Conflict in the Balkans from the late nineteenth century, as nationalists aimed to shake off Ottoman rule with the help of European powers, became important both as a long- and short-term factor explaining the outbreak of *World War I*.

(See also *Berlin, Congress of; Disraeli, Benjamin*.)

economic policy: for much of the nineteenth and twentieth centuries, government policy was concentrated on ensuring conditions which would maximise Britain's advantages in world trade. The commercial expansion of the late eighteenth century, which saw British goods penetrating Asia and the Americas in ever larger numbers, was followed by an Industrial Revolution in which the leading sector was cotton. By the mid-1830s textile goods produced 71 per cent of all Britain's export revenue and manufactured goods were running at more than 90 per cent of Britain's total exports. The dominant economic policy during the middle years of the nineteenth century (the so-called Victorian boom) was *laissez-faire*, whereby Britain reduced and, in most cases, removed tariff barriers to enable manufacturers and traders to reap a competitive advantage based on British technological advantages as the first industrial nation and well-established naval supremacy. Even at the height of the boom, however, the value of imports to Britain always exceeded the value of exports, the difference being made good by the sale of 'invisibles' – services, insurance and the like.

During the last quarter of the nineteenth century, competition from industrial competitors – especially the *United States* and Germany – bit hard, leading to widespread depression, especially in the agricultural sector. Meanwhile, US Gross Domestic Product exceeded British for the first time in the 1890s. This led to a reappraisal of economic objectives with some, notably *Joseph Chamberlain*, calling for a policy of *imperial preference* based on Britain's massive and far-flung *empire* to replace one of free trade grounded in what might be termed an 'industrial preference' which no longer existed. Free trade, however, remained the cornerstone of economic policy until *World War I*, although capital was being exported at an ever quicker rate.

The British economy in the inter-war period was characterised by substantial increases in the service and light industrial sector (especially *electronics* and synthetic materials) while *staple industries,* traditionally reliant upon exports (especially coal mining, *shipbuilding* and *textiles*), were ever harder hit, first by foreign competition, second by a pound set at an artificially high level when Britain went back onto the *gold standard* in 1925 and later by the effects of the Wall Street Crash. Economic volatility led to a reappraisal of overall policy, with increasing concern paid to unemployment levels (which exceeded 20 per cent in the early 1930s). Britain finally went off the gold standard in 1931 and implemented a form of imperial preference at the same time. The theories of *John Maynard Keynes*, calling for governments to adopt a more interventionist strategy to stimulate domestic demand, were widely debated in the late 1920s and 1930s. They were not influential in government until the 1940s, however.

From 1945 onwards, however, governments became increasingly interventionist, attempting to 'manage' the economy by stimulating growth and minimising *unemployment.* Until the late 1960s, these policies had success. Economic growth was substantial during a long post-war boom and domestic living standards increased more rapidly than ever before. Long-term problems remained, however, largely masked during the boom. British exporters were not, overall, regaining markets lost in the 1920s and 1930s while domestic consumers showed an alarming preference for foreign over domestic manufactured goods. After an *oil crisis*, precipitated by the Arab–Israeli war in 1973, brought massively increased fuel prices, *inflation* surfaced as the key economic problem. Wholesale and retail prices rose by almost four times between 1963 and 1978; the retail price index showed an annual increase of almost 27 per cent between August 1974 and 1975. The general trend also was for wages, buttressed by a strong *trade union* movement, to outstrip prices, which further fuelled inflation. Management of the British economy was partly taken out of government hands when a large loan was provided by the International Monetary Fund in 1976. Thereafter, *Keynesian* demand management became increasingly unfashionable. The Labour government of 1976–79 reduced expenditure and tried also to reduce the trade deficit.

This process was accelerated by the election of a Conservative government under *Margaret Thatcher* in 1979. Thatcher pursued a policy of *monetarism* which placed a much lower priority on levels of unemployment and a much higher one on deflation, reducing public sector expenditure, 'sound money' and 'squeezing inflation out of the system'. The policy in some respects represented a return to *laissez-faire* and the Gladstonian liberalism of free trade and financial orthodoxy. It produced mixed results. Unemployment, as intended for the short term, rose rapidly but Britain also lost about one quarter of its manufacturing capacity during a slump from 1979 to 1981. Both international competitiveness and economic growth rates began to increase, albeit slowly, later in the 1980s but overall taxation levels were higher by the 1990s than the late 1970s and Britain's long-term economic decline relative to other nations was not halted.

(See also *devaluation; gold standard; overseas trade.*)

Eden, Anthony (1st Earl of Avon): *Conservative* politician and *Prime Minister.* Born in 1897, he entered Parliament in 1923 as MP for Warwick and Leamington, a constituency he represented without a break until his retirement in 1957. He developed a strong interest in foreign affairs, and particularly the Middle East, and served as a junior minister at the Foreign Office in the 1920s and early 1930s. His major offices were:

- Lord Privy Seal, 1933–35
- Foreign Secretary, 1935–38, 1940–45, 1951–55
- Secretary for the Dominions, 1939–40
- Prime Minister, 1955–57

Eden was always sceptical about the policy of *appeasement* but remained in Chamberlain's government until he resigned over its official recognition of Italian occupation of Abyssinia. Thereafter, he was always close to *Winston Churchill*, who chose him as his successor. His succession to the premiership was, therefore, widely expected, but his brief tenure of office proved disastrous. His judgement probably impaired during recovery from an operation, he believed that the nationalist Egyptian leader, Gamal Nasser, was another Hitler whose aggressive actions needed to be curbed by force. The ensuing Anglo-French attack on *Suez* in support of Israel was arranged secretly and without the knowledge of the United States, which disapproved. Eden had to abort the invasion and, in the public outcry which followed, resigned, never to hold office again. It is unusual for a senior politician's experience to be so overwhelmingly slanted towards foreign affairs and this made Eden's fate doubly ironic, if not tragic. He lived on in retirement until his death in 1977, having been created a peer in 1961.

Education Act, 1870: Act which extended education provision to the poor. Often known as *Forster*'s Act, its main terms were:

- school boards, elected by ratepayers, were established with powers to raise funds for schools by charging rates
- these boards were obliged to provide elementary school accommodation (usually up to age 13) where there was insufficient provision
- *board schools* thus created would charge fees, but these could be remitted in case of poverty
- boards could make byelaws requiring children to attend school, but the Act did not itself make schooling compulsory (education became compulsory to age 10 in 1880 and free in 1891)
- schools received an annual parliamentary grant and were subject to inspections by Her Majesty's Inspectors

Although more than 5,000 new schools were created by this Act, it did not take over the large number of existing church schools, usually known as 'national' or 'voluntary' schools. In practice, most of the new schools were in towns, where there was frequent rivalry with church schools.

Education Act, 1902: education legislation which ended the role of school boards. Compulsory education had been extended to eleven years in 1893 and twelve in 1899. Church schools complained that board schools were often better funded, and some school boards had used the 1870 Act to introduce more extensive educational provision for older pupils than had been envisaged under the 1870 Act (see *Cockerton judgement*). The Conservative government therefore changed the basis of school provision. The Act is often referred to as the *Balfour* Act and its main terms were:

- school boards were abolished and their powers were transferred to *counties*, county boroughs and larger boroughs, each of which had to appoint local education authorities
- these LEAs created education committees to manage the provision of education in state schools
- education beyond elementary level could be provided but only to the amount provided by levying a 2d rate in the counties and a 1d rate in the county boroughs and boroughs. This limited provision nevertheless enabled local authorities to provide some secondary education
- voluntary (church) schools could be supported by LEAs in addition to receiving a government grant (this provision annoyed the nonconformists who argued that government should not support education provided by any one religious denomination)

Education Act, 1918: usually termed the '*Fisher* Act'. Its main terms were:

- raising the school leaving age to 14
- the formal abolition of any remaining fees for elementary education
- the provision of part-time continuing education for pupils aged 14–18.

This provision, which Fisher saw as the cornerstone of educational expansion, rapidly became a dead letter in most areas since education was one of the key areas affected by the 'Geddes Axe' of 1921

Education Act, 1944: usually termed the '*Butler* Act', it provided the framework for massive educational expansion in the second half of the twentieth century. Its main terms were:

- raising the school leaving age to 15
- introducing free, compulsory secondary education in schools of three types:
  - grammar schools for academic children who passed an examination, usually at age 11
  - technical schools for children who showed pronounced practical ability
  - 'modern' schools which did not fit into either of the other categories
- voluntary schools were confirmed as part of the rate-supported state sector and would retain their religious affiliations. All schools had to include an act of religious worship each day

The Act, although it allowed able children from economically disadvantaged backgrounds to progress through the educational system as far as university, thus greatly improving access to higher education, rapidly ran into criticism, not least from the teaching profession. Technical schools proved unpopular and relatively few were built. Widespread opposition built up to the principle of selecting pupils by ability at the age of eleven, particularly when it became apparent that resources for grammar schools usually greatly exceeded those for modern schools. The entry qualifications, set by local education authorities, also differed. In some areas, a much larger proportion of children 'passed the eleven-plus' and thus went to grammar schools than in others.

In 1965, the Labour government enacted legislation requiring local authorities to create 'comprehensive schools' which did not select on ability. The Conservative government increased the school leaving age to 16 in 1973. The majority of state secondary schools were converted to 'comprehensives' between 1965 and 1980 but a number of authorities retained grammar schools and the comprehensive system never became fully comprehensive.

education, state: see *state education*

Edward VII: King of Great Britain and Ireland from 1901 to 1910. Born in 1841, the eldest son, and second child, of Queen *Victoria* and Prince *Albert*, he married Princess Alexandra of Denmark in 1863. He disappointed and irritated both parents. He revealed too little of a serious nature in his youth to please his father, while his mother became increasingly aghast as rumours of his sexual profligacy filtered to her through court and other fashionable circles. Victoria effectively debarred him from any important duties during her long reign and he was politically frustrated. That Edward was feckless, self-indulgent and easily distracted cannot be denied but he was also patron of a number of charities and artistic and scientific ventures. He also travelled widely and got to know leading members of other royal families on a personal basis, not too difficult a task since his mother's other children had married into most of them. When he finally became King, he wished to continue to use his personal skills to help broker agreements between the European powers. He never threatened constitutional conventions, since ministers negotiated and signed the treaties. However, his good offices and easy geniality often created an atmosphere in which the diplomats could do their work. He could, for example, claim some credit for easing the way towards improving Anglo-French relations during the *ententes* of 1904–7. He tried hard behind the scenes to defuse those constitutional tensions in 1909–10 which led to the *Parliament Act* in 1911. He died in 1910 before the crisis was over.

(See also *monarchy.*)

Edward VIII: King of the United Kingdom, 1936, thereafter Duke of Windsor. Born in 1894, the eldest son of the then Prince George (later *George V*) and Princess Mary, he was created Prince of Wales in 1911. He worked hard as Prince, becoming a popular figure and showing considerable sympathy for the plight of the unemployed. His private life, however, caused increasing concern to the political establishment, especially after he became King in January 1936. There was much precedent for the casual philandering in which he indulged, but his relationship with the American divorcee Wallis Simpson careered out of political control and his determination to marry her caused the *Abdication Crisis*. Never politically astute, he minimised whatever chances he had of keeping the throne by lack of caution, stubbornness, bluster and poor choice of advice. His translation to Duke of Windsor on his abdication in December 1936 and his subsequent exile were both smoothly effected on a political level, but they left deep wounds within the royal family which never healed. Mrs Simpson, whom he married in France in 1937, was ostracised and the Duke felt bitter towards his brother and, especially, his brother's wife, Queen Elizabeth, until his death. He acted in the insultingly inappropriate post of Governor of the Bahamas during *World War II* but there is evidence that the Government, aware of fascist, pro-German sympathies, wanted him kept as far away from Britain as possible. He died in 1972, still unreconciled to the remainder of the House of Windsor, whose dukedom he had resentfully held for so long.

(See also *monarchy.*)

El Alamein, Battle of: decisive engagement fought in North Africa during *World War II* between 23 October and 4 November 1942, between the Allied Eighth Army under *Montgomery* and the German commander Erwin Rommel. Montgomery wore down the German army and forced its retreat. The Allied victory paved the way for the Allied landings in French North Africa which led to the expulsion of the Axis powers (Germany and Italy) from the area.

electric power: relatively cheap, efficient and, above all, plentiful source of energy which has transformed British society from the late nineteenth century onwards. After the discovery of electricity in the 1830s and the work of *Michael Faraday*, the industry developed from the discovery of the filament bulb by Swan and Edison in 1878. Electric street lighting appeared in 1881 and by the end of the 1880s the discovery in the USA of the alternating current machine opened up new possibilities for the use of electric power. Electric motors came into widespread use during the early twentieth century and the electronics industry grew rapidly between the wars, ancillary in part to the development of the motor car industry. A national grid, to supply power throughout the country, was completed in 1938.

The ability of the industry to provide huge amounts of power has revolutionised life in the home as well as at work. Many of the changes which provided a degree of freedom for women in the home by reducing the extent of manual labour – vacuum cleaners, refrigerators and washing machines – are electrically powered. The electricity industry was nationalised in 1947 and organised into generation and retail distribution centres. Most generation of electricity was in coal-fired stations from the 1940s to the 1960s, when gas, oil and, latterly, nuclear generation offered effective competition. The industry was privatised in the 1980s as part of *Margaret Thatcher*'s policy to return the key utilities to private ownership.

elementary schools: name given to board schools and national schools in the later nineteenth and early twentieth centuries providing basic education up to school leaving age. See *Education Acts*. Elementary schools were phased out from the later 1920s and increasingly replaced by separate primary and secondary schools normally taking children up to, and beyond, eleven years respectively.

eleven-plus: unofficial name for the tests taken by schoolchildren, normally at age eleven, to determine whether they proceeded from primary school to grammar or secondary modern schools. See *Education Act, 1944*.

Elgar, Edward: British composer. Born at Broadheath, near Worcester, into a Catholic family in 1857, he showed early talent but his career did not blossom until the composition of his oratorio 'The Dream of Gerontius' (1900). A large number of romantic works, in the German tradition but with a quite distinctive voice, followed before World War I, including two symphonies, a violin concerto and a number of orchestral pieces, including 'The Enigma Variations'. His reputation, based on the popularity of his 'Pomp and Circumstance' marches, is of a confident, patriotic composer who gave the people 'good tunes'. The reality is more complex. Elgar felt himself for many years socially underprivileged and there is much more melancholy than bombast in his best music. This is particularly the case with the four string works he composed immediately after World War I (which devastated him, since so much of his inspiration came from the German tradition) culminating in the haunting 'Cello Concerto'. After the death of his wife in 1920, he was a broken man and composed very little. He died in 1934, having fair claim to be considered Britain's greatest – and certainly most popular – composer of serious music.

Eliot, George, also Mary Ann Evans: novelist. Born in 1819, she was first attracted to philosophy and lived for a time with the positivist philosopher G H Lewes. She adopted a male pseudonym as a novelist, partly because she believed it would aid her career and partly to deflect attention from her relationship with Lewes. She wrote many novels, including 'Silas Marner' (1861) and 'Middlemarch' (1872). Her work is characterised by acute social and psychological observation as well as controlled narrative power. She died in 1890.

Eliot, Thomas Stearns (normally T S): poet and playwright. Born in the United States in 1888, he took up British citizenship soon after he arrived in 1915. An astringent critic and both a pessimistic and a conservative writer, his best known poems are 'The Love Song of J Arthur Prufrock' (1915), 'The Wasteland' (1922) and 'The Four Quartets' (1935–42). His best known play is 'The Cocktail Party' (1949). Much of his best work has a religious inspiration. He was awarded the Nobel Prize for Literature in 1948. Ironically for such a fastidious writer, one of his rare forays into light verse, 'Old Possum's Book of Practical Cats' (1939), was turned by Andrew

Lloyd Webber into the massively successful musical 'Cats'. Financial considerations apart, it is doubtful if the ascetic Eliot, who died in 1965, would have approved.

Elizabeth II: Queen of the United Kingdom since 1952. Born in 1926, the elder daughter of George, Duke of York (later *George VI*) and Elizabeth Bowes-Lyon, she married Philip Mountbatten in 1947. During her reign she has shown particular interest in, and concern for, the British Commonwealth, of which she is titular head, and her knowledge of foreign affairs generally has always impressed, and on occasion surprised, the ten prime ministers who had served her by the end of the century. She has a reputation for great conscientiousness. She took the decision to make the monarchy more accessible to the mass media in the 1960s, when she allowed a documentary film to be made, showing some private (though inevitably carefully staged) aspects of the life of the royal family. It is doubtful whether this decision was wise in the longer term.

Although key ceremonial events, such as the investiture of Charles as Prince of Wales in 1969 and the royal marriages of three of her four children, were occasions for lavish official celebration and displays of loyalty to the monarchy, the tabloid newspapers recognised that royal tittle-tattle and trivia were a sure source of high sales and easy profit. The sometimes immature, often wayward and attention-seeking, behaviour of the Queen's children, and more particularly their spouses, was treated as soap opera by an intrusive press and brought the institution of monarchy into increasing disrepute. There was little that was new in royal excesses but they were no longer hid from public view by a respectful press. The irony has been that Elizabeth II, whose reputation as a dutiful constitutional monarch stands at least as high as that of any twentieth-century monarch, has nevertheless presided over a spectacular decline in respect for the royal family as a whole. She was criticised for failing to catch the national mood in the aftermath of the death of her daughter-in-law Diana, Princess of Wales, in August 1997.

By the late 1990s, preference for a *republican* system of government was expressed by a substantial minority of British citizens, a phenomenon which had not surfaced since the self-indulgently long years of Queen *Victoria's* mourning for Prince *Albert* in the 1860s.

(See also *newspapers; television.*)

emigration: the process of leaving the mother country. Emigration has always been an important, but under-studied, element in British social history. It was particularly important during the nineteenth century when millions of people left Britain and Ireland. For most of the nineteenth and twentieth centuries (the 1930s are the main exception) emigration has exceeded immigration, usually by very large margins.

The main reasons for emigration were:

- desire for a new life with better opportunities of regular employment and/or land ownership
- availability of large amounts of unsettled or undersettled land in the United States and the colonies, especially *Canada, Australia* and *New Zealand*
- fleeing from unemployment and overpopulation at home
- fleeing from famine and disease (this was an especially important reason for Irish emigration from the 1840s)

- forced emigration through *transportation*
- incentives provided by government in terms of cash for 'assisted passages'. Between 1846 and 1869 almost 340,000 emigrants left England and Wales on assisted passages, though this represented only about 7 per cent of the total

Most emigrants were young, the most common age group being 15–40. The total number of emigrants was huge. It has been estimated that 11.4 million left Britain as emigrants between 1815 and 1930 and 7.3 million left Ireland. In terms of proportions, Irish emigration was more extensive. From the 1850s to the 1880s, about 14 Irish folk per thousand of the population emigrated; at the same time the British proportion veered between 2.6 and 5.6 per thousand. The proportion of emigrants went up at the end of the nineteenth century during the so-called Great Depression. It fell dramatically in the 1920s as opportunities abroad lessened and some countries introduced immigrant tariffs, before increasing again immediately after *World War II.*

(See also *immigration; Ireland; Irish Potato Famine; Wakefield, Edward Gibbon.*)

The Last of England, 1852–55 – Ford Madox Brown 1821–93
Birmingham Museums and Art Gallery

Empire, British: from the early seventeenth century to the late nineteenth, Britain acquired territories in all continents of the world. Its acquisitions in *India* and Africa in the second half of the nineteenth century made it comfortably both the largest and the widest flung empire in world history. At the outbreak of *World War I*, the United Kingdom, with fewer than 50 million inhabitants, ruled more than 400 million in territory which stretched over more than 11 million square miles. Inevitably, over such a long period, acquisitions occurred for a variety of reasons: settlement of previously 'uncivilised' territory, conquest and forcible annexation. Although Britain acquired and settled most of its territories in North America, *Australia, New Zealand* and India between about 1650 and 1850, it established commercial supremacy short of outright annexation in many other areas, notably Latin America and parts of the Middle East.

New South Wales

Penang
Malacca
Singapore

Bengal
Madras
India
Ceylon
Maldives
Fort York
Bombay
Laccadives
Chagos
Seychelles
Mauritius

Ionian Islands
Malta

Heligoland

Cape Colony

Niger
St Helena
Gold Coast
Ascension

British
Isles

Gambia
Sierra Leone

Labrador
Newfoundland

Bermuda
St Lucia
Tobago
Trinidad
Barbados

Bahamas
Jamaica
British
Guiana

Canada

British Honduras

◼ The British Empire 1820
△ British gains as a result
of the Napoleonic Wars
▨ Territory claimed by the
United States

British Empire, 1820

The main period of acquisition was 1880–1914 when Britain participated in a European 'scramble' to annex much of the African continent, partly through hope of commercial gain but partly in order to match the territorial ambitions of the other great powers. At the same time, the old 'white' colonies gained increasing independence and eventually self-governing dominion status. Along with territorial acquisition went a form of cultural imperialism whereby the mission was to civilise and Christianise the indigenous peoples, providing them with high-quality administration and a framework of Western law.

Loyalty to the idea of empire proved remarkably tenacious, especially in the mother country. The armed forces of the dominions and other territories in the Empire played an important role in both world wars. After 1918, however, when even more territory came Britain's way through the *League of Nations* mandates system, it became increasingly clear that maintaining an empire was overstretching increasingly limited British resources. Nationalist movements increasingly clamoured for independence and a process of remarkably rapid decolonisation began with independence for *India* and the newly created Muslim state of *Pakistan* in 1947. By the late 1960s, few territories remained under direct British rule. Southern *Rhodesia*, where the white minority maintained a rearguard action against majority rule in the 1960s and 1970s, attained independence as the black majority state of Zimbabwe in 1980.

(See Figures on pages 88 and 90. See also *Commonwealth, British; Nigeria; Singapore*.)

Employers and Workmen Act, 1875: important legislation affecting *trade unions* passed during Disraeli's government of 1874–80. By it:

- workers who broke contracts with employers, by striking or in any other way, could no longer face criminal charges and possible imprisonment for the offence
- the legal position of employers and employees was made the same: breach of contract became a civil matter for workers as well as employers. Either side could be fined on conviction

Employers' Liability Act, 1880: legislation which reduced the disparity of treatment between employers and employees. By it, employers could be sued by employees on grounds of negligence, for example by not ensuring adequate safety of machinery or by imposing working practices which exposed them to danger.

Endowed Schools Act, 1868: important legislation regulating Britain's public schools passed at the beginning of *Gladstone's* first government (1868–74). Acting on the recommendations of the *Taunton* and *Clarendon* Royal Commissions, its principal terms were:

- the appointment of three commissioners to review, and if necessary revise, the legal basis of all independent schools, paying attention to their financial basis
- charitable bequests were reviewed in order to make them more appropriate for sustaining education

Engels, Friederich: German-born writer and socialist. Born in 1820, the son of a wealthy German cotton manufacturer, he came to England on the family firm's business and stayed to study the operation of industry during the early stages of the

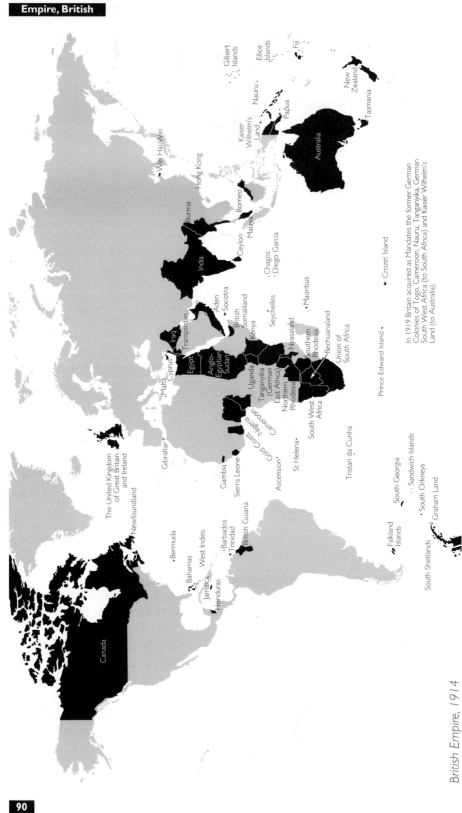

Gilbert Islands
Ellice Islands
Fiji
Kaiser Wilhelm's Land
Nauru
Papua
New Zealand
Tasmania
Australia
We Hai Wei
Hong Kong
Burma
Borneo
Malaya
Ceylon
India
Chagos
Diego Garcia
Mauritius
Crozet Island
Aden
Socotra
British Somaliland
Iraq
Transjordan
Kenya
Seychelles
Nyasaland
Bechuanaland
Cyprus
Egypt
Anglo-Egyptian Sudan
Uganda
Southern Rhodesia
Union of South Africa
Prince Edward Island
Malta
Tanganyika (German East Africa)
Northern Rhodesia
South West Africa
Gibraltar
Cameroon
Nigeria
Gold Coast
St Helena
Tristan da Cunha
Gambia
Sierra Leone
Ascension
The United Kingdom of Great Britain and Ireland
British Guiana
South Georgia
Sandwich Islands
South Orkneys
Graham Land
Newfoundland
Bermuda
West Indies
Barbados
Trinidad
Bahamas
Jamaica
Honduras
Falkland Islands
South Shetlands
Canada

In 1919 Britain acquired as Mandates the former German Colonies of Togo, Cameroon, Nauru, Tanganyika, German South West Africa (to South Africa) and Kaiser Wilhelm's Land (to Australia).

British Empire, 1914

Industrial Revolution. His most famous work was 'The Condition of the Working Classes in England in 1844' (1845), written as a young man in Manchester, which provided a devastating attack on employers and on the effects of industrial capitalism. His empirical work influenced the communist theorist Karl Marx, and together they wrote 'The Communist Manifesto' in 1848. Engels's money was used to support Marx's research and writings; the two were close friends for many years. He edited and translated much of Marx's work (which was written mostly in German) after his death. Engels died in 1895.

(See also *Marxism.*)

engineering industry: aspect of manufacturing concerned with machines, transport and the metals used in them. Effective machinery was crucial to the success of the *Industrial Revolution.* Developments in *iron* technology during the eighteenth century had been vital for the development of machinery and in the development of steam power, but the importance of engineering grew rapidly after the development of steam-powered railway engines in the 1820s. The engineering revolution of the 1850s and 1860s transformed many communities, especially the old metals towns around Birmingham and the Black Country (South Staffordshire), Sheffield and in ports and shipbuilding centres such as Newcastle on Tyne and the then new towns of Barrow in Furness and Middlesborough. Engineering also revolutionised the technology of arms manufacturing, from which many fortunes were made in the later nineteenth century. In the twentieth century, electronic engineering first rivalled, and then surpassed, earlier mechanical forms and many of the old shipbuilding, transport and metals industries suffered badly during the inter-war period. Electronic technology became ever more important to the engineering industry after 1945 and, from the 1960s onwards, more successful engineering firms became foreign-owned.

(See also *Armstrong, William; Trevithick, Richard; Stephenson, George; Stephenson, Robert; Watt, James.*)

ententes: literally meaning 'understanding' in French, the word is used collectively for diplomatic agreements, usually implying a coming together of nations which had previously been either enemies or on bad terms with each other. The term is most usually applied to the series of agreements between Britain and France from 1904 to 1907: the 'ententes cordiales' (friendly understandings). Both nations had become suspicious of German expansion which threatened French borders on the east and also continued British naval supremacy. The French and British governments came to a series of understandings about the foreign territories. Thus France agreed to Britain's dominant imperial interest in Egypt, whereas the British respected French influence in Morocco. In consequence, and despite German attempt to draw a wedge between them, the British supported French claims to control Morocco at the Algeciras Conference (Spain) in 1906. Britain also supported France when German gunboats were sent to the Moroccan port of Agadir in 1911 in the hope of weakening French control of the North African Mediterranean coast. The ententes survived to 1914 and into World War I. Thus, although these were more informal understandings than definite treaties, they helped determine the main power blocs which fought against each other from 1914 to 1918.

(See also *Edward VII.*)

entrepreneur: leader/organiser of a business. The term is frequently used in economic history to describe the owner and manager of a firm in the early industrial period. Pioneer entrepreneurs like *Richard Arkwright* or *Josiah Wedgwood* not only owned their companies but managed them directly, organising production, chasing markets and taking all high-level decisions from recruitment to risk. Inevitably, as the size of businesses increased, so functions became more specialised, a development accelerated by the advent of joint-stock companies in which ownership was transferred to shareholders. There is also a debate about the quality of entrepreneurship, some economic historians arguing that declining quality among organiser/managers was an important reason for Britain's loss of competitive edge in world markets from the 1870s. Others hold that this was a relatively unimportant factor when set against competition from nations, like the United States, which were both larger and had a wider range of natural resources.

(See also *Industrial Revolution.*)

Episcopal Church (Scotland): Church organised by bishops. After 1688, the Episcopal Church in Scotland lost its status as the established Church to the *Presbyterian Church.* In the nineteenth century, the Church had close links with the high Anglican *Oxford Movement.*

Equal Opportunities Commission: organisation set up by statute in 1975 to promote equal pay for equal work for men and women and also to reduce, and eventually eliminate, all forms of discrimination based on race and gender.

(See also *Race Relations Acts.*)

evacuation: the movement of children and, sometimes, their mothers from urban industrial areas to the countryside and smaller towns. It began in 1939 as a precaution against German air bombardments, which were expected (as eventually happened) to target the main centres of industry and commerce. Evacuation had wider social consequences. Since many evacuated children came from lower-class homes, the predominantly middle-class families with whom they stayed learned much at first hand of poverty, deprivation and different social standards. Some have argued that the experience made a radical welfare programme after the end of World War II more palatable to taxpayers, though the process of adjustment and mutual understanding was painful in many cases at the time.

(See also *World War II; welfare state.*)

evangelicalism: religious beliefs grounded in Protestantism, specifically the beliefs that the Bible offers direct lessons in moral behaviour and that a Christian should undergo a process of positive conversion. It is not in itself a religious faith, like Calvinism or Catholicism, but influences attitudes within a number of Protestant churches. In British history, the evangelical movement within the *Church of England* helped both to raise standards within the Church and to concentrate its attention on a range of social issues, not least *slavery* and *education* for the poor. Two of the most important evangelicals in early nineteenth-century Britain, *William Wilberforce* and the *7th Earl of Shaftesbury* came from the evangelical wing of the Church of England. The *Methodist Church* of the late eighteenth and early nineteenth centuries was also imbued with evangelical attitudes, notably religious conversion.

Factory Acts: legislation passed, mostly during the nineteenth century, with the intention of regulating eligibility to work in, and hours of, factory labour. The *Industrial Revolution* created a new demand for labour, especially in the textile and mining industries, which was partially satisfied by employing women and children. Pressure from humanitarian reformers led to the passing of a range of legislation designed to protect children and, to a lesser extent, women from exploitation. Reformers frequently found themselves in difficulties because calling for regulation went against the prevailing climate of opinion which held that manufacturers should be free to organise their businesses as they saw fit. Specific instances of factory legislation are dealt with elsewhere (see *child labour; Employers and Workmen Act; Employers' Liability Act; Mines Act; Ten Hours Bill; Trade Unions; Women, legal status of*) but the nineteenth century saw greater state intervention and more regulation. It should not be thought that views on the factory question were determined by one's social background and economic position. Some of the most fervent supporters of factory legislation, like *Sir Robert Peel snr* and *John Fielden*, were themselves factory owners. Likewise, many landowners, with no liking for industrialism, nevertheless opposed central regulation as restricting Englishmen's liberties. The main arguments for and against Factory Acts were:

For: humanitarian reformers, opponents of industrialism

- conditions in factories were harsh, if not downright brutal
- employers were inclined to work their employees too hard and for too little pay
- women and children needed special protection, since they were not free agents
- industrial work took place in enclosed factories, not in the open as with rural work
- employers put profit before everything else

Against: many factory owners and supporters of laissez-faire

- it was a basic principle that employers should organise and manage their concerns as they saw fit. They took the risks
- humanitarians greatly exaggerated the so-called abuses of the factory system
- employers needed to work their employees long hours because profit margins were tight. Often clear profit was made only in the last hour
- there was nothing special about factories. Regulation should apply to all workplaces, or none

family allowances:. although limited payments were made to families of demobilised soldiers in 1919, the first mass payment of family allowances was made under the Act of 1945 which provided a payment of 5 shillings (25p) a week for every child after the first and without a *means test*. Allowances were paid direct to the mother as a means of ensuring that the benefits went directly to the child. This was a central plank in the *welfare* system put in place by the Labour government of 1945–50 and was widely supported as a means of reducing poverty in large families. They had been advocated as early as 1792 by the radical writer Thomas Paine. Benefits increased to 8 shillings (40p) in 1952, 10 shillings (50p) in 1956 and 75p for the second child and £1 for subsequent ones in 1968. Allowances were termed 'child benefit' in 1975 and payments were made for all children.

(See also *Beveridge, William; National Insurance.*)

Faraday, Michael: physicist and pioneer of electronics. Born into a poor family in 1791, he worked with Sir Humphry *Davy*. He discovered electro-magnetic induction in 1831 and the rotation of light by magnetism in 1845. His work laid the foundation for the development of the dynamo and his theory that the atom was the basis of force in the natural world proved immensely significant to the development of science in the later nineteenth century and beyond. He died in 1867.

(See also *electric power.*)

fascism: political beliefs which lack internal coherence but which revolve around ideas of discipline, obedience, order and subordination of the individual to the needs of the State, often as interpreted by a great leader. European history was turned upside down by fascism and its near-ally, national socialism, in the inter-war period, but the strain proved both less virulent and less durable when it crossed to Great Britain. However, a British Union of Fascists was formed by a disaffected Labour MP, *Sir Oswald Mosley*, in 1931, taking that name in 1932. It did not put up candidates in general elections, but its activities led to riots in the East End of London in 1935–36, largely on account of the BUF's hatred of Jews (anti-Semitism). The Public Order Act of 1936 restricted BUF activity and the organisation was formally banned at the beginning of World War II in 1940.

Faulkner, Brian: Ulster Unionist politician. Born in 1921, he emerged to prominence quickly after the sectarian troubles broke out in Northern Ireland in 1968. His main offices were:

- *Prime Minister* of Northern Ireland, 1971–72
- Leader of the Unionist Party, 1974–76
- Chief Executive of the Power-Sharing Administration, 1974

In close alliance with the British government, he tried in the early 1970s to pursue moderate Unionist policies designed to be acceptable to moderate Catholics and thus defuse tensions. Centrifugal tendencies within Northern Ireland politics in the early 1970s destroyed any hopes of compromise between wholesale nationalism and unbending unionism. His own Unionist Party disowned Faulkner's concessions to the Catholics and his attempts all came to nothing. He died in 1977.

(See also *Ireland; Ulster; Ulster Unionist Party.*)

Fawcett, Dame Millicent: feminist campaigner and women's suffrage leader. She was born in 1847, the sister of *Elizabeth Garrett Anderson*. She campaigned for many women's causes, including full property rights for married women, access for women to university and the right for women to vote. She became President of the *National Union of Women's Suffrage Societies*. She opposed violence to achieve political objectives, however, and disagreed with leading *suffragettes*. She argued that giving women the vote would improve the quality not only of British politics but of domestic and family life. She died in 1929.

(See also *Davison, Emily; Pankhursts; women: legal and occupational status of.*)

Fenian Movement: Irish nationalist organisation. An underground organisation, it was founded in the late 1850s by James Stephens. Its aim was to secure an independent Ireland and it was committed to violence to achieve this objective. It organised terrorist activities in London and Manchester in 1867, involving the death of a policeman and the death of 20 people when Clerkenwell prison was attacked. It had close links with the United States and the *Irish Republican Brotherhood*.

(See also *Ireland; Irish Republican Army; Sinn Fein.*)

Festival of Britain, 1951: national festival held on the hundredth anniversary of the *Great Exhibition*. It was held on London's South Bank, and involved the building of a permanent concert hall, the Royal Festival Hall. For some, the celebrations meant the symbolic ending of Labour's age of post-war austerity. For others, it was a piece of frivolous self-indulgence which the nation could not afford and anyway offered an embarrassing contrast with Britain's role in the world a hundred years earlier.

Fielden, John: cotton manufacturer, humanitarian reformer and politician. Born in 1784, his cotton mill was in Todmorden, on the Lancashire–Yorkshire border. He developed an interest in radical politics, linked especially to support for factory reform. He was strongly opposed to *laissez-faire* and central direction by the State. He attacked the new *Poor Law* of 1834 as an example of both. He served as MP from 1832 to 1847 during which period he agitated constantly for a reduction in the hours of factory work. The *Ten Hours Act* of 1847 owes much to his tireless prompting.

(See also *Industrial Revolution; Shaftesbury, Earl of.*)

'First of June, Glorious': naval battle fought on 1 June 1794 during the *French Revolutionary Wars*. It was won in the Atlantic by the British navy under the Commander-in-Chief of the Channel Fleet, Admiral Richard Howe, after a keen battle from which the French navy retreated in good order.

'first past the post': term used to describe the electoral system used in British *general elections*. Under it, the candidate with the highest number of votes automatically wins. It has been criticised because it makes no allowance for the size of the votes for other candidates or for the proportion of the vote which the winning candidate has. Opponents prefer a system of 'proportional representation' whereby the share of the vote is taken into account and voters are allowed to express their preferences in order, rather than voting just for one candidate. Defenders of 'first past the post' argue that it produces a decisive outcome which the electorate can understand. It also forces electors to state a clear preference rather than 'hedging their bets'.

First World War: see *World War I*

Fisher, H A L (Herbert Albert Laurents): academic and politician. Born in 1865, he trained as an historian and wrote a famous 'History of Europe' (1935). He was asked by *Lloyd George* to join his wartime government in 1916 and stayed on in office until the *Prime Minister* resigned in 1922. His foremost political achievement was the *Education Act* of 1918. After leaving politics, he returned to academic life, becoming Warden of New College Oxford. He died in 1940.

Fisher, John (Baron Fisher of Kilverstone): British naval reformer and Admiral. Born in Ceylon in 1841, he worked mines and torpedoes for the navy in the 1870s. He introduced a number of reforms as Commander-in-Chief of the Mediterranean fleet at the turn of the century and, especially, as First Sea Lord from 1904 to 1910 when he introduced dreadnoughts and built up the navy to meet the growing challenge from Germany. He received a peerage in 1909 and intended to retire but came back at the invitation of *Winston Churchill* at the beginning of *World War I*. He disagreed with the Government over the importance of the *Dardanelles* campaign in 1915 and resigned. He died in 1920.

Fitt (Gerard (Gerry)), Baron: Northern Ireland politician. Born into a Catholic family in 1926, he went into politics and represented the moderate wing of Catholicism as MP for West Belfast. In this capacity, he organised civil rights protests in the late 1960s. He formed, and led, the Social Democratic and Labour Party from 1970 to 1979 and worked with Unionist politicians, such as *Terence O'Neill* and *Brian Faulkner*, in order to achieve a peaceful resolution of the difficulties in Northern Ireland. The target of frequent assassination attempts, he won the respect of politicians of all parties for his courage, honesty and determination to meet both violence and sectarian hatred with reasoned argument. He accepted a peerage in 1983.

(See also *Ireland; Irish Republican Army*.)

Fleming, Alexander: doctor and bacteriologist. Born in Ayrshire, Scotland in 1881. He worked on anti-bacterial agents and discovered lysozyme in 1922. He is most celebrated for his discovery – in partially accidental circumstances – of penicillin, a fungus growing on decaying organic matter. This opened the way for the development of antibiotics which dramatically reduced mortality for a number of diseases including tuberculosis and syphilis. Fleming received a Nobel Prize in 1945 jointly with the Australian-born pathologist, Howard Florey, who had developed the anti-bacterial properties of penicillin. He died in 1955.

football: see *Association Football; Rugby League Football; Rugby Union Football*

Forster, E M (Edward Morgan): novelist. He was born in 1879 and wrote novels which showed an acute sense both of place and of social observation. His most famous books, 'A Room with a View' (1908), 'Howard's End' (1910) and 'A Passage to India' (1924) were all filmed in the 1980s in representations which themselves signified a renaissance in British *cinema* with the accent on lavish, romantic work which nevertheless emphasised minute observation of character.

Fox, Charles James: *Whig* politician. Born into an aristocratic Whig family in 1749, he soon rose to prominence as one of the leaders of the Whigs who opposed *George III's* attempt to break the domination of the Whig Party. He was in charge of foreign affairs three times, in 1782, 1783 and 1806 but was usually out of office during his political maturity, opposing *William Pitt the Younger* both in peace, during the 1780s, and in war from 1793. During the *French Revolutionary Wars*, he attempted to protect the liberties of citizens against legislation passed by Pitt to harry British supporters of French revolutionary principles. His stand proved unpopular with the propertied classes, however, and Pitt's alliance with the *Duke of Portland* in 1794 provided the *Prime Minister* with a huge parliamentary majority against which Fox could not prevail. He returned to office as part of a coalition known as the Ministry of All the Talents (1806–7) but died in office at the end of 1806, a few months after his great rival.

(See also *Napoleonic Wars; Whig Party*.)

Fox-Talbot, William Henry: pioneer of photography. Born in Dorset in 1800, he became an MP in 1833 but was mostly interested in experiments. These led to the discovery of photography by exposing sheets of paper, soaked in salt, to light which became fixed after being exposed to silver nitrate. He first called the process 'photogenic drawing', emphasising the importance of light. He announced his discoveries in 1839 and thereafter worked to perfect his techniques. He died in 1877.

franchise: term meaning the right to vote. Thus franchise reformers were those who campaigned to increase the number of voters.

(See also *parliamentary reform; Reform Acts; suffragettes.*)

Free Church of Scotland: Church which rejected an official, or state, religion. It was formed in 1843 during the so-called 'disruption' of the Scottish Church when almost half of the membership and clergy of the established Church of Scotland left ('seceded') to form their own Church, with the emphasis on *evangelicalism* and Calvinist doctrine. Many of those who left were from, or represented communities dominated by, the urban middle classes. The Free Church was, in some senses, an assertion of independence from a landowning elite and so had social, as well as religious, implications.

(See also *Episcopal Church, Scotland.*)

free trade: economic doctrine based on the theory that removal of trading barriers between countries would lower prices (because of free competition), thus increasing the overall volume of commerce and improving national prosperity. The theory was formulated by the Scottish eighteenth-century political philosopher, Adam Smith (1726–90) in his book 'Wealth of Nations' (1776). The ideas interested the younger *Pitt* in the 1780s and the *Liverpool* government of the 1820s reduced tariffs on a number of goods. Free-trade ideas seemed to link with British interests during the early stages of the *Industrial Revolution* when Britain had a virtual monopoly of industrial production in some areas. The most decisive steps towards free trade were taken by *Peel's* government during the budgets of 1842 and 1845 and, especially, in the highly controversial repeal of the *Corn Laws* (1846). The repeal by *Russell's* government in 1849 of the *Navigation Acts* made Britain effectively a country committed to free trade and for the next half-century its guiding principles seemed to be an unshakeable orthodoxy of government policy. It was far from clear, however, that free trade operated in British interests when other nations, with greater natural resources, were able to out-sell Britain.

Britain has been in relative economic decline since the 1870s and some economic historians argue that one reason is that the country clung to an inappropriate economic ideology for too long. The government formally abandoned free trade as a guiding principle in 1931–32, in the depths of the worldwide Depression, and for much of the twentieth-century government priorities have been to managing the economy in order to maximise productivity and reduce unemployment.

Britain's joining the European Economic Community in 1973 can be seen as further recognition that free trade was not a government objective. Within the EC, member states work to reduce, or remove, tariffs but they were highly protective of the Community against other economic and political organisations and they operate price-support mechanisms which operate against the laws of supply and demand.

Margaret Thatcher, who attempted to reverse the economic trends of the previous 40 years by reducing government intervention in economic affairs and promoting free-trade ideas, found the protective aspects of the EC irksome. Overall, however, belief in free trade as an economic panacea has not recovered from the blows it took during the inter-war Depression.

(See also *Chamberlain, Joseph; Conservative Party; laissez-faire; Huskisson, William; Cobden; Cobden–Chevalier Treaty.*)

French Revolution: political revolution in France in 1789 which led in 1793 to the execution of the French King, Louis XVI, the end of absolute monarchical rule and the establishment of a republic. Its importance in British history derives from the political influence and example it offered. For those who wanted reform of the old, aristocratic-dominated system of government, notions of 'liberty, equality and fraternity' were highly attractive not just in the immediate aftermath of the revolution but for much of the first half of the nineteenth century. For defenders of the old system, acceptance of what they called 'French principles' spelled the end of civilisation as they knew it. Most property owners feared the French Revolution rather than applauded it, and its 'terror phase' (1792–94) was used as an awful warning against any dealings with 'Jacobins and atheists' infected by the French 'disease'. Probably, the impact of the French Revolution delayed the achievement of *parliamentary reform* as well as polarising society on issues of political principle.

(See also *Canning, George; Pitt the Younger; Fox, Charles James; French Revolutionary Wars; Liverpool, Earl of.*)

French Revolutionary Wars: wars between Britain, with several allies, against France, 1793–1802. The *French Revolution* alarmed the established monarchies and empires of Europe and war between France and Austria and Prussia had broken out in April 1792. Britain initially refused to join the war but did so in February 1793.

Causes of the War

1 French war successes against the Austrians led to their occupation of the southern Netherlands. This threatened Britain since a hostile power now occupied so much of the NW Europe coastline

2 French occupation threatened established British trade routes via the River Scheldt

3 growing fears that French revolutionary ideas might be imposed elsewhere in Europe by force

The war lasted for almost nine years but it was a fitful and, at times, confused struggle involving various alliances and few decisive land battles involving British troops. Overall, however, Britain was on the defensive and depended upon its naval supremacy to survive. French military might usually proved too much for Britain's allies and, at times, Britain faced France alone.

Main alliances against France

I First coalition
February 1793: Britain; Prussia (left 1795); Spain (left 1795); Austria (made separate peace with France 1797); Sardinia (1796)

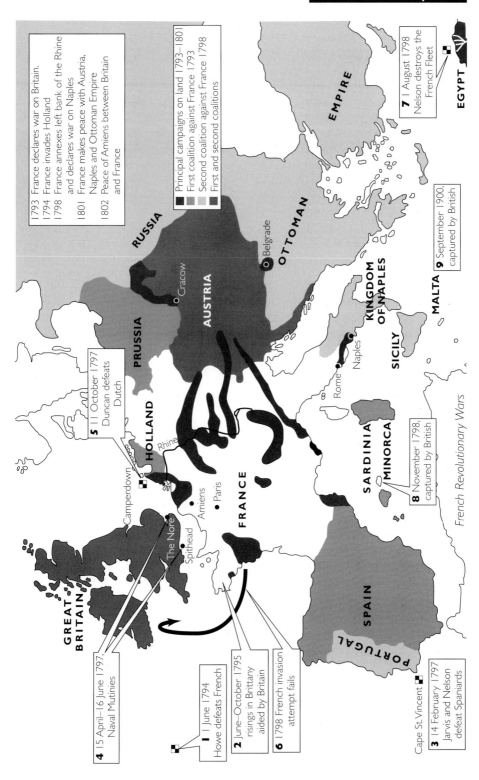

1793 France declares war on Britain.
1794 France invades Holland
1798 France annexes left bank of the Rhine and declares war on Naples
1801 France makes peace with Austria, Naples and Ottoman Empire
1802 Peace of Amiens between Britain and France

Principal campaigns on land 1793–1801
First coalition against France 1793
Second coalition against France 1798
First and second coalitions

7 1 August 1798 Nelson destroys the French Fleet

EGYPT

EMPIRE

OTTOMAN

RUSSIA

Belgrade

Cracow

AUSTRIA

PRUSSIA

5 11 October 1797 Duncan defeats Dutch

HOLLAND

Rhine

Camperdown

Amiens

The Nore

Spithead

• Paris

FRANCE

GREAT BRITAIN

4 15 April–16 June 1797, Naval Mutinies

KINGDOM OF NAPLES

SICILY

Naples

Rome

MALTA

9 September 1900, captured by British

SARDINIA

MINORCA

8 November 1798, captured by British

SPAIN

PORTUGAL

Cape St.Vincent

3 14 February 1797 Jarvis and Nelson defeat Spaniards

1 1 June 1794 Howe defeats French

2 June–October 1795 risings in Brittany aided by Britain

6 1798 French invasion attempt fails

French Revolutionary Wars

2 Second coalition

June 1799: Britain; Russia (left 1800); Austria (left 1801); Turkey; Portugal (left 1801); Naples (left 1801)

Theatres of War

I Europe

1793   Duke of York defeated at Hondschoote

1795   Britain tries to aid French counter-revolutionaries at Quiberon Bay but the expedition is unsuccessful. Meanwhile Prussia makes peace and French-dominated Batavian Republic (Holland) declares war on Britain

1796   Spain declares war on Britain

1797   Austria makes peace with France at Campo Formio: Britain isolated

1798   alliance made between Britain and Russia

1800   Britain captures Malta – armed neutrality established between Russia, Sweden, Denmark and Prussia against Britain's right to search foreign ships

1801   after naval victories, the armed neutrality breaks up

2 West Indies and other islands

1794   Britain captures Martinique, St Lucia, Seychelles and Guadeloupe, but French recapture Guadeloupe

1795   Ceylon captured from the Dutch

1796   St Lucia and Grenada captured from the French

1797   Trinidad captured

3 Main naval engagements

1794   *First of June* (against the French)

1797   *St Vincent* (against the Spanish); *Camperdown* (against the Dutch)

1798   *Nile* (otherwise known as Aboukir Bay, against the French in Egypt)

1799   blockade of Batavian Republic (Holland)

1801   *Copenhagen* (forced Denmark to a truce)

4 Egypt

1798   French expedition begins under Napoleon

1799   Napoleon's siege of Acre broken by British and Turkish forces

1801   France defeated near Alexandria; Cairo captured by Abercromby

In so far as a general pattern can be distinguished, it is that Britain, which expended large sums on subsidies to Allies in Europe, got poor value for money, throwing doubt on the validity of the war strategy of *Pitt the Younger*. Britain was much more successful in the West Indies, although large numbers of troops were lost to yellow fever, and especially on the seas. Britain could not be invaded because of its naval strength. Peace was eventually negotiated at the *Treaty of Amiens* but no fundamental matters were determined and few believed that the peace would prove permanent.

(See Figure on page 99. See also *Napoleonic Wars; Peninsular War.*)

French, Sir John (Viscount French, 1st Earl of Ypres): army commander. Born in 1852, he served with distinction in South Africa during the *Second Boer War*. He became Commander-in-Chief of the *British Expeditionary Force* in 1914 and was in charge at the *Battle of the Marne*. Poor relations with the French contributed to his being replaced by *Haig* at the end of 1915, whereupon he became Commander-in-Chief of the Home Forces. He was Lord Lieutenant of *Ireland*, 1918–21, during the difficult final period of that country's union with Great Britain. He was not a great success in that office. His earldom was conferred in 1922 and he died in 1925.

(See also *World War I*.)

friendly societies: mutual benefit and insurance societies which collected funds in the form of subscriptions and paid out benefits. Originating in the later eighteenth century, they became perhaps the most important of the *self-help* organisations for the secure working classes and lower-middle classes in Victorian Britain. By law, their rules had to be published and acceptable (1793) and a register of all societies was kept (from 1846). By the 1870s, they had more than 4 million members and more than 6½ million at the outbreak of *World War I*. Members subscribed usually small amounts which built up into a fund on which they could draw in times of need, usually in the form of sickness or unemployment benefit. They could also be used to provide pensions or help to a family after the birth of a child. They were particularly numerous in the industrial North of England. The names many adopted – such as 'The Royal Order of Ancient Shepherds' and 'Hearts of Oak' indicated the importance of both religion and respectability for their members. The State used many of their ideas and also their administration when introducing *National Insurance* in 1911. As the State increased its *welfare* responsibilities, the importance of friendly societies declined but they remained as a repository for small savings in the late twentieth century, though under increasing competitive pressure from large financial institutions.

(See also *building societies*.)

Fry, Elizabeth: philanthropist and prison reformer. Born into the wealthy Gurney banking family in 1780, she founded hostels for the homeless and contributed to an extensive range of charities. She took an interest in prison conditions, especially those experienced by women and children, after an inspection of Newgate prison in 1813. She formed prisoners' aid societies and campaigned to increase the nation's awareness of the squalor of much prison life. Her work was partly responsible for reforms in the 1820s. She died in 1845.

(See also *evangelicalism; Gaols Act; Peel, Sir Robert, Jnr; prison reform movement*.)

G

Gaitskell, Hugh: Labour politician. Born in 1906, he was educated at Winchester and Oxford and while an undergraduate supported strikers during the *General Strike*. He became MP during the Labour landslide of 1945. His major offices were:

- Minister of Fuel and Power, 1947–50
- Chancellor of the Exchequer, 1950–51
- Leader of the Labour Party and Leader of the Opposition, 1955–63

He quickly established his credentials on the right wing of the party and is perhaps best remembered for his titanic battles with *Aneurin Bevan*, the left's standard bearer, whom he defeated for the leadership on *Attlee*'s resignation. These battles between very different characters frequently deflected the party from the task of defeating the *Conservatives*, who won a large election victory in 1959. After this Gaitskell attempted to reform the *Labour Party* and, especially, tried – without success – to remove 'Clause 4' – the commitment to nationalisation – from its constitution. On this, and also on *unilateralism* (a battle he won), he was opposed vigorously by Bevan during 1959–60. He seemed very likely to win the next election, due in 1963 or 1964, and thus become *Prime Minister*, but was struck down by a severe virus and died in 1963.

(See also *Labour Party; Brown, George; trade unions; Wilson, Harold*.)

Gaols Act, 1823: reformist prison legislation. Introduced by *Sir Robert Peel* as Home Secretary, it provided for:

- women prisoners to have women gaolers
- gaolers to receive agreed wages
- use of irons for prisoners, only with the approval of magistrates

The legislation owed much to the campaigns of *Elizabeth Fry* but did not provide for inspectors which greatly reduced its practical effectiveness.

(See also *prison reform movement*.)

'garden cities': new towns or communities characterised by planned layout and space. Two early prototypes were the industrial settlements of Levers at Port Sunlight (1890) and Cadbury at Bournville (1891). However, garden cities proper were designed to house far more people. The early examples were designed to house over-spill from London. The first was Letchworth (Hertfordshire) in 1903 followed by Welwyn Garden City (Hertfordshire) in 1920.

(See also *housing; new towns*.)

gas industry: one of the main providers of energy in nineteenth- and twentieth-century Britain. The technology for producing gas from coal had been developed at the end of the eighteenth century. Its main purpose in the nineteenth century was, first, in the provision of street lighting and later in domestic lighting and cooking. Samuel Clegg developed technology enabling large amounts of gas to be stored in gasholders and the use of gas greatly increased from the 1830s, thereby increasing the need for *coal*. Gas came into widespread industrial use in the twentieth century and traditional gas production technology was revolutionised by the discovery of natural gas in the North Sea in the late 1960s.

(See also *Industrial Revolution.*)

Gas Workers' Strike, 1889: along with the *Dockers' Strike*, this was one of the key events leading to the development of *new unions*. A gas workers' union had been founded in 1888 and it successfully demanded reductions of hours to a maximum eight-hour working day without loss of pay.

(See also *trade unions.*)

Gaskell, Elizabeth: novelist. Born in 1810 and brought up in Lancashire, she made her name by writing novels with an acute sense of place. A favourite theme was the Industrial Revolution and its effects on working people. Both 'Mary Barton' (1848) and 'North and South' (1854) took a sympathetic view of the plight and privations of working people oppressed by manufacturers. She also wrote 'Cranford' (1853), based on the small Cheshire town of Knutsford. She died in 1865.

(See also *Dickens, Charles; housing; Industrial Revolution.*)

general elections: in modern times, the means of choosing governments by electing members of the *House of Commons*. Before 1832, however, general elections rarely changed governments. They were a means of electing Members of *Parliament* on an individual basis, rather than as representatives of a particular party. Only with the advent of party politics in reasonably modern form did general elections become more important. Landmark elections were those of:

- 1841, when *Peel's* Conservatives for the first time overturned a majority held by *Melbourne's* Whigs, the first occasion on which this had been done
- 1868, when *Gladstone's* *Liberals* defeated *Disraeli's* Conservatives and Disraeli resigned before the newly elected Parliament met. This was a symbolic recognition of the new importance of the electorate

In the twentieth century, general elections usually produced decisive results, with a Liberal 'landslide' (very large majority) in 1906, a Conservative one in 1983 and two Labour landslides in 1945 and 1997. Qualifications to vote were altered by the various *Reform Acts* passed between 1832 and 1969. The right to dissolve Parliament and call a general election theoretically resides with the monarch but in virtually all cases, the monarch will accept the advice of the outgoing *prime minister* that Parliament be dissolved. This could be at any time, but general elections before 1911 had to be held at least once every seven years and from 1911 every five years. This rule was suspended, however, during both *world wars*.

(See Figure on page 104. See also *parliamentary reform.*)

General Strike: a national stoppage of work called by the *Trades Union Congress* in support of coal miners who were on strike for better wages. The strike lasted from 4 to 12 May 1926 and was widely supported by trade unionists, especially in transport and heavy industry. The army and police did not join the strike and supported the Government. Government used *propaganda*, not least in their special strike newspaper 'British Gazette', urging that the strike was unconstitutional and a direct challenge to the authority of government. Despite initial solidarity, the TUC failed to provide strong leadership and called the strike off without any concessions by the

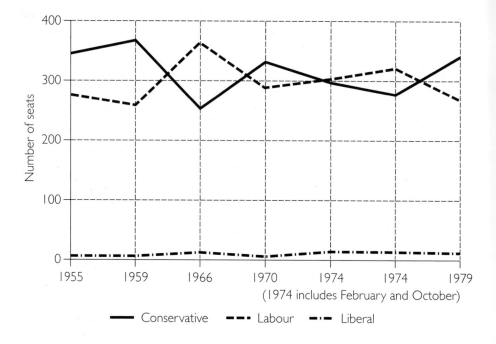

Numbers of seats won in general elections 1955–79

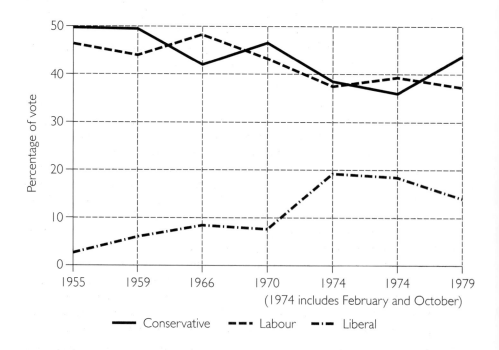

Percentage of vote won in general elections 1955–79

coal owners. The miners remained on strike but were forced back to work five months later without any success. The strike was a great blow to the trade unions which lost both confidence and membership.

(See Figure on page 106. See also *Baldwin, Stanley; Cook, Arthur James, Churchill, Winston; Trade Union Act, 1927; trade unions.*)

George III: King of Great Britain and Ireland from 1760 to 1820 and the third monarch of the Hanoverian dynasty. He was born in England in 1738, the first Hanoverian monarch to be so, and he succeeded to the throne on the death of his grandfather, George II, his father, Frederick Prince of Wales, having died in 1751. His mother, Princess Augusta of Saxe-Gotha, was a dominant influence on him in his early years. The first part of his reign involved a struggle with the *Whig* politicians, in which the King asserted his right to choose his own ministers, and the loss of the American colonies. From 1783, he moved more into the background of politics since he had, in the *Younger Pitt*, a *Prime Minister* he approved of and who could also command majorities in the *House of Commons*. He did, however, retain strong opinions. He wholly supported Pitt in his opposition to *radicalism* in the wake of the *French Revolution* but he opposed him on *Catholic emancipation,* a policy he considered against his coronation oath.

The later years of his reign were dominated by external dangers, especially the *French Revolutionary* and *Napoleonic Wars,* and by inner turmoil. He also became prone to bouts of mental instability, the most famous episode of which occurred in 1788 and precipitated a political crisis. From 1811, he was declared permanently unfit to rule and his son succeeded him as Prince Regent. When fit, he was a highly dutiful monarch, whose very conscientiousness helped to cause conflict with politicians. He was also devoted to his wife and, based on his genuine love for farming and the English countryside, liked to believe that he was a typical landowner with the attitudes, beliefs and patriotic instincts of an Englishman. He died in 1820.

(See also *George IV; Fox, Charles James.*)

George IV: King of the United Kingdom from 1820 to 1830 and the fourth monarch of the Hanoverian dynasty. He was born in 1762, the eldest son of *George III* and Queen Caroline of Mecklenburgh-Strelitz. He was an important political figure for much of his adult life, although not for reasons which reflect credit on the institution of monarchy. During his period, both as Prince Regent (1811–20) and King, he was the subject of fierce criticism for his self-indulgent lifestyle and lack of political judgement. From his late teenage years, he developed a reputation both for sexual licence and for wasteful expenditure and had frequent disagreements with his father. He contracted a secret, and illegal, marriage in 1785 to the Catholic Maria Fitzherbert and the relationship apparently continued until 1811. In 1795, he married *Caroline* of Brunswick, by whom he had a daughter, Charlotte, who predeceased him in 1817. His official marriage was a complete disaster and became a public scandal in 1820 when he tried, without success, to divorce her. Against the advice of his ministers, he thus opened the monarchy to ridicule as the sexual and other excesses of a deeply unattractive couple became the sport of journalists and cartoonists.

Despite early support for the *Whigs,* as both Regent and King he sustained anti-reformist *Tory* ministries in office. He frequently disagreed with his *Prime Minister,*

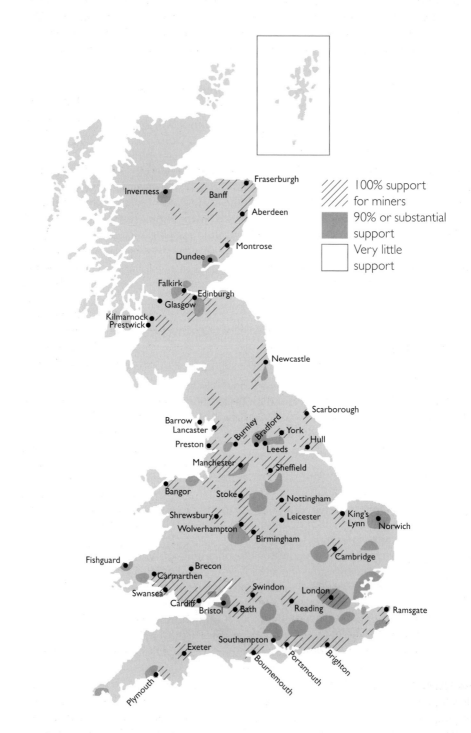

100% support
for miners

90% or substantial
support

Very little
support

Fraserburgh

Inverness

Banff

Aberdeen

Montrose

Dundee

Falkirk

Edinburgh

Glasgow

Kilmarnock
Prestwick

Newcastle

Scarborough

Barrow
Lancaster

Burnley

Bradford

York

Hull

Preston

Leeds

Manchester

Sheffield

Bangor

Stoke

Nottingham

Shrewsbury

Leicester

King's
Lynn

Norwich

Wolverhampton

Birmingham

Cambridge

Fishguard

Brecon

Carmarthen

Swansea

Swindon

London

Cardiff

Bristol

Bath

Reading

Ramsgate

Exeter

Southampton

Bournemouth

Portsmouth

Brighton

Plymouth

General Strike

Lord Liverpool, and was forced to accept ministers in Liverpool's government, notably *George Canning*, of whom he disapproved. During his reign, the principle of *Cabinet* government gained strength and this accelerated the decline in the independent powers of the monarchy. The fact that George was not publicly respected also contributed to this decline.

George was not without an aesthetic taste, which he indulged with characteristic excess. He was a patron of the arts, especially architecture, and the so-called *Regency* style owes at least something to his support. He refurbished Buckingham Palace, rebuilt Windsor Castle and built an ornate oriental palace called the Brighton Pavilion, a town he made fashionable. He died in 1830.

George V: King of the United Kingdom and Emperor of India from 1910 to 1936. Born in 1865, the second son of *Edward VII* and Princess Alexandra, he became heir to the throne in the first year of his father's reign on the death of his elder brother, the Duke of Clarence. He had trained as a naval officer and he saw active service from 1877 to 1892. Determined that he would not suffer the political neglect of his own period as heir to the throne, Edward VII included George in political affairs. He became King with a good training in the responsibilities of a constitutional monarch. These he discharged conscientiously while taking some discreet initiatives. He travelled to India in 1911 for the 'Durbar' (public ceremonial headed by the ruler), the first monarch to do so. He did not jib at appointing the first *Labour* government in 1924, even though *Ramsay MacDonald* did not have a parliamentary majority. He was also influential in MacDonald's appointment to head the coalition government of 1931. He also began the traditional of annual royal radio messages to the Commonwealth in 1932. He died at the beginning of 1936, soon after celebrating his silver jubilee.

George VI: King of the United Kingdom (1936–52) and Emperor of India (1936–47). Born in 1895 the second son of Prince George (later *George V*) and Princess Mary of Teck. Like his father, he had not originally been expected to succeed and, like him also, he received a naval training and saw active service during *World War I*. As Duke of York in the 1920s, he instituted camps for deprived boys and was President of the Boys' Welfare Association. He was thrust into the role of King because of the *Abdication Crisis*. He was not prepared for the role, embarrassed at his stammer and initially doubted whether he would be able to discharge his duties adequately. He proved an effective national symbol during *World War II* when he refused to quit Buckingham Palace as his main residence during the *Blitz* and travelled to meet soldiers on active service. He died of lung cancer in 1952.

Ghent, Treaty of (1814): treaty ending the *Anglo-American War*. Its main terms were:

- Britain retains islands in Passmaquoddy Bay, off Maine. Otherwise all conquests during the war returned to their original owners
- US claims for wartime commercial loss abandoned; but existing problems over fishing rights and navigation not solved

Gielgud, Sir John: British actor. Born in London into an acting family in 1904, he developed to be one of the greatest Shakespearean actors of the twentieth century, playing virtually all of the leading roles with distinction. He was particularly renowned for the beauty of his voice and its use in verse-speaking. His range was wide. He appeared in a very large number of films and television dramas. He had the rare distinction of having a West End theatre named after him in 1994.

Gilbert, Sir William Schwenck: humorous writer and collaborator with Sir Arthur *Sullivan* in the satirical and melodious Gilbert and Sullivan light operas. He was born in 1836 and worked as a clerk in the Privy Council office and as a barrister before turning to the writing which made his reputation. He published 'Bab Ballads' in 1869, before his collaboration with Sullivan began. Beginning with the now lost 'Thespis' (1871), the pair had immense success with operas such as 'HMS Pinafore' (1878), 'The Mikado' (1885), The 'Yeomen of the Guard' (1888) and 'The Gondoliers' (1889). The humour of the operettas was often extremely pointed; Gilbertian targets included the law, party politics and business. Queen *Victoria* believed that he kept Sullivan from writing the serious music he was capable of and would not knight him. That honour was bestowed by *Edward VII* in 1907. He died in a swimming accident at his home in 1911.

Gladstone, William Ewart: Tory, Peelite and Liberal politician and *Prime Minister.* Perhaps the outstanding political figure in the nineteenth century, he was born in Liverpool in 1809 into a prosperous trading family. He entered Parliament in 1832 at the first election held after the passage of the great *Reform Act.* In his early years he was a strong, anti-reform Tory and supporter of the *Church of England.* He first achieved *Cabinet* office in 1843 under Sir Robert *Peel.* His major offices were:

- President of the Board of Trade, 1843–45
- Secretary for War and the Colonies, 1845–46
- Chancellor of the Exchequer, 1852–55, 1859–66
- *Prime Minister,* 1868–74, 1880–85, 1886, 1892–94
- Leader of the Liberal Party, 1867–75, 1880–94

Gladstone's mentor was Peel and, despite the later twists in his political fortunes and loyalties, he always placed near the top of his priorities the disciplines of effective administration, low taxation and free trade which he had absorbed in Peel's ministry of 1841–6. Throughout his career, however, his conscience influenced his political attitudes. He briefly resigned from Peel's government in 1845 over a money grant to the Irish Catholic seminary at *Maynooth.* He resigned with Peel over the *Corn Laws,* leaving the Conservatives never to return, although his ultimate political destination was not clear for some years and *Derby* made several overtures to him in the 1850s to join his governments. He established himself as the ablest of the Peelites as Chancellor in *Aberdeen*'s Peelite government, a post he retained under *Palmerston* and *Russell* after he finally made his decision in 1859 to join the Liberals.

His leadership of the Liberal Party produced much administrative and legislative achievement but he was never an easy colleague. He was by temperament a believer in *aristocratic* government as 'government by the best' whereas the Liberal Party was becoming increasingly influenced by the *nonconformists* and the urban middle classes. His relations with Joseph *Chamberlain* were not close and his leadership style was not consensual. He chose large issues – administrative reform and low taxation during his first government; a solution to the Irish question increasingly in his later administrations – and expected his party to follow him. For someone at the centre of affairs for so long, he also threatened to resign surprisingly frequently in order to devote himself to private study, religion and writing. He did resign the Liberal leadership in 1875, coming back to the centre of political life with his famous attack on *Disraeli*'s policy over the 'Bulgarian atrocities'. The last decade of his political life was dominated by the question of *Ireland*. His conversion to *Home Rule* required a massive adjustment from the Liberal Party and, not surprisingly, it led to a decisive split in 1886. Gladstone was unable to win a Commons majority for Home Rule in 1886 and found his Home Rule Bill, successful in the Commons in 1893, blocked by the Lords. He resigned soon afterwards and died in 1898.

Gladstone was a controversial politician. His extraordinary energy and high intellectual abilities were unchallengeable. However, his party management lacked subtlety and his critics believed that he was quite unable to compromise in the interests of party unity. Like Peel, he put vital issues before the health of his party and would brook no debate on what issues were really 'vital'. Likewise his clashes with Disraeli in the 1870s were only partly about policy; they were at least as much about morality and attitudes to political life. He had a genuine dislike for the Conservative leader, considering him frivolous, untrustworthy and immoral. He epitomised Victorian earnestness, seriousness and high moral purpose.

(See also *Eastern Question; economic policy; laissez-faire*.)

Goderich (Robinson, Frederick (1st Earl of Ripon)), Viscount : *Tory* politician and *Prime Minister*. Born into a political family in 1782, he became MP in 1806 and first held office in the Tory government of Spencer *Perceval* in 1809. He held a number of economic posts in the first part of *Liverpool*'s government. His major offices were:

- Chancellor of the Exchequer, 1823–27
- Secretary at War, 1827
- Prime Minister, 1827–28
- Secretary for the Colonies, 1830–33
- Lord Privy Seal, 1833–34
- President of the Board of Trade, 1841–43
- President of the Board of Control, 1843–46

As can be seen, Goderich held a number of offices, mostly concerned with trade and finance, over a long period and in both Tory and Whig governments. As Chancellor of the Exchequer, under his commoner's name of Frederick Robinson, he worked closely with William *Huskisson* in reducing the number of tariffs on British goods and implementing a policy of free trade. At a time of expanding trade opportunities, he earned the nickname 'Prosperity Robinson'. He served in *Canning*'s brief ministry of 1827 before becoming Prime Minister himself, at the initiative of *George IV*, who seems to have thought that he could exercise greater direct influence by appointing a pliant minister. He proved as ineffective a leader as he had been a competent subordinate and quickly resigned, being the only Prime Minister never to have defended his policies in a parliamentary session. Like many Canningite *Tories*, he refused to serve *Wellington* as Prime Minister and was a member of Grey's *Whig* government of 1830–34. He returned to the Tories and held two financial ministries under *Peel*. He was created Viscount Goderich in 1827 and first Earl of Ripon in 1833.

(See also *free trade; laissez-faire*.)

gold standard: means of securing a nation's currency by tying its value to the price of gold and thus preventing large and unpredictable fluctuations in the value of a currency. Banks have an obligation, at least in theory, to exchange their notes for their exact value in gold. *Pitt* the Younger's need for money during the *French Revolutionary Wars* led to the issue of notes from the Bank of England not tied to any external value. During the financial crisis immediately after the wars, the *House of Commons* set up a Bullion Committee in 1819 under the chairmanship of Robert *Peel*, which recommended a return to a fixed value for the pound. This was achieved by 1821 and the British government was then effectively on a gold standard, which remained in place until the outbreak of *World War I*. *Baldwin*'s government went back on the gold standard in 1925, but at the over-valued level of $4.86 to the pound. During the economic crisis of 1931, the coalition government came off the gold standard again, whereupon the value of the pound immediately fell by about 30 per cent. At the end of *World War II*, reliance on gold as a fixed value reduced as the leading industrial nations, in a conference held at Bretton Woods (New Hampshire, USA) agreed on a new system of international exchange rates based on the value of the US dollar.

(See also *devaluation; Churchill, Winston; economic policy*.)

Graham, Sir James: Whig, Tory and Peelite politician. Born in 1792, he became an MP in 1826. He joined *Grey*'s *Whig* cabinet in 1830. His major offices were:

- First Lord of the Admiralty, 1830–34, 1852–55
- Home Secretary, 1841–46

Like many Liberal *Tories* he preferred working with a Whig administration to one committed against reform but, with *Stanley*, he left the Whigs on the *Catholic* Church revenues issues in 1834. He was an effective administrator both at the Admiralty, where he introduced many reforms, and the Home Office. He was a loyal and able lieutenant to *Peel*, sharing his beliefs in cheap and efficient government. He left office with him in 1846 and remained a leading Peelite thereafter. He returned to the Admiralty in *Aberdeen*'s Peelite coalition but did not hold Cabinet office after 1855. He died in 1861.

(See also *Conservative Party; Chartists; navy*.)

Grand National Consolidated Trades Union: early example of a *trade union* which attempted to recruit members from across the trades and to admit the unskilled. It was founded in 1834 and was closely linked to the *co-operative* ideas of *Robert Owen*. The union was a pioneer venture, since almost all unions were of one particular craft and most of them highly localised. It attracted about half a million supporters, few of whom, however, actually paid the subscriptions they owed. The union, therefore, had very little chance of success and collapsed when its treasurer ran off with its funds. It is best remembered as an early attempt at ambitious labour organisation, rather than as a successful experiment in union organisation.

(See also *Tolpuddle Martyrs*.)

'Great Britain' (SS): the first iron, screw-propeller steamship. Designed by *Isambard Kingdom Brunel* in Bristol, it was launched in 1843. At 3,200 tons, it was the largest ship of the day and could cross the Atlantic in fourteen days.

(See also *'Great Eastern'; 'Great Western'; steamships*.)

Great Depression: name frequently given to the downswing in the economy during the last quarter of the nineteenth century and conventionally dated to the years 1873–1896. It is important to distinguish this from the worldwide 'Great Depression' which followed the Wall Street Crash of 1929. This depression affected Britain, and particularly its agricultural and heavy industry sectors. Contemporaries were sure that Britain was experiencing a depression and many publications from the 1870s and 1880s warned that both Germany and the United States were now both outpacing and outselling Britain. Economic historians have been much less sure of the extent of the depression. The most important issues are:

- **agriculture:** the arable (corn-growing) sector was very heavily hit. The total acreage sown with corn declined from 3.6 million in 1871 to 1.7 million in 1901. This caused many landowners severe distress and many were forced to sell up. It greatly affected the *aristocracy*, particularly those who were dependent on arable land for their profits. However, the pastoral sector of agriculture was subject to much less severe falls in prices. In general the north and west of the country was affected far less than the south and east

- **industry:** many goods became more difficult to sell in world markets but there was no sustained fall-off in production. Britain seemed to experience only a relative decline. In other words, production in this period continued to increase but a very long period, during which Britain began to do less well than its industrial competitors, set in

- **living standards:** a time in which many agriculturalists and businessmen found themselves in difficulties coincided with good times for many working people. They benefited from the lower prices (especially for food but for many manufactured goods as well). Many British people benefited from a better and more varied *diet.* Death rates also fell

Overall, although this was a period of substantial adjustment and also of social change, it is difficult to argue that it was the 'Great Depression' which many later Victorians thought it to be.

(See also *Industrial Revolution.*)

'Great Eastern' (SS): steamship of revolutionary design by *Isambard Kingdom Brunel.* It incorporated the first steering engine and was the largest ship in the world, at nearly 19,000 tons, when it was launched in 1858, having taken almost five years to build. It helped to lay a cable across the Atlantic but, like many ambitious prototypes, was never a commercial success, being overtaken by more refined designs in the 1870s. It was scrapped in 1888.

(See also *'Great Britain'; 'Great Western'; steamships.*)

Great Exhibition: international exhibition held in Hyde Park, London, during 1851. Its full title – 'The Great Exhibition of the Works of Industry of all Nations' – indicates its purpose. However, since Britain was the first industrial nation of the world, the exhibition also contrived to show off Britain's pre-eminence. Its centrepiece was the huge *Crystal Palace*, designed by Joseph Paxton. The exhibition was planned by a committee, including Prince *Albert,* and it included more than 14,000 exhibits. More than 6 million visitors came to see it, many on pioneering railway excursion trains, and from its profits land was bought in London's South Kensington where more permanent educational attractions were established, especially the Natural History, Victoria and Albert and Science Museums.

(See also *Festival of Britain; Industrial Revolution.*)

'Great Western' (SS): pioneer paddle steamship designed by *Isambard Kingdom Brunel* and launched in 1838. At almost 1,800 tons, it was the first steamship designed to travel across the Atlantic, which it crossed in fifteen days.

(See also *'Great Britain'; 'Great Eastern'; steamships.*).

Greater London Council: reorganised local authority for London which came into effect in 1965. The old *London County Council*'s educational responsibilities were taken over by a new 'Inner London Education Authority. Thirty-two boroughs, formed from the old LCC and from Middlesex, were created to govern the Capital. It was abolished by the *Thatcher* government in 1986, largely because its predominantly left-wing complexion was frustrating many of Thatcher's local government policies.

(See also *Education Act, 1870; local government; Thatcherism.*)

Grenville (William), 1st Baron: *Whig* and *Tory* politician and *Prime Minister*. Born in 1759 into a well-established Whig political family, and the son of the senior minister George Grenville, he became an MP in 1782 and almost immediately Chief Secretary for Ireland. He served in *Pitt*'s peacetime administration of the 1780s. His major offices were:

- Home Secretary, 1790–1
- Foreign Secretary, 1791–1801
- Prime Minister, 1806–7

He was a close confidant of Pitt and supported the anti-*reformist* coalition with the Duke of *Portland* in 1794. He did much of the detailed, and thankless, work of trying to stitch together anti-French coalitions during the *French Revolutionary Wars.* He resigned with Pitt over *Catholic emancipation* in 1801 but did not return to office with him in 1804, arguing that Charles James *Fox* should be brought into government – a demand which neither Pitt nor *George III* would countenance. His brief period as Prime Minister was not successful, since the so-called 'Ministry of all the Talents' was not especially talented and contained too many divergent beliefs. He remained close to the centre of political life for many more years, though he never held office again. He acted almost as an eighteenth-century Whig leader of a political family grouping, known to contemporaries as 'the Grenvillites'. He hoped for a return to office, though only on his own terms and his support for Catholic emancipation disqualified him in the eyes of both George III and the Prince Regent. He co-operated with Earl *Grey* in opposing Lord *Liverpool* after 1812, but the alliance was never close. Grenville was no great lover of liberties at times of political danger. His group supported Liverpool in his anti-reformist legislation of 1817–19 and members of his grouping finally accepted office under Liverpool's Tory government in 1822. He died in 1834.

(See also *Tory Party.*)

Grey (Charles), 2nd Earl: *Whig* politician and *Prime Minister.* He was born in Northumberland in 1764 into an aristocratic north-eastern family and became MP for Northumberland in 1786. He was one of the leaders of the small group of Foxite

Whigs who opposed *Pitt*'s anti-reformist policies in the 1790s, and was a leading light in the Society of the Friends of the People, an aristocratic pro-reform group. In 1793 and 1797 he introduced two Bills for *parliamentary reform*. His major offices were:

- First Lord of the Admiralty, 1806
- Foreign Secretary, 1806–7
- Prime Minister, 1830–34

Grey's limited ministerial career is explained by the fact that, in practice (although the title 'Leader of the Opposition' did not yet exist) he led the Whigs during the long years of *Tory* supremacy under first Pitt and then *Liverpool*. He remained consistent to principles of *parliamentary reform*, although often reluctantly, since he recognised that this position reduced his prospects of office. He became Prime Minister on the resignation of the Duke of *Wellington* and his ministry is primarily remembered for passing the *Reform Act* of 1832. His ministry also abolished *slavery* in the *British Empire*. Having succeeded to his peerage in 1807, he was Prime Minister from the *House of Lords*. He resigned over internal disagreements about the Catholic question in *Ireland*, an issue which would see the break up of the Whig and Liberal-Tory coalition which had been in existence since 1827 and which made the revival of the Tory Party in the 1830s much easier.

(See also *aristocracy; Peel, Sir Robert*.)

Grey, Sir Edward: Liberal politician. He was born in 1862 and became the youngest MP in the Commons when he was elected for Berwick-upon-Tweed in 1885. His ministerial experience was almost all in foreign affairs. During the disagreements within the *Liberal* Party over foreign and imperial affairs, he was a strong *imperialist* and supported the *Boer War* of 1899–1902. His major office was:

- Foreign Secretary, 1905–16

In this position, he did much to improve relations with France during the period of the *ententes*, and his support for France over the Algeciras (1905) and Morocco (1911) crises concerned the pacifist wing of his party, which accused him of being too anti-German. He is the author of one of the most famous quotations about the outbreak of *World War I*: 'The lamps are going out all over Europe; we shall not see them lit again in our lifetime'. Always loyal to *Asquith*, he resigned with him in December 1916 and retired from British political life. His high reputation as a diplomat, however, earned him the post of first President of the *League of Nations* in 1918. He was also a keen birdwatcher and published a best-seller on the subject in 1925. Ennobled as Viscount Grey of Fallodon in 1916, he died in 1933.

Grimond, Jo: Liberal politician. He was born in 1913 and trained as a lawyer, practising as a barrister before being elected MP for Orkney and Shetland in 1950 and holding the seat without a break until 1983. He became leader of the *Liberal Party* in 1956 and helped revive Liberal Party fortunes, most notably via high-profile by-election successes during the increasingly unpopular *Conservative* government in the late 1950s and early 1960s. Grimond's main platform was the established Liberal one of individual liberty and responsibility but, as a Scottish MP, he was also an early advocate of a separate parliament for Scotland. His effective platform oratory and personal popularity contributed to a rise in Liberal fortunes, but this should not be exaggerated. The Liberals had six MPs when he became leader and only twelve when he resigned in 1967. Although the Liberal vote in general elections had more than trebled, it still only commanded 8.5 per cent support in the *general election* of 1966. He returned briefly to the leadership as a caretaker in 1976 after the disgrace of *Jeremy Thorpe*, and retired from Parliament in 1983. He died in 1993.

(See also *Davies, Clement; Steel, David.*)

Gross Domestic Product: usually abbreviated to GDP, it is defined as the money value of all the goods and services produced in the country. Economists have used it as an indicator of Britain's performance both over time and in relation to other countries. GDP data has shown, among other things, that:

- in relative terms, it increased about six times between 1870 and 1989
- this growth was most rapid after *World War II*; between 1950 and 1989 it increased two-and-a-half times. Over the twentieth century as a whole, growth has been much greater than in any previous century
- Over the period 1870–1989, the performance of Britain's main competitors – the USA, Germany, Japan and France – has been better. Britain has therefore been in economic decline relative to other countries
- Britain invests a smaller proportion of its income than most of its main competitors. In the 1960s and 1970s, for example, the Japanese invested almost twice as much as the British, while the West Germans invested about 30 per cent more

Such statistics can mislead, of course, but as a general guide GDP evidence suggests that British economic performance in the twentieth century has been strong in relation to previous centuries but worryingly weak in comparison with other industrial nations.

(See also *economic policy; inflation; free trade; Keynes, J M; laissez-faire.*)

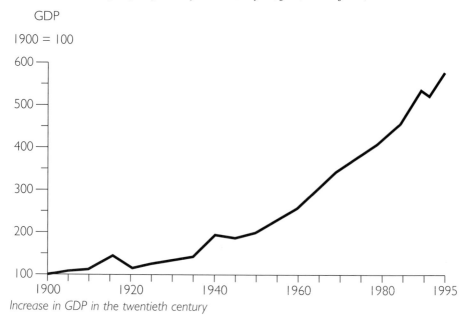

Increase in GDP in the twentieth century

gunboat diplomacy: phrase coined to describe negotiation carried out under threat of superior power. It can also imply bullying. It has become associated with the aggressive foreign policy of Viscount *Palmerston* in the 1850s, and especially over his threat to the Greeks during the *Don Pacifico* affair of 1850. The phrase may seem particularly apt in the case of Great Britain, whose power rested so largely in the nineteenth century upon its unchallengeable navy. The phrase was used, with less than perfect historical accuracy, by Aneurin *Bevan* when criticising Winston *Churchill*'s foreign policy in October 1951: 'he is still fighting Blenheim [a battle fought by Churchill's ancestor the Duke of Marlborough, but on land and in 1704!] again. His only answer to a difficult situation is send a gunboat'.

(See also *Liberal Party*; *Victoria*.)

H

habeas corpus: Latin phrase literally meaning 'You have the body'. It has a much more precise legal meaning which is important in criminal cases. By the Habeas Corpus Amendment Act of 1679, those who were being detained on suspicion of an offence had to be brought before a judicial court with cause shown as to why he or she had been detained. This is an important civil liberty, since it means that defendants cannot be held indefinitely without charge and/or trial. During the late eighteenth and early nineteenth centuries, the Act was often suspended by Parliament for brief periods, as in 1794, 1817 and 1819, to allow the authorities to round up suspects (usually *radicals* and *parliamentary reformers* or *Chartists*) and hold them without charge until the political discontents which had made radicalism dangerous to the authorities had passed. The suspension of habeas corpus became a well-used, and effective, tactic for managing political disaffection without creating martyrs.

Haig, Sir Douglas (1st Earl): British Commander-in-Chief in France from 1915. Born in 1881 into the Scotch whisky family, he saw action in the Sudan with *Kitchener* in 1898 and during the *Boer War* before helping to implement *Haldane*'s army reforms from 1906 to 1909. As Commander-in-Chief he believed in wearing down the enemy and has been widely blamed for the inflexibility of his tactics at the *Somme* and *Paschendaele* and for the apparent indifference with which he viewed enormous casualties for limited gain. He was the central figure of hate in Joan Littlewood's anti-war satire 'Oh, What a Lovely War' which was made into a film in 1969. Haig did, however, win a decisive victory at Amiens in 1918 which hastened the end of the war. His relations with the *Prime Minister, Lloyd George*, were frequently poor. He was ennobled at the end of the war and devoted the remainder of his life to helping organise the British Legion and the annual 'Poppy Days' or 'Haig Fund' for ex-servicemen and women and their families. He died in 1922.

(See also *French, Sir John; World War I.*)

Haldane (Richard), 1st Viscount (from 1911): *Liberal* and, later, *Labour* politician. Born in 1856, he was educated in Germany before becoming an MP in 1879. He was also a successful barrister and took an interest in the funding of higher education during a time of substantial university expansion in the first decade of the twentieth century. His major offices were:

- Secretary of State for War, 1905–12
- Lord Chancellor, 1912–15, 1924

Though he enjoyed the rare distinction of serving both Liberal and Labour governments as its Chief Law Officer, Haldane is best remembered for his army reforms. These owed much to his study of German practice. The main features of his reforms from 1906 to 1909 were:

- the creation of an Officer Training Corps
- the establishment of an Imperial General Staff
- turning the militia into a fully developed territorial army reserve
- the creation of a British Expeditionary Force

These reforms proved vital during *World War I* but he was dismissed from *Asquith*'s government in 1915 on suspicion of excessive sympathy for Germany. Like many middle-class intellectuals, he left the *Liberals* after the party split and joined the *Labour* Party, which he led in the Lords at the end of his life. He died in 1928.

Halifax (Wood, Edward (Lord Irwin (1925)), 3rd Viscount)) 1st Earl of: *Conservative* MP, colonial administrator and diplomat. Born in 1881 into a *Liberal* political family, he was Conservative MP for Ripon from 1910 to 1925. An effective administrator and supreme political 'insider', he served in high office of one kind or another almost continuously from 1922 to 1940. His main offices were:

- President of the Board of Education, 1922–24, 1932–35
- Minister of Agriculture, 1924–25
- Viceroy of India, 1926–31
- Secretary for War, 1935
- Lord Privy Seal, 1935–37
- Lord President of the Council, 1937–38
- Foreign Secretary, 1938–40
- Ambassador to the United States, 1941–46

As Viceroy of *India*, he was faced with the growth of a nationalist movement. He had some sympathy with Gandhi's objectives and especially his attempt to achieve political change without violence. He did, however, imprison him after widespread civil disturbance in 1930. He served all three prime ministers during the coalition government of 1931–40 and became associated with support for *Chamberlain*'s policies of *appeasement*. He replaced *Anthony Eden* when he resigned the foreign secretaryship on the question. Like Chamberlain, also, however, he was far from sure that war with Hitler could be avoided.

He was, for many Conservatives, a far more eligible candidate as *Prime Minister* in 1940 than *Winston Churchill*, but refused in the national interest to stand against him. As British Ambassador, he played an effective role as intermediary with F D Roosevelt and in ensuring that there should be no misunderstanding within the vital US alliance from the end of 1941 onwards. He became an Earl in 1944 and died in 1946.

(See also *World War II*.)

handloom weavers: textile workers who operated handlooms rather than the powerlooms which were introduced into British factories from the 1780s onwards. Traditionally, a highly skilled and politically literate group of workers, they had to face, first, a great influx of semi-skilled workers into their trade during the transitional period in the early nineteenth century when spinning had been mechanised but weaving not and, second, the much more widespread use of power looms from the 1820s. These two factors produced severely reduced wages and increasingly widespread unemployment. Many weavers were strong supporters of *parliamentary reform* and, later, *Chartism*. It has been estimated that the number of handloom weavers fell from almost a quarter of a million to 40,000 during the second quarter of the nineteenth century. Though some weavers in specialised forms of textile manufacture continued to flourish, the great majority suffered sharply deteriorating conditions. Some social historians see their plight as symbolic of the disruption caused during the early stages of industrialism; others point out that they were not replaced overnight and that they remained a respected, and important, working group at least until the 1830s.

(See *Industrial Revolution; cotton industry; woollen industry.*)

Hanoverian dynasty: royal family which provided Britain's monarchs from 1714 to 1837 in the persons, successively, of George I (1714–27), George II (1727–60), *George III* (1760–1820), *George IV* (1820–30) and *William IV* (1830–37). It provided the British royal house, largely for domestic political reasons concerned with the need for Protestant monarchs to keep out the Catholic Stuarts but, as a dynasty, it was little loved. The first two Georges were all too obviously German, rather than British, in their interests and sympathies. The third was conscientious, loyal and dutiful, though obstinate and frequently lacking perception. George IV was self-indulgent, profligate and lacked political sense. William IV had not been trained for kingship and dismissed a ministry which had a clear majority in the *House of Commons*. During the later stages of the dynasty both the independent power of, and popular respect for, the monarch declined sharply.

Harcourt, Sir William: lawyer and Liberal politician. Born in 1827. He was a distinguished international lawyer who became a *Liberal* MP in 1868. His temperament and abilities suited *Gladstone*'s concern for administrative reform and, despite misgivings, he supported his leader over *Ireland* and *Home Rule* policy in the mid-1880s. His major offices were:

- Solicitor General, 1873–74
- Home Secretary, 1880–85
- Chancellor of the Exchequer, 1886 and 1892–95
- Leader of the Liberal Party, 1896–98

He is best remembered as the Chancellor who first introduced death duties on the estates of the wealthy, in 1894. It is widely thought that he would have been the party's choice to succeed Gladstone as *Prime Minister* in 1894 until Queen *Victoria* took a hand and 'recommended' Lord *Rosebery* instead. He retired from active politics in 1898 and died in 1904.

Hardie, James Keir: Labour politician and first leader of the party. He was born in Lanarkshire in 1856 and worked as a miner, becoming Secretary of the Scottish Miners' Federation in 1886. He joined the newly founded Labour Party in Scotland in 1888 and became leader of the *Independent Labour Party* in 1893. He became the first Labour MP when elected in 1892 and he was elected to Parliament again in 1900 as MP for the Welsh mining constituency of Merthyr Tydfil. He became leader of the *Labour Representation Committee* in 1900.

Throughout his career he typified the interests and abilities of self-improving working men. He learned organisational skills in the trade union movement. He had a lifelong commitment to education as a form of both self-improvement and moral advance. He was an *evangelical nonconformist* who supported the *Temperance Movement* and he put both fire and flair into the early Labour Party, supporting a range of reformist causes throughout his career, including women's *suffrage*. He perhaps lacked necessary political skills, including the ability to trim some beliefs to prevailing opinion. He disagreed with many in the party over *World War I*, since he was a pacifist.

He died in 1915, having done more than any other individual to make the Labour Party into a credible political force. Though he never held high office himself, he facilitated the careers of many Labour politicians who did.

(See also *Labour Party*.)

Hardy, Thomas: novelist and poet. Born in 1840 in Dorset, his novels always had a strong sense of the Wessex countryside he knew so well, and where he lived virtually all his life. His most famous novels were 'Far from the Madding Crowd' (1874), 'The Mayor of Casterbridge' (1886) and 'Tess of the Durbevilles' (1891). His predominant themes were pessimistic ones, dealing with noble characters crushed by life's mischances and malign fate. His most celebrated verse drama was 'The Dynasts' (1903–8). He died in 1928.

Harmsworth, Alfred: see *Northcliffe*

Harmsworth, Harold: see *Rothermere*

Harney, George Julian: journalist, *radical* politician and *Chartist* leader. Born in 1817, he worked in the shop of Henry Hetherington, a leading radical journalist and editor of 'Poor Man's Guardian'. As a Chartist, he rejected the arguments of those who believed that political change could come from argument and debate. He urged the importance of 'physical force' – the use of violence – to gain real advantages for working men. He wrote for the 'Northern Star', which he edited in its last years. He was much more interested in international socialism than most Chartists, and produced the first English translation of Marx and Engels's 'Communist Manifesto' in 1850. He supported socialism for the rest of his life and died in 1897.

(See also *O'Connor, Feargus*.)

Harris, Sir Arthur: Commander-in-Chief of RAF Bomber Command, 1942–45. Harris had a controversial career. Born in 1892, he served in the Royal Flying Corps during *World War I*. In *World War II* he used 'strategic bombing' not only to attack enemy industrial and military targets but, more widely, to destroy morale by widespread 'fire-bombing' which would inevitably kill large numbers of civilians. The tactic earned him the title 'Bomber Harris'. His ideas were employed by the RAF to devastating effect in air raids on Hamburg and Dresden, though he himself did not select the targets. In military terms, his strategy was undoubtedly effective, though distressing to recall once the war was safely over.

Though he was ennobled in 1953, he did not receive the usual military honours accorded to someone who had played such a decisive wartime role. To some degree at least, he suffered from official hypocrisy from politicians and civil servants who willed the end (complete victory over Germany) but were prepared to see as scapegoats those who provided the embarrassing means. Harris died in 1984.

Hartington, Marquess of: see *Devonshire, 8th Duke of*

Haw-Haw, Lord: see *Joyce, William*

Healey, Denis: Labour politician. He was born in Yorkshire in 1917 and was a Labour Member of Parliament continuously from 1945 to 1992 before accepting a peerage. His main offices were:

- Defence Secretary, 1964–70
- Chancellor of the Exchequer, 1974–79
- Deputy Leader of the Labour Party, 1980–83

A highly intelligent politician with a wide range of interests, he was a robust controversialist who proved an effective minister. During the severe splits which affected the *Labour Party* after electoral defeat in 1979, he was the leading champion of its right wing. He was defeated for the party leadership in 1980 but did not join the Social Democratic Party when it broke away from the party in 1981.

Heath, Edward: Conservative politician and *Prime Minister*. He was born in Kent into a lower-middle class family in 1916 and entered Parliament in 1950. His early experience was in the Whips office. His main offices were:

- Minister of Labour, 1959–60
- Lord Privy Seal, 1960–63
- Secretary of State for Industry and Trade, 1963–64
- Leader of the Opposition, 1965–70 and 1974–75
- Prime Minister, 1970–74

He was the first *Conservative Party* leader to be formally elected to the post. His prime ministership is best remembered for Britain's entry into the European Economic Community and he has always been a strong supporter of closer European unity, a stance which made him deeply unpopular with the leadership during the 1980s. Attempted industrial and economic reforms early in his prime ministership were not sustained and its latter stages were associated with growing industrial unrest. Strikes in 1973 led to widespread power cuts, industrial disruption and the establishment of a power-saving three-day working week. He called a *general election* in February 1974 during a bitter miners' strike on the slogan 'Who governs Britain?'. He won a slightly larger share of the popular vote than the Labour Party but fewer seats and resigned. He was defeated by *Margaret Thatcher* in a leadership election one year later.

Unlike many defeated party leaders, he has remained in the *House of Commons* as an active backbencher in Parliament for more than twenty years, frequently speaking out to the embarrassment of a party leadership which moved strongly rightwards after 1979. He had an active life away from politics, as a talented musician and an experienced yachtsman.

(See also *trade unions*.)

Henderson, Arthur: Labour politician. Born in the North-East in 1862, he trained as a skilled iron worker and represented the Iron Workers' Union. He was a Newcastle-on-Tyne city councillor before becoming Labour MP for Barnard Castle in 1903. He was a member of *Lloyd George*'s War Cabinet in 1916–17. His other major offices were:

- Secretary of the Labour Party, 1911–34
- President of the Board of Education, 1915–16
- Paymaster General, 1916
- Home Secretary, 1924
- Foreign Secretary, 1929–31

He is best remembered as the moderniser of the *Labour Party*. He was the chief architect of the new constitution of 1918 which enabled it to function as a mass party. He was strongly opposed to Bolshevism and helped to move the party away from full socialism and towards moderate reformism. He refused to follow *MacDonald* and *Snowden* into the coalition of 1931 and acted as stop-gap leader of the party in 1931–32 before becoming President of the World Disarmament Conference from 1932 to 1935. He died in 1935.

Herbert, Sidney: Conservative and Peelite politician. Born in 1810 the son of the Earl of Pembroke, he was a loyal supporter of *Sir Robert Peel* who, like *Gladstone*, ended his political career in the *Liberal Party*. His major offices were:

- Secretary for War, 1845–46, 1852–54, 1859–61
- Secretary for the Colonies, 1855

He learned from Peel, with whom he left office in 1846, many lessons in administrative efficiency. He was critical of the 'stereotyped system of economy in military affairs' which threatened the war effort in the Crimea. He was perhaps the *Peelite* most amenable to a permanent fusion with the Whigs and helped to persuade Gladstone to throw in his lot with *Palmerston* at the important meeting in 1859. He died in 1861.

(See also *Crimean War.*)

high farming: term used in agriculture to describe farming using both scientific and business principles to maximise yields and productivity. It is often used to describe farming practices in the generation after the repeal of the *Corn Laws*, conventionally 1850–73, when farmers attempted to compensate for the loss of protected prices for corn by adopting rational methods in a competitive environment. The term was coined by the agricultural writer James Caird.

High-Church: name generally given to that grouping within the *Church of England* which was closer to the doctrines and practices of the *Roman Catholic* church. High-Churchmen tended to rely on authority, especially that of the church hierarchy, and to give less prominence to scripture than Low-Churchmen and *evangelicals*. In the nineteenth century, High-Churchmen were often associated with the *Oxford Movement*.

Highland clearances: the procedure whereby crofters and other small peasant farmers in the Highlands of Scotland were forcibly removed by landowners in order to enable landowners to introduce improved agriculture, usually sheep farming. The process began in the second half of the eighteenth century when Catholic peasants were removed from their smallholdings after the failure of the Jacobite rising of 1745–46. It was greatly accelerated for economic, rather than political, reasons in the years 1780–1820. The sense of outrage felt by many was heightened by the fact that many landowners most associated with wholesale clearances were either lowland Scots or, like the Duke of Sutherland, English. There being little alternative employment for those cleared, the process led to substantial emigration, especially to Canada and Australia.

Hill, Charles (Lord Hill of Luton): doctor, broadcaster and Conservative politician. Born in 1904, and trained in medicine, he became nationally famous for his radio broadcasts in the 1940s. He was dubbed 'The Radio Doctor' for his practical advice, including 'Wise Eating in Wartime' and he built up an immensely loyal following, indicating the growing power of a mass medium of communication. He was

Secretary of the British Medical Association from 1944 to 1950 before becoming a Conservative MP (1950–63). He reached ministerial office, his main posts being:

- Postmaster General, 1955–57
- Chancellor of the Duchy of Lancaster, 1957–61
- Minister of Housing, 1961–62

He returned to broadcasting in the much more elevated guise of Chairman of the Board of Governors of the *British Broadcasting Corporation* (1967–72). He died in 1989.

(See also *Conservative Party; radio.*)

Hill, Octavia: *housing* reformer. She was born in 1838, the grand-daughter of the public health expert Thomas Southwood Smith, and became interested in social reforms while teaching in the Marylebone district of London. She concentrated on housing reforms. She believed that good quality accommodation and moral improvement went hand in hand and that state assistance was not necessary. The system she developed required those who benefited from her charity to show that they could become 'respectable'. She took over property owned by the *Church of England* and selected tenants with care, and did not allow rent arrears to accumulate. She later became one of the founders of the *National Trust.* She died in 1912.

Hill, Rowland: teacher and domestic administrator. Born in 1795, the son of a pioneering Birmingham school teacher who invented a system of shorthand, his own early career also focused on teaching, where he experimented with new methods and the abolition of corporal punishment. He went to Australia in the 1830s where he helped in the early colonisation of South Australia. He is most famous, however, for the invention of the penny postage stamp. His invention was put into use from 1840. In the years 1846–64, he was Secretary to the Postmaster General, in which capacity he introduced many reforms in post office procedure. He died in 1879.

Hoare, Sir Samuel (1st Viscount Templewood): Conservative politician. He was born in 1880 and became MP for Chelsea in 1910, a constituency he represented continuously until 1944. His major offices were:

- Secretary of State for India, 1931–35
- Foreign Secretary, 1935
- First Lord of the Admiralty, 1936–37
- Home Secretary, 1937–39
- Lord Privy Seal, 1939–40

He was a competent, undemonstrative minister in the offices he held but he is best remembered for the *Hoare–Laval Pact,* which caused his speedy resignation from the Foreign Office. He supported *appeasement* and served in *Chamberlain*'s War Cabinet before *Churchill* sent him as Ambassador to neutral, but fascist, Spain, where he performed a delicate balancing act with some success in the years 1940–44. Ennobled in 1944, he died in 1959.

(See also *World War II.*)

Hoare–Laval Pact: agreement made in 1935 between the foreign ministers of Britain and France to resolve the crisis caused by Benito Mussolini's invasion of Abyssinia (Ethiopia). The pact proposed that:

- Italy should be granted two-thirds of the territory of Abyssinia
- Abyssinia's rights over the remaining third, and an outlet to the Red Sea, should be guaranteed by the *League of Nations*

Both countries, but especially France, had sound reasons to avoid conflict with Italy. However, when news of the pact leaked out it was widely denounced as *appeasement* of Mussolini. Both *Hoare* and Laval were forced to resign their offices. Hoare, however, slipped quickly into another *Cabinet* post and continued his ministerial career.

Hobhouse, Leonard Trelawny: philosopher and journalist. Born in 1864 and educated at Oxford, he wrote extensively on philosophical and social questions, especially for an increased role for the State in *social policy*. He became London University's first professor of sociology in 1907 and served in that post until his death in 1929.

(See also *Liberal Party; welfare state.*)

Hobson, J A: economist and *Liberal* political theorist. Born in 1858, he developed ideas which proved influential with progressive Liberals at the beginning of the twentieth century. He argued that many social and economic problems were caused by inadequate economic activity and 'under consumption'. He also advocated an extension of social welfare and taxation policies which redistributed wealth from the rich towards the poor. He is perhaps best remembered for his book 'Imperialism' (1902) which argued that the phenomenon was at root a desperate search by the industrialised nations for scarce economic resources. It greatly influenced the thinking of the Russian Bolshevik leader Lenin. He died in 1940.

(See also *imperialism; Liberal Party; Lloyd George.*)

Holland House: town house in Kensington, south-west London, which acted as the hub of political and social affairs for the leading *Whig* family, the Foxes, in the eighteenth and early nineteenth centuries.

(See also *Fox, Charles James.*)

Home, Lord: see *Douglas-Home, Alec*

Home Rule Bill, 1886: proposed legislation intended by *Gladstone* to give independence in home affairs to *Ireland*. Its main terms were:

- an Irish parliament, comprising 204 MPs, 28 peers and 75 members elected on a property qualification
- this parliament would control a separate Irish executive
- Parliament could pass any domestic Bills but could not interfere with the rights of the Crown
- Parliament could not legislate on foreign matters or on armed services
- no Irish MPs would be elected to serve in the Westminster parliament

The Bill was defeated in the Commons by 343 votes to 313. The majority included 93 Whigs and Chamberlainite Liberal radicals.

(See also *Act of Union; Home Rule Bill, 1893; Ireland; Chamberlain, Joseph; Devonshire, 8th Duke of.*)

Home Rule Bill, 1893: proposed legislation intended by *Gladstone* to give independence in home affairs to Ireland. Its main terms were:

- an Irish parliament would be set up with 'two bodies':
  - Legislative Assembly of 103 members
  - Legislative Council of 48 members elected by ratepayers with property worth at least £20 a year, which would veto for two years Bills passed by the assembly
- the powers of the parliament would be virtually the same as those proposed in 1886, except that rights over land legislation (for three years), customs and excise would remain with Westminster
- 80 Irish MPs would continue to serve at Westminster, where they would be able to vote on imperial and Irish affairs

This Bill passed through the Commons by a majority of 43 votes in September 1893 but was rejected in the Lords a week later by the massive majority of 419–41. It was *Gladstone*'s last attempt at Home Rule.

(See also *Act of Union; Home Rule Bill, 1886; Ireland; Redmond, John*.)

'homes for heroes': slogan implying *Lloyd George*'s commitment to widespread social reform for those who had fought in *World War I*. As with so many political quotations which are 'remembered' by later generations, this is inaccurate. What Lloyd George actually said, in a speech during the general election campaign on 23 November 1918, was: 'What is our task? To make Britain a fit country for heroes to live in'.

(See also *Liberal Party; housing; welfare state*.)

homosexuality, state attitudes to: from 1534 to 1967, male homosexual acts were illegal and homosexuals were liable to imprisonment. In 1885, legislation clarified their illegality, even when performed in private. Pressure for a change in the law increased in the 1950s. The success of the Basil Dearden film 'Victim' (1961), starring Dirk Bogarde, which emphasised the dangers of blackmail, increased that pressure. The Sexual Offences Act, 1967 decriminalised homosexual acts in private between adults in England and Wales. Legislation affecting Northern Ireland and Scotland followed in the 1980s.

(See also *Wolfenden Report*.)

Hone, William: publisher of radical literature. He was born in 1780 and published much material attacking the established order and advocating both free thought and *parliamentary reform*. He was tried on a charge of corrupting public morals with his writings during an increase in radical activity in 1817, but the jury refused to acquit.

(See also *radicalism*.)

Hong Kong: territory on the southern tip of China which was a British Crown Colony from 1842 to 1997. The British occupied the territory in 1841 and retained it at the end of the first of the *Opium Wars*. The adjacent Kowloon was similarly granted to Britain in 1860 and the New Territories occupied on a 99-year lease in July 1898. The area became an extremely important British colony and developed both as a centre for the British Asian trade and a strategic naval base in the South China Sea. After *World War II*, the population increased very rapidly, reaching 3.6 million by 1963. A range of industries grew up around shipping while commerce and financial services also expanded very rapidly. The Chinese communist government, which took power in 1949, refused to accept the validity of any of the nineteenth-century treaties and announced its attention of assimilating the whole of Hong Kong into the Chinese Empire when the New Territories lease expired in 1997. Margaret *Thatcher* signed a treaty in 1984 accepting this, although the Chinese seemed to accept that Hong Kong could continue to develop its capitalist, commercial infrastructure. A senior *Conservative* politician, Chris Patten, relieved of his British parliamentary seat at the general election of 1992, was despatched to Hong Kong as a high-profile Governor-General to see out British rule, which duly ended at midnight on 30 June 1997.

(See also *Nanking, Treaty of.*)

Hornby v. Close: decisions in 1866–67 affecting the legal status of trade unions. Justices of the peace in Bradford, Yorkshire, declared in 1866 that trade unions did not come under legislation of 1855 affecting *friendly societies.* The important consequence of this was that they were unable to protect their funds from fraudulent use. Thus, when the Bradford Boilermakers tried to recover funds from a defaulting treasurer, their action failed. The Queen's Bench confirmed this Bradford Justices' decision in 1867. The effect was to make *trade unions* vulnerable to almost any financial action. The decision was reversed by the Trade Union Act and Criminal Law Amendment Act passed by *Gladstone*'s Liberal government in 1871.

(See also *Conspiracy and Protection of Property Act; Liberal Party.*)

housing: important social question in the nineteenth and twentieth centuries.

Nineteenth century

The rapid growth of towns in the first half of the nineteenth century required the rapid construction of houses. As doctors and social investigators quickly recognised, poor-quality housing of high density was a major cause of illness and premature death. This was a central theme both of the Parliamentary Select Committee on the health of towns (1840) and of *Chadwick*'s famous 'Sanitary Report' (1842). Local authorities lacked both the economic resources and the power to improve matters significantly and most legislation in the second half of the nineteenth century, such as the *Torrens Act,* 1868 and the *Artisans' Dwellings Act,* 1875, was more concerned with slum clearance than with house building. Slum clearance was of limited use for many of the working classes who could not afford regular rent anyway, and still less the rents needed to occupy houses which satisfied sanitary standards.

Attention was concentrated on the housing question by propaganda books such as 'The Bitter Cry of Outcast London' (1883) and by a Royal Commission on the Housing of the Working Classes (1885). Legislation, however, remained limited in its effects. The Housing of the Working Classes Act, 1890 brought together useful regulations but did not give local authorities the resources to build their own houses.

Early twentieth century

Significant improvements in housing followed the ending of *World War I* and the widespread recognition that housing was the most underdeveloped area of social concern. Both the *Addison* and *Wheatley* Acts encouraged new house building. The housing situation was transformed during the wars. During the 1920s more than 1.6 million houses were built and in the so-called 'depressed' 1930s, aided by cheap raw materials and abundant labour, this total rose to 2.9 million. Roughly 30 per cent of this was publicly owned in the form of *council houses.*

Later twentieth century

The *Labour government* introduced fresh subsidies for house building in 1946 and legislation was also passed in 1949 to enable rents to be fixed in the hope of reducing exploitation of vulnerable tenants by profiteering landlords. In the 1950s and 1960s, housing became a dominant political issue for both parties. In the '50s, 2.8 million new houses were built; in the '60s, for the first time, more than 300,000 houses were completed in every year totalling more than 3.6 million in all. The proportion of houses which were owner-occupied, rather than rented, had been increasing significantly since the '30s. By 1989, almost two-thirds of all houses were owned (albeit on mortgages in most cases) by the people who occupied them, one of the largest proportions in the world.

The scale of improvement during the twentieth century may be gauged by comparing the increase in population with that of housing. In 1901, there were about 6.7 million houses in England and Wales for a population of 32.5 million, a ratio of 1 house to every 4.85 citizens. By 1981, the population of England and Wales had risen to 49.15 m but the housing stock had increased to 17.75 m, a ratio now of 1 house to every 2.76 citizens. Since the facilities in those houses – more rooms, reliable running water, indoor toilets and the rest – had immeasurably improved, we may conclude that the housing revolution has had as large an impact on living standards as any other factor in the twentieth century.

(See also *public health; Charity Organisation Society; Hill, Octavia; 'homes for heroes'*.)

Housman, A E: poet and classical scholar. Born in Worcestershire in 1859, a virtual contemporary of the Worcestershire composer Edward *Elgar*, his art has some striking parallels. It draws inspiration from the local countryside and it is filled with a wistful melancholy. Housman's most famous set of poems 'A Shropshire Lad' (1896) evokes both a countryside he knew well and also a mood of nostalgia and pessimism for what he famously called 'a land of lost content'. In many ways, it foreshadowed the irreversible changes in British society which *World War I* would bring. After the war, he composed the melancholy 'Last Poems' (1922). He was successively Professor of Latin at London and Cambridge Universities. He died in Somerset in 1936.

Hudson, George: railway manager and entrepreneur. Known as the 'railway king', he was born in 1800 and had already made a fortune out of banking and the linen trade before he became manager of the York and North Midland Railway Company in 1839. He at first profited hugely from speculation in railways ('railway mania') during the 1840s, invested in land and became MP for Sunderland at a by-election in 1845. His business dealings were always dubious, however, and he was convicted of fraud in 1849. He lost most of his money in the early 1850s and left the country in 1854. His work was not all dishonest and destructive, however. His business flair encouraged successful amalgamations of railway companies and a consequent rationalisation of lines. He died in 1871.

(See also *railways; Stephenson, George*.)

Huskisson, William: *Tory* politician. He was born in 1770 and entered Parliament in 1796. An intellectual convert to the ideas of *Jeremy Bentham*, he served in minor treasury office in the *Addington* and *Portland* governments. He believed in modest protection for the landed interest and removal of tariff barriers as an impediment to trade. Although he held only junior office in the first years of *Liverpool*'s government, his influence on economic policy was substantial, not least in trade policy and the return to the *gold standard*. His major offices were:

- President of the Board of Trade, 1823–27
- Secretary for War and the Colonies, 1827–28

During the 1820s, he significantly reduced the number of tariffs and contributed substantially to making Britain a free-trade nation. He resigned from *Wellington*'s government, along with other so-called 'Liberal-Tories' in 1828, but would almost certainly have achieved high office with the change of government in 1830. However, he was killed by a freak railway accident at the opening of the Liverpool and Manchester passenger railway in September 1830, two months before Wellington's government fell. He was one of the most intelligent and influential politicians of the age.

(See also *free trade; Goderich, Viscount; Peel, Sir Robert; Tory Party.*)

I

'Illustrated London News': weekly newspaper which relied heavily on pictures. Published from 1842, it was the first newspaper in Britain to make consistent use of visual images, including artists' sketches, drawings and, soon, photographs to strengthen the message of the written word. It proved popular in the second half of the nineteenth and early twentieth centuries, representing an important change in the format of newspapers.

immigration: movement into the country from overseas. For most of the nineteenth and twentieth centuries the numbers of immigrants into Britain have not been particularly large. The Irish migrated to Britain in very large numbers in the first half of the nineteenth century. According to the 1861 census there were more than 800,000 Irish-born living in Britain, and they formed almost one-quarter of the population of Liverpool at the time. In the late nineteenth and early twentieth centuries, many Jews, fleeing from persecution in Russia and other parts of eastern Europe, migrated to Britain, many of them settling in London's East End.

Immigration was greatly restricted after *World War I* by the Aliens Act, 1919, and did not increase significantly until after *World War II*. From the late 1940s first West Indians and, from the later 1950s, Asians from the old British Empire came to Britain to escape poorly functioning economies and in search of work. They also filled readily identifiable skill shortages. The number of immigrants living in the United Kingdom increased fourfold in the years 1961 to 1991 from 600,000 to 2,635,000. Immigration became a highly controversial political topic from the late 1950s onwards. The trend of government legislation, beginning with the Commonwealth Immigrants Act, 1962, has been to restrict entry and to try to ensure equality of opportunity and treatment for immigrants and their families who have settled in Britain. After the 1971 Immigration Act, immigration from non-white Commonwealth countries virtually ended.

(See also *Commonwealth; Race Relations Acts.*)

imperial preference: trading policy based on using the *British Empire* as a resource. Associated with *Joseph Chamberlain*, imperial preference was based on Britain's trading with its Empire at low tariffs while the colonies and dominions would do the same. Nations outside this relationship would pay full duties on imports and exports. The policy was an attempt to recover the British competitive edge in world trade but it was highly controversial since the official policy of British governments remained one of *free trade*. The policy divided the *Conservative Party* from 1903, was a major reason for its loss of power in the *general election* of 1906, and was not introduced in Chamberlain's lifetime. A version of it, however, was implemented by the *National Government* in 1932.

(See also *Import Duties Act, 1932.*)

imperialism: using the acquisition of territories as a political and/or economic resource to increase the power of the State. Britain had been acquiring territories outside Europe since the late sixteenth century but the term usually refers in a

British context to the rapid colonisation, especially in Africa, in the late nineteenth and early twentieth centuries. During the years of decolonisation, and since, imperialism has been used loosely as a term implying unthinking abuse. Although it can indeed imply heedless or arrogant domination by an established power over less developed ones, the dominant imperial ethic as understood by late nineteenth-century imperialists was very different. It included:

- a sense of duty, whereby the imperial power governed in part to provide education, material benefits and modernisation
- improvement of government structures, including spreading principles of representative democracy. Imperial territories were used as a training ground for British administrators schooled in the ethic of discipline, team spirit, self-sacrifice and leadership by example
- bringing Christianity to those who had not previously been exposed to its example. The role of *missionaries* in imperial history is very important

(See *Africa, Scramble for; Empire, British; Chamberlain, Joseph; Curzon, 1st Marquess; Milner (Alfred), Viscount.*)

Import Duties Act, 1932: legislation which formally ended Britain's commitment to a policy of *free trade*. It was passed by the *National Government* during the worst period of the inter-war Depression and its aims were to stimulate domestic production and reduce unemployment. Its main terms were:

- imposition of import duties (tariffs) on most goods coming into Britain
- duties were levied at a lower rate on goods coming from the Commonwealth after an agreement reached by Commonwealth states at a conference held in the same year at Ottawa (Canada)

The effect of this Act was to introduce a form of *imperial preference*.

'In Place of Strife': title of a *White Paper* introduced by the Labour government in 1969 to reform laws concerning *trade unions*. It was associated primarily with *Barbara Castle*, who was then Minister for Employment and Productivity and it stirred up furious controversy within the *Labour Party*. The context was the increasing influence of trade unions during the long period of post-war economic boom when wage levels of unionised workers were increasing more quickly than prices. Castle and the Prime Minister, *Harold Wilson*, argued that effective working relations between Labour and its close allies in the trade union movement nevertheless required a legal framework if the Government were to have an effective economic policy. Opponents argued that the interference of the law would poison relations between party and unions. The opponents, among whom the future Prime Minister *James Callaghan* was prominent, won the argument within the party, although the withdrawal of the key proposal in the White Paper was widely seen as a victory for the unions against the elected Government and probably contributed to Labour's defeat in the *general election* of 1970.

(See also *Conservative Party*.)

income tax: direct tax on both earned and unearned income.

Nineteenth century

Income taxes were not part of government revenue until 1799 when *William Pitt the Younger* introduced them as a means of raising money for the French Wars. It proved a very good revenue-earner but the Government was forced to withdraw it in 1816 when backbenchers, who believed in less control from central government and feared the growth of an inquiring tax-collecting bureaucracy, reminded *Liverpool* that it had been introduced only as a wartime emergency.

The tax was introduced again, this time permanently, by *Sir Robert Peel* in 1842 at the rate of 7d (3p) in the pound on incomes of more than £150 a year. By 1850 it was producing ten per cent of government revenue and proving very difficult to repeal, despite the intention of both *Gladstone* and *Disraeli* to get rid of it. Gladstone fought the losing election of 1874 on a proposal to abolish income tax.

Twentieth century

For a century afterwards, the general tendency of income tax was, first, to rise, and second, to be used as a means of redistributing income and providing welfare for needy sections of the community. The standard rate of income tax was one shilling (5p) in the pound in 1901, four shillings (20p) in 1930, ten shillings (50p) during *World War II* and 8s 6d (42½p) in 1959. From 1909, and *Lloyd George*'s so-called 'People's Budget', a higher rate – soon called 'supertax' – was levied in higher incomes to pay both for increased defence needs and social welfare programmes. During World War II this higher rate reached 19s 6d (97½p) in the pound; after the war it was frequently as high as 80p. By the 1940s, income tax was producing about one-third of all government income. By 1979, however, the new *Conservative* government under *Margaret Thatcher* was changing taxation priorities, shifting the emphasis away from direct taxes such as income tax towards *indirect taxation*.

(See also *economic policy; Keynes, J M.*)

incomes policies: name given collectively to the range of initiatives taken by Conservative and Labour governments, mostly from the late 1940s to the late 1970s, to manage the economy by restraining wage demands. The pronounced tendency of wages to rise more quickly than prices both squeezed employers' profits (thus reducing the capacity for some firms to increase their size by reinvestment) and fuelled the pressures of *inflation*. Effective policies required agreement between Government and *trade unions*, based on mutual trust. The Government would discuss with unions what levels of wage increase the country could 'afford' and hope to set a target which unions would accept. Incomes policies were rarely successful for long and produced great embarrassments and political problems, especially for the *Labour Party* which was funded to a large extent by trade union subscriptions. Substantial union victories over the *Heath*, *Wilson* and *Callaghan* governments during the 1970s produced widespread disillusion and the incoming *Thatcher* government of 1979 decided to abandon them. It relied on wage levels determined, not by negotiation, but 'market forces' in a deflationary climate to produce more 'rational' economic policies based on sound money.

(See also *economic policy; 'In Place of Strife'.*)

Independent Labour Party: political party founded at a conference held in 1893. Its objective was to improve the position of working people by striving for the election of working-class MPs. It took the lead in forming the Labour Representation Committee (later *Labour Party*) in 1900, hoping that this would make *trade unions* more willing to abandon long-standing alliances with the *Liberal Party.* Some of the leading figures in the early Labour Party, such as *Keir Hardie* and *Ramsay MacDonald* were also members of the ILP. Many of its members were also pacifist at the outbreak of *World War I.* The ILP, while co-operating closely with the Labour Party, maintained a separate identity. During the 1920s, it tended to be to the left of Labour, with many socialist members. Under the fiery leadership of the Scottish left-winger James Maxton, it was bitterly opposed to the Labour Party's joining a *National Government* in 1931. It separated from the Labour Party in 1932 and adopted increasingly *Marxist* policies. Three ILP members were elected at the *general election* of 1945, but after Maxton's death a year later the party ceased to have any significant separate existence. It was formally incorporated within the Labour Party in 1975.

India: extensive sub-continent under British control until independence in 1947. The nature of British rule, however, was not simple. Control was exercised directly in some parts of India and in others through influence over notionally independent princes ('niazams', 'nawabs', 'mehtars', 'walis' and 'mirs'). Also, until 1857, British government of India remained in the hands of the East India Company (EIC) a trading company originally established at the end of the sixteenth century whose influence greatly increased in the second half of the eighteenth century as it had taken on both military and governmental functions in defence of British interests.

Situation at the end of the eighteenth century

British interest in India was based on trade. India was the gateway to profitable and exotic Asian markets. Britain traded in tea, calicoes and opium from India and China and found in India a ready market for manufactured goods, especially woollen textiles. During the eighteenth century, as the previously dominant Mughal Empire declined, it became easier for both Britain and France to extend their influence. During the Seven Years War (1756–63) conflict between the two European nations resulted in Britain's acquiring an unchallengeably dominant position and from this both trading influence and territorial controls developed, especially around the main EIC trading bases of Bombay, Calcutta and Madras.

- In 1784, *Pitt's* government passed an India Act. This formalised the involvement of the British government by establishing a Board of Control to superintend the work of the Company in matters of administration, finance, diplomacy and war
- Marquess Cornwallis, as Governor-General from 1786, increased both the efficiency and the military strength of the Company
- During the 1790s, conflict with the French resumed in India. In 1791–92, a hostile ruler, Tippu Sultan of Mysore, had been defeated by Cornwallis and further extensions of territory followed. In 1799, to prevent a potentially damaging alliance between Tippu Sultan and the French, the British attacked Tippu's fortress of Seringapatam. Mysore was petitioned between the British and Indian rulers friendly to Britain. British control over southern India was in practice established

The first half of the nineteenth century

In this period British rule in India expanded steadily. The main developments were:

1813	a new EIC Charter from the British government removed the Company's trading monopoly and confirmed its administrative and governmental functions
1813	a new Governor-General, the Marquess of Hastings, arrived in India. This heralded fresh expansion
1814–16	frontier war with the Gurkhas in Nepal ended in Gurkha defeat and the establishment of another relationship of dependence, whereby the Gurkhas retained nominal independence but effectively under British control
1817–18	long-standing conflicts with the Pindaris finally resolved and the Marathas also defeated. British control around Poona also extended
1823–26	wars with *Burma* led to further extensions of British territory in the sub-continent
1828–35	Governor-Generalship of Lord William Cavendish Bentinck: British attacks on 'uncivilised' Indian customs such as 'Suttee' (the burning of widows on their husbands' funeral pyres) began. The 'thuggee' (Indians who robbed and killed in the name of the Hindu goddess Kali) suppressed. English educational methods introduced to India and English established as the official language
1833	the EIC lost its trading concession to China and was now a purely administrative organisation
1838–42	First Afghan Wars – precipitated by British fear of Russian expansion in the area. British, allied to the Sikhs, attempted to replace the hostile local ruler with a British 'puppet'. The wars went badly. After early successes Kabul, the Afghan capital, was lost and a British force of 20,000 massacred in 1842
1843	after Battle of Meeanee, Sind was annexed to the British-dominated territory of Bombay
1845–46 and 1848–49	Sikh Wars – British attempted to extend territory in north-west India. General Sir Hugh Gough defeated the Sikhs at Mudki (December 1845). Two further British victories forced the Sikhs to acknowledge British control over the Punjab. Sikh rebellion in 1848–49 put down by Gough at Gujarat (Febuary 1849). The Sikhs acknowledged loyalty to British rule

Second half of the nineteenth century

1848–55	Marquess of Dalhousie Governor-General. He continued the process of Westernising India, including railway construction and expansion of the leading ports. He also extended British territory. Administration of EIC further centralised
1852	Pegu (Burma) annexed
1856–62	Governor-Generalship of *Charles Canning*
1857–58	*Indian Mutiny*
1858	*Government of India Act*
1861	Penal Code revised
1876	symbolic, as well as practical, recognition that India was the 'jewel in the imperial crown' as Queen *Victoria* was proclaimed Empress of India
1878–80	Second Afghan Wars: there was further fear of Russian expansion and British moved against Afghan ruler, Sher Ali, who was favouring the

Russians. Sher Ali forced to flee but was replaced by Abdurrahman, who had received Russian support but was not hostile to the British. British recognised him as King and upheld him against Ayub Khan in a brief civil war. General Roberts defeated Ayub Khan at Kandahar (September 1880)

1880–84 Lord Ripon Viceroy introduced reforms including some local self-government, expanded educational opportunities for Indians and abolished censorship. He proposed that Indian judges should be able to try British subjects accused of crimes and encountered much hostility

This period witnessed much political turmoil but it should not be forgotten that it was also the time when British power was at its peak and when the Indian economy was substantially modernised. The contribution of India to British exports and also, via the expansion of towns and the building of an extensive railway system, to its continued industrial expansion was massive.

First half of the twentieth century

This period is dominated by increasing pressure for *Indian Independence* and the main changes concern initiatives and responses designed to involve Indians, both Hindu and Muslim, in administration, government and policy.

1899 Lord *Curzon* Viceroy. Further administrative reforms and attempts to settle
to 1905 remaining border disputes peacefully

1909 Morley–Minto Reforms, leading from a new Government of India Act. Increased Indian participation in government decision making and places on the Viceroy's Council

1911 Delhi Durbar attended by *George V*; Indian capital transferred from Calcutta to Delhi

1918 'Montagu–Chelmsford Report' produced by the Secretary of State for India, Edwin Montagu, and the Viceroy of India (1916–21), Lord Chelmsford. It proposed increased regional self-government, although British officials were to retain 'reserved powers'. These recommendations mostly incorporated within:

1919 Government of India Act – provided for a majority of Indians to sit on the Legislative Council and on provincial councils, though taxation and law and order powers remained largely in the hands of non-Indians

1921–26 Rufus *Isaacs* attempted, as Viceroy of India, to continue with reforms against backdrop of rising nationalist agitation

1927–30 Simon Commission reviewed workings of Government of India Act and recommended regional government be wholly in the hands of Indians, while discussions should proceed with a view to transferring central power

1935 Government of India Act: introduced a federal structure of government, which recognised the independence of Indian princedoms. Central government remained under control of the Viceroy

(See also *Empire, British; Churchill, Winston; Cripps, Stafford; imperialism; Industrial Revolution; trade, overseas.*)

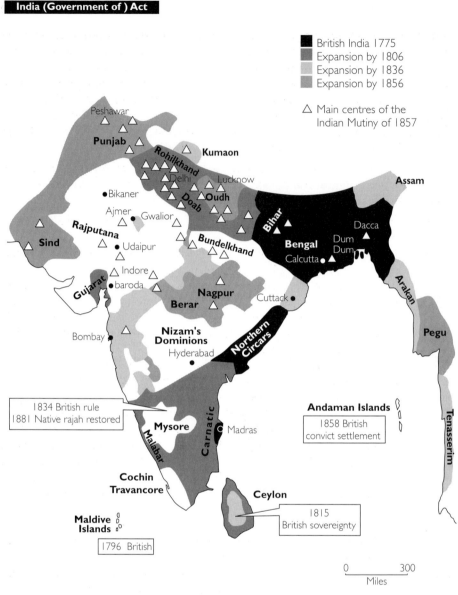

British India 1775
Expansion by 1806
Expansion by 1836
Expansion by 1856

△ Main centres of the Indian Mutiny of 1857

1834 British rule
1881 Native rajah restored

Andaman Islands
1858 British convict settlement

Ceylon
1815 British sovereignty

Maldive Islands
1796 British

0 ——— 300
Miles

British expansion in India

India (Government of) Act, 1858: legislation passed in the wake of the *Indian Mutiny* in an attempt to settle the country. Its main terms were:

- East India Company disbanded
- responsibility for government transferred to a new India Department, headed by a Secretary of State
- Governor-General's office replaced by a Viceroy with extensive powers on behalf of the British government
- Legislative Council established for India

(See also *India; Indian Mutiny.*)

Indian independence: process by which India achieved self-government. Pressure for political independence was intermittent throughout the second half of the nineteenth century and the so-called *Indian Mutiny* was only the most serious of many challenges to British authority in the sub-continent. Pressure for independence grew after the first meeting of the Indian National Congress in 1885, although the Congress initially only petitioned the Viceroy and did not yet make demands for full independence. Congress was overwhelmingly a Hindu party. A separate Muslim League, also calling for independence, was formed in 1906.

While the British attempted reforms and permitted considerable self-government in the period before *World War II* (see *India*), demands for independence were not assuaged. Key developments were:

1892	formation of a radical group within Congress, led by Gangadhar Tilak, demanding independence. It countenanced acts of terrorism
1908	new Congress constitution approved calling for similar political arrangements to those enjoyed by the white *dominions*
1919	after days of rioting in the Sikh holy city of Amritsar, British troops, under the orders of General R E H Dyer, opened fire on demonstrators who had refused to disperse under laws banning such assemblies. About 400 Indians were killed. The incident increased determination within Congress to press for independence
1920	Leader of Congress, Mohandas Gandhi, began a programme of non-co-operation and passive resistance with the British authorities
1930–32	after substantial protests, including those against the salt tax which provoked riots, a 'Round-Table' Conference was held in London, which led to the Government of India Act, 1935, promising eventual dominion status
1936	at general elections, Congress was elected to power in most provinces. Alarm that Muslim interests were not being safeguarded started to grow. Muslim leader Mohammad Jinnah began campaigns against Congress, and the prospect of civil war between Muslim and Hindu began to grow
1942	*Stafford Cripps*, on a mission to quell discontent in India during *World War II*, offered India dominion status. Congress rejected the offered, demanding full independence. Extensive civil disobedience during the remainder of the war and immediately afterwards
1946	New British Labour government conceded independence, but the danger of civil war was now real. Congress refused to agree to partition, which was the demand of the Muslim League
1947	India's last Viceroy, *Earl Mountbatten* appointed to effect transfer of power. British government approved partition despite the objections of Congress

Independence became reality on 15 August 1947, and the new independent Muslim state of Pakistan was created at the same time. The new states were born in bloodshed; there were many massacres and other atrocities resulting in about 250,000 deaths. Almost eleven million Hindu and Muslim refugees were created by a settlement which left them in the 'wrong' countries.

JUDGMENT, OF SOLOMON?
22nd May, 1947. Mr. Attlee is trying to find a solution to the Indian Problem.

The News Chronicle *looks at the problem of India.*

Indian Mutiny, 1857: rebellion, largely within the army in Bengal, against British authority in India.

The main reasons for its outbreak were:

- resentment at the reforms of Dalhousie which were extending not only British controls but British culture within India
- fear that the predominantly Hindu population would be compulsorily converted to Christianity. The work of the *missionaries* was regarded as too aggressive
- resentment that British army traditions were being insensitively imposed on Indian warriors. The rumour that Indian soldiers within the British army ('sepoys') were being issued with rifle cartridges greased with cow fat symbolised Indian anger. The cow is a sacred animal to the Hindu

After a smaller mutiny in February, a more widespread rebellion began in Meerut in May 1857, following which the mutinous regiments captured Delhi. Europeans were massacred at Delhi and Cawnpore and the rebellion spread down the Ganges valley. Sir Colin Campbell led the British forces in the recapture of key strategic points. The rebellion was ended by the summer of 1858.

The Mutiny shocked the British, whose reprisals were severe. It led directly both to constitutional changes (including the establishment of the post of Viceroy) and to reforms in the army.

(See also *India; India Act, 1858.*)

indirect taxation: description given to taxes which are levied not 'directly' on earned and unearned income, but 'indirectly' as consumers buy goods or services. Before 1973, the most common form of indirect tax was 'purchase tax'; it was replaced by *value added tax* which covers a wider range of goods. Thus whenever a consumer buys a gallon of petrol, or pays for a hotel room, part of the bill – sometimes, as with petrol, a very substantial part – is taken up by tax. Since consumers rarely calculate the precise value of the taxation component in any price they pay, indirect taxes tend to be more popular than direct taxes which clearly, and openly, reduce income.

(See also *direct taxation; economic policy.*)

Industrial Revolution: name normally given to the interlinked changes in means of production, and consequent economic growth, which took place between about 1780 and 1850 and which made Britain the world's first industrial nation. The term 'Industrial Revolution' was first used by the French communist writer Auguste Blanqui in 1837 in order to suggest that the changes in the British economy had been as great as the political changes which took place in France from 1789. It did not come into widespread use, however, until the 1880s. The changes which seem to justify the term 'revolution' include:

- the development of factories employing large numbers of people working at machines
- the appearance of machinery which resulted from numerous technological innovations, especially in the textile industry, such as the flying shuttle, spinning jenny and water frame
- a massive expansion in the capacity to produce manufactured goods
- the development of a mass market for the new industrial products
- massive growth in the use of natural resources, particularly coal and steam power. These changes stimulated similarly great changes in metals industries, particularly iron
- an associated revolution in transport – involving roads, canals and railways – which enabled goods to be moved much more quickly and cheaply, thus sustaining the mass market
- associated social changes involving not only the creation of new jobs but, in many cases, a redefinition in the relationship between employer and employee. These often involved longer hours of work and greater discipline. Some argued that the process also saw the emergence of two classes hostile to each other: the working class and the middle (or employing) class
- the rapid expansion of population in industrial towns and a relative decline in the importance of agriculture within the economy

No one disputes, first, that crucially important economic and social changes took place in the late eighteenth and early nineteenth centuries or, second, that they gave Britain a vitally important lead over other nations which did much to make Britain the leading power in the world in the middle of the nineteenth century. Not all economic and social historians believe that they deserve to be described as a 'revolution'. In recent years, some have argued that the changes were more 'evolutionary' than revolutionary. The main arguments against the use of the term are:

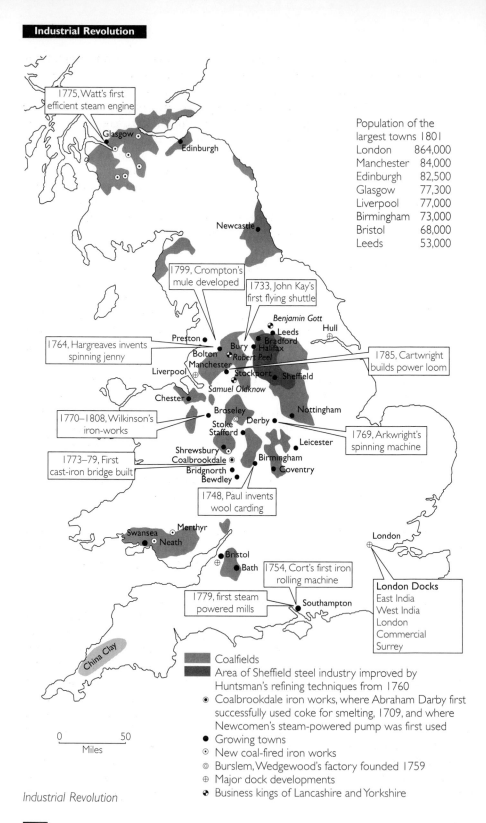

1775, Watt's first efficient steam engine

Glasgow

Edinburgh

Population of the largest towns 1801
London   864,000
Manchester 84,000
Edinburgh   82,500
Glasgow   77,300
Liverpool   77,000
Birmingham 73,000
Bristol   68,000
Leeds   53,000

Newcastle

1799, Crompton's mule developed

1733, John Kay's first flying shuttle

Benjamin Gott

Leeds   Hull
Bradford
1764, Hargreaves invents spinning jenny

Preston
Bury   Halifax
Bolton Robert Peel
Manchester   1785, Cartwright builds power loom
Liverpool
Stockport   Sheffield

Samuel Oldknow

Chester

Broseley   Nottingham
Stoke   Derby
1770–1808, Wilkinson's iron-works
Stafford
Leicester   1769, Arkwright's spinning machine
Shrewsbury
1773–79, First cast-iron bridge built
Coalbrookdale
Bridgnorth   Birmingham
Bewdley   Coventry

1748, Paul invents wool carding

Merthyr
Swansea
Neath   London

1754, Cort's first iron rolling machine
Bristol
Bath
1779, first steam powered mills
Southampton

London Docks
East India
West India
London
Commercial
Surrey

China Clay

Coalfields
Area of Sheffield steel industry improved by Huntsman's refining techniques from 1760
⊙ Coalbrookdale iron works, where Abraham Darby first successfully used coke for smelting, 1709, and where Newcomen's steam-powered pump was first used
● Growing towns
⊙ New coal-fired iron works
◎ Burslem, Wedgewood's factory founded 1759
⊕ Major dock developments
♠ Business kings of Lancashire and Yorkshire

0   50
Miles

Industrial Revolution

- the rate of economic growth did not 'take off' into a new dimension from the late eighteenth century, but grew steadily throughout the eighteenth and nineteenth centuries. This was not a 'revolutionary' performance
- many important innovations, for example, in the iron industry, had taken place at the beginning of the eighteenth century and some much earlier. Machinery of various types was in widespread use well before the so-called 'Industrial Revolution'
- the 'monster' factories and great concentrations of population took place only in well-defined areas of the country, transforming parts of Lancashire, west Yorkshire and Lanarkshire. Some have talked about a 'textile revolution' rather than an Industrial Revolution. Even here, older forms of handcraft production proved remarkably tenacious. *Handloom weavers*, for example, were still found in the 1850s. Furthermore, many of the textile factories were small, employing fewer than 200 workers. The so-called Industrial Revolution, therefore, was a regional, rather than a national, affair and change occurred at different rates in different places
- some of the most radical economic and social changes took place after 1850, with the development of new shipping and metals towns, such as Barrow-in-Furness and Middlesborough and with the creation or great expansion of railway towns like Crewe, Swindon and Wolverton. Some historians have talked of a 'metals revolution' in the second half of the nineteenth century following on from a 'textiles revolution' in the first. London also remained a town of small workshops, rather than large factories, until the end of the nineteenth century. This appears to emphasise that the Industrial Revolution was anything but a sudden affair

Although these arguments have considerable force, the predominant weight of opinion holds that the term still has value, if only as a means of explaining Britain's distinctive development.

(See Figure on page 138. See also *Agricultural Revolution; artisans; canals; class consciousness; cotton industry; electric power; engineering industry; Gross Domestic Product; iron industry; laissez-faire; railways; retailing industry; staple industries; steam power; water frame; water power.*)

inflation: the phenomenon whereby the purchasing power of money is reduced. It became the central concern of *economic policy* for much of the 1960s and 1970s when wage levels ran ahead of prices, thus increasing the living standards of those who were earning but threatening those who lived on fixed income, such as pensions and savings. The general tendency has been for the value of money to decline, but the rate of decline accelerated alarmingly from the 1950s. £1 at 1900 prices was worth only 10s10d (54½p) by 1939, 3s11d (19½p) by 1960 and only 3½p by 1980. The peak year for inflation proved to be 1975, when a rate of 26.9 per cent was recorded. *Margaret Thatcher* introduced policies of deflation from 1979, which eventually reduced inflation rates but at the cost of substantially increased unemployed and the loss of much capacity by manufacturing industry. Inevitably, also, price rises over long periods of time are much greater in certain areas than in others. Thus, while the cost of a foreign holiday, in money terms, went up by a factor of only fourteen in the years

1947–97, that of a year's road tax on a motor car increased 145 times in the same period. The salary of a primary school head teacher, similarly, increased by exactly twice the amount (46-fold) of that of a medical general practitioner (23-fold).

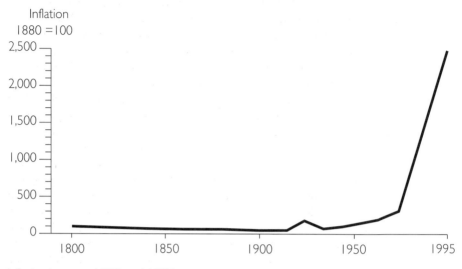

Inflation between 1800 and 1995

Invergordon Mutiny: non-violent refusal by sailors on fifteen ships of the Atlantic Fleet in the Cromarty Firth (Scotland) in September 1931 to accept naval duty in protest against pay cuts imposed by the *National Government* as part of the wider economy measures during the economic crisis. The sailors won a lower pay cut but the action increased nervousness on international money markets and was one of the factors which determined the Government to come off the gold standard.

(See also*MacDonald, Ramsay; Naval Mutinies, 1797.*)

Ireland: For all of the nineteenth century and the first 21 years of the twentieth century, the whole of Ireland was yoked to Great Britain in a *'United Kingdom* of Great Britain and Ireland'.

Nineteenth century

The problems presented by the Union proved long-lasting and what British politicians termed 'the Irish question' was frequently a dominant concern, especially during the later stages of *Gladstone*'s political career. 'Public opinion' is a notoriously difficult thing to gauge in the era before opinion polling, and especially so in a predominantly rural population with a high degree of illiteracy, but it is very unlikely that many in Ireland outside the privileged classes and the *Presbyterian* Protestants in the North saw value in the Union at any time. Reasons for discontent were many, but the most important were:

- **religious differences:** about 80 per cent of Ireland was Catholic but, until 1869, the established Church of Ireland was Anglican. The majority of Protestants were not Anglican but Presbyterian. They were concentrated in the more industrialised part of the country and were strongly anti-Catholic

- **political resentment:** much of the power was exercised by a small elite, predominantly Protestant, and located in Dublin. Nationalist politicians argued that the Union had been imposed by force and bribery after a failed rebellion in 1798. It never had the consent of the Irish people
- **economic disadvantage:** Ireland's was a rural society which shared very little in the economic growth which brought substantial benefits to the rest of the United Kingdom. During the *Industrial Revolution* only the shipyards of Belfast and the linen industry of the North-East enjoyed much prosperity.
- **absentee landownership:** many of Ireland's wealthiest and most powerful landowners were not Irish at all but English or Scottish. Nationalists objected that a small number of privileged non-Irish were draining Ireland of prosperity and organising farming, especially the lucrative Irish cattle trade, for the benefit of themselves and of Britain, but not of Ireland
- **population pressure:** while Ireland's population until 1845 was growing as fast as that of Britain, the lack of industry and economic development caused much more misery since few jobs existed outside agriculture and peasant landholdings were becoming increasingly unviable. Quite extensive *emigration* had already begun before the *Irish Potato Famine* of 1845–47. After it, the Irish population continued to decline until the early twentieth century, reducing the prospects of economic revival. The contrast between Ireland and the rest of the United Kingdom became ever more stark
- **a sense of betrayal:** after the Famine, Irish nationalist leaders argued that this disaster had been caused by British neglect, proof that the British were not committed to the Union for any other reason than national defence and *imperialism*

These views were not universally held within Ireland, but a succession of British political leaders were unable to win Ireland over to the Union. *Sir Robert Peel* attempted to do so, first by persuading *Wellington* of the need for full Roman *Catholic emancipation* in 1829 after the campaigns of *Daniel O'Connell* and the Catholic Association in 1829 and, second, by giving financial support to Roman Catholic colleges in the hope of building up an educated Roman Catholic *middle class* which could see benefit from the Union. *Gladstone* introduced church and land reforms in the years 1869 and 1881 before committing his party to Irish *Home Rule*. He was, of course, responding to growing nationalist pressure, including an increasingly assertive nationalist presence at Westminster, led by *Charles Stewart Parnell*, the concerted pressure of the Land League and terrorism orchestrated by the *Fenian Movement*.

Twentieth century

The *Liberal Party* returned to Home Rule at the beginning of the twentieth century, by which time it was very clear that Protestants in *Ulster* would fight to remain part of the Union. After the second *general election* of 1910, Irish nationalist MPs held the balance of power at Westminster. *Asquith*'s government had reason, therefore, to use nationalist votes to pass a third Home Rule Bill through the Commons in 1912, being prepared to use the *Parliament Act* of 1911 to over-ride continued opposition in the House of Lords before *World War I* intervened. Rebellion and widespread civil unrest continued during the war and immediately afterwards, leading eventually to Home Rule for southern and western Ireland from 1922.

Home Rule brought civil war between those who accepted, and those who rejected, the *Anglo-Irish Treaty*. Thereafter, the new Irish Free State distanced itself from Britain, eventually declaring itself a Republic. In the North, a Protestant-dominated Parliament (*Stormont*) ruled from 1922 to 1972. By the late 1960s, civil rights protests led by Catholics arguing that they were being systematically discriminated against, led to conflict and to the intervention of British troops in 1969. The *Irish Republican Army* conducted terrorist campaigns from the late 1960s, aimed at removing British troops from Ireland as a necessary prelude to their main objective: a fully united Ireland. *Northern Ireland* has been a centre of sectarian conflict which it has not proved possible to resolve, largely because of entrenched positions taken by both sides. Most Protestants are desperate to remain part of the United Kingdom and fear for their position within a united Ireland which would inevitably be dominated by Catholics. Many Catholics, and especially those in the paramilitary organisations, reject the validity of the division of Ireland in 1921. Attempts at power-sharing between the Protestant majority and Catholic minority from the early 1970s to the late 1990s had little success until a fresh agreement supported by UK and Irish governments and by *Sinn Fein* and the *Ulster Unionists* was signed in April 1998. The agreement was endorsed by 71 per cent of Northern Ireland's population and the first elections for a fresh assembly were held in June. At root, most Protestants wish to remain part of the UK; most Catholics want to be part of a united Ireland. A compromise between irreconcilable positions is never easy.

(See also *Act of Union, 1800; Easter Rising; Home Rule Bills, 1886 and 1893; Ireland (Government of) Act, 1921; Ireland Act, 1949; Northern Ireland; Phoenix Park murders; Roman Catholicism; Sinn Fein; Ulster; Ulster Defence Association; Ulster Volunteer Force.*)

Ireland Act, 1949: legislation passed by the United Kingdom government to regulate relations within Ireland. It stated that the constitutional position of Northern Ireland within the United Kingdom would not be altered without the express consent of *Stormont*. The general principle of this legislation has been maintained although after the abolition of Stormont in 1972, the ground shifted somewhat. UK governments confirmed that the status of Northern Ireland would not be altered without the consent of a majority of the electorate. In a highly charged atmosphere where so much political allegiance was determined on religious lines and where the inbuilt Protestant majority progressively decreased after 1922, what this guarantee precisely meant remained open to doubt.

Ireland (Government of) Act, 1921: proposals for a settlement of conflict in Ireland. It proposed:

- two parliaments, both with extensive self-government, but stopping short of complete independence
- one parliament would represent the six counties of the North
- one parliament would represent the remaining twenty-six counties
- a Council of Ireland would be established to administer a range of matters on which there was agreement between the two parliaments
- recognising the importance of religious divisions, both parliaments were to be elected by proportional representation

The proposals were rejected as inadequate by the Irish Dáil.
(See also *Ireland; Anglo-Irish Treaty, 1921*.)

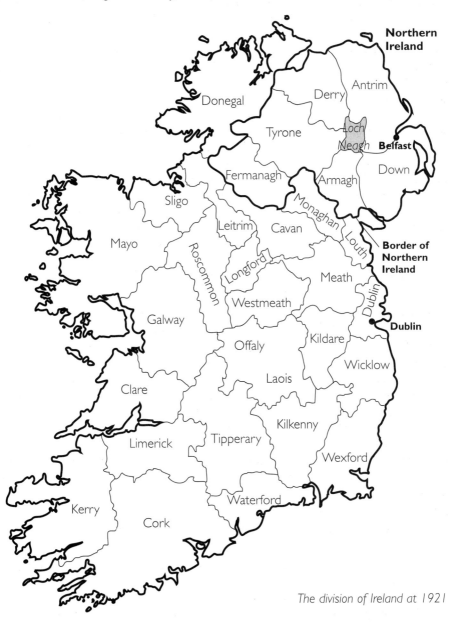

The division of Ireland at 1921

Irish Potato Famine: catastrophic failure of the potato crop in both 1845 and 1846. It was caused by a form of rot. The crop's deficiency in 1846 was about 75 per cent. The combination of two deficient harvests had such serious consequences because of the overwhelming dependence on the potato of so many of the Irish peasantry. It has been estimated that the famine killed about one million Irishmen. Almost one million more emigrated during the same period. Between 1845 and 1851, the Irish population fell from an estimated 8.3 million to 6.5 million and then continued to fall until the early twentieth century. The British government response had initial success. *Peel* imported Indian meal and established food depots, although the low cost of imported food was still beyond the resources of many peasants. The famine was also the occasion, if not the cause, of the repeal of the *Corn Laws*. The *Russell* government was less successful. It was persuaded that things were improving more quickly than was actually the case and abandoned public works schemes, relying instead on inadequate soup kitchens. Nationalists made much of the alleged heartlessness, ignorance and inadequacy of British reaction and there is no doubt that the Famine remained an event of huge significance for the future course of events in Ireland. The strong support for Irish nationalism from many East Coast states of the USA has much to do with the fact that so many emigrants from the Famine settled there.

Irish Republican Army (IRA): nationalist military organisation, which was first known as the Irish Volunteers and took its present name in 1919. It supported the Dáil during the rebellion against the British government in 1919–21. Relatively muted from the mid-1920s to the mid-1960s, despite a bombing campaign in the late 1950s and early 1960s, it emerged as a significant force once more during the 'troubles' which began in *Northern Ireland* in the late 1960s. When the Catholic civil rights movement failed to gain significant concessions from the Protestant leadership, the 'provisional' wing of the IRA, which had split from the official wing, began a terrorist campaign notionally on behalf of the Catholics but with the wider objective of a united Ireland. The 'Provos', as they were widely known, established substantial power bases in Catholic areas of Northern Ireland, especially west Belfast. Funded in significant part by Catholic sympathisers in the United States, the IRA was able to sustain an effective terrorist campaigns.

(See also *Ireland; United States of America.*)

Irish Republican Brotherhood: lesser known name for the *Fenian Movement*.

iron industry: basic industry of the British *Industrial Revolution*. The key developments in iron technology took place in the eighteenth century. First, Abraham Darby perfected a technique for smelting iron from coal in 1709 and in 1784 Henry Cort invented a 'puddling and rolling' process for using coke for making bar iron from pig iron. Iron contributed greatly to the expansion of British exports just before and during the Industrial Revolution. Iron production could now be concentrated in industrial areas, and the main metal centres of the Industrial Revolution were the West Midlands (around Birmingham and South Staffordshire), South Wales (especially Merthyr Tydfil) and central Scotland (in the Clyde and Forth valleys). The expansion of the industry was facilitated by transport developments, especially *canals, railways* and shipbuilding and also by the expansion of the *housing* industry.

(See also *steel industry.*)

Irving, Sir Henry: the most celebrated actor and theatre manager of the Victorian age. Born in 1838, he specialised in playing dramatic Shakespearean roles. He was an outstanding Hamlet, which he played on more than two hundred occasions in the 1870s. He became the first actor to be knighted when Queen *Victoria* honoured him in 1895. He died in 1902.

Isaacs, Rufus (1st Marquess of Reading): lawyer, Liberal politician and diplomat. Born in 1860 into the family of a Jewish merchant, after initial failure in finance, he trained as a lawyer and became Liberal MP in 1903. His main offices were:

- Solicitor General, 1910–12
- Attorney General, 1912–13
- Lord Chief Justice, 1913–21
- Viceroy of India, 1921–26
- Foreign Secretary, 1931

His career was a colourful, as well as a varied, one. A friend of *Lloyd George*, he was on the fringes of the Marconi financial scandal which made his appointment as Lord Chief Justice a controversial one. Eyebrows were also raised when he was briefly sent to the United States as Ambassador with a brief to negotiate a loan. He died in 1935.

Isherwood, Christopher: novelist. Born in 1904, he is best known for two novels, 'Mr Norris Changes Trains' (1935) and 'Goodbye to Berlin' (1939) written from his experiences as an English tutor in Berlin during the last years of the Weimar government. His novels inspired the musical 'Cabaret' which was made into a film in 1972 and which epitomised the sleaze and excess against which many Germans revolted when they voted for the Nazi Party. He worked on verse plays with W H Auden. He emigrated to the United States in 1940 and died in California in 1986.

J

Jameson Raid: important factor in events leading to the outbreak of the Second *Boer War*. Dr Storr Jameson was an administrator for the British South Africa Company who, on 29 December 1895, led about 470 men on an expedition to help the non-Boers in their attempt to overthrow the Boer government of Paul Kruger. In this he was supported by *Cecil Rhodes,* who wanted Transvaal to be annexed to the *British Empire.* The raid failed and, when Rhodes's involvement in the expedition was known, he was forced to resign. The Colonial Secretary, *Joseph Chamberlain,* officially reprimanded Jameson but he almost certainly knew about the raid and supported it secretly. The episode was significant because it destroyed any faith the Boer government had in the British. When Kruger received a telegram of congratulation from the German Kaiser, Wilhelm II, he felt that he could expect German support in a war against the British.

(See also *Anglo-German rivalry, 1890–1914.*)

Jarrow March: hunger march by 200 unemployed workers from the south Tyneside shipyard of Jarrow to London in November 1936. It was led by the local MP Ellen Wilkinson but was intended as a non-political demonstration of the plight of those in an area where unemployment during the Depression was particularly severe. It became a symbol of the helplessness and misery of those who were without work through no fault of their own.

(See also *economic policy; unemployment.*)

Jellicoe (John), 1st Earl: naval commander. Born in 1859, he saw duty during the *Boxer rebellion* of 1900. He played an important part in re-equipping the fleet before *World War I*, when he was appointed Commander of the British Grand Fleet. He commanded the British fleet at the *Battle of Jutland* after which he was removed from command and in December 1916 became First Sea Lord of the Admiralty. He was dismissed by *Lloyd George* in December 1917 largely because he had not developed an effective strategy to combat German U-boats. He served as Governor-General of New Zealand from 1920 to 1924, received his peerage in 1925 and died in 1935.

Jenkinson, Robert Banks: see *Liverpool, 2nd Earl of*

Jews: people of Hebrew descent, whose religion is Judaism. Jews have played an important part in British commercial and intellectual life since the medieval period and numbered about half-a-million at the end of the twentieth century. During the eighteenth century, they played an important part in the growth of London as the world's financial capital. Moves to help them become naturalised British citizens in 1753 were dropped, however, after public hostility. During the first half of the nineteenth century, the Jews in Britain numbered about 12,000, disproportionately concentrated among the financial and commercial middle classes in London, Leeds and Manchester. Francis Goldsmid became the first practising Jew to receive a baronetcy in 1841 and both Lionel Rothschild and David Salomons were elected to become MPs in 1847 and 1851, but were prohibited from taking their seats because they could not honestly swear a Christian oath. This restriction was only removed in 1858.

The situation was transformed in the late nineteenth century with the massive *immigration* of Jews from Russia and Poland, fleeing from persecution in their homelands. Unlike the indigenous Jewish population, most of the immigrants were poor. Many settled in London's East End. By 1901, the number of Jews recorded in the census exceeded 80,000. The size of this influx created difficulties of absorption, disruption of the working-class housing market and anti-immigrant hostility. A 'British Brothers' League' was founded which mobilised working-class support against the Jews. The *Conservative* government responded by passing an Aliens Act in 1905, restricting further immigration. Anti-Jewish hostility was also a prime focus of *Mosley*'s British Union of Fascists during the 1930s, but declined after *World War II* as the main targets of anti-immigrant hostility became arrivals from Asia, West Africa and the West Indies.

(See also *fascism.*)

jingoism: a form of extreme patriotism. It was coined during the *Bulgarian Crisis* of 1876–8 when it seemed likely that Britain might go to war. A popular music hall song stated: 'We don't want to fight, but by jingo if we do: we've got the men, we've got the ships, we've got the money too'. The term came into popular use to describe any unthinking support for one's country, usually in an aggressive context. It has also been a powerful political tool, which the *Conservatives* have exploited on at least two occasions: during the *Boer* and Falklands Wars. It is widely believed that the result of the general elections of 1900 and 1983, or at least the size of the Conservative majorities, owed much to jingoism. In both elections, the popular press was overwhelmingly pro-war.

Jones, Ernest: Chartist and journalist. He was born in 1816 and grew up in Germany before coming to Britain at the beginning of the *Chartist* outbreaks. He became a prominent Chartist, who used his journalistic skills, especially on the 'People's Paper' to support 'physical force'. His analysis of the plight of working people was greatly influenced by socialism and he supported international socialism in the 1850s, before becoming part of the movement to achieve a second *Reform Act* in 1867. He died in 1869.

(See also *radicalism; parliamentary reform.*)

Joseph, Sir Keith (Baron Joseph): Conservative politician. Born into a comfortable Jewish family in London in 1918, he trained as a lawyer and became an MP in 1956. His major offices were:

- Secretary of State for Social Services, 1970–74
- Secretary of State for Industry, 1979–81
- Secretary of State for Education and Science, 1981–86

He was an influential figure as one of the leading advocates of *monetarism* and did much to educate *Margaret Thatcher* to the need for a radical new economic policy to take Conservatism forward after the defeat of *Heath*'s government in 1974. He might well have challenged for the Conservative leadership in place of Thatcher in 1975 had he not made an unwise speech which appeared to call for compulsory birth control among the lower classes of society. He was a thinking politician, much liked by those with whom he worked but lacking ruthlessness and, perhaps, decisiveness too. He was ennobled in 1987 and died in 1996.

Joyce, William (Lord Haw Haw): US Nazi sympathiser and broadcaster. He was born the son of an Irish-American in 1909. His fame derives exclusively from the propaganda broadcasts which he made from Germany in an attempt to weaken the resolve of the British people during *World War II*. His nickname derives from the odd, affectedly superior, accent he used in his broadcasts in an attempt to convey authority. He was arrested at the end of the war when it was decided (dubiously, since he was not a British citizen) that he could be tried for treason. Predictably found guilty, he was executed in 1946.

Justices of the Peace: non-specialist law officers, often called magistrates. Until the nineteenth century Justices of the Peace (JPs) were the key figures in local government, drawn from the ranks of the gentry and smaller but respectable landowners, who tried a range of legal cases in local courts. Until the establishment of *county councils*, they discharged a wide range of legal and administrative functions. To be a JP was a sign of respectability as well as authority in a local area. JPs have remained an essential, if idiosyncratic, element in the British legal system. Not trained in the law (though they may draw upon the expert legal advice available), they sit in 'magistrates' courts' and decide a range of smaller offences, having the power to imprison those convicted. The magistrates' court also remains the first court before which those charged with more serious offences appear.

Jutland, Battle of: naval battle between the British Grand Fleet and German High Seas Fleet during *World War I*. Fought in the North Sea on 31 May 1916, it was the first major battle in which the British navy had been engaged since the decisive victory at *Trafalgar* in 1805. The Germans had been trying to avoid a major battle against superior forces but were lured out by Admiral Beatty. The battle did not produce the decisive victory which the British needed, and probably expected. Indeed, British casualties were the greater and the British attack was marred by poor communications between Beatty and *Jellicoe* which enabled the German force to escape a decisive bombardment. Nevertheless, the battle did not help the Germans to destroy the economically damaging naval blockade. Britain therefore remained the better equipped for a fight to the finish in a long war.

K

Kay-Shuttleworth, James: doctor and educational reformer. Born James Kay, he trained as a doctor in Edinburgh, marrying into the wealthy east Lancashire landed Shuttleworth family. During his work in Manchester, he wrote about the connection between dirt and disease in the poorer quarters of the city in a pioneering study which led to his greater involvement in social questions. He became an assistant Poor Law commissioner in 1835 and wrote perceptively on the training of pauper children. This led to his appointment as the first secretary to the Committee of the Privy Council on Education in 1839. In this post he exercised a decisive influence on the early development of state-supported education for the poor. He established a teacher-training college in Battersea in 1840, which became a prototype for the state system of pupil teachers, whereby able children from national schools were given the opportunity to train as teachers themselves. This was instituted from 1846. He objected violently to the confinement of elementary education represented by the *Revised Code* of 1862, which he considered 'utterly inconsistent with all preceding national policy'. He died in 1877.

(See also *Education Acts; Lowe, Robert; Newcastle Commission; Poor Laws.*)

Keats, John: poet. Born in London in 1795, he trained as a doctor but became perhaps the most purely 'Romantic' of the English poets of his age, appealing to the senses and drawing on nature for inspiration. His most famous poems are 'Endymion' (1818) and the various 'Odes' (1819), including 'To a Nightingale'. He frequently expressed his Romantic perceptions in letters to friends and acquaintances, declaring 'O, for a life of sensations rather than of thought' and his affinity to nature in utterances such as 'The roaring of the wind is my wife and the stars through the window pane are my children'. Just before he died he wrote to a friend: 'I have loved the principle of beauty in all things'. He died of tuberculosis in 1821.

(See also *Byron, Lord; Shelley, Percy Bysshe.*)

Keble, John: Anglican clergyman and hymn writer. Born in 1792, he was an important influence on the development of the *Oxford Movement*, his 'Assize Sermon' in 1833 attacking the Whig government's proposals for church reform in Ireland (see *Whigs*). Keble's vision was of a more spiritual Church of England and it was echoed by many others who were anxious to emphasise the ritual and liturgy of the Church. He was also an accomplished poet, holding the Oxford professorship of poetry from 1831 to 1835. His 'The Christian Year' (1827) formed the basis of several well-known hymns, including 'Blessed are the Pure in Heart' and 'New Every Morning is the Love'. After moving to become vicar of a rural parish in Hampshire in 1835, he was less in the public eye and died in 1866.

(See also *Church of England; Roman Catholicism.*)

Kellogg-Briand Pact, 1928: diplomatic agreement. Signed in London by the US Secretary of State and the French Foreign Minister, the countries renounced war and declared that they would resolve disagreements by negotiation. The pact was widened to, first, nine nations (including Britain) and then to 65 but it had no practical effect during the increased tensions of the 1930s.

(See also *appeasement; League of Nations.*)

Kenya: African republic within the Commonwealth and former British colony. It was colonised by the British East Africa Company in 1887 and taken over by the Crown in stages as British East Africa. The whole territory was formally placed under Colonial Office protection in 1905 and was renamed Kenya in 1920. It experienced substantial agricultural and commercial development and attracted many immigrants from *India*. Resentment by local Kikuyu tribesmen began in the 1920s and developed into a full-scale nationalist movement led by Jomo Kenyatta. In the 1950s, nationalist Mau Mau terrorism developed and Kenyatta was sentenced to life imprisonment. He was released in 1961, however, and became the first President of independent Kenya in 1963, leading a one-party state.

(See also *Africa, Scramble for; Empire, British; Commonwealth, British.*)

Keynes, John Maynard: economist. Perhaps the twentieth century's most influential economic theorist, he was born in Cambridge in 1883. As a young man, he joined the India Office and became editor of the 'Economics Journal' in 1912. He also worked in the Treasury where he was involving in developing policies to combat *unemployment*. He is best known for his reinterpretation of the function of demand in the economy, as developed in two major works 'Treatise on Money' (1930) and 'General Theory of Employment, Interest and Money' (1936), but his range of interests in mathematics, philosophy, the arts and the stock market was phenomenal. He produced a devastating critique of the *Treaty of Versailles* which ended *World War I* in 'The Economic Consequences of the Peace' (1919), which argued that the harsh terms imposed on Germany would destabilise one of the world's major economies with incalculable consequences. During *World War II*, he became a Director of the Bank of England and was one of the leading British representative at the Bretton Woods Conference on post-war monetary stability in 1944. He was also a member of the *Bloomsbury Group* and became the first Chairman of the Arts Council just before his death in 1946.

(See also *Keynesian economics.*)

Keynesian economics: based on theories of economic management developed by *J M Keynes*. Its main thrust was to attack the suppositions of the classical economists that the economy was self-regulating and that interference by government (whatever the beneficent intentions) would have malign consequences. The key beliefs of Keynesian economics were:

- government had a key role to play in stimulating the economy
- by pumping money into the economy, it could create jobs which would reduce unemployment
- those now in employment would not require benefit. Because they were in work, they would consume goods, thus stimulating demand elsewhere in the economy
- governments should, therefore, be prepared to invest in order to create jobs during a recession with the aim of maximising economic output
- the result might be a government deficit, but this was a lesser evil when weighed against the balance of advantage produced by full employment in an active economy geared to produce growth

These ideas, which had been developed during the 1930s, did not become widely influential on government policy until the end of *World War II* but was then the dominant economic philosophy in the developed, non-communist world until the early 1970s. British government policy was dominated by the need to avoid mass unemployment and, until the early 1970s, this aim was successful. Keynesian economics were increasingly challenged by professional economists from the 1960s and fell out of favour when international agreements on currencies broke down and governments were grappling with crippling economic deficits leading to inflation.

(See also *economic policy; laissez-faire; monetarism.*)

Khaki election, 1900: popular name given to the British *general election* fought during the Second *Boer War*. The main issue in the election was support for the war – 'Khaki' referred to the uniforms of British soldiers. The *Conservative Party* exploited both its own growing reputation as the patriotic party and divisions within the *Liberal Party* to win a large majority. Although it only had a lead of 6.5 per cent over the Liberals, the electoral system translated this into 402 seats won, as against only 184 by the Liberals and gave the Conservatives an overall majority of 134 seats.

(See also *Baden-Powell, Robert.*)

Kingsley, Charles: Anglican clergyman, novelist and social reformer. Born in 1819, he developed a keen interest in social reform and *co-operative* schemes to improve the lot of working people. This encouraged him to take the lead in a movement called 'Christian socialism' which aimed in the late 1840s and early 1850s to make Christians more aware of the need for mutual co-operation. Though he was sympathetic to the needs of working people and understood why they joined protest movements such as *Chartism*, he hoped that his type of Christianity would persuade people to trust property owners and the clergy to do what was right in the interests of the whole community. His novels 'Yeast' (1848) and 'Alton Locke' (1850) both presented sympathetic accounts of working people but he is best known for his collection of children's stories, 'The Water Babies' (1863). He was a vigorous religious controversialist and strongly anti-Catholic. He launched a celebrated attack on Victorian Britain's most famous convert to *Roman Catholicism*, Cardinal Newman. He died in 1875.

(See also *Church of England; Newman (John Henry), Cardinal.*)

Kipling, Rudyard: novelist and poet. Born in India in 1865, he is often considered the main literary apologist of the *British Empire*. The early part of his career was spent in India, where he worked as a journalist and it inspired much of his writing, notably the novel 'Kim' (1901), many of the children's 'Just So' stories and several poems about Empire. His best work evinces a directness, immediacy and genius for the simple, telling phrase which tends not to find favour with literary critics but is much admired by ordinary folk. His poem about duty and manhood 'If' is perhaps the most popular, and most extensively quoted, in the language. His sympathy with Empire is obvious but it is never unthinking and shows a knowledgeable sympathy with indigenous peoples – a sympathy he extended in 'Tommy' (1892) to the ordinary British soldier, whom he considered to be often unintelligently and insensitively led. He saw Empire as a mission and referred to taking up 'the white man's burden' both to civilise and to educate. He won the Nobel Prize for Literature in 1907 but declined all honours within Britain. His cousin was the Conservative Prime Minister *Stanley Baldwin*. He died in 1936.

Kitchener, Herbert Horatio (1st Earl Kitchener of Khartoum): army commander. Born in 1850, he saw extensive duty in North Africa, including acting as General Gordon's intelligence officer in 1884. During the 1890s he:

- rebuilt the Egyptian army (1892–96) under British control
- reconquered the Sudan (1896–98)
- became Governor-General of Sudan and rebuilt its capital, Khartoum
- acted as Lord Roberts's Chief of Staff during the Second *Boer War*, during which time he helped to end guerilla resistance

From 1902 to 1909 he was Commander-in-Chief in India where he had numerous conflicts with *Curzon*.

From 1914 to 1916 he was Secretary of State for War, where he pursued an independent line, frequently annoying his Cabinet colleagues. Appreciating, against popular opinion, that *World War I* would not be quickly won, he began planning for a long conflict, including a major recruitment campaign to supplement Britain's highly trained, but small, regular forces. His face stares boldly out of the recruiting poster which reads: 'Your country needs You'. He was drowned in 1916 when the cruiser 'HMS Hampshire', in which he was travelling to attend a conference in Russia, struck a mine and sank. He was not an easy man, often quarrelling and unable to see the virtue of compromise. On major strategic military issues, however, his judgement usually proved correct.

Korean War, 1950–53: war which involved British troops as part of a *United Nations* force. The territory of Korea, which had been under Japanese rule during *World War II,* was divided into North (under Soviet Russian influence) and South (under US influence) in 1945. In 1950, the communist North invaded the South, hoping to reunite the country under communist leadership. The United Nations Security Council sent forces to repel the invasion. Initially, the UN forces were successful. The North was invaded and its capital, Pynong-yang captured in October 1950. Chinese communist forces came to the aid of the North and drove UN forces south early in 1951. Lengthy, but mostly fruitless fighting ensued, before an Armistice was signed in July 1953, setting an agreed, permanent, border between North and South Korea at the 38th parallel of latitude.

(See also *Marxism*.)

L

labour aristocracy: term used by some social historians to describe better off working people, especially in Victorian Britain. The term is a controversial one, largely because of the use which has been made of it. It is not clear that a 'labour aristocracy' ever existed as a distinct social group with its own, separate values, although some historians stress factors such as a 'respectable' life-style, which involved the male breadwinner supporting his wife and children, moderation, especially in the use of alcohol and a commitment to improvement by hard work, education and thrift. Others suggest that these values were not specific to one economic group within the working class and also that the differences apparent among workers from different trades are so marked that they should not be linked together as possessing shared values and aspirations.

Some *Marxist* commentators have also suggested that the values of the labour aristocracy linked them more closely with the middle classes and thus divorced them from their 'natural' allegiance with other working people – the proletariat. Some have even suggested that the labour aristocracy prevented a revolution in Britain by failing to use its superior skills and education to lead the workers in a struggle against the economic oppressors in the middle and upper classes. Few now hold this view.

Recognising that the category is problematic, it is nevertheless possible to identify characteristics enjoyed by about fifteen to twenty per cent of working men which might set them apart, economically if not politically or culturally, from the remainder of workers. This is because so much labour in Victorian Britain was sporadic and casual and because so many were vulnerable to trade depressions or to reduced employment opportunities during the winter. The phrase refers almost exclusively to working men, rather than to women. Such men had:

- the ability to use a skill (probably acquired through apprenticeship) to command high wages through scarcity value. In mid-Victorian Britain good wages for working men were about £3 a week
- regular employment all the year round. The majority of working people in Victorian Britain were vulnerable to frequent periods of short time or *unemployment*
- the ability to insure themselves against the hazards of life, often by investment of regular sums in members of *friendly societies*
- bargaining power for wages and working conditions as members of skilled workers' *trade unions*
- the ability to pay rent regularly to occupy decent quality housing
- good standards of literacy and a commitment to education

(See also *class consciousness; Industrial Revolution; trade unions.*)

labour exchanges: organisations which existed to provide information about, and access to, jobs for those seeking work. Exchanges organised by *trade unions* and others had developed during the nineteenth century to provide work. These normally operated on a trade-by-trade basis and so had restricted general usefulness. During the economic slump of 1903–5, the Government had established 'distress commit-tees' to organise public relief, including appeals for charity to tide people over a crisis. However, the studies of *William Beveridge* revealed that such initiatives did not do much to help those who were normally in regular work, being mostly used by casual workers and those who were under-employed even when trade was good. His ideas were influential with the *Liberal* government which had taken office in 1905 and helped to produce the Labour Exchanges Act, 1909 which directly targeted those normally in regular employment by setting up 'exchanges' where they could obtain information about vacancies.

(See also *Churchill, Winston; National Insurance; unemployment.*)

Labour Party: national political party organised largely by, and for the benefit of, working people.

1900–18

It was founded, as the *Labour Representation Committee*, in 1900 by agreement between the *Independent Labour Party*, the *Social Democratic Federation*, the Fabian Society and various trade union supporters. It won two seats only in the *general election* of that year but an electoral arrangement with the Liberals in 1903, known as the MacDonald–Gladstone Pact, ensured that Labour candidates were not opposed in several winnable seats at the next election, in 1906. In consequence, Labour won 30 seats in that year. The defection of several unions in 1908–10, notably of the mineworkers, from their previously well-established allegiance to the *Liberal Party* gave the new party greater strength and 40 and 42 seats at the two general elections of 1910. Until 1914, however, the party was very much a minority one, fielding fewer than 80 candidates. Its fortunes were transformed during and immediately after World War 1 for three main reasons:

- the Liberal Party was split and two separate Liberal groupings fought the general election of 1918. Despite winning only 63 seats, Labour was installed as the official opposition since the party had won more seats than the 'opposition' Liberals led by *Asquith*, and since *Sinn Fein*, which won more seats, had no interest in loyalty to the United Kingdom political system
- Labour leaders, notably *Arthur Henderson*, gained senior ministerial experience as members of *Lloyd George*'s War Cabinet. The party thus gained credibility as a potential government
- the party was thoroughly re-organised and given a new constitution in 1918, with the aim of becoming a truly national party. It fielded 388 candidates in the 1918 general election and always more than 400 in each election thereafter

1918–45

During this period, the party had mixed fortunes. It formed a minority government on two occasions, in 1924 and 1929–31. Its leadership distanced itself from Bolshevism and presented the party as in the mainstream of British politics. Labour permanently supplanted the Liberals as the main alternative to the *Conservative Party* and it proved that it could attract mass support at general elections. After 1918, it never won fewer than four million votes and in 1929, when it won more seats than any other party (288), though not an overall majority, it attracted almost 8.4 million votes. On the other hand, its progress was hampered first by the failure of the *General Strike* and the anti-trade-union legislation which followed. Labour was heavily dependent on the unions for the financial support necessary to make it a mass, national party. It also split in 1931, when some senior ministers, notably *Ramsay MacDonald* and *Philip Snowden* accepted the King's request to join a *National Government* when the bulk of the party was determined not to join and to go back into opposition. In the election of 1935, the party won only 142 seats, although still polling more than eight million votes.

Since 1945

In 1945, the party won a huge parliamentary majority, winning 393 seats and polling almost twelve million votes. In part the beneficiary of long-term resentment at what was seen as the mismanagement of the National Government, Labour also promised a wide range of reforms, which it provided by nationalisation of many heavy industries and the creation of the *welfare state*. It was re-elected by a small majority in 1950 and defeated a year later. The 1950s saw bitter disputes between left-wingers, led by *Aneurin Bevan* and the party leadership, under the control of *Hugh Gaitskell* from 1955. From 1964, when it won a narrow victory under *Harold Wilson*, to 1979, Labour was in power for all but three-and-a-half years, though this was a period of uncertainty and division. The promised modernisation of Britain failed to take place and the governments of Wilson and *Callaghan* failed to solve deep-seated problems. The perceived excessive influence of the trade union movement also alienated many Labour supporters and uncommitted voters and it was no surprise when Labour lost power in 1979 after a winter punctuated by highly publicised strikes.

Labour Representation Committee: the original name taken by the *Labour Party* when it was formed at a conference of socialist groups and trade unionists in London 1900. It won two seats in the general election of 1900 but increased that number to 29 in 1906 following the electoral pact made between Herbert Gladstone and *Ramsay MacDonald*. It changed its name to the Labour Party in 1906.

laissez-faire: economic policy and political philosophy based on *free trade*, low taxation and a very limited role for the State. Associated with the economic ideas of Adam Smith and the political philosophy of *Jeremy Bentham* and the *utilitarians*, it strongly influenced government policy in the Victorian period. The predominant arguments advanced in support of a laissez-faire position were:

- individuals should be free to control their own lives and makes their own decisions, constrained only by the consequences of those decisions for the lives of others. When they negotiate, as for example, on wages, prices or contracts, they do so as free agents
- a free market, unconfined by tariffs, tolls or other governmental restrictions, is best for stimulating competition, innovation and growth, from which consumers benefit
- the role of the State should be minimised. It has a duty to defend the nation and to provide a framework within which the liberty of law-abiding citizens is guaranteed. It may also intervene to protect the interests of citizens who are not free agents (as, for example, in Victorian Britain women

and children) or – in the wider interests of liberty and opportunity for the citizen – to provide a measure of public health and education, but such interventions should be limited
- acting on these precepts, the needs of the State in peacetime are limited. Accordingly, governments should exercise financial prudence, ensuring that its income and expenditure are kept in balance. Government taxation needs are limited. Governments acting on laissez-faire principles would keep taxation – especially direct taxation on income and wealth – as low as possible

Some historians have argued that Britain came as close as is feasible to being a 'laissez-faire' state in the period 1830–70, after which relative economic decline and the increasing recognition that poverty and unemployment were not necessarily the fault of individuals caused a reappraisal of the functions of the State and the development of social and, later, welfare legislation.

(See also *Gladstone, William; Peel, Sir Robert, Jnr.*)

Lamb, Lady Caroline: novelist. Born in 1785, she married William Lamb, later the Prime Minister *Viscount Melbourne*, in 1801. The marriage was never successful and Lady Caroline is best known for her romantic association with Lord *Byron*, which he ended in 1813 and from which she never properly recovered. Her description of him as committed to her journal in 1812 – 'Mad, bad, and dangerous to know' – has entered the language as a pithy summary of character. Her novels, including 'Glenarvon' (1816), were little read by contemporaries.

Lancaster House Agreement: Peace agreement of December 1979 which ended internal war in Southern *Rhodesia* between the unofficial white government, headed by Ian Smith, and black guerilla groups. It was agreed that there should be free elections to choose a government for the country. The agreement ended the period of white minority colonial rule under Ian Smith. After the elections, Britain confirmed the independence of Southern Rhodesia (which became 'Zimbabwe' on independence) after elections had been held. This happened in 1980.

(See also *Empire, British; Thatcher, Margaret.*)

Lansbury, George: Labour politician and journalist. Born in 1859, he was a socialist and pacifist who became active in local politics in London's East End. He edited Labour's 'Daily Herald' newspapers from 1919 to 1922. In 1921 he helped to organise a protest – called 'Poplarism' – when the local authority in Poplar refused to raise rates, which local councillors said the people could not afford – to help deal with an economic crisis. He was an MP from 1910 to 1912 and again from 1922. His major offices were:

- Minister for Works, 1929–31
- Leader of the Labour Party, 1932–35

Like the majority of the party, he broke with MacDonald over the formation of a *National Government* in 1931. His leadership of the party was characterised by personal honesty and kindness, but his pacifist views were increasingly exposed during a time when Italy and Germany were under the control of aggressive dictators. He died in 1940.

(See also *Labour Party.*)

Lansdowne (Henry), 5th Marquess: *Liberal*, later *Unionist*, politician. Born into a famous *Whig* family in 1845, he served in minor office under *Gladstone* in 1872–74 and 1880 but was one of the first Liberals to resign on account of Gladstone's Irish policy. His career as Conservative Unionist was largely concerned with foreign and colonial affairs, but, as leader of the *Conservatives* in the Lords, he led the opposition to the Liberals' *Parliament Act*. His major offices were:

- Governor-General of Canada, 1883–88
- Viceroy of India, 1888–94
- Secretary of State for War, 1895–1900
- Foreign Secretary, 1900–5

During the First World War, he was a member of the coalition War Cabinet and was severely criticised for suggesting in 1916 and 1917 that Britain should make peace with Germany. He died in 1927.

(See also *Balfour, Arthur; Canada; India; Lloyd George, David; Salisbury, Marquess of.*)

Lawrence, David Herbert (usually known as D H): novelist. Born in Nottinghamshire in 1885, he wrote a number of novels drawing on his background as a miner's son who became a schoolmaster. Famous among them are the partly autobiographical 'Sons and Lovers' (1913), 'The Rainbow' (1916) and 'Women in Love' (1921). His most notorious, though certainly not his finest, novel is 'Lady Chatterley's Lover' (1928) which was the subject of a famous obscenity trial in London as recently as 1960. He died in France in 1930.

Lawrence, Thomas Edward (usually known as T E): soldier, archaeologist and author. Better known as 'Lawrence of Arabia', he was born in North Wales in 1888. He got to know the Middle East through archaeological work before *World War I* and joined the Arab Bureau in *Egypt* during the war. In 1916, he became British military adviser to the Arabs who were rebelling against the Turks. In this capacity he was close to Prince Feisal, son of the Sherif of Mecca. He helped to train the Arab forces and was present when the Red Sea port of Aqaba was captured by the Arabs in 1917. He was present as Feisal's adviser at the post-war peace conferences, where he attempted, but failed, to secure pledges from the great powers that the Arabs could have their independence. He became a member of the Colonial Office, with special responsibility for the Middle East, in 1921. His account of the Arab struggle for freedom, 'The Seven Pillars of Wisdom' (1926), became a classic. In quixotic changes of career, and of name, he joined the Royal Air Force as J H Ross in 1922 and the Royal Tank Corps as T E Shaw in 1923. He was killed in a motor cycle accident in 1935. His posthumous fame was greatly increased by the success of David Lean's romanticised film 'Lawrence of Arabia' (1962).

League of Nations: international peace organisation established after *World War I*. The establishment of a League to settle future international disputes was written into the peace treaties. Britain was one of only two great powers (France being the other) which remained a member until its formal dissolution in 1945, although it had ceased to have any rationale once *World War II* broke out. Although Britain was a mainstay of the League, which had considerable successes in the 1920s, British policy did not always further League objectives. The invasion of Abyssinia by the Italian dictator Benito Mussolini in 1935 was condemned by the League and economic sanctions imposed. Because of British and French support for *appeasement*, however, the sanctions worked poorly and did not deter Mussolini. Appeasement contributed significantly to the failure of the League in the 1930s.

leisure: time spent not at work. How ordinary people spent their leisure time has been an increasing subject of study by social historians in recent years.

Nineteenth century

Work in an industrial society placed a much higher value on order, regularity, discipline and timing than that required on the land. The division between work and leisure thus became sharper. Industrial work also usually required longer hours, making time available for leisure and recreation doubly valued. Furthermore, many of the traditional forms of leisure, developed in rural societies, had depended upon space which was not available in rapidly growing, and crowded, Victorian towns. Governing and middle-class elites feared a breakdown in public order if traditional leisure activities, such as bull-running and bear-baiting, were allowed to continue. Local legislation increasingly banned old leisure forms as liable to lead on to riotous and drunken behaviour. Much attention was given by the respectable classes to the development of what has been called '*rational recreation*'. This included the provision of parks for walking and 'taking the air', where games such as football were usually prohibited, *public libraries* and lecture and classical music concert series. These activities did attract many improving working men but most continued to seek entertainment, and solace, in beer shops and public houses, which remained almost entirely male preserves. During the second half of the nineteenth century, leisure developed into a significant industry in its own right. Statutory Bank Holidays, from 1871, agreed Saturday half-holidays and rising living standards made possible such developments as:

- professional sport, especially *Association Football*
- holidays at the seaside. *Railways* were particularly important in taking people to rapidly growing resorts such as Blackpool and Morecambe in Lancashire, Scarborough in Yorkshire and Skegness in Lincolnshire. These places catered both for 'day-trippers' and those who would stay for a week, usually coinciding with traditional holiday periods
- *music halls* where both the wealthy and the more humble were entertained by a variety of 'turns'. Successful halls offered both a variety of entrance prices and large quantities of drink

1900–45

Leisure time lengthened in the twentieth century as technological and other developments contributed to making it both richer and more diverse. The main changes in leisure were the development of:

- the *cinema*, which became the main working-class leisure activity in the 1930s
- broadcasting, both *radio* from the 1920s and *television* from the 1930s. Television remained relatively expensive, however, and did not become a mass medium for entertainment and information until the 1950s
- purpose-built holiday camps in seaside resorts, where accommodation and entertainment were all provided for an inclusive charge. The first holiday

camp was established at Skegness by Billy Butlin in 1936 and camps were enormously popular over the next 40 years

- an international culture in popular music. Popular music was influenced in the 1920s by the example of jazz and other rhythms from the United States. Broadcasting and film created international 'stars' while new rhythms attracted huge audiences to the dance hall

Since 1945

The themes of international entertainment and diversity have both been heavily accented since the end of *World War II*. Fuelled by longer holidays and rapidly rising living standards, the main developments have been:

- the emergence of popular music as a distinctive youth sub-culture, often in defiance of traditional authority. The emergence of 'rock-and-roll' from the mid-1950s placed ever greater emphasis on insistent rhythm and volume at the expense of both lyrics and melody. Almost all popular music came to be written in common (4/4) time, whereas much popular music in the early twentieth century had been in waltz (3/4) time
- the growth of the foreign 'package tour' industry, with an 'all-in' price for air travel and accommodation. Air travel, in the 1930s and 1940s, the privilege of the wealthy few, became democratised from the later 1950s. Ordinary people could travel to places where sun and warm seas were guaranteed. Not surprisingly, the domestic seaside industry found the competition increasingly severe

(See also *Industrial Revolution; tourist industry.*)

lend lease: the mechanism whereby supplies of armaments and raw materials were supplied to Britain and other Allies by the *United States* during *World War II*. Goods were 'lent' with payment due only at some unspecified date after the War. The system came into operation in March 1941 and enabled the USA to offer support to the anti-Nazi war effort before it formally entered the war. The system continued until September 1945, by which time Britain had received goods and supplies worth about $30 million. The system cemented Anglo-US commerce and, indirectly, led to the ending of the policy of Commonwealth trade preference.

(See also *overseas trade.*)

Liberal National Party: name given to the group of 23 Liberal MPs who broke with the party in 1931 to help form the *National Government*. Their numbers increased to 35 at the *general election* of 1931, but splits soon emerged. The followers of *Herbert Samuel* left the Government in 1932 in protest at its abandonment of *free trade*. Followers of *Sir John Simon* remained in the coalition and won 35 seats in the election of 1935. After *World War II*, the grouping moved closer to the *Conservative Party*. Following an agreement with the Conservatives in 1947, the party changed its name to 'National Liberal' and became increasingly indistinguishable from the larger party. The last two National Liberal MPs were elected in 1966.

(See also *Liberal Party.*)

Liberal Party: national political party which developed during the nineteenth century from increasing links between the *Whigs* and *radical* political groupings. There is no universally agreed date from which the Liberal Party can be said to exist. Some date it from the *Lichfield House Compact* of 1835; more would agree that an integrated party existed after a meeting at Willis's Rooms in June 1859 when a group of *Peelites*, most importantly *William Gladstone*, radicals and Whig politicians agreed upon an anti-*Conservative* alliance to defeat the government of the Earl of *Derby*. This ended a period of political uncertainty and inaugurated one of 26 years during which the new grouping, led first by *Palmerston* and then by *Russell*, Gladstone and *Hartington*, was out of office for only eight.

1850s–1914

The party, although frequently in office in this period, was never a united grouping. Certain broad policy agreements can, however, be discerned. These included:

- support for *free trade*
- belief in efficient, cheap government, characterised by low taxation
- support for a range of reforms, particularly in administration and *state education*
- concern for the interests of the *nonconformists*. Although most of the leaders of the party were landowners and *Anglicans*, many Liberal supporters, particularly in Scotland, Wales and Midland and northern towns in England were nonconformists

Differences within the party were, in part, explained by its social and regional divisions. A party led by aristocrats and other large landowners, predominantly in England, had difficulty empathising with urban nonconformists and with growing distinctiveness in Scotland and Wales. Further, many of the radicals who looked to the Liberals to advance their interests were interested in a narrow range of issues – secular education, or *temperance* reform, for example. They were uneasy colleagues in a party which encompassed a wide range of issues. The main disagreements in this period, however, were two:

- over *Ireland*, and especially Gladstone's *Home Rule* policy. This led to widespread defection and the development of *Liberal Unionism* from the mid-1880s
- over *imperialism*, and particularly policy towards *South Africa* and the Second *Boer War*, when the party was divided between an 'imperialist' and a 'pacifist' wing

Both disagreements helped to explain long periods of opposition in the 1880s, 1890s and early 1900s before the party reunited over free trade and won a large general election victory in 1906. The Liberal governments of 1905–14, led first by *Campbell-Bannerman* and, from 1908, by *Asquith*, enacted a substantial measure of social, *National Insurance* and *welfare* reforms, driven by a progressive wing responding to the investigations of *Charles Booth* and *Seebohm Rowntree*.

From 1914

The Liberal Party never formed a government after *Asquith*'s resignation in 1916 and *Lloyd George*, who headed coalition governments, was the last Liberal to be Prime Minister. No Liberal politician has served in government since 1945. In terms of power, therefore, the twentieth century has seen what is probably an irreversible decline in a once great political party. Historians have offered numerous explanations for this important phenomenon. Among the most important are:

- continued splits within the party. Asquith and Lloyd George split in 1916 and their supporters were in two camps during the crucial years 1916–22 when the *Labour Party* was installed as 'the official opposition'. The party split again after 1931. The 'Liberal National Party' (sometimes known either as National Liberals or 'Simonites') under *Sir John Simon* joined *Ramsay MacDonald's National Government*. After 1935, they effectively became *Conservatives* as continued members of the National Government
- decline in support for both free trade and nonconformity in the early twentieth century. This deprived the Liberals of much of their reformist energy
- divisions within the party – exposed by *World War I* – over the morality of fighting war on a large scale. The Liberals had always contained a small, but significant, minority of pacifists
- growing polarisation among the great economic power groups. The Conservatives had emerged in the late nineteenth century as the dominant party of the business interests while the new Labour Party had the support of most *trade unions* by 1914. In an age of mass politics, these two parties could call on large, institutional sources of finance to fight elections. The Liberals, who disproportionately retained the loyalty of the professional middle classes – lecturers, lawyers and the like – found it increasingly difficult to compete with the two other main parties on financial terms
- the strong discrimination of the '*first past the post*' electoral system against minority parties, which can gain millions of votes but few seats because their support tends to spread more evenly across parliamentary seats. In the general election of 1929, for example, the Liberals gained 5.3 million votes, against 8.6 million for the Conservatives and 8.3 million for Labour. Yet the Liberals won only 59 seats to the Conservatives' 260 and Labour's 288. In February 1974, it won nineteen per cent of the vote but only fourteen (2.2 per cent) seats. In 1983, the alliance of Liberals and the new Social Democratic Party gained 26 per cent of the popular vote and 23 seats, while Labour gained 28 per cent and 209 seats

Although Liberals had important influence in *coalition governments* in the twentieth century, therefore, they have made relatively little impact on the struggle for power. They tended to do well in by-elections, and developed a specialism between the late 1950s and the late 1990s in winning seats in prosperous areas at by-elections from the Conservatives. Almost invariably, those seats were won back by the Conservatives at the next general election. Only at the election of 1997, when there was substantial evidence of anti-Conservative *tactical voting*, did the Liberals win more than forty seats for the first time since 1929.

Liberal Unionists: name given to *Liberal* politicians who left the party over *Gladstone's* policy of Irish *Home Rule* in 1886. Very few returned to the party, most supporting the *Conservative Party* from the early 1890s. The leaders of this breakaway group were *Joseph Chamberlain*, from the progressive wing of liberalism, and the *Marquis of Hartington* from the old *Whig* grouping. Liberal Unionists formally merged with the Conservative Party in 1912 after which the latter became officially known as 'the Conservative and Unionist Party'.

Lib–Lab Pact, 1977: agreement between *David Steel* as leader of the *Liberal Party* and the *Labour* Prime Minister, *James Callaghan*. The pact enabled the Government to defeat a *Conservative* motion of no confidence in March 1977 by 322 votes to 298, but it had few committed supporters on either side and was regarded as a short-term measure. Steel withdrew formally from it in 1978 and the Liberals voted against the Government after its plans for national assemblies for Scotland and Wales foundered early in 1979. The Government was defeated by 311 votes to 310 in another Conservative vote of no confidence on 28 March 1979 and a general election followed.

Lib–Labs: working men who supported the Liberal Party either in the party organisation or as MPs. The first Lib–Lab MPs were Alexander MacDonald and James Burt, both very loyal to Gladstone's leadership. Until the mine workers left the Liberals in 1909, more working men in unions supported the Liberals than the new Labour Party. However, the difficulty which many politically-minded trade unions found in being adopted as Liberal candidates caused a drift into the Independent Labour Party and the Labour Party in the 1890s and 1900s.

libraries, public: collections of books and other reading matter intended for free access. Support for public libraries grew in the 1840s partly as a means of raising the standard of knowledge and education in the growing towns and partly as a civic good from which all citizens could benefit. The principle that knowledge should be freely available to all who sought it was central to the ethic of moral and educational improvement embraced by so many of the Victorian middle and upper working classes. Public libraries were established in many large towns in the later 1840s and a parliamentary select committee of 1849 recommended the expansion of library provision. The Public Libraries Act, 1850, allowed local authorities to set aside the product of a half-penny rate for establishing libraries. This sum was increased to one penny in 1855. All restrictions were removed by the Public Libraries Act, 1919, which gave county councils the power to establish library services throughout the county.

(See also *leisure; rational recreation*.)

Licensing Act, 1872: legislation passed during *Gladstone's* first government concerning regulation of alcoholic drink. By it:

- local magistrates were given powers to grant licences to public houses and to institute checks for fair dealing, including powers to deal with watering or other adulteration of drink
- public houses had to close not later than 11 p.m., except in London where they might remain open until midnight

The measure was a compromise which displeased both the *Liberal Party*'s *temperance* reformers, who wanted tighter regulation and the brewing trade, and many working men, who wanted less – or none. It proved electorally unpopular. Gladstone ascribed his defeat in the 1874 general election, writing to his brother: 'We have been borne down in a torrent of gin and beer'.

(See also *Conservative Party*.)

Lichfield House Compact: arrangement made at the London home of Lord Lichfield in February 1835. Its purpose was to unite *Whigs, radicals* and Irish nationalists under *Daniel O'Connell* to bring down *Peel's minority government.* This was achieved, and *Melbourne* resumed office. However, the arrangement was greeted with suspicion by many electors and did the Whigs little good in the longer term.

Limited Liabilities Act, 1855: legislation governing public companies. By it, individual investors in a properly registered company which failed could only be made responsible for the amount they had put into the company and not the company's entire debts. The legislation was developed further by the Joint Stock Companies Act, 1856, and the Companies Act, 1862. Its main strength lay in the protection which it gave to investors. This greatly developed public confidence, stimulated investment and increased the importance of the London Stock Exchange, which was developing as the world's leading money market. Its main weakness was that it provided a safety net for company directors to 'wind up' companies which were in difficulty but not insolvent as a tactical device and start up new businesses. This usually ensured that small investors lost money while those in charge escaped the full effects of bad, or sometimes even fraudulent, management.

(See also *Industrial Revolution.*)

Liverpool (Jenkinson, Robert Banks (to 1803) (Lord Hawkesbury, (1803–8)), 2nd Earl of: *Tory* politician and *Prime Minister.* Born in 1770, the son of Charles Jenkinson, one of *George III's* main political advisers and a minister under *Pitt the Younger,* he was educated at Cambridge and destined for a political career. He became an MP in 1790, was loyal to Pitt the Younger throughout the 1790s and spent almost all of his adult life in government office. His main offices were:

- President of the Board of Control, 1799–1801
- Foreign Secretary, 1801–4
- Home Secretary, 1804–6, 1808–9
- Secretary for War and the Colonies, 1809–12
- Prime Minister, 1812–27

Liverpool was an efficient minister who mastered the detail of a number of departments. His career before he became Prime Minister was not spectacular and it did have embarrassments. He helped negotiate the unsuccessful *Treaty of Amiens* in 1802 and also bore responsibility for the *Walcheren Expedition* of 1809. He lacked the charisma of *Canning* and the personal diplomatic authority of *Castlereagh* but he was considered a more congenial departmental colleague than either and this made it easier to succeed to the prime ministership after the assassination of *Spencer Perceval,* although he was not the first choice of the *Prince Regent.*

Policies

His basic political position was anti-reformist. He had been present as a young man at the fall of the Bastille and the later excesses of the *French Revolution* only confirmed his distaste for political change based on theory rather than maturity and experience. His hostile response to the resurgence of *radicalism* in 1815–20 was entirely predictable because he believed in the old order and the supremacy of the landed interest. He usually maintained good relations with landowning backbenchers in the *House of Commons.* He could not, however, persuade them to maintain the *income tax* in 1816 once the *Napoleonic Wars* were over. It has been conventional to divide his long prime ministership into two phases: a 'reactionary' one lasting till 1822 and then, associated with a major reshuffle of ministers in 1821–23, a 'Liberal Tory' phase. Although much of the early phase was associated with the suppression of political radicalism and much of the later with economic and administrative reforms and moves in the direction of *laissez-faire*, the division is thoroughly misleading. Liverpool never underwent a major change of mind or political attitude. His career was, in some respects, a mirror image of that of the Younger Pitt, whose leadership he tried to emulate. He followed Pitt in his belief that trade liberalisation would increase national prosperity and, like him, he developed good relations with the business classes. Also, like Pitt, he put national security before everything else when he believed it to be threatened. The calmer conditions of the 1820s, therefore, enabled him, prodded by sharper minds like those of *Huskisson* and *Peel*, to develop further both the trading and administrative reforms begun by Pitt in the 1780s.

Reputation

No one since Liverpool has held the office of Prime Minister for a longer period and only two predecessors – Robert Walpole and the Younger Pitt – had longer service overall. Yet his reputation has suffered from the wounding, and unfair, jibe of *Benjamin Disraeli* in his novel 'Coningsby' that he was 'the Arch-Mediocrity'. In recent years, historians have re-assessed him more favourably, pointing out his ability to keep a talented, but quarrelsome, group of ministers united under his leadership, his successful battle of wills with *George IV*, his extraordinary knowledge of the governmental machine and his successful, and remarkably scandal-free, private life. All these have their place, but the pendulum should not be allowed to swing too far. Liverpool lacked dynamism and his objectives were mostly negative ones. He offered no positive direction on the big issue of the 1820s, *Catholic emancipation*, which sharply divided his Cabinet and led to the break up of the Tory Party after his death. Above all, he wanted to preserve the pre-eminence of the landed interest during a time of turbulent change. Moreover, he was a fussy manager who could become obsessed with detail and sometimes lost sight of the larger picture. He was incapacitated by a severe stroke early in 1827, resigned office and died a year later.

(See also *economic policy; French Revolutionary Wars; Tory Party.*)

Livingstone, David: missionary and explorer. Born in Lanarkshire (Scotland) in 1813, he trained as a doctor by being sent to Bechuanaland in southern Africa by the London Missionary Society. He then worked to spread Christianity to Africans further north, exploring the continent from west to east, and building up a British presence in Nyasaland in the 1860s. His explorations involved the discovery by white men of Lakes Ngami and Nysasa and the Victoria Falls. He disappeared into the African interior for a long period in the second half of the 1860s, being located eventually by the shores of Lake Tanganyiki by the US journalist Henry Morton Stanley in the nineteenth century's most famous greeting: 'Dr Livingstone, I presume?'. He died in 1873 in land which was shortly to become northern Rhodesia. His exploits, and his Christian example, became hugely influential in the literature given to late Victorian children where he was presented as an example of fearlessness, heroism and self-sacrifice.

(See also *missionaries.*)

Lloyd (John), Selwyn: *Conservative* politician. Born in 1904, he was a *Liberal* early in his political career but he transferred to the Conservatives in 1929. He is best known for his role in the *Suez Crisis* in 1956, where he supported *Eden's* policy to break Nasser and stop Egyptian nationalisation of the canal. He was later sacked by *Macmillan* during his purge of Cabinet ministers in 1962 before returning to office under Hume. His major offices were:

- Minister of Defence, 1955
- Foreign Secretary, 1955–57
- Chancellor of the Exchequer, 1960–62
- Lord Privy Seal and Leader of the House of Commons, 1963–64
- Speaker of the Commons, 1971–76

He died in 1978.

(See also *Commons, House of; economic policy.*)

Lloyd George, David: Liberal politician and Prime Minister. The most self-consciously Welsh politician of the first half of the twentieth century was actually born in Manchester in 1863 before moving to North Wales as a young child. He trained as a solicitor and became MP for Caenarfon Boroughs in 1890, holding the seat without a break until his death in 1945. He came to national prominence as a Liberal MP who attacked the landowning elite and then in opposition to Britain's involvement in the Second *Boer War*. He entered the Cabinet in December 1905 at the beginning of the *Campbell-Bannerman's* government. His major offices were:

- President of the Board of Trade, 1905–8
- Chancellor of the Exchequer, 1908–15
- Minister of Munitions, 1915–16
- Secretary for War, 1916
- Prime Minister, 1916–22
- Leader of the Liberal Party, 1926–31

His achievements were enormous and he has claim to be considered the most successful Prime Minister of the twentieth century but he was a figure of controversy. He did not come from a privileged financial background, like most of his Cabinet colleagues, and was often associated with schemes to make money, not all of them entirely savoury. He was widely regarded as untrustworthy by political allies and enemies alike. The noted Liberal wit, Margot Asquith, said that 'He couldn't see a belt without hitting below it'. His career was threatened by his association with the so-called 'Marconi scandal' in 1913 and the 'selling of peerages' after *World War I* in order to build up a personal political fund at once showed Lloyd George's contempt for the institution of aristocracy and his eye for financial advantage. His energy was legendary and his private life colourful. He kept both a mistress, Frances Stevenson, and a wife for many years and had many other affairs at a time when public disclosure would have ruined him. His very public falling-out with *Asquith* whom, in effect, he deposed for the prime ministership at the end of 1916 caused a split within the *Liberal Party* which had catastrophic consequences. What could not be denied – indeed it was an aspect of the man's controversy – was his enormous political flair and sheer ability. He was a brilliant orator with a keen sense of political opportunity. He turned the 'People's Budget' of 1909 to political advantage by linking it both to rearmament and an attack on the 'idle rich'. His practical achievements were substantial, including the first system of *National Insurance* in 1911. He was an enormous success as Minister of Munitions, using unorthodox methods to provide the armaments Britain needed on the Western Front. His major innovation as Prime Minister was the creation of a streamlined War Cabinet which could respond to military intelligence and take decisions speedily. He received much credit for winning the war and was not seriously challenged as leader when the post-war coalition was formed. He played a decisive part in the peace negotiations which followed World War I, when he tried to temper extreme French demands for vengeance against Germany. He proved remarkably flexible and adroit in the crucial negotiations which led to the creation of the Irish Free State. The abiding weakness of his political position, however, was that he was a political prisoner of the *Conservatives* who comprised an overwhelming majority in his coalition government. When they withdrew their support for him, after the *Chanak Crisis* in 1922, he was forced to resign and never held government office again.

He became Liberal leader after Asquith's retirement and attempted to rebuild his party's fortunes by giving it a new direction. He used the ideas of Liberal progressives, such as *Beveridge* and *Keynes*, to advocate in 'Britain's Industrial Future' (1928) state intervention in roads, housing and electricity in order to stimulate the economy and reduce *unemployment*. The *general election* of 1929 revealed, however, that third parties can get large numbers of votes and nowhere near an equivalent proportion of parliamentary seats. Lloyd George failed to break the new mould of British politics and Liberal decline continued. Had he not been ill with prostate trouble during the crucial weeks surrounding the formation of the *National Government* under *Ramsay MacDonald*, there is little doubt that he would have returned to office in 1931 but what proved to be Lloyd George's last chance of office passed. He died in 1945.

(See also *Ireland; Labour Party; Versailles, Treaty of.*)

local government: government operating at a level below that of Westminster. Until the early nineteenth century, central government played almost no role in local administration. However, the changes brought about by a growing population, urbanisation and by the *Industrial Revolution* caused central government to enact legislation. This was intended to rationalise and improve old structures based on a rural society and on controls exercised almost on a personal basis by landowners and other men of property over the majority of the population.

Before 1888

Local government in England and Wales was based on a large, and confusing, number of units from the 'shires' (counties) downward to the parish. Many, such as the meeting of parish ratepayers known as the 'vestry' (of which there were about 13,000 in 1800), could be dominated by one or two large landowners who appointed all local officials. The basic unit of local administration in both church and other matters, however, was the parish. This was responsible at the beginning of the nineteenth century for the administration of *Poor Laws* and also highways. Men with sufficient property would be appointed *Justices of the Peace* with power over a wide range of offences.

Rationalisation occurred in stages during the nineteenth century. Poor Law administration was transferred from individual parishes to new Poor Law Unions in 1834. Local government in the urban areas was revolutionised by the *Municipal*

Corporations Act in 1835. Public order provision was radically changed by the *Police* Acts. *Public health* came under increasingly centralised supervision from the 1830s. By the 1880s, therefore, central government was increasingly directing the nature of local provision.

From 1888

Local government rationalisation began in 1888 with the creation of *county councils* and *county boroughs*. Their functions were extensive. From the early twentieth century they included administration and supervision of:

- public order
- sanitation, public health and hospitals
- most highways
- state education
- housing, planning and social services

They were funded by rates. Below these were created in 1894 other tiers of local government: parish, rural district, urban district and municipal borough councils. The basic principle was election of councillors who would serve for three years. County councils and county boroughs elected from among their members more senior councillors, called 'aldermen' who served for six years. In Scotland, a similar system operated, although some local government functions were exercised directly by the Scottish Office, created in 1885 as a separate tier of administration and responsible to central government. In 1894 a Local Government Board was established for Scotland.

The general trend was for local government to absorb greater responsibilities and for rates to increase to accommodate these. Substantial changes were made both to the organisation and responsibilities of local government from the early 1970s. The main ones were:

- the Local Government Act of 1972 rationalised provision in England and Wales, giving new functions (taken from the lower tiers of local administration) to reorganised county councils and six 'metropolitan counties' for the large conurbations. Outside London, 39 county and six metropolitan counties replaced the previous 83 county councils, and some new counties – such as Avon and Humberside – were created. Below them operated only two tiers of administration: district and parish councils
- the creation in Scotland from 1975 of nine administrative 'regions', of which Strathclyde – based on Glasgow – was much the largest. These regions were subdivided into 53 districts with their own elected councils

(See also *Greater London Council; Lord-Lieutenant; London County Council; Parish Councils Act; Thatcher, Margaret Hilda and Thatcherism.*)

Locarno Pact, 1925: treaty signed by Britain, France, Germany, Italy and Belgium to provide mutual security. It was an attempt to stabilise the position of the leading European powers and establish a permanent basis for agreement. Its main features were:

- confirmation of the borders between Germany, France and Belgium
- agreement that the Rhineland should remain demilitarised

Although nothing was said about Germany's eastern borders, the pact was widely hailed at the time as an indication that the powers which had fought one another in *World War I* had now reached an honourable and permanent agreement.

(See also *appeasement; Versailles, Treaty of; World War II.*)

London County Council: the authority which governed the capital city from 1888 to 1965. It was established under the Local Government Act, setting boundaries which formally brought into the capital previously separate communities such as Hampstead, Hackney and Wandsworth and taking over some areas previously administered by Middlesex, Kent and Surrey. The Act also created 28 subordinate borough councils. Its first chairman was the later *Liberal* Prime Minister, the *Earl of Rosebery* and control of the LCC, as it was known, was first in Liberal hands, then *Conservative* and from 1934, *Labour*, who developed policies of municipal socialism under *Herbert Morrison*. It was administered after 1922 from a purpose-built County Hall on the south bank of the Thames.

(See also *Greater London Council; local government.*)

London, Treaty of (1915): secret agreement during *World War I* which brought Italy into the war on the side of Britain, France and Russia. The Allies agreed that, after the war, Italy should gain territory from the Austro-Hungarian Empire. The earmarked territory was in what became Yugoslavia, and, although Italy gained some additional territory in 1919–20, it did not get all that the Allies had promised. This proved to be one of many factors which increased Italian resentment in the years leading up to the seizure of power by Benito Mussolini.

Lord-Lieutenant: the royal representative in each county. An appointment of major importance in the sixteenth century when the Tudor monarchs could not be entirely sure of local loyalty, the duties of the Lord-Lieutenant declined in importance during the seventeenth and eighteenth centuries, although they continued to preside over county *Justices of the Peace* and had considerable influence over their appointment. With the creation of *county councils*, their political significance dwindled almost to nothing. Frequently members of the aristocracy, they retain some social significance but their duties in the late twentieth century are purely honorary.

(See also *local government.*)

Lords, House of: upper chamber of Parliament. In 1800, it comprised hereditary peers of the realm (the aristocracy), princes in the royal family and the 26 bishops of the Church of England. Originally the more important of the two Houses comprising in medieval times the barons and princes of the church, by 1800 the Lords was acknowledged as of subordinate status. This was because the Commons had during the seventeenth century gained control over finance, especially the power to raise taxes. While the Lords could amend Commons finance bills, it would not initiate them. The Lords, however, was still of great importance for two reasons:

- it could veto any bill passed in the Commons
- many of the country's leading politicians were peers of the realm and could still influence the composition of the House of Commons, even after the *Reform Act* of 1832. Peers were frequently prime ministers, including the *Marquess of Salisbury* as late as 1902

Usually, the Lords did not seek to frustrate the clearly expressed will of the Commons. They were, however, goaded into a challenge by the People's Budget of 1909. This led to the *Parliament Act* in 1911 which reduced their powers. The composition of the Lords was changed in 1958 with the creation of life peerages for persons either of high distinction or political value to one of the political parties or, very occasionally, both. Since 1958, proceedings in the Lords have usually been dominated by life peers, who attend debates more regularly and are unofficially known as 'working peers'. All peers retain the right to attend the Lords, however, and certain controversial issues (proposals to abolish foxhunting being one) can be guaranteed to bring normally 'non-political' peers into the upper chamber in force to defend what they see as essential aspects of rural life.

(See also *Parliament, English.*)

Lovett, William: Chartist. Born in Cornwall in 1800, he was apprenticed as a cabinet maker and, like many well-educated skilled workers, he took up radical politics. He was a founder of the London Working Man's Association and helped to draft the People's Charter. Although he served a brief term of imprisonment in 1839 for publishing an attack on the new *police* which angered the authorities, he was perhaps one of the staunchest believers in 'moral-force' *Chartism*. He believed that working people should earn the respect of their social superiors by education, *self-help* and *temperance*. He continued to support all of these causes after Chartism declined and also worked with *Liberal* radicals to oppose warlike policies, especially those of *Palmerston*, and to promote international understanding. He died in 1877.

(See also *radicalism.*)

Low-Church: term used to describe those in the *Church of England* who supported *evangelicalism* or who emphasised the importance of Bible readings and the teachings of the scriptures over ritual, tradition and authority. In the nineteenth century, Low-churchmen opposed the *Roman Catholic* church and the *Oxford Movement.*

Lowe, Robert: *Liberal* politician and journalist. Born in 1811 into a prosperous *Church of England* family, he emigrated in 1842 to New South Wales (Australia) and served on that state's legislature. He returned to Britain in 1850 and became a Liberal MP in 1852. He quickly proved himself an effective administrator and helped to draft limited liability legislation. His major offices were:

- Vice-President of the Board of Education, 1859–64
- Chancellor of the Exchequer, 1868–73
- Home Secretary, 1873–74

He is perhaps best known for the *Revised Code of Education* in 1862 which introduced 'payment by results', reduced the cost of the Government's education budget and angered *Kay-Shuttleworth*. He was also leader of the *Adullamites*, who opposed the Liberal Reform Bill in 1866. By contemporaries he was known both for the clarity of his views on *free trade*, education, the evils of democracy and the virtues of low taxation and also for the sarcasm which he was prone to employ in expressing them. His belittling reference in *Parliament* to the new voters of 1867 is famous: 'I believe it will be absolutely necessary that you should prevail on our future masters to learn their letters'. He was created Viscount Sherbrooke in 1880 and died in 1882.

(See also *Bright, John; Limited Liabilities Act, 1855; Reform Act, 1867.*)

Luddites: description used to describe those who, between 1811 and 1816, destroyed industrial machinery in Yorkshire, Lancashire, Nottinghamshire, Leicestershire and Derbyshire, usually under cover of darkness. Their name derives from a wholly mythical figure who is supposed to have led them: Ned Ludd. Luddism is widely misused as a derogatory term covering those opposed to all progress who strike out blindly at everything new or unfamiliar. The early nineteenth century Luddites were skilled men. They opposed only specific types of machinery which threatened their livelihoods. In the East Midlands, for example, they were stocking-makers and attacked shearing frames which made inferior products in large numbers. Their activities need to be seen against a background of high prices and widespread unemployment towards the end of the *Napoleonic Wars*. Since they were protected by local communities which sympathised with their activities, they proved difficult for the authorities to catch. Charlotte Brontë's novel 'Shirley' is concerned with Luddite activity in Yorkshire.

(See also *apprenticeship; artisans; Industrial Revolution.*)

'Lyons v. Wilkins': legal case of 1896 concerning trade union rights. Lyons secured an injunction stopping a small union of leather workers from picketing his work-place. The union argued before the High Court that they were acting within the law as it stood after 1875 but the Court ruled against them.

(See also *Conspiracy and Protection of Property Act, 1875; trade unions.*)

Lytton (Constance), Lady: *suffragette.* Born into an aristocratic family in 1869, she joined the *Women's Social and Political Union* in 1908, and participated in militant activity. She was imprisoned but refused to accept forcible feeding and was released. She disguised herself as a working-class suffragette from Liverpool, named 'Jane Warton', in order to be rearrested and to demonstrate that the prison authorities treated women of humble birth more brutally than they did aristocrats. She publicised her findings, but *World War I* prevented their implications from being fully debated. She died in 1923.

Lytton, Edward Bulwer: diplomat, poet and politician. Born in 1831, he was appointed Viceroy of *India* by *Disraeli* in 1875, which post he held until 1880. During his term of office he organised the 'Durbar' at which *Victoria* was proclaimed Empress of India in 1877. His policies on the north-eastern borders were in part responsible for the outbreak of war with the Afghans in 1878. He died in 1891.

Macaulay, Thomas Babington: *Whig* politician and historian. Born in 1800, the son of a leading anti-*slavery* campaigner, he was educated at Cambridge and trained as a lawyer. He contributed many articles to the Whig journal 'Edinburgh Review' and became a Whig MP in 1830. He was Secretary of the Board of Control for India and helped to draft its penal code in the 1840s. His major offices were:

- Secretary for War, 1839–41
- Paymaster General, 1846–47

He is best known, however, for his historical writings – particularly 'The Lays of Ancient Rome' (1842) and 'History of England', the first volume of which was published in 1848 and which he continued writing until his death in 1859.

MacDonald, Alexander: trade unionist. Born in Scotland in 1821, he worked as a miner before managing to pay for a degree course at Glasgow University. He piloted proposals for trade union reform in the 1860s and, like most skilled workers' leaders, looked to the *Liberal Party* to produce the necessary legislation. He is best known as one of the two first working men elected to Parliament, as a Liberal MP in 1874. He died in 1881.

(See also *Lib–Labs*.)

MacDonald, James Ramsay: Labour politician and Prime Minister. Born the illegitimate son of a farm worker in 1866, he became as a pupil teacher before moving to London in the 1880s and working as private secretary to a *Liberal* MP. He failed to gain nomination for a Liberal seat and this influenced his decision to join the *Independent Labour Party* in the 1890s. MacDonald was a crucial figure in the organisation both of the ILP and the *Labour Party*, and negotiated a crucial pact with Herbert Gladstone in 1903 whereby the Liberal and Labour parties agreed not to oppose one another in certain parliamentary constituencies. This gave the Labour Party a crucial toe-hold in Parliament after the election of 1906. He became a Labour MP in 1906 and remained an MP, with one break from 1918 to 1922, until his death in 1937. His major offices were:

- Secretary of the Labour Party, 1900–12
- Leader of the Labour Party, 1911–14, 1922–31
- Prime Minister and Foreign Secretary, 1924
- Prime Minister, 1929–35
- Lord President of the Council, 1935–37

He proved himself both a skilful orator and a capable organiser and his route to high office would probably have been speedier had he not resigned the leadership of the Labour Party because of his pacifist views in 1914 and lost his parliamentary seat in 1918. Both as leader of the party and as Prime Minister in the two minority governments of 1924 and 1929–31, he showed himself both a moderate and a supporter of orthodox *economic policy* which angered supporters who wanted more full-blooded *socialist* policy to be attempted. MacDonald's view was that the Labour Party had to demonstrate its respectability in order to confirm its position as one of the two leading political parties in the country. This, he argued, would appeal both to the electorate and to the political establishment. His view appeared to be vindicated when *George V* showed no qualms about asking a working man's party to form a government. MacDonald was first bitterly attacked within, and then forced out of, the party in 1931. First, he committed the party to severe expenditure cuts, which included reductions in unemployment benefit. Then he accepted the King's invitation to continue as Prime Minister but now at the head of a National Government.

Personally, he seems to have been deeply unhappy for most of the last 25 years of his life. His adored wife died in 1911 and he never truly recovered. His frequent disagreements with members of the party he had done so much to establish grieved him and he was sensitive to criticism both that he was a social climber whose radicalism was neutralised by easy flattery from the establishment and that he was indecisive. *Winston Churchill* famously called him 'the boneless wonder' in 1931. He does seem to have suffered from a kind of identity crisis. He confided to a friend in 1930: 'If God were to come to me and say, 'Ramsay, would you rather be a country gentleman than a Prime Minister?' I should reply, 'Please God, a country gentleman'. The socialist intellectual Harold Laski scornfully said of him at the time of his split with the Labour Party: 'He is leading the gentlemen of England, and there is no price he would not pay for that'.

(See also *MI5*.)

MacLeod, Iain: *Conservative* politician. He was born in 1913, joined *R A Butler* in the Conservative research department after *World War II* and became an MP in 1950. His major offices were:

- Minister of Health, 1952–55
- Minister of Labour, 1955–59
- Secretary of State for the Colonies, 1959–61
- Leader of the House of Commons, 1961–63
- Chairman of the Conservative Party, 1961–63
- Chancellor of the Exchequer, 1970

A disciple of Butler, he positioned himself on the left of the Conservative Party and tried throughout his career to consolidate its reformist instincts. He implemented change leading to the independence of many Black Commonwealth nations, following up *Macmillan*'s *'wind of change' speech*. This antagonised many on the right of the party. The fifth Marquess of Salisbury confirmed a long-standing prejudice against brainpower in some sections of the Conservative Party in 1961 when he famously called MacLeod 'too clever by half'. He turned his cleverness to journalism as editor of the Conservative magazine 'The Spectator' from 1963 to 1965. He died suddenly only a month after becoming Chancellor in *Heath*'s government in June 1970.

Macmillan, Harold (Earl of Stockton): *Conservative* politician and Prime Minister. Born in 1894 into a successful Scottish publishing family and, like *Winston Churchill*, with a mother from the United States, he was educated at Eton and Oxford. He was severely wounded during active service in *World War I*. He became MP for Stockton (County Durham) in 1924 and his experience as a North-East MP set him apart from most Conservatives. He was receptive to the ideas of *J M Keynes* and in 1938 published 'The Middle Way' which advocated government expenditure to stimulate the economy. Views such as this, and his undisguised opposition to *appeasement* and especially the *Munich Agreement*, made him an unlikely candidate for promotion until *Churchill* took over as Prime Minister in 1940. His major offices were:

- Minister of Supply, 1940–42
- Minister with responsibility for the war in North Africa (resident there), 1942–45
- Secretary for Air, 1945
- Minister for Housing and Local Government, 1951–54
- Minister of Defence, 1954–55
- Foreign Secretary, 1955
- Chancellor of the Exchequer, 1955–57
- Leader of the Conservative Party, 1957–63
- Prime Minister, 1957–63

His time in North Africa, where he worked well with the US general Eisenhower, was successful and he was established as an important figure in the party by the end of the war. He lost his Stockton seat in the *Labour* landslide of 1945 but soon returned for the safe seat of Bromley. As *Housing* Minister, he won wide acclaim within the party for exceeding its target of building more than 300,000 houses a year. He fell out with *Eden* over foreign affairs. Being moved to the chancellorship during a time of economic boom almost certainly saved his career since the *Suez Crisis* proved a graveyard for the political reputations of those involved in policy making, not least Eden. Macmillan was preferred to *R A Butler* for the party leadership and prime ministership when Eden resigned. His prime ministership was characterised by two main themes:

- **economic prosperity.** He announced in a speech in July 1957: 'Let's be frank about it: most of our people have never had it so good', and the Conservative election victory of 1959 was widely attributed to a feeling of economic wellbeing and Macmillan was christened 'Supermac' by the popular press
- **decolonisation**, which proceeded rapidly both before and after his famous *'wind of change' speech* at Cape Town (South Africa) proclaiming the awareness of a new African 'national consciousness' in February 1960

The later years of his premiership, however, were not successful. Decolonisation posed more problems than answers, giving rise to the US Secretary of State Dean Acheson's famous aphorism in December 1962: 'Great Britain has lost an empire and has not yet found a role'. Economic performance was patchy. Too many imports and high wage demands fuelled inflation, leading to so-called 'stop–go' policies suggesting a wider uncertainty. Political unpopularity led Macmillan to sack almost half his Cabinet in July 1962 in the so-called 'Night of the Long Knives'. When Macmillan suddenly resigned on grounds of ill-health in the autumn of 1963, his precipitate departure led to an ugly and blatant power struggle for the succession played out during a party conference. It was resolved in highly contentious circumstances, leading to ministerial resignations which almost certainly doomed the Conservatives to electoral defeat the following year.

These later years dented Macmillan's reputation for unflappability and effortless wit which was anyway a facade. As he later admitted, he was never as confident as he seemed and was frequently physically sick before he made major speeches, which were far from the impromptu performances they appeared. His personal life was not happy. His wife had a long-standing and, within political circles, well-known affair with a prominent colleague. He was wracked by self-doubt and found solace in reading nineteenth-century literature. He survived his illness and lived on until 1986, alert enough to offer penetrating criticisism of what he considered the crude excesses of *Thatcherism* in the last years of his life. He accepted an hereditary earldom on his 90th birthday in 1984.

(See also *Conservative Party; economic policy; housing; Keynesian economics; MacLeod, Iain.*)

Mafeking, Relief of: important action during the Second *Boer War*. Mafeking was a town in the north of Cape Province which, while defended by *Baden-Powell*, was besieged by the Boers under Cronje for seven months. It was relieved on 17 May 1900 by British troops led by Lord Roberts, Plumer and Mahon to immense relief and joy in Britain. The relief seemed to turn the tide of the war and the Conservatives capitalised on the waves of patriotic enthusiasm in the *Khaki election* which took place a few months later.

Major, John: Conservative politician and Prime Minister. Born in London in 1943, he first worked in a bank and became a member of the Greater London Council before becoming MP for the safe seat of Huntingdon in 1979. Due in more or less equal measure to an open, pleasant personality, political shrewdness and good fortune, his career progressed very rapidly during the *Thatcher* years. After working in the Whips office from 1983 to 1985, his major offices were:

- Minister for Health and Social Security, 1985–87
- Chief Secretary to the Treasury, 1987–89
- Foreign Secretary, 1989
- Chancellor of the Exchequer, 1989–90
- Prime Minister, 1990–97
- Leader of the Conservative Party, 1990–97

He was not in any office other than that of Prime Minister long enough to leave a distinctive impression but his brief tenure of the Foreign Office did not impress officials, while, as Chancellor, he persuaded Thatcher to join the European Community's Exchange Rate Mechanism in 1990 but at too high a rate. His introduction of a new tax-exempt savings scheme, the TESSA, did, however, prove popular.

His prime ministership was long (only *Asquith* and Thatcher have served a longer continuous period in the twentieth century) but inglorious. He won a narrow, but unexpected, victory at the *general election* of 1992, shrewdly exploiting his personal charm and his ability to suggest that the *Labour Party* was still tainted with the extremist follies it exhibited in the early 1980s. Thereafter, however, matters went rapidly downhill. The central plank of government *economic policy* – currency stability based on membership of the Exchange Rate Mechanism – was severed when currency speculators forced Britain's withdrawal from it at huge financial cost and with maximum humiliation to the Prime Minister and his Chancellor of the Exchequer, Norman Lamont. The Government's reputation with the public never recovered and Major's government lost every by-election it fought, many by devastating majorities in previously safe Conservative seats. By 1996, he was forced to rely for a continued majority on covert support from the *Ulster Unionists*, which only drove the final nail into the coffin of his plans to settle the problems of Northern Ireland. Ironically, the British economy recovered steadily after 1992, but on the basis of policies which Major had said before being forced out of ERM he could never support. The political capital he could make from economic improvement was, therefore, minimal.

His party became fractious during the 1990s when it was deeply divided on the question of Europe. As the so-called 'Euro-sceptics' (who were not 'sceptical' at all; they knew that they hated Europe with a passion) gained the upper hand in the party, so Major was forced to trim his government's policies leaving Britain even more isolated within the European Union. Almost openly defied by members of his own Cabinet, he provoked a leadership challenge in 1995 in an attempt to reassert his control over this party. He won the contest but not any wider respect. Sniping over his leadership continued. He launched a 'back-to-basics' movement designed to emphasise core values in family, education and morality and was rewarded by a string of tabloid revelations about the sexual indiscretions of his own ministers, while investigative journalism had revealed by 1996 that a number of Conservative MPs were selling political services and receiving assorted 'favours' from business interests while concealing their extensive, and dubious, gains. Major was forced to fight the general election of 1997 against a background of 'sleaze' and with the reputation of weakness as a leader, in sharp contrast to that of his predecessor, Margaret Thatcher. He campaigned in support of a truly 'United Kingdom' and against Labour proposals for devolved government in Scotland and Wales. He was rewarded by an unprecedented 'wipe-out' in which the Conservatives won no seats at all in either country. The election overall was lost by a majority larger than any fought between contending political parties since the very different circumstances immediately after the *Reform Act* of 1832. Major resigned the party leadership immediately.

(See also *Conservative Party*.)

Malta: small island in the eastern Mediterranean, south of Sicily and east of Tunisia. Its main value, since its acquisition at the end of the *Napoleonic Wars*, was strategic. It acted for many years as the navy's main Mediterranean base. During *World War II*, it was subject to constant bombardment and blockade, especially by Italy which wanted to capture the island and improve its own supply route to Africa. The bombardment was unsuccessful and *George VI* awarded the island a collective George Cross (GC) in recognition of its citizens' bravery. The island became independent in 1964, declared itself a republic in 1974 and the British base there finally closed in 1979.

Malthus (Thomas), Reverend: Anglican clergyman and political economist. Born in 1766, he held a curacy in Surrey for many years and, from 1805, was Professor of History and Moral Economy at the East India Company college at Haileybury. He is primarily remembered for his publication 'An Essay on the Principle of Population as it Affects the Future Improvement of Society', which was first published in 1798 and revised in 1803. It argued that the general tendency was for population to increase and, eventually, to outrun the means of feeding itself. At this point a 'check' – in the form of epidemic disease, famine or war – would intervene and reduce the population to sustainable levels. In the second edition, he gave greater emphasis to the possibilities of collective self-restraint as a means of achieving a proper balance, probably by later marriage or sexual abstinence. His message was particularly pertinent coming as it did at the time of the first *census* which revealed how rapidly the population of the United Kingdom had been growing. In particular, his ideas fuelled the increasingly controversial debates on the *Poor Laws* and influenced the thinking of those who advocated 'less eligibility' as the guiding principle for poverty relief which would force labourers to go out and search for work. He died in 1834, the year in which the Poor Law Amendment Act reached the statute book.

(See also *economic policy; Chadwick, Edwin; Senior, Nassau.*)

'Manchester school': name rather colloquially given to believers in *free trade* and *laissez-faire* in the middle years of the nineteenth century. The title, originally coined as a term of abuse by *Benjamin Disraeli* who wanted to suggest that its range of support was narrow and sectional, is appropriate enough for two reasons. The most effective publicists for the cause were *John Bright* and *Richard Cobden*, supporters of the Manchester-based *Anti-Corn Law League*. Also, cotton manufacturers and traders were among the chief beneficiaries of free trade, since the efficiency of their production techniques enabled them to reach new markets and to undercut competition.

(See also *economic policy.*)

Marne, Battles of (September 1914 and July to August 1918): battles on the Western Front during *World War I*. The first battle, fought by the French and the *British Expeditionary Force*, halted the German progress through France and indirectly led to the establishment of a long stalemate of trench warfare. The second saw the bold German offensive of spring 1918 successfully checked. It had important consequences, effectively ending the last German strike for victory after which German troops were driven back.

Marquis, Frederick James: see *Woolton, 1st Earl of*

Marshall, Alfred: economist. Born in London in 1842, and educated at Cambridge, he became the most influential British economist of his generation. His main publication, 'Principles of Economics' (1890), was remarkably wide-ranging and remained the main statement of what came to be called 'neo-classical' orthodoxy before the publications of *J M Keynes*, whose work he influenced. His work on the economics of welfare and state involvement related directly to the concerns of progressives within the *Liberal Party* who were concerned with advancing the role of the State to secure material benefits in the lives of ordinary citizens. He died in 1924.

(See also *economic policy.*)

Marshall Plan: Strategy to advance the economic recovery of Europe after the end of *World War II*. This US plan, which carries the name of President Truman's Secretary of State, George C Marshall, was launched in 1947. Under it European nations received about $15 billion in grants from 1948 to 1952, Britain receiving about ten per cent of the total aid available. Its main purpose was not altruistic but to ensure that the countries of Western Europe would be able to resist any further expansionist activity from the Soviet Union or the remainder of the communist bloc.

Martineau, Harriet: political economist and novelist. Born into a Unitarian family in 1802, her main reputation is based on the effective popularisation of *laissez-faire* ideas in works such as 'Illustrations of Political Economy' (1832–34). She spent time in the United States, where she supported the abolition of *slavery*, and the Middle East. She wrote on a wide range of subjects, from history to mesmerism, informed by a broadly liberal and rationalist perspective. Her novels for adults and children are rarely read nowadays. Perhaps the best of them is 'Deerbrook' (1839). She died in 1876.

(See also *economic policy; Mill, James; Ricardo, David; Senior, Nassau; slavery, abolition of.*)

Marx-Aveling, Eleanor: Socialist writer and agitator. Born the daughter of Karl Marx in 1855, she was brought up in London and spent much time among working people there in the 1880s, in particular with recently arrived Jewish immigrants. She was a leading advocate of the expansion of unskilled workers' trade unions and, particularly, of the importance of women workers to such organisations. She produced a tract on women's rights, 'The Woman Question' in 1886. She was unhappily married to a fellow socialist, Edward Aveling, and committed suicide in 1898.

(See also *Marxism; socialism; trade unions.*)

Marxism: a political doctrine developed by the German political philosopher Karl Marx (1818–83) and rooted in the belief that man's actions are determined by the way the economic and productive forces in a given society operate. Marx and his collaborator *Friedrich Engels* developed the view that capitalist forms of production, which massively increased during the *Industrial Revolution*, led to the exploitation of labour by those owning capital. This analysis, based largely on the study of Britain in the mid-nineteenth century, led to the view that the dynamic of history would eventually lead to successful revolution by the industrial masses – the proletariat – against their capitalist oppressors and the establishment of a beneficent dictatorship by this proletariat based on an equal distribution of the means of production, distribution and exchange. Though developed from the British experience, neither Marxism nor communism has achieved significant political success in the United Kingdom. Its intellectual influence during the twentieth century, however, was huge not least among a school of Marxist historians which developed during the 1950s and 1960s and included scholars such as Christopher Hill, Eric Hobsbawm and Edward Thompson.

(See also *class consciousness; socialism; trade unions.*)

Match Girls' Strike, 1888: labour dispute in London which helped the development of unskilled workers' trade unionism. The match girls of Bryant and May's factory went on strike to achieve higher wages but their dangerous working conditions were effectively exploited by *Annie Besant* to bring the strike to national attention. The strike was successful and, in July 1888, the women won a wage rise.

(See also *trade unions.*)

materialism: a political doctrine closely associated with *Marxism* which holds that political, social and cultural beliefs are determined by an individual's relationship to forms of economic production. Those holding materialist beliefs thus argue that the dominant forces for historical change are economic rather than other factors such as the role of the individual or the structure of society. Materialists argue that these are subordinate elements, largely determined by wider economic structures.

Maudling, Reginald: Conservative politician. Born in 1917, he was educated at Oxford, trained as a barrister and became an MP in 1950. His major offices were:

- Paymaster-General, 1957–59
- President of the Board of Trade, 1959–61
- Secretary of State for the Colonies, 1961–62
- Chancellor of the Exchequer, 1962–64
- Home Secretary, 1970–72

Always on the left wing of the Conservative Party, he made steady progress up the ministerial ladder during the party's long period in office from 1951 to 1964. He was narrowly defeated by *Edward Heath* in the first election for the party leadership in 1965. He resigned suddenly from office in 1972 when accusations were made that he had received money from the corrupt architect John Poulson.

May Committee, 1931: body set up by the Labour government under the chairmanship of Sir George May to consider the consequences of the virtual collapse of the British export market in the wake of the Wall Street Crash. This contributed to a massive *balance of payments* deficit. The Committee predicted that this deficit would reach £120 million and recommended cuts in expenditure totalling £96 million, including a twenty per cent cut in unemployment benefit. The majority of the Government could not accept this and it broke up to be replaced by a *National Government* under *Ramsay MacDonald* while the *Labour Party* as a whole went into opposition. The National Government imposed many of these cuts.

(See also *economic policy; unemployment.*)

Mayhew, Henry: journalist and social investigator. He was born in 1812. His articles appeared in the 'Morning Chronicle', many of which were later published in his famous work 'London Labour and the London Poor'. His investigations threw light both on the extent to which London's economy depended on the work of unskilled and casual labourers, and also on the problems this created for poor families. His approach was journalistic rather than scientific and doubts exist about the typicality of much of his material. However, both the vividness of his descriptions and the evident knowledge which underpins the characterisations both compel respect. He died in 1877.

(See also *class consciousness; laissez-faire.*)

means test: measure which attempted to define real need of families for relief. It was introduced by the *National Government* in 1931 as a measure to reduce government expenditure and remained in place until the outbreak of *World War II*. All applicants who had exhausted their entitlement to *unemployment* benefit had to have their income assessed by local Public Assistance Committees, which considered all forms of family income as well as the value of furniture and other household effects. Almost 20 per cent of applicants failed the 'test' and were refused relief. Means-testing was widely resented. Many poor families hated intrusions into privacy which assessment entailed and also the apparently casual unfairnesses and inequity which resulted. It helped to make the experience of life on '*the dole*' even more humiliating.

(See also *economic policy; May Committee; National Insurance.*)

mechanics' institutes: organisations for *self-help* and mutual aid provided both by, and for, working people. They emerged both in Scotland and England in the first quarter of the nineteenth century and expanded rapidly in numbers in the years to 1860, by which point they are estimated to have had about 200,000 members. The London Mechanics' Institute, founded in 1823, eventually became Birkbeck College, an important outlet for the higher education of working men. Funded by a mixture of subscriptions, legacies and donations, the institutes provided a range of 'improving' activities, including lectures, evening classes on academic and vocational subjects and *library* facilities. By no means used exclusively by skilled working men, they were, nevertheless, male-dominated and an integral part of what might be called the Victorian 'culture of improvement'. Some working men were undoubtedly encouraged by the work of the institutes to feel satisfied with their lot and a few social historians have argued that the institutes represented a form of 'social control' whereby the middle classes sought to neutralise the threat from working people in the early stages of the *Industrial Revolution*. Their work, however, was just as likely to encourage a *radical* cast of mind and to furnish working people with sophisticated arguments for both political, industrial and social change. Their increasing emphasis on education made many the forerunners of technical colleges and night schools at the end of the nineteenth century.

(See also *Education Act, 1870; parliamentary reform; trade unions.*)

Melbourne (Lamb, William), 2nd Viscount: *Whig* politician and Prime Minister. Born in 1779 into a successful legal family which had bought land and acquired a peerage, he became an MP in 1806. He initially supported *Charles James Fox* and was always a Whig, but he was never an active reformer. A very able man with a wide range of interests, he always affected not to be particularly interested in politics and certainly not in power but, as with most politicians, this was in large part a conceit. His turbulent marriage to Lady Caroline Lamb (née Ponsonby) absorbed much of his energy and contributed substantially to a deeper melancholy below the surface of a languid aristocratic demeanour. The main reason, however, that it took him so long to reach high office, in comparison with contemporaries such as *Canning, Huskisson* and *Peel*, was that he had remained within the Whig Party during a time of overwhelming *Tory Party* dominance. His major offices were:

- Chief Secretary for Ireland, 1827–28
- Home Secretary, 1830–34
- Prime Minister, 1830–34, 1835–41

He acted as a restraint on some of the more radical Whigs during the reform crisis of 1830–2 and, as Home Secretary, was active in pursuing the trade unionists of *Tolpuddle*. His succession to the prime ministership was uncontroversial but his long tenure of the office produced controversy enough. He became the last Prime Minister to be dismissed by the will of the monarch when he offended *William IV* over giving a senior appointment to *Lord John Russell*. The manner of his return to office in 1835 after stitching together the *Lichfield House Compact* did little for the long-term stability of his government or for its electoral popularity. Although he epitomised aristocratic caution, his administration was regarded with suspicion because of its links with *radicals* and Irish nationalists. The ministry also lacked evident direction in its later years when a large financial deficit mounted and Peel effectively attacked its competence. Overall, however, the low reputation of Melbourne's ministry is undeserved. It passed many important reforms, not least the *Municipal Corporations Act*. A series of reforms of the *Church of England* also helped to stabilise that institution and reduce the threat of *disestablishment*. His relationship with Queen *Victoria* after she came to the throne in 1837 was very close. He taught her much about the responsiblities of a constitutional monarch. Melbourne's government was roundly defeated in the *general election* of 1841 and he resigned immediately. Already tired of political life, he suffered a stroke in 1842 and remained incapacitated until his death in 1848.

mercantilism: an economic doctrine formulated in the seventeenth century which held that a powerful state needed a favourable balance of trade – i.e., to earn more from exporting goods than it paid from importing them. This doctrine led to protection of one state's trade against another, usually by the establishment of customs duties on imported goods. Mercantilism was challenged during the European enlightenment, especially by the Scottish philosopher Adam Smith. It was progressively abandoned in Britain from the late eighteenth century in favour of trade liberalisation and, eventually, *free trade* and *laissez-faire*.

(See also *economic policy; Navigation Acts*.)

merchant banks: specialised financial agencies which provided a range of services both for private individuals and governments. Among their most important functions were:

- dealing in foreign exchange
- negotiating loans and other financial deals for government and large private clients
- issuing financial bonds; buying and selling stocks and shares on behalf of others
- particularly in the second half of the twentieth century, managing pension and other investment funds

Some of the larger merchant banks, such as Baring and Rothschild, operating from London, made Britain the world's main provider of financial services during the nineteenth century.

(See also *Bank of England; economic policy*.)

Merchant Shipping Acts: legislation to regulate carriage of cargoes. From a range of legislation passed during the nineteenth century, the following stand out:

1850   legislation requiring ships' officers to be properly trained and to prevent exploitation of sailors

1876   legislation requiring the marking of a ship. If it were dangerously overloaded the line would not be visible and it could not legally embark on a voyage

(See also *Plimsoll, Samuel*.)

Methodist Church: nonconformist sect originally founded by John Wesley in the early 1740s, but as a group within the *Church of England*. It was forced out of the established Church by opposition from within the Church hierarchy. At Wesley's death in 1791, there were approximately 58,000 Methodists. Numbers thereafter continued to increase rapidly. By 1820, Methodism numbered 220,000 members and by 1870, with 600,000 members, it accounted for about thirteen per cent of all church members in Britain. From the 1790s, however, it was divided into various separate groups. The most important of these were:

Wesleyan Methodists

Led by Jabez Bunting in the early nineteenth century, this branch proved increasing attractive to the middle classes and some from the upper working classes. The church was highly organised into separate 'circuits' and 'districts'. It was very anxious to ensure that it was considered respectable and many of its members were strongly anti-reformist in the first half of the nineteenth century. Others, however, drew parallels from the organisation of their church in trade union work and in a number of polit-cial organisations, notably *Chartism*. Methodist organisation also went hand in hand with education, thrift and a variety of *self-help* strategies. The Wesleyans built a large number of substantial churches which emphasised their substance and importance. These were especially numerous in northern and midland towns and, overall, formed about two-thirds of all Methodists in 1850. In terms of doctrine, the Wesleyan message was not very different from that of the evangelical wing of the Church of England.

Primitive Methodists

Formed after a series of revivalist meetings beginning in north Staffordshire from 1808, Primitive Methodism was at first led by Hugh Bourne and William Clowes and seceded from the main body of Methodism in 1812. It emphasised *evangelicalism* and developed a range of emotional messages designed to secure religious conversion. It proved attractive to many in the working classes. Nicknamed 'Tom Paine Methodists', many 'Prims' were both trade unionists and local preachers. The sect gained a reputation for political *radicalism* and was much the largest Methodist group after the Wesleyans with about a quarter of overall Methodist membership by 1870.

There were also splits between Wesleyan Methodists and both the 'Protestant Methodists' (1827) and the so-called 'Church of Wesleyan Reformers' (1849). Formal reunification took place between various groups in 1857 and 1907 but complete unification was achieved only in 1932 with the establishment of the 'Methodist Church of Great Britain'. By 1851, the Methodists had developed as the most numerous non-conformist religious group. Methodism's association with temperance reform was also significant, emphasising the movement's seriousness and also its commitment to moral reformation and educational advance among both the working and the urban middle classes.

(See also *class consciousness; dissenter; nonconformity; Temperance Movement.*)

Metropolitan Police: professional police force operating within London. This, the first professional police force in Great Britain, was established during *Sir Robert Peel's* period of office as Home Secretary in 1829. The police were recruited under the leadership of two 'Metropolitan Police Commissioners' who reported to the Home Secretary. Though the 'Met', as it came to be known, always remained separate from other police forces, its early working provided a blueprint for other urban and rural police forces created over the next thirty years.

(See also *police.*)

MI5: British security system responsible for operations within Great Britain. It was formed in 1905 and expanded as 'Division 5 of the British Directorate of Military Intelligence'. Its major work has been with political groups threatening the stability of the State. Most of these have been extremist groups such as *fascists, communists* and cells of the *Irish Republican Army*. Its work is shrouded in secrecy and has frequently attracted the criticism of groups concerned with political liberties who have asserted that the organisation, which formally reports to the Home Secretary, is insufficiently accountable and has initiated surveillance activity on those who present no threat to the security of the State.

MI6: British security system responsible for surveillance and security operations out-side Great Britain. It was formed in 1911 by Captain Mansfield Cumming (generally known as 'C', which initial gave the inspiration for Ian Fleming's creation 'M' in the James Bond novels). Once formally known as 'Division 6 of the British Directorate of Military Intelligence', it operates as the overseas intelligence counterpart to MI5. Active in both *world wars* and also during the so-called 'Cold War' between the capitalist and communist systems from 1945 to the 1980s, its credibility was severely dented by the revelation that several of its senior personnel had been double agents. Inevitably, speculation also turned on others whose treachery was never proved.

middle classes: social category, including those whose wealth and status falls below that of the *aristocracy* and above those whose livelihood depends upon physical labour, and who are normally called the 'working classes'. The term is a highly con-tentious and problematic one on definitional and other grounds. Two general statements can be made with certainty, however. First, more people consider them-selves 'middle-class' than would be accorded that status according to official categorisation based upon occupation. Second, the proportion of the middle classes within the population as a whole has increased substantially in the second half of the twentieth century as the need for physical labour has been reduced by the develop-ment of increasingly sophisticated electronic technology and as the need for a range of professional and commercial services has increased in an increasingly diverse, sophisticated and wealthy society. It is difficult to define the middle classes in terms of function but two broad categories are distinguishable:

- **the industrial and commercial middle classes:** these are concerned pri-marily with buying, selling and trading. They encompass great manufacturers, traders and bankers at one end of the spectrum of wealth and small shopkeepers at the other. Either directly or indirectly, their income derives from profit and the size of that income is often related to the prevailing economic climate

- **the professional middle classes:** these are concerned primarily with the provision of a range of services. The number and diversity of these services increase as the wealth of society as a whole increases. As with the industri-al and commercial classes, a wide variety of income was observable from successful barristers and specialist doctors at one end of the scale, to poor clergy, ordinary schoolteachers and nurses at the other. In one way or another, the professional middle classes sell specialist skills, their status and income usually depending both upon the rarity of the specialism and on the need of society for the service on offer. In general, professionals working for central or local government were less generously rewarded than those working in the private sector, though disparities during the twentieth century were in part moderated by the greater security of employment in the so-called 'public sector' of the economy

Definitions, therefore, are difficult. So are statements about 'ideology'. Broadly, the middle classes, having acquired a degree of status, respectability or wealth under a given political system are disposed to wish to see that system continue. In voting terms, during the second half of the twentieth century, it has been estimated that about four times as many in the middle classes normally voted Conservative than Labour. Ideologically, however, the middle class is more diverse and less 'conservative' than may at first sight appear. The following points are relevant:

- during the nineteenth century, a large number of the middle classes, especially in the industrial and commercial towns of the Midlands and North of England, were religious *dissenter*s. Since dissenters suffered both political and social disabilities, they could hardly be considered unthinking conformists or conservatives. Most voted Liberal and many supported a range of reformist causes, especially in education and *temperance reform*
- some of society's most trenchant critics came from the professional middle classes, rather than the working classes. Educational and intellectual advantages partly explain this. So also does a relative security of employment, enabling many in this category not only the intellectual capacity to appraise society from first principles and to suggest changes and improvements but also the economic security which ensured that they would not be the first casualties of an economic downturn
- even among the industrial and commercial middle classes of Victorian Britain, the pursuit of profit was far from the only imperative. Many successful businessmen were substantial philanthropists and contributors to a wide range of charities. Others took on the leadership and organisation of societies or political duties which were not paid but which were 'expected' from people of their status and which represented a contribution to society as a whole. Such societies as the *Anti-Corn Law League* were pressure groups which aimed at freeing business and industry from constraints which threatened profit and expansion, it is true. However, many middle-class supporters of *free trade* also believed that this would benefit all members of society by increasing economic growth and thus providing more jobs

(See also *class consciousness; laissez-faire.*)

Mill, James: philosopher, political economist and father of *John Stuart Mill*. Born in 1773, he was greatly influenced by the ideas of *Jeremy Bentham* and helped to form the group of 'philosophic radicals' who both publicised and developed his ideas. His 'Essay on Government' (1820) argued the case for representative democracy as a superior system to monarchy or aristocracy, although he was sceptical about the influence of an under-educated working class. He died in 1836.

(See also *utilitarianism.*)

Mill, John Stuart: philosopher and son of *James Mill*. Born in 1806, his early thinking was, not surprisingly, influenced by his father and the 'philosophic radicals'. As he developed, however, he began to argue that *utilitarianism* was too theoretical and dehumanising a belief-system, at least as applied by politicians dominated by ideas of *laissez-faire* and low taxation. His book 'On Liberty' (1859) emphasised the importance of individual freedom: 'The only purpose for which power can be rightfully exercised over any member of a civilised community, against his will, is to prevent harm to others'. He also defended the notion of contending political parties in a free society: 'A party of order and stability, and a party of progress or reform, are both necessary elements of a healthy state of political life'. He also produced a treatise on 'Utilitarianism' (1861). He was MP from 1865 to 1868, when he became one of the earliest male advocates of a female suffrage, a cause advocated also in his 'Subjection of Women' (1869). He died in 1873.

(See also *Bentham, Jeremy; free trade; suffragists.*)

Milner (Alfred), Viscount: colonial administrator and imperialist. Born into a British family in Germany in 1854, he was educated at Tübingen and Oxford Universities and trained as a lawyer before becoming a colonial administrator in *Egypt* and then High Commissioner for *South Africa* from 1897 to 1905 (and thus during the Second *Boer War*). He worked to bring the South African states closer together and to rebuild the country's economy after the war. He supported the *Liberal Party* but was on its *imperialist* wing, opposing both Lloyd George's budget and Irish *Home Rule*. Later in his career, he held high political office, as:

- Member of Lloyd George's War Cabinet, 1916–18
- Secretary for the Colonies, 1919–21

He was created Viscount in 1902 and died in 1925.

(See also *Curzon, 1st Marquess; imperialism.*)

Mines Act, 1842: industrial legislation to regulate working conditions in the mining industry. Enacted after a number of investigations and considerable pressure from factory reformers and humanitarians, its main terms were:

- women and children under ten years were prohibited from working underground in mines
- a Mines Inspectorate was established to supervise implementation of the legislation

(See also *Factory Acts; Shaftesbury, 7th Earl of.*)

Ministry of all the Talents: see *Talents, Ministry of all the*

minority government: situation which occurs when no parliamentary party has an overall majority in the House of Commons but one party chooses to try to govern without forming a *coalition*. In the nature of things, such governments are rare and usually of short duration. The best known examples in the nineteenth century are the three *Derby* minority *Conservative* governments of 1852, 1858–59 and 1866–68. In the twentieth century, neither of the first two Labour governments, headed by *Ramsay MacDonald* in 1924 and 1929–31, had a majority. In the post-war period, the Labour government headed by *Harold Wilson* from March to October 1974 was a minority one and *Callaghan*'s Labour government of 1976–79 lacked an overall majority for much of its duration, though kept in office in 1977–78 by a pact with the *Liberal* Party.

(See also *Labour Party; Lib–Lab Pact; Parliament.*)

missionaries: Christian workers, usually ordained, whose function was to convert others to their faith. Christian missions expanded rapidly from the end of the eighteenth century, the main agencies being the Baptist Missionary Society (1792), the London Missionary Society (Congregationalist, 1795), the Church Missionary Society (1799) and the Wesleyan Missionary Society (1813). Additionally, the British and Foreign Bible Society (1804) distributed bibles and other Christian literature throughout the Empire. The work of missionaries received great attention and publicity through the career of *David Livingstone* but, in addition to Africa, extensive missionary work was undertaken throughout the Empire and further afield, including China. Scots, perhaps because of their strong evangelical and educational traditions, were particularly prominent in British missionary work. For most of the nineteenth century, missionaries worked to establish, and then direct, churches. Many worked closely with colonial governors and administrators, seeing the Christian message as an essential element in British *imperialism*. In the twentieth century, however, the emphasis shifted towards establishing religious communities which would then be self-governing. A World Missionary Conference was held in Scotland in 1910 and the inter-denominational message of later missionary activity was emphasised in the foundation of the World Council of Churches in 1948.

(See also *Church of England; evangelicalism; nonconformity.*)

monarchy: technically government controlled by a single ruler, who usually inherits the position by birth according to strict rules of succession ('hereditary monarchy'). By the nineteenth century, however, monarchs in the United Kingdom had limited powers. They could, in theory, both appoint ministers and veto any legislation passed by Parliament. In practice, the first power was almost extinguished and the second never used. Britain had become a 'constitutional monarchy' whose main function was to provide continuity, someone to act for the nation on ceremonial occasions and also a figurehead for the population to respect. The famous writer on constitutional matters, Walter Bagehot, declared in 'The English Constitution' (1867) that 'The Sovereign has, under a constitutional monarchy, such as ours, three rights – the right to be consulted, the right to encourage and the right to warn'. Intelligently exercised, these rights have proved sufficient to give monarchs considerable influence, especially when reigns are long ones and monarchs (to whom *prime minister*s conventionally report at least once every week during parliamentary sessions) experienced. Also, when political parties are more or less evenly represented in the *House of Commons,* decisions about who should properly form either a *minority* or a *coalition government* can also give the monarch genuine power, although this is exercised discreetly, out of the public eye and after extensive guidance by courtiers and political and constitutional experts.

As Bagehot perceived, however, the main buttress of a successful constitutional monarchy is popular respect. He argued that ordinary people wish to have an individual above politics, whose position is usually unchallenged and not the subject of continuous argument or debate: 'The best reason why monarchy is a strong government is that it is an intelligible government. The mass of mankind understand it, and they hardly anywhere in the world understand any other'.

Theory and practice in the history of the nineteenth- and twentieth-century monarchies have not always gone hand in hand. *George IV* inspired no respect whatever and even Queen *Victoria*, immensely popular and respected for most of her reign, was subject to substantial criticism during the 1860s and early 1870s during a long period of mourning for *Prince Albert*, when she discharged few civic duties and was not regularly seen. The most successful constitutional monarchs of the twentieth century have been *George V* and *George VI*. It is surely significant that both were on the throne during world wars, providing a national symbol and rallying point. *Elizabeth II*, whose reign began amid a welter of popularity and obsequious deference in which the press played a nauseating part, presided in the 1980s and 1990s over a period of sharply declining monarchical fortunes. Again media influence was decisive. The press, in particular, exposed the activities of many junior members of the royal family to merciless scrutiny; editors of popular newspapers knew that 'royal stories' guaranteed high sales. The activities were not in themselves remarkable. Exceedingly wealthy and privileged individuals with no clearly defined roles are liable to spend extravagantly and act indulgently, if only to ward off boredom. Before the 1970s, however, what was routine behaviour for many in the upper classes was only rarely exposed to such intrusive enquiry. A monarchy which tabloid newspapers are determined to turn into a soap opera is not one which can either meet Bagehot's criteria or inspire uncritical respect. By the end of the century, increasing criticism was being heard that the British monarchy was 'out of touch' with the needs of ordinary people. *Republicanism*, though still a minority belief, became a more respectable political creed than ever before.

(See also *democracy; Edward VIII; George III; Lords, House of; William IV.*)

Mond–Turner talks: negotiations between trade union leaders and industrialists held in 1928. The leading figures were Sir Alfred Mond, an ex-Liberal minister then a Conservative MP, who was a successful businessman in the chemical industry and Ben Turner, then Chairman of the *Trades Union Congress.* The talks were an attempt to rebuild constructive relations after the industrial disputes which culminated in the *General Strike* and the Government's response after its defeat, the *Trades Union Act, 1927.* The talks achieved little in specific terms, but they did confirm that channels of communication between industry and labour could be used to mutual benefit.

(See also *trade unions.*)

monetarism: economic doctrine which developed in opposition to *Keynesian economics.* Associated particularly with the US economist Milton Friedman, founder of the so-called 'Chicago School' in the 1950s, its main objective was to direct *economic policy* by rigid government control of the supply of money. Linked in one important sense to the economic liberalism and *laissez-faire* of Victorian Britain, its political importance grew in Britain from the mid-1970s when governments felt that the most severe economic problem they faced was *inflation.* Monetarists argued that, since the quantity of money in circulation was crucial to levels of economic activity, strict controls would produce a better balance and 'squeeze inflation out of the system'. Reliance on Keynesianism had seen governments, in effect, print money to help economic activity and to minimise *unemployment* levels. Monetarists argued that the main consequence of this had been dangerously high inflation levels. The *Conservative Party* was converted to an economic policy based on monetarism by *Sir Keith Joseph* and monetarism was the keynote of *Thatcherism* at least in the years 1979–85. It was particularly controversial since an inevitable immediate by-product of monetarism was economic depression and sharply rising unemployment.

(See also *Labour Party; Thatcher, Margaret Hilda; trade unions.*)

monitorial system: common teaching method in nineteenth-century schools. Associated with Andrew Bell and Joseph Lancaster at the beginning of the nineteenth century, its main aim was to select able pupils from schools provided for the poor and train them to teach pupils in their turn. Initially, they would be 'monitors' – hence the name. The system was hierarchical. It gave able pupils something of a career path while also encouraging the spread of knowledge and understanding at relatively low cost. It was widely adopted in elementary schools in the second half of the nineteenth century.

(See also *Education Act, 1870; elementary schools.*)

Mons, Battle of: fought on 23 August 1914 at the beginning of *World War I*. It was the first European battle fought by the British since the *Crimean War*. Though heavily outnumbered and forced to retreat, the *British Expeditionary Force* and French forces produced the first check to the massive and rapid German thrust through Belgium and Northern France.

(See also *Marne, Battles of the.*)

Montagu–Chelmsford Report: British government initiative, published in 1919, which produced reforms to the government of *India*. The report was produced by Edwin Montagu, Secretary of State for India, and Lord Chelmsford, the Viceroy. Its main objective, which failed, was to increase Indian confidence in the government to reduce support for nationalism and independence. The British government acted on the proposals and the main effects on government in India were:

- the creation of a Parliament, with two Houses, which could pass laws for the internal government for India
- some sensitive areas were deemed 'reserved' and would still be determined by British colonial governors, officials or administrators
- the British executive could not be removed by the Indian parliament
- in times of emergency, the Viceroy could govern by decree

(See also *Curzon, 1st Marquess; Indian Independence; Simon, Viscount.*)

Monte-Cassino, Battle of: battle during World War II fought south of Rome between October 1943 and May 1944. The Germans were holding the monastery of Monte-Cassino as a key point in its so-called 'Gustav line' against advancing Allied forces. The Allied bombardment eventually broke the line, though at the cost of destroying the ancient monastery. The Allies were then able to march on Rome and inflict a key defeat on the Germans and Italians.

Montgomery, Bernard (Viscount Montgomery of Alamein): British army leader during *World War II*. Born in 1887 the son of a bishop, he saw service in *World War I*, and was severely injured at Ypres. He came to national prominence when, as a general in charge of the British Eighth Army, he defeated the Germans at *El Alamein* in 1942, forcing their surrender in North Africa in 1943. He was also in command in Sicily and southern Italy as the push northwards began. He was in charge of the attack on the Germans in Normandy after the successful *D-Day* landings and at *Arnhem*. He took the surrender of the German forces on Lüneburg Heath in 1945. Undeniably a soldier of great strategic gifts, he was also a difficult man, much given to arrogance and uncritical reliance on his own detailed planning. His lack of either flexibility or self-criticism had both military and political repercussions. He was criticised for relative neglect of Allied troops not under his direct command and also for not responding to opportunities as they presented themselves. His relations with the US general Eisenhower were notoriously difficult, giving rise to greater problems within the Allied forces in 1944 than were necessary. He was ennobled in 1946 and died in 1979.

More, Hannah: Evangelical writer and teacher. Born in Somerset in 1745, she became a great ally of the growing *evangelical* campaign within the *Church of England*. She founded schools in which she trained poor children to read and to be obedient, but not to write (which facility she considered dangerous in the lower orders). She allied herself with the majority conservative group in the aftermath of the *French Revolution* and produced both 'Village Politics' (1792) and a large number of extremely highly selling 'Cheap Repository Tracts' (1795–98). The purpose of both was straightforward: to warn ordinary folk about the dangers of support for new doctrines of liberty and democracy and to encourage them to be obedient to their betters – who knew best. The money she earned by her writing she used in supporting a range of educational and other charitable causes. She died in 1833.

(See also *Pitt the Younger, William; Wilberforce, William.*)

Morris, William: poet, craftsman and socialist. Born in 1834 and educated at Oxford he abandoned an intended career in the *Church of England* for the creative arts. He was a leading member of the *Pre-Raphaelite Brotherhood*, specialising particularly in furniture and interior design. He became increasingly influenced by *socialism,* joining the *Social Democratic Federation* before forming a breakaway Socialist League. His later writings advocated a return to the purity of rural England and an attack on industrial society and its values. He formed the Society for the Protection of Rural Buildings. His best known book is probably 'News from Nowhere' (1891). He died in 1896.

(See also *Industrial Revolution; Marxism.*)

Morris, William (1st Viscount Nuffield): industrialist and philanthropist. Born in 1877 in humble circumstances, he first worked in a bicycle shop before he established a very early car factory at Cowley, on the outskirts of Oxford. He was a pioneer of mass production. Morris Motors became easily the biggest-selling British car manufacturer between the two world wars. He founded Nuffield College, Oxford in 1937 as a centre for postgraduate research and also established the Nuffield Research Foundation in 1943, while also supporting hospitals and medical research. He received many honours, notably his viscountcy in 1938. He died in 1963.

(See also *Industrial Revolution; motor car industry.*)

Morrison, Herbert: Labour politician. He was born in 1888 and came to prominence in London Labour politics, being Secretary of the London Labour Party in 1915, and, from 1934 to 1940, leader of the London County Council. He was first an MP in 1923. His major offices in national politics were:

- Minister of Transport, 1929–31
- Minister of Supply, 1940

- Home Secretary, 1940–45 (and member of the War Cabinet, 1942–45)
- Deputy Prime Minister (and Leader of the Commons, 1945–51)
- Foreign Secretary, 1951
- Deputy Leader of the Labour Party, 1951–55

He was twice defeated for the leadership, by *Attlee* in 1935 and *Gaitskell* in 1955. An effective minister, especially in home affairs, and a pugnacious character, he rather relished his reputation as a 'rough diamond'. Popular with some, he was fiercely critical of the Labour left. Once, famously, when a colleague said that *Aneurin Bevan* was 'his own worst enemy', Morrison replied: 'Not while I'm alive, he ain't'.

(See also *Labour Party*.)

Mosley, Sir Oswald: *Conservative*, Independent, *Labour* and fascist politician. Born into an aristocratic family in 1896, he served in the Royal Flying Corps during *World War I* before becoming the youngest MP in the Commons on his first election as a Conservative in 1918. He quickly impressed himself on the House both as an orator and also as a restless spirit anxious to find an outlet both for his energies and his own sense of self-importance. He moved between parties in an attempt to advance what he saw as 'progress' and served for a time as Chancellor of the Duchy of Lancaster in *MacDonald's* government of 1929–31 before resigning over policy disagreements on unemployment. He left the party and formed the so-called 'New Party' in 1931 before founding the British Union of Fascists in 1932. He led the fascists in marches through London and used his oratorical powers to rally support for strong leadership, using Hitler as a model of how a country could be regenerated. Like him, he played strongly on hatred of the *Jews* (anti-Semitism). The party, however, failed to win a seat in Parliament. He was interned from 1940 to 1943. After the war, he campaigned against Commonwealth *immigration*, and for entry into the European Economic Community, which he thought Britain should lead. He died in 1960.

motor car industry: the most important new industry to develop in Britain in the first half of the twentieth century. Before 1914, motor cars were a luxury for the rich but the country was already producing 35,000 of them a year with both Rolls Royce and Morris Motors established market leaders. By 1925, Morris was making 25,000 cars a year. The main period of expansion took place between 1918 and the late 1960s. By the 1930s, Austin was established as the main rival to Morris and Ford had established a large assembly plant at Dagenham (Essex). The years immediately after *World War II* saw British car manufacturers export more than half its output, earning vital foreign currency for the British economy. However, from the mid-1950s, export performance tailed off and the domestic market was increasingly penetrated by overseas vehicles, especially from Japan and Germany. Austin and Morris merged in 1952 to produce the British Motor Corporation and, in 1968, British Leyland but mergers were insufficient to meet overseas competition from car manufacturers with more streamlined production methods, less overmanning and fewer industrial disputes. British Leyland was first nationalised and then privatised but the ever-growing demand for cars continued to be satisfied more by imports than by domestic production. The 1980s saw the end of a British car industry as such since motor car production was in the hands of foreign-owned companies such as Ford General Motors, Peugeot, Honda and Nissan. By the end of the century, more than 30 million cars were on British roads. Issues such as pollution by car engines and an inadequate road structure were beginning to make an impact, although the perception that car-ownership represented freedom as well as status made environment-protecting policies directed at a switch to public transport difficult to implement. Arguably, the success of the motor car industry produced greater changes in the lifestyles and opportunities of ordinary people than any other in the twentieth century.

(See also *Morris, William; motorways; nationalisation.*)

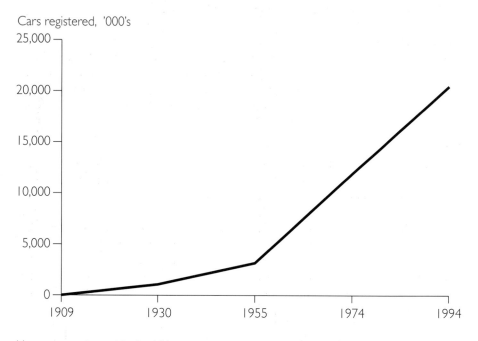

Cars registered, '000's

Motor cars registered in the UK

motorways: specific roads dedicated to long-distance, trunk traffic on which separate regulations apply. Motorways had been discussed as early as the first decade of the twentieth century but progress in Britain was slow relative to other European countries, especially Germany and its Autobahn programme in the 1930s. The first section of British motorway was a small section of the M6 which by-passed Preston in 1958 and the M1 from London to Watford Gap (near Rugby) was opened in 1959. The mileage of motorways did not exceed 1,000 until 1975 and stood at almost 2,000 miles at the end of the century. Motorways have generated extra traffic and critics have argued that the benefits they produce for travellers in urban areas are relatively short-term. However, motorways have initiated or accelerated important social changes. Among these are:

- the ability to live at greater distance from the workplace
- the transfer of industries to locations near the motorway network. This has produced a greater concentration of industry in the Midlands and south-east of England, which have disproportionate motorway provision

- greater safety. Motorways are heavily used and accidents on them tend to have serious consequences because of the speed of traffic. However, there are far fewer accidents per motorway mile than on other trunk roads

(See also *motor industry.*)

Mountbatten, Lord Louis (Viscount and 1st Earl Mountbatten of Burma): naval commander and statesman. He was born the son of Prince Louis of Battenberg in 1900, and saw naval service during *World War I* and in *World War II* was Allied commander with responsibility for South-East Asia, which involved the recapture of Burma and Malaya from the Japanese. He was appointed Viceroy of *India* by *Attlee* in 1947 with a brief to prepare the country for independence in the shortest possible time. This mission he accomplished, but not without much Indian bloodshed. He was First Sea Lord from 1955 to 1959 and Chief of the Defence Staff from 1959 to 1965. He was uncle to Prince Philip, husband of Queen Elizabeth, and his relations with their eldest son, Prince Charles, were especially close. He was killed by an *IRA* bomb in Northern Ireland in 1979.

(See also *monarchy.*)

Munich Agreement, 1938: name given to the negotiations between *Neville Chamberlain* and Adolf Hitler which ended with Britain's agreement that Czechoslovakia should be required to surrender the Sudetenland (the German-speaking part of the country) to the Germans. Chamberlain returned to Britain informing the nation from Downing Street: 'I believe it is peace for our time'. The agreement was enormously popular in Britain at the time but came to be seen within a few months, when Hitler occupied the whole of Czechoslovakia in March 1939 anyway, as a tragic failure – the high watermark of the policy of *appeasement*. It is far from clear that the Munich Agreement was as odious as critics such as *Winston Churchill* said, or that Chamberlain actually believed that peace had been secured. The agreement gave the country much-needed time for a massive rearmament programme so that, when *World War II* broke out, it was not so unprepared as might have been the case.

(See also *Eden, Anthony; Halifax, 1st Earl of.*)

Municipal Corporations Act, 1835: legislation enabling a rationalisation of local government in the towns to take place in England and Wales. Passed by *Melbourne*'s *Whig* government in some ways as the counterpart to the *Reform Act* of 1832, it enabled local authorities to be elected which were much more representative and did away with many ancient forms of *local government*, such as the select vestry. Its main terms were:

- it replaced 178 local 'closed' boroughs with elected borough corporations
- councillors were elected every three years by local ratepayers, and chose their own mayors and aldermen
- corporations could take over functions of the local improvement commissions
- corporations could levy rates to finance expenditure
- councils formed watch committees for protection of persons and property and could also establish borough *police* forces

The Act was largely 'permissive' – that is, it enabled local authorities to take up new powers but did not require them to do so. Most authorities were careful in their expenditure but they did pay increasing attention to *public health*. Over the next half century, the Act made possible a large number of new initiatives, increased the extent of representative government and also gave new opportunities for smaller property owners to participate, both as voters and councillors, in representative government.

(See also *democracy*.)

Munitions, Ministry of: new government department set up in 1915 during *World War I*. Its main function was to supply British troops with adequate numbers of guns, mortars and tanks. The first minister was *David Lloyd George*. By the end of the war, three million workers were employed under its supervision. Its work represented not only a break with tradition to meet unprecedented new circumstances but was also a powerful indication of the potential of the State to effect decisive change when it took control of an industrial sector of the economy. It was renamed the Ministry of Supply in 1919 and abolished, its work completed, in 1921.

music halls: places of entertainment which developed, particularly in the larger industrial and commercial towns, from the 1840s onwards. By 1875, thanks to the tireless efforts of entrepreneurs such as Charles Morton, London alone supported more than 200 music halls. They began as local forms of entertainment but later developed as a showcase for national talent. In the late nineteenth and early twentieth centuries, they made national celebrities of artists such as Marie Lloyd, Harry Lauder and Dan Leno. The halls attracted people of all social classes who were attracted by a range of other benefits, such as the availability of drink and, in some places, prostitutes. The 'halls' were challenged for popular support, and eventually defeated by the advent first of the *cinema* and later *television*.

(See also *leisure*.)

N

Namier, Sir Lewis: historian. Born in 1888, he came to Britain as a young man when his Polish–Russian parents emigrated. His historical research was grounded in the eighteenth century and his method involved the detailed study of influential people in their political and social contexts. Building up a picture from minutely researched detail, he established a school of historical thinking entirely opposed to that of *Marxism* since it emphasised the importance of individuals, rather than impersonal economic forces, in dictating change. His best known work, 'The Structure of Politics at the Accession of *George III*' (1929) inspired many to emulate his approach and its thinking informed that massive work of minute and diligent scholarship, 'The History of Parliament' which provides information about every MP, every constituency and every electoral contest. He died in 1960.

Nanking, Treaty of (1842): peace treaty signed at the end of the Anglo-Chinese war of 1839–42. Its main terms were:

- the Chinese government ceded *Hong Kong* to Britain
- Britain gained access to the Chinese ports of Shanghai, Amoy, Ningpo and Foochow
- China paid compensation for confiscated opium and for many costs of the war

(See also *Opium Wars.*)

Napier, Sir Charles: soldier. Born in 1782 into a family with *Whig Party* connections, he enjoyed a colourful and varied career which saw active service in the *Peninsular* and *Anglo-American wars* before involvement in the Greek liberation movement in the 1820s and in the North of England during the Chartist disturbances of the early 1840s. He is best known for his service in *India* which involved the conquest of the province of Sind. This he announced in a famous Latin pun: 'Peccavi' – which translates as 'I have sinned'. Since the conquest involved his own considerable enrichment from the profits of loot, the erudite joke was true in both senses. He was Commander-in-Chief of the army in India from 1849 to 1851 and died in 1853.

(See also *Chartism.*)

Napoleonic Wars: wars between Britain, with several allies, against France from 1803 to 1815. They are best seen as a continuation of the conflict which had begun in 1793. Neither side trusted the other to be bound by the *Amiens treaty* and Britain (not having reduced its military and naval forces) declared war in May 1803.

Causes of the War:

- mutual hostility between France and Britain. Napoleon refused to evacuate Holland; Britain, likewise, did not quit Malta
- France took over Piedmont and Elba. Britain remained concerned about its trading position and military bases in the Mediterranean

The war fell into three main phases:

1803–6   Napoleon consolidated and extended French military dominance in Europe while Britain confirmed its naval supremacy, rendering a French invasion all but impossible

1806–12 period dominated by economic warfare between the two powers, although France continued its dominance virtually throughout Europe. Britain opened up a new front in the *Peninsular War* in 1808

1812–15 France's invasion of Russia led to defeat and substantial military loss. New coalitions against a weakened France brought victories in 1813. Napoleon was forced to flee in 1814, but returned to launch a 'hundred days campaign' with a revived French army before final defeat at the *Battle of Waterloo*

Main alliances against France:

- **Third Coalition** (**Treaty of St Petersburg, April 1805**): Britain, Russia, Austria (made separate peace with France, December 1805)
- **Treaty of Orebro**, **July 1812:** Britain; Russia and Sweden
- **Treaty of Reichenbach**, **June 1813:** Britain, Russia and Prussia
- **Treaty of Chaumont**, **March 1814:** Britain, Russia, Prussia and Austria

Theatres of War:

1 Europe:

1803   France occupied Hanover

1805   France won decisive victories over Austrians at Ulm and Austrians and Russians at Austerlitz. French power in Europe unquestioned

1806   Prussians defeated by France at Jena

1807   Russia made peace with France by Treaty of Tilsit

1808   France invaded Spain and Britain sent an expeditionary force there, thus beginning the Peninsular War – effectively a war within the wider war

1809   British expedition to Holland in support of Austria (now back in the war) failed: the Walcheren expedition

1812   Napoleon invaded Russia and captured Moscow but was eventually forced to retreat with 500,000 casualties.

1813   Napoleon defeated Russia and Prussia at battles of Lutzen and Bautzen but suffered a major defeat later in the year at Leipzig. His own alliance system, based largely on conquest and threat, fell apart. Wellington crossed Pyrenees into France

1814   Allies captured Paris; Napoleon fled. War seemed to be over

1815   Napoleon returned from exile but was defeated by British and Prussian troops at Waterloo

2 West Indies and other islands:

1803   Britain occupied St Lucia, Tobago and Dutch Guiana

1810   Britain occupied Guadeloupe

1811   Britain occupied Java

3 Main naval engagements:

1804   Captain Moore sank Spanish commercial convoy off Cadiz. Spain declared war on Britain

1805   off Cape *Trafalgar*, Admiral *Nelson* defeated French and Spanish fleet

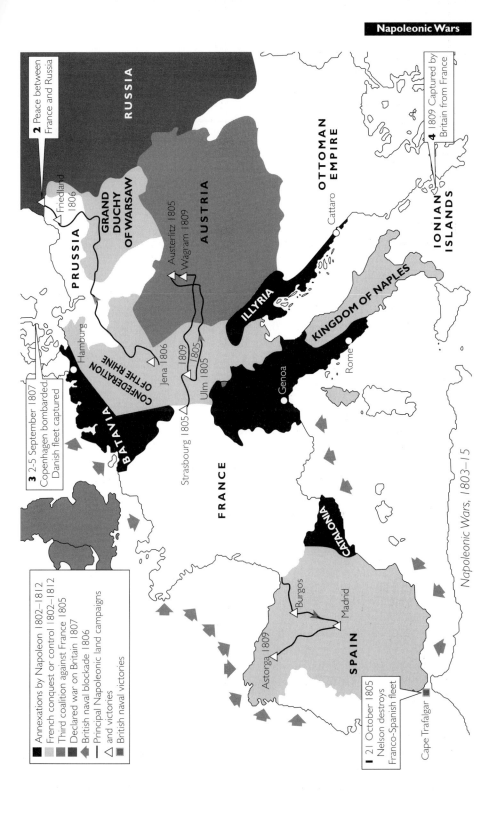

Napoleonic Wars, 1803–15

2 Peace between France and Russia

Friedland 1806

RUSSIA

PRUSSIA

GRAND DUCHY OF WARSAW

AUSTRIA

Austerlitz 1805
Wagram 1809

4 1809 Captured by Britain from France

OTTOMAN EMPIRE

Cattaro

IONIAN ISLANDS

Hamburg

Jena 1806

1809

1805

Ulm 1805

Strasbourg 1805

CONFEDERATION OF THE RHINE

BATAVIA

ILLYRIA

Genoa

Rome

KINGDOM OF NAPLES

FRANCE

3 2–5 September 1807
Copenhagen bombarded.
Danish fleet captured

- Annexations by Napoleon 1802–1812
- French conquest or control 1802–1812
- Third coalition against France 1805
- Declared war on Britain 1807
- British naval blockade 1806
- Principal Napoleonic land campaigns and victories
- British naval victories

CATALONIA

Burgos

Madrid

Astorga 1809

SPAIN

1 21 October 1805
Nelson destroys
Franco-Spanish fleet

Cape Trafalgar

under Admiral Villeneuve: the decisive naval engagement of the war

1807 Britain bombarded Copenhagen to prevent Napoleon using Danish fleet against Britain. Denmark declared war on Britain

4 Economic warfare:

1806 Napoleon issued the Berlin Decrees in November, closing European ports under French control to British trade. This began the *continental system*

1807 Britain responded with Orders in Council. November: France invaded Portugal, which had refused to invoke the continental system. Further 'Orders' issued by British government declaring that all European ports from which Britain was excluded were to be blockaded. Napoleon responded in December with the 'Milan Decrees'

1809 Orders in Council extended to cover USA

1810 Sweden joined the continental system

Considerable similarities exist with the French Revolutionary Wars. Again, Britain offered subsidies to Prussians, Austrians and Russians. Again their value was reduced by Napoleon's apparent ability, before 1812, to win any land battle in continental Europe at will. Again Britain relied on its naval strength to secure itself against invasion. The main differences, however, were that:

- the war became economic after 1806 and this caused enormous difficulties for Britain, especially in the period 1809–12 when food prices and unemployment at home were alike high. However, ultimately, the early industrial British economy proved stronger than the French
- economic warfare led to a further conflict with the United States, the *Anglo-American war* of 1812–15
- Napoleon overstretched French resources with the invasion of Russia. French decline after 1812 was rapid

The wars ended in clear French defeat. The formal peace treaties were, first, the Peace of Paris, 1814, and then the *Congress of Vienna* in 1815.

(See Figure on page 195. See also *Anglo-American Wars; French Revolutionary Wars; Paris, Treaties of (1814–15); Peninsular War.*)

Nash, John: architect. He was born in 1752 and made his reputation in Wales as the designer of elegant houses for the gentry. He worked extensively with the landscape designer Humphrey Repton on a number of projects in the early nineteenth century but is best known for his work with the Prince Regent (later *George IV*), especially in the design of buildings around Regent's Park. He was also responsible for Marble Arch, for that extraordinarily idiosyncratic Western vision of the Orient, the Brighton Pavilion and for substantial extensions to Buckingham Palace. His style was rooted in classical traditions but strongly influenced by India and Egypt. He died in 1835.

Nasmyth, James: inventor and engineer. Born in 1808, he is best known for inventing the steam hammer in 1839 which removed a previous production blockage in the manufacture of large iron bars. This was important for the massive expansion of the *iron industry* in the second half of the nineteenth century. He also invented a steam pile driver and a hydraulic punching machine. He died in 1891.

(See also *engineering industry; Industrial Revolution.*)

National Assistance Act, 1948: legislation passed by *Attlee's Labour* government with the intention of obliterating memory of the hated *dole*. The basis of the *welfare state* created in the later 1940s was insurance provision. However, the Government also installed a 'safety net' to help those who had exceeded their entitlement under insurance. This Act provided cash payments for those who could be proved to be in real need.

National Front: right-wing political party founded in 1966. In some respects, the natural successor to *fascism*, its main aims were:

- a halt to the *immigration* of black citizens from the Commonwealth
- to develop a programme of repatriating (sending back to their original homes) immigrants who had arrived since the 1940s
- to ensure that Britain did not join the European Economic Community, and to urge Britain's withdrawal after it did

The party was openly racist and received what support it did in working-class areas of some large cities, especially London and especially among young males who were attracted to it by the possibilities of violence it afforded. It campaigned in parliamentary elections during the 1970s but won no seats. It had little more success in local elections, but its often menacing presence won it considerable publicity. Increasingly tough laws on immigration removed much of the party's rationale anyway, but it split in 1982 when John Tyndall formed a separate 'British National Party' which had no more success in attracting support.

National Government: *coalition government* which ruled Britain from 1931 to 1940 under the prime ministership of *Ramsay MacDonald* (1931–35), *Stanley Baldwin* (1935–37) and *Neville Chamberlain* (1937–40). Although the name suggests, and was at the time intended to imply, national support for agreed policies, the reality is rather more complex. It was formed to deal with the problem of national debt and economic crisis which had been worsened by the Wall Street Crash. However, it did not have the support of the *Labour Party*, the official opposition. Those few senior Labour politicians who joined it were expelled from the party. The 1935 general election also demonstrated that the opposition retained substantial popular support. Nor were its policies especially consensual. Although the Government finally abandoned *free trade* as the guiding *economic policy*, its attitudes to *unemployment* and to improving Britain's economic performance were both cautious and conservative. Given the high degree of social misery, particularly in the industrial North of England and Scotland in the 1930s, they were highly controversial. Nor was foreign policy any less controversial. *Appeasement* was popular, at least until the end of 1938, but it was ferociously attacked in some quarters. In reality, the National Government was a coalition dominated by the *Conservative Party*, following policies which had the support of many in what might be termed 'the establishment' but which were coming under increasing attack by economic thinkers in the Labour and *Liberal* parties.

(See also *Churchill, Winston; Eden, Anthony; Keynesian economics*.)

National Health Service Act, 1946: legislation passed during *Attlee's Labour* government. Closely following the principles of the *Beveridge Report*, it developed the principles under which the National Health Service (NHS) operated from July 1948. Its main terms were:

- free access to medical service, through general practitioners (GPs), and free medical prescriptions
- free hospital care
- free dental and eye (optical) services
- existing hospitals, previously voluntary or local-authority run, now came into the NHS
- doctors working within the NHS could link their work with private practice available only to fee-paying patients

(See also *Bevan, Aneurin; welfare state.*)

National Health Service, operation of: the NHS was the keystone of the *welfare state* and tinkering with it proved politically risky. Its operation, however, hardly lived up to the idealistic visions of its creators in the 1940s. The main reason was cost. *Beveridge* had argued that a scheme which needed to be funded by insurance and taxation would actually lessen as the health of the nation improved. He was proved wrong on three main grounds:

- a massive backlog of necessary treatment had built up in the late 1930s and 1940s when those who could not afford treatment now exercised their rights under the new legislation
- the NHS structure was intrinsically costly and became more so as doctors and medical administrators argued for improvements in treatment. Since the principle of the NHS was equal access to necessary treatment and since the cost of treatment increased with technological sophistication and medical advance, overall expenditure continued to rise
- in the longer term, the NHS was a victim of its own success. Improved medical care, allied to improved living standards in the 1950s and 1960s, ensured that life expectancy increased. The much larger proportion of citizens surviving beyond the age of eighty substantially raised the cost of long-term care (see Figure on page 199)

To a degree, such costs could be absorbed by the considerable economic growth of the 1950s and 1960s. However, the first breach in the principle of free treatment was made as early as 1951 with the introduction of charges for prescriptions, dental and ophthalmic treatment. The real costs of such services continued to increase thereafter. Burdens on the taxpayer became ever more substantial from the 1970s and the NHS became a prime candidate for rationalisation after Thatcher came to power.

National Insurance Act, 1911: legislation passed during *Asquith's Liberal* government of 1905–15. Masterminded by *David Lloyd George*, the Act partially took over the functions of *friendly societies* and other mutual aid organisations to provide insurance for workers against:

- sickness
- unemployment

The key principles of the legislation were that benefits would be:

- self-financing (the State would be part of the scheme but its commitment would be clearly costed in contributing to a notional 'insurance fund') and
- available to all in the relevant categories. They would not be means-tested

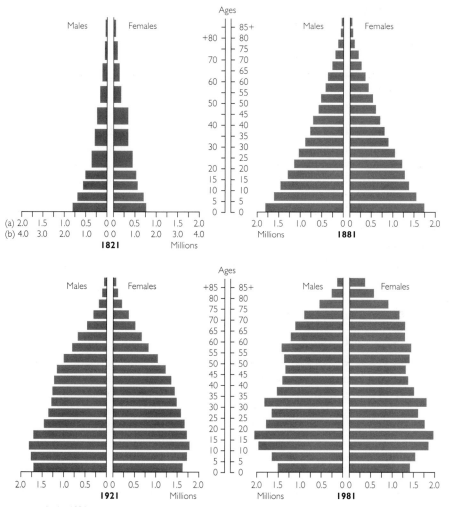

In the 1821 'pyramid', scale (a) represents the age group 0–20 and scale (b), age groups from 20–80+

National Health Service – bar charts showing increase in numbers of people living into old age

and citizens would feel no shame in applying for benefit under a scheme to which they had been contributing

The scheme was funded by contributions from three sources:

- the employee (who paid 4d (1½p) a week into the fund)
- the employer (who paid 3d (1p))
- the State (which paid 2d (½p))

Lloyd George could thus claim that individuals would receive '9d for 4d'. In the early years, the scheme operated only in those industries deemed most vulnerable, especially to seasonal unemployment, and it insured only the worker, not family or dependants. It did, however, represent the beginnings of a non-means-tested, universal benefits scheme. It grew steadily until the outbreak of *World War II*, the most significant development being the incorporation of state *old age pensions* in 1925.

(See also *Beveridge, William; Churchill, Winston; National Insurance Act, 1946; welfare state.*)

National Insurance Act, 1946: legislation passed during *Attlee*'s *Labour* government as part of the creation of the *welfare state*. Its essential principle was universality; all citizens were to be covered by its provisions. The legislation was accordingly designed to close up the gaps left by state insurance schemes as they had operated since 1911. It operated on the same contributory principle as *Lloyd George*'s legislation of 1911 but it was not anticipated that it would be invariably self-financing. The State committed itself to making up shortfalls through taxation. The range of benefits on offer was also much wider than in 1911. Insurance now covered:

- unemployment
- sickness
- maternity benefits for mothers
- widows' benefits
- old age pensions

Overall, the Act put in place the basic social security benefits which have been at the heart of welfare-state provision.

(See also *Beveridge Report.*)

National Liberal Party: see *Liberal National Party*

National Parks Act, 1949: legislation during *Attlee*'s *Labour* government. It set up a National Parks Commission which would identify, and designate as protected from most forms of industrial and commercial development, areas of outstanding natural beauty. The first to be set up was the Peak District National Park in 1951. This was followed by the Lake District, Snowdonia and Dartmoor the same year and then the Pembrokeshire Coast and North York Moors (1952), Yorkshire Dales and Exmoor (1954), rural Northumberland (1956), the Brecon Beacons (1957) and Norfolk Broads.

(See also *leisure; tourist industry.*)

national service: a form of *conscription* into the armed services. It was introduced at the beginning of *World War II* and continued into peacetime by the National Service Act, 1947. Under it, males over the age of eighteen were required to undertake one year's military service. This was increased to eighteen months in 1948 and two years in 1950. The system was scaled down by the *Conservative* government in 1957 and abolished in 1960. It was highly controversial.

Arguments for:

- it provided useful work and training for young men
- it inculcated a sense of self-discipline, concern for others and team spirit
- it could raise self-esteem among the less able who had found formal education a dis-spiriting experience
- it provided a ready-made military reserve which could be called upon at need, as during the *Korean War* and converted a few conscripts into willing volunteers for longer service in the armed forces

Arguments against:

- it was a fundamental invasion of personal liberty in peacetime
- it produced a large number of discontented and frustrated recruits who opposed the system, resented military discipline and were of very little practical use to the armed services anyway
- for those with further education, apprenticeship or job-specific training, it introduced an unnecessary delay which might have serious consequences both for motivation and career prospects
- especially for brighter recruits, the lack of an obvious rationale for the routine tasks of the armed forces, repetitive drilling and obeying commands without question was frustrating, mind-numbing and demeaning

National Trust: organisation devoted to the preservation of 'places of historic interest and natural beauty'. It was founded in 1895, its main supporters being *Octavia Hill* and Canon H D Rawnsley. It began as a private organisation but its work was supported by legislation for England and Wales in 1907 and for Scotland (where a separate trust had been formed in 1926) in 1931. Its funds are used for the acquisition and preservation of both buildings and landscape and it played a key role in preserving buildings abandoned by the *aristocracy* when the costs of upkeep became too great, from the inter-war period onwards. In the 1980s and 1990s, its educational functions received increased attention as effective preservation became seen, in part, as dependent on raising popular consciousness about the value of key elements in national heritage.

(See also *leisure; tourist industry.*)

National Unemployed Workers' Movement: organisation founded by the *Communist Party* in 1921 to protect the interests of unemployed workers. It organised hunger marches and other demonstrations in the inter-war period, while also opposing what it saw as the inadequacy and discrimination of government *unemployment* policy. Its membership was never large; at its height it probably did not exceed 20,000. However, its propaganda influence was considerable, despite opposition both from the *Conservative* and *Labour* parties and, during the 1930s, the *National Government* which saw it as a front for communism. It was wound up in 1939 on the outbreak of *World War II.*

(See also *economic policy.*)

National Union of Women's Suffrage Societies (NUWSS): organisation formed in 1897 to co-ordinate the activities of political organisations agitating for 'votes for women'. It had about 500,000 members on the outbreak of *World War I*, when it was producing a successful journal, 'The Common Cause'. Inevitably, however, its impact was reduced by the fact that women's organisations had developed different tactics to promote their cause and gave primary attention to these rather than to an 'umbrella' organisation.

(See also *suffragettes; suffragists; Women's Social and Political Union.*)

nationalisation: policy which involves state ownership, organisation and control of industries and utilities. It became associated with the *Labour Party* which had argued that national regeneration depended upon greater state controls. The so-called

'Clause IV' of the party's constitution committed it, at least in theory, to 'common ownership of the means of production' from 1918 to 1995. However, important moves towards common ownership had been made before Labour formed its first majority government in 1945. The experiences of both *world wars* showed how effectively the State could take control of the means of production both to maximise armaments production and to organise the country's defence against attack. Important nationalisation initiatives were also taken by the *Conservative Party* in creating the Central Electricity Board (1926) and the *British Broadcasting Corporation* (1927), while the *National Government* also created a publicly owned London Passenger Transport Board (1933) and the British Overseas Airways Corporation (1939).

The Labour nationalisation programme during its governments of 1945–51 proceeded as follows:

1946 the *Bank of England* and civil aviation
1947 coal, Cable & Wireless
1948 public transport
1949 electricity and gas
1951 iron and steel

Nationalisation normally involved creating boards to run the industries and this led to criticism that they were insufficiently accountable. Nationalisation was a controversial policy but the extent of party conflict which it generated should not be exaggerated. Labour took good care to offer shareholders ample compensation for their lost property when industries were taken into public ownership. Furthermore, many of the industries actually nationalised – coal and the railways were prime examples – had been in a poor state for much of the pre-war period, producing losses and leading to widespread *unemployment*.

The Conservatives in the 1950s committed themselves to a 'mixed economy' (whereby industry is partly in private and partly in public ownership) and undid very little of the Labour nationalisation programme. Only iron and steel became a 'political football', being denationalised in 1951 and renationalised by Labour in 1967.

In the 1970s, further nationalisation took place under both parties but only in order to salvage what were considered prestige companies and industries which would otherwise have gone into liquidation and also in order to avoid raising unemployment rates. This explains the nationalisation of Rolls Royce in 1971, British Leyland in 1975 and the shipbuilding industry in 1977.

Thinking nationalised industries both less efficient than those in the public sector, and anyway an outmoded legacy of *Marxist* thinking, the governments of *Margaret Thatcher* were determined to return nationalised industries to private ownership and this policy was pursued with vigour throughout the 1980s and continued under *John Major* in the early 1990s.

(See also *economic policy*.)

Naval Mutinies, 1797: the refusal of British fleets anchored at Spithead and the Nore to accept normal naval discipline during the spring and early summer of a critical year of the *French Revolutionary Wars*. The main causes of the mutinies were poor conditions and low pay and the mutineers demanded improvements in both. However, both the Government and the naval authorities were concerned that the mutineers had become 'infected' with what they called 'French principles' of *democracy* and equality. This was a factor in the Nore mutiny, whose leader, Richard Parker, was a self-confessed advocate of the ideas of Tom Paine. The threat of a French invasion during 1797 was real and the navy felt that it could not afford merely to crush the mutinies. Thus, although some leading mutineers were executed, the mutinies themselves did lead to increased pay and better conditions, although life on men-of-war remained extremely harsh and unpalatable, especially for those who had recently been forcibly recruited in large numbers from civilian life.

(See also *Camperdown, Battle of (1797); Napoleonic Wars.*)

Navigation Acts: legislation designed to advantage British trade against foreign competition by placing duties on imports. Fierce 'protectionist' duties had been placed on goods by the Acts of 1651, 1660, 1661 and 1663 in an attempt to break the commercial supremacy of the Dutch. These came under increasing attack during the late eighteenth and early nineteenth centuries when Adam Smith's *free trade* doctrines were gaining ever wider support. Also, British need for *overseas trade* during the *French Revolutionary* and *Napoleonic wars* meant that a policy of protection worked strongly against Britain's interests. In consequence, the Acts fell largely into disuse before they were finally abolished by an Act of repeal in 1849.

(See also *mercantilism; laissez-faire.*)

navvies: colloquial name given to those 'navigators' who worked on constructing the canals and, especially, the railways of Britain from the late eighteenth century onwards. The time of peak demand coincided with that of acute labour shortage, and later famine, in *Ireland* and a large proportion of navvies were young Irishmen attracted by the prospect of reasonable pay and able to move around the country as construction work required. Navvies lodged in shanty towns which gained a reputations for disreputable, and often drunken, behaviour.

(See also *canals; railways.*)

Nelson, Horatio (Viscount and Sicilian Duke of Brontë): naval commander. Born the son of an Anglican clergyman in Norfolk in 1758, he joined the navy at the age of twelve and saw service in both the East and West Indies and in the Arctic. He owed the range of his experience partly to family connections, but he impressed almost all of the superiors with whom he came into contact with his exceptional dedication to duty and his flair. Some also commented on a certain foolhardiness in one who used unorthodox methods, teetering in some cases on the edge of insubordination. He gained rapid promotion via service in the Mediterranean from 1793 and became an Admiral in 1797. He suffered a number of injuries while on active service:

1794	at Calvi, Corsica: he lost an eye	
1797	at St Vincent: an internal rupture	
1797	at Santa Cruz (Canaries): he lost his right arm	
1798	at *Battle of the Nile*: severe head wound, probably contributing to some mental instability	

He had decisive victories at the Nile and also at *Copenhagen* but he is best remembered for two things:

- his romantic attachment to Lady Emma Hamilton, wife of Sir William Hamilton, British emissary to the kingdoms of Naples and Sicily, which occurred during Nelson's involvement in the politics of the two states at the turn of the century
- when commander of the Mediterranean fleet (1803–5) his decisive victory over the French and Spanish fleets at *Trafalgar* at which battle he was fatally wounded

He was a difficult and headstrong colleague who became a national hero. He was given a barony after his success at the Nile and became a viscount after the Battle of Copenhagen. His grasp of strategy and his willingness to attempt the unexpected earned decisive victories during the *French Revolutionary* and *Napoleonic wars* which made a substantial contribution to Britain's ability to sustain the war effort at times when defeat seemed probable.

'new model' unions: term used by *Sidney* and *Beatrice Webb* at the end of the nineteenth century to describe *trade unions* organised by skilled workers. The supposed 'model' was the Amalgamated Society of Engineers, founded in 1851, which developed a national organisation, had high subscription rates and used its labour scarcity to negotiate good wages and conditions from employers. The Webbs had in mind the skilled workers' reaction to the collapse of the Grand National Consolidated Trades Union in 1834 but skilled workers had dominated trade unionism at least since unions had been legalised in 1824–25 and would continue to do so until the late 1880s. There was nothing particularly novel about the foundation of the engineers' union, although it accelerated the trend towards national, rather than local, organisation.

(See also *new unions; skilled workers.*)

New Party: organisation formed by *Oswald Mosley* after he left the *Labour Party* in 1930. It campaigned on policies designed to reduce unemployment. Its life was brief. It fielded 24 candidates in the 1931 *general election*, winning 0.2 per cent of the total vote. Its failure was one factor which persuaded Mosley to abandon parliamentary politics and establish a *fascist* party in Britain.

new towns: term used to describe towns created under the New Towns Act, 1946. Their models were the so-called 'garden cities', most notably Letchworth (1903) and Welwyn (1920) which had been created to relieve congestion in London. After *World War II* the need was for more extensive 'overspill' developments and also for the creation of purpose-built urban environments to meet the needs of urban society ravaged by bombing. The Act established 'new town development corporations' with extensive powers both to develop entirely new urban environments and to extend existing villages and small towns. New towns created within commuting distance of London included Basildon (Essex), Crawley (Sussex) and Stevenage (Hertfordshire), but the largest of all was Milton Keynes (Buckinghamshire), established in 1967. County Durham established three new towns, Newton Aycliffe, Peterlee and Washington. 'Satellite' new towns outside existing conurbations included Skelmersdale (for Liverpool) and Redditch (in Worcestershire, for Birmingham).

The six Scottish new towns were Cumbernauld, East Kilbride, Glenrothes, Irvine, Livingstone and Stonehouse.

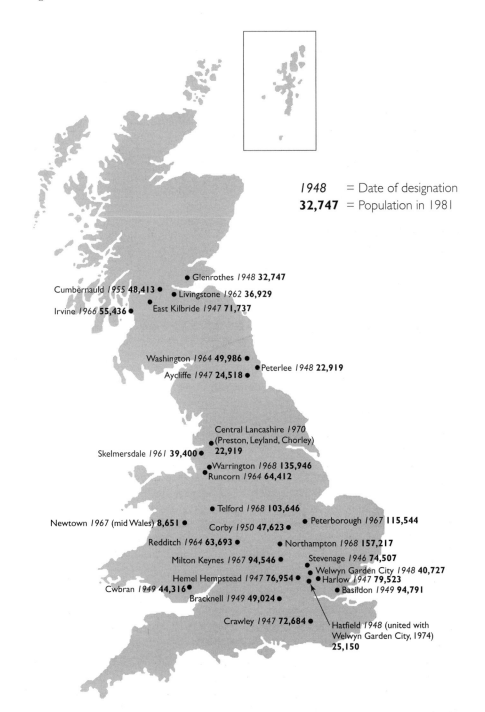

1948 = Date of designation
32,747 = Population in 1981

Glenrothes *1948* **32,747**
Cumbernauld *1955* **48,413**
Livingstone *1962* **36,929**
Irvine *1966* **55,436**
East Kilbride *1947* **71,737**

Washington *1964* **49,986**
Peterlee *1948* **22,919**
Aycliffe *1947* **24,518**

Central Lancashire *1970*
(Preston, Leyland, Chorley)
22,919
Skelmersdale *1961* **39,400**
Warrington *1968* **135,946**
Runcorn *1964* **64,412**

Telford *1968* **103,646**
Newtown *1967* (mid Wales) **8,651**
Peterborough *1967* **115,544**
Corby *1950* **47,623**
Redditch *1964* **63,693**
Northampton *1968* **157,217**
Milton Keynes *1967* **94,546**
Stevenage *1946* **74,507**
Welwyn Garden City *1948* **40,727**
Hemel Hempstead *1947* **76,954**
Harlow *1947* **79,523**
Cwbran *1949* **44,316**
Basildon *1949* **94,791**
Bracknell *1949* **49,024**

Crawley *1947* **72,684**
Hatfield *1948* (united with
Welwyn Garden City, 1974)
25,150

new unions: term conventionally applied to *trade unions* of unskilled workers which developed from the late 1880s. Contrasted with so-called '*new model unions*' by appealing to all and by their low entry fees, these unions often developed out of successful strikes, such as those by the *dock* and *gas* workers and also by the *match girls*. Although, after the first flush of success, they needed support and organisational assistance from established union leaders, these 'new unions' provided the catalyst which made trade unionism into a mass movement of working people. Before the late 1880s, the total membership of trade unions was about half-a-million. By the outbreak of *World War I*, this had expanded to over four million. A significant minority of this membership was women who had been virtually excluded from trade unionism for most of the nineteenth century.

New Zealand: former British colony and dominion comprising two main islands (north and south) in the South Pacific ocean. Although Captain Cook visited the islands on three occasions, the first British settlement was of missionaries in 1814. In the 1820s and 1830s about 2000 Europeans were based there involved in trading and land acquisition. This led to substantial disorder, both between settlers and with the indigenous Maori population. In 1837, a New Zealand Association was formed, supported by both *Durham* and *Edward Gibbon Wakefield*, to promote settlement. The *Whig* government agreed reluctantly to annexing the territory in 1840, partly to protect Maori and British citizens from further violence and partly to forestall unwanted French colonisation. It was established as a colony in its own right in 1841.

As settlement increased, especially after the discovery of gold in Otago in 1852, the Maoris felt increasingly threatened and unprotected and a number of wars resulted which were not concluded until 1872. The colony developed as a successful exporter of wool and dairy produce and had considerable, European-dominated, self-government from 1846 when its first colonial constitution was agreed. The country was divided into six provinces in 1852 and representative government was acquired in 1856. New Zealand became a self-governing dominion in 1907, when its population was about one million.

(See also *Empire, British; Commonwealth, British; Waitangi, Treaty of.*)

Newcastle Commission: Royal Commission, sitting under the chairmanship of the 5th Duke of Newcastle, from 1858 to 1861, to consider the state of education for working people. Its main concern was the rising cost of education to the State, through government grants made to *Church of England* and *nonconformist* schools but it was also concerned at the variable quality and lack of overall direction in education. It recommended that:

- school boards be established to regularise educational provision in all towns of more than 40,000 population
- a system of basic examination to test the quality of education in state-supported schools be established
- the level of grants should be dependent on demonstration of satisfactory performance, both in terms of attendance and examination results

Palmerston's Liberal government refused to set up school boards but introduced the *Revised Code* in 1862 which adopted the Commission's other recommendations.

(See also *Clarendon Commission; Education Act, 1870; Kay-Shuttleworth, James; Lowe, Robert; state education; Taunton Commission.*)

Newcastle Programme: programme of radical reforms adopted by the Liberal Party when in opposition in 1891. The context for this initiative was the loss of many previous Liberal members and supporters after *Gladstone*'s declaration of support for Irish *Home Rule* and the need to unite those who remained in the party behind a credible programme of reform. Since many of those who had left were the less reform-inclined *Whigs*, this should have been relatively easy, but the programme lacked coherence, giving the impression to many observers that it was a hastily compiled 'shopping list' whose real purpose had been to prevent further defections. In addition to continued support for Home Rule, the main elements in the programme were:

- land reform, so that landowners were more heavily taxed on 'unearned income'
- the establishment of district and parish councils
- the abolition of plural voting (people having more than one vote because they qualified both as individuals and as ratepayers)
- payment of MPs and parliaments elected at least once every three years
- *disestablishment* of the Churches of Wales and Scotland
- local vetoes on the sale of drink

Later Liberal governments acted on many of these proposals but they had little immediate impact. They reflected the extent to which the *Liberal Party* was now dependent on support from the *nonconformist middle classes* and was also disproportionately influential in Scotland and Wales. It alarmed many middle-class voters and proved to be a strong indicator of the extent to which the *Conservative Party* was now seen by most property owners as the sounder party to support.

Newman (John Henry), Cardinal: clergyman who converted from the *Church of England* to the Roman Catholic church. Born in 1801, he was Vicar of the Oxford University Church from 1828 and became increasingly influential in the High-Church, Anglo-Catholic *Oxford Movement*. He wrote many books and articles and his famous 'Tract 90' (1841) argued that one of the Church of England's 'Thirty-nine Articles of Faith' (originally drawn up in the reign of Elizabeth I) was supported by decisions made at much the same time by the Roman Catholic reformist Council of Trent. There was thus no reason why the Church of England should not join with Catholicism. This argument provoked furious controversy which saw Newman leave the Church of England and be received into the Roman Catholic church in 1845. Most of his fellow 'Tractarians' (so called from the 'Tracts' in which Anglo-Catholics argued their position) remained within the state Church. Newman became a very active Catholic, founding 'oratories' in London and Birmingham and a new Catholic university in Dublin in 1854. He wrote hymns and an extended religious poem 'The Dream of Gerontius' which later inspired the Catholic composer *Edward Elgar* to produce his most famous oratorio. He also engaged in religious controversy with the 'Christian socialist' *Charles Kingsley* in the 1860s, an intellectual battle which led to the appearance of his 'Apologia pro vita sua' (defence of the principles on which he had lived his life). He was made a cardinal by Pope Pius IX in 1877 and died in 1891.

newspapers: publications which provide news, comment, entertainment and advertisement to a wide audience. The first newspapers were produced in the seventeenth century and a considerable expansion occurred in the eighteenth century, with the development of a large number of regional newspapers.

Early nineteenth century

By the beginning of the nineteenth century, more than 100 regional newspapers were published in England alone. They were frequently subject to taxes which aimed to put them outside the price range of skilled working people, who, during the *French* and *Napoleonic wars*, were reading *radical* newspapers in large numbers and supporting *parliamentary reform* and attacks on the *aristocracy*. Radical writers, with some justice, called these 'taxes on knowledge' and produced 'unstamped newspapers' (that is, those which were published without paying these taxes and, thus, in defiance of the law). Radical newspapers, such as *Cobbett's 'Political Register'* in the 1810s or the *Chartist 'Northern Star'* in the 1840s greatly outsold more 'loyal' or 'establishment' newspapers such as '*The Times*' or the 'Morning Chronicle'. The abolition of newspaper taxes increased their circulation, a development also encouraged by the growth of literacy resulting from the expansion of education after the 1830s.

Later nineteenth century

Newspaper owners knew that there were profits to be made by publishing newspapers whose purpose was at least as much to entertain as to inform, or by presenting news in a more dramatic, or popular, manner. This perception lay behind the so-called 'newspaper revolution' usually associated with *Alfred Harmsworth* and the arrival of papers such as the '*Daily Mail'*. Changes in the market for newspapers preceded Harmsworth and newspapers such as 'Reynolds' Magazine' had been publishing lurid stories of crime since the 1840s. George Newnes's 'Tit Bits' (1881) also preceded Harmsworth's career. The emergence of mass-circulation dailies revolutionised not only the market but also the technology of newspaper production.

Twentieth century

The market for newspapers became increasingly polarised between 'quality' papers, such as 'The Times', 'Daily Telegraph' and 'Manchester Guardian' and 'popular' ones, led by the 'Daily Mail', 'Daily Express' and 'Daily Mirror'. Not surprisingly, there was a broad social imbalance in newspaper readerships. The better educated and the middle classes tended to read the 'qualities' and, for a time between the *world wars*, it was said that any leading figure had to know what was in 'The Times'. The working classes tended to read popular newspapers, although some who wished to have more depth of information and analysis would buy a 'quality'. Until the 1960s, however, the popular newspapers placed the main emphasis upon providing their readers with news.

Broader changes within the media, involving the development of *television* as an important vehicle for news, changes in newspaper ownership (including the emergence of multi-national news corporations such as that headed by Rupert Murdoch) and also social changes increased the division between newspapers. Quality newspapers tended to increase in size, offering more 'investigative' journalism and 'in-depth' analysis. Newspapers such as the 'Daily Mail' and the 'Daily Express' presented news but in lesser depth and, sometimes, rather more sensationally. From the 1960s, they tended to be seen as 'middle-market' newspapers. The main change was the development of popular newspapers which openly placed the emphasis on entertainment. Newspapers such as 'The Sun', 'The Star' and even the 'Daily Mirror' (which had been an effective campaigning journal in the 1940s and 1950s) gave over the great bulk of their space to pictures, to information about the world of popular entertainment, especially soap operas, the lives of the royal family (which they increasingly pictured as a form of soap-opera anyway) and sport. Politics hardly featured, except when politicians were involved in scandal one kind or another, or in the approach to general elections, when editors and proprietors would urge support for one political party or another, often in the same terms, and with as little rationale, as support for a football team. Critics argued that such crudities debased the political process. Such observations had no effect on sales. These papers had huge circulations. At the end of the twentieth century, newspaper circulations were under pressure from competition by television and the Internet. The extraordinary range and diversity of newspapers in Britain remained, however, a distinctive feature of its society.

(See also *class consciousness; middle classes; Rothermere, Viscount.*)

Nigeria: former British colony in West Africa and member of the *British Commonwealth*. Britain first became interested in the territory in the late seventeenth and early eighteenth centuries for trading purposes, including the trading of slaves, cocoa and palm oil. Britain annexed Lagos in 1853 when anxious to end the slave trade in the region. It intervened in tribal rivalries in the 1850s, formally annexing much of the territory in 1861. As *missionaries* and explorers opened up further land away from the coast, so other European powers became involved in the area and colonial territorial boundaries were established by treaties with France and Germany in 1890. Further territory run by the Royal Niger Company was added to the *British Empire* in 1900. Only in 1914 was the more heavily populated north added to the south as an integrated colony. Religious, economic and tribal rivalries remained, however, not least because the south of the colony was so much more prosperous than the north. The country gained independence in 1960 with these tensions unresolved.

(See also *Africa, Scramble for; slavery.*)

Nightingale, Florence: pioneer of the nursing profession. Born into a wealthy family in 1820, she was educated in classical subjects and found herself frustrated by the limited opportunities for work available to her. She used money from her family to found an Institution for Sick Gentlewomen in London in 1853 and went to the Crimea in 1854 to head a nursing team at the invitation of the Prime Minister, *Aberdeen*. She worked at Scutari not under army discipline, where her organisation, attention to details of cleanliness and sanitation and willingness to work long hours all contributed to a massive fall in the death rate from battle wounds. Her work gained her the affectionate title: 'Lady of the Lamp', though she was anxious to avoid any sentimentalisation of her work. She was invalided back to Britain herself in 1856, but continued to devote herself to nursing and to providing worthwhile careers for women. She established a nursing school at St Thomas's Hospital in 1860, helped to reform army medical services and made suggestions for the improvement of sanitation and medical care in *India*. She turned nursing into a true profession, her work being instrumental in establishing guides to good practice. She was much more concerned to see nursing established as a proper career for women than she was to see women get the vote. She died in 1910.

(See also *suffragettes; women, legal and occupational status of.*)

Nile, Battle of the: naval engagement during the *French Revolutionary Wars*, otherwise known as the Battle of Aboukir Bay. Fought on 1 and 2 August 1798, a small British fleet under the command of *Nelson* caught the French fleet under Brueys unawares, attacked at night and annihilated it. One of the most decisive naval battles of the French wars, its strategic importance was substantial. It left Napoleon's army in Egypt stranded without supplies and precipitated his retreat from North Africa.

nonconformity: name given to those Protestants in England who did not accept the doctrines of the *Church of England*. Since the Church of England was the established church, nonconformists experienced discrimination in terms of status and in political and educational matters. Until the repeal of the *Test and Corporations Act* in 1828, nonconformists were not entitled to hold public office in central or local government. They used their new legal rights to good effect in many towns. After the passing of the *Municipal Corporations Act* in 1835, many councils were dominated by *middle-class* nonconformists. Nonconformists were also a vital source of strength for the *Liberal Party*. The religious census of 1851 also revealed that virtually one half of all church or chapel attendances on 'Census Sunday' had been to a nonconformist service. Restrictions continued to be placed on where they could marry and they were also supposed to pay tithes to an Anglican clergyman and church rates to support the upkeep of Anglican churches until 1868. The last significant civil restrictions on nonconformists concerned rights over burial and these were abolished in the 1880s. During the twentieth century, the number of nonconformists declined steadily as part of the wider process of secularisation and nonconformity also lost most of its nineteenth-century vigour and political influence.

(See also *dissenter, Methodist Church; secularism.*)

Nore Mutiny: see *Naval Mutinies, 1797*

Norman, Montagu (Lord Norman of St Clere): banker. Born in 1871, he was best known as Governor of the *Bank of England* during the period 1920–44. In this powerful position, he was a staunch (his opponents said obsessive) supporter of 'sound money', balanced budgets and the attempt to return Britain to the economic conditions which held before *World War I*. He advised *Winston Churchill*, who was not economically literate, to return to the gold standard at a high rate against the US dollar, which made British exports uncompetitive and contributed to high levels of unemployment. He also urged the Labour government to cut expenditure and reduce its financial deficit in 1931 in order to avoid a complete collapse of the currency, similar to that which had devastated Germany in 1923. His economic views were entirely opposed to those of reflationists such as *J M Keynes*. He was ennobled in 1943 and died in 1950.

(See also *Baldwin, Stanley; economic policy; MacDonald, Ramsay; National Government.*)

North America Act, 1867: constitutional settlement for *Canada*. By it:

- a federal 'dominion' of Canada was created comprising the territories of Ontario, Quebec, New Brunswick and Nova Scotia

- the new dominion had full internal self-government; the United Kingdom retained control only of foreign affairs

In 1870 Manitoba and the North-West Territories were added to Canada and British Columbia followed in 1871.

(See also *Commonwealth, British; Empire, British*.)

North Atlantic Treaty Organisation (NATO): alliance system negotiated by the Western powers in 1949. Dominated militarily and economically by the *United States of America*, its main purpose was to defend Western Europe against what was perceived as the growing threat of the Soviet Union and Eastern communism. There were twelve original signatories, of which the United Kingdom was one. NATO remained a formidable organisation throughout the period known as the 'Cold War' between East and West which lasted from 1945 until the 1980s, although relations were thawing from the mid-1970s. It contributed fully to the development of nuclear weapons as a means of deterring aggression. With the collapse of communism from 1989 to 1991, NATO's military activities were scaled down.

North Sea gas: otherwise known as 'natural gas', its main constituent is methane. It began to supersede coal gas from the 1970s and was by the end of the twentieth century the main source of gas in the United Kingdom. The main advantages of North Sea over coal gas are its lower toxicity and its greater efficiency in providing energy.

(See also *gas industry*.)

North Sea oil: large reserve of energy discovered in sedimentary rocks below the North Sea in 1969. Oil in usable quantities in the UK sector of the North Sea was discovered for the first time in 1975 and became one of the most important commodities for the British economy in the last quarter of the twentieth century. Britain, like other industrialised countries, had been increasingly large consumers of oil as the *motor car industry* expanded rapidly from the 1920s. Since oil had to be exported from politically unstable or sensitive areas, especially the Middle East, the dangers of inadequate supply or rapid price rises were ever-present and had created substantial problems, especially in the years 1967–73. North Sea oil was extracted by the multinational companies BP and Shell from 1975; by 1983, Britain was established as the fifth largest oil producer in the world and a net exporter of oil. Both the economic and political consequences were substantial. Although the development of Thatcherite economic policies in part obscured its effect, domestic oil production enormously eased endemic balance-of-payments problems, whereby Britain imported much more by value than it exported. The availability of North Sea oil enabled *Margaret Thatcher* to sustain policies of low direct taxation. Also, since most of the oil was produced offshore from Scotland, making Aberdeen one of the fastest growing and most prosperous cities of the 1970s and 1980s, North Sea oil was argued by Scottish nationalists to strengthen the case for independence from England. Nationalists used the image of 'Scotland's oil' to suggest a prosperous future for a small, but vigorous and economically independent country within the European Economic Community.

(See also *oil crisis, 1973–74*.)

Northcliffe (Harmsworth, Alfred), 1st Viscount: journalist and newspaper proprietor. Born in Ireland in 1865, he came to London as a boy and made his career in newspapers. He founded the *'Daily Mail'* and the 'Daily Mirror' and made a fortune from popular journalism early in the twentieth century and used it to make himself powerful both as a moulder of popular opinion and as a figure to whom politicians listened – sometimes fearfully. He was the first newspaper proprietor to demonstrate the power of the press in an age of mass communication and was ennobled by *Lloyd George* in 1917, largely for his mission to the United States which played a part in bringing that country into the war. Lord *Beaverbook* called him 'the greatest figure who ever strode down Fleet Street' and a popular joke which circulated just after the end of *World War I* epitomised his influence: 'Have you heard? The Prime Minister has resigned and Northcliffe has sent for the King'. His brother, Harold, Viscount *Rothermere* (1868–1940) continued the tradition of powerful 'press barons' after his death in 1922.

(See also *newspapers; Rothermere, Viscount.*)

Northcote, Sir Stafford (1st Earl of Iddesleigh): civil servant and Peelite and Conservative politician. Born in 1818, he was private secretary to *William Gladstone* in the 1840s and entered Parliament in 1855. He was one of the authors of the *Northcote–Trevelyan Report* on recruitment to the Civil Service. He joined the Conservative government at *Disraeli*'s persuasion in 1859 and thereafter became one of the party's most senior figures. His major offices were:

- President of the Board of Trade, 1866–67
- Secretary of State for India, 1867–68
- Chancellor of the Exchequer, 1874–80
- joint leader of the *Conservative Party* (with *Salisbury*), 1881–85
- Foreign Secretary, 1886

He was an amiable colleague and an effective minister. His tenure of joint leader of the party was less than happy because the Conservatives were anxious to make maximum impact in their opposition to Gladstone, not least over foreign affairs and *Ireland*, and Northcote's previously close personal association with him made this difficult. Salisbury was therefore anxious to ease him out of a central role. He gave him an earldom in 1885 and made it clear that his tenure of the office of Foreign Secretary would be only brief. Northcote, however, died very suddenly early in 1887.

(See also *Churchill, Lord Randolph; Home Rule Bill, 1886.*)

Northcote–Trevelyan Report: government report on the future of the *Civil Service*, compiled in 1853–54 by Sir Charles Trevelyan, an assistant secretary at the Treasury and Sir Stafford Northcote, who had been secretary to *William Gladstone*. It recommended the recruitment by competitive examination of two classes of civil servants, the 'intellectual' for the higher grades and the 'mechanical' for the lower. Its aim was to reduce the influence of patronage in the selection of government personnel and to improve the efficiency of the service. It led to the establishment of the Civil Service Commission in 1855.

(See also *Aberdeen, Earl of.*)

Northern Ireland: territory created in the north of *Ireland* by the *Anglo-Irish Treaty*. It comprised six counties: Antrim, Down, Armagh, Londonderry, Fermanagh and Tyrone and was somewhat smaller than the historic *Ulster*. Northern Ireland remained part of the *United Kingdom* when the remainder of Ireland became independent. The Northern Ireland Parliament, usually known as *Stormont*, was created by the *Government of Ireland Act, 1920*, as part of a constitutional settlement with three main elements:

- a Governor of the Province, appointed by the Crown
- most internal matters delegated to a Northern Ireland Parliament containing 52 elected members
- Northern Ireland sent twelve MPs to the UK *Parliament* (increased to seventeen after the 1979 general election and eighteen after the 1992 election to reflect the absence of Stormont)

As intended, the Northern Ireland government remained firmly loyal to the union with the United Kingdom and its institutions were dominated by Protestants. All six Northern Ireland prime ministers were from the *Ulster Unionist Party*, which never won fewer than 32 of the 52 Stormont seats in any of the twelve elections held in the years 1921–72. Unionists normally outnumbered nationalists by a ratio of about 4:1. Since similar Unionist and Protestant majorities obtained in local government, much discrimination against the *Roman Catholic* minority was encountered. Resentment by a Catholic community which felt itself underprivileged in matters of representation, housing and employment boiled over in the late 1960s when Catholic marches led to violence between what had become two entrenched communities.

The UK government's solution, after the violence of the late 1960s and early 1970s had claimed almost 1,000 lives, was to pass the 'Northern Ireland (Temporary Provisions) Act' in 1972. This suspended Stormont and intoduced direct rule from Westminster. A new UK *Cabinet* post, Secretary of State for Northern Ireland, was created and what rapidly became known as 'Direct Rule' was imposed. Attempts at power-sharing and constitutional rearrangement in 1974–76 failed. The government of Northern Ireland was put on a new footing based on power-sharing between the religious communities in 1998.

(See also *Faulkener, Brian; O'Neill, Terence; Ulster Volunteer Force*.)

'Northern Star': *Chartist* newspaper. Owned by *Feargus O'Connor* and published weekly from Leeds (1837–44) and London (1844–52), it became the leading organ of Chartist opinion and had higher circulation figures than other provincial journals for most of its life. At its peak, in 1839, it sold almost 50,000 copies, and outsold all other *newspapers*, but its actual readership was far higher. The purchase price, 4½d (2p), put it outside the scope of all but the wealthier sections of the working classes but it was also bought to be read more widely by others in pubs, reading rooms and even lecture halls. O'Connor gave his editors, William Hill, *George Julian Harney* and G A Fleming, free rein, encouraging diversity of opinion. In consequence, 'Northern Star' is much the most fruitful source of information about working-class politics, opinion and culture during the years of its publication.

Norton, Caroline: novelist and pioneer of women's rights. Born in 1808, the grand-daughter of the playwright Richard Brinsley Sheridan, she made a disastrous marriage to the aristocratic Hon. George Norton in 1827. From the results of this flowed many of her campaigns. He attempted to divorce her on what appears to have been a trumped-up charge of her adultery with the *Prime Minister* Lord *Melbourne* and continued to ill-treat her. He also tried to take control of her earnings as a writer. Her campaigns were responsible for the Custody of Infants Act, 1839, which gave courts the power to award custody of children to mothers of 'unblemished character' up to the age of seven years. She also campaigned for married women to have independent access to their own property which was achieved in a succession of Acts, beginning with the Married Woman's Property Act, 1870. Though little read nowadays, her most famous novel was 'Lost and Saved' (1863) which drew powerful attention to the 'double standard' obtaining in sexual behaviour for men (who were rarely punished for 'indiscretions') and women (who frequently were and whose lives were often entirely ruined). She died in 1877.

(See also *women, legal and occupational status of.*)

nuclear power: generation of power by controlled nuclear fission. Nuclear technology closely followed progress on nuclear weapons after *World War II.* The development of nuclear power came under the control of the Atomic Energy Authority and the first nuclear power station was opened on the remote Cumberland coast at Calder Hall (later Windscale and Sellafield) in 1956. Its power was generated by a reactor designed to produce plutonium for nuclear bombs. Eighteen so-called 'Magnox' reactors were built between 1956 and 1971, when production was switched to Advanced Cooled Reactors. For the Government, the potential advantage was the generation of limitless energy at low cost which would reduce, and eventually even remove, Britain's dependence on imported energy. The development of *North Sea oil*, the increasing revelation that the generation of nuclear energy could not be made entirely safe and spectacular disasters such as those at Three Mile Island (USA) and Chernobyl (USSR) all contributed to making it a much less attractive option from the 1980s. Furthermore, the costs of waste disposal and the decommissioning of now obsolete, but still nuclear reactive, plants proved much more costly and difficult than had originally been intended. Nuclear power therefore failed to fulfil the promise of the 1950s, 1960s and early 1970s.

Oastler, Richard: factory reformer and anti-Poor Law agitator. Born in Leeds in 1789, he worked for many years as the estate steward of a landowner near Halifax. He is perhaps best described as a 'Tory humanitarian'. He opposed many aspects of the new industrial society in which he lived and was especially critical of the new political economy of *laissez-faire* and *utilitarianism*. He was also a strong supporter of the *Church of England* and the monarchy. Like many Anglicans he was strongly anti-Catholic. He believed that those with wealth and privilege should take a proper concern for the lower orders, who, in their turn should be respectful (an attitude of 'paternalism and deference'). He campaigned for a maximum ten hours' day for factory employees and launched strong, satirical attacks on what he saw as the dehumanising effects of the Poor Law Amendment Act of 1834. Many of these were published in 'The Fleet Papers', a journal he wrote in the early 1840s from the Fleet prison where he had been placed for debt after losing his job because of his political campaigns. He died in 1861.

(See also *Catholic Emancipation Act, 1829; Factory Acts; Poor Laws; radicalism.*)

O'Brien, James (Bronterre): Chartist. Normally known as 'Bronterre' he was born in Ireland in 1805 and trained as a lawyer. He was one of the intellectually most able of Chartist leaders and was known as the 'Schoolmaster of Chartism'. He wrote well-argued and perceptive articles in both the 'Poor Man's Guardian', the leading *radical* journal of the 1830s, which he edited, and the '*Northern Star*'. After supporting 'physical force' in the early stages of the movement, he increasingly advocated *socialism* and the nationalisation of land as the best means of improving conditions for working people. He died in 1864.

(See also *Chartism; O'Connor, Feargus.*)

O'Connell, Daniel: Irish Catholic politician and nationalist. He was born into one of *Ireland*'s relatively few prosperous Catholic landowning families in 1775. He trained as a lawyer and practised successfully as a barrister. In 1823, he founded the Catholic Association which developed into a powerful pressure group which involved the *Roman Catholic* priesthood and posed a major threat to Protestant control of Ireland within the *United Kingdom*. It called for:

- *Catholic emancipation*
- an end to the payment of tithes to the (Anglican) Church of Ireland
- Repeal of the *Act of Union* – although it is important to note that he did not support full independence for Ireland. He wanted extensively devolved government, but envisaged Ireland as part of the *British Empire* and still a monarchy: 'one King, two countries' as he called it
- land reform favouring greater Catholic ownership

His victory in a by-election at County Clare in 1828 forced *Wellington* and *Peel* to concede Catholic emancipation in 1829 and this proved to be O'Connell's greatest achievement. He remained active as leader of an Irish nationalist group at Westminster in the 1830s and 1840s and supported extensions of the franchise, but his agreement with *Melbourne* to keep the *Whigs* in power after 1835 led him to support measures such as the Poor Law Amendment Act which distanced him from many British *radicals*. He did, however, support a wide range of reforms, including universal manhood suffrage and the abolition of *slavery*. He was Lord Mayor of Dublin in 1841–42. He formed the Repeal Association in 1841 which continued his struggle for the hated Act of Union and wrote articles in 'The Nation' arguing the repeal case. Trying to repeat his successes with the Catholic Association, he summoned a mass meeting at Clontarf in 1843 in the hope of threatening the British government into granting repeal but *Peel*'s government called his bluff and, never in support of violence in furtherance of political objectives, he backed away from confrontation. The *Irish Potato Famine* dominated his last years and he made many emotional appeals to the Government for aid. He died in 1847 while on a pilgrimage to see the Pope in Rome. In many ways he deserved this nickname of 'The Liberator', though to his supporters he was just as likely to be known as 'The Counsellor' in recognition of his high reputation as a lawyer. His powerful presence, immense moral authority and above all his organisational capacity ignited the flame of Irish nationalism which would not be extinguished.

(See also *Lichfield House Compact*.)

O'Connor, Feargus: Chartist leader. Like *Daniel O'Connell*, with whom he is often confused by students, he was an Irishman who practised as a lawyer, became a Westminster MP (he became the only Chartist Member of Parliament when elected for Nottingham in 1847) and led an important radical protest movement. He was, however, younger than O'Connell – he was born in 1794 – and O'Connell's Catholic Association, which he supported, was an inspiration to him. Unlike O'Connell, also, his main concern was with British, rather than Irish, politics. His ownership of the leading Chartist journal '*Northern Star*' gave him a strong base from which to preach the Chartist message and he was also an extremely powerful orator. His many critics, however, asserted that he used his skills as a speaker to arouse expectations among his followers which could not be met. He was a controversial figure both during his lifetime and afterwards. He was attacked from both sides of the Chartist movement. *William Lovett* and other 'moral-force' leaders attacked the violence of his speeches and his apparent lack of concern to educate working people to be worthy of the vote they sought. *Bronterre O'Brien* and *Ernest Jones* attacked him for not advocating *socialism* and for appearing to support, via his National Land Company (1845–51), an outmoded system of landownership. O'Connor's 'land plan' offered Chartists the opportunity of leaving the towns and becoming settled on rural smallholdings. O'Brien dismissively suggested that O'Connor was thus supporting 'the hellish principle of landlordism'. Many contemporaries believed that O'Connor's leadership was too self-centred, divided Chartism and weakened its impact. In recent years, more sympathetic historians have concentrated on his strengths as a leader and his tolerance (unlike some of his critics) of diverse opinions. Above all, they have pointed to his ability to convey powerful, straightforward messages which enthused whole sections of the working classes which had not previously been politically aware. The truth may lie in between these extremes. Modern historians have perhaps not sufficiently emphasised the lack of clarity in much of O'Connor's thought, his tendency to exaggerate and the lack of organisational ability to match his capacity to enthuse and make converts to Chartism. The decline of his latter years was sad. He never properly recovered from the failure of the last mass Chartist protest in 1848, which he led. He was declared insane in 1852 and died in 1855.

(See also *Chartism.*)

oil crisis, 1973–4: crisis caused by large increases in the price of oil exported from the Middle East. The immediate context was the failure of the Arab States in their war against Israel. Feeling that Israel was receiving too much support from the Western powers, and especially the *United States*, the Arab-dominaed Organisation of Petroleum Exporting Countries (OPEC) decided to use its economic power. It reduced production of oil and increased its price. After a long period since 1950 when oil-price stability had been one of the main reasons for the long post-war economic boom, the suddenness of the change caused crises in most Western countries, and especially in Britain where *inflation* was already a major difficulty. It also fuelled political instability in Britain and encouraged fundamental rethinking about the direction of *economic policy.*

(See also *Heath, Edward; Keynesian economics; monetarism; North Sea oil; Thatcherism; three-day week.*)

Old Age Pensions Act, 1908: legislation passed as part of the *Liberal* welfare reforms during *Asquith*'s government. The Act represented the climax of a campaign for financial support for old people which had gathered pace in the 1880s and 1890s, with the help of politicians such as *Joseph Chamberlain,* and was strengthened by revelations about the causes of poverty by *Charles Booth* and *Seebohm Rowntree.* The example of Germany, which had introduced pensions in the 1880s, was also important. Many different schemes were discussed and the situation was complicated by the fact that *friendly societies* had been making financial provision for those who had been able to pay contributions into a fund. The main features of the Liberal scheme were:

- it was 'non-contributory' (i.e., the government funded the scheme out of taxation rather than insurance payments)
- it was not payable until the age of 70 (many had urged a starting date of 65, but the Government was concerned about the overall cost of the scheme if support began too early)
- rates of payment were modest: a single person was entitled to 5s (25p) a week and a married couple to 7s 6d (37½p)
- payment was only made to those who:
  - earned less than £31.10s (£31.50) a year
  - had no criminal convictions, and
  - had never received help from the *Poor Law*

In all, about half-a-million pensioners were entitled to receive the first payments which became due on 1 January 1909.

The scheme proved too expensive to sustain and later pension changes, although reducing the qualification age to 65 (which was done by *Neville Chamberlain* in 1925), saw the cost transferred to National Insurance rather than being funded by taxation.

(See also *Lloyd George, David; National Insurance Act, 1911 and 1946; welfare state.*)

Olivier, Laurence (Baron Olivier of Brighton): actor and director. Born in 1907, he was widely considered the greatest actor of his generation. His range was wide and encompassed both theatre and film but he excelled in the more dramatic Shakesperean roles, such as Henry V and Richard III, both of which he transferred successfully to film. He established his Hollywood reputation playing the wild, romantic Heathcliff in 'Wuthering Heights' (1939) and his career tended on both film and screen to be most successful in parts which emphasised earthy sensuality, in contrast to that of his great rival *John Gielgud*. The most remarkable achievement of a patchy later career, in which (like Gielgud) he appeared in a number of films of dubious artistic merit, was the creation of the seedy vaudeville entertainer Archie Rice in John Osborne's 'The Entertainer' (1957). He transferred this role to film in 1960. He was dogged by ill-health in later years but became, in 1970, the first actor to be elevated to the peerage. He died in 1989.

Omdurman, Battle of: battle fought in the Sudan in September 1898. It represented the climax of a campaign to destroy the authority of the 'Mahdi', a religious leader who had challenged the government of British-controlled Egypt in the 1880s. In 1895, British forces under *Kitchener* began a campaign against the Dervishes and in 1898 captured the Mahdi's holy city of Omdurman, completely destroying his forces in the process.

(See also *Africa, Scramble for; Empire, British.*)

O'Neill, Terence (Baron O'Neill of the Maine): Unionist politician. Born into a prosperous Protestant landowning family in 1914, he became a Unionist MP in *Stormont* in 1946. As *Prime Minister* of Stormont from 1963, he attempted to bring about reforms against a background of increasing sectarian hostility between Protestants and Catholics and the growth of Catholic civil rights agitation. Aware of the need to avoid a split in his own party, he attempted to increase job prospects for Catholics by a policy geared to economic growth. When this failed to reduce tension, he introduced a five-point programme of political reform in local government, but this satisfied few. He resigned in 1969 at the point when the Unionist Party split and took little active part in Ulster politics thereafter. He died in 1990.

(See also *Democratic Unionist Party; Ireland; Paisley, Ian; Ulster Unionist Party.*)

Opium Wars: wars fought against China in 1839–42 and 1856–60 and sometimes known as the 'China Wars'. Trade between Britain and China had always been difficult, largely since Chinese emperors were reluctant to open their country to Western influences. Opium, however, had been regularly traded until 1839, when the Chinese tried to stop it and confiscated all of the substance held in warehouses in Canton.

1839–42

The Chinese fired on British warships, but were heavily outmatched by the large gunboats at the disposal of the East India Company. The British captured *Hong Kong* and were able to negotiate virtually their own terms at the *Treaty of Nanking* which gave them 'favoured-nation status' in commercial dealings with China.

1856–60

The background to this was civil war and virtual collapse of authority in much of China between 1850 and 1864. Many European powers tried to exploit the situation but the specific cause of the war was the arrest of the Chinese crew of the ship 'Arrow' in Canton habour on suspicion of piracy. The ship was registered in Hong Kong and flew the Union Flag. The British and French formally declared war in 1857, occupied Canton and forced China to accept The Treaty of Tien-Tsin in 1858. Its main terms were:

- the Chinese paid an indemnity (effectively a fine)
- the Chinese agreed to legalise the opium trade and open up more of their ports to the trade

In 1859, the British founded what proved to be a valuable naval base at Port Arthur. The Chinese having refused to accept British and French ministers into Peking, the two powers resumed hostilities and landed a force at Pei-Tang in 1860. This forced the Chinese to agree to a further treaty, the Treaty of Peking in 1860. Its main terms were:

- China ceded Kowloon, on the mainland opposite Hong Kong, to Britain
- China agreed to abide by the Treaty of Tien-Tsin

Hostilities were not quite concluded. The British in 1860 destroyed the Imperial Summer Palace in Peking in reprisal for earlier Chinese atrocities.

(See also *Empire, British; trade, overseas.*)

Orange Order: political order in defence of *Ulster* Protestantism. Originally founded in 1795 to celebrate William III's victory at the Battle of the Boyne (1690) and the end of the Catholic James II's attempt to re-establish himself on the throne, it rapidly developed links with the army and helped to put down the Irish rebellion of 1798. An attempt was made to ban it as too inflammatory in the 1820s but it was reconstituted and became in the second half of the nineteenth century the main agency celebrating the supremacy of Protestantism in Ireland. As the movement for *Home Rule*, it associated itself with the *Ulster Unionist Party* and has held marches in the towns of Northern Ireland each year in celebration of the victory at the Boyne. Its membership was exclusively Protestant and it had some of the social functions of a semi-secret or Masonic society. From the time of the 'Troubles' in the late 1960s, Orange activity has been seen by many Catholics as inflammatory, while Orangemen argue that their marches are peaceful and represent a fundamental civil right in a free society.

(See also *Ireland.*)

Orwell, George (Eric Blair): novelist and socialist. He was born in *India* in 1903, the son of a senior civil servant, he served in the police department of the colony of Burma in the 1920s before coming to Britain and developing his career as a writer. He was a humanitarian socialist who became frustrated at the bureaucratic, dehumanising aspects of communism as practised in the Soviet Union. He satirised a soul-less, controlled future in '1984', published in 1949, while his most famous novel, 'Animal Farm' (1945) is an allegory about control and the use of power. He also served in the anti-fascist army during the Spanish Civil War and used his experiences as the basis of 'Homage to Catalonia' (1938). In 'The Road to Wigan Pier' (1937), he wrote a bleak, and mostly factual, account of the experience of unemployment and destitution in the North of England during the 1930s. He died in 1950.

Osborne Judgement, 1909: legal case concerning trade union rights. It arose because a Liberal-supporting member of the Association of Railway Servants sued his union for deducting part of his membership subscription and using it to help fund the infant *Labour Party*. The *House of Lords* ruled that trade unions were not entitled to use any part of their funds to support a political party. The decision was reversed by the *Trade Union Act, 1913* but the question of using union funds for party-political purposes remained a controversial one for the remainder of the twentieth century.

(See also *Liberal Party; trade unions; Trade Dispute and Trade Unions Acts, 1927.*)

'Overlord', Operation: code name given to the Allied operation, which took place from 6 June to 25 August 1944, to land troops on the beaches of Normandy and thus begin the campaign to recapture France and then invade Germany which was crucial to Germany's defeat in *World War II.*

(See also *Montgomery, Bernard.*)

overseas trade: see, *trade, overseas*

Owen, Robert: manufacturer, philanthropist and socialist thinker. Born in Wales in 1771, he moved to Scotland where he made his fortune as a cotton manufacturer in Lancashire and Lanarkshre. His Clydeside factory at New Lanark he developed into a model industrial community, with good quality housing, modern sanitation and a system of education for factory children. In 'A New View of Society' (1813) he propounded the revolutionary doctrine that man's attitude and beliefs were shaped by environment and circumstances and that society should be organised on what he called 'the co-operative principle'. Social advance could only be achieved if masters and workers co-operated for mutual benefit. These ideas became the foundation of the *Co-operative Movement.* They were also influential in the experiment in mass trade unionism which was known as the Grand National Consolidated Trades Union (1834). He died in 1858.

(See also *Factory Acts; trade unions; socialism.*)

Owen, Wilfred: poet. Born in 1893, he volunteered for service in *World War I* in 1915. He was severely wounded at the *Battle of the Somme* and invalided back to Britain. When he returned to duty, he met, and was greatly influenced by, *Siegfried Sassoon.* He began writing poems about the war which are both searing in their intensity and haunting in their evocation of life on the Western Front. The best known are 'Anthem for Doomed Youth' and 'Futility'. His poems formed the basis of *Benjamin Britten*'s 'War Requiem' (1962): 'My subject is War and the pity of War. The poetry is in the pity'. He was killed in action in November 1918, one week before the Armistice which stopped the fighting.

Anthem for Doomed Youth

What passing-bells for these who die as cattle?
– Only the monstrous anger of the guns.
Only the stuttering rifles' rapid rattle
Can patter out their hasty orisons.
No mockeries now for them; no prayers nor bells;
Nor any voice of mourning save the choirs, –
The shrill, demented choirs of wailing shells;
And bugles calling for them from sad shires.

What candles may be held to speed them all?
Not in the hands of boys but in their eyes
Shall shine the holy glimmers of goodbyes.
The pallor of girls' brows shall be their pall;
Their flowers the tenderness of patient minds,
And each slow dusk a drawing-down of blinds.

Oxford Movement: religious movement of the 1830s and 1840s, originally based in the University of Oxford. Its main purpose was to emphasise the importance of liturgy and ritual within the *Church of England* and to combat what it saw as the growing strength of the *evangelical* movement. It was launched by a sermon delivered by *John Keble* in 1833. The other leaders of the movement were *John Henry Newman* and Edward Pusey. Pusey became famous for taking monastic vows within the Anglican communion. They produced a number of so-called 'Tracts for the Times', which spread their message, and also founded 'The Guardian' in 1846, a newspaper in support of High-Church Anglicanism. The movement stimulated much vigorous controversy within the Church and, although it gave the movement great fame during a religious age, it is not clear that this was to benefit of the Church of England. Newman was famously transferred into the *Roman Catholic* church but most others remained on the 'High-Church' wing of the Church of England. By the last quarter of the nineteenth century, they increasingly called themselves 'Anglo-Catholics'.

P

pacifism: the belief that the use of force is not justified to achieve political goals. In British history it is associated with the Quakers, a nonconformist sect which developed in the 1650s, and with the attitude of conscientious objectors during the two *world wars*. In the late 1950s and 1960s, the term was also used to describe supporters of the Campaign for Nuclear Disarmament. Although their objection was to particular types of weapon, CND attracted many pacifists.

Paisley, Ian: Unionist politician and Presbyterian clergyman. Born in 1926, he made his reputation as a powerful preacher and orator and then as the leading spokesman of uncompromising opposition to any agreement with Roman Catholics and nationalists over the future of Northern Ireland. He became Unionist MP for the strongly Protestant area of North Antrim in 1970 and led the breakaway *Democratic Unionist Party* from 1971. In this capacity, he has opposed all attempts to resolve problems in Northern Ireland other than on the basis of deciding policy on the basis of the in-built Protestant majority in the province. His rhetoric and his support among working-class Protestants was instrumental in ensuring first that a workers' strike destroyed the experiment in power-sharing in 1974 and then that the Anglo-Irish agreement for the future of Northern Ireland made in 1985 between *Margaret Thatcher* and the Irish *Prime Minister* Garrett Fitzgerald had no practical effect. His powerful preaching draws on a nineteenth-century tradition of Presbyterian *evangelicalism*.

(See also *Faulkner, Brian; Ireland; O'Neill, Terence; Roman Catholicism; Ulster.*)

Pakistan: independent Muslim state which was part of *India* until independence in 1947. The Muslims, under M A Jinnah, began pressing in the 1930s for an independence separate from Hindu-dominated India. This pressure bore fruit, albeit in tragic circumstances. Britain's withdrawal from India after the end of *World War II* was very rapid and the last Viceroy, *Mountbatten*, was more concerned that Britain grant independence than to ensure a peaceful transfer of power. The creation of Pakistan was crude. Those areas in the north-west with an inbuilt Muslim majority – Sind, Baluchistan and the north-west frontier province – became part of the new Pakistan as did the east of Bengal and the west of Punjab. However, the forcible splitting of these two large territories produced violence on a dramatic scale. It has been estimated that about half-a-million people died and many more refugees were created. Furthermore, Pakistan was split into two culturally and geographically different portions, with more than 1,000 miles of Indian territory separating them.

(See also *Commonwealth, British; Empire, British; India.*)

Palestine: an area of the Middle East which the *Jews* from the late nineteenth century claimed as their homeland. Britain's involvement in the Palestine question grew after the *Balfour Declaration* of 1917 which committed the Government to support for a separate Jewish territory in the area. General Allenby captured Palestine from the Turks at the end of the *World War 1* and Britain governed it under a 'mandate' from the *League of Nations* from 1922. Jewish nationalists, known as Zionists, increasingly opposed British rule which ended with the creation of a separate state of Israel in 1948.

(See also *Zionism.*)

Palmerston (Henry John Temple), 3rd Viscount: *Tory,* then *Whig* and *Liberal,* politician and *Prime Minister.* Born in 1784, he was educated at Edinburgh and Cambridge before becoming an MP in 1807. Although he was a peer, he was able to sit in the *House of Commons* because his peerage was an Irish one and, according to the terms of the *Act of Union,* Irish peers were entitled to sit in the lower House. His parliamentary and ministerial records were remarkable. He remained in the Commons without a break for 58 years until his death in 1865 and he was a minister of the crown for 48 of those years. His major offices were:

- Secretary at War, 1809–28
- Foreign Secretary, 1830–34, 1835–41, 1846–51
- Home Secretary, 1852–55
- Prime Minister, 1855–58 and 1859–65

Although he received junior office as early as 1807, he first came to prominence as a Tory supporter of *Canning,* leaving the Tory Party with Huskisson and other 'Liberal Tories' over disagreement with *Wellington.* He joined *Grey's* Whig government in 1830, although anything but a fervent supporter of *parliamentary reform* and remained in the Whig or Liberal Party for the remainder of his life. His foreign policy closely followed the principles of Canning and, like him, he saw public opinion as a key element in sustaining political power. Within the small world of political elites he was far from universally popular. Many, including Queen *Victoria,* saw him as a cheap showman who played far too much to the crowd, talked too much about 'patriotism' and tried to keep control of foreign policy very much to himself and out of the hands of ministerial colleagues. This characteristic led to his dismissal as Foreign Secretary in 1851 when he congratulated Louis Napoleon on his take-over of power in France without first consulting either the Queen or the Prime Minister, Lord John Russell. The main principles underlying his foreign policy, apart from the over-riding one of attempting to safeguard British interests, were trying to maintain a balance of forces within Europe. To this end, he helped to negotiate the independence of Belgium in 1839 while ensuring that France did not control the new country, thus maintaining British trading interests in the Mediterranean. This often involved supporting the Turks, with whom trade greatly increased suspicion of, and opposition to, Russia in the middle years of the century. This was largely because of Russia's attempts to wrest control of the eastern Mediterranean from the Turks.

He was out of office when the *Crimean War* began, which worked to his advantage and paved the way for his becoming Prime Minister. In that office, he helped to shape the modern Liberal Party by welcoming *Gladstone* into his government in 1859. He was never, however, an enthusiastic domestic reformer, frequently asking why it was necessary to fill up the statute book with new laws. He continued to superintend foreign affairs, though he failed to get the better of the powerful Prussian minister Bismarck at the end of his career, leaving the details of domestic policy to Gladstone and Sir George Grey. He approved of law taxation and *free trade.* His private life was intensely colourful; he maintained mistresses into old age and his numerous affairs were the talk of London society for more than half a century. He became one of a very small number of prime ministers to die in office when he expired in 1865.

(See also *Huskisson, William; Empire, British; Opium Wars.*)

Pankhurst, Christobel: *suffragette* daughter of *Emmeline Pankhurst* with whom she founded the *Women's Social and Political Union* in 1903. Born in 1880, she trained as a lawyer but was refused admission to Lincoln's Inn on grounds of her sex. She was arrested for direct suffragette action and edited the WSPU newspaper 'The Suffragette'. After *World War I*, she emigrated to the United States. She died in 1958.

(See also *Cat and Mouse Act, 1913; Sylvia Pankhurst.*)

Pankhurst, Emmeline: *suffragette.* She was born in 1858, the daughter of a Manchester cotton manufacturer and developed an interest in radical politics, joining the Fabian Society in the 1880s and the *Independent Labour Party* in the 1890s. She could not persuade the ILP to take up the cause of votes for women and founded the *Women's Social and Political Union* in Manchester in 1903 with her daughter *Christobel Pankhurst.* She proved an excellent speaker and a good organiser. Like many suffragettes, she was imprisoned for taking direct action. She broke into the lobby of the House of Commons in 1908 and began a campaign of attacking property. Breaking windows became a favoured suffragette tactic in the years leading up to *World War I.* She was arrested in 1913 for attempting to bomb the house of the Chancellor of the Exchequer, *David Lloyd George,* refused food and fell foul of the *Cat and Mouse Act.* She abandoned militancy on the outbreak of war and helped in military and nursing recruitment campaigns. After the vote was won, she supported the *Conservative Party,* standing for election to Parliament in 1926. She died in 1928.

(See also *Pankhurst, Sylvia; suffragists.*)

Pankhurst, Sylvia: *suffragette.* The daughter of *Emmeline Pankhurst* and the sister of *Christobel,* she was born in 1882. Her artistic training proved useful to the suffrage cause since she helped to design suffragette posters. Unlike her mother and sister, she took a pacifist position during *World War I* and edited 'Workers' Dreadnought', a journal which ironically took its title from the *dreadnought* battleship while campaigning for both *socialism* and *pacifism.* Her work after the end of the war was concentrated in London's East End, where she helped unemployed women and established clinics and education for nursery-age children. Her international contacts took her both to Russia, where she met Lenin and to Abyssinia, where she opposed Mussolini's fascist regime. She died in 1960.

Paris, Treaties of (1814–15): peace agreements at the end of the *Napoleonic Wars.* Separate agreements were necessary because of Napoleon's unexpected return from exile after his defeat in 1814 to continue the war. The main terms of the treaties, which maintained peace between the great powers in Europe for forty years, were:

- France was forced to give up the territories of Saar, Landau and Savoy
- an allied army of occupation was to remain in France for five years
- Britain retained Malta and Heligoland
- Britain established a protectorate over the Ionian islands
- the allies agreed to act together to maintain the settlement if France should attempt to challenge it

- the allies agreed to meet regularly to discuss the workings of the settlement and to iron out difficulties (*congress system*)

(See also *Castlereagh, Viscount; French Revolutionary Wars; Vienna, Congress of.*)

Paris, Treaty of (1856): peace agreement at the end of the *Crimean War*. Its main terms were:

- Britain and Russia agreed to sustain the independence of the Turkish Empire
- Russian forts at Sebastopol and Odessa were to be dismantled
- the Black Sea was declared a neutral zone
- the Danubian principalities were transferred from Russian protection and became a Turkish responsibility. All the powers agreed to respect the rights of the Danubians
- control of navigation on the River Danube was to be given to a European commission
- Russia gave up part of Southern Bessarabia, which was transferred to control of Moldavia

(See also *Aberdeen, Earl of; Palmerston, Viscount.*)

Parish Councils Act, 1894: local-government legislation passed by *Gladstone's* Liberal government. Its main terms were:

- separate urban and rural district councils established for all communities of more than 300 people
- women could both vote for, and serve on, these new councils

The legislation was highly controversial because it seemed to deprive traditional rulers of local communities, such as the village squire and the parson, of their old responsibilities. Opposition by the *Conservative Party* ensured that the amount of money available to the new councils would be limited. Revenue from rates on agricultural land, a major source of parish council income, was reduced after 1895, thus further reducing the scope for decisive action by the new councils. Nevertheless, they remained in place under local government reform in 1972.

(See also *county boroughs; county councils; local government; Municipal Corporations Act, 1835; Newcastle Programme.*)

Parliament Act, 1911: legislation which restricted the power of the *House of Lords*. The Lords rejected *Lloyd George's* so-called People's Budget in 1909, resulting in a constitutional crisis. After the *Liberal Party* won two *general elections* in 1910, though narrowly, it introduced this legislation. The Lords agreed to its passage (by 131 votes to 114) only once it became known that *George V* would create sufficient new peers favourable to the legislation to enable it to pass rather than have the will of an elected lower house permanently frustrated.

Its main terms were:

- the Lords could delay the passage of so-called 'money bills' (dealing with finance) for no more than one month. The *House of Commons* was the judge of what constituted money bills

- the Lords could delay the passage of other legislation for a maximum of two years
- the maximum length of a parliament's life was reduced from seven years to five

The Act governed relations between the two Houses of Parliament thereafter, although in 1949 the 'delaying power' of the Lords was reduced from two years to one.

(See also *Asquith, Henry; Lansdowne, 5th Marquess; Parliament.*)

Parliament, English: representative assembly sitting at Westminster with powers to pass laws binding on citizens. Its origins are medieval, when it offered advice and, before long, voted taxes for the use of the monarch. Developments in the seventeenth century confirmed its control, first, over finance and later, over other areas of public policy. By the beginning of the nineteenth century, Parliament clearly had greater overall powers than the monarch. Developments during the nineteenth century confirmed its control over virtually all aspects of public life. Rights which remained theoretically in the hands of the monarch, such as those to veto legislation passed by Parliament and to choose ministers, were either never exercised or so severely restricted as to be of almost no practical effect. In reality, Parliament, rather than the monarch, was 'sovereign' by the middle of the nineteenth century, and has remained so. Parliament is divided into two Houses, the *House of Commons* and the *House of Lords*. The former is elected, though the basis of elections has changed (see *parliamentary reform* and *Reform Acts.*). The latter originally comprised only royal princes, hereditary peers, and bishops of the *Church of England*. From 1958, it has included 'life peers', persons appointed theoretically by the monarch, but on the advice of the *Prime Minister*. As with relations between Parliament and the *monarchy*, the balance of power between the two Houses has changed over time. Already established by the eighteenth century as in control of finance, the powers of the House of Lords have further reduced while those of the Commons have increased. By the end of the twentieth century, the Lords are largely a so-called 'revising chamber' – that is, they have the often useful function of scrutinising legislation in detail and suggesting amendments, but they exercise very little independent power.

Since the late eighteenth century, control of Parliament has lain in the hands of political parties. The number of members elected as 'independents' declined sharply in the first half of the nineteenth century and independent MPs have been a real rarity during the twentieth century. The effective struggle for power, therefore, is between political parties at *general elections*. Discipline of parties at Westminster has become increasingly strict, such that few MPs are willing to challenge their party leaderships. Some have seen this as a significant reduction in the independence of Parliament, not least since voters at elections (at least theoretically) vote for real individuals and not for disembodied parties.

After an Act of Union in 1707, Scotland gave up its rights to a separate parliament and elected Scottish MPs to a new British Parliament. Wales did not have a strong tradition of separate parliaments and, after Union with England in 1536, it sent MPs to the English Pparliament. From 1801 to 1922, when Ireland and Great Britain were linked in a 'United Kingdom' Ireland sent MPs to the 'UK' Parliament.

(See also *devolution; Parliament Act, 1911; Stormont.*)

parliamentary reform: general process whereby changes were made to the qualifications for voting in parliamentary elections and also to those places which were entitled to send MPs to Parliament. Pressure for change had been building up since the second half of the eighteenth century. This was for three main reasons:

- opposition leaders felt that the existing system enabled the King and his ministers to exert greater control over the political process. Increasing charges of 'corruption' and 'improper management' of Parliament were heard from the late 1760s onwards. Opposition *Whigs* were in the forefront of calls for parliamentary reform from the 1770s and 1780s
- the rapid commercial and industrial changes of the period made the obvious anomalies in the old system seem ever more stark. None of Birmingham, Leeds, Manchester or Sheffield were parliamentary boroughs before 1832, for example, and so could not send members directly to Parliament. Also, the presence of antique boroughs, which had either ceased to have any function at all (such as Dunwich in Suffolk which had largely slipped into the sea) or which had a derisorily small number of voters, drew increasing criticism. Some places were much more highly represented than others. Cornwall sent 44 members to Parliament while Lancashire, increasingly industrial and full of centres of population, sent only fourteen
- skilled workers and others who did not have the right to vote were campaigning for change. The *French Revolution* gave a great boost to *radicals* and parliamentary reformers

Once reform was enacted in 1832, it proved to be the first of many such reforms which eventually created a parliamentary democracy based upon universal suffrage (votes for all adults) and constituencies of roughly equal size.

(See also *pocket boroughs*; *Reform Acts, 1832, 1867, 1884, 1918.*)

Parnell, Charles Stewart: Irish nationalist. Born into a Protestant landowning family in County Wicklow (Ireland), he entered Parliament in a by-election in 1875. He supported *Isaac Butt*'s Home Rule Party and became President of the Irish Land League in 1879 which called for rent reductions for Irish tenants. He became a pioneer of the policy of non-co-operation with the process of government when he obstructed business in the Commons by deliberately long speeches and other delaying tactics. In 1880 he became leader of the Home Rule Party in the Commons. He was a brilliantly effective speaker and his personal charm and negotiating skills added to the strength of his leadership. However, he never properly reconciled the conflicts within his party and he never truly convinced those who believed that a nationalist party should be lead by a Roman Catholic. His leadership was a delicate balancing act between outright support for violence, which the radicals in his party wanted, and maintaining lines of communication with British politicians, which he considered vital to achieve *Home Rule*. The so-called Kilmainham Treaty, which he negotiated with the Prime Minister, *Gladstone*, in 1882 promised an end to violence in return for government commitment to offer help to tenants in arrears with their rent during the agricultural depression. The pressure he was able to sustain in the following years was a major factor in persuading Gladstone to adopt Home Rule.

After Gladstone's bill of 1886 failed, however, he was criticised by many supporters for maintaining too close an alliance with the Liberal Party and for visiting Ireland too seldom. His career was ruined when during 1889 to 1890 he was cited by her husband as Kittie O'Shea's lover in a divorce case. Gladstone and the Liberals made it clear that he should resign and his attempt to retain the leadership of the Home Rule Party succeeded only in splitting it. He married Kittie O'Shea after her divorce but died shortly afterwards, in 1891.

(See also *Ireland.*)

Passchendaele, Battle of: battle from July to November 1917 during the later stages of *World War I*, sometimes known as the Third Battle of Ypres. It resulted from an initiative by the British commander, *Douglas Haig,* who attempted to inflict a major defeat on the German forces by driving them from their defences in southern Belgium to the coast. During long periods on the offensive, the weather was bad making movement all but impossible. Stiff German resistance also ensured that the British objective would not be achieved. More than a-quarter-of-a-million British casualties resulted. The failure added to criticism that Haig was prepared to sacrifice men in huge numbers for little or no result.

paternalism: often extended to 'paternalism and deference', this represented an informal system of organisation in which both rich and poor acknowledged their respective positions in society. The rich would look after the poor by providing charity and other forms of support to those in economic distress. The poor recognised the right of their social superiors to exercise authority over them and followed their lead. The system was best attuned to small-scale societies, as in villages, where personal contact across the classes was relatively common. It was supported by many *Tory* humanitarians, particularly those opposed to the changes and dislocations of the *Industrial Revolution.* The benefits of the system were often either exaggerated or romanticised and it was increasingly challenged by *laissez-faire* and the *free market* economy during the nineteenth century.

payment by results: the main recommendation of the *Newcastle Commission* on education, and embodied in the *Revised Code* of 1862. Under the system, schools supported by government grant received for each enrolled pupil:

- 4s (20p) on evidence shown of a satisfactory attendance record
- 8s (40p) on evidence that he or she could pass basic tests in English reading and writing and in arithmetic

The purpose of the scheme, which survived until 1897, was to give schools incentive to achieve higher standards in basic subjects. It achieved another basic objective, which was to reduce the cost of education expenditure. It was widely criticised, however, as requiring excessive concentration on a narrow range of subjects and encouraging rote-learning of facts rather than wider understanding of the subjects.

(See also *Education Act, 1870; Kay-Shuttleworth, James; Lowe, Robert.*)

Pearse, Patrick: Irish nationalist. He was born in 1879, the son of an English craftsman, and trained as a lawyer. He joined the *Irish Republican Brotherhood* and became a founder member of the so-called 'Irish Volunteers' in 1913 who wished to achieve independence by violent action. During the *Easter Rising* of 1916, he proclaimed the Irish

Republic from the steps of the central Post Office in Dublin and was named as the Republic's first President. He was arrested after the failure of the Rising and executed. (See also *Home Rule, Ireland.*)

Peel, Sir Robert, Jnr: Tory/Conservative politician and *Prime Minister.* Born into a successful manufacturing family (see *Sir Robert Peel, Snr*) in 1788, he was educated at Harrow and Oxford before becoming a Tory MP in 1809. His political career was spent at, or near, the centre of power. His major offices were:

- Chief Secretary for Ireland, 1812–18
- Home Secretary, 1822–27, 1828–30
- Leader of the Tory/Conservative Party, 1834–46
- Prime Minister, 1834–35, 1841–46

Like most politicians of his generation, he was brought up to fear the influence of the *French Revolution* and to support a government committed to sustaining public order. Unlike most, however, he was not born into an established landed family and his slight Lancashire accent remained a sore point all his life. It caused some snobbish comment and made a naturally shy man more defensive than he might otherwise have been.

He staunchly supported the Protestant ascendancy in Ireland as Chief Secretary, earning from *Daniel O'Connell* the title 'Orange Peel'. As Home Secretary, he supported public order but, during a period of general economic prosperity, was able to give priority to administrative reforms, including a wholesale revision of the criminal law and the establishment of a professional police force for London. He refused to serve *Canning* in 1827, because the new Prime Minister supported Catholic Association. In 1829, however, as Home Secretary in *Wellington*'s administration, he advised the Prime Minister to enact him for fear of civil war and the destruction of the *Act of Union.* This decision was to haunt him all his life, because those on the right of the party never forgave him for what they considered an act of treachery. He opposed *parliamentary reform* up to the passage of the *Reform Act* in 1832 but committed his party to retaining it when he unexpectedly became Prime Minister of a minority administration in 1834. From 1835 to 1841, his energies were devoted to building up the Tory Party after its huge electoral defeat in 1832, while also supporting *Melbourne's Whig* government when it passed legislation which he judged would strengthen and defend the established order against attacks from radical politicians. In the process of educating his party to accept what he called necessary reforms and 'the correction of proved abuses', he encouraged some to talk of a reformulated '*Conservative Party*' as a more flexible successor to the *Tory Party.*

His government of 1841–46 is remembered for three main achievements:

- the restoration of the nation's finances and the establishment of a government surplus
- a steady reduction in the number and size of tariffs, as part of a commitment to an economic policy of *free trade*
- the repeal of the *Corn Laws*

This final achievement entailed the break-up of the party because roughly two-thirds of Conservative MPs refused to support a policy which they considered a betrayal of the landed interest. Right-wing Conservatives (or Tories) accused Peel of a double betrayal, both of the Protestant interest, in 1829, and the landed interest in 1846. Led by *Benjamin Disraeli* and Lord George Bentinck, they forced Peel to choose between support for a party he had done much to revive, and support for a policy he believed essential to national prosperity. In choosing the latter, he destroyed his party but became much more popular in the country than ever before. Frequently considered aloof, arrogant and opposed to the interests of working people, he was now lauded for giving them 'cheap bread'. His last years were spent above the political fray, but nevertheless involved in giving informal (and, apparently, much valued) advice to his Liberal successors on economic management. When he died suddenly, as the result of a riding accident in 1850, the outpouring of public grief was remarkable.

His administrative skills and his grasp of both the specific details and the broad objectives of economic policy were recognised by all, but his political abilities were the subject of fierce controversy both at the time and by historians subsequently. His opponents criticised him for arrogance, lack of sensitivity and a determination to push ahead with policies which had limited support. His supporters argued that his was the decisive contribution to modernising the Conservative Party and establishing its political viability in the industrial age while also asserting that he was one of the chief architects of mid-Victorian prosperity.

(See also *Graham, Sir James; Grey, Earl; laissez-faire.*)

Peel, Sir Robert, Snr: industrialist and *Tory* politician. Born into a farming family in 1750, he established a successful cotton weaving business in Bury (Lancashire). His success in this enabled him to buy an estate in south Staffordshire in 1790 which he used, in part, as a base for his own political career and those of his sons, Robert (the future Prime Minister) and Jonathan. As an MP, he opposed *parliamentary reform* and took up a range of causes, most notably factory reform. As an employer himself, he had become concerned at the degree of exploitation suffered by young children in textile factories. The *Factory Act* of 1819 bears his name as its main sponsor. The Act prohibited children under nine years from working in cotton factories and pre-scribed a maximum working day for those of nine to sixteen years. It was of limited effect, however, because no inspectors were appointed to enforce the legislation. He died in 1830.

(See also *cotton industry; Industrial Revolution.*)

penal servitude: form of punishment introduced by two parliamentary Acts in 1853 and 1857 as a replacement for *transportation*. Convicted prisoners sentenced to penal servitude in specified institutions – Dartmoor, Parkhurst, Peterhead and Aylesbury – at which they performed various forms of labour (often referred to as 'hard labour'). Convicts who were well-behaved and discharged the tasks they were given could earn shorter sentences before they were released. The system survived until 1949.

Peninsular War: conflict fought in the Iberian Peninsula (Spain and Portugal) from 1808 to 1814 as part of the *Napoleonic Wars*. It proved a long and, for the British, frequently defensive struggle but British troops, well provisioned by sea, resisted all French attempts to drive them out. The French were forced to divert resources which could have been used further east, not least in Russia in 1812.

Napoleon later referred to the Peninsula as his 'Spanish ulcer' which contributed significantly to his defeat.

Causes of the War:

- Britain sent troops to Spain in 1808 to aid a revolt which had broken out against Napoleon's attempt to put his brother Joseph Bonaparte on the Spanish throne. Britain was glad to have the opportunity of committing land forces to a part of Europe which Napoleon did not completely control
- defending the Iberian peninsula against Napoleon was also a way of keeping ports open and thus reducing the effect of his *continental system.* British forces were led by Sir Arthur Wellesley, later Duke of *Wellington*

Main events in the War:

1808 Wellesley defeated the French at Battle of Vimiero (August) in Portugal, but French army were permitted to retreat in good order by the Convention of Cintra. French troops captured Madrid (December)

1809 Sir John Moore invaded Spain but was forced to retreat before fighting a defensive action at Corunna at which he was killed but most of his army was evacuated by sea. British troops defeated French at Oporto: French troops retreated from Portugal. Wellington defeated French in Spain at Battle of Talavera (July)

1810 France captured Portuguese forts at Ciudad Rodrigo and Almeida. Wellington forced to retreat but won a battle at Busaco (September) before retreating to fortifications at 'the lines of Torres Vedras'

1811 Wellington won defensive action against the French at Fuentes d'Onoro and recaptured Almeida

1812 Wellington recaptured fortress of Ciudad Rodrigo (January) and advanced to take Badajoz (April) and Salamanca (July). Long period of defence finally turned to attack. Madrid captured from French (August). Wellington forced to retreat from Burgos (October)

1813 Wellington captured Vitoria (June) and was then able to cross Pyrenees and enter France (October)

(See also *Anglo-American Wars; French Revolutionary Wars.*)

Perceval, Spencer: *Tory* politician and *Prime Minister.* Born in 1762, the son of the Earl of Egmont, he trained as a lawyer and was involved in prosecuting the radical leaders Thomas Paine and J Home Tooke. He became an MP supporting the government of *William Pitt* in 1796. His major offices were:

- Solicitor General, 1801–2
- Attorney General, 1802–6
- Chancellor of the Exchequer, 1807–9
- Prime Minister, 1809–12

For most of his life he was associated with the evangelical wing of the *Church of England* and disapproved both of gambling and excessive drinking. He was a good performer in Parliament, successfully defending the increasingly unpopular *Addington* government, and he had a good eye for detail. Although his succession to the office of Prime Minister was hotly contested and owed much to the support of

George III, who approved of his transparent honesty and decency, his period in office was mostly successful. He established effective control over the *House of Commons,* successfully continuing Pitt's sternly anti-reformist policies and he laid the foundations for the long prime ministership of his successor, Liverpool. He was not able, however, to turn the tide of the *Napoleonic Wars* and his final years were dogged by economic crisis. One of the casualties of that crisis, the deranged overseas trader John Bellingham, took his revenge on Perceval by assassinating him in the lobby of the House of Commons in May 1812. Perceval remains the only British Prime Minister to suffer assassination.

(See also *Canning, George; Castlereagh, Viscount; evangelicalism; Portland, Duke of; Tory Party.*)

Peterloo Massacre, 1819: name given to the attack by the Manchester Yeomanry on a crowd, probably about 50,000 strong, assembled in St Peter's Fields, Manchester (the site of the present St Peter's Square) to hear a speech on *parliamentary reform* delivered by the *radical* leader Henry 'Orator' Hunt. An attempt to arrest Hunt provoked a wholesale attack on the crowd and resulted in eleven deaths and about 400 injuries, including those of women and children. The event gravely embarrassed *Liverpool's* government, which was forced to defend the actions of a local militia which had clearly panicked. It made radical leaders martyrs and seems to have converted many, not least among the *middle classes,* to the justice of the reformers' case. The spirit of 'Peterloo' (a nickname coined in ironic reference to *Wellington's* great military victory at the *Battle of Waterloo*) was frequently invoked by the radicals in the years before the *Reform Act of 1832* and also by the *Chartists* a decade later.

Phoenix Park murders: the political assassinations, on 6 May 1882, by an Irish nationalist terrorist group of the newly arrived Chief Secretary for Ireland, Lord Frederick Cavendish and his under-secretary Thomas Burke. The assassins were never caught. The murders provoked outrage in Britain and a burst of coercive legislation in *Ireland* which the *Prime Minister Gladstone* believed would not solve the increasingly difficult Anglo-Irish political situation.

(See also *Irish Republican Brotherhood; Irish Republican Army; Parnell, Charles Stewart.*)

Phoney War: term originally coined by a US journalist to describe the period during *World War II* between the fall of Poland in September 1939 and the German attack on Norway in April 1940 when there was little fighting.

Pitt the Younger, William: politician and *Prime Minister.* Conventionally described by most textbooks as a 'Tory', especially after his coalition with the *Duke of Portland* in 1794, it was a term he resisted, preferring to see himself as the King's minister governing in the national interest and calling himself an 'independent *Whig*'. He was born in 1759 at the time when his father, the elder Pitt, later Earl of Chatham, was enjoying his greatest period of success as Prime Minister during the Seven Years' War (1756–63). He was educated at Cambridge and trained as a lawyer but entered Parliament in 1781 and devoted the remainder of his life to politics. His major offices were:

- Chancellor of the Exchequer, 1782–83
- Prime Minister, 1783–1801 and 1804–6

In his early years, he established the reputation of a reformer, attacking the government of Lord North during the last years of the War of American Independence and then the coalition government of North with *Charles James Fox*. He came to office in December 1783 as Britain's youngest Prime Minister (age 24) when *George III* turned to him in desperation after dismissing the Fox–North coalition. Pitt's reputation for ability, even at so young an age, and his lack of close association with discredited politicians served him well in the general election of 1784 when he gained a majority in the House of Commons.

Pitt's prime ministership is conventionally divided into peacetime (1783–93) and wartime (1793–1801) phases.

1783–93

During this period, Pitt consolidated his reputation as both an administrative and financial reformer. He placed the nation's finances on a safer footing, managing the national debt more securely and introducing short-term taxes to reduce debts run up during the war against the American colonists. He also cut some tariff duties, arranged trade treaties with France and Ireland and ended Britain's diplomatic isolation after the wars by taking the country into a triple alliance with Holland and Prussia in 1788.

He also supported a measure of *parliamentary reform* but was unable to carry it through the *House of Commons*. He also refused to support measures of relief for *nononformists* when the opposition Whigs introduced a bill to repeal the Test and Corporation Acts. Although normally secure in his hold over the Commons, his lack of party support made him vulnerable if the King's support was not forthcoming. He was almost forced to resign when the King became mentally incapacitated in 1788 and a 'regency crisis' occurred when it seemed likely that Prince George, a supporter of Portland and Charles James Fox, would become regent.

1793–1801

The period of the *French Revolutionary Wars* is usually seen as the less successful part of Pitt's prime ministership. Both his overall war strategy, including the nation's initial unpreparedness, and his reliance on weak allies in Europe have attracted much criticism. However, Britain remained the only undefeated Allied nation, its navy proving an effective shield against invasion. Pitt was also able to steer the nation through huge financial crises during the late 1790s, and to introduce a radical new *income tax* to help pay for the cost. Pitt's political position was strengthened by the war. The Pitt–Portland coalition secured large majorities and the challenge of the *radicals* was successfully beaten off. Pitt eventually resigned in 1801 not because he had lost the confidence of Parliament but because the King would not allow him to enact *Catholic emancipation* as a means of sweetening the *Act of Union* for the majority of Irishmen.

1804–6

Pitt's last period in office is not specially memorable, although it did include *Nelson*'s victory at *Trafalgar* which finally removed any threat of a French invasion. Although only 45 when he replaced *Addington*, his health was poor, partly because of consistent overwork and partly as a result of heavy drinking, which certainly contributed to his increasingly severe health problems and, indeed, probably killed him in January 1806.

The conventional image of Pitt is of a man of high ability who sacrificed himself by overwork in the national interest at a time of great danger. The reality, as always, is more complex. He seems to have enjoyed little personal happiness and may have sublimated his unhappiness in work. Like *Peel* in the next generation, he was a master of detail and used his superior knowledge to win parliamentary debates, usually managing to convince the independent MPs of his position. He maintained a good working relationship with his ministers, and he certainly paid attention to training talented juniors like *Canning, Castlereagh* and the future *Earl of Liverpool*, though he seems to have been intimate with few. He never married and the homosexual community in the 1990s asserted that he was gay. The evidence on this is far from conclusive.

Place, Francis: radical politician. Born in 1771, he was apprenticed as a tailor. As a skilled artisan, he helped to form the radical London Corresponding Society. He supported the extension of the franchise to working men all his life but he believed that the vote had to be earned by education and by sober behaviour. He himself built up a huge and impressive library of improving and radical literature. Few radical causes of the day lacked his support. He was an extremely good organiser and lobbyist and used these skills to obtain the repeal of the *Combination Acts* and the legalisation of trade unions in 1824. He also helped draft the petition which was turned into the 'People's Charter' in 1838. His own career seemed to show the virtue of hard work and improvement. He became a prosperous London shopkeeper and master tailor. He died in 1854.

(See also *Chartism; radicalism; Reform Act, 1832; trade unions.*)

Plaid Cymru: political party dedicated to the achievement of independence for Wales. It was founded in 1925 by John Saunders Lewis but made little political impact at Westminster before *World War II*. Its first parliamentary seat was won at a by-election in Carmarthen in 1966 but since 1974 it has usually returned two or three Welsh MPs, winning between eight and twelve per cent of the popular vote. The party has always been much stronger in rural central and, especially, northern Wales than in the more heavily populated southern industrial areas.

(See also *Scottish National Party.*)

Plimsoll line: marking compulsorily placed on a ship's side indicating the maximum level of displacement of water for a ship laden with cargo.

(See also *Merchant Shipping Acts; Plimsoll, Samuel.*)

Plimsoll, Samuel: radical *Liberal* politician. A member of the Congregational *nonconformist* church, he was born in Bristol in 1824 and acted as Secretary to the 1851 Great Exhibition. As a successful coal merchant in London, he acquired extensive knowledge of the coastal shipping trade and began to work for the implementation of safeguards to protect merchant shipping and its cargoes. He became a Liberal MP in 1868 and campaigned for the establishment of a Royal Commission to examine the question. The *Merchant Shipping Act* of 1876 was a direct consequence. Plimsoll left Parliament in 1880 but continued his interest in the shipping industry and in ship workers' trade unionism. He died in 1898.

pluralism: a term from political and social science suggesting division of powers between different authorities or the co-existence of different attitudes or forms of belief. It is generally associated with democratic states and with toleration of a range of beliefs. It thus links closely with traditions of liberalism which developed during the nineteenth century.

pocket boroughs: name used to describe parliamentary boroughs, especially before the *Reform Act* of 1832, in which a patron had a usually controlling interest. The borough was thus said to be in the 'pocket' of its proprietor. The majority of such boroughs had small electorates but not all of them were entirely at the disposal of one man. Real electoral contests in such boroughs were not infrequent and patrons nearly always had to spend money and attend to the interests and concerns of the voters if they were to retain their influence. It has been estimated that as many as 300 seats in England and Wales were subject to a degree of influence by patrons, who were usually large landowners.

(See also *rotten boroughs.*)

Polaris: nuclear weapons designed to be fired from submarines. They were manufactured in the United States and supplied to Britain after 1962 as a key part of the country's nuclear defences. The system was in operation until replaced by the Trident series during the 1990s.

police: agency by which civil order is maintained. The *aristocracy* and others in the social elite in the eighteenth and early nineteenth centuries were mostly opposed to the creation of a professional police force arguing that it represented 'foreign' influences, especially excessive centralisation of power by the Government. They felt that order should be most appropriately maintained in the localities and, if possible, on the basis of local knowledge. The *Industrial Revolution* and the growth of *population* made this an increasingly unrealistic position. Calls for more police protection grew and legislation was enacted to enable borough and county authorities to establish professional police forces. The *Metropolitan Police*, established in 1829, created a model for developments elsewhere and the *Municipal Corporations Act* in 1835 provided an appropriate administrative framework within which the principle of policing could be extended.

The 1839 County Police Act:

- enabled county police forces to be established under the control of police committees supervised by justices of the peace
- required the costs of establishing a force to be met locally out of rates
- was 'permissive' – i.e., there was no requirement to establish county forces

The 1856 County and Borough Police Act:

- made the establishment of police forces compulsory in both borough and county authorities
- introduced a central inspectorate, reporting to the Home Office, to monitor efficiency
- authorised central government grants for those noted as efficient

A similar Act concerning policing in Scotland was passed in 1857 and by 1860, about 200 police authorities were in existence.

The main operations of the police soon settled into solving crime and maintaining public order. The principles of local organisation and control with some central supervision were established, except for the Metropolitan Police which reported directly to the Home Secretary. The crime detection side of police work became more professionalised with the establishment of the Criminal Investigation Department in 1878 and the subsequent interchange of information between police forces. The most controversial aspects of police work have tended to involve keeping order during strikes. During the most notable incidents, for example, the industrial unrest of 1910–14 and 1918–20, the *General Strike* of 1926 and the bitter miners' strike of 1984–85, the police have been accused of siding with 'the authorities' against 'the people'.

'Political Register': radical newspaper published in the years 1802–36. Edited by *William Cobbett* it was the most extreme, and probably the most influential, radical *newspaper* of the pre-*Chartist* era. It began publication in 1802 in support of the Government but Cobbett switched its allegiance in 1804, after which it consistently called for *parliamentary reform* and an end to what Cobbett called the 'old corruption' of the existing political system.

poll books: forms of register kept in parliamentary constituencies which inscribed the names of those voting in elections before the *Reform Act* of 1832. Not all of the books survive but, where they do, historians can identify the names of voters and also the political party they voted for. In some ways, therefore, more can be learned about the political allegiance of voters in the old political system than under one in which elections are conducted by secret ballot.

(See also *House of Commons; Parliament.*)

poll tax: technically, a tax levied on each person in the population. The term was first coined to describe a levy on all people over the age of fourteen made in 1377 at the beginning of the reign of Richard II. However, in recent years it became the normal means of describing what was more officially known as the Community Charge, introduced in highly controversial circumstances at the end of the prime ministership of *Margaret Thatcher.*

(See also *local government.*)

Poor Law Amendment Act, 1834: legislation which changed the basis of Poor Law provision and introduced a degree of central control over Poor Law provision. Its main terms were:

- the introduction of a centralised 'Poor Law Commission' which developed overall principles governing Poor Law provision
- local election of 'Poor Law Guardians' who became the administrators of poor relief in each Poor Law Union; they replaced 'overseers of the poor'
- parishes were grouped into 'Poor Law Unions' to help efficient use of resources, especially the capital costs involved in building new 'Poor Law Workhouses'
- the central appointment of assistant commissioners to supervise the introduction of the new system

Additionally, the new legislation worked on the principle of 'less eligibility'. This was intended to act as a deterrent to those who were poor to seek relief until they had exhausted all opportunities for supporting themselves. The fit were supposed to receive relief ('be relieved', in the terminology of the time) in workhouses, where conditions were intended to be less favourable (or less 'eligible') than labourers could find from the lowest paid employment which gave them independence.

Many administrative changes were made to the system during the remainder of the nineteenth century, but the principles of deterrence and concern for economy remained paramount. Accordingly, being required to 'go into the workhouse' became an enormous stigma which the respectable poor would seek to avoid at all costs. The image of the workhouse was one of harshness, severity and lack of individuality.

(See also *Poor Laws*.)

Poor Laws: means of supporting the poor when they were unable to support themselves. After 1601, the principle that each parish had a duty to 'relieve' the poor was established. Funding to support Poor Law provision was obtained through a rate levied on all property owners, the amount payable was intended to be proportional to the value of the property they occupied. An individual had a right to poor relief in the parish where he or she was born or where 'settled', usually after being resident in a place for more than one year.

The old system worked tolerably efficiently until a rise in population combined with poor harvests put increasing strain on both the poor and ratepayers. Between 1775 and 1818 the cost of relieving the poor increased from £2 million to almost £8 million. The practice of subsidising inadequate wages to maintain a labourer and family (known as the Speenhamland system after the Berkshire village where it was first adopted in 1795) became widespread. This was widely criticised, especially by political economists like *David Ricardo, Thomas Malthus* and *Nassau Senior*, who argued that it offered labourers no incentive to find work for themselves. Rising costs, declining agricultural profitability from the second decade of the nineteenth century and the assault from economists and *utilitarians* led to the establishment of a Royal Commission on the Poor Laws whose report in 1834 led to the passage of the highly controversial *Poor Law Amendment Act.*

The New Poor Law, as it was known, though regularly amended in administrative detail for the remainder of the century, remained the basis of state poverty relief until the early twentieth century. Then the *Liberal Party's* welfare reforms, especially the introduction of *old age pensions* and *national insurance*, in the years 1906–14 reduced the scope of the Poor Law. Extensions of welfare provision in the 1920s rendered a separate Poor Law unnecessary. Its remaining functions were transferred to county and county borough councils in 1929, when the post of Poor Law Guardian was abolished.

(See also *Bentham, Jeremy; Chamberlain, Neville; Lloyd George, David.*)

Poor Laws, Royal Commission on (1908–9): government commission which made recommendations on the future of the *Poor Laws.* Its members comprised some of the most eminent and experienced men and women in the field of social policy, including C S Loch, Helen Bosanquet and *Octavia Hill* of the *Charity Organisation Society, Charles Booth* and *Beatrice Webb* and although all the commissioners agreed that reforms were necessary, they were fundamentally divided on the way forward:

- the Majority Report recommended that the basic principles of the *Poor Law Amendment Act, 1834* – including 'less eligibility' – should remain. A reformed Poor Law should exercise overall responsibility for relief. Administration, however, should be transferred to *county councils* and *county boroughs*
- the Minority Report wanted a much more radical solution which would recognise that the causes of poverty were not wholly – indeed, frequently not at all – the responsibility of the individual but were bound up with changing economic conditions, which affected employment prospects, wage levels and many other factors over which workers had no control. Accordingly, the Poor Laws, which were thoroughly hated by most poor people as harsh, demeaning and discriminatory, should be abolished. Instead, local authorities should deal with problems in separate departments, covering pensions, education and health

The *Liberal* government, noting the depth of division within the Commission and with plans anyway of its own for pensions and *national insurance*, did not act on the Commission's recommendations. The Poor Law continued until 1929, although its role and functions dwindled.

popular culture: description given to the study of the products consumed by, and the achievements and customs of, ordinary folk. It is often distinguished from 'elite culture', which is concerned with the manners of, products consumed and tastes enjoyed by those with power and influence. Popular culture has been increasingly studied by historians since the 1980s as part of the expansion of social history and other forms of history 'from below'. Historians have studied both the entertainments, including sport, *music halls* and *cinema* and popular music enjoyed by working people and other aspects of lifestyle. Some historians argue that popular culture is a valid, and neglected, route into understanding society and that our understanding of the past has been distorted by undue emphasis on the lives of the great and powerful.

population: the changing size of Britain's population is one of the most important factors governing social life and economic development. Throughout the nineteenth and twentieth centuries, British population has grown, and usually very quickly in comparison with previous centuries. Sustained population growth began from the late 1720s and continued, though at varying rates, until the last quarter of the twentieth century, when it levelled out. The most rapid period was the first half of the nineteenth century, when the population of Britain almost doubled. Between the first census of 1801 and the end of the twentieth century British population increased more than five-fold from 10.5 million to approximately 54 million.

The population history of Ireland, which was part of the United Kingdom from 1801 to 1922, is quite different. Although it grew from approximately 5.5 million to 8.2 million between 1801 and 1841, the *Irish Potato Famine* proved to be a long-term catastrophe, the population falling continuously until, and beyond, the creation of the Irish Free State. The population of Ireland only sustained a recovery from the 1940s, albeit a slow one. The population of Northern Ireland increased from 1.2 million in 1931 to 1.6 million in 1991.

The graph below shows the main changes in the population of Britain (which does not include Ireland).

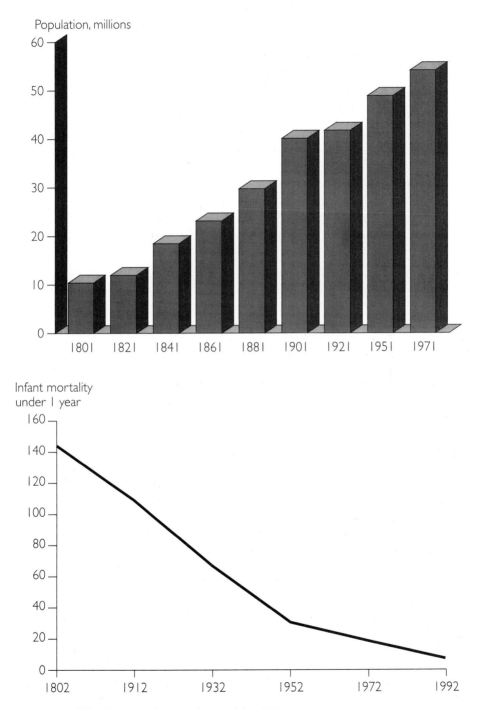

Population – UK infant mortality per thousand live births

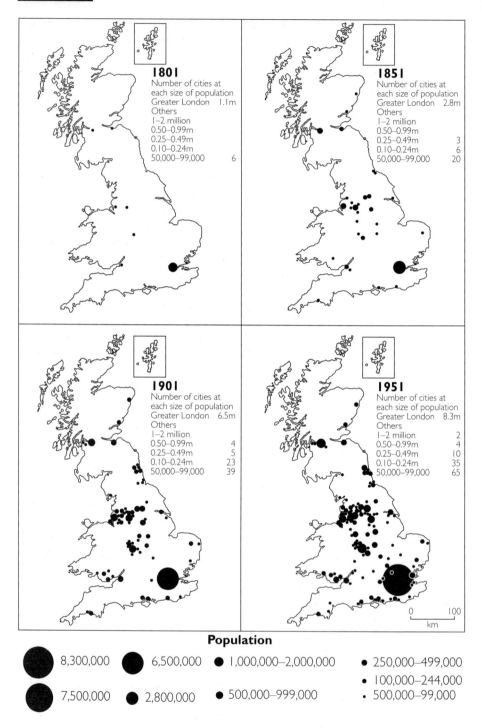

Population

● 8,300,000	● 6,500,000	● 1,000,000–2,000,000	• 250,000–499,000
			• 100,000–244,000
● 7,500,000	● 2,800,000	● 500,000–999,000	· 500,000–99,000

Population – growth of cities

Portland (Bentinck, William Cavendish), 3rd Duke of: *Whig* politician and *Prime Minister*. Born in 1738 into one of the richest and best-connected of Whig families. He became an MP in 1761, before succeeding to the dukedom in 1762. He became leader of the Whig opposition to the government of Lord North in 1782 and his major offices after that point were:

- Prime Minister, 1783 and 1807–9
- Home Secretary, 1794–1801
- Lord President of the Council, 1801–5
- Minister without Portfolio, 1805–6

His first period as Prime Minister was purely nominal, real power being exercised by *Charles James Fox* and Lord North. During his second period in office, his health was not good and he did little more than preside over a Cabinet including such important figures as *Canning, Castlereagh* and the future Lord *Liverpool*. His lack of decisive leadership was remarked on by political supporters and opponents alike and may have contributed to the festering enmity between Castlereagh and Canning which led to a duel between them just before Portland resigned. His main importance as a politician was as the leading 'conservative Whig' who began to sympathise with *Pitt's* policies from 1792 and who led the majority of the Whigs at Westminster into an active coalition with him in 1794. Many historians have seen this as the true rebirth of the *Tory Party* and it certainly isolated Fox and the small rump of reformist Whigs. In this role, as Home Secretary, he was a leading advocate of repression of *radicalism*, including suspension of *habeas corpus* and new legislation which prohibited the calling of large political meetings. He died shortly after resigning as Prime Minister in 1809.

Post Office: organisation for the transmission of mail. Originally developed as a means of carrying the monarch's messages, the service was expanded during the seventeenth and eighteenth centuries with penny posts established in most large towns and free transmission of post from London for Members of Parliament. Stage coaches were transmitting mail on a regular basis between larger towns by the end of the eighteenth century. In the nineteenth and twentieth centuries, the most important developments were:

1840	the expansion of a public mail service with the adoption of a 'penny post' for transmission of letters on the principle proposed by Rowland Hill. The post became a state monopoly
1849	first introduction of a post for books
1850s	introduction of the first pillar boxes, the idea of *Anthony Trollope*
1861	introduction by *William Gladstone* of a savings bank attached to post offices, to facilitate small savings
1870	introduction of a reduced rate of post for newspapers and postcards 1870; telegraph services added to the work of the General Post Office
1890	telephone services added to the work of the General Post Office; it became a monopoly in 1892
1969	General Post Office ceased to be a department of government, becoming just The Post Office
1981	telephone services split from Post Office services

1984 telephone service privatised, becoming British Telecom and open to competition

(See also *Thatcher, Margaret Hilda.*)

Potsdam Conference: meeting of the victorious powers in July to August 1945, after the end of *World War II*. The British leaders were first *Churchill* and *Eden* and, after the *Labour Party*'s election victory of 1945, *Attlee* and *Ernest Bevin*. The main business concerned redrawing the boundaries of Germany, giving Poland more territory, extending its western borders, and agreeing *reparations* to be paid by Germany. The conference revealed substantial disagreements between the Western powers and the Soviet Union, which would shortly widen into 'Cold War', especially between the USA and the USSR.

'pound in your pocket': famous phrase coined by *Harold Wilson* as *Prime Minister* in 1969 in a broadcast explaining the consequences of the *devaluation* of the pound. He tried to convince his audience that the devaluation would not affect the prices people paid for goods. Since this was transparently untrue for that increasing proportion of goods imported from abroad, the phrase stuck among the political classes as a slogan epitomising the half-truths politicians frequently resort to in order to gain acceptance for politically embarrassing policies.

Powell, J Enoch: *Conservative* politician. He was born in Birmingham in 1912 and became a *Conservative* MP in 1950. He had impressive academic credentials as a classicist, becoming Professor of Greek at the University of Sydney at the extremely young age of 25. During the 1950s and 1960s, he became associated with right-wing economic policies, based on the stability of the pound. His major offices were:

- Financial Secretary to the Treasury, 1957–60
- Minister of Health, 1960–63

When he refused to serve as a minister under Lord *Home*, many believed that he was preparing himself for a leadership challenge at a later date. This happened, but he attracted very small support and never held office again.

Many of his economic ideas challenged *Keynesianism* and anticipated the economic policies of *Margaret Thatcher* during the 1980s. He is best known, however, for his strong opposition to *immigration*, especially from the Black *Commonwealth*, delivering a speech which combined his classical learning – 'I see the River Tiber foaming with much blood' – with crude populism, urging the British to resist immigration to avoid social breakdown and even, potentially, civil war. *Edward Heath* sacked him from the shadow Cabinet and he eventually left the *Conservative Party*, gaining election as *Unionist* MP for South Down in 1974, holding the seat until his retirement from politics in 1987. His later career symbolised another of his passions, held with a characteristic combination of remorseless logic and limited common sense, that of the integrity of the *United Kingdom*. He died in 1998.

(See also *Thatcherism.*)

power loom: invention to mechanise the weaving process of textile production. It was patented by Edmund Cartwright in 1785 but did not come into widespread use in the main textile areas until the mid-1820s. It had considerable importance for two main reasons:

- it removed what had previously been a substantial technological logjam, whereby cotton spinning had been successfully mechanised from the 1760s, but weaving not
- its widespread adoption spelled a long period of decline and deprivation for one of the most skilled, and heavily politicised groups of workers, the *handloom weavers*

(See also *Chartism; Industrial Revolution.*)

prefabricated houses (prefabs): one-storey, purpose built dwellings designed to basic standards to replace houses destroyed by enemy action during *World War II* and help meet an acute *housing* shortage. About 150,000 were built in the years 1945–50. Most remained in use well into the 1960s and 1970s, despite having been built as temporary accommodation.

Pre-Raphaelite Brotherhood: a group of artists, writers and critics who took their inspiration from the Renaissance art and aesthetic sense of fifteenth-century Italy, before the time of the artist Raphael. Founded in 1848, their artistic statements were critical of what they saw as the materialism and vulgarity of Victorian Britain. They took their inspiration from nature, often allied to strong Christian themes. Leading members included the artists John Everett Millais, William Holman Hunt and *Dante Gabriel Rossetti* and the artist and critic *John Ruskin*. Later supporters, sometimes known as the 'second brotherhood', included Edward Burne Jones and *William Morris*. The brotherhood was sometimes known simply as 'PRB' after its initials.

Presbyterianism: Christian religious belief based on the ideas of the sixteenth-century religious reformer, John Calvin. Its organisation was based on the notion that church ministers (Presbyters) made decisions equally in councils (presbyteries) and so was non-hierarchical. It was an important branch of Puritanism in both England and Scotland. It remained so both in Scotland and in the north of Ireland (after 1922, *Northern Ireland*) throughout the nineteenth and twentieth centuries. In Northern Ireland it became associated with strong anti-Catholicism. After the Restoration of 1660 in England, however, it declined in importance. Despite the formal re-establishment of a Presbyterian church in 1844, numbers remained very small. It united with the Congregationalists in 1972 to become the 'United Reformed Church'.

(See also *Church of England; Roman Catholicism; Ulster.*)

Prime Minister, office of: the senior political post in the United Kingdom government. Its holder chooses ministers, including those senior ministers who sit in the Cabinet, which the Prime Minister chairs. The Prime Minister reports directly to the monarch on government business and policies and, during parliamentary sessions, answers questions from MPs in the House of Commons twice every week. Either directly or indirectly, the Prime Minister also influences the appointment of many who run government agencies. Britain does not have a written constitution which precisely specifies the role and functions of leading political figures. The office of Prime Minister has therefore evolved over roughly 250 years. Robert Walpole, who served from 1721 to 1742, is generally recognised as the first Prime Minister, though he never acknowledged that he was, as he put it, 'sole and prime minister'. Formal recognition of the title, indeed, came very late, through the Ministers of the Crown Act, 1937.

During the eighteenth century, the monarch chose individuals who might hold office so long as they commanded the confidence of Parliament, but who could still be dismissed. This happened to *Pitt the Younger* over a disagreement with *George III* on *Catholic emancipation* in 1801 and to *Melbourne*, whose judgement *William IV* distrusted, as late as 1834. Many prime ministers were peers rather than commoners. As late as 1902, a Prime Minister – the *Marquess of Salisbury* – sat in the *House of Lords*.

During the twentieth century it has become accepted that a Prime Minister must be a member of the House of Commons. One peer, *Lord Home*, resigned his peerage in 1963 in order to become Prime Minister, as Sir Alec Douglas Home. From the early nineteenth century onwards, the monarch's power to choose a Prime Minister effectively disappeared. As party disciplines became tighter, so prime ministers either already were, or immediately became, leaders of one of the two major political parties. Which party could command a majority in the Commons was determined by the electorate at *general elections*. The powers actually exercised by the Prime Minister may vary according to the temperament and personality of the occupant. Some, like *Stanley Baldwin* in the 1930s and *Clement Attlee* in the 1940s, preferred to act primarily as chairmen of groups of senior ministers, effectively only first among equals, delegating much independent power. Others, such as *Margaret Thatcher* in the 1980s, chose to present themselves as dominant leaders, delegating less and attempting to master much more of the detailed work of ministries.

It is generally agreed that the powers of the office have increased, especially since 1945. One recent study calculated that the number of governmental files going directly to the Prime Minister's office more than doubled between 1945 and 1965 and the rate of increase is unlikely to have slackened since. Increasingly, the post of Prime Minister is presented both at party conferences and in the media as if the occupant exercised presidential powers. In reality, however, prime ministerial power remains limited by the need both to remain acceptable to a political party, and especially its Members of Parliament and to the electorate. A recent instance of this is the case of *John Major* who, after winning an election in 1992, felt that he did not have the power to dismiss ministers with whom he fundamentally disagreed, and who were causing damaging party disunity, because of the strength of their support within the *Conservative Party*.

Primrose League: an organisation within the *Conservative Party*, founded by *Lord Randolph Churchill* and John Eldon Gorst in 1883 in memory of *Disraeli* and named after his favourite flower. It was committed to maintaining his 'one-nation' Tory beliefs in an age of large electorates, rather than letting the party revert to excessive reliance on the landed interest. It became an effective fund-raising organisation with more than one million members by the early 1890s.

Prince Regent: see *George IV*

prison reform movement: movement of the late eighteenth and early nineteenth centuries, associated with John Howard and *Elizabeth Fry*, to improve prison administration and remove widespread corruption within the system. Its main legislative achievements were:

- the *Gaols Act, 1823*
- the Prisons Act, 1853, which appointed prison inspectors for the first time

(See also *economic policy*; *Thatcherism*.)

Privy Council: a body offering advice to the monarch. From its origins during the reign of Henry VIII, the council became less important as the role of Parliament increased and as specialised departments of government (such as the Treasury) evolved separate functions in the seventeenth and eighteenth centuries. The *Cabinet* developed originally as a specific committee of the Council, whose functions rapidly became dominant in the formation of government policy. The Privy Council survives, its numbers now swollen to more than 400 members, since privy councillors, once appointed, serve until they die. All Cabinet members remain on the Privy Council which also includes a wide range of other interests. Its specific function remains to advise the Government though now on a range of specialised legal or constitutional matters, but much of its work is either ceremonial or formal.

(See also *monarchy*; *Prime Minister*.)

Profumo scandal: sexual affair, with political undertones, which weakened *Harold Macmillan*'s government from 1962 to 1963. John Profumo, then Minister for War, had been conducting an affair with a prostitute, Christine Keeler, who (unknown to him) had also been having sexual relations with a USSR military attaché based in the United Kingdom. Profumo lied both to the Prime Minister and to Parliament, but was found out and had to resign. The possible security angle invested the affair with greater significance than it might otherwise have had but its true importance proba-bly lies in the poor light it cast on a government which was already experiencing political difficulties. Macmillan, in particular, appeared unduly credulous for having believed Profumo and also, perhaps, out of touch and behind the times. Profumo's social circle also encompassed others in powerful positions with sexual liaisons well known both within Westminster and to the newspapers.

progressive Liberals: name given to members of the *Liberal Party* at the end of the nineteenth century who wished to use the power of the State to reduce inequalities between the social classes and to establish a range of insurance, pensions and other social benefits for the working classes. Many had absorbed the lessons of *Charles Booth* about the causes of poverty in Victorian society. Originally founded in 1889 to fight seats for the new *London County Council*, the progressives had increasing influence on policy-making within the Liberal Party, especially during the government of *H H Asquith* (1908–16).

(See also *Churchill, Winston*; *Lloyd George, David*.)

progressives: see *progressive Liberals*

prostitution: the provision of sexual services for money, usually by women. During the nineteenth century, an age of rapid urban expansion when more Puritanical 'Victorian' standards became dominant, attempts were made to regulate the trade and subject prostitutes to regular medical examination (see *Contagious Diseases Acts*), but there is no evidence that it controlled the trade. For many working-class girls, especially those outside a conventional family, it became a vital source of income, though a risky one, since prostitutes had little or no redress against violence or worse.

As in the eighteenth century, higher-class prostitutes (often known as 'courtesans') plied their trade among the wealthy and well-connected. Propertied middle- and upper-class men frequently consorted with prostitutes, though they were forced to do so less openly than in the eighteenth century. The Criminal Law Amendment Act, 1885, introduced new restrictions. By it:

- brothels (places at which sex was 'sold') were declared illegal
- the age of sexual consent was set at sixteen years
- new penalties were introduced for homosexual behaviour

The Act merely made the trade less open, and thus more difficult for the police to detect. Legislation passed during a more liberal moral climate in the second half of the twentieth century, such as the Street Offences Act, 1959, has been similarly ineffective, producing different consequences from those intended by legislators. In practice, individual police forces have to take decisions on how to deal with offences such as 'soliciting' for sexual trade and 'street crawling', knowing that legislation is a very blunt instrument indeed with which to deal with human nature and desire.

(See also *Wolfenden Report.*)

public health: the health of the community at large. This emerged as a problem only in the early nineteenth century when rapid urban growth created conditions which many contemporaries recognised were harmful to health. These included:

- poor standards of *housing*
- overcrowding in tenement blocks
- inadequate sanitation and poor water supplies

Additionally, a widespread outbreak of *cholera* in 1831–32 focused specific attention on the effects of epidemic disease on an overcrowded population. Death rates among infants were particularly high. In some large towns in the 1830s and 1840s, one child in every four born alive had died by the age of five.

In the early 1840s, *Edwin Chadwick* produced an influential study which associated poor environmental conditions with high death rates. This led to the establishment of a Royal Commission on the Health of Towns in 1844–45 and then to the first major Public Health Act in 1848. Its main terms were:

- a central Board of Health was established, responsible to Parliament
- local boards of health could be established on the petition of not fewer than ten per cent of ratepayers
- local boards of health must be established when the death rate in a town exceeded 23 per thousand of the population (as against a national average of 21 per thousand)
- the work of the by now numerous local boards established by individual legislation was not affected by this Act

Developments over the next decade showed how unpopular central direction in matters of public health had become. The Board was wound up by the Local Government Act and Public Health Act of 1858 and its functions were transferred to a newly established Local Government Act Office. The statistics did not show that the Board of Health had effected any significant improvement in death rates. Only in 1866, by the Sanitary Act, were uniform and compulsory basic standards put in place

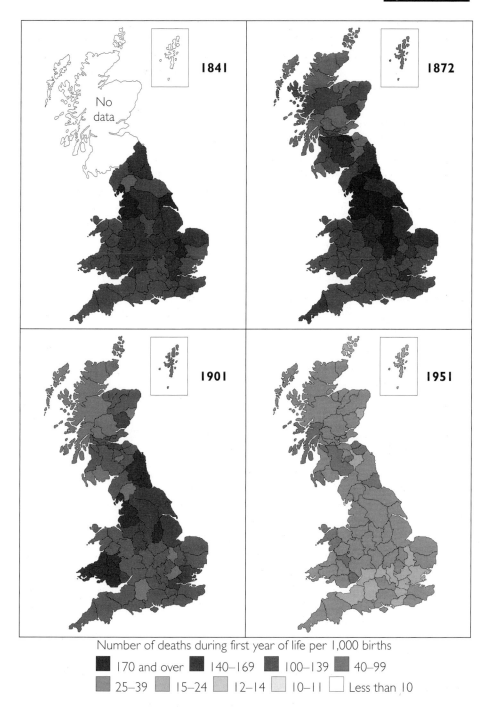

Number of deaths during first year of life per 1,000 births

■ 170 and over ■ 140–169 ■ 100–139 ■ 40–99
■ 25–39 ■ 15–24 ■ 12–14 ■ 10–11 □ Less than 10

Public health – infant mortality

and only in 1872 did local boards have to appoint a medical officer of health with the responsibility of reporting on standards. During the last quarter of the nineteenth century, standards began slowly to improve, then more rapidly in the years before 1914 as the State took a more direct role in providing welfare services and *national insurance*. Public health improvements occurred first in less crowded and wealthier areas.

In the twentieth century, as housing standards began to improve and overcrowding became less severe, public health provision concentrated more on mitigating the effects of epidemics by giving advice on the management of infectious disease, by facilitating inoculation campaigns and by supervising standards of food hygiene.

(See also *Kay-Shuttleworth, James: Simon, Sir John; Liberal Party; welfare state*.)

public schools: non-state schools, funded by a combination of charitable endowments and fees paid by parents. Because these endowments originally enabled some members of the ordinary public to receive an education, they became known as 'public', though they are in reality private or 'independent' of the state system. Many, like Eton and Winchester, date from medieval times. From the 1840s a large number of new schools were founded. Many, like Lancing, Radley and Rossall, were Anglican (*Church of England*) foundations often on principles of 'muscular Christianity' stressing the link between a healthy body and a clear mind. Most were for boys, but the Girls' Public Day Schools Commission began to create girls' schools from the 1860s, of which one of the most famous was the North London Collegiate School. Public schools educated the children of the middle and upper classes. The nine most famous were the subject of a report from the *Clarendon Commission* and the remainder was investigated by the *Taunton Commission*.

During the twentieth century, public schools were frequently attacked by the Labour Party, which argued that they were seats of privilege at which a social elite was educated in ways which reinforced social distinctions. Educating about seven per cent of the population, they gained for their pupils a much larger proportion of places at the older universities, especially Oxford and Cambridge. However, plans for abolition during the Labour governments of 1964–70 and 1974–79 never came to fruition and the Labour government elected in 1997 attempted to raise educational standards generally, rather than attacking the independent schools.

(See also *Arnold, Thomas*.)

pupil–teacher scheme: system for training teachers in schools supported by public grant. It was established by the Committee of the Privy Council on Education in 1846. Under it, the old 'monitorial' system of teaching, whereby older pupils instructed younger ones, was dropped. It was replaced by a new training scheme which set minimum standards for teaching staff. It proved an avenue of opportunity for able working-class pupils to acquire some degree of professional training. It proved successful but expensive. Its rapid expansion was one of the main reasons why the Revised Code of Education was introduced in 1862 in order to save taxpayers' money.

(See also *Education Acts; Kay-Shuttleworth, James; Lowe, Robert*.)

Q

Quebec Conferences, 1943–44: meetings between the US President F D Roosevelt and the British *Prime Minister Winston Churchill* to agree on strategy during *World War II*. The conference in 1943 committed the Allies to support for the development of an atomic bomb and also established a South-East Asia Command to co-ordinate the war against the Japanese in *Burma*. In 1944, the British agreed to send a fleet to help the USA in the war at sea against Japan.

Queenston Heights, Battle of (1812): first significant engagement in the *Anglo-American War*, which took place in Canada when British forces under Sir Isaac Brock repulsed a force of 1,000 US troops which had crossed the Niagara river and climbed the heights. Almost all of the US troops were forced to surrender. Brock was killed in the battle.

R

Race Relations Acts: legislation passed by *Labour* governments in 1965, 1968 and 1976 in the wake of widespread *immigration*, especially from the West Indies and the Indian sub-continent. The intention was to promote racial harmony. By the Act of 1965:

- discrimination in public places, such as restaurants, was made illegal
- incitement to racial hatred was for the first time made an offence
- a Race Relations Board was established with powers to investigate complaints about racial discrimination on grounds of race

The Act of 1968:

- extended the scope of the Race Relations Board
- established a Community Relations Commission to promote racial harmony

The Act of 1976 was intended to strengthen previous legislation. By it:

- discrimination in employment, training or education was made illegal
- the definition of discrimination extended to include victimisation and forms of indirect preference for one race over another
- a Commission for Racial Equality was established with greater powers than predecessor bodies to promote 'equality of opportunity and good relations'. Its first Chairman was Sir David Lane

Although each of these pieces of legislation was passed by Labour governments, none was opposed by the *Conservative* Party. Both parties, however, firmly opposed further immigration especially from the Black *Commonwealth* and the Conservatives' Nationality Act in 1981 (based on Labour Party policy documents of 1976 and 1977) removed automatic right of British citizenship from all people born in the country.

Race-relations legislation has created a framework which formally outlaws discrimination. However, most of the indicators of living standards and unemployment show that children of immigrants entering Britain in the 1950s and 1960s fare worse than those from other backgrounds.

(See also *Powell, J Enoch.*)

radicalism: the desire to effect change as a result of analysing the root of a particular problem. In our period, it is more frequently associated with the nineteenth than with the twentieth century. Radicalism is usually associated with the movement for political reform, especially the movement for *parliamentary reform* and democracy associated with *artisans* and *middle-class* reformers in the late eighteenth and early nineteenth centuries. Other forms of radicalism from the same period can, however, be readily identified:

- 'philosophical radicalism', associated with the ideas of *Jeremy Bentham*, urged reforms in government based on *utilitarian* principles and is also associated with *laissez-faire*
- '*Manchester school* radicalism', associated particularly with *Richard Cobden* and *John Bright*, was concerned with achieving *free trade*. It also tended to be

anti-aristocratic, most of its adherents believing that *aristocracy* was a form of government which impeded progress and did not adequately reward merit

- 'single-issue' radicals are more difficult to categorise. They supported causes which required a fundamental shift in policy. Among the most significant were those who sought moral reformation or political improvement through the *Temperance Movement*, *disestablishment* of the *Church of England*, secular education, a *republican* form of government and the like

In the second half of the nineteenth century, most shades of radical opinion found a more or less comfortable home within the *Liberal Party*. Since their views on single issues clouded wider judgement of political priority, they were frequently difficult to unite into a coherent policy programme, as *Gladstone* discovered.

(See also *Anti-Corn Law League*; *Bradlaugh, Charles*; *Chartism*; *Dilke, Charles*; *Newcastle Programme*; *Place, Francis*.)

radio: form of broadcasting based on sound rather than vision. The technology for radio broadcasting depended upon the discovery of electromagnetic waves, which eliminated the need for cables, and the development of the thermionic valve which could transmit speech. The first broadcasts were made during 1922 by the Marconi Company as '2MT' broadcasting from Chelmsford and '2LO' broadcasting from Marconi House. These were the prelude to the establishment of a monopoly by the British Broadcasting Company, licensed by The *Post Office*, which took over operations in November 1922, with *John Reith* as Managing Director, a post he held until 1938. The 'BBC' became the *British Broadcasting Corporation* in 1927, by which time the great majority of the public could receive broadcasts from a network of transmitters. It was established as a non-profit-making organisation funded by a licence bought by owners of radio sets.

BBC radio broadcasts were immensely popular, but the content was controlled by Reith to provide a carefully calculated mixture of information, education, instruction and entertainment. For Reith, entertainment was less important than moral improvement and he revelled in great set-piece occasions, such as the announcement of important events or annual Christmas broadcasts by the reigning monarch, beginning with that by *George V* in 1932. Although radio became less overtly moralistic after *World War II*, Reith's legacy was an enduring one, especially while the BBC retained a monopoly. 'The Third Programme' (from 1967, 'Radio 3'), founded in 1946, owed much to Reithian principles. It broadcast serious music, plays, poetry, political and philosophical lectures and discussions, bringing the best of uncompromising high culture into domestic living space. Although it attracted only very small audiences, together with 'the Home Service' (from 1967, 'Radio 4'), it provided high-quality broadcasting which became the envy of the world while also operating as a kind of unofficial university of the airwaves for those who wished to improve their knowledge and understanding. Together with the BBC World Service, it sustained a level of broadcasting excellence at a time when British power and influence in other fields was in rapid retreat.

Radio broadcasting was forced to adapt rapidly to a commercial world when the BBC's monopoly ended in 1973. Competitors in 'Independent Local Radio' were far less interested in quality than in mass appeal and their aggressive style and unsophisticated vigour compelled a response from the BBC. An ever larger gap developed between its 'popular', music-based programmes mainly for the young ('Radio 1', which began broadcasting in 1967) and for the middle-aged and elderly ('The Light Programme', founded in 1945 – 'Radio 2' from 1967) on the one hand and the more serious, speech- and high-culture-based programmes (Radios 3 and 4) which it continued to offer, mostly to well-educated middle-class audiences.

In the last twenty years of the century, radio broadcasting became much more diverse in both its scope and the audience at which it aimed. Both commercial and BBC radio developed local and community-based networks, broadcasting much more local and regional news, providing regular 'updates' on traffic and travel interspersed with ubiquitous popular music which cost little to transmit. Channels largely, or wholly, devoted to sport also emerged, led by BBC's Radio 5 launched in 1990. Radio became less concerned with transmitting, and enhancing, a national culture than with providing cheap, reliable information – noise moderated by news, its critics might say.

(See also *British Broadcasting Corporation; television.*)

Raffles, Sir Stamford: colonial administrator. He was born on board ship off Jamaica in 1781 and rose rapidly to prominence as an employee of the East India Company. He was instrumental in the capture of Java from the Dutch in 1811 during the *Napoleonic Wars* but was criticised in Britain for his administration of public lands during the time of British occupation (1811–14). After returning to the far east, he took up an administrative post in Sumatra, and urged British occupation of *Singapore* as security against Dutch ambitions in the area. Singapore was taken over by the British in 1819 and Raffles acted as its governor until 1824, laying its foundations as a key strategic and economic base. A keen naturalist, he also became the first President of the Royal Zoological Society. He died in 1826.

ragged schools: elementary schools for poor children. The first schools which eventually had this title were founded by John Pounds, a shoemaker from Portsmouth, in 1818. They charged no fees and attempted to provide children with basic literacy and schooling, becoming most common in London. In 1844 the Earl of *Shaftesbury* took up the presidency of a newly founded 'Ragged School Union'. By 1870, at which point the schools were mostly absorbed into the new state-supported *Board Schools,* approximately 360 ragged schools were in existence in England and Wales, 60 per cent of them in the capital.

(See also *Education Act, 1870.*)

Raglan (Fitzroy, James Henry Somerset), 1st Baron: soldier. Born in 1788, he saw service with *Wellington* during the *Peninsular War.* He was Secretary of the Horse Guards from 1827 to 1852 and then became Commander of the British Army. In this capacity, he commanded the forces in the *Crimean War.* He proved a weak and indecisive leader and much of the widespread criticism of British performance centred on his incompetence. He died of dysentery while on active service in 1855.

(See also *Balaclava, Battle of; Cardigan, Earl of.*)

railways: the fastest and most efficient form of long-distance inland transport in the nineteenth and early twentieth centuries. Carriages conveyed on wheels moving along fixed track were in operation from the early seventeenth century, when they were horse-drawn. 'Wagon ways' were extensively developed in the North-East of England in the century after 1660. The first commercially effective steam locomotives, working on the ideas of James Watt and Richard Trevithick, were demonstrated by Matthew Murray and John Blenkinsop at Middleton Colliery, near Leeds, in 1812. The first public steam railway sanctioned by Parliament to carry both passengers and goods was the Stockton and Darlington opened in 1825, but it was dominated by the conveyance of coal and was only thirty miles long. The Liverpool to Manchester Railway (1830) was designed for steam haulage throughout and was, from the beginning, committed to passenger traffic. After its success, the development of railway transport was extremely rapid. The main advantages of railway transport in the nineteenth century were:

- speedier and more efficient transport
- opportunities for associated industries, particularly coal and iron, to grow
- new opportunities for investment. Many fortunes were made from wise investment in railway stock, though many small investors had their fingers badly burned by investing when stock was high and just before a price fall
- opportunities for migration, both within the country and to the main ports
- opportunity to work at a greater distance from home and 'commute' by train to and from work
- the creation of new towns, existing as rail and engineering centres. Examples are Crewe, Swindon and Wolverton
- reducing the amount of time taken on travel. The advent of railways also made people more 'clock-conscious' and ended the keeping of different times within the British Isles
- expanded *leisure* opportunities, both for 'day trips' to the seaside and for longer holidays

The main developments were:
1830–70

1831	Garnkirk and Glasgow Railway became the first line to be opened in Scotland
1837	railway opened by Grand Junction company from Warrington to Birmingham
1838	Grand Junction Railway completed from London to Birmingham
1837–40	first burst of so-called 'railway mania', characterised by huge investment and large number of projects begun
1840s	many railway companies have early success but are forced into merger to ensure future viability. About 200 separate companies were running services in 1843; this had reduced to 22 by 1850
1840	1,500 miles of railway track were open
1841	first line in Wales opened (Cardiff to Merthyr); Thomas Cook organised the first passenger excursion train, from Loughborough to Leicester, for a *temperance* fête. Broad-gauge railway from London to Bristol, designed by *I K Brunel*, opened
1842	railway opened from Edinburgh to Glasgow

1844	Railways Act created a separate Railways Board with powers of inspection and regulation. The Act required cheap ('parliamentary') trains to run at least once a day with a fare no higher than one penny a mile to encouraging 'commuting'
1846	creation of the London and North-Western Railway by mergers of smaller companies, to take customers from London to Carlisle
1846–47	second burst of 'railway mania'
1848	completion of first direct route from London to Glasgow (on the route of the 'West Coast Main Line')
1850	6,084 miles of track were open. London to Edinburgh direct route opened (later called the 'East Coast Main Line')
1851	*Great Exhibition* proved a great boost to railway traffic, through trips and excursions
1860	9,000 miles of track were open. All major cities connected to the rail network by this date and process of linking smaller, rural communities is well advanced
1862–65	third burst of 'railway mania'
1863	opening of Metropolitan Railway's first track from Paddington to Farringdon Street began the London Underground Railway, which was steadily extended
1870	13,562 miles of track were open

Since 1870

1873	first 'sleeper service' run by the North British Railway between Glasgow and London King's Cross
1876	opening of 72 miles of largely moorland railway from Settle to Carlisle, owned by the Midland Railway, completed another route from London to Glasgow
1886	Severn Railway Tunnel opened, connecting the South-West to South Wales. It was the longest railway tunnel in Britain (outside London Underground) and, at that time, the longest underwater tunnel in the world
1897	first continuous all-night service opened between Liverpool Street and Walthamstow
1923	extensive amalgamations resulted in the creation of four major companies: the Southern Railway; the Great Western Railway; London Midland and Scottish Railway; London and North-Eastern Railway
1932	at 22,243 miles, the British railway system reached its greatest extent; 20,267 of this was on the 'standard gauge'
1935	first railway station to service an airport was opened by Southern Railways at Gatwick
1947	*nationalisation* of the system by the Transport Act. British Railways formally took over service on 1 January 1948
1960	18,369 miles of track were open. Between 1948 and 1962, the system contracted by about ten per cent
1963	publication of 'The Reshaping of British Railways' by Richard Beeching. This recommended a severe reduction in the railway system and the closure

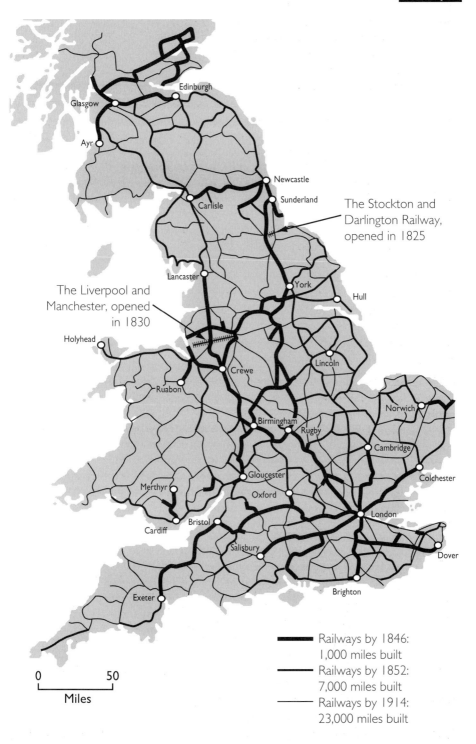

The Stockton and Darlington Railway, opened in 1825

The Liverpool and Manchester, opened in 1830

Railways by 1846: 1,000 miles built

Railways by 1852: 7,000 miles built

Railways by 1914: 23,000 miles built

Glasgow
Edinburgh
Ayr
Newcastle
Carlisle
Sunderland
Lancaster
York
Hull
Holyhead
Crewe
Lincoln
Ruabon
Birmingham
Norwich
Rugby
Cambridge
Gloucester
Colchester
Merthyr
Oxford
London
Cardiff
Bristol
Salisbury
Dover
Exeter
Brighton

0   50
Miles

Railways built between 1825 and 1914

of 2,000 stations. Although amended in detail, it began a period of planned reduction of services

1970   system reduced to 11,799 miles

1980   system reduced to 10,964 miles

1994   British Rail privatised and the system was sold off to a number of different companies

The railway system fell into decline in the second half of the twentieth century. The main reasons for this were:

- increasing competition from the motor car, which proved more flexible. Car ownership also proved a potent status symbol for many
- increasing competition in the leisure industry from aeroplanes. The 'package tour industry' could take holidays to guaranteed sun
- government policy which systematically favoured road over rail transport at least from the 1950s. In the 1980s, also, *Thatcherism*'s obsessional concern to reduce public subsidies meant that the British railway network received less priority than most other forms of transport
- loss of morale among both workers and management as government policy moved towards privatisation which few wanted and most prophesied would be a disaster

(See Figure on page 255. See also *canals; immigration; Industrial Revolution; transportation; tourist industry.*)

Rathbone, Eleanor: feminist social reformer and politician. Born in 1872 into a prosperous family from Liverpool, she soon took up a number of *radical* causes, including baby clinics, women's suffrage, and extended rights for women in India. Her campaign for *family allowances* resulted from her experience during *World War I* when she saw the value of small payments made directly to women rather than to the head of the household. She sat as an independent MP from 1929 until her death in 1946. She opposed *Neville Chamberlain* and *appeasement* and warmly supported the proposals of *William Beveridge*, being particularly concerned to ensure that the benefits his reforms presaged would go particularly to women and children.

(See also *public health; social policy; suffragettes; Women's Social and Political Union.*)

'rational recreation': name given by social historians to forms of *leisure* intended either to improve the mind or to refresh the spirit. This was the objective behind several schemes in Victorian Britain, such as the establishment of *public libraries* or public parks in urban areas. These contrasted with baser forms of entertainment which might threaten public order or peace. Many of these involved drink, dancing or vigorous sports played by large numbers of men in the necessarily confined spaces of towns and cities.

Rebecca Riots: a form of protest, particularly in the west of Wales, and concentrated in 1842–43. Some saw the riots as part of the general *Chartist* disturbances but their targets were specifically rural ones. Turnpike gates and toll houses were attacked at night by people in disguise, frequently wearing women's clothes. Their name was taken from a reference in the Bible (Genesis, xxiv v.60): 'the seed of Rebecca shall possess the gates of her enemies'. Other forms of disturbance included attacks on the new *Poor Law workhouses.* As with *Luddism* in the first decade of the nineteenth century, the Government deployed many troops in usually vain attempts to hunt down rioters who were well-protected by their local communities. The protests also had a nationalist tinge. In particular, rioters objected to paying tithes to provide for clergy of the *Church of England.* The rioters' protests had some success. In 1844, *Peel's* government passed an Act which reduced turnpike tolls.

(See also *Swing Riots.*)

'Red Clydeside': name given to *trade unionists* in the *engineering* and *shipbuilding* industries and to *socialist* politicians around Glasgow who had campaigned for improved wages and better conditions and against bringing in unskilled workers during *World War I.* Immediately after *World War I,* during a short post-war economic boom, they organised many strikes and demonstrations.

(See also *syndicalism.*)

Redistribution Act, 1885: legislation which reduced the discrepancy between the size of parliamentary constituencies and related constituencies to population size. It thus brought much closer the *Chartist* objective of 'equal electoral districts', although the Government specifically rejected the principle of absolute equality in the size of constituencies. The main changes involved:

- the loss of many smaller boroughs, especially in England and Ireland, and the creation of new boroughs in centres of population. The boroughs disfranchised had their representation transferred to the counties of which they were geographically a part. In all, 132 borough seats were disfranchised and 138 new seats created
- the allocation of ten extra seats to Scotland; these went in part to the counties and in part to the cities of Glasgow, Edinburgh and Aberdeen
- the allocation of far more seats to the main centres of population in England. Of the 106 new seats created, the London area received forty
- the allocation of proportionately more seats to Scotland, Ireland and Wales all of which had been under-represented before 1885

(See also *parliamentary reform; Reform Act, 1884.*)

Redmond, John: Irish nationalist politician. Born in County Wexford in 1856, he trained as a lawyer and became clerk of the *House of Commons* in 1880. He took over the leadership of the Nationalists at Westminster from *Charles Stewart Parnell* in 1891 after Parnell was forced to resign but his leadership lacked Parnell's charisma and determination. Many in Ireland also accused him of being too willing to compromise with the *Liberal Party,* especially after 1910 when the nationalists held the balance of power in the Commons. He also accepted proposals for a partition of Ireland at independence, which caused further nationalist resentment. His credibility was further damaged by his failure to anticipate the *Easter Rising* in 1916. He died in 1918 before the full power of *Sinn Fein,* which he had always distrusted, was revealed. Essentially, Redmond was a democratic politician facing political events which many nationalists believed could now be resolved only by violence.

(See also *Carson, Edward; Ireland; Lloyd George, David.*)

referendum: device whereby the electorate is asked a specific question on a matter of national importance. Referenda (the correct plural form of 'referendum') are a recent device. They do not bind *Parliament* but their results, when decisive, have guided or (much more commonly) confirmed, the views of the government of the day. Referenda, in truth, have usually been employed in support of a particular political strategy. The government controls the form in which the question is asked, and this is crucial. Especially when opinion is almost evenly divided, precise wording is of first importance. The most significant referenda were those held over Britain's membership of the European Economic Community in 1975 and on Scottish and Welsh devolution in 1997. In the former case, the referendum took place after Britain's membership was an established fact and was a political device to quieten political opposition to continued membership within the then governing *Labour Party*. In the latter case, Scottish and Welsh electorates were asked by a government recently elected by a large majority to confirm support for a policy which had formed part of the Labour Party's election manifesto. In these cases, the governments got the results they wanted. A much weaker Labour government in 1979, without a majority of its own and severely constrained by difficulties and dissension within the party, failed to secure sufficient support in referenda on Scottish and Welsh devolution. It has usually been *Conservative Party* policy to oppose referenda. Opponents argue that Members of Parliament are elected to represent their constituents and to vote on their behalf on questions both large and small. Since there is no clear guidance on the kinds of issue which might be 'offered' to the electorate in the form of a referendum, the danger that the device is exploited for reasons of governing party convenience, rather than because it genuinely wants to know what the electorate thinks, is considerable.

(See also *devolution; Parliament; Commons, House of.*)

Reform Act, 1832: first of the nineteenth-century Acts which changed rules governing both the composition of, and the eligibility to vote for members of, the House of *Commons*. It was passed by the *Whig* government under *Earl Grey*. The main changes it introduced were:

- 56 old parliamentary boroughs lost both their MPs; 30 others lost one of their two
- 22 new boroughs were created with two members and 20 with one. Most of these new boroughs were in the main centres of population
- the number of English county constituencies was increased from 80 to 144
- a standard qualification to vote was introduced in the boroughs. Men occupying property worth £10 a year could vote. Those entitled to vote before 1832 kept this right while they lived
- in counties, owners of land worth £2 a year (40 shillings) retained their right to vote; after a Tory amendment (the Chandos Amendment) was passed in the *House of Lords*, tenants who occupied land worth £50 a year could also vote

It has been estimated that the Act increased the number of voters from about 440,000 to 652,000, but the proportion of voters increased more in some places than others. In Scotland, for example, the number increased from about 4,000 to 65,000.

The Act did not change the nation's rulers and did not give power to the middle classes. The *aristocracy* remained dominant in both government and Parliament. However, the Act did make Parliament more responsive to pressure from outside.

(See also *parliamentary reform*.)

Changes in England and Wales as a result of the 1832 Reform Act

Boroughs

Boroughs lost or gained members as follows:

Lost one member

Arundel	Eye	Lyme Regis	Rye	Weymouth &
Ashburton	Grimsby	Malmesbury	Shaftesbury	Melcombe
Calne	Helston	Midhurst	St Ives	Wilton
Christchurch	Horsham	Morpeth	Thirsk	Woodstock
Clitheroe	Hythe	Northallerton	Wallingford	
Dartmouth	Launceston	Petersfield	Wareham	
Droitwich	Liskeard	Reigate	Westbury	

Lost both members and now disfranchised

Aldbrough	Camelford	Heytesbury	Newtown	Stockbridge
Aldeburgh	Castle Rising	Higham Ferrers	Okehampton	Tregony
Amersham	Corfe Castle	Hinden	Old Sarum	Wendover
Appleby	Downton	Ilchester	Orford	Weobley
Beer Alston	Dunwich	Lostwithiel	Plympton Erle	West Looe
Bishop's Castle	East Grinstead	Ludgershall	Queenborough	Whitchurch
Bletchingley	East Looe	Milborne Port	Saltash	Winchelsea
Boroughbridge	Fowey	Minehead	Seaford	Wootton
Bossiney	Gatton	Mitchell	St Germains	Bassett
Brackley	Great Bedwyn	New Romney	St Mawes	Yarmouth
Bramber	Haslemere	Newport	St Michael	
Callington	Hedon	Newton	Steyning	

New boroughs gaining one member

Ashton-under-	Dudley	Kidderminster	Swansea	Whitby
Lyne	Frome	Methyr Tydfil	Tynemouth	Whitehaven
Bury	Gateshead	Rochdale	Wakefield	
Chatham	Huddersfield	Salford	Walsall	
Cheltenham	Kendal	South Shields	Warrington	

New boroughs gaining two members

Birmingham	Devonport	Leeds	Sheffield	Tower Hamlets
Blackburn	Finsbury	Macclesfield	Stockport	Wolverhampton
Bolton	Greenwich	Manchester	Stoke-on-Trent	
Bradford	Halifax	Marylebone	Stroud	
Brighton	Lambeth	Oldham	Sunderland	

Counties

All English counties now returned four MPs, instead of two previously, except the following:

Yorkshire	6	Dorset	3	Bedfordshire	2	Rutland	2
Berkshire	3	Herefordshire	3	Huntingdonshire	2	Westmorland	2
Buckinghamshire	3	Hertfordshire	3	Middlesex	2	Isle of Wight	1
Cambridgeshire	3	Oxfordshire	3	Monmouth	2		

All Welsh counties continued to send one MP to Parliament, except the following:

Glamorgan	2	Carmarthen	2	Denbigh	2

In addition, Merthyr Tydfil and Swansea became new one-member seats

Reform Act, 1867: second of the nineteenth-century Acts which changed rules governing both the composition of, and the eligibility to vote for members of, the House of *Commons*. It was passed by the *Conservative* government under the *Earl of Derby*. The main changes it introduced were:

- in parliamentary boroughs with populations of less than 10,000, three lost both their MPs, 35 lost one of their two and four lost the single MP they had possessed
- two new double-member boroughs and nine new single-member boroughs were created. Birmingham, Leeds, Liverpool and Manchester all now elected three MPs. Two boroughs (Merthyr Tydfil and Salford) received a second MP
- ten counties, plus Yorkshire's West Riding, received two more seats and Lancashire was given three more. The University of London was given one MP
- in parliamentary boroughs adult male owners and occupiers of dwelling houses could vote if they could establish continuous residence for at least twelve months. Lodgers could vote if they occupied lodgings worth at least £10 a year and if they could establish continuous residence for at least twelve months
- in county constituencies, adult males who owned or held on long leases (60 years or more) property worth £5 a year, or occupied land worth £12 a year could vote

Overall, the number of voters increased from about 1.1 million to 2.0 million. The Act was largely the work of *Benjamin Disraeli* and no one knew how it would work. The Earl of Derby, voicing common concerns among the propertied classes about the voting extensions particularly in the boroughs, talked about its being 'a leap in the dark'. It certainly created working-class majorities in a number of urban constituencies and it required the political parties to organise themselves much more professionally but it did not produce radical change in the way the country was governed, although the number of MPs from the middle classes continued to grow. The residence qualifications reduced the potential number of working-class voters substantially.

(See also *parliamentary reform; Reform Act (Scotland), 1868*.)

Reform Act (Scotland), 1868: this Act closely followed the changes effected in England and Wales the previous year. The large Scottish cities of Glasgow and Dundee gained an extra MP as did the most populous counties, Aberdeenshire, Ayrshire and Lanarkshire. The property qualification in the Scottish counties was set at £14 not £12. The proportion of male voters in Scotland was broadly similar to that in England and Wales.

(See also *parliamentary reform; Reform Act, 1867*.)

Reform Act, 1884: third of the nineteenth-century Acts which changed rules governing eligibility to vote for members of the *House of Commons*. It was passed by the *Liberal* government under *William Gladstone*. The main changes it introduced were:

- the ending of different qualifications to vote in borough and county seats. The qualification was now set at that agreed for English and Welsh boroughs in 1867

- those who occupied land or, in towns, tenements worth £10 a year could vote

The changes brought about need to be linked to the *Redistribution Act* of 1885.

(See also *parliamentary reform*.)

Reform Act, 1918: first of the twentieth-century Acts which changed rules governing eligibility to vote for members of the *House of Commons* and which redistributed parliamentary seats. It was passed by the *coalition* government under *David Lloyd George*. The main changes it introduced were:

- the abolition of property qualifications for voting; this permitted a large number of adult men to vote for the first time
- the enfranchisement of women aged 30 years and over on the same basis as men
- parliamentary candidates were required to pay a deposit of £150 which would be returned if they received at least one-eighth of the votes
- for the first time, all the voting in parliamentary elections was to be held on a single day
- an increase in the number of parliamentary constituencies to 707; this number was reduced to 615 when the Irish Free State was created in 1922

This legislation increased the number of people entitled to vote from 7.7 million to 21.8 million and thus created overwhelmingly the largest increase in voting numbers in British history. It increased the proportion of adults entitled to vote from approximately 28 per cent to approximately 78 per cent.

Three further changes to the rules for voting were made during the twentieth century:

- The Equal Franchise Act, 1928, extended the right to vote to women of 21 and above
- The Representation of the People Act, 1948, abolished separate rights to vote based on a business qualification or a degree from one of the ancient universities. This finally established the principle of 'one person, one vote'
- The Representation of the People Act, 1969, reduced the voting age from 21 to 18

Regency: name given to a style of architecture and dress developed in the early nineteenth century during, and often under the patronage of, the Prince Regent, later *George IV*. Following on from the neo-classical designs of eighteenth century town houses and assembly rooms, its most prominent feature is the large, opulent houses of brick and stone built in terraces. Examples are those in Bath, Leamington Spa and London. The name is also associated with Regent Street and Regent's Park in central London and with the lifestyle of friends of the Regent, notably George Bryan 'Beau' Brummel (1778–1840), who threw large parties and posed as an arbiter of taste and fashion in the second decade of the nineteenth century.

(See also *Nash, John*.)

Reith, John (1st Baron Reith of Stonehaven): pioneer broadcaster. Born the son of a Church of Scotland minister in Aberdeenshire in 1889, he retained from his family background a high moral seriousness. This he invested into his career as the first General Manager of the *British Broadcasting Corporation*, a post he held from 1922 to 1938. His mission was to instruct and to improve the minds of the listeners to his programmes and he saw *radio* as a superb vehicle for education. Entertainment, though important, had a subordinate role in his vision. His imprint on the BBC was huge, lasting until the early 1960s. Reith had a much shorter, and less effective, career in politics. He entered Parliament in 1939, and quickly achieved ministerial status. His major offices were:

- Minister of Information, 1940, in *Chamberlain*'s government
- Minister of Transport, 1940 in *Churchill*'s government
- Minister of Works and Buildings, 1940–42

Churchill, however, found his high-minded seriousness a considerable trial to his patience and dismissed him in 1942. Though he lived until 1971, his post-war career lacked direction and he became increasingly disillusioned. Both radio and *television* have been utterly transformed since Reith's day and it is easy to poke fun at this austere, anachronistic and arrogant man. However, his contribution to making the BBC the world's pre-eminent broadcasting company in the first fifty years of its life was decisive.

Rent Legislation: Acts of Parliament passed to protect tenants from excessive rents or other forms of exploitation by landlords. The most important Acts were those of:

1915 the Liberal government of Asquith, which imposed maximum levels of rent after a number of 'rent strikes' and other forms of civil unrest, particularly in Glasgow

1957 the Conservative government of Macmillan, which ended the system of rent controls on most houses owned by private landlords, rather than councils. The aim was to improve the efficiency of the rented housing market

1965 the Labour government of Wilson, which repealed the 1957 Act, which had encouraged some private landlords to exploit the system, especially to the disadvantage of those renting unfurnished property usually near the bottom of the housing market. The new Act introduced rent controls over unfurnished, privately-rented property

reparations: name given to payments to be made by Germany for costs incurred by the Allies during *World War I*. The justification for these charges, originally set in 1919 at £13.4 million but reduced in 1921 to £6.6 million, was that Germany had been responsible for the outbreak of the war. Most of the payments were to be made to France. Germany's unwillingness and, after the collapse of its currency, inability to pay remained a festering sore in international relations during the 1920s. The amounts due were further reduced and, following the worldwide economic crash in 1929–31, cancelled in 1932. They are widely believed to have been one of the main reasons why extremist parties grew to challenge the democratic 'Weimar Government' in Germany.

(See also *Keynes, J M.*)

republicanism: system of government not headed by a monarch. Britain has only once in its history been a republic (from 1649 to 1660) and the experiment was not a happy one. Although most of the established European monarchies disappeared, as a result of revolution or defeat in war, between 1789 and 1918, Britain remained a monarchy. Support for republicanism was usually low, although a significant move-ment developed during the 1860s, when Queen *Victoria* shut herself away during a long period of mourning for the death of her husband Prince *Albert* and in the 1990s, in reaction to the heavily-publicised waste, immaturity and profligacy of Queen *Elizabeth II*'s children and their spouses. In general, however, republicanism has had very little support in Britain because the monarchy proved to be an adaptable insti-tution. Queen *Victoria* and her successors have abandoned all claim to direct policy, acting publicly as heads of state on ceremonial and other public functions and, more privately, to give advice when asked by the government of the day.

retailing industry: economic activity which developed to meet the needs of con-sumers. Although the increasing wealth of late eighteenth- and early nineteenth-century society saw a great upsurge in demand for a range of foodstuffs and manufactured goods, the basis of retailing remained that of personal contact between purchaser and shopkeeper, or stall-holder, at one of the regular fairs or in a 'market town'. Market towns, many of them now small villages, were the vital medi-um of exchange and it was rare for them to be more than ten to fifteen miles apart. The growth of population overall and the densities found in the leading industrial and commercial towns forced a substantial change in patterns of buying and selling. The main developments from the 1840s have been:

- the growth of department stores. Beginning with Whiteley's in Bayswater and Harrods in Knightbridge, these provided a range of goods mostly for middle- and upper-class shoppers. From the 1880s, as living standards for the working classes increased when prices fell, stores such as Marks and Spencer (which began as a penny bazaar run by Jewish traders in Leeds) and F W Woolworth (a firm established first in the United States) became established

- in the growing suburbs, the establishment of 'corner-shops'. Often inti-mately tied to the economics of the local community (shopkeepers were forced to give credit to reliable customers during depressions or periods of local unemployment as a strategy for staying in business) and responsive to social shifts, they became a permanent part of the retailing scene. When challenged first by growing city-centre stores offering a wider range of goods at keener prices and later by 'out-of-town' sites, they responded by maintaining the convenience of local stores (available to supply the goods which a customer may have forgotten when shopping in the town centre) and longer opening hours. The phrase 'open all hours', while never liter-ally true, was indicative of the small shops' willingness to trade on convenience, personal knowledge of customers and availability

- the establishment of specialist retail outlets, such as Lipton's grocers (a range of stores developed from a successful initial shop in Glasgow), the 'Home and Colonial' stores and Dewhurst's butchers. These firms were able to supply a large variety of products at keenly competitive prices and expanded their activities substantially during the 1930s as Britain began to recover from the worldwide Depression

- the development of 'multiple-stores', sometimes known as 'hypermarkets' from the 1960s. Many of the largest stores solved problems of space by establishing premises in 'out-of-town' sites. These flourished because of customers' increasing ability, and willingness, to use cars to travel for shopping. In the 1980s and 1990s, huge complexes appeared, such as the 'Metro-Centre' in Gateshead, serving Tyneside but attracting visitors from much further afield (and supporting a regular bus service from Whitehaven almost seventy miles away), Meadowhall on the northern fringes of Sheffield, Trafford Park to the south of Manchester, and Thurrock, in Essex. Such sites commanded high rents from the stores which traded in them but flourished because they offered almost limitless choice, the convenience of obtaining everything from weekly groceries to entire Christmas shopping extravagances and – increasingly important as pressures on space in towns grew – free parking

Until the late nineteenth century, shopworkers were not protected by any legislation restricting hours or conditions of labour. The Shop Hours Act of 1886 stated that shopworkers were not to work more than 74 hours in any one week. It was very difficult to police, however, and hours of work for many shopworkers remained extremely long. Local government regulations imposed somewhat greater constraints on shopowners after 1912 but the fact that many small shops were staffed by their owners ensured the continuation of a 'long-hours' tradition in the retail trade throughout the twentieth century.

(See also *Co-operative Movement; Industrial Revolution; Rochdale Pioneers.*)

Revised Code of Education: change of policy, introduced in 1862, for the funding of schools supported by government grants. Associated with *Robert Lowe*, Vice-President of the Council on Education in *Palmerston*'s *Liberal* government, it rationalised the grant-awarding system but its main purpose was to reduce the cost of state-supported education. In effect, the Code determined the basic curriculum taught. By it:

- the grant was to be paid direct to school managers but its size was determined by satisfactory performance by pupils in tests on reading, writing and arithmetic. Grants were not determined by aptitude in any other subject
- two-thirds of the grant were based on test performance and one-third on pupil attendance
- state inspectors administered the tests

(See also *elementary schools; Kay-Shuttleworth, James; Newcastle Commission on Education.*)

'Revolt of the Field': name given to strike activity by agricultural labourers in 1874 under the leadership of *Joseph Arch*, whose National Agricultural Labourers' Union had rapidly gathered more than 80,000 members. A lock-out of labourers by tenants and landowners broke the strike and reduced the power of the labourers' union.

(See also *Agricultural Gangs Act; Great Depression.*)

Rhodes, Cecil: adventurer, imperialist and educational benefactor. Born in 1853, he journeyed to Natal to help in his brother's cotton enterprise there but made his fortune in diamond mining. He returned to study in Oxford in 1873 already a rich man and returned to Africa in 1880, founding the de Beers mining company. He diversified into gold in the 1880s, enhancing his wealth, which he increasingly put at the service of expanding Britain's Empire. He wished to create a federation of South Africa, harmonising British and Dutch interests and acquired Bechuanaland for Cape Colony in 1884. He founded the British South Africa Company in 1887, in territory which became known as *Rhodesia* and was expanded in territory after a war against Matabele chiefs in 1893–94. He became *Prime Minister* of Cape Province in 1890 but was forced to resign in 1896 after the failure of the *Jameson Raid*, in which he had been implicated. He died after a long illness in 1902, leaving in his will a large legacy to fund 'Rhodes Scholarships' originally intended to benefit young members of the British Empire, Germans and US citizens. Rhodes's methods were frequently unscrupulous and his relations with the indigenous peoples of southern Africa have attracted criticism from many historians. His commitment to the ideal of Empire was absolute and his career symbolises the ambiguities of *imperialism.*

(See also *Chamberlain, Joseph; Empire, British; imperialism; Rhodesia; South Africa.*)

Rhodesia: territory in east, southern Africa first colonised by *Cecil Rhodes* and the British South Africa Company in the 1890s. The territory was rich in mineral deposits, with extensive resources of copper in the north. With Nyasaland, it briefly formed the 'Central African Federation' in the 1950s until black hostility to prolonged white dominance led to its break-up. The northern portion of the territory became independent as Zambia in 1964 under the leadership of Kenneth Kaunda, but the south resisted majority rule, issuing a '*unilateral declaration of independence*' from Britain as Southern Rhodesia in 1965. White minority rule under the *Prime Minister*ship of Ian Smith was maintained against massive hostility from the *Commonwealth* until 1979 when *Margaret Thatcher*'s government negotiated a peaceful settlement between blacks and whites, leading to the establishment of an independent 'Zimbabwe' in 1980 under black majority rule. Its first Prime Minister was the Marxist intellectual Robert Mugabe.

(See also *decolonisation; imperialism; Scramble for Africa; Wilson, Harold.*)

Ricardo, David: economic theorist and *radical* politician. Born in 1772 into a wealthy Jewish banking family, he used the time which his lack of financial dependence afforded to mastering economic theory. Heavily influenced by Adam Smith's 'Wealth of Nations' (1776), and perhaps his most gifted disciple, Ricardo exerted great influence on economic policy in the first half of the nineteenth century. His most important contributions were probably:

- the development of a 'law of comparative cost' which argued the value of free trade in international competition
- the argument that the *Corn Law* of 1815, against the tenets of *free trade*, engendered social disharmony by advantaging landowners at the expense of manufacturers and labourers
- the 'labour theory of value' as a key factor determining the prices of manufactured and other products. This in turn influenced Karl Marx, attracted by the notion that it was labour which was the determinant of value in a free market
- his attack on the unreformed *Poor Laws*. He argued that, unchecked, the cost of relieving the poor would increase exponentially, swallowing up rent and destroying rural society

He wrote numerous articles on political economy in the 'Edinburgh Review' and became an independent MP at a by-election in 1819. He died in 1823.

(See also *laissez-faire; Malthus, Thomas.*)

Rickman, John: demographer and statistician. He was born in 1771 and is best known for his work on the first official *census* of *population* published in 1801. This included estimates of population during the previous century which, based on parish registers, have proved surprisingly accurate in the light of much more sophisticated later research. He also directed the next three censuses, compiled statistical information about Poor Law expenditure and administration from 1831 to 1836 and indexed the *House of Commons* journals. He died in 1840.

Ripon, Earl of: see *Goderich*

Robbins Report, 1963: policy report on the future of higher education chaired by the economist Lionel Robbins. It recommended a substantial expansion of higher education, including the creation of six new universities and increased intakes for all the others. In its wake the Universities of East Anglia, Coleraine, Essex, Lancaster, Stirling, Sussex, Warwick and York were all created under royal charter during the years 1964–67 while the total number of university students doubled within a decade. Robbins's target of 60 *universities* by 1980 was not met but the wider vision of expansion was amply achieved as a university education became an attainable goal for a much larger proportion of the population. In the 50 years after *World War II* the number of universities increased from 17 to 103, most of the new institutions being created or renamed as universities in the 1960s and 1990s. The nature of university education changed radically as the cost of higher education per student was squeezed downwards, especially from the 1980s.

(See also *Macmillan, Harold; Wilson, Harold.*)

Robinson, Frederick: see *Goderich*

Rochdale Pioneers: name given collectively to 28 members of the organisation which founded a shop in Toad Lane, Rochdale in 1844. The principle of trading was that profits should be shared out among members of the society. It caught on rapidly as the *Co-operative Movement* which had more than 450 shops, mainly in the North of England, by the mid-1860s. It was an important example of the principle of working-class improvement through *self-help.*

Rolling Stones: British rock musicians particularly popular in the late 1960s and 1970s. Their frequently loud and aggressive music combined with a stage act which, through the gyrations of the lead singer Mick Jagger, was often sexually suggestive made them into one of the youth icons of the age, symbolising a reaction against convention and conformity.

(See also *Beatles, the; popular culture.*)

Roman Catholicism: faith of those who believe in the supreme religious authority of the Pope (the Bishop of Rome; hence the name) and the traditional teachings of a Church which traces its ancestry back to St Peter, the first Pope. The state religion of England had parted company from Roman Catholicism during the so-called 'Reformation' of Henry VIII in the 1530s, from which eventually emerged the *Church of England,* and Catholicism was long associated both in the public mind and among many members of the propertied elite as synonymous with absolute monarchies and lack of freedom. This helps explain the political disabilities under which the one to two per cent of the English Catholic population, many of whom were concentrated in the west of Lancashire, laboured until into the nineteenth century. Numbers of Catholics in Britain increased rapidly because of *immigration* from predominantly Catholic Ireland even before the *Irish Potato Famine*, and accelerated still more after it. By the time of the religious census of 1851, about 700,000 people in Britain were Catholics with particularly large concentrations of Irish-born in Liverpool, London, Glasgow and Manchester. Anti-Catholic hostility in working-class areas led to frequent disturbances, most notably the riots in Stockport (north Cheshire) in 1852 and anti-Catholicism was almost certainly an important factor in the revival of the *Conservative Party* in northern industrial areas after the *Reform Act* of 1867. The *Liberal* government of *Lord John Russell* permitted the hierarchy of the Roman Catholic church to be restored to England in 1850, amid much popular hostility, but this development helped the long, and in some places painfully slow, process of assimilation. Only in the second half of the twentieth century did anti-Catholic prejudice finally abate, with hostility in some quarters transferred to more recent immigrants.

(See also *Catholic Emancipation Act, 1829; Newman, John Henry.*)

Romilly, Sir Samuel: *Whig* politician and legal reformer. Born in 1757, the son of a London jeweller from a French Protestant family which had fled from religious persecution in France at the end of the seventeenth century, he produced an influential book advocating law reform, 'Thoughts on Executive Justice' in 1786. He was influenced by the ideas of the eighteenth-century Enlightenment, especially Rousseau and Mirabeau, the French revolutionary leader, and defended a number of men accused of treason or sedition during *Pitt*'s attack on *artisan radicalism* in the 1790s. He was an MP from 1806 to 1818 but his only important office was Solicitor General in 1806–7 during the *Ministry of all the Talents*. He was nearly always in opposition to predominantly anti-reformist *Tory* governments. He was instrumental in removing capital punishment as a possible penalty for a number of relatively trivial offences in 1808 and 1811, thereby setting a precedent for *Sir Robert Peel* to follow in the 1820s. He was also a supporter of the abolition of *slavery*. By the time that he committed suicide in 1818, very soon after the death of his wife, he was a leading member of the Whig Party, with some prospect of becoming party leader.

Rosebery (Primrose, Archibald Philip), 5th Earl of: *Liberal* politician, *Prime Minister* and author. He was born in 1847 into an established Scottish aristocratic family and was the son of a *Whig* MP. He had great intellectual ability, considerable charm and was a persuasive public speaker. However, a rich man's fondness for gambling with high stakes, his passion for horse-racing and breeding (as an owner, he won the Derby three times) which he certainly preferred to politics, and a lack of durability all combined to prevent him from achieving everything in political life of which he might have been capable. His background and lifestyle made him a figure of suspicion, as leader of a political party with a very important Puritan, *nonconformist* element. His career was a diverse one. He succeeded to the earldom on the death of his grandfather in 1868, and his personal fortune was assured when he married the daughter, and heiress, of the banking millionaire Baron de Rothschild in 1878. He refused junior office under *Gladstone* both in 1872 and 1880 and in 1883 declined a seat in the Cabinet with responsibility for Scottish affairs. His main offices were:

- Lord Privy Seal, 1885
- Foreign Secretary, 1886, 1892–94
- Chairman of *London County Council*, 1889 – the first to hold this office – and 1892
- Prime Minister, 1894–5
- Leader of the Liberal Party, 1894–6, and Leader of the Opposition, 1895–96

He first became Foreign Secretary because *Home Rule* had deprived Gladstone of many of the old *Whigs* in the *House of Lords*. Rosebery proved a capable Foreign Secretary, not least because of his sympathy for the *British Empire* and his direct knowledge of it. He visited Australia and New Zealand in 1883 and India in 1886–7. He became a strong imperialist but, unlike many in his party who took this position, was also a keen reformer, taking an interest in local government and also being one of the first leading politicians to develop a programme of House of Lords reform. His period as Prime Minister was brief and not particularly memorable, except perhaps for making apparent the severe splits within the party. Rosebery, for example, wished to withdraw the Liberal commitment to Home Rule and opposed punitive taxation such as *Harcourt*'s death duties. Rather than continue to fight against opposition, he resigned immediately after a defeat on a minor matter concerning defence – the supply of cordite to the army. The resulting general election saw a substantial Liberal defeat and it took the party more than a decade to return to office.

His retirement was long, and often interrupted by attempts to deflect *Campbell-Bannerman* and *Asquith*'s governments from some of its reformist programme. He vigorously opposed *Lloyd George*'s budget of 1909. He now preferred writing, however, producing short political biographies of the younger *Pitt* and Napoleon Bonaparte, a sympathetic study of his political opponent Lord *Randolph Churchill* and, in 1910, a longer study of the elder Pitt, Earl of Chatham. He refused office for the last time when Lloyd George formed his wartime government in 1916, endured many years of ill-health from 1918 and died in 1929.

(See also *imperialism*.)

Ross, Sir John: Arctic and Antarctic explorer. Born in 1800, he joined the navy in 1812 and went on his first Arctic expedition in 1818. With his uncle, James Ross, he discovered the Magnetic Pole. During the late 1830s and 1840s he led expeditions to the Antarctic, probably penetrating further south than any explorer before the twentieth century. He died in 1862.

Rossetti, Dante Gabriel: poet and artist. Born in 1828, he became a leading member of the *Pre-Raphaelite Brotherhood*. His painting 'The Girlhood of Mary Virgin' was the first to bear the inscription 'PRB'. Later in life, he moved away from the brotherhood. His main inspiration was his model Elizabeth Siddal, whom he later married. He died in 1882.

Rothermere (Harmsworth, Harold), 1st Viscount: newspaper owner and younger brother of *Alfred Harmsworth, Viscount Northcliffe*. Born in 1868, he was more adept at financial management than his brother and was initially less interested in publicity. He played a full part in making both the '*Daily Mail*' and the 'Daily Mirror' financially successful and was primarily responsible for launching the visually striking 'Sunday Pictorial', aimed at the mass market, in 1915. He took charge of Associated Newspapers in 1922 and, ironically in view of his early career, became much more controversial than his brother had been when he changed the Mail's editorial line to support first Mussolini in Italy and then Hitler in Germany. He also supported *Mosley*'s British Union of Fascists. He served briefly in *Lloyd George*'s War Cabinet as Air Minister (1917–18). He died in 1940.

(See also *Baldwin, Stanley; newspapers.*)

rotten boroughs: name colloquially given in the late eighteenth and the early nineteenth centuries to parliamentary boroughs which had very few voters and which were effectively in the control either of the *monarchy* or a landed 'patron'. The name derives from a famous description by the elder *Pitt* in which he criticised what he called 'the rotten part of the constitution'. Most of these boroughs, like Old Sarum in Wiltshire, were in the South of England with a particular concentration in Cornwall where boroughs like East and West Looe and Fowey rarely put voters to the trouble of actually having to turn out for an election. Most rotten boroughs were abolished by the *Reform Act* of 1832.

(See also *Commons, House of; Parliament.*)

Rowntree, (Benjamin) Seebohm: pioneer social investigator and industrialist. Born in 1871, the son of Joseph Rowntree, a Quaker chocolate manufacturer from York who was also a philanthropist, he took over the family business and directed it successfully as its chairman from 1923 to 1941. He is best remembered, however, for his work in investigating poverty in York. His researches, begun in 1897, were published in 1901 as 'Poverty: A Study in Town Life'. Drawing on some of the methodology used by *Charles Booth* for London, his conclusions about the extent of poverty in a provincial town which was not as heavily industrialised as many were nevertheless remarkably similar to Booth's for the capital. His evidence was therefore taken as a strong indication that the poverty problem and its causes were not specific to the capital. He produced two later sociological studies of York in 1936 and 1950 and updated his conclusions about the city in 'Poverty and Progress' (1941). A supporter of the *Liberal Party*, he was increasingly active in the formulation of social policy. He served in the welfare department of *Lloyd George*'s Ministry of Munitions and, in the inter-war period, advocated *family allowances* and better quality *housing* as two of the key elements necessary to reduce poverty and raise self-esteem among working-class families. He died in 1954.

(See also *Chamberlain, Neville; welfare state.*)

Rugby League Football: the professional offshoot of *Rugby Union Football.* A number of clubs especially from the North-West of England broke away from the Union in 1895 and formed a separate league which was known as the Rugby Football League from 1922. Played in teams of thirteen, and with rules which made game-slowing scrums rarer, it developed as a very popular professional game attracting large crowds in the industrial areas of Lancashire and Yorkshire but had only a limited following in the South. Competition was keen and the annual challenge cup final, held at Wembley, became one of the key sporting events in the calendar. The game spread to France, Australia and New Zealand and international 'test matches' followed. It also provided the focus for one of the most successful, and depressing, 'social-realist' films of the 1960s, 'This Sporting Life' (1961). At least until the 1980s, the social distinction between the 'League' and 'Union' codes was very marked, the former remaining an overwhelmingly working-class sport. Because of the financial rewards available, however, it was able to attract a number of successful Rugby Union players, especially from South Wales, into the professional game.

Rugby Union Football: team game for fifteen players based on the principle of holding, and running with, an oval ball. It is generally supposed to have begun at Rugby School when William Webb Ellis picked up a football in 1823 and ran with it, but many other explanations of its origins exist. It quickly established a hold, especially in the rapidly growing *public schools,* and a Rugby Union Code was agreed for England in 1871, with Scotland, Wales and Ireland following over the next decade. International matches were also played from the 1870s. The breakaway of the *Rugby League* allowed the Union Code to confirm its preference for amateurism and, in England, support for the game was much stronger among the middle than the working classes and in the South than the North. In South Wales, however, Rugby Union continued as a predominantly working-class sport, both in schools and among adult teams. The strong edge to international games between England and Wales, especially after 1945, owed something to Welsh national sentiment but something also to the resentment felt in parts of Wales against what was seen as effete, English middle-class social domination of Britain. Amateurism became increasingly difficult to maintain as a sporting ideal in an age of growing commercialism, especially when television was prepared to pay large fees for the privilege of televising important matches. The Union game became openly professional in 1995, rather than covertly so as in the previous two decades, and a fresh competitive edge to club rugby was given by the creation of two leagues for the leading clubs with promotion and relegation each season.

Ruskin, John: art critic and social commentator. Born in 1819, the son of a prosperous wine merchant, he learned about art at first hand, like many wealthy youths, on tours of Europe. He was greatly influenced by the innovative style of *J M W Turner,* whose work he praised in the first of his many important books of art criticism, 'Modern Painters' (1843). In the mid-Victorian period, he championed the *Pre-Raphaelites* and saw art as a means of restoring what he considered a morality lost to the rampant chase for material success in an industrial society. This theme he developed in a number of lectures delivered in the 1850s and 1860s and he also wrote a number of articles attacking industrial values and calling for social reforms in leading journals such as the 'Cornhill Magazine'. He believed, as he wrote in 'Time and Tide' (1867), that 'The first duty of a state is to see that every child born therein shall be well housed, clothed, fed and educated, till it attain years of discretion'. He moved to Coniston in the Lake District in 1871, where, while drawing continuing inspiration from nature, he encouraged ancient craftsmanship and the spirit of philanthropy. His later years were troubled by bouts of insanity. In his last decade, he had effectively withdrawn from the Victorian world which he had striven both to educate and to change. He died in 1890.

(See also *Industrial Revolution.*)

Russell, Bertrand (3rd Earl): mathematician, philosopher and political thinker. Born in 1872, the grandson of *Lord John Russell*, he was educated at Cambridge where he studied mathematics and produced 'Principles of Mathematics' (1910). Mathematics, he argued, 'possesses not only truth, but supreme beauty – a beauty cold and austere, like that of sculpture'. He produced numerous works on Western philosophy which earned him the Order of Merit in 1945 and the Nobel Prize for Literature in 1950. He opposed *World War I* on principle, supporting the cause of *conscientious objectors* and was briefly imprisoned in 1918 for his unpatriotic writings. In 1958, he became the first President of the *Campaign for Nuclear Disarmament*. Long-lived, like many of his family, he died at the age of 98 in 1970.

Russell, Lord John (1st Earl): *Whig* and *Liberal* politician and *Prime Minister*. Born into an aristocratic *Whig* family in 1792 as the third son of the Earl of Bedford, he was educated at Westminster School and Edinburgh University before becoming an MP in 1813. His major offices were:

- Paymaster General of the Forces, 1831–34
- Home Secretary, 1835–39
- Secretary for War and the Colonies, 1839–41
- Prime Minister, 1846–52 and 1865–66
- Foreign Secretary, 1852–53 and 1859–65
- Lord President of the Council, 1854–55
- Secretary for the Colonies, 1855

Russell's ministerial career was long and frequently controversial. He was a clever, but rather intolerant, man who (like many Whigs) believed in his right to provide leadership but not always in the benefits of consultation or compromise. His long-standing personal rivalry with *Palmerston* was a frequent topic of conversation within the political classes. The two men were similar in age and frequently contenders for high office. Their rivalry was the more piquant in that the two men agreed on a number of issues, not least support for nationalist movements in Europe, and especially Italy. Russell, however, was always a much keener supporter of *parliamentary reform* than his rival. Russell supported many domestic reforms, taking a leading role in the repeal of the *Test and Corporation Acts* in 1828, before helping draft the first Reform Bill in 1831 which proposed much more extensive changes than most MPs of the time had anticipated – or desired. Like many Whigs also, he favoured reform only under careful supervision from the upper classes. He believed, for a time, that the 1832 *Reform Act* represented the final solution of 'a great constitutional question' and, although his practical effectiveness as Home Secretary after 1835 was frequently criticised, he was certainly an implacable opponent of *Chartism*. As *Prime Minister*, his Ecclesiastical Titles Act of 1851 showed that he was prepared to pander to the anti-Catholicism of his Anglican backbenchers rather than sustain the normal Whig commitment to religious toleration.

Neither of his periods as Prime Minister was especially successful. Though the first was long-lasting, he worked for much of the time in the long shadow cast by *Robert Peel*, who retained much greater authority out of office than Russell had in it. His second period as Prime Minister, following the death of Palmerston, involved leadership from the *House of Lords* as Earl Russell, his earldom having been conferred by Queen

Victoria in 1861. It was brought to an end by a rebellion within a section of the *Liberal Party* against his proposals for a second parliamentary reform Act. After his resignation in 1866, Russell did not hold office again. He died in 1878, an old and somewhat embittered man who believed that he had not been blessed with the achievement his high talents warranted.

(See also *Crimean War; Lowe Robert; parliamentary reform, 1867; United States of America.*)

Russell, William Howard: journalist. Born in 1820, his fame derives from the war despatches he sent back to Britain from the *Crimea* for publication in '*The Times*' in the years 1854–6. They showed both insight and compassion, bringing home to civilians the horrors and practical squalor of war, as well as its glories. His reports also had political significance since they revealed massive incompetence within the British military leadership. His report on the Charge of the Light Brigade during the *Battle of Balaclava*, which referred to Britain's 'thin red streak tipped with a line of steel' inspired *Tennyson*'s famous poem on the subject. He also brought to public attention the heroic deeds of Mary Seacole, a Jamaican mulatto woman, in ministering to troops on the battle field. He died in 1907.

Sadler, Michael Thomas: landowner, *Tory* politician and factory reformer. Born in 1780, he represented the Yorkshire borough of Aldburgh and became suspicious of the ambitions and priorities of factory owners in that county. He was one of the leaders of the early factory reform movement, making it a popular cause among Tory MPs and other humanitarians hostile to the *Industrial Revolution*. His pressure led to the formation of a select committee which investigated the extent and abuses of child labour in textile factories. His opponents had no difficulty in demonstrating that he had used slanted evidence but his work was responsible for putting the question onto the political agenda, leading to the first inspected *Factory Act* in 1833. His parliamentary seat of Aldburgh disappeared under the terms of the *Reform Act* of 1832 and he did not sit in the new Parliament. He died in 1835.

(See also *child labour; Peel, Sir Robert, Snr; Shaftesbury, 7th Earl of.*)

Salisbury (Gascoyne-Cecil, Robert), 3rd Marquess of: Conservative politician and *Prime Minister*. Born in 1830 into one of the premier aristocratic families of Great Britain he was an MP (bearing the courtesy title Viscount Cranborne) from 1853 to 1869, succeeding to the title of Marquess, and a seat in the *House of Lords*. His main offices were:

- Secretary of State for India, 1866–67 and 1874–76
- Foreign Secretary, 1878–80, 1887–92 and 1895–1900
- Leader of the Conservative Party, 1881–1902 (from 1881–85 jointly with *Stafford Northcote*)
- Prime Minister, 1885–86, 1886–92, 1895–1902

From rather unpromising beginnings as a politician who seemed to be more interested in opposing measures than in creative activity, Salisbury became one of the most significant leaders of the *Conservative Party*, whose contribution has tended to be under-valued, partly on grounds of personality. He was a shy man who did not create a clear 'image' as readily, in their different ways, as either *Gladstone* or *Disraeli* and he put many of his thoughts more easily onto paper – he was a successful journalist contributing regular articles to the Conservative journal the 'Quarterly Review' – than into stirring political speeches. His main contributions to Conservatism may be identified as:

- offering a safe haven for *Liberal Unionists* and helping to prepare the way for their eventual absorption into the Conservative Party. His exploitation of divisions within the *Liberal Party* was extremely effective
- his recognition of the importance of effective *local government* and his determination that the Conservative Party should use changes here to build an effective power base
- his opposition to *Home Rule* for *Ireland*, which was presented in part as a determination to preserve the *British Empire* and to protect the interests of property owners. This was in tune with the views of many rising property owners. Salisbury's government was associated with what was called 'Villa

Toryism', which anchored many small property owners in the urban suburbs to the Conservative Party
- his foreign policy, which was aimed at preserving British interests including support for further acquisitions during the *Scramble for Africa*. This also
proved electorally popular

His earlier career was not especially distinguished and he came first to the public eye
in opposing Disraeli's *Parliamentary Reform Bill* in 1867, which led to his resignation.
He also proved a difficult colleague early in Disraeli's second government, when he
opposed a bill on public worship, because he believed that it threatened the interests
of the *Church of England*. As Foreign Secretary, however, he was an important figure
at the *Congress of Berlin*.

Although keenly aware of factors which worked to his party's advantage, he was not
particularly interested in domestic politics and mostly relied on the advice and recommendations of his departmental ministers. It is significant that, rather than
linking his title as *Prime Minister* to the more normal additional rank of 'First Lord of
the Treasury' – which symbolised the Prime Minister's overall responsibility for economic policy – he served for the most part as his own Foreign Secretary. He was not
a naturally trusting man, preferring to work with relatives (especially his nephew
Arthur Balfour) and he could be ruthless with opponents. In one sense he was an
anachronism, being the last man to govern as Prime Minister from the House of
Lords and maintaining a strong attachment to many old *Tory* values. In another, he
was remarkably far-sighted and shrewd. He prepared the ground for his nephew's
succession to the prime ministership and died in 1903, a year after his resignation.

(See also *imperialism*; *Chamberlain, Joseph*; *South Africa*.)

Salt, Titus: industrialist, philanthropist and Liberal politician. Born in 1803, he was
a woollen spinner before making his fortune in adapting imported woollens to the
growing women's fashion market. In 1853, he began the building of a 'model' mill
at Saltaire, near Bingley (Yorkshire) which he intended to be a working social community as well as a place of work. In it, he placed a United Reformed church (1868)
and high school (1868), a hospital and an alms house. He built high-quality *housing*
for his workforce. Seven-hundred-and-seventy-five houses were erected in the 1860s,
all with drainage, gas and water. They were built at a cost of £120 each and rented for
2s 4d (12p) a week. Most of the houses remained in good repair at the end of the
twentieth century. He was mayor of Bradford in 1848 and its *radical Liberal* Member
of Parliament from 1859 to 1861. He contributed lavishly to a number of charities,
especially in Yorkshire, was knighted in 1869 and died in 1876.

(See also *Industrial Revolution*; *woollen industry*.)

Samuel (Herbert), 1st Viscount: *Liberal* politician. He was born into a prosperous Jewish banking family in 1870 and became a Liberal MP in 1902, serving in the
Commons until losing his seat in 1918 and then again from 1929 to 1937. His major
offices were:

- Chancellor of the Duchy of Lancaster, 1909–10, 1915–16
- Postmaster General, 1910–14
- Home Secretary, 1916 and 1931–32

- High Commissioner in Palestine, 1920–25
- Leader of the Liberal Party, 1931–40

His political career as an orthodox, perhaps old-fashioned, Liberal was long but never distinguished and he was not universally respected. He did, however, discharge a wide range of functions, including detailed work on the Children Act of 1908, work in the mandated territory of Palestine and the chairing of a commission on the coal mining industry in 1925–26. His commission, which recommended wage cuts, helped to cause the *General Strike*. As acting leader of the Liberals, he negotiated Liberal entry to the *National Government* headed by *Ramsay MacDonald* in 1931, but resigned from it the following year when the Government abandoned *free trade*, a long-established Liberal belief. He led a group of 'Samuelites' until 1935 before becoming a peer in 1937. He led the Liberals in the *House of Lords* from 1944 to 1955, not an especially onerous task, and lived on until 1963.

(See also *Asquith, Henry*.)

Sassoon, Siegfried: poet and novelist. Born in 1886 into a successful banking family with extensive interests in *India*, he served as a commissioned officer during *World War I* about which he wrote a number of powerful, bitter anti-war poems. Among his most famous writings are 'Counterattack' (1918) and 'Memoirs of a Foxhunting Man' (1928). He died in 1967.

(See also *Brooke, Rupert; Owen, Wilfred*.)

Saxe-Coburg: name of the United Kingdom royal house from 1901 to 1917. The name derives from the German duchy of *Prince Albert*, consort of Queen *Victoria*. Albert was the second son of the Duke of Saxe-Coburg-Gotha. Victoria's mother, Mary Louisa Victoria, was also from Saxe-Coburg. *Edward VII*, Prince Albert's and Queen Victoria's eldest son and *George V*, their grandson, bore the name, which appropriately reflected the strongly Germanic nature of the British monarchy after 1714. German associations were, however, an embarrassment during *World War I* and George V changed the name of the royal house to the much more English-sounding 'Windsor' in 1917.

school meals: the provision of meals at lunchtime for school pupils. Local authorities were given the power to provide these as part of the Education (Provision of Meals) Act passed by the Liberal government in 1906. In general, those authorities who took up the opportunity came from areas with high levels of poverty, where school meals greatly enhanced the quality of children's diets. By 1939, roughly half of all local education authorities provided a school-meals service. This proportion increased during *World War II* when high nutritional standards were vital and continued to go up until the late 1960s.

Scott, Sir Walter: poet and novelist. Born in 1771, he practised as a lawyer and wrote extensively both in prose and poetry. He is particularly remembered for those novels, such as 'Waverley' (1814), 'Rob Roy' (1817) and 'Heart of Midlothian' (1818), which recreated the Scottish past and celebrated its traditions. Earlier in his career, he wrote narrative poems, of which the most impressive is probably 'Marmion' (1808). He also contributed numerous articles to the *Whig* journal the 'Edinburgh Review'. Much of his output was published anonymously and he did not admit authorship of the novels until 1827. His novels were extremely successful and he used much of the profits to build 'Abbotsford' in which property he housed numerous artefacts and memorabilia, mostly celebrating Scotland. He lived in substantial comfort until bankruptcy after the collapse of a publishing firm with which he was associated in 1825. He died in 1832.

Scottish Church Secession: the breakaway in 1843 of approximately 395 ministers of the Church of Scotland and a large minority of its lay members to form a separate evangelical *Free Church of Scotland*. This was the culmination of a decade of religious controversy between so-called 'moderates' and 'evangelicals' but the conflict was also overlain with both class and nationalist elements. Landowning Scots tended to be strongly Anglicised and favoured moderation in worship, whereas many of the urban middle classes resented both excessive deference to English ways and the barely concealed hostility towards *evangelicalism* of both the *Whig* government headed by *Melbourne* and its successor, the *Conservative* government of *Peel*.

(See also *Church of England*.)

Scottish National Party: political party formed out of two smaller groups in 1934 to press for independence for Scotland. It won its first parliamentary seat at the *general election* of 1945 but had little success until an upsurge of nationalist feeling in Scotland in the late 1960s and early 1970s, which coincided with the discovery of large quantities of *North Sea oil* to which nationalists laid claim as 'Scotland's oil'. Exploiting much more widespread support within Scotland for legislative *devolution*, the party won eleven seats in the October 1974 general election and, at 840,000, more than 30 per cent of the popular vote. Support for the party declined after Scottish devolution proposals narrowly failed to win sufficient popular support in 1979. In general elections from 1979 to 1992, the party never won more than three seats. In the election of 1983, its vote slumped to 330,000. Popular support, however, revived in the later 1980s when many Scots felt that *Margaret Thatcher*'s government showed scant interest in, or respect for, Scotland's distinctive culture or needs.

'Scramble for Africa': name colloquially given to the process whereby European powers laid claim to territories in Africa as part of their growing colonial empires. The process began in the late 1870s, when Germany and Belgium began to challenge what they regarded as the excessive influence held by Britain on the continent, recognising the enormous economic potential of colonisation. The peak decade for colonial acquisition, which often merely regularised what had previously been informal arrangements, was the 1890s and the Scramble has been seen as one of many causes of the international rivalry which contributed to the outbreak of *World War I*.

(See also *Empire, British*; *imperialism*.)

Scutari: site of the main barracks on the Black Sea during the *Crimean War*. It was from here that *Florence Nightingale* established her nursing regime for the wounded which had such long-term influence on the development of the nursing profession.

Sealion, Operation: codename given to the German plan for the invasion of Britain during *World War II*. The Germans attempted to execute it in 1940 but were frustrated by the failure to gain necessary command of the skies during the *Battle of*

Britain. The operation was abandoned in September 1940 and developments in the war never made it feasible to resume the attempt.

(See also *Blitz.*)

Second World War: see *World War II*

secularism: movement characterised by belief that everything necessary for a fulfilling life can be found within the natural and material world. Secularists thus deny the existence of God or life after death. Secularism should be distinguished from atheism in that the latter merely holds that God does not exist whereas secularism developed as an alternative ethical system based on rationalism and the self-sufficiency of humankind. The movement was given impulse by the Liberal journalist George Jacob Holyoake (1817–1906), editor of the journal 'Reasoner' which published from 1846 to 1861. Numerous 'secular societies' were founded in the 1850s. Leadership of the secularists passed to the much more charismatic *Charles Bradlaugh* during the 1860s. Secularism excited furious antagonism from all Christian sects in the 1860s and 1870s. By the 1880s, the movement was in decline, although the National Secular Society has continued throughout the twentieth century to campaign for a number of causes, notably the *disestablishment* of the *Church of England* and the abolition of compulsory acts of religious worship in schools, required under the *Education Act* of 1944. Ironically, the principles underlying secularism have received much more widespread acceptance in the increasingly materialist culture of the late twentieth century when secularism has ceased to have significant influence as a pressure group.

self-help: the belief that individuals should rely on their own efforts, rather than outside agencies such as charities or the State, to relieve poverty and improve their life chances. It was a dominant ideology of *Victorian* Britain, linking closely with *laissez-faire* and *free-trade*. The term received widespread currency with the publication of the book 'Self-Help' by *Samuel Smiles* in 1859. The book, arguing that material improvement was open to all who disciplined themselves to hard work and thrift, became a best-seller and made Smiles's fortune. The doctrine has often been considered as the ideal counterpart to the values of the dominant *middle classes* and so, in some ways, it was. However, it was a precept much valued also by skilled workers who were able to use labour scarcity and *trade union* organisation to improve their conditions and claim that 'respectability' which was such a mark of esteem during the nineteenth century.

Senior, Nassau: political economist and lawyer. Born the son of a *Church of England* clergyman in 1790, he became Professor of Political Economy at Oxford University in 1825. Much of his intellectual energy was given up to criticising the unreformed *Poor Law* and he worked with *Edwin Chadwick* to produce the influential Poor Law Report of 1834 which established the principles of 'less eligibility' and increased workhouse provision established by the *Poor Law Amendment Act*. His work contributed to the growing influence of *laissez-faire* and *utilitarianism* which causes he promoted in a number of cogently argued articles which appeared in the 'Edinburgh Review' and the 'Quarterly Review'. He died in 1864.

(See also *Bentham, Jeremy.*)

Sevres, Treaty of (1920): peace settlement between the victorious Allies and Turkey after the end of *World War I*. By it, territory previously held by the Ottoman Empire was taken from it:

- an area on the Asian side of the Dardanelles was to be neutralised
- much of Thrace and the Aegean coast of Asia minor was given to Greece
- remaining territories were divided between British, Italian and French spheres of influence

The treaty was considered harsh and demeaning by the Turks and was a direct cause of the *Chanak crisis*.

sexually transmitted diseases: the most common of these in the nineteenth and early twentieth centuries were gonorrhoea and syphilis, both of which could have serious long-term consequences, the latter especially so. It is generally believed that the premature decline and death of Lord *Randolph Churchill* was due to syphilis. It was to deal with the so-called 'venereal diseases' in naval dockyards that governments in the 1860s passed the *Contagious Diseases Acts*. The Government was also very concerned about the spread of gonorrhea and syphilis during *World War I* when it urged on troops the use of primitive condoms.

Treatment for syphilis, which could be passed on to unborn children and which, unchecked, invariably led to madness and premature death, was painful and not in any way sure. Doses of mercury were the main means of treatment until the early twentieth century when Salvarsan was introduced. The most effective treatment, however, was penicillin but it was not available for syphilis until the 1940s.

Sexually transmitted diseases remained common after *World War II* but were more controllable thanks to modern medicine, specialist clinics and greater awareness of their causes. It was the widespread feeling in the developed world that these diseases were coming under control which made the advent and rapid spread of AIDS (Acquired Immune Deficiency Syndrome) from the early 1980s so alarming.

(See also *prostitution*.)

Shaftesbury (Cooper, Anthony Ashley (Lord Ashley)), 7th Earl of: *Tory* politician, philanthropist and humanitarian reformer. He was a strict *evangelical* Christian who attempted to live his life according to the precepts of the Bible. He supported *Factory Acts* restricting the powers of factory owners over their work force and he was instrumental in securing the *Mines Act* in 1842. He was also involved in a wide range of Christian causes, including the Lord's Day Observance Society and better quality *housing* for the working classes. Like many humanitarians, he was a Tory who was opposed both to extensions of the *franchise* and also to the rapid progress of the *Industrial Revolution*. He believed in a society run on principles of *paternalism*.

(See also *child labour; Peel, Sir Robert; slavery*.)

Shaw, George Bernard: playwright and critic. He was born in Dublin in 1856 but spent most of his life in London where he studied political ideas and became a supporter of gradual (so-called 'Fabian') socialism. He supported women's rights, attacked orthodox religion and opposed *World War I*. He is best known as a playwright, and many of his plays, among the most famous of which are 'The Devil's Disciple' (1897) 'Pygmalion' (1916) and 'St Joan' (1924), include much social comment. He received the Nobel Prize for Literature in 1925. He was also a trenchant music critic, who wrote under the pen-name of 'Corno di Basetto', and championed the music of the then highly controversial German composer Richard Wagner. His plays have fluctuated in popularity. There is no denying their acuteness and commitment but some have found them too long-winded and a vehicle for *secular* preaching rather than dramatic power.

'Sheffield outrages', 1867: violent disturbances carried out in South Yorkshire by *trade unionists* against both employers and non-unionists who threatened the wages of skilled workers. They caused some concern among the governing classes partly because they came apparently suddenly after a long period of relatively little social unrest and partly because they coincided with violent activity by Irishmen in the *Fenian Movement.*

Shelley, Mary Wollstonecraft: novelist. Born in 1797, the daughter of *Mary Wollstonecraft* and the philosopher William Godwin and, from 1816, wife of the poet *Percy Bysshe Shelley.* She is best known for her 'Gothic' story 'Frankenstein' (1818), which spawned a large number of profitable horror films in the twentieth century. She was also a prolific writer on a number of issues. She died in 1851.

Shelley, Percy Bysshe: poet. Born the son of a substantial landowner and *Whig* MP in 1792, he turned quickly to poetry and became one of the leading figures of the Romantic movement. His best known works are 'Ode to the West Wind' (1819), 'Prometheus Unbound' (1820) and 'To a Skylark' (1820). Like many other Romantic poets, he was attracted to *radical* politics, believing that most of the evils of society were caused by a corrupt and unrepresentative *Parliament.* He lived from 1818 in Italy and died in a boating accident in 1822.

(See also *Byron, Lord; Keats, John.*)

shipping industry: one of the biggest, and most profitable, of Britain's industries in the nineteenth and early twentieth centuries. Shipping had been at the heart of the country's commerce from the medieval period, but it flourished with the development of *iron* and innovations in *engineering* from the second half of the eighteenth century. After 1850, steam and iron replaced wood and sail in the larger carrying ships. Because of the need of *steamships* for coal, many of the key shipping areas – the North-East at the estuaries of the Tyne, Wear and Tees, the Mersey estuary at Liverpool and Birkenhead, and the Clyde estuary in west-central Scotland – were located near to coalfields. Shipbuilding on the Lagan estuary in Belfast developed as far the biggest industry in Ireland before *World War I.* In the years 1910–14 Britain produced 60 per cent of all the world's ships and the Royal Navy was by far the largest in the world.

The industry was very severely affected by a collapse in world markets after 1920 and the areas which supported shipbuilding became some of the most depressed of all during the inter-war slump. In the early 1930s, unemployment at *Jarrow*, a small town on the south bank of the Tyne, reached 74 per cent. The industry revived in preparation for *World War II* and remained profitable for a time after the war. In the 1950s, Britain was the third largest exporter of ships behind West Germany and Japan, but demand slumped. Weak management and poor industrial relations saw slip many opportunities to keep up with latest technology. Order books emptied as contracts for new developments, such as large oil tankers, went elsewhere, and especially to Japan. By the end of the 1970s many dockyards faced closure. A much smaller shipping industry survived at the end of the twentieth century when new investment in water-front sites redeveloped old dockyards into luxury apartments, hotels and marinas.

(See also *Industrial Revolution; steel industry.*)

shops: see *retailing industry*

Sickert, Walter: artist. Born in Munich (Bavaria) in 1860, he moved to England with his parents in 1868. He studied art at the Slade school before becoming an assistant to James Whistler who, with the French impressionist Degas, became a major influence on his art. He is generally considered to have been one of the few significant English impressionist artists, remembered mostly for his paintings of working-class urban life and for music hall scenes.

Sidmouth, Viscount: see *Addington, Henry*

Simon, Sir John Allsebrooke (1st Viscount Simon): *Liberal* politician and lawyer. He was born into a modest Jewish family in Manchester in 1873, and rose rapidly on the basis of his intellectual brilliance both at Oxford University and as a young barrister after being called to the bar in 1899. He first became an MP during the Liberal landslide at the *general election* of 1906 and his political career developed equally rapidly thereafter. His major offices were:

- Attorney-General, 1913–15
- Home Secretary, 1915–16, 1935–37
- Foreign Secretary, 1931–35
- Chancellor of the Exchequer, 1937–40
- Lord Chancellor, 1940–45

In addition, he chaired an important commission on the government of *India* in 1927–30. Very few men have held such a wide range of senior political offices over such a long period but his career was dogged by controversy. He was undoubtedly hampered by splits within the Liberal Party, to which he was a prime contributor, and he never got on with *Lloyd George*. His career stalled after he resigned from the Government because, like many Liberals, he was temperamentally and intellectually opposed to the carnage caused by *World War I*. It is not surprising that he lost his seat in the general election of 1918, not having been given Lloyd George's famous *coupon*. He returned to Parliament at the next general election in 1922.

He fell out with Lloyd George again during the last months of the *Labour* government of 1929–31 when he called for a national coalition. His elevation to the foreign secretaryship in *MacDonald*'s coalition government was in part a recognition of his seniority as leader of the *Liberal National Party* (sometimes called 'the Simonites'), which had split from Lloyd George's Liberals. In this office, he advised against firm action to restrain Japan's aggression against Manchuria, pursued policies designed to avoid conflict with the European dictators and was later regarded as one of the main architects of *appeasement*. The fact that the fierce anti-appeaser *Winston Churchill* was prepared to give him high office during *World War II*, albeit one which carried no responsibility for war policy, is testimony to his high reputation for administrative efficiency and intellectual grasp. He almost entirely lacked the common touch, however, being both ill at ease with many parliamentary colleagues and spectacularly ill-suited to communicating via the increasingly influential mass media. He died in 1954.

(See also *Asquith, H H; Liberal Party.*)

Simpson, Wallis (Duchess of Windsor): wife of *Edward VIII.* Born into a wealthy East-Coast United States family in 1896, she married twice before coming to London with her second husband, Edward Simpson, in 1928. She met Edward as Prince of Wales in 1930 and became his mistress in 1934. The affair, well-known and widely gossiped about in high-society circles, was deliberately concealed from the British public by newspaper proprietors until the very last weeks of what had become the *Abdication Crisis.* Edward was by 1936 hopelessly in love with Mrs Simpson and determined to marry her whatever the cost. The couple eventually married in France in 1937, with no other members of the British royal family present. When the dukedom of Windsor was created for Edward, his wife was denied the honourary title 'Her Royal Highness' by a vengeful royal establishment, led by Edward's brother *George VI,* who had never wanted to succeed to the throne, and his wife Elizabeth. Edward and Wallis lived happily until Edward's death in 1972, although the marriage produced no children. She died, still unreconciled to the royal family, in 1986.

Singapore: large trading port and strategic base in South-East Asia which operated as a British colony from 1819 to 1942 and from 1945 to 1959. Situated on the China Sea, it was founded in 1819 by *Stamford Raffles* and became increasingly important to British trading interests in the far east, largely because of rubber, tin and, later, oil. It became a Crown Colony formally in 1867 and its strategic influence increased in 1921 with the establishment of a new naval base. Captured by the Japanese in 1942 during *World War II,* it reverted to Britain in 1945. It was granted self-government in 1959 and joined the *British Commonwealth* in 1965.

(See also *Empire, British; trade, overseas.*)

Sinn Fein: Irish nationalist political party. The name, translated from the Gaelic, means 'ourselves alone' and the party was founded by the nationalist leader and journalist Arthur Griffith at the beginning of the twentieth century, adopting its formal title in 1907. Its original objectives were:

- an independent republican Ireland, to be achieved by passive resistance rather than rebellion
- the development of separate cultural identity

The organisation was involved in the *Easter Rising* in 1916 and won 73 of the 108 seats at the *general election* of 1918 and declared itself the government of Ireland in 1919. The party split over the outcome of the Anglo-Irish treaty. After a further split on whether to participate in the new Dáil (Parliament) in the Irish Free State it lost popular support. It has been intimately involved with the *Irish Republican Army* (IRA) since the recurrence of violence in Northern Ireland from the late 1960s. It has participated in elections in the 1980s and 1990s, winning parliamentary seats at Westminster. It has always been held in deep suspicion by the *Unionist* community in Northern Ireland which has always argued that the party is nothing more than a veil of political legitimacy thrown over IRA violence.

skilled workers: see *labour aristocracy*

slave trade, abolition of (1807): the climax of a campaign mounted for more than half a century by *evangelicals* against the trade in slaves from West Africa. Though France and Portugal were also heavily involved, Britain dominated the slave trade, exporting more than one million slaves in the 25 years before abolition. Liverpool alone accounted for almost one-half of the total value of the European slave trade at the end of the eighteenth century. Those who opposed the trade concentrated on the:

- immorality and indignity of the institution of slavery
- conditions under which slaves were transported in the so-called 'triangular trade' from Africa, through British ports (especially Liverpool, Glasgow, London and Bristol) to the Americas
- excessive profits made by slavers: profits of 100 per cent were by no means rare on a successful trip
- waste and inefficiency involved in using slaves. Slavery distorted the market for labour, an increasingly important argument when *free-trade* ideas were becoming more influential

The main pro-slavery arguments, heard particularly in the ports where the trade was carried on, and from MPs representing those ports, were that:

- the trade was vital to the nation's economy and provided Britain with important commodities, such as cotton, tobacco, sugar and rum, at reasonable prices. Ending the trade would jeopardise not only commercial prosperity but also living standards
- abolition in Britain would not stop the trade, merely transfer it to the advantage of Britain's competitors
- anti-slavery supporters grossly exaggerated the profits which slavers made and ignored the risks involved. Ships were frequently lost or damaged on the hazardous voyages
- anti-slavery supporters picked untypically horrible stories of overcrowding and abuse and passed these off as normal
- slavery was a normal condition in Africa and the Americas. Slavery, far from being barbaric, was integral to the most civilised ancient states

An anti-slave trade Bill was introduced in Parliament in 1782 and became an annual event thereafter, until the trade was finally abolished by an Act passed by the so-called Ministry of all the Talents in 1806. It took effect the following year. Other countries did initially profit, but the trade was abolished in France, Spain and Portugal from 1819 to 1830.

(See also *Empire, British; Industrial Revolution; slavery, abolition of; trade, overseas; Wilberforce, William.*)

slavery, abolition of (1833): after the abolition of the *slave trade, evangelicals* and other humanitarian reformers maintained the pressure for a complete abolition of the institution of slavery anywhere in the British Empire. Court judgements in the 1770s both in England and Scotland had established that slavery contracts were not enforceable within Britain itself. However, these judgements did not apply to the territories of Britain's growing *Empire*. The leading campaigner against slavery was the

Yorkshire evangelical and *Tory* MP, *William Wilberforce*. Slavery was abolished everywhere in the British Empire in the year he died.

Slim, William (Viscount Slim of Yarralumba): soldier. He was born in 1891 and joined the Army in 1914, fighting at Gallipoli and in Mesopotamia. As commander of the First Burma Corps, he developed effective defensive tactics to check the advance of the Japanese during *World War II* and was later commander of the Fourteenth Army. He won a notable victory against the Japanese at Kohima-Imphal in 1944 which paved the way, under *Mountbatten*, for the recapture of Burma. A much less abrasive and self-regarding figure than many Allied commanders during *World War II*, he held a number of distinguished positions after its end, notably Chief of the Imperial General Staff (1948–42) and Governor-General of Australia (1953–60). He died in 1970.

Smiles, Samuel: doctor, administrator, journalist and economic populariser. Born in 1812, Smiles is remembered almost exclusively for his famous book 'Self-Help', published in 1859. Reprinted in numerous editions, it sold 250,000 copies and made Smiles's own fortune. Its popularity derived from the direct, uncomplicated way in which it advanced the dominant values of *laissez-faire*, by chronicling the careers of leading industrialists, like *Titus Salt*, and other self-made men. His views about self-improvement also spoke directly to the aspirations of both skilled workers and those in the lower middle classes. He produced a less successful, but still influential book, 'Thrift' in 1875. He deserves recognition for more than his skillful writing. He was also a *radical* sympathiser, who supported an extension of the franchise and he was also active in supporting the interests of *nonconformists*. He died in 1904.

(See also *self-help*.)

Smith, Frederick E (1st Lord Birkenhead): lawyer, *Conservative* politician and administrator. Almost invariably known as 'F E ', he was born in 1872 and practised as a barrister in Liverpool before being elected that city's MP in 1906. He was a leading *Unionist* sympathiser during the debates over *Ireland* between 1910 and 1914 and later played a leading role in negotiating the terms of the *Anglo-Irish* treaty of 1921. His major offices were:

- Attorney-General, 1915–19
- Lord Chancellor, 1919–22
- Secretary of State for India, 1924–28

In addition to his work on Ireland, he was an active law-reformer and a successful writer. His political career suffered when he opposed the Conservative Party's decision to break with *Lloyd George* in 1922 and he refused to join *Bonar Law*'s government. His waspish oratory and pointed writing were somewhat dulled by a combination of drink and disillusion in later years. He died in 1930.

Smith, John: *Labour* politician. Born in 1938, he trained and practised as a lawyer before becoming a Labour MP in 1970. His major offices were:

- Secretary of State for Trade, 1978–79
- Leader of the Labour Party, 1992–94

Like almost all Labour politicians of the time, he became embroiled in the turmoil of the battle between left and right. Though firmly on the right of the party, he did not contemplate leaving it to join the Social Democratic Party and he assisted Neil Kinnock in his modernisation programme during the second half of the 1980s. He died suddenly of a heart-attack in 1994, thus being denied the opportunity to win a general election and become *Prime Minister.*

(See also *Blair, Tony; Labour Party.*)

Smith, Sydney: clergyman, journalist and essayist. Born in 1771, he never held high office in either politics or the church but he exerted great influence through his witty and effective writings. He was a *Whig* sympathiser and helped to found the 'Edinburgh Review' in 1802. Among the causes he supported in his writings were:

- *Catholic emancipation*
- reform of the game laws which he believed symbolised unearned and unworthy landowner privileges
- abolition of the *slave trade* and *slavery*

He was a rector of the *Church of England* first in Yorkshire and then in Somerset. He passed ironic comment on his powers as a preacher thus: 'While I am in the pulpit, I have the pleasure of seeing my audience nod approbation while they sleep'. He died in 1845.

Smith, William Henry: newsagent and politician. Invariably known as 'W H Smith', he was born in 1825 the son of a successful newsagent and bookseller. He greatly extended the business in the second half of the nineteenth century, linking his shops with the expanding *railway* network and establishing lending *libraries* in some shops. He thus became a central figure in *retailing* revolution which saw some names, like Boots and Liptons, dominate particular sectors. He was first a supporter of the *Liberal* Party but moved away from the party and was elected as a 'Liberal–Conservative' MP for Westminster in 1868. He soon declared his support for *Disraeli*, however, and his major offices were held as a Conservative:

- First Lord of the Admiralty, 1877–80
- Secretary of State for War, 1885, 1886–87
- First Lord of the Treasury, 1887–91

He died in 1891.

Snowden, Philip (1st Viscount Snowden): *Labour* politician. Born into a Yorkshire weaving family in 1864, he was one of the founders of the *Independent Labour Party* before becoming MP for Blackburn (Lancashire) in 1906. He is a good example of the type of self-improving working man who would probably have been a *Gladstonian Liberal* had he been born a few years earlier. His beliefs encompassed *free trade*, temperance reform, thrift, *pacifism* and *self-help*. He believed in a kind of ethical *socialism* and believed, unlike many late nineteenth century Liberals, that the number of working men in Parliament should be greatly increased but he did not believe in revolution or even direct attacks on the State. He opposed *World War I* and was out of Parliament from 1918 to 1922, returning as member for Colne Valley. His major offices were:

- Chancellor of the Exchequer, 1924 and 1929–31
- Lord Privy Seal, 1931–32

He worked well with *Ramsay MacDonald* but opposed the *General Strike* in 1926. His financial policies were always orthodox. Like Gladstone, he believed in balanced budgets and offered little to deal with the growing economic problems of the late 1920s and early 1930s. He willingly supported MacDonald and accepted a peerage when the *National Government* was formed. His falling-out with the Labour Party was bitter; he accused it in 1931 of turning to 'Bolshevism'. He resigned from the National Government in 1932 when it abandoned free trade and never held political office again. He died in 1937.

Social Democratic and Labour Party: non-violent *Catholic* political party in Northern Ireland. It was formed in 1971 during the early stages of the political troubles in the province and campaigned vigorously first under *Gerry Fitt* and, from 1979 under the leadership of John Hume for civil rights and equal political opportunities for the minority community. It participated in the brief power-sharing initiative in 1973–74 and its failure probably lost the party support among many of the Catholic working class, who increasingly looked to *Sinn Fein* and to the *IRA* for leadership. Its influence has continued, however, and it played an important role in the Anglo-Irish agreement of 1985. It has remained the leading non-violent Catholic organisation, but its support has swung increasingly towards the middle classes and its authority has become ever more dependent upon the leadership of John Hume.

(See also *Ireland*; *Ulster*.)

Social Democratic Federation: *socialist* political party. Founded by H M Hyndman in 1881, it was one of the earliest socialist organisations in Britain but it never had the support of either Marx or Engels and it soon suffered important defections. It helped organise a number of impressive political demonstrations of working men during the 1880s and was one of the organisations which helped found the *Labour Party* in 1900. Its influence declined thereafter, and most of its active members eventually transferred their allegiance to the *Communist Party* after *World War I*.

social policy: activities designed to use the power both of the State and of private organisations to effect improvements in society, usually by attending to the needs of its least privileged members. All actions to this end can be considered as 'social policy' but the term came into common use only in the twentieth century when governments began to use a range of policies to protect citizens by extending education, and through *national insurance* and *pensions*. After *World War I*, attention was increasingly directed towards *housing* policy and, during and after *World War II*, to the creation of a *National Health Service* and a *welfare state*. Most advocates of an active social policy have also argued the importance of using taxation to redistribute wealth from the richer to the poorer classes. 'Social policy' was particularly fashionable from the 1940s to the mid-1970s, but then came under increasing attack on grounds both of cost and ideology. *Thatcherism* advocated a shift in emphasis back towards *self-help* and moral improvement rather than a reliance on outside agencies. The experience of the twentieth century has suggested that, while limited emphasis by government on social policies will ensure that inequalities in society will widen, often with significant consequences for crime and public order, even costly and effectively targeted social policies cannot eradicate poverty.

(See Figure on page 286.)

socialism: political doctrine, rooted in economic organisation, which places reliance on common ownership and collective activity, rather than individualism and

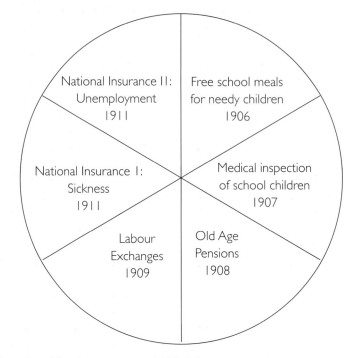

Social policy of the Liberal governments, 1905–14

reliance on the market place to determine wages and profits. The most common definition of socialism derives from Marx and *Engels* and relates to the 'collective ownership of the means of production, distribution and exchange'. However, practical socialism in Britain owed more to the ideas of *Robert Owen* and emphasised community and collective trading, especially through the *Co-operative Movement*. Socialist societies in the 1880s and 1890s attracted small, if committed, memberships often dominated by the intellectual *middle classes*. These societies were frequently divided on whether they believed in violent revolution as a means to achieve their socialist ends. Clause 4 of the *Labour Party*'s constitution of 1918 formally committed the party to collective ownership and the *nationalisation* policies of *Attlee*'s governments of 1945–51 worked within this framework. However, the Labour Party was frequently divided on the extent to which it believed in socialism defined as wholesale collective ownership, rather than a less ideological commitment to reform and improvement. Socialism had much less support within an established political party in Britain in the late nineteenth and early twentieth centuries than in many other industrial European countries, notably Germany. The reasons for this have been much debated but centre on:

- longer established political traditions of *radical* liberalism which acted as a focus for political change, and
- an established *trade unionism* tradition, rooted in the experiences of *artisans*, of working within an established political system. Linked first to the

> *Liberal Party*, this tradition was transferred in the years before 1914 to a non-revolutionary *Labour Party*

(See also *Communist Party*.)

Somme, Battle of the (1916): battle fought in northern France, on the Western Front, during *World War I*. The strategy of General Douglas *Haig* was to use a major offensive, backed for the first time by tanks, to break through the German lines, end the stalemate of trench warfare and bring the war to a speedy conclusion. It failed. On the first day of the offensive, 1 July, almost 60,000 British troops were killed. The battle continued until 18 November, involving almost one-million casualties from Britain, France and Germany, and the maximum advance achieved was eight miles. The battle is usually considered not only a failure but a turning point in the perception of war to one of tragic and futile sacrifice. It is possible, however, that the effort of defending positions at enormous cost had greater long-term effects on the German war effort than was apparent at the time. Controversy over the significance of the battle continues.

South Africa: a union of four states within the *British Empire*, created in 1910. Two of the states, Cape Colony and Natal, had been British colonies and self-governing since 1872 and 1893 respectively. The other two, Transvaal and the Orange Free State, had formerly been Boer Republics, with strong Dutch connections. The new state had a Boer majority and a predominantly Boer parliament and developed policies designed to exploit the rich natural resources of the state (especially gold, minerals and good farming land) in the main interests of the whites, who formed about 20 per cent of the total population in the 1920s. Despite some friction between whites of Dutch and British origin, South Africa became part of the British Commonwealth in 1931. White supremacy became official government policy as 'apartheid' after the victory of the Nationalists in 1948. This led to increasing tension with the *Commonwealth*. South Africa left the Commonwealth in 1961 to become a republic, returning only after majority rule was established in 1994.

(See also *Boer Wars*.)

'Speenhamland system': form of poor relief which became common after 1795. It was not introduced as the result of an Act of Parliament but on an initiative by Berkshire magistrates responding to rapidly rising food prices. To meet the real threat of starvation, they introduced new scales which varied with the price of grain and also with the size of the family seeking relief. The system spread throughout much of southern and eastern England, though it was frequently costly. It was at the heart of the attack by political economists and other opponents of the *Poor Laws*, who suggested that it encouraged the poor to have more children, thus making the situation worse.

(See also *Malthus, Thomas; Poor Law Amendment Act*.)

spinning jenny: important piece of pioneer machinery developed by James Hargreaves in 1766. It allowed cotton spinners to spin multiple threads, thus greatly speeding up productivity. Spinning jennies could be used in domestic industry and had spread rapidly throughout Lancashire and Lanarkshire by the end of the eighteenth century. They were also introduced into early textile factories.

(See also *cotton industry; Industrial Revolution*.)

Spithead Mutiny: see *Naval Mutinies*

St Germain, Treaty of (1919): peace treaty signed by the victorious Allies of *World War I* with Austria. By it the old Austro-Hungarian Empire of the Habsburg family was dismantled:

- Slovenia, Bosnia-Herzegovina and Dalmatia went to a new 'Yugoslavia'
- Bohemia and Moravia went to a new 'Czechoslovakia'
- South Tyrol went to Italy
- Galicia went to Poland
- Bukovina went to Romania
- Austria and Germany were formally forbidden to unite
- Austria was liable to reparations on grounds of war guilt
- the Austrian army was limited to a maximum of 30,000 men

(See also *Versailles, Treaty of.*)

'stagflation': term coined by economists in the 1960s to describe the simultaneous occurrence of two unfavourable phenomena which had formerly been considered mutually exclusive:

- economic stagnation, in which growth is either very slow or non-existent, and often associated with increased *unemployment*
- *inflation*, in which the value of money declines

Stanley, Henry Morton: African explorer, journalist and imperialist. Born in extreme poverty in Wales in 1841, he joined the staff of the US journal 'New York Herald' in 1857 and was sent by it in 1871 to try to discover the missing *David Livingstone*. He is best known for his famous introduction on their meeting at Lake Tanganyika: 'Dr Livingstone, I presume'. He also journeyed across Africa from 1874 to 1877 and, in the pay of King Leopold of the Belgians, established the Congo Free State in the early 1880s. He died in 1904.

(See also *imperialism.*)

staple industries: originally a term applied to the wool industry, which medieval kings singled out for taxation, its usage extended in the nineteenth and early twentieth centuries to include all industries basic to Britain's employment pattern and export performance from the *Industrial Revolution* onwards. It usually included not only textiles but also coal, *iron* and *steel* and *shipping*. These were the industries which came under greatest pressure during the Depression of the inter-war period.

state education: term used to describe education provided, or financially supported, by government rather than by charity or by the private sector of the economy. It is usually said to have begun in 1833 when a parliamentary grant of £20,000 was voted to help *Church of England* and *nonconformist* organisations to build schools for children of the poor. A separate administrative organisation, the Committee of the Privy Council on Education, was established in 1839 which appointed Inspectors ('Her Majesty's Inspectors') whose task was to report on the quality and range of education provided in state-aided schools and to make recommendations for improvement. After 1846, a teacher-training scheme was also in place.

A new phase in state provision was begun with the *Education Act* of 1870 and state education expanded rapidly thereafter. It is important to stress, however, that central government had relatively direct involvement. So-called 'state schools' were usually funded by ratepayers through 'local education authorities' after the *Education Act* of 1902. After the *Education Act* of 1944 made compulsory 'primary' and 'secondary' education to age fifteen, between 90 per cent and 95 per cent of children have been educated in state schools, the remainder going outside the state system, notably to the confusing-titled 'public schools'.

(See also *Education Acts; Kay-Shuttleworth, James; Lowe, Robert; Revised Code of Education.*)

steam power: the technique of using the pressure generated by boiled water to provide movement was first developed by Thomas Savery in 1698, while the Dartmouth (Devon) ironmonger Thomas Newcomen created 'steam engines' for pumping water from coal pits in 1712. The potential of steam power was greatly increased by *James Watt*'s invention of a 'steam condenser' in 1769. From the early nineteenth century, when about 2,500 steam engines were in use, steam power became the foundation of much mechanised power. The invention in 1802 of a high-pressure engine by Richard Trevithick was of immediate value for coal mining. During the nineteenth century, steam engines were used mainly in:

- mining, for drainage
- textiles (the *cotton* and *woollen* industries especially), for powering spinning and weaving machines
- *transport*, especially *railways* and *steamships*

The development of steam power also gave a huge boost to the coal industry, which provided most of the heat needed to generate steam. Steam power was characteristic of the so-called 'second phase' of the *Industrial Revolution* in which heavy industries expanded very rapidly. This process was further accelerated in 1884 by the development of the 'rotary steam engine' by Charles Parsons. These engines, which worked with blades rather than pistons, enabled higher speeds to be achieved with far less vibration and helped the *shipping* industry to develop faster vessels.

(See also *Brunel, I K; Stephenson, George; Stephenson, Robert.*)

steamships: increasingly large ships used for transatlantic and intercontinental trade from the second half of the nineteenth century. Although smaller steamships had made an appearance early in the nineteenth century to challenge sail, the characteristic large ocean-going vessels were developed only from the 1840s. The total British tonnage of sailing ships exceeded that of steamships until the early 1880s. Steamships worked mainly out of the ports of London, Hull and Glasgow. Glasgow and the Clyde estuary were especially important. On the eve of *World War I*, Clydeside built one-third of the world's ships.

Since they provided their own power, steamships could run to a timetable, rather than being dependent on the vagaries of the wind, and they were normally much faster than sailships. They revolutionised overseas trade after 1850 and were an important element in the growing international rivalry in the years leading up to World War I. The main technological developments associated with nineteenth century steamships were:

- using iron plates in constructing ships' hulls. This provided added strength, enabling ships to be long and narrow yet water-resistant. They could also accommodate larger engines without vibration damaging the structure

- using iron plates in boiler construction allowed the use of much higher steam pressure, allowing more powerful engines to be operated
- using screw propellers rather than external paddle boxes. This allowed ships to be laid immediately alongside in port. Goods could be moved onto such ships much more quickly

Thus, the development of steamships was strongly associated with the growth of the *iron* and *steel* industries in what some economic historians have seen as a 'second Industrial Revolution' superseding the textile revolution after 1850.

Ships trebled in tonnage size between the late 1840s and the late 1880s, but during the 1880s the design of ships was revolutionised again with the development of triple-compound engines. This facilitated the development of very large ships, especially prestige passenger liners such as 'Aquitania' (1914) which weighed 47,000 tons. With the success of huge lines, steamship-ownership became concentrated in the hands of a few firms, such as British India, Cunard and P & O. The total tonnage of British steamships increased from 1.5 million to 10.9 million between the early 1870s and the early 1910s and the proportion of shipping powered by steam rose from 26 per cent to 92 per cent.

Along with its close ally, the coal industry, British *shipping* suffered dramatically in the inter-war period when the market for international cargo ships plummeted and the shipbuilding industry contributed substantially to rising *unemployment* figures in the 1920s and 1930s.

(See also *Brunel, I K; 'Great Eastern'; 'Great Western'.*)

Steel, David: Liberal Party politician. Born in Scotland in 1938, he became the youngest MP in the *House of Commons* when he won a by-election in 1963 at the age of 25. Fluent, personable and a good deal tougher than his agreeable manner suggested, his political career included a number of successes. He pioneered the first Abortion Bill through Parliament in 1967 and he served as leader of the Liberal Party from 1976 to 1988, helping in the process to rebuild the party's image in the wake of the resignation of Jeremy Thorpe.

His political influence is best seen in helping to forge the *Lib–Lab Pact* of 1977–78 and thus keeping *Callaghan*'s Labour government in power for perhaps two years longer than might otherwise have been the case.

If, as with all other Liberal leaders since *Asquith,* heading a Liberal government proved an unrealistic objective, he nevertheless exercised greater power than most and contributed much to increasing the standing of the Liberal Party as a substantial and viable 'third force' in British politics. He retired from the *House of Commons* in 1992.

(See also *Grimond, Jo.*)

steel industry: metals industry closely linked to *iron* which developed rapidly in the second half of the nineteenth century after Sir Henry Bessemer introduced a process in 1856 which superseded iron puddling and removed impurities from pig iron. The technology of steel production was further advanced first by the Siemens 'Open-Hearth' process (1856–57), which enabled a greater range of hardness to be achieved, and then by the development of the Gilchrist 'basic process' in 1879 which was able to absorb phosphorous from iron. The major steel-producing centres of the country were Middlesborough (which was, in effect, a new industrial town in later Victorian Britain) and Sheffield. The industry endured relative decline from the last quarter of the nineteenth century. It was first *nationalised* as British Steel by the *Labour Party* in 1949 and then denationalised soon after the *Conservatives* were elected into government in 1951.

(See also *economic policy; Great Depression; Industrial Revolution.*)

Stephens, Joseph Rayner: Chartist sympathiser and *Tory radical.* Born in 1805, he became a *Methodist* minister in 1829 but was suspended for advocating *disestablishment* of the *Church of England.* He was a brilliant orator who attacked the *Poor Law Amendment Act* in the 1830s and, like many others in the North of England, was led from this into support for *Chartism.* He also supported a range of humanitarian causes, notably the *Ten Hours Movement.* He died in 1879.

Stephenson, George: engineer. Born in humble circumstances in the North-East in 1781, he produced a number of technological innovations, including a safety lamp for miners and steam locomotives, which established his reputation. He was Superintendent Engineer of the pioneer Stockton and Darlington Railway in the 1820s, and his steam engine 'Rocket' which was demonstrated to huge success in 1829 convinced many important investors that the future of the *railway* industry lay in the rapid development of steam engines. He died in 1848.

(See also *engineering industry; railways.*)

Stephenson, Robert: engineer. The son of *George Stephenson*, he was born in 1803 and worked on engineering projects, notably the steam engine 'Rocket', with his father. He worked as civil engineer on a number of railway projects in the 1830s and 1840s. He emerged from his father's shadow by designing a large number of major engineering structures, notably the dramatic High Level Bridge over the Tyne at Newcastle (1849) and the tubular bridge over the Menai Straits to Anglesey (1850). He also worked in Canada in the later 1850s. He was Conservative MP for Whitby (Yorkshire) from 1847 until his death in 1859.

(See also *engineering industry; Hudson, George; railways.*)

Stevenson, Robert Louis: novelist. He was born in 1850 and studied both engineering and law before becoming a full-time writer. His romantic and adventure novels and 'Treasure Island' (1883) and 'Kidnapped' (1886) made both his fame and his fortune. He also wrote the intriguing psychological story 'The Strange Case of Dr Jekyll and Mr Hyde' (1886). He was a frequent traveller to warmer climes, partly as a means of improving his never robust health. He settled with his family on the Pacific island of Samoa, where he died in 1894.

Stopes, Marie: biologist and pioneer of birth control. Born in 1880, her early career was as a brilliant research scientist who contributed to a new form of classifying ancient plants. Her fame, however, derived from the publication of two controversial books – 'Married Love' (1918) on female sexual fulfilment in marriage and 'Wise Parenthood' (1918) which advocated birth control. Her books sold in huge quantities but upset moralists and the *Roman Catholic* church. She founded Britain's first birth-control clinic in Holloway (London) in 1921. She defended her position in print, on public platforms and in the law courts. She alienated even some of her supporters by her arrogance and lack of tolerance towards the opinions of others. Some also accused her of seeking publicity not so much for her causes but for its own sake, but her impact on the social development of Britain – and particularly Britain's women – is undeniable. She died in 1958.

'stop–go': name given to rapid shifts in government management of the economy between the 1950s and the early 1970s. Although this was a period of unprecedented economic growth, it was also one during which Britain's relative position in world trading continued to decline. Politicians of both the *Labour* and *Conservative* parties found themselves unable to manage stable economic growth, since after a period of expansion ('go'), which nearly always involved excessive imports of foreign manufactured goods, the economy 'overheated', bringing excessive wage demands and rising levels of *inflation*. To keep inflation in check, governments were forced to introduce curbs on expenditure, usually in the form of higher interest rates (making borrowing more expensive) and also higher rates of taxation. The process began again when the economy had 'cooled down'. Stop–go had an important political dimension, since Chancellors of the Exchequer were usually asked to try to intervene in the economy to ensure that periods of 'go', associated not only with economic expansion but with rising spending levels and general feelings of consumer well-being, occurred during the period which preceded *general elections*. The economy could then be 'cooled down' when the election was safely won. 'Stop–go' was widely condemned, not least by businessmen who disliked rapid shifts in economic policy which, they argued, made it difficult for them to plan their investment strategies with confidence.

(See also *economic policy; Keynesian economics.*)

Stormont: officially the name of the *Northern Ireland* parliament building in Belfast, it became more generally associated with the government of Northern Ireland, which had a separate, Protestant-dominated, parliament from 1922 until 1972 when the British *Conservative* government substituted direct rule for *Ulster* from Westminster. The parliament building itself was not occupied until 1932.

(See also *Ireland.*)

Strachey, Lytton: writer. Born in 1880, he became a prominent member of the *Bloomsbury Group*. He is best known for his collection of essays 'Eminent Victorians' (1918) which were a landmark in criticism and subjected 'Victorianism' to one of its most sustained attacks. He also produced a lucid and entertaining, but historically suspect, study of 'Queen Victoria' (1921). He died in 1921.

(See also *Keynes, John Maynard; Victoria.*)

Straits, Convention of the (1841): diplomatic agreement designed to ensure stability in the near east. The 'straits' in question were the Bosphorous and the Dardanelles. The signatories to the Convention were Britain, France, Russia, the Austro-Hungarian Empire, Prussia, Naples, Sardinia and Turkey. By the agreement:

- the independence of Turkey (Ottoman Empire) was guaranteed by the other powers
- during time of peace, Turkey would permit free passage to merchant ships
- during war, Turkey might close the Straits to any power it wished

(See also *Palmerston, Viscount.*)

strike weapon: the withdrawal of labour by working people with the intention of extracting concessions from employers. The word 'strike' has a naval origin: sailing ships could not move with their main masts 'struck', or lowered. *Trade unions* have always had the strike weapon as a means of attempted coercion, but it has not been used as frequently as many think. It is a fairly blunt weapon, and tends to produce decisive results. Strikes which fail have frequently done defeated unions substantial long-term damage. Thus, skilled workers in the nineteenth century usually preferred negotiation and compromise to the withdrawal of labour. The so-called 'new unions' of the late nineteenth century, on the other hand, were forged out of successful strikes, for example, by *dockers* and *gas workers*.

During the twentieth century, the main periods of strike activity were:

1910–14 when 4,568 separate disputes were recorded and more than 80 million working days lost
1919–21 3,722 disputes and 147 million working days lost
1926 the *General Strike* – 162 million working days lost

After *World War II*, the general trend was for a large number of disputes most of which were settled quickly, often because employers retreated in the face of concerted union activity. In 1970, for example, 3,906 separate stoppages were recorded but they lost only eleven million working days. The frequent disputes of the 1970s lost the unions public sympathy as the feeling grew that unelected unions were exercising as much power over the economy as the elected government. *Margaret Thatcher*'s legislation against unions had widespread support and the miners' strike of 1984–85, which was lost, proved to be the last high-profile lengthy strike mounted by a major trade union in the twentieth century.

(See also *Citrine, Walter; Cook, A J.*)

Suez Crisis, 1956: the Suez canal, linking the Mediterranean to the Red Sea was opened in 1869. Britain gained a substantial interest in it through *Disraeli*'s purchase of canal shares in 1875 and British troops protected the waterway from 1883 onwards. In July 1956, after British and US funding arrangements for a new Egyptian dam broke down, the Egyptian leader Gamel Abdul Nasser nationalised the canal contrary to a leasing agreement. Britain and France sent troops to Port Said in November 1956 but were forced to withdraw after the United States' hostility had been made clear. Nasser's control over the canal remained complete. The crisis destroyed the prime ministership of *Anthony Eden* but also had wider implications. It demonstrated that Britain and France no longer had the international power they had claimed before *World War II* and could not stand alone against United States opinion. For many, the crisis represented the end of the era of British imperial greatness.

(See also *Empire, British; imperialism.*)

suffragettes: name given to supporters of the *Women's Suffrage and Political Union* (WSPU) who campaigned for women to have the right to vote and were prepared to use violence and other forms of direct action to achieve their objective. They were active from 1903, when the WSPU was founded to 1914. Their leaders included *Emmeline* and *Christabel Pankhurst.* The main methods employed by suffragettes were:

- interrupting political meetings by anti-suffrage speakers

- attacking property, particularly breaking windows and setting fire to pillar boxes
- intervening in parliamentary by-elections
- trying to interrupt public events, such as the Derby in 1913 – see *Emily Davison*
- when imprisoned, refusing food and inviting martyrdom

These tactics were controversial. Some argued that they brought suffrage campaigners vital publicity. Others believed that they provoked antagonism in some powerful places and delayed the achievement of the vote until the end of *World War I*. Suffragettes abandoned their militant campaign in 1914 and contributed towards the war effort.

(See also *suffragists*.)

IS THIS RIGHT?

THE OPEN MARKET

Woman. Why can't I have an umbrella too?

Voter. You can't. You ought to stop at home.

Woman. Stop at home indeed! I have my Living to earn.

Printed and published by the Artists' Suffrage League, 259 King's Road, Chelsea.

Contemporary cartoon illustrating the suffragettes' cause

suffragists: name often given to non-militant supporters of 'votes for women'. The suffrage campaign in practice began in 1867 with the formation of the London Society for Women's Suffrage, a central committee being established five years later to co-ordinate activity. In 1897, the National Union of Women's Suffrage Societies (NUWSS) was formed. The suffrage campaign was dominated by well-educated *middle-class* women, although a number of working-class women, especially textile *trade unionists* in Lancashire, were also strong supporters of the campaign. It was against the apparent lack of success by non-violent methods that the *Pankhursts* and other members of the *Women's Political and Social Union* reacted after 1903.

(See also *suffragettes*.)

Sullivan, Sir Arthur: composer. Born in London in 1842, he was trained at the Royal Academy of Music and seemed set for a career in serious music. However, his collaboration with *W S Gilbert*, which began with the one-act operetta 'Trial by Jury' (1875) and continued with such major 'hits' as 'HMS Pinafore' (1878), 'Iolanthe' (1882), 'The Mikado' (1885), 'The Yeomen of the Guard' (1888) and 'The Gondoliers' (1889) transformed both his bank balance and his reputation. These 'Gilbert and Sullivan' operas depend in equal measure on pointed social satire (provided by Gilbert's well-informed wit) and easy, but skilful, melody (provided by Sullivan, drawing upon examples provided by earlier composers such as Mendelssohn and Donizetti). Queen *Victoria*, who conferred a knighthood on him in 1883, urged him to write a 'grand opera, Sir Arthur: you would do it so well'. He obliged with his 'romantic opera' 'Ivanhoe' (1891), based loosely on the novel by *Sir Walter Scott*, but it has not endured as have the operettas and does not deserve to. His collaboration with Gilbert, which he frequently regretted during a tempestuous creative relationship since he felt that it trivialised his talents, has ensured his long-term reputation. He died in 1900.

Sunday schools: schools which provided not only religious instruction but also basic education in reading and writing for poor children. The Methodists established a number in the 1770s but the development of the Sunday school movement is usually associated with Robert Raikes of Gloucester, who took children out of church and provided separate instruction and worship for them. A Sunday School Society was founded in 1785 and developed in 1803 into the Sunday School Union. Both *Church of England* and *nonconformist* churches established Sunday schools which, from the 1790s, were also concerned to ensure that the *radical* challenges of the *French Revolution* were seen off by teachers who stressed order and obedience to established authority. About a-quarter-of-a-million children were being educated in Sunday schools by 1800 and the number increased to almost six million by the 1880s. By then, the extension of day schools had reduced the importance of Sunday schools except in their primary purpose of providing religious instruction.

(See also *Education Acts; More, Hannah*.)

sweated labour: name given to work done by labourers, often women, who worked long hours carrying out usually unskilled and repetitive tasks for low rates of pay. Many worked in the textile trades, as seamstresses, alterers or repairers, either from home or in small workshops. During the nineteenth century, they were not protected by the *Factory Acts*. Some women took up such work only when their families were in poverty and it was almost impossible to provide any protection from *trade unions*. However, successful industrial production depended to a large extent upon a very large pool of labour which was sometimes employed (in times of trade boom) and sometimes not (in times of slump). A parliamentary select committee of 1890 investigated low-paid workers in a range of trades, including clothes-makers, dockers and unskilled workers in the hardware trades. The Trade Boards Act of 1909, passed by *Asquith's Liberal* government, offered some support in the form of wage boards to determine wages in wholesale tailoring, lace-making and chain-making. The number of such boards was increased in the inter-war period and their functions transferred by the *Labour* government in 1945 to wages councils.

(See also *Industrial Revolution; labour exchanges*.)

Swing Riots: name given to disturbances by agricultural labourers, mostly in southern and eastern England in 1830 and 1831. The name was taken from the mythical leader of the labourers, 'Captain Swing'. The riots occurred at the end of a long period of declining wages and less secure employment for rural workers. In the 1820s, 'threshing machines' began to be introduced which threatened the already limited amount of work available for arable labourers (workers in the corn growing areas). The disturbances took various forms including:

- destruction of threshing machines
- threatening letters to farmers and clergymen, which accused them of paying starvation wages or not offering comfort and support to the weakest in the community
- burning hayricks

The riots disturbed the Government, partly because there was so much unrest in Britain at the time, concerned with agitation for *parliamentary reform* and partly because rural labourers were considered one of the loyalist sections of the early industrial workforce. Many were prosecuted. On conviction, some were executed and many *transported* to Australia.

Sykes–Picot Agreement, 1916: secret agreement, named after the two main negotiators, between Britain and France over the fate of the Ottoman Empire if the Allies were victorious in *World War I*. Both powers would take over Turkish territory:

- Britain would have direct control of territory in lower Iraq and a small part of Palestine and indirect control of northern Mesopotamia
- France would have direct control of the coast of Northern Syria and indirect control of southern Mesopotamia

The agreement conflicted with promises made by both powers about Arab independence after the fall of the Ottoman Empire and was never fully implemented. It was one of many factors which increased the lack of trust between the Arab world and the Western powers in the first part of the twentieth century.

(See also *Balfour Declaration*.)

syndicalism: a form of militant trade unionism. Its main objectives were:

- worker control of industry on *socialist* principles
- the development of a few very large industrial unions representing a number of trades, rather than separate craft-based labour organisations
- to destroy capitalism by mounting a series of challenges, mostly in the form of aggressive strikes, using the collective power of large numbers of workers to ensure victory

Syndicalism thus rejected working through political parties, the route favoured by most British trade unions, either through the *Liberal Party* before the first decade of the twentieth century and the *Labour Party* from the early twentieth century onwards. At the Trades Union Congress of 1912 – the peak pre-*World War I* year for *strike* action – the unions rejected syndicalist calls to abandon links with the Labour Party. Imported from France and the United States, its most prominent advocate in Britain was Thomas Mann who publicised his views in the journal 'Industrial Syndicalist'.

Syndicalism was only briefly influential in Britain but was one of the factors explaining the militancy of labour relations in the years 1910–14.

(See also *strike weapon*.)

Synge, John Millington: Irish playwright. Invariably known as 'J M Synge', he was born near Dublin in 1871. He studied the Irish language in Dublin and music in Germany and was heavily influenced by W B Yeats, who advised him to develop his writing by studying distinctively Irish speech patterns. These were reflected in his plays, notably 'The Playboy of the Western World' (1907), his best-known work which became a symbol of revived interest in Irish culture. He was also Director of Dublin's famous Abbey Theatre, from 1904 to his death in 1909. This post further increased his influence on later Irish dramatists. His writings were controversial. His determination to convey what he saw as the whole truth about 'Irishness' annoyed many nationalists who wished to portray a more soft-grained and romantic image hardened only by conflict with Britain.

(See also *Ireland*.)

T

tactical voting: name given to voting at elections which aims to ensure the defeat of an unfavoured candidate. Under *'first past the post'*, a candidate who is unpopular with the majority of the electorate may be elected because votes for other candidates are relatively evenly spread. Tactical voting maximises the possibility of defeating an unpopular candidate. Electors vote not necessarily for their favourite candidate but for the candidate most likely to defeat the least favoured candidate. The size of *Labour*'s majority in the general election of 1997 was almost certainly increased by widespread tactical voting. *Liberal* supporters in seats where Labour was the main challenger to the *Conservatives* would vote Labour to defeat the Conservatives. In the South-West of England, where the Liberals were the main challengers, many natural Labour supporters voted Liberal with the same objective. Objectors to tactical voting argue that it is a cynical manoeuvre which perverts the main purpose of an election, which is to vote for a favoured candidate or party. Supporters respond, first, that it is just as acceptable to vote <u>against</u> an unpopular candidate as to <u>support</u> a popular one and, second, that tactical voting may be a valid means of reducing the distortions produced by 'first past the post'.

Taff Vale Case, 1901–2: legal judgement which jeopardised the funding of *trade unions*. After a trade dispute between the Amalgamated Society of Railway Societies and the Taff Vale Railway Company in South Wales in 1901, the employers took their case to the House of Lords where they received a judgement that the union was liable to pay for losses incurred during the strike. In December 1902 the union was forced to pay £43,000 damages and costs. The judgement seemed to overturn a crucial part of the Trade Union Act, 1871, which protected union funds from claims during a strike. *Ramsay MacDonald* used the opportunity to argue to trade unionists that they clearly needed the protection of a political party dedicated to the interests of working men. In 1906 *Asquith*'s *Liberal* government passed the *Trades Disputes Act* which in effect reversed the Lords' judgement.

Talents, Ministry of all the: name colloquially given to the coalition government of 1806–7 which took office after the death of *William Pitt the Younger*. Its leaders were *Charles James Fox*, who died before it fell, and *William Grenville* and it also included the former *Prime Minister Henry Addington* (now Viscount Sidmouth). The ministry was not especially 'talented' and fell, as the younger Pitt's had in 1801 over the question of *Catholic emancipation*, which *George III* still refused to allow. The real beneficiaries were those left out of the ministry, particularly the younger supporters of Pitt, such as *Liverpool* and *Castlereagh*. They formed the core of the new ministry, headed by the Duke of *Portland* in 1807. Nevertheless, the 'Talents' gave the *Whigs* their only taste of office during a long period of opposition which stretched from 1784 to 1830.

Tariff Reform League: organisation founded by *Joseph Chamberlain* in 1903 to campaign for a policy of *imperial preference* rather than *free trade*. It survived only until Chamberlain's stroke in 1906 and it never managed to convince the *Conservative* government under *Balfour* to abandon the long-standing commitment to *free trade*. It did, however, split the Conservative Party and contributed to its very heavy defeat at the *general election* of 1906.

(See also *laissez-faire, Liberal Party.*)

Taunton Commission: Royal Commission on education which sat from 1864 to 1867. Its main task was to report on the state of secondary education in England and Wales. Finding that provision for education beyond elementary level was very limited, it recommended the foundation of a large number of secondary schools in towns which lacked them. The schools would be funded by ratepayers. The government rejected the proposal for two main reasons:

- it feared increasing expenditure on education at a time when government was trying to cut costs
- it was suspicious of the principle of allowing large numbers of children from humble homes to receive the kind of education which could give them higher expectations of a career than society was likely to be able to meet

(See also *Clarendon Commission; Education Act, 1870; Education Act, 1902; Lowe, Robert; Newcastle Commission; Revised Code of Education.*)

Tawney, Richard Henry: historian, educationist and socialist thinker. Invariably known as 'R H Tawney', he was born in 1880 and had a varied career. To historians, he is best known for his novel interpretation of the Reformation, in 'Religion and the Rise of Capitalism' (1926), and as Professor of Economic History at the London School of Economics from 1931. He did much to promote the study of economic history as a separate academic discipline. He was, however, also a key figure in the *Workers' Educational Association,* giving tutorial classes in Manchester and Rochdale from 1908 to 1914. He wrote extensively on increasing access to education at all stages of life. Although he stood as a Labour candidate in three general elections in 1918, 1922 and 1924, he was never elected. His educational writings, however, influenced *Labour Party* thinking as did his analyses of a society he found profoundly unequal, 'The Acquisitive Society' (1921) and 'Equality' (1931). He died in 1962.

(See also *socialism.*)

Tedder, Sir Arthur (1st Baron Tedder of Glenguin): senior figure in the Royal Air Force. He was born in 1890 and served in the army during *World War I* before devoting the remainder of his career to the air force. He played an important role in *World War II* first as commander of the RAF in the Middle East from 1941 to 1943, then in charge of Allied air forces in the Mediterranean and then as Deputy Supreme Commander of *Operation Overlord* in 1944, during which he worked very successfully with US General Eisenhower. His use of air forces to interrupt the flow of supplies from enemy countries to the fighting fronts proved of immense value to the war effort. He received a peerage when he became Marshal of the Royal Air Force in 1946 and served in this capacity until 1955. He died in 1967.

(See also *Montgomery, Bernard.*)

'Teddy boys': name given to groups of youths who dressed distinctively in the 1950s in fashions some of which owed an origin to the Edwardian period (1901–10) – hence 'Teddy' as a brief nickname for 'Edward'. They wore drain-pipe trousers and kept their hair very well oiled. To older generations, they represented rebellion against authority and conformist values. Many were also lovers of the new types of popular music which emphasised rhythm ('beat') against melody and form and some were associated with threatening behaviour and violence.

(See also *popular culture.*)

television: form of broadcasting using both sound and vision. The first television experiments were made in the late 1920s by *John Logie Baird* based on the cathode ray tube, an invention of the late 1890s which converted light and shade into electrical signals and had remained under-developed. The first experimental television broadcast was made in 1929. In the early 1930s, Electrical and Musical Industries (EMI) were competing with Baird to fashion an effective system and the EMI system, based on 405 lines, was found to be the more effective. The world's first regular television service began broadcasting from Alexandra Palace, London, in November 1936 but the new medium remained a luxury item for the upper and upper middle classes until the early 1950s. Television coverage of the coronation of *Elizabeth II* proved to be a decisive spur to popularising the medium. By the end of the 1950s, television had superseded *radio* as the primary medium of mass communication. In 1958, the number of radio and television combined licences (8 million) exceeded radio-only licences (6.5 million) for the first time.

From the 1950s, also, television was beginning to lose its reputation for seriousness and sober presentation. The BBC was a public-service broadcaster and the challenge presented by the commercial stations which began broadcasting under the Independent Television Authority (ITA) in 1955 was substantial. Independent television programmes tended to be oriented more towards entertainment and the BBC, in order to compete for audiences, began to popularise much more of its own output. Scope for this increased with the creation of a new channel, BBC2, in 1962, since the BBC tended to put more of its 'popular' programmes onto BBC1 and its more serious and experimental work onto BBC2. Quite quickly, BBC1 was capturing about 90 per cent of the BBC audience. A similar division occurred in independent television with the creation of the more 'upmarket' Channel 4 in 1982. A fifth terrestrial British network, Channel 5, emphasising entertainment, especially for the young, began broadcasting in 1997. All channels made substantial use of *United States* programmes as a significant element in their entertainment output. Some saw this as part of the increasing 'globalisation' (by which they meant 'Americanisation') of culture.

The technical quality of television was enhanced from 1962 with the development of a clearer '625-line' broadcasting system. This was adaptable for colour transmissions, which began on BBC2 in July 1967. The emergence of video recorders in the late 1970s gave viewers more flexibility and satellite broadcasting from 1989 vastly greater choice to those willing, and able, to pay subscriptions. The most assiduous early purchasers of satellite systems were from the lower socio-economic groups. The satellite and cable companies, though they had some excellent news coverage and information programmes and also broadcast a large range of radio programmes free from interference, sold their systems much more on the basis of sport and feature films not yet available to the terrestrial channels.

By the 1980s, television was entrenched as far the most popular form of entertainment in Britain, while people increasingly gained their news and other forms of information from television rather than radio or *newspapers*. Politicians also paid much more attention to the immediacy of the television 'image' than to closely argued statements intended to be read and digested at leisure. The medium's contribution to, and reflection of, changing tastes in *popular culture* was likewise immense.

(See also *Reith, John*.)

Telford, Thomas: civil engineer. He was born the son of a Dumfriesshire shepherd in 1757 and was apprenticed to a stonemason where his immense talents began to show themselves. He left Scotland for London in the early 1780s and was working on the Portsmouth dockyards by 1784. He pioneered new forms of road construction which were more weather-resistant. He designed more than 1,000 miles of road in the Scottish Highlands between the early 1800s and the mid-1820s. He also created a new road from Shrewsbury to Holyhead in the first decade of the nineteenth century.

He was also active in *canal* and bridge design. He created the Caledonian Canal in the Scottish Highlands in 1822. This major engineering feat created a navigable route between Fort William and Fort Augustus by linking Lochs Linnhe, Lochy, Oich and Ness. He also completed the Birmingham and Liverpool canal in 1835. He also pioneered the use of suspension bridges in North Wales. He died in 1834, just as the *railway* age was getting underway.

(See also *Brunel, I K*; *engineering industry*; *Industrial Revolution*.)

Temperance Movement: pressure group designed to restrict the sale and consumption of alcohol and to promote 'teetotalism'. It grew out of the British and Foreign Temperance Society, which was established in 1831. Other important temperance societies were the National Temperance Society (1842) and the United Kingdom Alliance (1853). Temperance exerted a substantial influence in Victorian Britain. The moral case against drink was strong, since many men kept their families deprived by immoderate spending on alcohol immediately after receiving their pay. Temperance was promoted as a major agency of respectability and upward social mobility for the working classes and the conversion of many *Methodists* to the temperance cause linked it strongly with the growth of religious *nonconformity*. Propaganda against 'the demon drink' was effectively deployed by many societies and a number of sentimental Victorian ballads, such as 'Father's a Drunkard and Mother is Dead', had a powerful impact on national consciousness. Many *radicals* within the *Liberal Party* were powerful advocates of temperance. Because of this, drink became an important item on the political agenda, nonconformist Liberals being frequent temperance advocates while the brewing trade looked to the *Conservative Party* for support. The societies also had an impact on legislation. Acts of 1869 and 1904 imposed stricter controls on licensing of alcoholic drink. *Gladstone* believed that his very mild Licensing Act of 1872, which disappointed Liberal radicals, nevertheless fatally weakened his government since it enabled the Conservatives to argue that he was depriving the working man of access to well-earned beer.

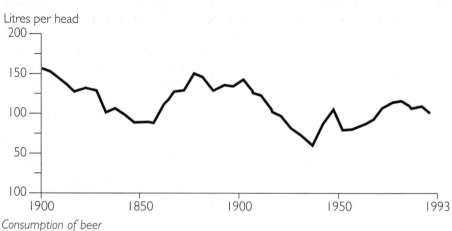

Litres per head

Consumption of beer

Litres per head

Consumption of spirits

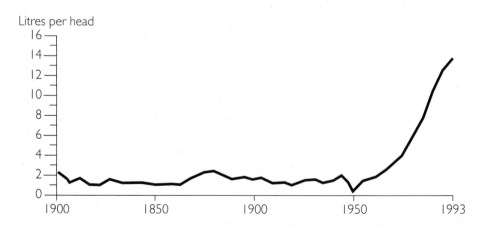

Litres per head

Consumption of wine

Ten Hours Movement: pressure group of the early nineteenth century to restrict hours of work in factories. It was widely supported, both by humanitarian reformers within the *Tory* Party who were hostile to factory owners, and by *radicals* and working-class political leaders. Although mostly associated in Parliament with the tireless efforts of the 7th *Earl of Shaftesbury* in the 1830s and 1840s, it was strongly supported outside Parliament by leaders such as *John Fielden, Richard Oastler* and *J R Stephens*. The Ten Hours Movement was very strong in industrial Lancashire and Yorkshire in the 1830s and 1840s and had important links to *Chartism*. Restrictions on hours of labour were strongly resisted by some factory owners and also *political economists* who argued in favour of *laissez-faire*. The Ten Hours Act of 1847 provided the desired shortening of hours of work for women and children in textile factories. Adult males were, in practice, not required to work more than ten hours a day after amending legislation in 1853.

(See also *child labour; Factory Acts.*)

Tennyson (Alfred), Baron: poet. Born the son of a Lincolnshire clergyman in 1809, he was educated at Cambridge and first made his mark with 'The Lady of Shalott' published in 1832 as part of a collection of poems. He published regularly throughout a long life, his inspiration often coming from historical and mythological subjects such as 'Idylls of the King' (1859). His poems did not always please literary critics either at the time or subsequently. Many, being direct, heroic and simple, established a public popularity which the critics could not challenge. His best known poems are probably 'In Memoriam' which he wrote in 1833, but did not publish until 1850, to commemorate the death of a close boyhood friend, Arthur Henry Hallam, 'The Charge of the Light Brigade' (1854) and 'Maud: a Monodrama' (1855). These last two provide two of the most-quoted extracts in English literature: 'Into the valley of Death Rode the six-hundred' and 'Come into the garden, Maud'. Well-connected to leading politicians and the court, he was a natural choice to succeed *Wordsworth* as poet laureate in 1850 and enjoyed his official duties. He was given a peerage in 1884 and died in 1892.

(See also *Charge of the Light Brigade; Crimean War.*)

Test and Corporation Acts, Repeal of (1828): these Acts, passed in 1661 and 1673 in the reign of Charles II debarred non-members of the *Church of England* from holding public office in either central or local government. Religious *nonconformists* had campaigned against them for much of the eighteenth century, often with the support of influential *Whig* politicians, but without effect. Their formal repeal, after a motion promoted by the Whig *Lord John Russell* and not formally opposed by *Wellington*'s government was in part symbolic since many nonconformists had found ways around the legislation. It did, however, have considerable political significance. Support for the Church of England was one of the key planks of *Tory Party* belief at the time and their repeal caused considerable resentment among die-hard Tories. It contributed to the increasing disunity which tore the party apart in the years 1828–30 and led to their eventual replacement by the Whigs under *Earl Grey*.

(See also *Catholic Emancipation Act, 1829.*)

Thackeray, William Makepeace: journalist and novelist. Born in India, the son of an official of the East India Company in 1811, he was educated at Cambridge before embarking on a career in journalism, a decision largely forced on him by his father's bankruptcy in 1833. He wrote for '*The Times*', 'Fraser's Magazine' and 'Punch' and later became the first editor of 'Cornhill Magazine' in 1860. Much his best known novel is the elegant social satire 'Vanity Fair' (1848) but he also wrote 'Barry Lydon' (1842) and 'Pendennis' (1850). Like *Dickens*, many of his novels first appeared in serialised form. He travelled and lectured in Europe and the United States in the 1850s and died in 1863.

Thatcher, Margaret Hilda (Lady Thatcher of Kesteven): *Conservative* politician and *Prime Minister*. Born the daughter of a *Methodist* grocer in Grantham (Lincolnshire) in 1925, she was educated at Oxford, where she studied chemistry, before taking up the law as a profession. She was first elected to the *House of Commons* in 1959 and achieved junior office under *Macmillan* in 1961. Her major offices were:

- Secretary of State for Education and Science, 1970–74
- Leader of the Conservative Party, 1975–90
- Prime Minister, 1979–90

Thatcher quickly earned a reputation for both hard work and mastery of detail, attributes which made her an effective opposition spokesperson during the *Labour governments* of 1964–70 headed by *Harold Wilson*. She was similarly an efficient Education Secretary under *Edward Heath*, during which time she increased the number of comprehensive schools in England and Wales more substantially than any other holder of the office. She was not widely considered to be of leadership quality in the early 1970s and owed her advance to a combination of good fortune and political bravery. She had absorbed economic ideas attacking the *Keynesian* consensus from *Sir Keith Joseph* and agreed to challenge Heath for the leadership after his two election defeats of 1974 only when Joseph stood aside. She proved a competent leader of the opposition but the *general election* victory of 1979 owed more to Labour mistakes and divisions than it did to Thatcher's leadership.

As *Prime Minister*, however, she proved strong, brave, decisive and, at least politically, successful. The longest serving prime minister of the twentieth century, she succeeded in changing *economic policy* in radical ways while, over time, marginalising her opponents within the party. She was the most popular Conservative leader of the twentieth century among ordinary party members and her successful prosecution of the highly controversial Falklands War of 1982 won her substantial national popularity as a victorious defender of Britain's national interests.

Her political career was undoubtedly helped by being faced by an opposition at some times almost equally divided between the *Labour* and *Liberal/Social Democratic* parties. This was an important factor in the *general elections* of 1983 and 1987. She used her good fortune in this respect, however, to reshape the agenda of British politics, making it very difficult for politicians of whatever party to support increased taxation and shifting the centre-ground of British politics several notches to the right.

Thatcher herself was never interested in the centre ground. Though politically very astute, she abominated 'consensus', considering herself a 'conviction politician'. As such she proved immensely controversial, provoking at least as much hatred among her opponents (which included left-wing Conservatives as well as Labour and Liberal politicians) as hero-worship among her supporters. After her third election victory in

1987, her political sensitivities seemed increasingly to desert her and she did not realise the damage which was being done to her position by support for the highly controversial Community Charge, or 'poll tax'. She was eventually forced to resign in November 1990 after a powerful challenge to her leadership by Michael Heseltine convinced the majority of her Cabinet colleagues that her position was irreparably damaged. She never accepted his analysis and felt that she had been stabbed in the back, never having been rejected by the British electorate. She was awarded the by now rare distinction of an hereditary peerage by her successor *John Major* in 1992 after deciding not to seek re-election to the *House of Commons*. She spent much of her time thereafter in overseas lecture tours, particularly to the United States, where her fame and popularity guaranteed her enormous fees. Meanwhile, she slipped gradually, if gracelessly, from the British political scene, apparently convinced that she had earned the right to retire at a time of her own choosing.

(See also *Thatcherism.*)

Thatcherism: the name given to the ideas and policies associated with *Margaret Thatcher*, especially as *Prime Minister* from 1979 to 1990. It is unique for a British party leader to be associated by name with a body of theory. In practice, however, Thatcherism, though electorally potent, was intellectually incoherent. It was not based on a single consistent body of economic or political theory but drew on a number of theories to reinforce personal values, assumptions and beliefs. The name is associated primarily, however, with beliefs and attitudes opposed to the previous consensus on government policies for regulating the economy and for promoting welfare policies. Dominant beliefs in Thatcherism were:

- low government expenditure
- low levels of direct taxation
- promoting self-help, individual initiative and private enterprise
- support for law and order and the police
- patriotism and opposition to directives from the European community
- attacks on what were perceived as entrenched interest groups such as trade unions and many professions

The economic ideas were not new: most derived from Victorian liberalism with its concern for *laissez-faire*. Twentieth century economists such as F A Hayek and Milton Friedman, in attacking *Keynesian* economics, greatly influenced *Conservative* thinking in the 1970s and 1980s. Elements of Thatcherism, particularly those associated with populism and strong leadership, helped the Conservatives to three successive election victories (1979, 1983 and 1987) under Thatcher, who always tempered some of the theoretical extremes of Thatcherism in the interests of electoral popularity. The policies themselves did not reduce levels of personal taxation overall, though they certainly increased the gap between rich and poor. Nor did they arrest Britain's relative economic decline. It is possible, however, that the patriotic aspects helped to raise Britain's standing in the world.

theatre of war: technical term meaning areas where war is carried on. It is often useful to distinguish between different 'theatres' during wars fought in different territories.

(See *French Revolutionary Wars; World War I; World War II.*)

Thomas, James Henry: trade unionist and Labour politician. Usually known as 'Jimmy' or 'J H', he was born in 1874, was President of the Amalgamated Society of Railway Servants in 1905–6 and played an important role in the national railway *strike* of 1911. He was parliamentary general secretary of the National Union of Railwaymen from 1919 to 1931 and President of the *Trades Union Congress* in 1920. He became a *Labour* MP in 1910, representing Derby continuously until 1936. He first became a minister in the *MacDonald* Labour government of 1924. His major offices were:

- Colonial Secretary, 1924, 1931–36
- Lord Privy Seal, 1929–30 (with a brief to handle the unemployment crisis)
- Secretary for the Dominions, 1930–1, 1931–36

His career was a colourful one. Like many trade unionists on the right wing of the Labour Party, he opted to remain in government in 1931 and, along with MacDonald and *Snowden*, he was expelled from the party and forced also to give up his trade union responsibilities. Often indiscreet when drunk (a not infrequent occurrence), he eventually let slip some budget secrets in 1936 and was forced to resign. He died in 1949.

(See also *railways*.)

Thorpe, Jeremy: lawyer and *Liberal* politician. He was born in 1929 and was educated at Eton and Oxford. He practised as a barrister before becoming a Liberal MP in 1959. He succeeded *Jo Grimond* as leader of the party in 1967 and saw the party's share of the popular vote treble from approximately two million to six million in the general election of February 1974. He was generally accounted a successful leader: articulate, clear-headed and plausible but his political career ended in tragedy after he was accused of having a homosexual relationship. He resigned the leadership in 1976 and his parliamentary seat in 1979, after which he was tried, and acquitted, of conspiring to murder his previous lover. In later life he developed Parkinson's disease.

(See also *Steel, David*.)

three-day week: restriction of industrial production to three days in a working week in 1973. It was the response by the *Conservative Prime Minister Edward Heath* to a long ban on overtime by coal miners and also to a rapid increase in the price of oil from the Middle East. Its purpose was energy conservation and it was accompanied by speed restrictions for cars and reduced hours of *television*. The measures did not solve the industrial dispute, which led to Heath's decision to call a *general election* in February 1974. When he lost power, the incoming *Labour* government of *Harold Wilson* made a deal with the miners and ended the three-day week.

'Times, The': newspaper. It was founded in 1785 as the 'Daily Universal Register', changing to its more famous title in 1788. It is the world's oldest almost continuously running newspaper, although production was halted during a bitter strike in 1984–85. The paper's reputation grew during the editorship of John Walter in the 1830s and 1840s and it became the unofficial newspaper of authority and of the upper classes. Its court and appointments pages were scoured for information about the great and good of the Victorian era. Its reputation diminished somewhat in the later nineteenth century and it was rescued in 1908 by *Viscount Rothermere*.

Tippett, Sir Michael: composer. Born in London in 1905 but of Cornish origins. He was trained at the Royal School of Music. His music was conservative in its early phase but became increasingly individualistic from the later 1930s. He is best known for his oratorio 'A Child of our Time' (1941) and his operas 'A Midsummer Marriage' (1952) and 'King Priam' (1961). His music is not particularly accessible and it has not drawn the audiences which *Britten* had achieved by the end of his life but it is both powerful and mystical. He was a *socialist* and *pacifist* by conviction and he was imprisoned as a *conscientious objector* during *World War II*. This probably explains why, despite worldwide recognition of his musical distinction, he did not receive a knighthood until 1966. He received the Order of Merit, the most distinguished club in the United Kingdom with a maximum membership of 24, in 1983. He died in 1998.

Tolpuddle Martyrs: name given to a group of six agricultural labourers and *trade unionists* from the village of Tolpuddle (Dorset) who were prosecuted in 1834 for taking oaths of loyalty to the union, a practice which had been declared illegal by legislation of 1797 passed during the *French Revolutionary Wars*. Their leader was George Loveless, a *Methodist* local preacher. On conviction, the labourers were sentenced to seven years' *transportation* to *Australia*. The *Whig* Home Secretary of the time, *Viscount Melbourne*, was a strong believer in traditional authority and did not want to see the Tolpuddle incident as the beginning of another episode of widespread agricultural unrest. This influenced the decision to prosecute, but the result was counterproductive. The harsh sentences meted out to essentially mild-mannered and generally law-abiding men were widely condemned and they provided the trade union movement with 'martyrs' whose stand against injustice would be celebrated for more than a century as an example to all of the dignity and nobility of working-class organisation.

(See also *Grand National Consolidated Trades Union*.)

Torrens Act, 1868: legislation on *housing* and sanitary reform. Taking its name from the promoter of the legislation, the Irish landowner and MP William McCullagh Torrens (1836–94), it attempted to improve housing conditions by giving local authorities power to pull down dwellings with no proper drainage or water closet. It was not extensively used but often made things worse when it was. This was because local authorities lacked the funds (and often the political will) to erect alternative accommodation and many of the poorer working classes could not afford to rent sanitary accommodation anyway.

(See also *Artisans' Dwellings Act, 1875; local government*.)

Tory Party: political party, the predecessor of the *Conservative* Party. The name 'Tory' was taken from the Gaelic 'Toraidgh', meaning bandit and was used originally as a term of abuse to describe those who supported Charles II's attempt to keep his brother as successor to the throne during the so-called 'Exclusion Crisis' of 1678–81. The Tories were mostly out of office after the Hanoverian succession in 1714, but their fortunes revived in reaction to the *French Revolution* when the *Prime Minister, William Pitt the Younger* and the *Duke of Portland* made an alliance to defend the country against both the ideological and the military threat from France. The so-called 'Pitt–Portland' coalition of 1794 is seen by many as marking the origin of the modern Conservative Party. The main beliefs of the Tory Party in the late eighteenth and early nineteenth centuries were:

- support for established authority, which included emphasising the role of the monarch as its symbol
- support for the *Church of England* as an important pillar of authority and, because of its status as the 'established church' a further symbol of national unity
- hostility to religious toleration. Although Pitt attempted to persuade *George III* to grant *Roman Catholic emancipation* at the time of the *Act of Union* between Britain and Ireland, this was largely for political reasons. He wanted to see Catholic Ireland loyal in the wars against revolutionary France and would have liked to see Irish Catholic officers fighting in the British army. Religious toleration was never popular in the party as a whole, however, and became a source of considerable dispute during the 1820s
- opposition to most forms of reform, especially parliamentary reform. The Tories believed that concessions on this issue would weaken the State and leave it vulnerable to being taken over by the lower orders, or even to revolution

Pitt never accepted that he was a Tory and the term came into common use only during the long government of *Lord Liverpool* which attempted to continue the policies of Pitt. It was sustained in office from 1812 to 1827, partly with support from *George IV* but mostly because of continued fears within the propertied classes about the dangers of reform. After Liverpool's resignation and death, the party rapidly split into factions. One group joined the *Whigs* while another, the 'Ultra Tories', seemed to ready to die in the last ditch against proposals for *parliamentary reform*. *Wellington*'s government was forced into resignation in 1830 and the Tories suffered one of their biggest election defeats in 1832. It was in rebuilding the party, under *Peel*, that the Tories, now committed to 'moderate reform' and to 'the correction of proved abuses' increasingly took up the title 'Conservative'.

(See also *French Revolutionary Wars; Napoleonic Wars; Perceval, Spencer; Whigs.*)

tourist industry: the urge to travel in search of *leisure* and information about places unfamiliar is closely linked to both income and to means of transportation. It is not surprising, therefore, that, although aristocrats and others with means made long trips in the seventeenth and eighteenth centuries, a full-blown tourist industry should have developed from the mid-nineteenth century and in the age of the *railway*. The work of *Thomas Cook* in offering cheap, organised tours both within Britain and, from the late 1850s to Europe, is of central importance. The tourist industry expanded more quickly with the development in the twentieth century, first, of motor cars and then of aeroplanes. After 1945, when most of Britain's established industries were in relative decline, or facing stringent foreign competition, tourism became an increasingly valuable source of income. By the 1980s, with increasingly cheap air fares and a hotel and accommodation market which had both expanded and adapted, tourism had become one of Britain's largest industries. Tourists were attracted by the diversity of the country, by its rich cultural and historical legacy and also by the fact that the value of the pound sterling was usually declining against currencies such as the US dollar, German mark and Japanese yen, so that these tourists got increasingly good value for money.

Tourism has generated anguished debate. Two main arguments for controlling tourism have been advanced:

- environmentalists have argued that beauty and natural habitats alike are threatened by large influxes of visitors not all of whom have the cultural sensitivity to understand and respect what they are seeing. Sometimes the nature of the tourist attraction is fundamentally changed
- others have pointed out how narrow is the geographical range of many foreign tourists. 'Package tours' of Britain rarely stray far beyond London, Stratford-on-Avon, Edinburgh, York and the Lake District, many of which places became immensely over-crowded in the 1980s and 1990s, particularly in summer months

On the other side of the argument, enthusiasts for tourism have noted that tourism:

- generates much new employment, and
- has become a major stimulant to the economy

Tractarianism: see *Oxford Movement*

Trade Boards Acts, 1909 and 1913: legislation passed by *Asquith's Liberal* government to regulate conditions in industries which had previously had little or no legal interference. The Act of 1909 created 'trade boards' on which sat representatives of employers and workers for:

- tailoring
- chain making
- paper box making
- lace finishing

The boards set minimum wages for employment in these trades. The 1913 Act refined and extended the system. Some spectacular wage gains were recorded. In chain making, for example, basic wage rates increased by about 50 per cent between 1911 and 1914.

(See also *Booth, Charles; Churchill, Winston; sweated labour.*)

Trade Disputes and Trade Unions Act, 1927: legislation during *Baldwin's Conservative* government which followed the *trade unions'* defeat in the *General Strike.* By it:

- sympathetic strikes in support of workers in other trades and unions were declared illegal
- restrictions were placed on the political activities of trade unions
- workers had to make a positive decision to 'contract in' to a union's political fund. Previously, members were deemed to have agreed to a portion of their membership subscriptions being placed in a political fund unless they specifically stated their objection ('contracting out')

This Act was repealed in its entirety by *Attlee's Labour* government by the Trades Unions Act of 1946.

trade, overseas: the trade of goods and services between countries has always been one of the main sources of income and economic development. Overseas trade was vital to Britain's emergence as a world power in the eighteenth century, as previous dependence on markets in Northern Europe expanded rapidly to include southern Europe, the Americas, India and other parts of Asia.

The main pattern of overseas trade in the late eighteenth and early nineteenth centuries was for Britain to import raw materials and foodstuffs and to export manufactured goods. The value of British exports increased from £13.5 million to £184 million between the mid-1780s and the late-1860s. During the same period, manufactured goods made up between 82 per cent and 91 per cent of Britain's total exports by value, while textile raw materials (mostly cottons) and food made up between 63 per cent and 71 per cent of total imports. Statistics like these explain why Britain was called 'the workshop of the world' in the heyday of its *Industrial Revolution.*

Since the 1870s, the balance of trade shifted. Britain had always imported by value more than it exported but more than made up the difference by *shipping,* banking, insurance and carrying the goods of other nations. The growth of other industrial economies in the last quarter of the nineteenth century, however, presented a much more severe challenge. By 1912, for example, Britain had a trade deficit of £82 million with one of its major competitors, the *United States.* While the US share of world manufactured exports increased from 2.8 per cent to 12.6 per cent in the years 1880–1913, the United Kingdom share fell from 41.4 per cent to 29.9 per cent. Many were beginning to argue that *free trade* was no longer a sensible policy since, in the words of one cartoon from the *Tariff Reform League:* 'Free imports have made Britain the dumping ground of all nations'.

After *World War I,* Britain's overseas trading position was further weakened by the collapse of many of its *staple industries.* Throughout the inter-war period, imports ran strongly ahead of exports and overseas trade was particularly slack in the 1930s. The world economic recovery of the 1950s and 1960s saw Britain participating effectively, particularly in the export of electronic goods and the products of the *motor car industry.* The *balance of payments* often showed a surplus in Britain's favour in these years. Worrying deficits began to accumulate from the late 1960s, however, partly because of the international rise in oil prices in the early 1970s and partly because of the success of the so-called 'tiger economies' of Hong Kong, Singapore, South Korea and Taiwan in capturing larger proportions of world markets. The collapse of the British car industry put further strain on its overseas trading position. As an indicator, among other things, of its weakening overseas trade position, the value of the pound against the dollar went down from $2.80 in 1965 to $1.75 in 1977.

The immense success in overseas trade generally enjoyed by Britain from the 1780s to the 1860s and the usually less successful years which have followed are, overall, a useful indicator of Britain's changing position as a world power.

(See also *Chamberlain, Joseph; economic policy; imperial preference; Thatcherism.*)

Trade Union Act, 1913: legislation passed during *Asquith's Liberal* government which reversed the *Osborne Judgement.* By it, unions were permitted to collect funds for political purposes.

(See also *trade unions.*)

trade unions: organisations of working people which aim to ensure better wages and conditions by collective action.

1800–50

At the beginning of the nineteenth century, all trade unions were illegal under the terms of the *Combination Acts* of 1799–1800, although many continued to exist, either by converting to *friendly societies* or by operating out of the eye of the authorities. The repeal of the Acts in 1824–25 made unions legal but under very severe constraint. A considerable amount of union activity took place over the next ten years, particularly the development of a 'general' union of workers, inspired by the ideas of *Robert Owen*. The collapse of the 'Grand National Consolidated Trades Union' in 1834 proved a substantial blow. Most of the unions which survived were regionally based and formed of skilled workers, such as joiners, carpenters, miners and engineers with genuine scarcity value and the ability to bargain with employers.

1850–1914

The development of nationally organised skilled workers' unions was facilitated by the founding of a successful 'new model' union, the Amalgamated Society of Engineers in 1851. Union membership remained very low and dominated by skilled working men until the last years of the nineteenth century. In the mid-1880s, unions had approximately half-a-million members and this number roughly doubled with the foundation of unskilled workers unions in the years 1888–91, following successful strikes by the *gas* and *dock* workers. By 1914, membership had swollen to over 4 million and, with the foundation of the *Labour Party* which union subscriptions were doing much to fund, unions were beginning to develop a political role which increased after *World War 1*. Unions, particularly in the mining and transport sectors, also organised several bitter strikes, influenced in part by *syndicalism*. In 1912, for example, almost 41 million working days were lost to strike action. Union membership, which peaked at 6.5 million in 1920, declined thereafter as first unemployment and then the failure of the *General Strike* reduced their power. Membership declined to 3.3 million in 1934 before recovering to almost 5 million by the outbreak of *World War II*.

1945–79

The post-war years, which saw a long economic boom and also *economic policy* dominated by *Keynesianism* and the determination to keep unemployment low, proved fertile ones for the movement. Membership exceeded eight million in 1952, ten million in 1971, and peaked at twelve million in 1980. Union representation in the Labour Party remained strong and the political influence of the unions in the 1960s and 1970s became increasingly controversial. They defeated proposals to curb their powers in 1969 (see *'In Place of Strife'*) and *Edward Heath* called, and lost, a general election in February 1974 asking the voters to decide whether it was the elected government or the unions which decided *economic policy*. The incoming Labour government, led by *Harold Wilson*, further protected the unions by introducing an Employment Protection Act in 1975 which gave workers protection against dismissal without good cause being shown by the employer and extended the scope of redundancy payments. Hostility to the union movement grew with the widespread feeling that its political influence in a Labour government was excessive. Heavily publicised strikes in 1978–9, after unions had refused to accept the Labour government's 'pay norm', contributed to the *Conservative* Party's general election victory in 1979.

Trades Disputes Act, 1906: legislation passed by the *Liberal* government of *Asquith* which protected *trade unions* from claims for loss and damage caused to employers during strikes.

(See also *Taff Vale Case.*)

Trades Union Congress: annual meeting to which representatives of all trade unions are invited. Known as 'the TUC.', it first met in Manchester in 1868 and, during the twentieth century, it co-ordinated the unions' growing political influence. During *World War I,* for example, it organised a 'strike truce' in support of the war effort and during the 1920s it gave support to unions fighting against wage cuts and longer hours, notably during the *General Strike* of 1926. During the 1930s, TUC influence over the *Labour Party* increased markedly as many union leaders calculated that the high proportion of Labour funds which the unions provided should win appropriate political recognition. The TUC influenced Labour's commitment to *nationalisation* during the *Attlee* government of 1945–51 but the peak of its power was probably during the *Wilson* and *Callaghan* Labour governments of 1974–79 when union support for pay policies was considered essential for the success of national *economic policy.*

(See also *Citrine, Walter; Murray, Len; trade unions; Woodcock, George.*)

Union members, '000s

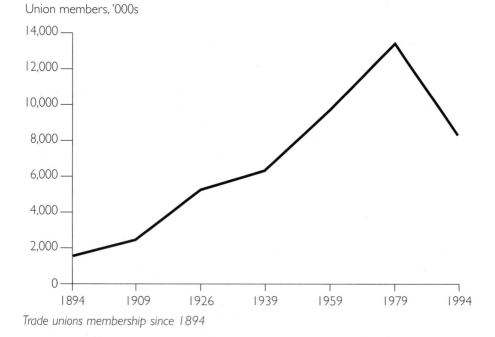

Trade unions membership since 1894

Trafalgar, Battle of: decisive naval battle during the *Napoleonic Wars* fought on 21 October 1805 twelve miles south-west of Cape Trafalgar between the coasts of southern Spain and Morocco. The British fleet under the command of *Admiral Nelson* defeated a combined French and Spanish fleet under the command of Admiral Villeneuve. The tactics used by Nelson were contrary to normal naval rules of engagement, since he attacked the enemy at right-angles rather than in parallel lines. Eighteen of the 33 French and Spanish ships were either destroyed or surrendered to the British and, because of storms in the days after the battle, only four eventually returned safely to port. About 500 British sailors (including Nelson himself) were killed and more than 2,000 French and Spanish. The victory was of immense strategic importance. It confirmed that Britain could not be successfully invaded by an enemy fleet, since Britain's command of the seas was now absolute. Britain did not fight another naval engagement against a European power until the *Battle of Jutland* in 1916.

transportation: form of punishment whereby convicted criminals were removed to either Australia or the Americas. It was in use in Britain from the 1650s to 1868 when it was abolished. It offered an alternative to execution for offences considered serious, but it was also used as an alternative to prison when prisons were not state-run and capacity was low. About 210,000 convicts were transported overall; 146,000 of these (73 per cent) went to *Australia* between 1788 and 1850, the first convict colony being at Port Jackson, Sydney. By the 1840s, New South Wales ceased to accept convicts as did Van Diemen's Land (Tasmania) in 1853. Transportation did offer real prospects of improvement for fortunate and diligent convicts but the conditions under which prisoners were moved and the regime they faced on arrival contributed to many early deaths also.

(See also *emigration*.)

Trenchard (Hugh), 1st Viscount: soldier, airman and policeman. Born in 1873, he became a soldier in 1893 before being seconded to the infant Royal Flying Corps in 1912. He took command of the RFC in France during *World War I*, rising to the rank of Major-General. His pressure was an important factor in the creation of a separate Royal Air Force in 1918, whose Chief of Air Staff he was from 1919 to 1929. He became Commissioner of the Metropolitan *Police* in 1931 and served until 1935. He became a Viscount in 1936 and died in 1956. His belief that a crushing bombing campaign would be crucial to the outcome of *World War II* was proved, in the event, to be, at best, a considerable oversimplification.

(See also *Churchill, Winston; Harris, Arthur.*)

Trent incident: see *United States*

Trevelyan, George Macaulay: historian. Born in 1876, the nephew of *T B Macaulay* and the son of George Otto, also a historian, he was Regius Professor of History at Cambridge University from 1927 and Master of Trinity College, Cambridge, from 1940 to 1951. He wrote widely, including a detailed study of the Italian nationalist leader Garibaldi and a three-volume study of England in the reign of Queen Anne, but he is best known for his 'English Social History' published in 1944, a very successful synthesis, even if few social historians would nowadays accept his own definition of social history: 'the history of a people with the politics left out'. He died in 1962.

Trevithick, Richard: engineer. Born in Cornwall in 1771, he produced a number of high-pressure condensing engines which were used both in mines and for early railways. He is credited with building the first steam passenger engine in 1801 and the first *railway* locomotive in 1804. He also invented a screw propeller. He was as weak a businessman as he was a fertile inventor and lost money both in England and Peru, to where he travelled in 1816. He returned from central America in 1827 and died in 1833.

(See also *Stephenson, George; Stephenson, Robert.*)

Trianon, Treaty of (June 1920): peace treaty signed by the victorious Allies at the end of *World War I* with Austria. It settled the boundaries of the newly independent state of Hungary, cutting its borders so that Hungary was shrunk to a central core of Magyar-speaking people. Hungary became approximately 30 per cent of its former size and its population was reduced from 21 million to about 8 million. About one-third of Magyars now lived outside Hungary. Of former Hungarian territory:

- Ruthenia and Slovakia went to the new state of Czechoslovakia
- Croatia went to Yugoslavia
- Transylvania went to Romania

(See also *Versailles, Treaty of.*)

'Triple Alliance': name given to the alliance of Britain's three most powerful unions, those of the miners, dockers and railwaymen. It was forged in 1911 and helped to co-ordinate a series of damaging *strikes* in the years 1911–14. The miners wished to use it again in their bitter struggle with the coal owners in 1921 but the other two unions refused to co-operate.

(See also *General Strike; Thomas J H; trade unions.*)

Trollope, Anthony: novelist and civil servant. Born in 1815, he is best known for two sets of novels. The eight so-called 'Barchester Novels' of 1855–67 are modelled on the life of Salisbury Cathedral and reveal, usually in an urbane and kindly fashion, the political and religious divisions within the *Church of England*. They contain, in Obadiah Slope from 'Barchester Towers', one of the greatest characterisations of grasping ambition and sanctimonious humbug in all of English literature. The five political novels begin with 'Phineas Finn' (1869) and depict the high political world of a *Whig Party* dominated by the fictional 'Duke of Omnium' (everything) in its last years. 'The Way We Live Now' (1875) is a sharp reminder that 'sleaze' and financial corruption in high places were as well known to the mid-Victorians as to those who lived through the 1990s. Trollope's reputation as a novelist has fallen in comparison to those of *Dickens* and *George Eliot* but he produced lucid and subtle narratives laced with much gentle satire and insight into character. He worked as an official in the *Post Office* and invented the pillar box. He died in 1882.

tuberculosis: serious infectious disease which attacks the respiratory and gastro-intestinal tract. Often called just 'TB', it spread very rapidly in Victorian Britain where rapid overcrowding and poor sanitation, especially in working-class areas, proved dangerously conducive. It was probably the biggest killer of adults in the Victorian period, with an average of more than 50,000 deaths a year. It was frequently treatable, but only with the rest (in sanatoria), fresh air and good food which were denied to most of its victims. Death rates declined with the improved living standards early in the twentieth century but it did not go into full retreat in Britain until the introduction of the BCG vaccine and the use of antibiotics after *World War II*.

Turner, J(oseph) M(allord) W(illiam): England's most innovative, and probably greatest, artist. Born the son of a barber in London in 1775, he trained at the Royal Academy and began to travel widely, painting a number of water-colours of English scenes before visiting Italy and moving to oils. He was amazingly prolific and his greatest works reveal new techniques for showing shade, colour and movement. He painted landscapes, such as 'Frosty Morning' (1813), classical subjects, as with 'Ulysses deriding Polyphemus' (1829), evocatively romantic ones such as 'The Fighting Temeraire' (1839) and modern inventions, notably 'Rain, Steam and Speed' (1844), a picture of a Great Western train crossing a bridge which anticipates impressionism. He was a solitary, and probably embittered, man who was not anxious to share his artistic insights. He died in 1851.

typhus: an acute infectious disease seen in several forms and borne either by the louse or the flea. It spread most rapidly in the insanitary and overcrowded conditions which prevailed in most of Britain's industrial towns in the early nineteenth century. It was common in both Britain and Ireland during the nineteenth century, with par- ticularly severe outbreaks in 1816–19 and 1836–42. About 100,000 people were killed by it in England in the late 1830s and early 1840s and the high mortality strength- ened *Edwin Chadwick*'s case for increased attention to sanitation and *public health*. Its seriousness declined in the second half of the nineteenth century, but a variant of the disease wreaked havoc on the Western Front during *World War I* as 'trench fever'.

(See also *cholera*; *Simon, Sir John*.)

U

Ulster: the most northerly of the four historic provinces of *Ireland*, the others being Connacht, Leinster and Munster. During the nineteenth century, its easterly part, around Belfast, became the only significant area of industrial development in the country with a prosperous *shipbuilding* industry and the largest centre of the linen industry in the *United Kingdom*. Principally because of the large number of Scottish and English settler families who arrived in the seventeenth century, this was the only part of Ireland to have a Protestant majority. The growth of nationalism was more strongly resisted here than anywhere else in Ireland and by the time of the *Home Rule* bills of the 1880s and 1890s, it was becoming clear that this part of Ireland would resist independence based on a *Roman Catholic* majority government. After strong *Ulster Unionist* resistance in the years before *World War I*, British politicians began to consider partition as the most practical solution to the increasingly pressing Irish problem. Thus, the *Anglo-Irish Treaty* of 1921 created a separate *Northern Ireland*, somewhat smaller in extent than historic Ulster with boundaries drawn to maintain a clear Protestant majority.

(See also *Carson, Edward; Northern Ireland; Redmond, John.*)

Ulster Defence Association: paramilitary pro-*Unionist* organisation formed in 1971 and committed to keeping *Northern Ireland* part of the *United Kingdom*. It engaged in a number of terrorist activities directed against *Roman Catholics* between the 1970s and the 1990s. It was instrumental in making the Protestant–Catholic power-sharing experiment of 1974 unworkable.

(See also *Ulster; Northern Ireland.*)

Ulster Defence Regiment (UDR): armed force established in *Northern Ireland* in 1970 to replace the *B-specials*. Both the *Northern Ireland* and *United Kingdom* governments wished it to be a non-denominational organisation but *Roman Catholics*, long suspicious of Protestant rule, were reluctant to join it. Numbering about 10,000 at its peak, it played an important part in the security of the Province in the 1970s and 1980s before being merged with the Royal Irish Regiment in 1992.

(See also *Ulster Special Constabulary.*)

Ulster Special Constabulary: auxiliary armed police force in *Northern Ireland* between 1920 and 1970. It originally comprised three elements:

- full-time officers: the so-called A-specials
- part-timers: the so-called *B-specials*
- volunteer reservists: the so-called C-specials

Both the A and C groups were disbanded in the 1920s, leaving the B-specials to help police the Province. Criticism that the B-specials favoured Protestants and discriminated against Catholics became widespread in the 1960s and was one of the reasons for increasing discontent within the Catholic community at the end of the 1960s.

Ulster Unionist Party: main Protestant-dominated political party of *Northern Ireland*. Originally formed in 1904 as the Ulster Unionist Council, it dominated the politics of *Stormont* in the years 1921–72. The party was led from 1921 to 1940 by Sir

James Craig, who had been instrumental in organising resistance to Irish independence from the North in the years before 1914. The party provided the bulk of the Northern Ireland representation in the *United Kingdom* Parliament. Its main religious support was found in the *Presbyterian Church*. For most of the *general elections* held between the 1920s and the 1960s, the Ulster Unionists – in active co-operation with the British *Conservative Party* – held nine or ten of the twelve Northern Ireland seats. The violence and disturbances of the late 1960s and early 1970s caused splits within the Unionist Party, broadly between those who wished to reach effective agreements with the *Catholic* minority in Northern Ireland and those who wanted to maintain a hard line. This was the basis of the split by *Ian Paisley*, who formed the *Democratic Unionist Party* in 1971. From the 1970s, the party still represented majority Protestant opinion in Northern Ireland, although its previously rock-solid position became much less secure not only because of splits but also because of the *United Kingdom*'s evident frustration with the existing political position.

(See also *O'Neill, Terence; Faulkner, Brian.*)

Ulster Volunteer Force (UVF): Protestant paramilitary force raised in 1913 to defend the *Union* against renewed proposals for *Home Rule*. It recruited very rapidly within *Ulster*, having an estimated 100,000 members on the outbreak of *World War I*. It organised a high-profile shipment of arms – the so-called 'Larne gun-running' of 1914. It ceased formal activity when war was declared but many of its members joined the *B-specials* in 1920. The title was readopted by Protestant loyalists in 1966 who carried out a number of sectarian killings. The organisation was formally banned by *Terence O'Neill* but continued to operate into the 1990s.

(See also *Carson, Edward; Ulster Defence Association.*)

unemployment: the situation of those who, wanting work, are unable to find it. Unemployment in the nineteenth and twentieth centuries has been both a personal tragedy and a cause of social discontent and disturbances. It is frustrating, therefore, that it is almost impossible to measure unemployment precisely. No official statistics covering the whole population exist before 1921 and they have been subject to endless refinement and political manipulation ever since. In the years 1979–96, for example, when unemployment was a key political issue, the governments of *Margaret Thatcher* and *John Major* changed the basis on which the statistics were calculated on 31 separate occasions. The usual consequence was to make the unemployment totals seem lower; statisticians and economic historians meanwhile find it almost impossible to make valid comparisons between like and like. Apart from political interference, other factors making unemployment difficult to quantify are:

- the frequent assumption that only full-time work counts as employment. Unemployment figures frequently understate the absence from the workforce of casual and part-time workers, and particularly women
- concentration on figures trade by trade rather than for the population as a whole. This also leads to under-estimation of unemployment levels in unskilled or casual occupations. It might also lead to an over-estimation when unemployment in a high-profile trade was particularly high. In the period 1841–42, for example, the *cotton* industry in Lancashire was in

severe depression when other trades, particularly building, were more buoyant

- regional variations. It is very rare for unemployment to be evenly spread across the *United Kingdom*. In the 1820s, for example, unemployment and under-employment amongst agricultural labourers in south-east England were particularly severe when much of industrial Britain had little unemployment. Similarly, in the 1930s, unemployment levels were much higher in the old industrial areas, such as north-east England or South Wales than they were in areas where new *electronic* industries were situated, such as the West Midlands or the South-East

- short-term variations. People out of work for short periods are rarely officially categorised as 'unemployed'

- the changing nature and structure of employment. The Victorian 'ideal' was the male 'breadwinner' whose full-time income catered for all of his family. Unemployment statistics followed this over-simple model. The structure of employment has constantly changed. Particularly in the later twentieth century, more people were being employed on short-term contracts. Unemployment statistics usually lag behind important shifts in occupational structure

Some broad conclusions about patterns of unemployment are, however, possible. Periods when unemployment was clearly an important national issue were:

1815–20	after the *Napoleonic Wars* when demobilised soldiers found it very difficult to get work
late 1830s and early 1840s	particularly because of depression in industrial occupations
1870s–90s	as part of the so-called *Great Depression* and particularly severe amongst agricultural labourers
1921–40	according to official figures unemployment never fell below 1.3 million and stood at 2.8 million and 2.9 million in 1931 and 1932 under the impact of the Wall Street Crash
1975–85	official figures show an increase from 1.1 million to 1.6 million 1975–78 and then much sharper rises associated with *Thatcherism* in the early 1980s, reaching a peak of 3.2 million in 1985. The true figures are almost certainly higher

The general trend since 1945 has been for historically low unemployment till the 1970s then sharp increases which, however, need to be seen against a radically changing overall structure of employment (see above).

(See Figure on page 319. See also *economic policies; unemployment legislation; Women, legal and occupational status of.*)

unemployment legislation (inter-war): the long-term Depression of the inter-war period produced the first systematic attempt by government to tackle unemployment. Its main planks were:

- **changes in *National Insurance* benefit:** this was increased from 7s (35p) a week to 15s (75p) in 1920 and to 18s (90p) in 1924. It was reduced in cost-cutting exercises in 1928 and 1931

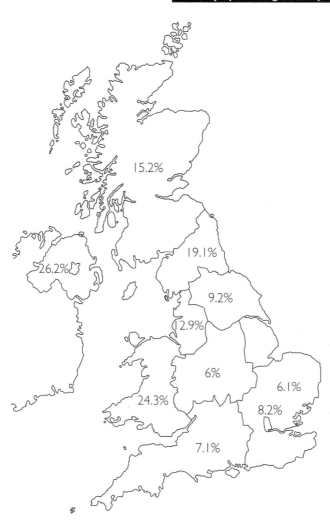

15.2%

26.2%

19.1%

9.2%

2.9%

6%

6.1%

24.3%

8.2%

7.1%

The distribution of unemployment in 1937

- **Unemployment Insurance Act, 1927:** this provided a new scheme, allowing for benefits without limit of time when appropriate insurance contributions had been made
- **Unemployment Insurance Act, 1930:** passed in the depths of the Depression, this removed the previous restriction that the unemployed should be 'genuinely seeking work'. Receipt of benefit was subject to a *means test*. In 1931, responsibility for the long-term unemployed was transferred from the insurance scheme directly to the treasury
- **Unemployment Act, 1934:** created an Unemployment Assistance Board to deal with the long-term unemployed who had exhausted insurance benefit. The Act made a clear distinction between:
  - 'unemployment benefit' which was 'earned' through insurance contribution, and

> – 'unemployment assistance' which the new board handled through means tests

(See also *unemployment; welfare state*.)

Unilateral Declaration of Independence (UDI): literally, this means a decision taken by a state of its own accord to declare itself independent. In British history, however, it relates only to the decision taken by the white minority government of Ian Smith in Southern *Rhodesia* in 1965 to assert independence in the hope of permanently staving off the black majority rule which was becoming the norm in Africa in the late 1950s and early 1960s. This decision angered the *Labour* government of *Harold Wilson* which instructed the *BBC* to refer to Southern Rhodesia as 'the illegal Smith regime', a silly and ineffectual piece of name calling which had no practical significance whatever. Smith's government survived until 1979.

(See also *Empire, British; imperialism*.)

unilateralism: belief, widely held within the *Campaign for Nuclear Disarmament* in the 1960s, that 'one side', in this case the *United Kingdom*, should declare its opposition to nuclear weapons and refuse to produce any more, irrespective of the policy pursued by other powers. Opposition to these weapons was particularly strong during the so-called 'Cold War' between the Soviet Union and the *United States* and especially so after the Cuban Missiles Crisis of October 1962 brought the world to the brink of nuclear war. CND beliefs were strong within the *Labour Party* between the late 1950s and the late 1980s, when unilateralism was one of the most important questions which divided the party. Most Labour Party leaders considered it a certain vote-loser at *general elections* and the *Conservative* Party was not slow to take advantage of the division. Unilateralism also caught hold amongst Labour-controlled local authorities. From the 1960s to the 1980s, it was not unusual for travellers to be redundantly informed that they were entering a 'nuclear-free zone' although, of course, the authorities had absolutely no power to make good their assertion and were indulging in what their opponents scornfully described as 'gesture politics'.

Union, Act of (1800): the legislative Union between Great Britain and *Ireland*. The resultant state was entitled the *United Kingdom* of Great Britain and Ireland and remained in being until the independence of Ireland, except for the six counties of the north, was agreed in 1921. Until 1782, legislation passed by the Irish parliament had to be ratified in Britain. From 1782 to 1800, Ireland enjoyed a wide degree of legislative independence but this period was characterised by increasing unrest, which ended with a full scale rebellion, with some French assistance, in 1798. Though easily put down, the rebellion caused many of the Protestant minority who controlled the Irish parliament to conclude that legislative independence was too risky. *Pitt's* government had come to the same view. Even a semi-independent Ireland was too great a risk when Britain was at war with France, which clearly saw Ireland as a back door to Britain. Thus, a combination of self-interest, persuasion and bribery induced members of the Irish parliament to vote to give up its separate existence. In consequence of the Act, 100 Irish MPs sat in the UK *House of Commons* – all of them Protestant – increasing its number to 658. Campaigns in Ireland, first to secure equal civil rights for Catholics and then to repeal the Union began almost immediately.

(See also *Catholic Emancipation Act; Castlereagh, Viscount; O'Connell, Daniel.*)

United Kingdom: name given to the nations of England, Scotland, Wales and, from 1801 to 1922, Ireland. The formal title was adopted as part of the Act of *Union* and confusion is frequently made between the UK (which includes Ireland or, from 1922, Northern Ireland) and Great Britain which includes England, Scotland and Wales only. Wales was formally linked to England in 1536, while Scotland voluntarily agreed to an Act of Union with England in 1707.

United Nations Organisation (UNO): international organisation established to secure peace between nations. It was formed in San Francisco in 1945, when Britain, as one of the world's leading powers at the time, became one of five permanent members of the organisation's Security Council with the right of *veto* over UN decisions. The other Security Council members were the *United States*, the USSR, China and France. Britain has retained its place, although declining influence on world affairs from the 1950s made that position look increasingly anomalous. Britain has played an active part in UN work, not least as a member of peace-keeping forces in *Cyprus* in the 1960s and Bosnia in the 1990s.

(See also *Suez Crisis*.)

United States of America, British relations with: the American colonies won their independence from Britain at the Treaty of Versailles in 1783 and formed themselves into a 'United States of America', with a written constitution guaranteeing rights to citizens, in 1787.

1783–1850

Relations between the two countries in these years were frequently strained, not least because the colonists had made alliances with France – Britain's leading colonial rival – and Spain during the War of Independence. However, *overseas trade* and industrial considerations forged close commercial links. From the 1790s, the southern states of the USA were the major suppliers of raw cotton to the new mills and factories of Lancashire and Lanarkshire, while the USA became a rapidly growing market for British manufactured goods. The *French Revolutionary* and *Napoleonic Wars* interrupted this trade and thus contributed to bringing about the *Anglo-American War* of 1812–15.

Relations improved after the end of the wars. The so-called Monroe Doctrine of 1823, which condemned European territorial interference in the American continent, accorded well with *Canning*'s foreign policy which emphasised commercial, rather than colonial, involvement by Britain in southern America. In 1842, also, by the *Webster–Ashburton Treaty* boundaries between British territory in *Canada* and the United States were agreed. In 1846, also, agreement was also reached with President Polk to settle the US's northern border with Canada on the 49th parallel of latitude. This gave Britain a sea coast on the Pacific Ocean and also Vancouver Island. These agreements resolving outstanding border disputes between the powers, and the growing British commitment to *free trade*, helped relations to become much closer.

1850–1914

Relations between the powers were reasonably quiet during this period, although the American Civil War of 1861–65 strained relations for a time. Within Britain, there was a conflict between moral and commercial considerations. Dominant British public opinion was opposed to slavery, although cheap and plentiful supplies of raw cotton came from the slave states of the south, which were fighting to maintain their legal status. The so-called 'cotton famine' in Lancashire resulted from interruptions to supply during the Civil War and it caused considerable *unemployment* and hardship within the textile districts.

Diplomatic relations were also damaged by the so-called 'Trent' incident of 1861. The British packet boat Trent was stopped by a Federal (Northern) warship and two Confederate (Southern) envoys were taken off it. The British *Prime Minister Palmerston* refused to supply the North with more weapons and war seemed likely until the Federal government backed down and released the envoys.

A further incident occurred during *Gladstone's* first government when the US government claimed compensation for damage done to its shipping during the Civil War by the 990-ton vessel 'Alambama', which had been built in Birkenhead by the Laird *shipbuilding* company for the Confederate forces in 1862. It did much damage, capturing and destroying numerous Federal ships and sinking a gunboat before being sunk itself in 1864. Gladstone settled the claim by agreeing in the Treaty of Washington, 1871, to paying the United States $15.5 million in compensation, a sum which many in Britain considered excessive.

Britain did not attempt to interfere when the United States began substantially to increase its own *navy* in the late 1890s, believing (quite correctly) that the main threats to Britain's security came from Europe.

1914–45

Relations in these years were dominated by United States' policy towards the European powers in *World War I* and *World War II* and by the implications in the inter-war period of the so-called US policy of 'isolationism'. This might more accurately be called isolation from powers outside the American continent since other American countries hardly felt that the US was maintaining a respectful distance from them.

The United States, which had many German as well as British immigrants, at first wished to maintain neutrality in World War I, but the Royal Navy disrupted US trade with Germany. When the Germans sank the liner 'Lusitania' in 1915, killing more than 100 US citizens, opinion moved against Germany. After President Wilson tried, and failed, to intervene to end the war in Europe, relations deteriorated and the US entered the war on the Allied side in April 1918.

US isolationism between the wars was not total. It hosted the *Washington Naval Agreement* in 1921, for example. Economically, furthermore, the US was now so powerful that any change in its position would have worldwide implications, as the Wall Street Crash demonstrated. However, the United States was absorbed with its own internal recovery plan – President Roosevelt's 'New Deal' – during the 1930s and it reaffirmed its neutrality to aggressive action by the European dictators, Hitler and Mussolini.

The US did not join Britain and its Allies at the outbreak of World War II. It did, however, supply arms to them on favourable terms in its so-called 'cash and carry' scheme. It entered the war at the end of 1941 when its Pacific interests were directly threatened by the Japanese attack on Pearl Harbor. US involvement in the last two-and-a-half years of the war, however, was decisive. Despite many rivalries and jealousies among the commanders, the alliance between Britain and the United States was very strong and it was US nuclear weapons which finally broke Japanese resistance in 1945.

Since 1945

The relationship between Britain and the United States became an increasingly unequal one after the end of World War II. The United States was now one of the two 'superpowers' engaged in a massive economic and ideological struggle with the other, the USSR. Britain was not a superpower and was engaged in a retreat from *Empire*. Nevertheless, the main focus of superpower rivalry was Europe and the United States valued Britain's contribution, not only to the defence of Western Europe but also its extensive Commonwealth connections, not least its worldwide network of military bases. The United States and Britain co-operated extensively in the *North Atlantic Treaty Organisation*.

It suited Britain to talk after 1945 about a 'special relationship' with the United States which transcended mere alliance and many in both the *Conservative* and *Labour* parties drew on the common language and strong cultural links between the powers to argue that Britain did not need to be a member of the European Economic Community and should look more naturally to the West for help and support.

It is true that at many points since 1945, the US–British alliance seemed specially strong. *Harold Macmillan* and President J F Kennedy forged a strong bond in the early 1960s. So, for ideological reasons, did the two right-wingers *Margaret Thatcher* and President Reagan. The United States supported Britain over the Falklands War in 1982 and the two worked closely in the Gulf War of 1990–1. Official intelligence was also closely co-ordinated with the two powers. However, the growing disparity in power, wealth and status meant that the two countries could not be remotely equal partners. President Eisenhower refused to support Britain and France during the *Suez crisis* and Dean Acheson's famous statement of 1962 that Britain had 'lost an Empire but has not yet found a role' indicated also that not all Americans felt the need even to pretend that the two nations were equal partners.

By the end of the twentieth century, few in the United States, and fewer than before in Britain, saw the Anglo-American relationship as particularly 'special'.

(See also *Churchill, Winston; cotton industry; imperialism; Thatcher, Margaret; Yalta Conference.*)

universities: institutions of higher education established for the purposes of teaching and research. At the beginning of the nineteenth century, England had only two Universities (Oxford and Cambridge), Scotland four (Aberdeen, Edinburgh, Glasgow and St Andrews), and Ireland one (Dublin). The first half of the nineteenth century saw a small number of new creations (University College London, 1828; the separate University of London, 1836; Durham, 1832 and Belfast, 1849). University College became the first higher-education institution in England to admit *nonconformists*. Between 1862 and 1909 universities were created in virtually all of Britain's main industrial and commercial cities, though some developed at first as university colleges preparing their students for external degrees of the University of London.

Between 1872 and 1923, the five constituent colleges of the University of Wales were created. Many of these universities were funded by bequests and legacies from leading industrialists, commercial figures and philanthropists and supported also by local authorities anxious to claim the prestige of universities in their cities.

The curricula of nineteenth-century universities were heavily slanted towards 'pure', rather than 'vocational' study and those of Oxford and Cambridge, in particular, emphasised the classics and divinity, many of their students becoming clergymen of the Church of England. In the 1870s, religious tests for university entrance were abolished (although Oxford and Cambridge continued to reserve a large number of scholarships to members of the Church of England). University education for women, pioneered from the late 1840s in 'extra-mural classes', also began. Women-only colleges were established in both Oxford and Cambridge, the first being Girton College, Cambridge in 1869.

The pace of university expansion slowed in the years 1910–45 when only a small number of university colleges were established, for example at Hull and Leicester. However, recognising the crucial importance of government funding, the University Grants Committee was established in 1919 to provide a national mechanism for the distribution of funds.

(See also *University Tests Act*.)

University Tests Act: legislation passed in 1871 during *Gladstone*'s first government. The *Liberal Party* was committed to administrative reform and to the sweeping away of what seemed to it inappropriate restrictions on freedom. This Act:

- allowed men of all creeds to apply for fellowships and other teaching posts at university. Previously, the majority of such posts – and all at Oxford and Cambridge – had been restricted to those who were members of the *Church of England* and subscribed to its Thirty-nine Articles of doctrine
- broadened access to universities by removing religious tests, although Universities were permitted to retain scholarships which were available only to members of the Church of England or to other specified groups.

(See also *universities*.)

utilitarianism: the political philosophy which holds that the over-riding principle of government is to secure the maximisation of happiness and benefit for as many citizens as possible. Actions might be judged by how usefully they contributed to increasing the store of human happiness. This was the supreme 'utility' – hence 'utilitarianism'. The philosophy has its origins in classical Greece, but is mostly associated in Britain with the ideas of *Jeremy Bentham*. It developed in mid-nineteenth-century Britain as a principle which guided *social policy*, especially in changes to the *Poor Laws* and in the proposals of *Edwin Chadwick* for *public health* and sanitary reforms. The aim was to make progress in policies by rational calculation based on evidence and research. As its critics were not slow to point out, however, policies which might increase the overall store of human happiness might also jeopardise the life chances of identifiable minorities who 'stood in the way of progress'.

(See also *laissez-faire; Mill, John Stuart; Senior, Nassau*.)

V

V1 and V2: German missile weapons launched against Britain towards the end of *World War II.*

- V1 was a small pilotless aircraft with a 130-mile range but which lacked direction and accuracy. It was also relatively easy to shoot down. Of 8,000 such weapons launched against London in 1944 only 2,000 found a target. They did, however, do damage to the invading forces in France and Holland after *D-Day*
- V2 was a much more sophisticated weapon. It was a ballistic rocket with a 200-mile range which descended vertically and arrived ahead of the sound it made. About 2,000 were fired at Britain in the autumn of 1944 and they caused substantial casualties

vaccination: technique of protecting against infection by injecting mild forms of disease and encouraging the body to develop its own defence mechanisms. It was developed by Edward Jenner in 1798 who used cowpox, a mild disease affecting cows (in Latin 'vacca' means cow: hence 'vaccination'), for injections which were proved to give protection against smallpox. The success of the technique led to legislation which proved very effective in lessening mortality from smallpox:

- 1840 Vaccination Act enabled local authorities to provide vaccination for the poor, the cost being borne by ratepayers
- 1853 Vaccination Act made vaccination compulsory for all children of school age

There was no serious smallpox epidemic in Britain after 1872.

Vaccination was developed in the twentieth century to give protection against a variety of serious diseases, notably diphtheria, whooping cough, measles and poliomyelitis. It also had some success in the fight against *tuberculosis.*

(See also *public health.*)

value added tax: a tax placed on sales and services, in effect adding to their cost to the consumer. It is therefore an '*indirect tax*' paid on consumption not on income. It was introduced into Britain in 1972 as preparation for the country's entry into the European Economic Community the following year. It replaced the earlier 'purchase tax'.

(See also *direct taxation; income tax.*)

Vansittart, Nicholas (Lord Bexley): *Tory* politician. He was born in 1766 and became an MP at the *general election* of 1796 supporting *Pitt the Younger's* wartime coalition. His major offices were:

- Chief Secretary to the Treasury, 1801–4 and 1806–7
- Chief Secretary for Ireland, 1805–6
- Chancellor of the Exchequer, 1812–23
- Chancellor of the Duchy of Lancaster, 1823–28

He gained considerable administrative experience and was well respected by *Addington* and *Liverpool,* the two *prime ministers* he served for the longest period. He was not, however, an able speaker and never dominated the *House of Commons.* He never developed an effective strategy for dealing with the mounting government debt after the end of the *Napoleonic Wars,* the lead in financial policy increasingly being taken by *William Huskisson.* He retired in 1828 and lived on until 1851.

Vaughan Williams, Ralph: composer. Born in 1872, he composed a great deal of music associated with the English countryside and with folk music. He is perhaps best known for his 'Fantasia on a Theme of Thomas Tallis' (1909), a piece which shows his indebtedness to the inspiration of sixteenth-century music. He also wrote the fantasia for violin 'The Lark Ascending' and another piece of 'programme music' (describing a scene or a place), 'Sinfonia Antarctica'. His music fell out of fashion after *World War II* and especially among the new generation of 'a-tonal' composers. One of them, Elizabeth Maconchy, famously lampooned his fondness of the countryside by calling Vaughan Williams's work 'cow-pat music'. He died in 1958.

V-bombers: Royal Air Force aircraft, named Valiants, Victors and Vulcans, which carried British nuclear weapons in the 1950s and early 1960s before being replaced by *Polaris.*

venereal disease: see *sexually transmitted diseases*

Vereeniging, Treaty of: see *Boer War, Second*

Versailles, Treaty of (1919): peace settlement made by the victorious Allies with Germany at the end of *World War I.* It is often, though wrongly, used to apply to all the peace treaties made with the defeated powers. This treaty has become one of the most controversial in European History. It was forced on Germany and its terms were deliberately harsh. Germany lost much territory (see below) but, worse, was effectively dismantled as a great military and imperial power. The British *Prime Minister David Lloyd George,* echoing even more vengeful sentiments from the French, pledged to 'make Germany pay' for starting the war, a highly controversial claim anyway. The Germans were also made to sign the peace in the very hall where they had proclaimed their own national state after defeating the French in 1871. Many Germans never accepted the validity of the Treaty and commentators have seen it as one of the main reasons for the rise to power of Hitler and the origins of *World War II.* By it:

- Germany gave back the territories of Alsace and Lorraine, captured in 1870–1, to France
- Germany gave up much territory in West Prussia and East Silesia to Poland, now recognised again as an independent state
- Germany gave up part of Upper Silesia to the newly independent Czechoslovakia
- Germany gave part of Schleswig to Denmark
- Germany gave up Memel to the newly independent Lithuania
- Germany gave up Eupen and Malmedy to Belgium
- German colonies in *Africa* were shared out under *League of Nations* mandates between Britain, France, Belgium and *South Africa*

- a new peace-keeping organisation, the League of Nations, came into existence
- the German army was limited to 100,000 men and its navy virtually dismantled
- the Rhineland was demilitarised
- Germany was forced to admit liability for beginning the war – the 'war guilt clause'. It was thus made to pay *'reparations'* for the damage done by its troops in France and Belgium. In 1920 reparation payments were fixed at the cripplingly high figure of 13.4 million German marks
- France occupied the mineral-rich Saar land

(See also *Keynes, John Maynard; St Germain, Treaty of; Trianon, Treaty of.*)

veto: the ability to render a proposal of no effect. In British history, the term is most frequently encountered in disputes between the *House of Commons* and the *House of Lords*, where the Lords' veto prevented *Home Rule* bills for *Ireland* from being passed before the outbreak of *World War I*. The *monarchy* also retains a theoretical veto over any legislation passed by *Parliament* but this has not been used since 1708 and it is difficult to envisage any circumstances in which it would be. Britain also, as a permanent member of the *United Nations* Security Council, retains a veto over UN resolutions.

(See also *Parliament Act, 1911.*)

Victoria: Queen of the United Kingdom from 1837 to 1901. She was born in 1819, the only child of the fourth son of the Duke of Kent (fourth son of *George III*) and Princess Victoria of *Saxe-Coburg*-Gotha but her father died before she was one year old. Since, by an odd quirk of fate, none of George III's elder children (*George IV*; Frederick Augustus, Duke of York, died 1827; *William IV*) had any legitimate children of their own, Victoria succeeded to the throne at the age of eighteen on William's death in 1837.

Her early political life was dominated by two powerful men, the Earl of *Melbourne*, who acted as her first tutor in political matters and whom she adored and, after her marriage, her husband Prince *Albert*, to whom she was absolutely devoted and to whom she bore nine children between November 1841 and April 1857. Reasonably intelligent and well-read, though often wilful, prejudiced and opinionated, she was usually happy to take her lead on political matters from Albert. Albert taught her to respect the talents of *Sir Robert Peel*, whom she had taken strongly against over the *Bedchamber Crisis* in 1839.

There is no doubt that the death of Albert in 1861 was a blow from which she never truly recovered during a widowhood which lasted more than forty years. She left Albert's rooms untouched as a mark more of veneration than respect and withdrew from public life for half a decade. She attracted considerable criticism both on the grounds of neglect of duty and, among those who knew about it, her ambiguous relationship with a Highland manservant, John Brown (who died in 1883). In the 1860s, a significant *republican* movement grew up. She was coaxed back into public life from the late 1860s, not least by the efforts of *Benjamin Disraeli* who flattered her shamelessly, manipulatively and with success. She grieved for his death in 1881. *Gladstone*, who preferred more direct, and more long-winded, approaches to negotiations with his sovereign, she did not like. She once famously complained that he addressed her as if she were 'a public meeting' and even described him as 'half-crazy'. She attempted, though without success, to prevent him from becoming *Prime Minister* for a second time in 1880.

The second half of her reign permanently fixed her reputation. The twentieth century has largely forgotten the insecure, well-meaning young Queen and grieving widow and has instead celebrated Victoria as matriarch (her children and grand-children mostly married into the leading royal houses of Europe substantially affecting the diplomacy of late nineteenth and early twentieth-century Europe in consequence), symbol of *Empire* (Disraeli characteristically engineered for her the title of 'Empress of *India*', which she adored and adopted from 1877) and mother of the nation. In late 1896, the year before her Diamond Jubilee, she exceeded George III's record as longest-reigning British monarch, and both this event (see Figure below) and the Golden Jubilee of 1887 were manufactured into enormous occasions for national celebration. Much of what is generally assumed to be centuries-old tradition and ceremony was invented in the 1880s to present Britain as the supreme industrial and imperial power of the world, ruled over by an infinitely experienced, gracious and wise monarch.

Queen Victoria's Diamond Jubilee, 1897

Inevitably, the reality was more complex. In one sense, Victoria, learning from Albert, symbolised many of the virtues of the improving *middle classes*. For most of her reign, she worked very hard on public duties and she read government papers carefully. Though she did not like her children very much and her grandchildren hardly at all, she did have a very happy and fulfilling marriage which could be used to symbolise the Victorian family ideal. She ate too much and became very fat in later life (a trait exaggerated by her small stature) but she was reasonably moderate in her habits overall (contrasting strongly with her wayward and self-indulgent eldest son *Edward VII*). Lacking aesthetic sensibility, she did not over-spend on artistic treasures as several of her predecessors had done. She hardly needed to. Royal relations and those from the far-flung corners of the *Empire* were happy to shower her with gifts. She developed a very strong sense of imperial identity and she gloried in Britain's international status. In 1900, after all, she was monarch to about a quarter of the world's population. She also remained narrow-minded and stubborn on many matters; she had very fixed views on her political dislikes and favourites. Nevertheless, she rarely, if ever, risked these prejudices compromising her role as a constitutional monarch. That she died, in January 1901, beloved of most of her subjects is beyond doubt.

(See also *imperialism; monarchy; Palmerston, Viscount; Salisbury, Marquess of.*)

Vienna, Congress of (1814–15): peace conference at the end of the *Napoleonic Wars*. It developed from the *Treaty of Paris* and aimed to produce post-war stability after the lengthy disruption brought about by more than twenty years of warfare. It began before Napoleon's escape from Elba which brought about the renewal of war. The main decisions reached at the congress were:

- a Quadruple Alliance between Britain, Russia, Austria and Prussia was signed
- all the old monarchies and empires in existence at the beginning of the *French Revolutionary War* were restored
- Belgium was merged with Holland to provide a stronger buffer state against any French expansion northwards
- a new German confederation of states was created, replacing Napoleon's, and led by Austria
- Prussia received more territory and Russia's influence over Finland was recognised
- French territory on the mainland of Europe reverted to that held in 1790 and an Allied army of occupation was installed until France had paid off an indemnity
- in the Italian states, Piedmont was strengthened and Austria acknowledged as the major power
- many of Britain's colonial conquests and acquisitions during the wars were confirmed. These were: the Cape of Good Hope, Ceylon, Tobago, St Lucia, Malta, Mauritius and Heligoland
- the powers agreed to meet regularly to discuss matters of mutual interest and concern

(See also *Castlereagh, Viscount; congress system.*)

Vincent, Henry: *Chartist.* Born in 1813, he trained as a printer and became an effective speaker and writer in the Chartist cause. He advocated moral improvement and was fiercely critical of the leadership of *Feargus O'Connor*. As an essential counterpart to the improvement of the working classes, he was also a supporter of the *Temperance Movement*. He died in 1876.

(See also *Lovett, William.*)

W

Waitangi, Treaty of: treaty signed in February 1840 on the north island of *New Zealand* by Captain William Hobson, on behalf of the British crown, and 46 Maori Chiefs. By it:

- the Chiefs agreed to grant sovereignty to Britain and were granted the privileges of British subjects
- Britain agreed to respect Maori rights to the possession of their lands, while reserving the right to buy them
- Britain granted the Maoris the full protection of the British crown

The treaty ensured that Britain, rather than France which had also become involved in the South Pacific, should become the European power in control of New Zealand. The Maoris soon complained that Britain was taking land to which they were not entitled and a series of wars broke out in the mid-1840s which did not end until 1872.

(See also *Empire, British; Wakefield, Edward Gibbon.*)

Wakefield, Edward Gibbon: colonial administrator. Born in 1796, after a colourful early history which involved abduction, a shotgun marriage and a three-year imprisonment in Newgate gaol, he became interested in the settlement of the Empire on which he lavished ferocious energies. He was sent to *Australia* in the late 1820s, where he wrote pamphlets on the best means of settlement, ended the system of free grants of land in New South Wales and played a part in ensuring that South Australia became a 'free state' when established in 1834 and not a penal settlement. He went with *Lord Durham* to *Canada* in 1838 and founded the New Zealand Land Company, which bought land from the Maoris and persuaded the British government to annex the country in 1840. He emigrated to *New Zealand* in 1853 and died in 1862.

(See also *Empire, British; imperialism; Waitangi, Treaty of.*)

Walcheren expedition: incident in 1809 during the *Napoleonic Wars*. The aim was to mount an expedition to Walcheren, an island in the Netherlands, capture it and use the territory as a base both for menacing Antwerp, trying to wrest control of it from Napoleon, and for urging people in the Netherlands and in the German states to rise up against Napoleon. Although a British army under Lord Chatham captured Walcheren, none of the more important objectives were achieved. Devastated by dysentery and meeting strong French resistance, the expedition was abandoned. It was widely seen as a blow to British morale, since the government of *Portland* had committed substantial resources to it. It was also the cause of a duel between *Castlereagh* and *Canning* after Castlereagh discovered that Canning had written a letter to the *Prime Minister* in which he strongly criticised his handling of the affair.

war poetry: collective name usually given to those who wrote about *World War I.* The most famous are *Rupert Brooke, Wilfred Owen* and *Siegfried Sassoon.* The themes highlighted in their work include the ideals of patriotism and self-sacrifice as in Brooke's '1914': 'Now, God be thanked Who has matched us with His hour and caught our youth, and waked us from sleeping'. These are contrasted with the brutal realities of mass destruction and the futile waste of young life. Sassoon's 'Suicide in the Trenches' pours scorn on 'You smug-faced crowds with kindling eye Who cheer when soldier lads march by. Sneak home and pray you'll never know The hell where youth and laughter go'. Owen summed up the overall mood in the Preface to his collection: 'My subject is war and the pity of war. The Poetry is in the pity'. *Benjamin Britten*'s 'War Requiem' (1962) takes much of its text from Owen's work.

Washington Naval Agreement, 1921–22: sometimes known as the 'Four Power Pact' between Britain, the *United States*, France and Japan, it was designed to prevent another naval arms race similar to that over *dreadnoughts* between Britain and Germany before *World War I*. Its main focus, however, was the Pacific Ocean rather than the Atlantic. By it:

- Britain, the United States and Japan agreed to limit their shipbuilding programme and to maintain fleets in respect of each other in the ratio 5:5:3
- France and Italy agreed to navy sizes roughly half that of Japan
- Britain and the United States agreed not to strengthen their naval fortifications in *Singapore* and Hawaii respectively

water frame: machine developed in the early stage of the *Industrial Revolution* and usually credited to Richard Arkwright, who patented it in 1769. This roller-spinning machine produced strong cotton thread which allowed cotton cloth to be woven for the first time. In 1779, Samuel Crompton combined the potential of both the water frame and Hargreaves's slightly earlier spinning jenny into a so-called 'spinning mule' which enabled mass production of yarn to take place in factories.

(See also *water power*.)

water power: important source of energy, especially in the early stages of the *Industrial Revolution*. Most of the early factories were powered by water, which explains their location. Most were situated in the countryside near to those fast-flowing rivers and streams which could move water wheels. This constraint was removed with the harnessing of *steam power* from the end of the eighteenth century, which enabled much greater concentration of factories in urban areas. Large and successful water-powered factories continued, however, until well into the second half of the nineteenth century.

In the twentieth century, water has been used to provide 'hydro-electric' power, particularly in parts of upland Britain, such as the Highlands of Scotland.

(See also *Armstrong, William; engineering; Watt, James*.)

Waterloo, Battle of: decisive battle fought in present-day Belgium on 18 June 1815 which ended the *Napoleonic Wars*. It was fought between a British army led by Arthur Wellesley, *Duke of Wellington*, allied to a Prussian army led by Marshal Blücher, against a French army led by Napoleon. The battle, which took place after an indecisive engagement two days earlier at Quatre Bras and lasted all day, involved late forces. Wellington commanded 67,000 men (about one-third of which were British) and Napoleon about 72,000. Blücher had 89,000 under his command and the Prussian army's arrival to support Wellington late in the day proved decisive after the French had captured a strategically important farmhouse at La Haye Sainte and were preparing a frontal assault on the British forces. Wellington himself later called the battle 'the nearest run thing you ever saw in your life'. The retreating French army was routed by chasing Prussian forces in the evening and late into the night, so that Napoleon was deprived of any opportunity to regroup.

Watt, James: inventor and engineer. Born in Scotland in 1736, he worked on *canal* development in the second half of the eighteenth century, but is best known for his work on developing steam engines. He patented a separate steam condenser using latent heat in 1769, rather than using a cylinder. He worked extensively on steam technology in the last quarter of the eighteenth century in partnership with the Birmingham businessman Matthew Boulton. Watt himself lacked business skills. As *Samuel Smiles* said of him, he would 'rather face a loaded cannon than settle an account or make a bargain'. His engines were expensive and initially did not sell well, but they led to a revolution in engine power crucial to mechanised production in the early stages of the *Industrial Revolution*. He died in 1809.

(See also *engineering industry; steam power.*)

Waugh, Evelyn: novelist. Born in 1903 the son of a successful publisher, his best novels, such as 'Decline and Fall' (1928) and 'Brideshead Revisited' (1945), took as their theme the old *aristocratic* order in retreat. He was a very witty writer and could be a savage satirist, although his best work (strongly influenced by conversion to *Roman Catholicism* in 1930) is more melancholic and wistful in its treatment of institutions under threat from a modern society with which he felt himself increasingly out of sympathy. Like many who affected aristocratic habits without coming from aristocratic backgrounds, he sometimes appeared extraordinarily snobbish and intolerant.

Wavell (Archibald Percival), 1st Earl: soldier. Born in 1883, he served in the *Boer War* and with Field Marshal Allenby in Palestine during *World War I*. His experience made him a natural choice as Commander-in-Chief of Allied forces in the Middle East (1939–41), where at the beginning of *World War II* he defeated the Italians in North *Africa* before being forced to retreat by Rommel. He was appointed Commander-in-Chief in India in 1941 and then also in the South-West Pacific. He attempted offensives against the Japanese in *Burma* but was not successful. He was Viceroy of *India* from 1943 to 1947 where he tried to repair increasingly difficult relationships between Hindu and Muslim while attempting to prolong British rule. He was made a viscount in 1943 and an earl in 1947. He died in 1950.

(See also *Churchill, Winston; Mountbatten, Viscount.*)

Webb, Beatrice: social reform and socialist, born as Martha Beatrice Potter in 1858, the daughter of a successful industrialist in Gloucester. She worked with *Charles Booth* on his famous study of the London poor before marrying *Sidney Webb* in 1892, thus forming what became one of the most famous partnerships in left-wing politics and social policy making. With her husband, she helped to found the London School of Economics in 1895 and was a member of the Royal Commission on the *Poor Laws* (1905–9). The Webbs' 'Minority Report', calling for the complete dismantling of the Poor Law, though not accepted by the *Liberal government* at the time, proved very influential in guiding social policy through the 1920s and 1930s. They visited the USSR in the 1930s and produced a wildly enthusiastic report on the Bolshevik regime in 'Soviet Communism: a New Civilisation' (1935) – just as Stalin's purges were getting underway. She died in 1943.

(See also *Labour Party; socialism.*)

Webb, Sidney (1st Baron Passfield): Labour politician and social reformer. He was born in 1859 and worked as a civil servant before joining the Fabian Society. He was elected to the *London County Council* in 1892, serving until 1910. Here he argued for reforms to improve the social conditions of the London poor. With his wife *Beatrice Webb*, he founded the left-wing journal the 'New Statesman' in 1913 and much of the remainder of his life was concerned with the *Labour Party*. He served on its executive committee from 1915 to 1925 and, with his wife, had an important hand in redrafting its constitution in 1918. He was a convinced *socialist*, but opposed revolution as a means to achieve social reorganisation. He coined the phrase 'the inevitability of gradualness' to describe his position when making his presidential address to the Labour Party in 1920. He became a Labour MP in 1922, representing the North-East mining constituency of Seaham until he received a peerage in 1929. His major offices were:

- President of the Board of Trade, 1924
- Secretary of the Dominions and Colonies, 1929–30
- Secretary for the Colonies, 1930–1

He and his wife were also prolific authors. They produced a 'History of Trade Unionism' in 1894 and the nine-volume 'English Local Government' from 1906 to 1929. He died in 1947.

(See also *Poor Laws*.)

Webster–Ashburton Treaty, 1842: treaty made during the administration of *Sir Robert Peel* between Britain and the *United States* over the border between the US state of Maine and the Canadian province of New Brunswick. This removed one of the main territorial obstacles to improved relations between the two powers.

(See also *Aberdeen, Earl of; Canada*.)

welfare state: name given to the system of benefits and pensions provided by the State to protect the health and welfare of citizens. It is generally said to have come into effect in Britain during the *Labour* government of 1945–50 headed by *Clement Attlee*, though the first distinctively 'welfare' policy by a British government was the establishment of old age pensions in 1908 under the *Liberal* government of *H H Asquith*. All three political parties supported *Beveridge*'s plans for welfare at the *general election* of 1945 and Labour largely implemented the Beveridge agenda. The creation in 1948 of a *National Health Service* giving free access to medical treatment for all was a central pillar since it recognised the principle of state response to need.

In some respects the welfare state became in the second half of the twentieth century a victim of its own success. As levels of health care improved, so a larger proportion of the population was able to survive into very old age. In their eighties and nineties, most people need much higher levels of care than in earlier life. Thus the welfare system was required to meet ever larger demands. In addition, the network of benefits became so extensive and so complex that it was susceptible to exploitation by those who either exaggerated their needs or otherwise made false claims. By the late 1990s, the social security budget had reached almost £100 billion a year and fraudulent claims were estimated at between five and six per cent of this. In 1997, the *Labour Prime Minister Tony Blair* was asserting that the welfare state had been 'left behind by economic and social change' and called for a 'fundamental change in (its) culture, attitude and practice ... to create a fairer and more efficient society'.

(See also *Bevan, Aneurin; Old Age Pensions Act, 1908; social policy.*)

Beveridge Report
1942

Family Allowances –
Maternity Benefits for
mothers
1946

Widows' benefits
1946

Free secondary
education
(Butler Act, 1944)

Unemployment
National
Assistance
1946

New National Health
Service hospitals
1948

Free access to
a medical
general
practitioner (GP)
1948

Free hospital
care
1948

Key features of the welfare state

Wellesley, Richard: colonial administrator and *Tory* politician. He was born in 1760, the eldest son of an Irish peer and became an MP in 1784. His major offices were:

- Member of the Board of Control for India, 1793–97
- Governor-General of India, 1797–1805
- Foreign Secretary, 1809–12
- Lord Lieutenant of Ireland, 1821–28 and 1833–34

During his tenure of the governor-generalship he brought more of *India* under British protection as a means of resisting the challenge of the French during the *French Revolutionary* and *Napoleonic Wars*. Hyderabad, Oudh and the Carnatic were all, in effect, annexed. His tenure of the foreign secretaryship was not happy. The war showed few successes before 1812 and his relations with other Cabinet ministers, including *Castlereagh*, the Secretary for War, were poor. Nevertheless, he hoped to succeed as *Prime Minister* in 1812 and was the *Prince Regent*'s choice before *Liverpool*.

Once more, his arrogance and lack of close political contacts told against him. He was a competent Secretary for Ireland and was firm in putting down terrorist activity. He disagreed with the policy of *Catholic emancipation* and resigned when his brother, *Wellington*, enacted it on *Peel's* advice. He retired from public life in 1835 and died in 1842.

Wellington (Wellesley, Arthur), 1st Duke of: soldier, Tory politician and *Prime Minister*. He was born in 1769. He made his reputation as a soldier in *India*, playing an important part in the capture of Mysore during the governor-generalship of his brother *Richard Wellesley*. He returned in 1805, becoming an MP in 1806. His major offices were:

- Chief Secretary for Ireland, 1807–9
- Commander of the British Army in the *Peninsular War*, 1808–14
- Commander-in-Chief of the British Forces, 1815
- Master General of the Ordnance, 1819–27
- Prime Minister, 1828–30, 1834
- Foreign Secretary, 1834–35
- Minister without Portfolio, 1841–46

His military abilities were very substantial. He was not a dashing commander, like Napoleon, but he had a shrewd and practical understanding of military possibilities and he fought some brilliant defensive actions in the Peninsula, before pushing out into France at tactically the right moment. His victories against the French in 1813–14 earned him his dukedom in 1814, but he became a national hero through his decisive victory at the *Battle of Waterloo*.

His career after Waterloo was close to the centre of political life. His joining *Liverpool's* government in 1818 gave it prestige and he worked closely with *Castlereagh*. He represented Britain at the Congress of Verona in 1822 when he opposed armed intervention in Spain. He was not widely considered a likely Prime Minister. He had shown little interest in domestic matters, though he could be relied upon to oppose *parliamentary reform* and any moves towards democracy with vigour. He became Prime Minister because the premature death of *Canning* and then the patent inadequacy of *Goderich* left the *Tory Party* in urgent need of strong, 'steady' leadership. This Wellington attempted to provide, but in difficult times for his party. Always considered, like his brother, a stalwart opponent of *Catholic emancipation*, he shocked the right wing of his party by agreeing to *Peel's* advice that it must be granted to stave off civil war in *Ireland*. Since the 'liberal' wing of the party, led by *Huskisson* and including *Palmerston*, had already left, Wellington's tenure of the leadership might be considered disastrous to party unity. His firm stance against parliamentary reform in 1830 failed to unite the party, and he was forced by dwindling majorities and lessening authority to resign in November 1830. He was briefly caretaker Prime Minister in 1834, and served Peel loyally throughout the years 1841–46. He was never remotely interested in the detailed administrative work so assiduously done by Peel's rising stars, *Gladstone* and *Graham*, but he lent the administration seniority and authority. Characteristically, he supported Peel over the highly controversial repeal of the *Corn Laws*, which helped the passage of the measure, though it could not preserve party unity.

It may seem ironic that a man so devoted to discipline and authority should have been involved in two measures so damaging to the historic party of order. Wellington, however, was never an unreflecting 'ultra-Tory'. He had a strong sense of the national interest and realised that, in industrial Britain, some change was necessary to preserve the essentials of *aristocratic* government. He died in 1852 and was mourned as a national hero.

(See also *Conservative Party; congress system.*)

Wells, H(erbert) G(eorge): novelist and *socialist*. He was born in 1866 and studied science, an interest which stayed with him through life and is reflected in some of his novels, such as 'The Time Machine' (1895) and 'The First Men on the Moon' (1901). His novels also demonstrate social awareness. 'Kipps' (1905) and 'The History of Mr Polly' (1910) both draw on his experiences as a lower *middle-class* boy from the south London suburbs. He was also an active member of the Fabian society, writing a number of pamphlets on topics of contemporary importance such as 'Socialism and the Family' (1907). He also stood as a *Labour Party* candidate. In later life, he was more concerned with social analysis and using the past to provide examples for future planning. His 'The Outline of History' (1920) called for reconciliation between nations and world peace. It reflected his strong support for the new *League of Nations*.

Welsh National Party: see *Plaid Cymru*

Wheatley Housing Act, 1924: legislation passed during the first minority *Labour* government and named after the Minister of Health, John Wheatley (1869–1930), an ex-miner and member of the *Independent Labour Party*. It:

- granted a subsidy of £9 per house for forty years to both local councils and private builders to stimulate house building for rent to the working classes
- was intended to run for fifteen years

The Bill passed with the help of the *Liberal Party* and the extent of the subsidy was reduced by the incoming *Conservative* government and abandoned during the economic crisis of 1932. However, it was a landmark in *housing* legislation because it provided a central government subsidy for council-house building for the first time. This was eagerly taken up; twice as many council houses were built in 1925 than 1924. By 1932, almost 700,000 public-sector houses had been built since the end of *World War I*.

(See also *Addison Housing Act, 1919.*)

Whigs: political party, the forerunner of the *Liberal Party*. The name derives from 'Whiggamore', originally a term of abuse used to describe supporters of James II's exclusion from succession to the throne during a constitutional crisis in 1678–81. Comprising large landowners, they had been the dominant political grouping for much of the eighteenth century but had split in 1794 when those opposing the *French Revolution* joined forces with the younger *Pitt*'s government to create an anti-reform coalition. The remaining Whigs, led now by *Charles James Fox*, carried what they believed to be the main traditions of Whiggery into the nineteenth century. These were:

- limited powers for the *monarchy*. The Whigs considered themselves the guardians of the 'Glorious Revolution of 1688' when James II was removed from the throne and Parliament placed more restrictions on what the monarchy could do without its consent

- support for reform of many kinds. Whigs were never *radicals* but liked to believe that they supported 'the people' in their demands for change. Who these 'people' were was never precisely defined, but it was a key element of Whiggery that they were in touch with the opinion of those not directly represented in Parliament and would respond to their needs. Thus, in the 1790s, the Whigs formed an 'Association of the Friends of the People' which supported *parliamentary reform*. During the period 1815–32, the Whigs developed links with the professional and commercial *middle classes*.
- support for religious toleration. Very few Whigs were themselves *nonconformists*, but many of their supporters were, particularly in the growing towns of early industrial Britain

Socially, the Whig leaders were very exclusive, being drawn from the ranks of an established *aristocracy*. The most prominent families were the Devonshires, Greys, Grenvilles and Russells. Holland House, the Kensington town house of Baron Holland, became the centre of Whig society in the first half of the nineteenth century where many high-level political decisions were made and important social contacts established. Whig social exclusivity, which frequently manifested itself as outrageous snobbery, and support for 'the people' often seemed incongruous and was frequently remarked upon by their opponents. The prevailing Whig view was, however, that by listening to the people, they could not only keep in touch with an increasingly important 'public opinion' but could seek to guide, filter and control its more dangerous elements, leaving the world safe for people of breeding, taste and natural leadership qualities.

The Whigs paid a high price for listening to public opinion in the first thirty years of the nineteenth century, when propertied opinion was mostly anti-reform. They were in office during this period only during the so-called 'Ministry of all the Talents' in 1806–7. Returned to office in 1830, during the reform crisis, *Grey's* government, which lasted until 1834, passed a *Reform Act* which attempted to produce substantial change and remove any danger of revolution. Both his government and those headed by *Melbourne* (1834 and 1835–41) enacted a substantial measure of reform, concerning *slavery*, the *Poor Laws*, *police* and the *Church of England* but their over-riding instincts were to preserve the essence of the old order, ruled by a landed elite, rather than to change. When the party began to use the name 'Liberal' to denote its broader base of support, it nevertheless tended still to be led by members of the aristocracy until the mid-1880s. *Gladstone's* government of 1868–74, for example, was one of the most aristocratic of the nineteenth century. The true spirit of Whiggery lived on vigorously in the early history of the Liberal Party.

(See also *Grenville, William; Parliament; Tories.*)

White Paper: name given to a government document in which firm proposals for legislation are published for discussion.

Wilberforce, William: *evangelical* and anti-*slavery* campaigner. Born in 1759, he was the son of a rich merchant in Hull. He was educated at Cambridge, where he met the *Younger Pitt*, who was of the same age and became a lifelong political friend and useful political contact. He became MP for Hull on his father's influence in 1780 and then for the prized county seat of Yorkshire, which he represented until 1812 when ill-health forced him to give it up in favour of the much less demanding small borough of Bramber. He remained an MP for this seat until he retired finally from public life in 1825.

He underwent a religious conversion in 1784 and thereafter devoted himself to evangelical religion and to charitable works. He wrote many pamphlets in which he urged the *Church of England* to adopt a more evangelical stance. His 'Practical View of Christianity' (1797) which distinguished between 'real' and nominal religious observance became a great publishing success. He was also involved in the founding of the Proclamation Society in 1787 which pressed for severe penalties against the publication of blasphemous or otherwise irreligious literature, and in the Society for Bettering the Condition of the Poor (1796). Like most evangelicals, he sought the improvement of the poor through example and good works and not through extended political rights. He opposed the extension of the franchise and loyally supported Pitt's anti-*radical* measures in the Commons.

His first began his campaigns against the *slave trade* in 1787 and kept the issue firmly before the public eye until abolition in 1807. He was the most celebrated figure behind the formation of the Anti-Slavery Society in 1823, though ill-health prevented him from taking an active part in its work. Slavery was abolished in the *British Empire* in 1833, the year he died.

Wilde, Oscar Fingall O'Flaherty Wills: novelist and playwright. Born in Dublin in 1854, the son of a surgeon, he made his reputation in England, first as a notable supporter of the aesthetic movement of the 1880s. He produced his famous fantasy novel 'The Picture of Dorian Gray' in 1891, and 'Salome' in 1893. His most famous plays are 'Lady Windermere's Fan' (1892) and 'The Importance of Being Earnest' (1895), both of which poke not always gentle fun at the conventions of upper-class late Victorian society. He was accused of sodomy by the Marquis of Queensbury, took libel action against him, was outwitted in court by *Edward Carson* and, when his action failed, imprisoned for two years for homosexuality. This experience, though it produced two fine poems, 'De Profundis' (1897) and 'The Ballad of Reading Gaol' (1898), broke him and he died living in shame under an assumed name in Paris in 1900.

Wilkinson, Ellen Cicely: *Labour* politician. She was born in 1891 and had both an active and a varied political career from a young age. She joined both the *Independent Labour Party* and the *suffragettes* before becoming a *trade unionist* and a member of the *Communist Party*, which she left to join the Labour Party in 1924. She was MP for Middlesborough from 1924 to 1931 and for Jarrow from 1935 to her death in 1947. As Member of Parliament for seats in the North-East, she developed a particularly close interest in the *unemployment* question and a strong sympathy for the unemployed. She led the famous *Jarrow March* and wrote about the town's experiences during the slump in 'The Town That was Murdered' (1939). She joined the war-time coalition government as a junior minister in the Home Office in 1940. From 1945 to 1947 she was Minister for Education, responsible for putting into effect *Butler's Education Act* of 1944.

(See also *economic policy*.)

William IV: King of the United Kingdom from 1830 to 1837. He was born the third son of *George III* in 1765. His early career was in the navy, which he joined in 1779 as a midshipman. Despite having limited talent, his position earned him the posts of Admiral of the Fleet (1811) and Lord High Admiral (1827). He married Princess Adelaide of Saxe-Meiningen in 1818, but the marriage was childless. He had been associated for more than twenty years from 1790 with the actress Dorothea Jordan by whom he had ten children. He came to the throne as the *parliamentary reform* crisis deepened. He was temperamentally opposed to reform and his handling of the crisis was not good. He first agreed with *Grey* to create a number of peers to pass Reform through the *House of Lords*, then changed his mind, leading to Grey's resignation and an unnecessary, and dangerous, crisis during the 'days of May' when the *Duke of Wellington* was trying to form a *Tory* government. In 1834, he became the last monarch to dismiss a government with a workable parliamentary majority, but his attempt to get rid of *Melbourne* and the *Whigs* had little success, since *Peel* was able to hold office for less than four months. Few politicians respected him and he could not substitute high ability for lack of relevant experience. He died in 1837, a month after his niece and heir, Princess *Victoria,* had her eighteenth birthday and was thus able to reign without a regency.

Wilson, (James) Harold (Lord Wilson of Rievaulx): *Labour* politician and *Prime Minister.* He was born to lower middle-class parents in Huddersfield in 1916 and was educated at Oxford University where he gained a first-class degree in Politics, Philosophy and Economics and was marked out as one of the ablest young scholars of his generation. He moved quickly into governmental circles, being appointed an economist in the Cabinet Secretariat in 1940. In 1945, he was elected as Labour MP for Ormskirk and his career continued to move quickly. His major offices were:

- President of the Board of Trade, 1947–51
- Leader of the Labour Party, 1963–76
- Prime Minister, 1964–70 and 1974–76

He resigned with *Aneurin Bevan* from *Attlee*'s government in 1951, just before it lost power, in a protest against the government defence policy and its implications for the *National Health Service.* This placed him on the left of the party, though little of his subsequent career suggested strong left-wing sympathies. He won the leadership by a narrow margin against *George Brown* after the unexpected death of *Hugh Gaitskell*.

He was seen at his best in 1963–64 when he harried first *Macmillan's* and then *Home's* governments unmercifully, criticising them as out of date and lacking purpose. Having won a narrow *general election* victory in 1964, he proved a disappointing Prime Minister. He had aroused expectations of modernisation and dynamic action, but few of these were fulfilled. The economy faltered and government seemed powerless to end the cycle of '*stop–go*' policies. The pound drifted downwards, forcing a *devaluation* in 1967 which severely weakened government credibility. *Unemployment* increased sharply, and damagingly, in the late 1960s. In foreign policy, the inability to stop *Southern Rhodesia*'s *Unilateral Declaration of Independence* in 1965 was a blow to prestige and Wilson's support for the *United States* during the Vietnam War earned much criticism inside the party. There were also major personality clashes between Wilson and Brown and many Cabinet ministers complained of Wilson's obsessive suspicion with plots against his leadership. The Labour Party lost power in 1970 and Wilson did not expect to become Prime Minister again.

He did so in unusual circumstances after *Heath* called a *general election* in February 1974 during the miners' *strike* which he narrowly lost. Wilson formed a minority administration, which he converted to one with a very small majority at a second general election in October 1974. Though his government resolved the miners' strike, it was widely seen to have done so by capitulating to the power of the *trade unions*. The country's basic economic problems were not addressed and Wilson, apparently tired of office, resigned in 1976. Since he had given no hint of resignation beyond a very narrow circle of advisers, it came as a considerable shock and numerous wild conspiracy theories circulated to explain his sudden departure. He remained a member of the *House of Commons* until the general election of 1983, when he was granted a peerage. He died in 1995.

Wilson's reputation as Prime Minister is low. It should be noted, however, that the Labour Party had become difficult to lead, with splits between left and right wings becoming ever wider. Wilson devoted much time (far too much, his critics have said) to devising strategies for keeping it together. That constitutional innovation, the *referendum* of 1975 on whether the United Kingdom should remain a member of the Common Market, was in reality a device to maintain a semblance of party unity.

(See also *James Callaghan; economic policy*.)

'wind of change' speech: speech made by *Harold Macmillan* as *Prime Minister* in 1960. He talked of 'national consciousness' as 'a wind of change blowing through this continent'. The speech was made to the parliament of *South Africa* and was intended to convey the message that Britain would participate fully in the process of *decolonisation*. The speech was widely criticised by white South Africans, most of whom supported their government's policy of apartheid. South Africa left the *Commonwealth* in 1961, intending to maintain 'white supremacy' as a structure which would withstand the winds of change.

Windsor, House of: the official name of the United Kingdom royal family since 1917. It has therefore been held successively by the monarchs *George V, Edward VIII, George VI* and *Elizabeth II*. The name was chosen because the strong German associations of British royalty since the *Hanoverian* succession of 1714 became an embarrassment during *World War I*. Given the scale and virulence of anti-German propaganda orchestrated by the Government since 1914, it is surprising that it took George V almost three years to renounce formally all German titles and adopt a new name associated with the largest royal castle, Windsor, beside the Thames in Berkshire.

(See also *Saxe-Coburg*.)

'winter of discontent': name given by the press to the winter of 1978/79 when *James Callaghan's Labour* government was assailed by a number of *strikes* after attempting to impose a national wage increase limit of five per cent, which the more powerful *trade unions* refused to accept. The winter was quite severe and the visual image of rubbish piled high in the streets and delayed burials was very powerful. It suggested a government out of control and played an important part in the *general election* victory of *Margaret Thatcher* in May 1979.

Wolfenden Report, 1957: Government Committee on Homosexual Offences and Prostitution, named after its Chairman, Sir John Wolfenden. It recommended that:

- homosexual activity should be decriminalised
- tighter regulations should be introduced to deter soliciting of prostitutes in public places and other activities offensive to public decency, but the law should not normally seek to punish sexual activity between adults which took place in private

The *Conservative* government responded with the Street Offences Act, 1959 – see *prostitution* – but refused to make homosexuality between consenting adults legal.

(See also *homosexuality*.)

Wollstonecraft, Mary: author. Born in 1759, she worked as a nurse and a governess before coming into a circle of *radical* political thinkers including Richard Price, Thomas Paine and William Godwin, whom she married in 1797. She wrote novels and tracts on education but is best known for 'A Vindication of the Rights of Woman', published in 1792. She took her title deliberately from Paine's famous radical work 'Rights of Man' (1791–92) and aimed to draw attention to the double standard which even radicals employed when they called for 'universal manhood *suffrage*'. She died in 1797, shortly after giving birth to her daughter Mary (later *Mary Shelley*). Her work proved influential for many feminist writers in the later nineteenth and twentieth centuries.

Wolseley, Sir Garnet Joseph (1st Viscount Wolseley): soldier and colonial administrator. Born in 1833, coming from an Irish military family, he had an extraordinarily varied career in three continents. He saw action in the *Crimean War*, was in *India* during the Mutiny of 1857 and served in the *Opium War* against China in 1860. He is best known, however, for his exploits in Africa. He led a military force against the Ashantis in 1873–74 after which the Gold Coast area was declared a British Crown Colony. He then established colonial governments in Transvaal and Zululand. He won national celebrity in 1882 when he crushed the revolt of Arabi Pasha against British rule, and he led the unsuccessful campaign to relieve General Gordon in Khartoum in 1884–85. He was created Viscount in 1885, was Commander-in-Chief in Ireland from 1890 to 1895 and, as Field Marshal, overall Commander-in-Chief of the British army from 1895 to 1899. He died in 1903.

(See also *Empire, British; imperialism*.)

women, legal and occupational status of: at the beginning of the nineteenth century, women's status was in every respect inferior to that of men. No woman could vote, for example, and a woman's property became the exclusive right of her husband on marriage, to dispose of as he wished. Women were not permitted to attend university. They were paid much less for work and the work they did nearly always had a lower status than that of men. In the *middle classes* and, increasingly, among skilled workers it was not considered 'respectable' for a wife to work. Instead, married women were encouraged to undertake voluntary and unpaid charitable work. About half-a-million did so by 1900 and some of the work, for example in soup kitchens or visiting the sick in slum areas, was emotionally and physically demanding. Culturally and educationally, women were encouraged to consider themselves separate from and, by strong implication, inferior to, men.

From the middle of the nineteenth century, the legal status of women began to improve although cultural assumptions were much slower to change. The main changes were:

1834 women could vote in elections for *Poor Law* guardians

1857 Matrimonial Causes Act: *divorce* became possible without need for private Act of Parliament

1869 Girton College, Cambridge, became the first university college for women students in England

1870 Married Women's Property Act gave women the right to keep their own earnings from employment after marriage

1870 *Education Act* permitted women ratepayers to vote for, and to serve on, the new school boards

1875 women could be elected as *Poor Law* guardians

1878 the legal status of 'judicial separation' – short of divorce but ensuring a physical distance between man and wife – was instituted

1882 women could keep property acquired before marriage separate from that of their husbands

1888 women could vote for the new *County Boroughs* and *County Councils*

1891 women not divorced or separated were no longer compelled to live with their husbands

1894 women could serve on urban and district councils

1902 after school boards were abolished in the *Education Act*, women's representation in educational organisation was guaranteed by requiring at least two women to serve on every local education authority

1918 women over the age of 30 could vote in parliamentary elections

1918 women were allowed to enter the legal profession and could become *Justices of the Peace*

1923 a wife could for the first time divorce her husband on grounds of adultery, the first of many pieces of legislation which challenged the so-called 'double standard' between man and wife – see *divorce laws*

1928 women over the age of 21 could vote in parliamentary elections

1955 women's pay in the Civil Service, local government and teaching made equal with men's over a six-year phasing-in period

1970 Equal Pay Act introduced the principle of equal pay for equal work and no discrimination over terms and conditions of employment on grounds of sex

1975 Employment Protection Act made dismissal on grounds of pregnancy illegal and employers were required to offer a contract of employment to a returning woman after pregnancy was over

1975 Sex Discrimination Act. Discrimination on grounds of sex was made illegal in any matter concerning employment, education, recreation and finance. The Equal Opportunities Commission was established to oversee operation of the legislation

It is important not to interpret the list above as securing equality for women. Many women before the 1960s were expected, or even required, to give up paid employment when they married and only rarely would their jobs be held for them until they wished to return after a pregnancy. After both *World Wars*, during which women had taken over many jobs normally taken by men, they were expected to relinquish more senior positions particularly when, as in the early 1920s, *unemployment* was on the increase. The general assumption, shared by many women, was that men should have priority when it came to skilled jobs, high pay and responsibility. For many of both sexes a married woman's 'proper' place remained in the home.

With war came greater equality of opportunity for women – but this was often relinquished when peace came.

Nor did equality of opportunity necessarily mean equality of pay. In the mid-1970s, women were being paid, on average, 34 per cent less than men for doing jobs of equivalent status. This differential had narrowed to 20 per cent by 1997, but progress towards eliminating it was slow.

On the other hand, and probably because employment patterns have changed, with less emphasis on permanent full-time work, women (traditionally used to job flexibility) have become more attractive as employees. In 1951, census figures suggested that women formed 31 per cent of the total labour force, while only 26 per cent of married women under 60 years of age were in paid employment. By 1981, women formed 40 per cent of the labour force and 62 per cent of married women under 60 were in paid employment. In 1996, for the first time, government statistics suggested that more women (11.25 million) were officially 'employed' than were men (11.24 million). This increase was particularly marked in the professional sector.

Almost 70 per cent of 450,000 new professional jobs created in the years 1981–96 were taken by women.

(See also *economic policy; local government; Reform Act, 1918; suffragettes; suffragists; unemployment.*)

Women's Social and Political Union (WSPU): the militant organisation founded by *Emmeline* and *Christobel Pankhurst* in 1903 in support of votes for women. Its activities, and the *radical* tone of its journal 'Votes for Women', made the women's *suffrage* question a much more urgent one for the *Liberal* government led by *H H Asquith*.

(See also *suffragists.*)

Wood, (Howard) Kingsley: *Conservative* politician. He was born in 1881 and was elected a Conservative MP for Woolwich in 1918, serving the same constituency continuously until his death in 1943. He was knighted in 1918 and his major offices were:

- Postmaster-General, 1931–35
- Minister of Health, 1935–38
- Minister for Air, 1938–40
- Lord Privy Seal, 1940
- Chancellor of the Exchequer, 1940–43

All of his *Cabinet* experience was within the *National Government* or in *Churchill's* wartime Cabinet, where he served from 1940 to 1942.

An efficient minister with a talent for innovation, he is best remembered for supervising the rapid build-up of air defences just before, and in the early months of, *World War II* and for introducing the PAYE ('pay as you earn') system of direct deduction of income tax from pay packets.

(See also *income tax.*)

Woodcock, George: trade union leader. Born near Preston (Lancashire) in 1904, he was educated in elementary school and worked as a cotton weaver before going to Ruskin College, the working man's college at Oxford before New College, where he took a first-class degree in Politics, Philosophy and Economics. For nearly all his working life he worked for the *Trades Union Congress*, being Assistant General Secretary from 1947 to 1960 and General Secretary from 1960 to 1969 when the trade union movement was near the peak of its influence. He was a respected figure on the right wing of the Labour movement, which made him a natural candidate to chair the Commission on Industrial Relations set up by *Harold Wilson's Labour* government in 1969. He died in 1979.

(See also *trade unions.*)

Woolf, Virginia: novelist. She was born in 1882, the daughter of Leslie Stephen. She became associated with the *Bloomsbury Group* and almost married *Lytton Strachey*. Her writing was 'modern' in that it moved away from conventional narrative style. Her most famous books are 'Mrs Dalloway' (1925), 'To the Lighthouse' (1927) and 'Orlando' (1929). 'A Room of One's Own' (1929) has been claimed as an important contribution to feminist literature. Prone to depression, she committed suicide by drowning in 1941.

woollen industry: for many centuries England's largest and richest industry. Wool production was centred in East Anglia, the western parts of Yorkshire and in the West of England. The supremacy of wool was challenged by the *cotton industry* from the late eighteenth century, which mechanised a little faster, became a factory-based industry somewhat earlier and contributed more to Britain's *overseas trade* during the nineteenth century. Whereas woollens contributed 30 per cent to the value of Britain's exports in the mid-1780s, this proportion had declined to twelve per cent by the mid-1850s.

Woollens, however, remained vital to Britain's economic performance. Much of the industry became concentrated from the early nineteenth century in Yorkshire. 'Worsted' production of long-stapled yard was based around Halifax, and Bradford developed as its commercial centre. 'Woollens', made from shorter fibres than worsteds, were concentrated a little further east, around Leeds and Wakefield. For much of the nineteenth century, the industry prospered and was able to meet the increasingly severe challenges from overseas from the 1880s. The twentieth century has been one of overall decline; this became especially rapid from the 1960s as the market turned increasingly to man-made fibres. The industry was hit hard by the worldwide slump during the inter-war period, although both tariffs and a recovery in the domestic market staved off its worst effects.

(See also *Industrial Revolution*.)

Woolton (Marquis Frederick James), 1st Earl of: businessman and *Conservative* politician. Born in 1883, he was educated at Manchester University. He became Chairman of John Lewis of Liverpool before being given a peerage in 1939 when he was brought into government early in *World War II* by *Neville Chamberlain* as a businessman with a reputation for achievement. His major offices were:

- Director-General of the Ministry of Supply, 1939–40
- Minister for Food, 1940–43
- Minister of Reconstruction 1943–45
- Chairman of the Conservative Party, 1946–55

Woolton was rapidly recognised as an extremely effective minister. He introduced wartime rationing and played a major part in adapting Britain to wartime conditions on the 'Home Front'. After the end of the war, with the *Conservative Party* in opposition, he remodelled its organisation as Chairman and was a major factor in the party's rapid recovery from what had been a shattering defeat in the *general election* of 1945.

(See also *Churchill, Winston*.)

Wordsworth, William: poet. He was born in Cockermouth, on the north-western fringes of the English Lake District in 1770 and lived most of his life in the Lakes, which provided inspiration for his romantic poetry. As a young man, he was involved in the *radical* political movement and supported *parliamentary reform*, but he became much more conservative in both spirit and politics in later life. His most famous poetry is contained in the collection 'Lyrical Ballads' (1798) and 'The Prelude', written over a long period from the beginning of the nineteenth century but not published until 1850, the year of his death. In later life, he was opposed to most physical manifestations of industrial 'progress'.

(See also *Coleridge, Samuel Taylor; Industrial Revolution*.)

Workers' Educational Association: organisation which sought to improve educational opportunities for working men, founded by Albert Mansbridge in Derby in

1903. It worked closely with the *trade unions* and also co-operated with university teachers who offered courses of higher-education standard. Many 'WEAs' became incorporated as 'Adult Education Departments' of *universities*. Among the distinguished academics who worked for the WEA were *R H Tawney* and E P Thompson.

workhouses: institutions where relief was given to many of those applying for *poor relief* and where, for those who were physically fit, work was required. About 2,000 workhouses existed in England and Wales at the beginning of the nineteenth century, but they became much more controversial after the *Poor Law Amendment Act* of 1834. This Act saw workhouses as part of the 'less eligibility' strategy and conditions were to be made deliberately harsh to deter applications for relief. Workhouses were also considered by many to be a less costly way of providing for the poor than 'outdoor relief'. In practice, much more relief (between 75 and 80 per cent of the total expended) continued to be provided in the form of outdoor relief. Partly because of a few highly publicised cases, such as the *Andover Scandal*, workhouses gained a reputation for brutality and inhumanity. This was largely undeserved. Workhouses were dreary, unexciting and uniform. Their heavy, forbidding architecture also symbolised the 'institution'; comparisons with prisons were frequently made. *Richard Oastler* deliberately referred to them as 'Poor Law Bastilles', making a direct comparison with the symbol of oppression in France before the Revolution of 1789. However, they were not places of systematic repression and terror. The 'terror' which the authorities wanted, and to a large extent achieved, was that of shame. Workhouses rapidly entered the public imagination as symbols of degradation and the 'respectable' poor would do almost anything – including resort to *prostitution* – to avoid being put into them. The symbolism continued into the twentieth century, when the Poor Law was gradually dismantled. Ironically, the workhouses themselves were often too solidly built to deserve demolition. Many survived, often as hospitals or other public buildings.

(See also *Malthus, Thomas; Chadwick, Edwin; Senior, Nassau.*)

Workmen's Compensation Acts: legislation which gave working people the right to claim compensation from employers in specific cases. In theory, workers could always take employers to court under common law but this was an expensive and uncertain process in which employers were usually at a large advantage. These Acts enabled workers to pursue their cases more cheaply by arbitration:

- **the 1897 Act** made employers liable to pay compensation to workers for injuries or accidents incurred in factories, mines, *railways* and quarries during the normal course of workers' duties
- **the 1906 Act** extended the scope of the previous Act by:
  - making it applicable across most trades, including merchant shipping, and
  - enabling workers to claim for industrially-related diseases

Further amendments were made, notably in 1925. The *National Insurance Act* of 1946 brought a new 'industrial injuries' scheme into effect giving still greater protection.

(See also *Conservative Party; Liberal Party; trade unions; welfare state.*)

World War I: war, sometimes known as 'The Great War', fought between 1914 and 1918. The war was between two sets of allies:

- Britain, France, Russia and Serbia, later joined by Japan (1914), Italy (1915), Portugal (1916), Romania (1916), the *United States* (1917), and Greece (1917)
- Germany, the Austro-Hungarian Empire, Turkey (1914), Bulgaria (1915) – sometimes known collectively as 'the Central Powers'

Britain's involvement in the war began on 4 August 1914 and ended with an armistice on 11 November 1918.

Causes of the War

1. In the long term, hostility had been building up between the major European powers on a number of fronts: economic (see *Great Depression*), colonial (see *Scramble for Africa; imperialism*), naval (see *dreadnoughts*) and military. In the 1890s and 1900s a number of alliances were signed between them which saw France and Britain edge closer together in the *ententes* while Germany had made alliances with the Austro-Hungarian Empire.

2. The Balkans had been an area of international tension since the 1870s (see *Berlin, Congress of*). The continued weakness of the Turkish Empire gave many opportunities for European states to interfere on behalf of countries wanting full independence and also to further their own strategic interests.

3. In the short term, the assassination of the heir to the Austro-Hungarian Empire, Archduke Franz Ferdinand by a Serbian nationalist on 28 June 1914, gave Austria–Hungary the excuse to declare war on Serbia, activating the alliance systems and leading to general war.

4. Britain's official reason for entering the war was Germany's invasion of neutral Belgium on 3 August 1914, to which Britain had been committed to defending since 1839. In reality, Britain had bigger interests to defend. It was part of the wider alliance system. It also feared German expansionism, which threatened:
   - the balance of power in Europe
   - its colonial empire, particularly in Africa
   - its long-established trade routes to Asia.

5. Though this remains controversial, historians have increasingly come to the view that German long-term planning under Kaiser Wilhelm II involved deliberate aggressive acts in order to make good its claims to great-power status. Germany had been a united nation only since 1871.

Britain's overall strategy in 1914

As with most of the wars fought since the Seven Years' War of 1756–63 (see *French Revolutionary Wars, Napoleonic Wars*) Britain wished to implement a three-pronged strategy; to:

- rely on European Allies to do the bulk of the land fighting against the enemy
- use naval supremacy both as the primary means of defence and also to weaken the enemy by starving it of supplies
- draw on the strength of its *Empire* to achieve supremacy outside Europe

The strategy proved fatally flawed, mainly because the initial strength of the German assault in Western Europe meant that France and Belgium were likely to be over-powered without substantial British involvement. Secondly, it was soon revealed that Britain's naval supremacy (assumed to be absolute since the *Battle of Trafalgar*) was not in practice unchallengeable.

Thus, Britain found itself sucked into a conflict of unparalleled ferocity and carnage, the outcome of which could not be predicted. At the beginning of the war it had 700,000 men under arms.

Theatres of War

Fighting during World War I was very complex. It is helpful to identify the following theatres of war, although British efforts were mostly concentrated on the Western Front and on the War at Sea.

I The Western Front in France and Belgium

1914

August	Germany, using its preconceived 'Schlieffen Plan' for capturing Paris by Christmas 1914, occupied Brussels and forced the Allies to retreat from Mons
September	Allies halted German advance at the first *Battle of Marne*
October	Germans captured Antwerp, Ghent and Lille
Oct–Nov	at first *Battle of Ypres*, German advance finally halted. Both sides 'dug in' in their positions in northern France and Belgium, protecting positions by trenches and barbed warfare. 'Trench warfare' began, along a line stretching from the Channel north-east of Dunkirk to the Swiss border

1915

January	heavy fighting at Soissons (Belgium)
March	Britain launched an offensive at Neuve Chapelle
April–May	Second Battle of Ypres
June	Allies captured Neuville
September	French offensive at Champagne was repulsed by the French

1916

January	first German 'Zeppelin' air raid on Paris
Feb–Dec	major battle at Verdun on the River Meuse: 650,000 soldiers killed in first four months
July	*Battle of the Somme* began in a major Anglo-French offensive. 20,000 British troops killed on 1 July, the first day of the battle
December	new British and French offensive on the Meuse

1917

March	some German withdrawals: Allies captured Bapaume and Péronne
April	Battle of Arras saw significant British advance, but Germans halted a French advance in Battle of the Aisne
May	British troops broke through German positions at Arras – the 'Hindenburg line'

Main Battles
1914 Oct–November *First Ypres* German gains
1915 March *Neuve Chapelle* British gains
1915 April–May *Second Ypres* British gains
1915 September *Loos* British gains
1916 July–November *Somme* British gains
1917 April *Vimy Ridge* Canadian gains
1917 April–May *Arras* British gains
1917 June *Messines* British gains
1917 July–October *Third Ypres* British gains
1917 November *Passchendaele* British gains
1917 November *Cambrai* British gains
1917 March–April *Kemmel* German gains
Somme German gains

A million British and Empire soldiers died and three million were wounded in the shaded areas shown on this map

Ostend

BELGIUM

Dunkirk

BELGIAN ARMY   **FLANDERS**

Passchendaele

Calais

NORTHERN BOUNDARY BRITISH EXPEDITIONARY FORCE

Ypres

Zonnebeke
Menin

Cassel

Kemmel

Wytschaete
Messines

St. Omer

Bailleul

Hazebrouck

Plogsteert

Boulogne

Armentieres
Bois Grenier

Lille

1914–15 Sir John French's headquarters

Neuve Chapelle   Aubers

Commanders-in-Chief
1914–15 Sir John French
1915–18 Sir Douglas Haig

Lillers

Béthune

FRANCE

Loos

Lens

Etaples

Montreuil

St. Pol

Vimy Ridge

1916–18 Sir Douglas Haig's headquarters

Arras

Cambrai

Le Crotoy

St Valery

Doullens

Bapaume

Thiepval

Abbeville

Albert

Headquarters of British lines of communication

River Somme

Péronne

SOUTHERN BOUNDARY BRITISH EXPEDITIONARY FORCE   Amiens **FRENCH ARMY**

0   10
Miles

The Empire forces included Indians, South Africans, Canadians, Australians and New Zealanders. Manual labour behind the lines was also done by the Chinese Labour Corps and the South African Native Labour Corps.

═══ Trench line by October 1914
▓ British gains
▓ German gains
△ Main hospital areas

The Western Front in World War I

July–Dec	Third Battle of Ypres (Passchendaele) gained five miles, but 35,000 British troops killed
Aug–Dec	French troops gained some territory in second Battle of Verdun
November	First US troops, under General Pershing, arrived on Western Front

1918

Mar–July	major German offensives in second Battle of the Somme and in Battle of the Lys. They made advances of about 40 miles, capturing Soissons. They were able to shell Paris from a distance of only 75 miles. However, key fortifications at Ypres, Arras and Amiens did not fall and the Allied lines held. 800,000 German casualties
July	Allied counter-offensive began; Marne crossed
August	Soissons recaptured by the French
September	German forces thrust back to Antwerp-Metz railway link
October	Cambrai, Le Cateau and Lille captured by the British
November	armistice terms agreed on 4th and signed on the 11th

2 The Eastern Front

1914

August	Russians advanced into East Prussia, but defeated by Germany at Battle of Tannenburg
September	German victory at Masurian Lakes drove Russians back from Prussia
October	battle for Warsaw: Germans forced to retreat from Poland
December	further German advance captures Lodz

1915

Feb–Oct	Austro-German attacks gained territory in western Russia
March	Russians captured Przrmysl (Poland)
April	German offensive in Courland and Lithuania began
June	Russian southern front in Poland destroyed and Przrmysl recaptured by Germans
August	Germans captured Warsaw and Brest-Litovsk
September	Germans captured Vilna

1916

January	Russians began an offensive in Galicia
June–Oct	Russian General Brusilov began a counter-offensive against Austro-Hungarian troops. It had immediate success, destroying much of the enemy army but German troops were withdrawn from France and halted the offensive

1917

March	after fall of Tsarist government, Russian provisional government guaranteed the independence of Poland
June	Russian Black Sea Fleet mutinied
July	Russians mounted a final offensive, capturing territory from Austria–Hungary around Stanislau. Russians could not continue the offensive after thousands of troops mutinied or deserted

August	Germans captured Czernowitz and began an attack on Riga
September	Germans captured the Latvian capital of Riga

1918

February	German offensive began on the Russian front and Ukraine signed peace with Germany
March	Germans occupied Kiev and Narva. Russians agreed to peace at Brest-Litovsk

3 The Southern Front, including the Balkans and Romania

1914

September	Russians invaded Hungary
December	Austrians captured Belgrade, but it was quickly recaptured by Serbia

1915

October	Austro-German troops captured Belgrade

1916

August	Romania declared war on Austria–Hungary and attacked Transylvania
December	Germans under Falkenhayn captured Bucharest

1918

May	Germans occupied Sebastopol; Romania signed peace with Central Powers
September	Allied forces made decisive break-through in Bulgaria, forcing Bulgaria to make peace with the Allies

4 The Turkish fronts, including the Dardanelles and North Africa and the Middle East

1915

February	Turkish attack on *Suez canal* rebuffed; British and French fleets bombarded Dardanelles
April	Anglo-French forces landed at Gallipoli but failed to achieve objectives
September	Turkish force defeated by British at Kut-el-Amara (Mesopotamia)

1916

January	British troops finally withdrew from Dardanelles
April	Turks captured Kut-el-Amara
June	Arab revolts against Turkey began in Hedjaz on the Red Sea. These were supported by the Allies
October	Allies occupied Athens

1917

January	Britain, France and Italy recognised independent Arab kingdom of Hedjaz
March	British army captured Baghdad and defeated Turks at Gaza
April	Turkish–German force repulsed the British at Gaza
November	Britain captured Gaza
December	General *Allenby* captured Jerusalem

The horror of the trenches of World War I

1918

March	Turks occupied Baku
September	Turkey abandoned Palestine to the British
November	Anglo-French forces recaptured Constantinople

5 The War at sea

1915

February	Germans began blockade of Britain, backed up by submarine warfare
March	British counter-blockade of Germany began
May	US vessel 'Gulflight' sunk by German submarines; 'Lusitania' sunk by Germans – many US lives lost and *United States* almost joined the war

1916

May	*Battle of Jutland* between British and German fleets
June	HMS 'Hampshire' sunk by Germans, General *Kitchener* killed

1917

January	Germany announced policy of unrestricted warfare to include sinking of neutral vessels
May–Dec	500 British merchant vessels sunk, jeopardising British chances of continuing the war
June	'Convoy system' introduced by Britain; more than 16,000 merchant vessels were protected by cruisers, destroyers and torpedo boats. This drastically reduced merchant shipping casualties

1918

October	Germany suspended submarine warfare
November	German fleet mutinied at Kiel

The sea war was extremely damaging. German submarines sank more than eleven million tons of Allied shipping, more than three-quarters of it British. Five-hundred merchant ships were sunk by the Germans from May to December 1917 alone.

The war overall was unprecedentedly costly. About 900,000 troops from Britain and its *Empire* were killed and 2 million were wounded. France had 1.4 million killed and 2.5 million wounded. Germany had 1.6 million killed and 4.2 million wounded. Overall casualties numbered more than 16 million.

(See also *League of Nations; Sevres, Treaty of; Trianon, Treaty of; Versailles, Treaty of*)

World War II: war fought between:

- Britain and its major Allies; France (conquered in 1940), the USSR (after being attacked by Germany in 1941), and the United States (after being attacked by Japan in 1941)
- Germany and its major allies; Italy (1940–43) – sometimes called 'the Axis Powers' and Japan (from 1941). From 1940 to 1944, also, Germany was in control of most of west and central Europe and could draw on their resources to fight the war

This was the first truly world war but some historians have cautioned against its being seen as just one conflict. The war which broke out between the United States and Japan in December 1941 had quite different causes from those which led Britain to declare war on Germany on 3 September 1939. Britain's involvement in the war with Germany in Europe lasted until 8 May 1945 (so-called VE – Victory in Europe – day) and with Japan until the latter's surrender on 15 August 1945 (so-called VJ – Victory in Japan – day).

Causes of the War

1 In the long term, many Germans had never accepted the legitimacy of the *Treaty of Versailles* and especially its harsh treatment of the country. Though much else was involved, frustration and anger with the post-*World War I* peace settlements were major factors in the rise to power in Germany of Adolf Hitler in January 1933 and, thus, of what followed from his policies.

2 Hitler's policy of reversing the Versailles settlement led to various challenges to Britain, France and the *League of Nations*. Hitler was not met with force in 1936 when he marched into the Rhineland, an area which had been demilitarised by the Treaty of Versailles. Many historians have argued that the policy of *appeasement* was a direct cause of World War II since it encouraged Hitler to believe that he could continue his aggressive policies without any effective response.

3 Hitler's expansion within Europe had involved the takeover of Austria in 1938 (the 'Anschluss'), followed by peaceful entry into Sudetenland after the agreement made at *Munich* in the autumn of 1938. This was followed, however, by further aggression. German troops marched into northern Czechoslovakia in March 1939, thus showing the futility of the Munich settlement. Britain and France were now convinced that they could not tolerate any further aggression by a leader who seemed hell-bent on domination of the European mainland, if not complete world power. Thus,

they agreed to defend Poland, if and when Hitler should seek to occupy it as the next stage of his expansionist programme based on destroying the Versailles settlement. Meanwhile Hitler signed a non-aggression agreement with Soviet Russia – the Ribbentrop–Molotov Pact – in August 1939.

4 German troops marched into Poland on 1 November 1939. Britain sent an ultimatum requiring the Germans to withdraw. When this was ignored, Britain declared war on Germany.

5 In 1941, Japan (having had important victories in a war against China which had begun in 1937) was looking to expand further. The *United States*, fearing for its influence in the Pacific, banned exports of oil and iron to Japan. Japan launched a series of attacks against British, US and Dutch territories in the Pacific. That on Pearl Harbor on 7 December brought the US into the war in alliance with Britain.

Main events of the War

1939

September	German troops defeated Poland, which was divided between Germany and the USSR
November	German U-boats launched successful attacks on British shipping

1940

February	Finland, threatened with annihilation, signed a peace treaty with Germany
April	Norway and Denmark attacked by Germany. British naval assistance ineffective
May	Belgium, Holland and Luxemburg invaded by Germany. Invasion of France began. British forces evacuated from *Dunkirk*
June	France surrendered and was governed by a 'puppet administration' – the 'Vichy Government'; Russians occupied Lithuania, Latvia and Estonia; Italy declared war on Britain, leading directly to war in the Italian colony of Libya in North Africa
July	*Battle of Britain* began
August	air raids on London began the *Blitz* (to 1941); Italians attacked British Somaliland from Abyssinia, forcing British withdrawal
October	Britain sent troops to Greece to support them against attack from Italy

1941

January	British counter-attacked in North Africa captured territory in Sudan and Eritrea
February	*Wavell's* army captured Benghazi; British troops invaded Italian Somaliland
March	British troops invaded Abyssinia; German troops in North Africa began counter-offensive
April	more British troops sent to Greece following a German ultimatum, but were forced to quit by German troops
May	Germans invaded Crete
June	British troops invaded Syria in attempt to defend Middle East against the Axis powers

	Germany invaded USSR, changing the focus of the war utterly
July	treaty of mutual assistance between Britain and the USSR signed
August	British and Russian troops invaded Iran
September	Germans captured Kiev
October	German attack on Moscow began, but failed to capture either it or Leningrad, despite commitment of huge resources
December	Britain and US declared war on Japan; US declared war on Italy and Germany; German commander Rommel retreated in face of Allied troops in North Africa; Japanese captured Hong Kong

1942

January	Japanese captured Kuala Lumpur and invaded *Burma*
February	British forces in Malaya retreated to *Singapore,* but Singapore quickly surrendered to Japanese. Japanese forced British withdrawal from Burma; Japanese landings on Java. In the Battle of the Java Sea, eleven of the fourteen Allied ships were lost and one Japanese
May	Rommel resumed attack in North Africa; Phillipines captured by Japanese
June	Japanese captured Mandalay (Burma); US–Japanese battle in Midway Islands (Pacific). Actual fighting at Midway was inconclusive but this battle ended Japanese naval supremacy in the Pacific
July	Rommel captured Tobruk, forcing British Eighth Army to retreat to El Alamein
October	*Battle of El Alamein* began, resulting in British success and recapture of Tobruk
November	Russian counter-offensive encircled German army in the east
December	British and Indian troops began offensive in Burma against Japanese; British Eighth Army recaptured Benghazi

1943

January	Germany began retreat from Caucasus. German commander von Paulus surrendered at Stalingrad; Eighth Army entered Tripoli. US had air and naval control of the Pacific and used it in 'island hopping', by which it landed on, and captured, whichever islands it wished, leaving those more strongly defended by the Japanese without supplies. This process proved very successful
March	heavy German attacks on Eighth army in Tunisia but these were repulsed
May	German army in Tunisia surrendered and Axis powers were effectively defeated in North Africa
July	new German offensive on Russian front; Allied attacks on Italy began in earnest with bombing of Rome. Italian dictator Mussolini fell from power
September	invasion of Italy began and enjoyed rapid success
October	in effect defeated by US and British troops, Italy declared war on Germany, but German troops there continued to resist fiercely

1944

January	Fifth Army launched attack on Germans east of Cassino
February	*Battle of Ánzio*
March	heavy Allied attacks on Monte Cassino
April	advancing Russians entered Romania; heavy Allied bombing of German cities began
May	Allies finally crushed German resistance in Italy
June	*D-Day* landings secured a bridgehead against Germany in Western Europe and began the last stage of the war; Battle of the Philippine Sea won by the US which could now attack Japan directly
July	Russians, after long and bitter campaigns against Germans, finally crossed into Poland
August	Eighth Army captured Florence (Italy); Russians captured Bucharest, capital of Romania and began invasion of Yugoslavia
September	liberation of Brussels (Belgium); unsuccessful Allied assault at *Arnhem*
October	US troops recaptured the Philippines after the Battle of Leyte Gulf; Russian troops invaded Hungary
November	Allies captured Strasbourg as they closed on German territory itself
December	*Battle of the Bulge* began

1945

January	new British offensive in Burma began; Russians reached the Oder and threatened German territory from the east
February	Russians captured Budapest and took Hungary; US invasion of Iwo Jima
March	Allied troops captured Cologne; British Fourteenth Army entered Mandalay (Burma); Russians crossed into Austria
April	US invasion of Okinawa began; US naval victory over Japanese at Kiyushu; Russian troops reached Berlin; US and USSR troops met up, effectively ending German resistance; Hitler committed suicide
May	formal German surrender; Russians captured Prague (Czechoslovakia)
June	Okinawa captured by the US
August	USSR declared war on Japan and invaded; US atomic bombs dropped on Hiroshima and Nagasaki; Japan surrendered, formally ending the war

Casualties among both combatants and civilians were immense. Weapons of destruction were more sophisticated, and in much wider use, than during World War I. The Nazi government murdered about six million Jews, most of them in concentration camps in Poland, in its crazed attempt to find its 'final solution' to the Jewish problem. In all, about fifteen million soldiers, sailors and airmen were killed and about 35 million civilians.

(See also *Chamberlain, Neville; Churchill, Winston; United Nations; Yalta Conference.*)

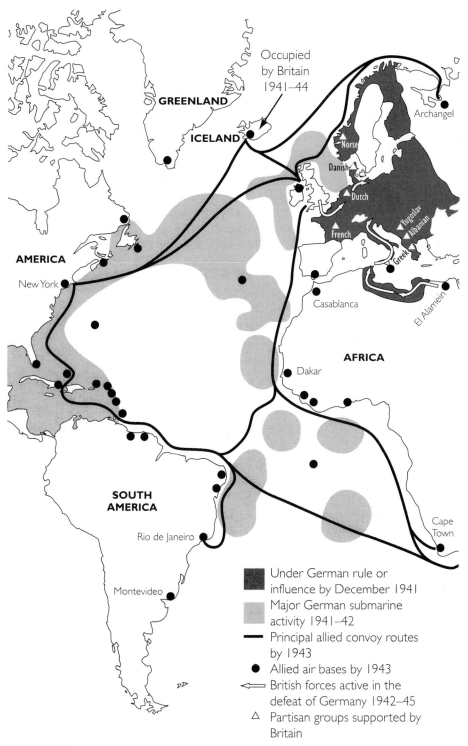

GREENLAND

Occupied
by Britain
1941–44

ICELAND

Archangel

Norse

Danish

Dutch

AMERICA

French

Yugoslav
Albanian

New York

Greek

Casablanca

El Alamein

AFRICA

Dakar

SOUTH
AMERICA

Cape
Town

Rio de Janeiro

Montevideo

◼ Under German rule or
influence by December 1941

▨ Major German submarine
activity 1941–42

━ Principal allied convoy routes
by 1943

● Allied air bases by 1943

⇐ British forces active in the
defeat of Germany 1942–45

△ Partisan groups supported by
Britain

World War II

Y

Yalta Conference: meeting in February 1945 of the three Allied leaders, *Winston Churchill*, F D Roosevelt and Joseph Stalin to determine the conditions on which peace could be established after the end of *World War II*. It proved particularly valuable to the Soviet Union and largely determined the shape of post-war Europe. By it, the Allies agreed:

- that only unconditional surrender by Germany would be acceptable
- the Allies would establish some kind of occupation over Germany but the details were left for further consideration
- Churchill and Roosevelt agreed that the Soviet Union should retain buffer states to protect it from any future attack from Germany. This became the warrant for the Soviet Union to establish communist regimes throughout most of eastern Europe
- the Soviet Union agreed to join the new *United Nations* and also to attack Japan after Germany had surrendered

Young England: romantic political movement of the 1840s formed by young *Tories* in opposition to the government of *Sir Robert Peel*. Its leading lights were Lord John Manners, George Smythe and, most famously, *Benjamin Disraeli*. It had no coherent ideology but was generally backward-looking and 'anti-modern', being fearful of the changes being wrought by the *Industrial Revolution*. It supported *aristocracy*, the way of life of the rural Englishmen and 'paternalism', whereby the wealthy acknowledged an obligation to care for the interests of the poor. It opposed the *Anti-Corn Law League* as an organisation of grasping businessmen and championed the cause of the urban poor. Disraeli's famous assertion in the novel 'Coningsby' (1844) that England was 'two nations' – the rich and the poor – comes directly from his Young England beliefs.

(See also *Conservative Party*.)

Young Ireland: political movement supporting Irish nationalism. It was founded in 1841 in opposition to the tactics of *Daniel O'Connell* and his 'Repeal Association'. It appealed to a more romantic strain of nationalism which it developed in a new journal 'The Nation', founded in 1842. Its leaders were Charles Gavan Duffy, the first editor of 'The Nation', Thomas Davis and John Dillon. The movement split from O'Connell irrevocably in 1846 on the issue of violence. Its leaders began to plan a rebellion against Britain, forming the 'Irish Confederation' in 1847 to co-ordinate action. A small and ineffective attempt was made in August after which the movement was in retreat, although its newspaper survived to become an important voice in the nineteenth-century struggle for independence.

(See also *Ireland; Home Rule; Roman Catholicism*.)

Young Men's Christian Association (YMCA): organisation to spread the message of Christianity, formed in 1844 by the *evangelical* George Williams. Its first president was the *Earl of Shaftesbury*. It became an international organisation in the mid-1850s and has concentrated on charitable work, though it is best remembered for the clean, cheap hostels in which men could lodge. The YMCA was particularly active in providing social services and charitable support during both *world wars*. The sister organisation, Young Women's Christian Association (YWCA), was founded in 1855 by Emma Robarts and Emily Kinnaird.

'You've never had it so good': political slogan, in widespread use during the *general election* of 1959. It described the rapidly increasing living standards enjoyed under the *Conservatives* in the 1950s. Like so many famous political quotations, it is in fact something of misquotation, adapted by the press in the interests of a good headline. The actual phrase used by the then *Prime Minister, Harold Macmillan,* in a speech at a party rally in Bedford in July 1957 more than two years before the election was: 'Let us be frank about it; most of our people have never had it so good'.

Ypres, Battles of: three battles fought in Belgium on the Western Front during *World War I.*

- October to November 1914: here the *British Expeditionary Force* was mostly destroyed in attempting to defend the town against heavy German bombardment
- April to May 1915: another German attack produced some success and withdrawal by French, British and Canadian troops
- July to November 1917: see *Passchendaele, Battle of* (its better-known name)

(See also *Haig, Douglas.*)

Zinoviev letter: perhaps a forgery, this letter had considerable impact on the outcome of the *general election* held on 29 October 1924. It was supposed to have been sent from Grigori Zinoviev to the British *Communist Party* urging it to make efforts to destabilise the British state. It was published in the press in October 1924 and was used by editors to suggest both that communism was a real danger to the stability of the British state and that the *Conservative Party* was the best safeguard against this threat. *Ramsay MacDonald*'s minority *Labour* government, in power since January 1924, had recognised the Soviet regime and this letter was used to suggest that Labour sympathies were, in reality, much more Bolshevik than the party liked to pretend. It is possible that the letter was deliberately leaked by British intelligence officers wishing the damage the Labour government.

ON THE LOAN TRAIL.

[In a document just disclosed by the British Foreign Office (apparently after considerable delay), M. ZINOVIEFF, a memb of the Bolshevist Dictatorship, urges the British Communist Party to use "the greatest possible energy" in securing the ratificatio of Mr. MacDonald's Anglo-Russian Treaty, in order to facilitate a scheme for "an armed insurrection" of the British proletariat.

Cartoon showing how many in the British press suggested, during the 1924 election campaign, that the Labour Party was just a front for communism

Zionism: militant movement in support of a separate homeland for the *Jews* in *Palestine*. It began among Russians exiled from their homeland in the 1880s. By 1914, almost 100,000 Jews were living in Palestine which was then part of the Turkish Empire. Britain considered that a Jewish homeland would be valuable to them since a friendly Jewish state might be useful in defence of the *Suez Canal*. Palestine became a British mandated territory under the *League of Nations* in 1922. British insistence that the creation of a Jewish state should not jeopardise the interests of Arabs living in Palestine caused much resentment among Zionists, especially after substantial immigration to Palestine by Jews fleeing from Hitler and the Nazis. During and after *World War II*, Zionist terrorist groups attacked the British because of their alleged support for Arab interests.

Zulu War, 1879: war between Britain and the Zulu peoples of southern Africa. It occurred after the discovery of diamonds in Transvaal in 1877. The policy of the *Conservative* colonial secretary, the Earl of Carnarvon, was to unite British colonies and Boer republics in a united '*South Africa*' to give settlers greater security. In 1878, the British required the Zulu King, Cetewayo, to disband his troops, since they constituted a threat to stability in the region. The Zulus, who had so far resisted conflict, now considered themselves threatened by crude provocation and declared war. The main incidents in the war were:

January	Zulu attack on the British army at Isalandwhana, virtually annihilating it
January	at Rorke's Drift, a small missionary station, British forces held out against a hugely superior Zulu force
March	at Nkambule, the Zulu force was overwhelmed by fresh British troops
July	Zulu capital of Ulundi captured by the British, ending the war

In the short term, Cetewayo was forced into exile and his lands divided among thirteen rival chiefs. By 1881, however, the Boers had asserted rights over parts of Zululand and the British incorporated the rest into the colony of Natal.

ANSWERING HISTORY QUESTIONS IN AN EXAMINATION

It is obviously vital to know the content of any history course you are studying but unless you can answer the questions which come up in an examination then much of your learning will have been in vain. The section which follows gives you useful tips, but the most important of all is that you should know *exactly* what will be required of you in the examination. You should know what syllabus you are entered for and what its demands are. You can readily get copies both of the syllabus and of past examination papers from the examination group. Ask your teacher which this is and make sure that you are directed to the right parts of the syllabus and to past papers. When you have seen past papers, you will know what to expect and you can face the examination with more confidence.

In history examinations, most questions are of one of two types: **document questions** and **essays**. Document questions are of different types depending on the examination group, and the syllabus for which you are entered. It is doubly important here to know what kinds of question you will be answering.

Specific hints on answering source questions

1 Most source questions are designed to test your understanding of the material you are given. Very often this understanding will link to your own knowledge. You must get practice in tackling questions with a particular focus or emphasis.

2 When you see a phrase like 'According to Document I … ', you should see that you have all that you need to answer the question from the document itself. Such questions are testing the skill of **comprehension**: can you understand what the document says? Can you put it in your own words? Can you use the information?

3 When you see a phrase like 'What can you tell from Document II?', you are being asked to draw conclusions from the document. The skill being tested is **inference**: can you work out a conclusion from material you are given in the examination? This is not the same skill as comprehension. You do need to understand what you are reading but you also have to work out (or 'infer') an attitude or position. You are being asked to 'read between the lines'.

4 Sometimes you are asked to make use of two, or more, documents. You are being asked to make an **analysis**. Can you work on different materials together and reach a conclusion?

5 When you are asked 'in what ways' the sources 'help to explain' something, you will still be working with the documents in the question but notice the word 'help'. It should suggest that your answer can be linked to your wider knowledge and understanding.

6 Sometimes you are asked 'how useful' the documents are for explaining a particular question or issue. The skill being tested here is called **source utility**: can you explain why sources are useful for a particular topic, explaining at the same time *in what ways* they are useful? Remember that

the information given about the sources – its 'provenance' – is useful here. You will be told that a document is of a particular type and you should use this information in your answer.

7 Most source questions end with a more general question which asks you to make an **historical judgement** based on your understanding of the documents in the question and also on your own knowledge. You will need plenty of practice at answering questions of this type. Remember that you will be expected to use *both* the sources *and* your own knowledge. You will have to *select* information very carefully.

8 Always read your documents *slowly* and *carefully* at first to make sure that you understand them. When you start doing this, you may find the language unfamiliar. Again, the answer is practice. You will gain confidence with experience and practice. You need to know how to 'get inside' the period you are studying. Make yourself familiar with the sources from the period you are studying. Don't lose heart when some words, or phrases, are unfamiliar. Ask your teacher; use a dictionary; keep plugging away. It all gets much easier with experience.

9 In answering document questions, you will almost certainly be asked not only to show understanding but also to draw conclusions. You may also be asked to comment on *how* the writer, speaker, cartoonist or artist is putting the message across.

10 Each sub-question will carry a maximum mark. The number of marks available is powerful clue about how much to write. In many examinations, the number of marks 'builds up' so that the last question is worth most. Make sure that you have arranged your time for the questions so that you leave plenty of time for the question with most marks.

11 Remember that in examinations, most candidates get more marks on document questions than on essays. You can do yourself a lot of good by remembering the basic rules relating to document questions. Marks can build up very nicely. But if you don't know the 'rules' of the question you risk throwing away marks where they can be easiest to gain.

Specific hints on answering essay questions

Essays are set in nearly all examinations. You need to develop skills in essay writing. Examiners frequently report that too many students go into their examinations uncertain about how to plan and write essays. The following tips should help you.

1 Examiners are always more interested in finding out how well you can direct your answer to the specific title of the essay than in weighing the amount of knowledge you might have. Only decide on a question when you are absolutely sure that you understand its focus. Sometimes an essay on a topic about which you know a little less may offer you a better focus than one on a topic which is very familiar but whose specific focus may be unfamiliar.

2 Remember the key word 'focus'.
   – If you are asked to focus on 'why' something happened, you are being asked a 'cause' question. Focus your answer on explanation of cause, not on telling the story.

- If you are asked 'how important' something is, you are being asked to make an historical judgement, which might be concerned with the importance of an individual, a specific event, or a set of circumstances. Again, tailor your answer accordingly.

- Examiners often use words like 'comment on' or 'discuss'. This is code for asking you what you think. You are being asked to provide an opinion about an individual, issue or event and to justify your opinion by selecting appropriate information from your own knowledge.

- Examiners also like making up quotations and asking you to 'comment', 'discuss' or to say 'how far you agree' with the statement. These quotations will often give part of the truth but not all of it. Perhaps the quotation may give an exaggerated view. Remember that the examiner will expect your view. It's not a bad idea to show that you understand that the opinion may be exaggerated as well as having some truth. 'Discuss' is an invitation to agree, or disagree but with properly selected information.

3 In answering questions, remember that there will be key words which always require you to pay them attention. If, for example, you are asked a questions such as 'How far do you agree that Disraeli's domestic policy in the years 1874–80 promised much but achieved little?', then you will obviously *select* the question on the basis of whether you know about Disraeli's domestic policy in these years. But you will get best marks if you comment on key words such as 'promise' – what *did* Disraeli promise? – and 'achieved' – did Disraeli's domestic policies actually *work*?

The key words will have been deliberately chosen by your examiner to provide you with a focus. Unless you can say something about each of them, you should probably looking for another question.

Planning an answer

You should certainly consider doing a **plan** of the essay you write. Why? It will help you to clarify the focus of an essay and then to carry it through. A well-planned essay will have organisation: it will be coherent, logical and will argue a case. It won't be as long as the example here, because this one plays with a number of ideas but it *will* help you focus your answer.

Most essays will have three identifiable elements. Each has a separate function. A useful plan might comprise:

1 an **introduction**: the purpose here is to not to offer general opening comments or to provide a lot of information you think you might forget later on. It has a precise function. The introduction should ideally show your examiner that you know what the main point of the question is. You might also want to offer a specific comment on one of the key words. From the example above you might say that Disraeli said a lot about the condition of the people before he came into office in 1874. He had therefore 'promised' things. The introduction should not be very substantial. A couple of paragraphs is usually ample.

2 a **main section**: this should be the longest of the three, comprising about three-quarters of the essay as a whole. Here you develop the main points you want to make. Remember to back up each point with specific information. An argument in history is only valid if it is supported by specific information or evidence. Don't rely on generalisation. In planning for this part of the essay, you should say something specific about *each* of the key words, thus showing that you are trying to meet the full demands of the question.

3 a **conclusion**: here you draw the threads together. Don't repeat yourself; there is not time. However, it is useful to show how the specific points made in the middle section lead to an overall conclusion. In the question above, you might want to argue that Disraeli seemed to offer plenty to help working people but, especially after 1875, he actually produced rather little. Much of what he did produce only consolidated what Gladstone had begun during his administration of 1868–74. You should actually 'conclude'. It's better to reach a definite judgement, even though you might usefully recognise that there are things to say on the other side of the case. Remember, history essays are about **argument** and **judgement** on the basis of evidence about the past, sensibly and appropriately selected. The conclusion should not be long. It might be a bit longer than the introduction, but three paragraphs will usually be plenty.

Some common questions about essays answered

- **How long?** Since essays normally have to be written in time varying between 45 minutes and an hour, they are not expected to be long. You will be judged on quality – especially relevance – and not on length. Remember, though, that it is difficult to sustain a logical structure throughout a very long essay. Three or four sides of average-sized writing is usually enough.

- **Should I spend the same amount of time on each essay?** Broadly, yes. Examiners will be instructed not to make any allowance for a very much weaker, or shorter, final answer on a paper. To do so would be unfair to other candidates who have taken the trouble to organise their time properly. Don't think that because you have made three good answers you can coast through the final one. If the questions have equal marks you should give them equal weight.

- **Do I use quotations?** Yes, but do beware. Before you use them, think of the checklist:
  - Can you remember the quote properly? Examiners may know the quotation anyway. If they don't, they may still check!
  - Can you say you made the quotation? Attributing one to the wrong historical figure – or the wrong historian – creates a worse impression than not using it.
  - Can you *use* your quotation sensibly? Far too many candidates drag quotations in for no better reason than that they have remembered them. There's no special merit in using a quotation which everyone else in your school or college will be using. Some hackneyed quotations are best avoided. Certainly many students place too much importance on

quotations. Good quotations might make an already good essay a bit better; they won't make a poor one good.

- **Should I write the question out before I start?** No; time is short and this is a waste of precious commodity. The examiner will have the question paper.
- **If the examiner doesn't agree with me, will I lose marks?** No. Examiners are instructed not to let their personal views affect their judgement. If you offer a plausible argument backed up with well-selected evidence, you will be given high credit. History essays are all about presenting a good argument; there are no *right* answers at this level.

SUBJECT INDEX

1 Parties, politics and political leaders 1780–1867

child labour
class consciousness
Coleridge, Samuel Taylor
cotton industry
Dickens, Charles
Engels, Friedrich
engineering industry
entrepreneurs
Factory Acts
Fielden, John
free trade
gas industry
Gaskell, Elizabeth
'Great Depression'
Great Exhibition
Gross Domestic Product
handloom weavers
high farming
Highland clearances
Hudson, George
Industrial Revolution
iron industry
labour aristocracy
leisure
Limited Liabilities Act, 1855
Luddites
'Manchester School'
Marxism
mechanics' institutes
middle classes
Mines Act, 1842
Morris, William
Morris, William (1st Viscount Nuffield)
Nasmyth, James
navvies
paternalism
Peel, Sir Robert, Senr
power loom
Railways
retailing industry
Ruskin, John
Sadler, Michael Thomas
Salt, Titus
Shaftesbury (Anthony Ashley Cooper,
    (Lord Ashley)), 7th Earl of
shipping industry
shops; see *retailing industry*
slave trade, abolition of (1807)
spinning jenny
staple industries
steam power

steamships
steel industry
Stephenson, George
Stephenson, Robert
sweated labour
Telford, Thomas
tourist industry
trade, overseas
Trevithick, Richard
typhus
water frame
water power
Watt, James
woollen industry

4 19th-century social and religious history

Agricultural Gangs Act, 1867
Andover Scandal
Arnold, Matthew
Artisans' and Labourers' Dwellings Act,
    1875
Barnardo, Thomas
Barnett, Samuel
Bentham, Jeremy
birth control
Booth, Charles
Booth, William
Bradlaugh, Charles
building societies
Carlyle, Thomas
Carpenter, Mary
census
Chadwick, Edwin
Charity Organisation Society
child labour
cholera
Church of England
Contagious Diseases Acts
contraception; see *birth control*
Dickens, Charles
diet
divorce laws
emigration
Employers' Liability Act, 1880
Engels, Friedrich
Episcopal Church (Scotland)
evangelicanism
Factory Acts
Free Church, Scotland

5 British foreign policy and international relations, 1783–1830

Queenston Heights, Battle of (1812)
Raffles, Sir Stamford
Raglan (Fitzroy, James Henry Somerset)
Singapore
slave trade, abolition of (1807)
slavery, abolition of (1833)
Spithead Mutiny; see *Naval Mutinies*
theatre of war
Tory Party
United States of America, British
   relations with
Vansittart, Nicholas (Lord Bexley)
Vienna, Congress of (1814–15)
Walcheren expedition
Waterloo, Battle of
Wellesley, Richard
Wellington (Wellesley, Arthur) 1st
   Duke of

6 Party politics and political leaders, 1867–1918

Addison, Christopher
aristocracy
Asquith, Herbert Henry
Balfour, Arthur
Barings Bank
Bonar Law, Andrew
Bradlaugh, Charles
Bright, John
Burns, John
Burt, Thomas
Campbell-Bannerman, Henry
Cardwell, Edward
Cecil, Robert Gascoyne; see *Salisbury,
   3rd Marquess of*
Chamberlain, Austen
Chamberlain, Joseph
Churchill, Winston Spencer
Churchill, Randolph
Commons, House of
Conservative Party
Corrupt and Illegal Practices Act, 1883
county boroughs
county councils
coupon election
Curzon, George Nathaniel
Derby, Edward Stanley
Devonshire, Spencer Cavendish
Dilke, Sir Charles
Disraeli, Benjamin

Edward VII
'first past the post'
George V
Gladstone, William Ewart
Grey, Sir Edward
Haldane (Richard), 1st Viscount
Halifax, Edward Wood
Harcourt, Sir William
Hardie, James Keir
Henderson, Arthur
Hobhouse, Leonard Trelawny
Independent Labour Party
India
Isaacs, Rufus
Jameson Raid
Jellicoe, John (1st Earl Jellicoe)
Khaki election, 1900
Labour Party
Labour Representation Committee
Lansdowne (Henry), 5th Marquess
Liberal Party
Liberal Unionists
Lib–Labs
Licensing Act, 1872
Lloyd George, David
local government
London County Council
Lords, House of
MacDonald, James Ramsay
Marxism
MI5
MI6
Milner, Alfred (Viscount)
monarchy
Morrison, Herbert
Munitions, Ministry of
Newcastle Programme
Northcote, Sir Stafford (1st Earl of
   Iddesleigh)
Old Age Pensions Act, 1908
Osborne Judgement, 1909
Parish Councils Act, 1894
Parliament Act, 1911
Parliament, English
Parnell, Charles Stewart
pluralism
poll books
Poor Laws
Poor Laws, Royal Commission on
   (1905–9)
Prime Minister, Office of

7 Trade unions and class relations, 1780–1914

8 British foreign policy and international relations, 1830–80

9 The political, economic and social roles of women

subject index

Monte-Cassino, Battle of (1943–44)
Montgomery, Bernard (Viscount
   Montgomery of Alamein)
Munitions, Ministry of
National Service
National Unemployed Workers'
   Movement
'Overlord', Operation
Owen, Wilfred
Passchendaele, Battle of (1917)
Phoney War
Quebec Conferences, 1943–4
reparations
Russell, Bertrand
'Sealion', Operation
Second World War; see *World War II*
shipping industry
Slim, William (Viscount Slim of
   Yarralumba)
Somme, Battle of the (1916)
Sykes–Picot Agreement, 1916
Tedder, Sir Arthur
theatre of war
Tippett, Sir Michael
Trenchard, Hugh (1st Viscount
   Trenchard)
V1 and V2
war poetry
World War I
World War II
Ypres, Battles of (1914, 1915, 1917)

12 Ireland

Anglo-Irish Treaty, 1921
Black and Tans
Bloody Sunday, 30 January, 1972
B-specials
Butt, Isaac
Carson, Edward
Collins, Michael
Davitt, Michael
Democratic Unionist Party
Easter Rising
Faulkner, Brian
Fenian movement
Fitt (Gerard (Gerry)), Baron
Home Rule Bill, 1886
Home Rule Bill, 1893
Ireland
Ireland Act, 1949

Ireland (Government of) Act, 1921
Irish Potato Famine
Irish Republican Army (IRA)
Irish Republican Brotherhood
Liberal Party
Liberal Unionists
Major, John
Northern Ireland
O'Connell, Daniel
O'Neill, Terence (Baron O'Neill of the
   Maine)
Orange Order
Paisley, Ian
Parnell, Charles Stewart
Pearse, Patrick
Phoenix Park murders
population
Sinn Fein
Stormont
Synge, John Millington
Ulster
Ulster Defence Association
Ulster Defence Regiment (UDR)
Ulster Special Constabulary
Ulster Unionist Party
Ulster Volunteer Force
Union, Act of (1800)
Young Ireland

13 Party politics and political leaders, 1918–45

Abdication Crisis
Attlee, Clement Richard
balance of payments
Baldwin, Stanley
Balfour, Arthur
Bevin, Ernest
Bonar Law, Andrew
Butler, R A
Chamberlain, Austen
Chamberlain, Neville
Chanak Crisis, 1921–22
Churchill, Winston Spencer
Common Wealth Party
Commons, House of
Communist Party
Conservative Party
Cook, Arthur James
Cripps, Stafford
Curzon, George Nathaniel

14 The making of the welfare state, 1906–51

15 Economy and society since 1918

16 British foreign policy and international relations since 1918

17 Party politics and political leaders since 1945

subject index

Further *Complete A–Z Handbooks* are available from Hodder & Stoughton. Why not use them to support your other A levels and Advanced GNVQs? All the *A–Zs* are written by experienced authors and Chief Examiners.

0 340 65467 8   *The Complete A–Z Business Studies* Second Edition £9.99
0 340 65489 9   *The Complete A–Z Geography Handbook* £9.99
0 340 64789 2   *The Complete A–Z Leisure, Travel and Tourism Handbook* £9.99
0 340 65832 0   *The Complete A–Z Sociology Handbook* £9.99
0 340 65490 2   *The Complete A–Z Psychology Handbook* £9.99
0 340 66985 3   *The Complete A–Z Economics and Business Studies Handbook* £9.99
0 340 66373 1   *The Complete A–Z Biology Handbook* £9.99
0 340 72513 3   *The Complete A–Z Chemistry Handbook* £9.99
0 340 68804 1   *The Complete A–Z Physics Handbook* £9.99
0 340 68803 3   *The Complete A–Z Mathematics Handbook* £9.99
0 340 67996 4   *The Complete A–Z 20th Century European History Handbook* £9.99
0 340 69131 X   *The Complete A–Z Media and Communication Studies Handbook* £9.99
0 340 68847 5   *The Complete A–Z Business Studies CD-ROM* £55.00 + VAT
0 340 69124 7   *The Complete A–Z Accounting Handbook* £9.99
0 340 72051 4   *The A–Z Business Studies Coursework Handbook* £6.99

All Hodder & Stoughton *Educational* books are available at your local bookshop, or can be ordered direct from the publisher. Just tick the titles you would like and complete the details below. Prices and availability are subject to change without prior notice.

Buy four books from the selection above and get free postage and packaging. Just send a cheque or postal order made payable to *Bookpoint Limited* to the value of the total cover price of four books. This should be sent to: Hodder & Stoughton *Educational,* 39 Milton Park, Abingdon, Oxon OX14 4TD, UK. EMail address: orders@bookpoint.co.uk. Alternatively, if you wish to buy fewer than four books, the following postage and packaging costs apply:

UK & BFPO: £4.30 for one book; £6.30 for two books; £8.30 for three books.
Overseas and Eire: £4.80 for one book; £7.10 for 2 or 3 books (surface mail).

If you would like to pay by credit card, our centre team would be delighted to take your order by telephone. Our direct line (44) 01235 400414 (lines open 9.00am–6.00pm, Monday to Saturday, with a 24 hour answering service). Alternatively you can send a fax to (44) 01235 400454.

Title _____ First name _____ Surname _____

Address _____

Postcode _____ Daytime telephone no. _____

If you would prefer to pay by credit card, please complete:

Please debit my Master Card / Access / Diner's Card / American Express (delete as applicable)

Card number _____ Expiry date _____ Signature _____

If you would not like to receive further information on our products, please tick the box ☐